JK
526
.E53
1984b

Elections '84

Poynter Institute for Media Studies
Library

DEC 20 '68

CONGRESSIONAL QUARTERLY INC.
1414 22ND STREET, N.W.
WASHINGTON, D.C. 20037

Congressional Quarterly Inc.

Congressional Quarterly Inc., an editorial research service and publishing company, serves clients in the fields of news, education, business and government. It combines Congressional Quarterly's coverage of Congress, government and politics with the more general subject range of an affiliated service, Editorial Research Reports.

Congressional Quarterly, founded in 1945 by Henrietta and Nelson Poynter, publishes the *Congressional Quarterly Weekly Report* and a variety of books, including college political science textbooks under the CQ Press imprint and public affairs paperbacks designed as timely reports to keep journalists, scholars and the public abreast of developing issues, events and trends. Recent public affairs titles include *Presidential Elections Since 1789, Third Edition, Employment in America* and *Defense Policy, Third Edition.* New CQ Press texts include *Interest Group Politics, Change and Continuity in the 1980 Elections, Revised Edition,* and *The Presidency and the American Political System.*

CQ also publishes information directories and reference volumes on the federal government, national elections and politics. They include the *Guide to Congress,* the *Guide to the Supreme Court,* the *Guide to U.S. Elections* and *Politics in America.* The *CQ Almanac,* a compendium of legislation for one session of Congress, is published each year. *Congress and the Nation,* a record of government for a presidential term, is published every four years.

CQ publishes *The Congressional Monitor,* a daily report on current and future activities of congressional committees, and several newsletters, including *Congressional Insight,* a weekly analysis of congressional action, and *Campaign Practices Reports,* a semimonthly update on campaign laws.

CQ conducts seminars and conferences on Congress, the legislative process, the federal budget, national elections and politics, and other current issues. CQ Direct Research performs contract research and maintains a reference library and query desk for clients.

Editorial Research Reports covers subjects beyond the specialized scope of Congressional Quarterly. It publishes reference material on foreign affairs, business, education, cultural affairs, national security, science and other topics of news interest. Founded in 1923, the service merged with Congressional Quarterly in 1956.

Copyright © 1984 Congressional Quarterly Inc.

All rights reserved. No part of this publication may be reproduced or transmitted in any form or by any means, electronic or mechanical, including photocopy, recording, or any information storage and retrieval system, without permission in writing from the publisher.

Printed in the United States of America

Library of Congress Cataloging in Publication Data

Main entry under title:

Elections '84

Includes bibliography and index.
1. Presidents — United States — Election — 1984. 2. United States. Congress — Elections, 1984. I. Congressional Quarterly, inc.
JK526 1984b.   324.973´0927   84-7109
ISBN 0-87187-310-9

Editor: Michael D. Wormser
Major Contributor: Rhodes Cook
Contributors: Donald F. Baldini, Alan Ehrenhalt, Jeremy Gaunt, Martha Gottron, Nancy Lammers, Steven Pressman, Margaret C. Thompson, Wayne Walker
Cover Design/Graphics: Robert Redding
Index: Twin Oaks Indexing Collective

Congressional Quarterly Inc.

Eugene Patterson *Editor and President*
Wayne P. Kelley *Publisher*
Peter A. Harkness *Deputy Publisher and Executive Editor*
Robert E. Cuthriell *Director, Research and Development*
Robert C. Hur *General Manager*
I.D. Fuller *Production Manager*
Maceo Mayo *Assistant Production Manager*
Sydney E. Garriss *Computer Services Manager*

Book Department

David R. Tarr *Director*
Joanne D. Daniels *Director, CQ Press*
John L. Moore *Assistant Director*
Kathryn C. Suarez *Marketing Director*
Mary W. Cohn *Associate Editor*
Michael D. Wormser *Associate Editor*
Barbara R. de Boinville *Senior Editor, CQ Press*
Nancy Lammers *Senior Editor*
Nola Healy Lynch *Developmental Editor, CQ Press*
Margaret C. Thompson *Senior Writer*
Carolyn Goldinger *Project Editor*
Mary McNeil *Project Editor/Design Coordinator*
Patricia M. Russotto *Project Editor*
Mary Ames Booker *Editorial Assistant*
Judith Aldock *Editorial Assistant*
Elizabeth H. Summers *Editorial Assistant*
Nancy A. Blanpied *Indexer*
Barbara A. March *Secretary*

Editor's Note. *Elections '84* provides a detailed description of the federal election process and the factors shaping the 1984 presidential and congressional elections. The book concentrates on this year's presidential election and includes chapters on previous presidential primaries and the 1984 delegate selection events, past presidents and their backgrounds, third-party challenges, background on presidential nominating conventions and information on the 1984 Republican and Democratic conventions, the electoral college and the popular vote for president. Other sections are devoted to the 1984 House, Senate and gubernatorial elections, outlooks on how the two parties are expected to fare, election-year lobbying and past and projected national voter turnout. The final section is devoted to campaign spending: the cost of running for public office and the role and impact of political action committee (PAC) contributions to election campaigns. An appendix provides additional data on previous presidential and congressional elections, the 1980 presidential nominating conventions and the Carter-Reagan contest and complete 1982 election results for governor, the House and the Senate. A selected bibliography and an index are included. *Elections '84* continues CQ's biennial coverage of federal elections and the U.S. electoral system.

Table of Contents

The 1984 Election 1
    The American Electorate 3
    Election-year Lobbying...................................... 7

Seeking the Presidency.. 11
    The Long Road to the White House.................... 13
    Third-party Challenges..................................... 17
    Presidential Backgrounds 22
    Presidential Primaries...................................... 27
    1984 Delegate Selection................................... 31
    Primary Results 46

National Nominating Conventions...................... 49
    Functions of Party Conventions 51
    Pre-convention Era, 1789-1828......................... 60
    National Party Conventions, 1831-1980.............. 65
    National Convention Information — 1980, 1984 68

Electing the President 77
    The Electoral College 79
    The Popular Vote 97

Congressional and Gubernatorial Elections 101
    The 1984 Congressional Elections..................... 103
    Senate Membership in the 98th Congress.............. 109
    House Membership in the 98th Congress............... 110
    Senate Elections 113

    House Elections.................................. 121
    House Districts for the 1980s..................... 125
    Gubernatorial Elections 129

Campaign Financing................................ 133
    Political Party Campaigning 135
    Controls on Political Spending..................... 147
    Incumbents' Campaign Funds — Jan. 1, 1984........ 156

Appendix 161
    1980 Presidential Primaries........................ 163
    1980 Presidential Nominating Conventions 170
    Results of Presidential Elections, 1860-1980 183
    Victorious Party in Presidential Elections............ 185
    1982 Elections for Governor, Senate, House......... 186
    Selected Bibliography 195

Index 199

The 1984 Election 1

The American Electorate 3
Election-year Lobbying. 7

Growing Franchise in the United States, 1930-84

Year	Estimated Population of Voting Age	Vote Cast for Presidential Electors Number	Vote Cast for Presidential Electors Percent	Vote Cast for U.S. Representatives Number	Vote Cast for U.S. Representatives Percent
1930	73,623,000	—	—	24,777,000	33.7
1932	75,768,000	39,732,000	52.4	37,657,000	49.7
1934	77,997,000	—	—	32,256,000	41.4
1936	80,174,000	45,643,000	56.9	42,886,000	53.5
1938	82,354,000	—	—	36,236,000	44.0
1940	84,728,000	49,900,000	58.9	46,951,000	55.4
1942	86,465,000	—	—	28,074,000	32.5
1944	85,654,000	47,977,000	56.0	45,103,000	52.7
1946	92,659,000	—	—	34,398,000	37.1
1948	95,573,000	48,794,000	51.1	45,933,000	48.1
1950	98,134,000	—	—	40,342,000	41.1
1952	99,929,000	61,551,000	61.6	57,571,000	57.6
1954	102,075,000	—	—	42,580,000	41.7
1956	104,515,000	62,027,000	59.3	58,428,000	55.9
1958	106,447,000	—	—	45,818,000	43.0
1960	109,672,000	68,838,000	63.1	64,133,000	58.7
1962	112,952,000	—	—	51,261,000	46.3
1964	114,090,000	70,645,000	61.8	65,886,000	57.8
1966	116,638,000	—	—	52,900,000	45.4
1968	120,285,000	73,212,000	60.7	66,109,000	55.2
1970	124,498,000	—	—	54,173,000	43.8
1972	140,068,000	77,625,000	55.4	71,188,000	50.9
1974	145,035,000	—	—	52,397,000	36.1
1976	150,127,000	81,603,000	54.4	74,419,000	49.6
1978	155,712,000	—	—	54,680,000	35.1
1980	162,761,000	86,515,221	53.2	72,796,000	45.4
1982	169,342,000	—	—	63,852,938	37.7
1984	173,936,000				

Source: Bureau of the Census, *Statistical Abstracts of the United States;* Congressional Quarterly, *Congress and the Nation* vol. 5; *Congressional Quarterly Weekly Report*, Oct. 30, 1982, p. 2749, and Feb. 19, 1983, p. 387.

The American Electorate

Probably no president since Franklin D. Roosevelt has done more to stimulate voter turnout than Ronald Reagan. But while Roosevelt attracted millions of new supporters to the Democratic Party, it is not so clear that Reagan's legacy will be a blessing to Republicans.

In 1980 Reagan was the catalyst for a GOP revival that captured the White House and the Senate. But in 1982 he was the target of a striking Democratic countersurge, spearheaded by low-income groups that traditionally had lagged in their participation at the polls.

The question for 1984 and the rest of the decade was whether this surge in the "have-not" vote would continue. Both parties had made plans for 1984 on the assumption that it was here to stay, a result of the arguments and emotions of the Reagan era.

"There is a polarization process going on," observed Richard Bond, director of political operations for the Republican National Committee (RNC). "The distinction between major party candidates is often blurred. But Reagan against any Democratic candidate is a stark contrast. You get a lot of people for you and a lot of people against you."

It would not be difficult for either party to cast the presidential election in apocalyptic terms. Democrats could argue that four more years of Reagan and his programs would make fundamental changes in federal policy that could be reversed only with great difficulty. A Reagan defeat would hold out the possibility that his conservative policies were no more than an interlude in a predominantly Democratic era.

"All the cards will be on the table for both sides," predicted Republican pollster Lance Tarrance. "The Reagan program is a restructuring of the federal role in American political life. The 'haves' and 'have-nots' are more sensitive to this election than to any since 1960."

Voter Turnout Upswing

The emergence of a huge new "have-not" vote had potentially historic significance for the Democratic Party.

Party leaders had looked longingly for years at the huge pool of working-class whites and blacks who all but opted out of the political process. Every voting study indicated that those people would favor Democratic candidates if they voted. But no contest in recent years had attracted their attention, and they created what political scientists referred to as a "hole" in the American electorate.

"The party of non-voters is concentrated among the poorest and most dependent social classes," political scientist Walter Dean Burnham wrote in 1981. "There is a huge hole in American participation much more sharply class-stratified than any recent election between Republican and Democrat."

All of the get-out-the-vote efforts endorsed by Democrats in the past decade, such as registration by post card and the Carter administration's Election Day registration plan, were offered with a clear sense of who were the non-voters.

But by 1980 that "hole" in the electorate seemed beyond the capacity of either party to fill. It remained for the 1982 elections to raise the issue anew.

The national turnout for House elections in 1982 was 64 million — nearly 10 million more than in 1978, the most recent previous midterm congressional election year. The upswing in voting represented a dramatic change from the preceding two decades, when the raw turnout in midterm elections was almost static.

Democrats were the clear beneficiaries. The vote for Democratic House candidates increased by more than six million, to 35.3 million in 1982 from 29.2 million in 1978. Republican voting, by contrast, grew by only three million, to 27.6 million in 1982 from 24.6 million in 1978. The remaining one million 1982 votes went to Libertarian and other third party candidates, independents and write-ins.

The bulk of the Democratic increase was provided by have-nots — blacks, struggling blue-collar workers and unemployed voters. "All these groups," claimed Ann Lewis, political director of the Democratic National Committee (DNC), "felt their own interests had been hurt by the Reagan administration. When people are convinced their interests are at stake, they will turn out and vote."

According to a post-election Census Bureau survey, whites continued to vote at a higher rate than blacks, white-collar workers at a higher level than blue-collar workers, and the employed more frequently than the unemployed. But the comparisons with 1978 were crucial. Blacks, blue-collar and unemployed voters all showed much sharper increases in their rate of voting participation than their higher-income counterparts.

The suddenly aroused have-nots were among the most staunchly Democratic voting blocs in 1982. Blacks, the unemployed and union households gave at least two-thirds of their votes to Democratic House candidates, according to ABC News Election Day polls.

Voter Registration Drives

The 1980s voter surge had some similarities to the one a half century ago, when the 1928 presidential candidacy of Democrat Alfred E. Smith lured millions of previously unregistered low-income voters into the Democratic Party. As an Irish Catholic from New York City, Smith drew to the Democratic Party masses of recent immigrants, many of whom were urban Catholics themselves.

That increase in the turnout was not sufficient to elect Smith president, largely because a second voting surge was taking place along with it. Southern white Protestants, antagonized by Smith's religion and urban roots, voted in large numbers for Republican Herbert Hoover. It was the worst Democratic showing in the South since Reconstruction.

But the burst of Southern Republicanism in 1928 was not the surge that was to be critical in American politics. Republicans' hopes of promptly expanding their Southern beachhead were dashed by the Depression. Meanwhile, the urban ethnic enthusiasm for Smith launched a national transformation of the Democrats from a minority party — rural and Southern-based — into a majority party with its heart in the Northern industrial states.

After the election of Reagan, Republicans speculated whether 1980 was to be the turning point in their emergence as the new majority party. By 1983, however, it was more common to hear Democratic strategists talking about whether the high-turnout 1982 election was a precursor, like the vote in 1928.

The Democratic National Committee was doing what it could to help that idea along. Seeking to maintain the momentum the party developed in 1982, the DNC in early 1983 unveiled plans for an ambitious $5 million voter registration drive aimed at the groups that contributed to Democratic success in 1982.

They had a large pool of potential voters to target. After the 1982 elections, the Census Bureau reported that 7.2 million blacks, 5.4 million unemployed, and nearly 12.5 million blue-collar workers of all races were not registered to vote. There were an estimated 2.5 million unregistered Hispanic citizens.

Black and Hispanic organizations and organized labor were fine-tuning the registration and get-out-the-vote efforts that were successful in 1982. The AFL-CIO Committee on Political Education had gathered computerized information on union members in all 50 states, with their addresses, phone numbers, registration status and voting places.

That attention to nuts-and-bolts politics in 1982 enabled organized labor to re-establish its influence in the heart of union strength, the large industrial states of the Frost Belt. Labor helped replace retiring GOP governors in Michigan, Ohio and Wisconsin with Democrats who had close ties to the labor movement. In several economically hard-hit congressional districts, the unions were instrumental in ousting Republican incumbents.

Importance of Blacks

One of the big surprises in 1982 was the heavy black turnout. One of the few generally agreed upon assumptions about 1984 was that black voting would continue to increase. While Hispanics were listed in the Census Bureau survey as voting in 1982 at a rate 1.8 percentage points higher than in 1978, and whites at a rate 2.6 percentage points higher, the black turnout rose a dramatic 5.8 percentage points, bringing it closer to the white turnout level than ever before. In nine states blacks were reported to have voted at a rate higher than whites. "The interest of blacks should remain high," predicted Curtis B. Gans, the director of the Committee for the Study of the American Electorate. "There is no way Reagan can turn their animosity around."

Intense opposition to Reagan, the economic recession and successes by blacks at the polls had combined to ignite the most active black registration effort since the 1960s. The result in 1982 was an unexpectedly strong Democratic showing even in places where moderate Republicans expected to win sizable portions of the black vote.

Heavy black turnouts in Chicago and Philadelphia nearly toppled GOP Govs. James R. Thompson of Illinois and Richard L. Thornburgh of Pennsylvania. Both had run well among black voters in 1978, before the Reagan presidency had begun.

In the South, a surge in the black vote helped Democrats gain two governorships in 1982 and retire several conservative GOP House members, including Albert Lee Smith Jr. of Alabama and five-term veteran Robert W. Daniel Jr. of Virginia.

In 1983 there was an even more important breakthrough for blacks. Rep. Harold Washington, D-Ill. (1981-83), capitalized on huge black registration gains in Chicago to win election as the city's first black mayor. His victory provided further impetus to black registration efforts across the country and fueled the talk of a black presidential candidate in the 1984 Democratic primaries. A black candidate for the White House, many civil rights leaders believed, would stimulate even more interest among blacks in registering to vote.

A variety of registration efforts were under way, ranging from the NAACP's "Breadbox-Ballotbox Voter Drive" — which sought out unregistered voters among persons waiting in line for free government cheese — to the Rev. Jesse Jackson's barnstorming in the South. Black leaders talked of registering 2.5 million new black voters by November 1984. Much of their activity would be focused in the South, where about half of the voting-age blacks lived. (Jackson formally announced his candidacy for the presidency on Nov. 3, 1983.)

While blatant barriers to black voter registration had been struck down in the 1960s and 1970s, subtle barriers remained. Jackson's complaints to the Justice Department about registration problems in Mississippi, including inconvenient courthouse hours and a dual registration system (requiring voters to register in both their hometown and county seat), brought a personal inspection tour by William Bradford Reynolds, the department's assistant attorney general for civil rights, and the dispatch of federal registrars to several heavily black rural counties.

Blacks comprised only 11 percent of the national voting-age population, but they were strategically located. There were more than one million voting-age blacks in four of the five largest electoral vote states (California, New York, Texas and Illinois). By carrying those four states, a candidate gained more than half of the electoral votes needed to win the White House.

But the full potential of the black vote in those states or in the South generally had yet to be realized. Blacks represented more than 20 percent of the voting-age population in six Southern states. In the same number of Southern states, the total of unregistered blacks exceeded Reagan's 1980 victory margin, according to the Joint Center for Political Studies.

White Countersurge?

Nevertheless, growing black political power did present some problems for the Democrats. There was the danger of intraparty friction between blacks and long-dominant whites in places where blacks were flexing their new political muscle. That was the case in 1983 in Chicago, where Washington capitalized on the registration of about 250,000 new black voters to upset two white candidates for the Democratic mayoral nomination. In the general election much of the white ethnic vote defected to Washington's GOP rival, creating some concern among Democratic officials that many of the white voters — long the backbone of the party in Illinois — might not return to the Democratic fold.

A heavy black registration surge sometimes has stimulated a white countersurge. That happened in 1983 in Philadelphia, where W. Wilson Goode, a veteran black city administrator, opposed former Mayor Frank L. Rizzo, a champion of the city's white ethnics, for the Democratic mayoral nomination. Democratic voter registration swelled by more than 200,000, a combination of blacks for Goode and whites primarily for Rizzo. Goode narrowly won the nomination.

It was likely there would be other white countersurges elsewhere. The specter of a growing monolith of black Democratic voters aroused elements of the New Right and their fundamentalist Christian allies to develop a registration drive of their own.

In early July 1983, GOP Sen. Jesse Helms of North Carolina and the Rev. Jerry Falwell of the Moral Majority announced plans for a nationwide campaign to register millions of conservative Americans. Falwell hoped that much of the effort would be led by conservative clergy in their churches. "We hope to get millions of conservative Americans registered to vote," he said. "If that happens, I think we'll see a change in government — the kind of government we deserve."

While not a very visible force in 1982, conservative Christians were a vital part of the Republican surge in 1980. They helped Reagan sweep most of the Southern states and helped elect GOP Senate candidates Jeremiah Denton in Alabama and Don Nickles in Oklahoma.

Falwell and Helms claimed their 1984 registration effort was directed at conservatives of both races, but several of their colleagues were more pointed in explaining the thrust of the registration drive. The registration of conservative Christians, said Lamarr Mooneyham, the chairman of the Moral Majority in North Carolina, "is the only way to keep a political blackmailer like the Rev. Jackson from acquiring the political clout that he needs to implement his racist agenda."

In a fund-raising letter for Helms' political arm, the National Congressional Club, Sen. John P. East, R-N.C., warned that "time is running out for us and Jesse Jackson's liberal army is growing."

Hispanic Mobilization

Hispanics were not so large a voting population as blacks, and they were extremely slow to mobilize. But, like blacks, Hispanics were strategically situated and could give the Democrats an important boost in 1984. Nationally, Hispanic groups were aiming to register one million new voters by November 1984, with their effort focused on California and Texas, where more than half the Hispanics of voting age lived.

Hispanics enjoyed their most dramatic success in 1982 in Texas, where they were a vital part of the united Democratic effort that ousted conservative GOP Gov. William Clements and elected the entire slate of statewide Democratic candidates. According to the San Antonio-based Southwest Voter Registration Education Project, the number of registered Hispanic voters within the state reached almost 320,000, nearly twice the number that were registered four years earlier. A remarkable 86 percent of Hispanics voted for Democratic gubernatorial candidate Mark White. Other Democratic statewide candidates drew even higher shares.

In 1983 New Mexico's newly elected Hispanic governor, Toney Anaya, took a leading role in seeking to increase the influence of his compatriots within the Democratic Party nationally. "The hands that traditionally have been used to pick the cotton and the lettuce," Anaya said, "can pick the next president of the United States." Named the head of a new group called Hispanic Force '84 shortly after his inauguration, Anaya spent much of his spare time in 1983 mobilizing the Hispanic vote. Among his stops was Denver, where Democratic state Rep. Federico Peña was elected in June 1983 as the city's first Hispanic mayor.

GOP Target: 'Baby-boomers'

The increased ballot box militancy of minority groups was causing GOP leaders some concern by early 1983. With the possible exception of fundamentalist Christians, they had no new, reliably Republican voting blocs to mobilize. The likely GOP voters for the most part already were active voters. "For every new vote the Republicans pick up from 1980," said Tarrance, "the Democrats pick up two. This election [1984] should be much closer than 1980."

As of July 1983 the RNC had not yet disclosed its registration plans for 1984, but a likely target was the group of young people in the 18-to-34-year-old range. It was not an easy target to focus on. The young in recent years had been swing voters, and they were a much less plausible source of support for the GOP than new black and Hispanic voters were for the Democrats. In 1980, according to the Gallup Poll, voters under 30 preferred Jimmy Carter to Reagan. Two years later, a majority voted for Democratic congressional candidates.

Still, GOP officials saw the young as a largely untapped voting bloc well worth cultivating. They were looking carefully at both the 18-to-24-year-olds and the "baby-boom" generation from 25 to 34. Republicans felt the latter group was more conservative than when it first entered the electorate, more concerned about jobs and economic security than liberal causes. "They are much more supportive of Reagan than one would suspect," said Bond. "There are millions of potential Republicans out there that have been lying fallow."

The fallow field of unregistered young people under 35 numbered 33.2 million. The young had registered and voted at a notoriously low rate for years, but many experts expected the voter turnout rate of that generation to increase.

There was evidence of a slight "baby-boom" awakening in 1982. That year, 25-to-34-year-olds reported voting at a rate 2.4 percentage points higher than in 1978. That

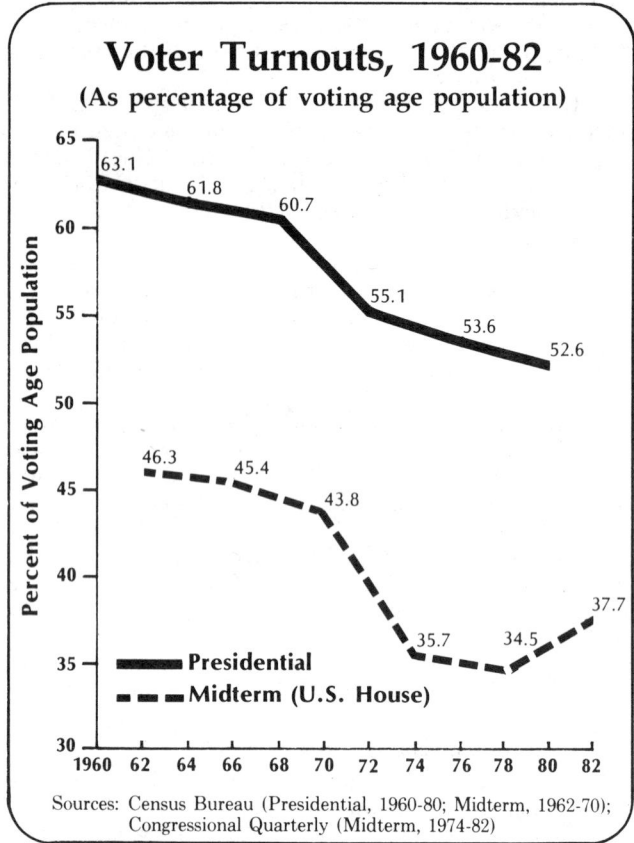

Sources: Census Bureau (Presidential, 1960-80; Midterm, 1962-70); Congressional Quarterly (Midterm, 1974-82)

figure was below the national rate of increase but still a significant jump.

Higher participation from that age group in the years ahead could ensure a continued voter upswing even if Reagan disappeared from the scene. That was what University of California political scientist Raymond E. Wolfinger predicted.

'Haves' vs. 'Have-nots'

But the real battle lines of the 1984 campaign were likely to be drawn between the "haves" and the "have-nots," with the voting participation of each group dependent on the condition of the economy.

Democrats insisted that the economic recovery taking place in 1983 was a "split-level" recovery, with conditions favoring the upper-middle class but with the disadvantaged in a state of continuing recession. The goal for Democratic strategists in 1984 was to convince millions of blue-collar voters that they were in the non-recovering class and should vote with the "have-nots."

Polls in 1983 showed some evidence that this argument might sell. In a June *Washington Post*-ABC News poll, families with annual incomes of more than $20,000 — roughly half the electorate — said they were optimistic that the economy was improving and voiced strong support for Reagan. But among families with annual incomes under $20,000 there was less optimism and more criticism of the president.

Reagan made deep inroads into the normally Democratic blue-collar vote in 1980, enabling him to sweep most of the Frost Belt industrial states that were key to any Democratic presidential victory. Nationally, the Gallup Poll reported that Reagan ran virtually even with Carter in blue-collar areas, trailing Carter by only 2 percentage points among all working-class voters and by just 7 percentage points among labor union families.

Reagan's combination of decisive leadership, a tough foreign policy stance and conservative social views could well allow him to keep a sizable chunk of the ethnic, blue-collar workers who backed him in 1980. "He has charismatic appeal," admitted Rick Scott, the political director of the Minnesota branch of the American Federation of State, County and Municipal Employees. "FDR didn't do that much to end the Depression, but his plain talk was appealing. Reagan has the same quality."

For many blue-collar workers, however, the key question in 1984 might be the same one Reagan asked with such effect in 1980: "Are you better off than you were four years ago?" According to a CBS-*New York Times* exit poll in 1980, blue-collar voters who believed their family's financial position was improving stayed with Carter by a margin of more than 3-to-1. But the larger group that felt its financial position was worse bolted to Reagan by a margin of 2-to-1.

Continued high unemployment in certain regions of the country remained a major problem for the Republicans in 1984, both as an issue and as a source of disgruntled voters. Between 1980 and 1982 the number of voting-age unemployed increased by nearly four million (to more than 10.7 million from 6.9 million). Barely one-third of such people voted in 1982, but the participation rate of the unemployed increased more sharply than that of any other group. While many were habitual voters who had recently been employed, the sharp increase in the turnout among the unemployed threw into doubt the argument that they were a negligible voting force too absorbed with their own personal problems to be involved in politics.

High unemployment could have a significant ripple effect, providing political motivation for workers who had not experienced unemployment but feared it. That was evident in 1982. "When workers are making good wages," explained Scott, "they think about vacation or snowmobiling. But when they are hard-pressed, they think about economic issues and the ballot box."

Election-Year Lobbying

With lawmaking giving way to election-year politics, Washington lobbyists and political strategists shifted their sights from Capitol Hill to the presidential and congressional campaigns.

Labor unions, business interests, women's groups, environmental organizations, the New Right and others usually had diverse interests but a common objective: to win votes in Washington by delivering votes next Election Day — November 6.

The nation's influential interest groups will play a big role in determining the next president as well as the House and Senate membership in the 99th Congress, which convenes in January 1985. They provide campaign cash and volunteers in return for the promise, or at least the hope, of support from the winners for their legislative efforts.

"Politics is not all that different from organizing," explains David A. Sweeney, legislative and political director for the International Brotherhood of Teamsters. "It goes back to [labor organizer Samuel] Gompers. You support your friends and defeat your enemies."

The aggressive political plans of special interest groups have given rise to charges that some politicians sell their political souls to lobbying groups in exchange for endorsements. For example, presidential hopeful Walter F. Mondale was attacked by other Democratic candidates and by President Ronald Reagan for making too many promises to organized labor. Mondale, in turn, criticized Reagan for being beholden only to high-income interests.

But the increased sniping at the start of the presidential campaign did not deter special interest groups from going ahead with their election-year plans. Many politicians found nothing wrong with that. "Whether it be the Iowa Pork Producers Association, the dairymen, the civil rights people or pro-life people, all are recognized interest groups that have concern for their issues," said Sen. Roger W. Jepsen, R-Iowa. "And the combination of these groups is what the country is all about."

Jepsen was counting on the help of those organizations that supported his conservative politics, while his challenger, liberal Democratic Rep. Tom Harkin, expected to receive the help of groups that opposed Jepsen.

Jepsen was one of many congressional incumbents targeted for election defeat by one or another interest group. Another, Rep. Don Ritter, R-Pa., was marked for defeat by environmental groups because of his 1982 support for changes in the nation's clean air laws. And women's groups were trying to replace the three-term Ritter with Jane Wells-Schooley, a former vice president of the National Organization for Women (NOW).

An 'Auction'

While interest groups waited to see which lawmakers would be returning to Capitol Hill in 1985, their political strategists were overshadowing the lobbyists by working to influence the election of a president, 33 senators and 435 representatives.

"It's an auction process out there," said Rep. Dick Durbin, D-Ill. "Why in the world should there be thousands of PACs out there, all scrambling to raise money, all trying to get involved in this process and all trying to have some sort of influence and access to a congressman?" But Durbin, a freshman Democrat from Springfield, knew the answer. After raising more than $200,000 in PAC money for his 1982 campaign, Durbin almost immediately began raising funds for his first re-election race. "The campaign never ends," he noted.

Women

For 13 years the National Organization for Women focused its efforts on lobbying for the proposed Equal Rights Amendment (ERA) to the Constitution, first in Congress and then in the state legislatures. When the deadline passed in 1982 without enough ratifying states, NOW plunged into a new lobbying campaign to start the process over again.

But to the frustration of NOW's leaders the House failed by six votes to approve the ERA in November 1983. NOW leaders said they would try to achieve through the ballot box what they were unable to win legislatively. They said they were tired of lobbying virtually all-male legislative bodies at the state and national levels. Aware that 20 of the 22 female members of the U.S. House of Representatives voted for the ERA in 1983, NOW's overall goal was to elect more women to national and state political offices.

"It is, as they say, the only game in town and the only way to make a difference," said NOW President Judy Goldsmith. "The only way for us to achieve real goals for women is to have women in those legislative seats making the decisions that affect all of us."

8 Elections '84

But finding enough female political candidates proved to be difficult. In 1982 only 5 percent of all congressional candidates were women. While that number was expected to increase in 1984, NOW still would have to endorse mostly male candidates.

In Illinois, for example, the 10,000-member state NOW chapter was supporting Rep. Paul Simon, who won the Democratic nomination for the U.S. Senate in the March 20 Illinois primary election. His GOP opponent was incumbent Sen. Charles H. Percy, who handily defeated Rep. Tom Corcoran. A local NOW chapter in Chicago also was supporting the re-election of Rep. Cardiss Collins, who turned back a strong challenge by Danny K. Davis, a Chicago alderman, in the Democratic primary.

Because the 3,000-member NOW organization in Chicago was not registered as a PAC under federal laws, it could not contribute money to congressional candidates. "I don't worry about buying and selling candidates because we can't afford to do that anyway," said Karen Wellisch, the chapter's executive director.

Although it was officially bipartisan, NOW was making no secret of its affinity for Democrats. It endorsed Mondale for president and wanted to see the Democrats regain control of the Senate.

Goldsmith, however, angrily disputed the charge that NOW had become an arm of the Democratic Party. "I'm getting increasingly tired of taking the rap for the Republicans' betrayal of women. Ronald Reagan's Republican Party has turned its back on women dramatically. To ignore that is not non-partisan. It's foolish."

The women's lobby probably will have to wait until 1985 to refocus Congress' attention on most of its legislative agenda. Besides the ERA, NOW and other women's groups were pushing for legislation to prohibit gender-based insurance rates and so-called economic equity measures such as changes in pension rights and stronger child support enforcement. Some of those proposals, including higher Individual Retirement Accounts (IRAs) for nonworking spouses, were considered to have a good chance of passing in the 98th Congress.

Labor

Largely because of the AFL-CIO's expensive drive to put Mondale in the White House, much of the attention given special interest politics in the 1984 election year focused on organized labor.

Many unions were joining together to try to defeat Ronald Reagan. "Whoever the Democratic nominee is will be of a belief . . . to implement a broad recovery program to mend the wounds and damage of the Reagan administration," said Ray Denison, the AFL-CIO's chief lobbyist.

Labor lobbyists did have specific legislation on their 1984 agenda, but there was little chance that Congress and the White House would pay much attention. In 1983 the House passed the so-called domestic content bill to boost the U.S. auto industry, a top priority of the United Auto Workers. But the Senate was not expected to go along. The AFL-CIO also was lobbying for the creation of a national industrial policy. But prospects for passage by Congress in 1984 were slim.

Labor lobbyists also were promoting legislation to prevent businesses from declaring bankruptcy as a union-busting tactic.

Union officials, however, were not optimistic about winning enactment of their legislative proposals without Democratic control of the White House and Congress. It was this realization that made unions willing to take the political risk of throwing so much effort into the 1984 presidential and congressional election campaigns.

"We're rolling the dice in terms of the primaries and the general election, and to a certain degree the strength of American labor is on the line in terms of whether we can deliver," said Gerald W. McEntee, president of the million-member American Federation of State, County and Municipal Employees (AFSCME).

Some union officials worried about a negative image regardless of the election's outcome. "If Mondale wins, it'll be the labor bosses that did it," said Ken Sharp, a political organizer in Chicago for the Communications Workers of America. "But if he loses, labor will be seen as having no clout. Either way, labor loses."

A number of unions were aiding the Mondale campaign in the presidential primaries and caucuses by running phone banks, getting union members named as convention delegates and turning out the labor vote.

Unions also were promising to pitch in for congressional candidates, especially those running for GOP-held Senate seats.

Jerry Clark, AFSCME's political director, said his union planned to work in such states as Tennessee, North Carolina and Iowa, where Democratic Senate contenders were thought to have a good chance to capture GOP seats.

One union that did not sign onto the Mondale bandwagon was the Teamsters. The 1.7-million-member union, which backed Reagan in 1980, did not plan to endorse a presidential candidate until after the party nominating conventions in the summer.

Teamsters President Jackie Presser, who pushed for the Reagan endorsement four years ago, said he thought Reagan was doing a good job. But Teamsters officials said such personal statements did not necessarily reflect what the union would do in 1984. At the congressional level, Sweeney predicted the vast bulk of the Teamsters' contributions and support would go to Democratic candidates.

Teachers

The 1984 presidential campaign brought the nation's two largest teachers' unions back into the same political camp.

The 580,000-member American Federation of Teachers (AFT), which was affiliated with the AFL-CIO, was supporting Mondale. In 1980 the AFT backed Sen. Edward M. Kennedy, D-Mass., in the presidential primaries. The larger National Education Association (NEA) supported Jimmy Carter. The NEA also is backing Mondale in 1984.

Despite its endorsement of Carter, about 40 percent of the teachers in the 1.7-million-member NEA voted for Reagan in 1980.

The NEA jumped into presidential politics for the first time in 1976, supporting Carter. Carter had won teachers' backing with his promise to establish a Cabinet-level Department of Education. In 1980 Reagan pledged to abolish the department. He did not actively pursue that promise, however, and is not likely to again make that pledge in 1984.

"Needless to say, we haven't gained much in the Reagan administration. So we don't stand to lose much in this election," said Yvonne Shafer, an NEA government relations specialist based in Minneapolis. She was dispatched to Iowa early in 1984 for NEA's all-out drive in behalf of Mondale in that state's Feb. 20 presidential caucuses.

Kenneth Melley, NEA's political director, said the organization had thrust itself into campaign politics "to enhance the position of education at the federal level." But he said the NEA was a credible lobbying force even before it first got involved in congressional campaigns in 1972.

Like other interest group officials, Melley was not worried about the teachers' lobby fading from sight if its candidates lost. "Win or lose, the NEA will still remain a visible presence in Congress," he maintained. The critical test for lobbying groups, however, was not whether they would remain visible after the elections, but whether they would be more influential on Capitol Hill after the votes were counted.

Throughout Reagan's term, teachers had fought against a proposed constitutional amendment to permit school prayer and legislation to provide tuition tax credits, both of which were backed by the administration and congressional conservatives. NEA and AFT lobbyists confronted those issues again in 1984, though it was unlikely Congress would pass either proposal. Looking ahead, the teachers hoped that generous promises of increased education funding made by Mondale and some of the other Democratic candidates would translate into legislative victory in 1985.

Business

While some lobbying groups hoped the 1984 presidential election would reverse the political trend begun in 1980, business lobbyists generally wanted to preserve the economic changes brought about by the Reagan administration and Congress.

The United States Chamber of Commerce, for example, in 1984 planned to support candidates who opposed tax increases and remained supportive of Reagan's economic policies. The country's major business groups were ecstatic when the administration won its huge tax cuts in 1981. Despite a Reagan-backed tax increase in 1982 and soaring federal deficits, most business groups remained loyal to Reagan's economic blueprint and would use it as a litmus test for congressional candidates.

Although the Chamber of Commerce considered itself bipartisan, it did not endorse any Democratic candidates in the 1982 House and Senate general elections. That brought a stinging rebuke from Rep. Tony Coelho, D-Calif., chairman of the Democratic Congressional Campaign Committee. The Chamber did back a few conservative Democrats in their primary campaigns against more liberal opponents.

"We will endorse Democrats in the general election [in 1984]," promised Neil Newhouse, the Chamber's political affairs director. "But there is a difference between what Tony Coelho thinks is a pro-business Democrat and what the U.S. Chamber of Commerce thinks is a pro-business Democrat," said Newhouse, who left the Chamber in the spring of 1984 to join Decision Making Inc., the polling firm of White House pollster Richard Wirthlin.

There were signs that Democrats recently were getting a better reception from business. In 1983 business lobbyists and large-corporation executives flocked to a dinner honoring Sen. Russell B. Long of Lousiana, the ranking Democrat on the Senate Finance Committee.

Many attended to pay homage to a senator important to their interests. Traditionally, the business community provided substantial political support to such tax-writing powers in Congress as the House Ways and Means Committee chairman, currently Dan Rostenkowski, D-Ill.

In addition, some officials probably figured the cost of the dinner was a good investment in case the Democrats regained Senate control and Long once again was in the chairman's seat at Finance. Whatever their reason, the dinner added $1 million to the coffers of the Democratic Senatorial Campaign Committee, headed by Sen. Lloyd Bentsen of Texas.

Other business officials found such behavior a little strange, however. "If you're worried about Republicans keeping the Senate, you don't go out and give the Democrats a million dollars," said one Chamber of Commerce staffer.

Bentsen aggressively courted business executives, getting them to open their wallets for Democrats in 1984. Newhouse said he had received more campaign pitches from Bentsen in six months than from the Republican Party in the last three years, suggesting the GOP might have been taking some business support for granted.

Republicans still stood to receive the lion's share of business contributions and endorsements in the 1984 congressional races. But in some parts of the country, business-backed Republicans might have trouble, even amid signs that economic recovery was proceeding nationally. "I'm responsible for Illinois, Indiana, Ohio, Michigan and Kentucky, some of the most exciting states where the economy is really booming," said Kent Haag of the Chamber of Commerce, his voice heavy with sarcasm.

Haag had reason to be dismayed. While the national unemployment rate dropped to 8 percent in January 1984, in Illinois it increased from 9.6 percent to 9.9 percent. In Michigan the rate dipped just slightly from 11.6 percent to 11.5 percent.

In 1982 Rep. Durbin, a freshman Democrat from Springfield, Ill., squeaked past his Republican opponent with a 1,410-vote victory. Since Durbin's district was relatively conservative, national business groups felt that they could help a Republican win back the seat in 1984. But Haag and other strategists conceded that Durbin solidified his hold, partially by cultivating local businesses.

The Chamber was going after another Illinois freshman, Democratic Rep. Lane Evans of Rock Island. Evans got only a 10 percent vote rating from the Chamber in 1983 while compiling a 94 percent rating from the AFL-CIO. "He's going to be a top target, there's just no doubt about that one," said Newhouse.

At the National Federation of Independent Business (NFIB), the goal in 1984 was to remold the House into its 1981 shape, where a coalition of Republicans and conservative Southern Democrats gave Reagan a working majority to pass his economic measures.

"What our money is trying to secure is a moderate to moderate-conservative Congress," said John J. Motley, deputy legislative director of the 560,000-member small business lobby.

NFIB's political action committee (PAC), first organized in 1980, expected to spend about $300,000 on the 1984 elections. The group distributed congressional voting scores, encouraged by a survey indicating that 65 percent of NFIB members used the scores to guide them on Election Day.

According to Motley, NFIB was planning a major effort in 1984 to re-elect Sen. Rudy Boschwitz, R-Minn., who was considered likely to face a tough Democratic challenge. NFIB also planned to help Sen. William L. Armstrong, R-Colo., and Rep. John Hiler, R-Ind.

Hiler, first elected in 1980, got a scare in 1982 when he was re-elected by fewer than 4,000 votes. He could face another tough campaign this time.

Motley was one of several business lobbyists who thought the business community was not as politically active as it should be. He told business officials the way to bolster the group's lobbying clout was to be more of a force on Election Day. "Our job is to draw that connection a little more closely. And we haven't done it yet," said Motley.

Environmental Groups

Lobbying groups for environmental issues also attempted to raise their political profile during the 1984 elections. Environmental activists were particularly angered by Reagan administration policies and appointments since 1981. "Our purpose is not just to spend a lot of money and get involved in politics. Our goal is to strengthen environmental legislation as much as we can," said Steven Pearlman, political policy director of the League of Conservation Voters (LCV).

The Northeast's concern about acid rain pollution already had developed into a major campaign issue even before the presidential primaries had begun.

At the congressional level, the Sierra Club's political arm was trying to defeat two House Republicans, Ritter, Pa., and Denny Smith, Ore., for what the group said were anti-environment positions.

In 1982 environmental groups got credit for helping re-elect two GOP Senate incumbents who were in tough races, Robert T. Stafford of Vermont and John H. Chafee of Rhode Island. In 1984, environmental groups faced a dilemma in New Hampshire's Senate race, where Republican incumbent Gordon J. Humphrey was likely to face Democratic Rep. Norman E. D'Amours.

Although D'Amours had a better overall environmental record, LCV and other groups credited Humphrey for improving his record, particularly with his active opposition to the Clinch River breeder reactor.

Confronted with the politically difficult choice between the two, the LCV board of directors Feb. 16 opted to delay a decision to endorse a candidate in the New Hampshire race. "If our purpose is to convince people that it is politically disadvantageous to vote against environmental legislation, that they better change the way they act and then they do, it is tough to go after them anyway," said Pearlman, referring to Humphrey.

But ignoring D'Amours also carried some risk. "If I win," D'Amours told one environmental group that explained its reluctance to endorse the Democrat, "I'll still vote for your legislation but I won't return your phone calls."

The New Right

For the New Right, the task was more complicated than having legislators return phone calls. Rather, religious and other conservative organizations that coalesced under the New Right banner hoped to give a political boost to their ambitious legislative agenda, which had not been realized during Reagan's first three years.

New Right lobbyists were optimistic after the 1980 elections swept Ronald Reagan into the White House and sent more social conservatives to Congress. Those election victories, they felt, promised progress for their efforts to ban abortion, return prayer to the public schools and "Christianize" the United States.

But to the sharp disappointment of New Right leaders, White House lobbyists did little to press congressional action on social issues. In addition, New Right allies in Congress discovered that the more moderate GOP leadership was not eager to spend much time on their causes.

"We need to have our supporters go to the wall and put pressure on Congress, and this is where Christians take the blame themselves," said Gary Jarmin, legislative director of Christian Voice, one of the New Right lobbying groups.

According to voting studies by Christian Voice, Congress was becoming more liberal not more conservative. In 1983 the collective House membership agreed with Christian Voice on a dozen selected issues 46 percent of the time. That compared to a 58 percent finding in 1982. Jarmin said the dip was due to the 58 freshman Democrats who were elected in 1982; they agreed with Christian Voice just 27 percent of the time in 1983.

New Right strategists acknowledged that the 1984 campaign would require more of a defensive action than one in which significant gains were expected. Most efforts would be devoted to re-electing some of their closest friends in Congress, including Sens. Jepsen and Jesse Helms, R-N.C.

And they also exhibited a pragmatic streak. Because GOP control of the Senate was crucial to their interests, New Right followers felt obliged to support party moderates such as Minnesota's Boschwitz.

There were limits to pragmatism, however. The Mid-America Conservative Political Action Committee (MACPAC) backed Rep. Corcoran in his campaign against Sen. Percy in the Illinois GOP Senate primary. What would MACPAC do if Percy, whose moderate Republicanism was anathema to much of the New Right, won renomination? "I seriously doubt," said MACPAC Chairman Leroy D. Corey, "that I can go to our members and say we ought to support Percy."

Seeking The Presidency ... 11

The Long Road to the White House 13
Third-party Challenges 17
Presidential Backgrounds 22
Presidential Primaries 27
1984 Delegate Selection 31
Primary Results 46

Presidents and Vice Presidents of the United States

President and Political Party	Born	Died	Age at inauguration	Native of—	Elected from—	Term of Service	Vice President
George Washington (F)*	1732	1799	57	Va.	Va.	April 30, 1789-March 4, 1793	John Adams
George Washington (F)			61			March 4, 1793-March 4, 1797	John Adams
John Adams (F)	1735	1826	61	Mass.	Mass.	March 4, 1797-March 4, 1801	Thomas Jefferson
Thomas Jefferson (D-R)	1743	1826	57	Va.	Va.	March 4, 1801-March 4, 1805	Aaron Burr
Thomas Jefferson (D-R)			61			March 4, 1805-March 4, 1809	George Clinton
James Madison (D-R)	1751	1836	57	Va.	Va.	March 4, 1809-March 4, 1813	George Clinton
James Madison (D-R)			61			March 4, 1813-March 4, 1817	Elbridge Gerry
James Monroe (D-R)	1758	1831	58	Va.	Va.	March 4, 1817-March 4, 1821	Daniel D. Tompkins
James Monroe (D-R)			62			March 4, 1821-March 4, 1825	Daniel D. Tompkins
John Q. Adams (N-R)	1767	1848	57	Mass.	Mass.	March 4, 1825-March 4, 1829	John C. Calhoun
Andrew Jackson (D)	1767	1845	61	S.C.	Tenn.	March 4, 1829-March 4, 1833	John C. Calhoun
Andrew Jackson (D)			65			March 4, 1833-March 4, 1837	Martin Van Buren
Martin Van Buren (D)	1782	1862	54	N.Y.	N.Y.	March 4, 1837-March 4, 1841	Richard M. Johnson
W. H. Harrison (W)	1773	1841	68	Va.	Ohio	March 4, 1841-April 4, 1841	John Tyler
John Tyler (W)	1790	1862	51	Va.	Va.	April 6, 1841-March 4, 1845	
James K. Polk (D)	1795	1849	49	N.C.	Tenn.	March 4, 1845-March 4, 1849	George M. Dallas
Zachary Taylor (W)	1784	1850	64	Va.	La.	March 4, 1849-July 9, 1850	Millard Fillmore
Millard Fillmore (W)	1800	1874	50	N.Y.	N.Y.	July 10, 1850-March 4, 1853	
Franklin Pierce (D)	1804	1869	48	N.H.	N.H.	March 4, 1853-March 4, 1857	William R. King
James Buchanan (D)	1791	1868	65	Pa.	Pa.	March 4, 1857-March 4, 1861	John C. Breckinridge
Abraham Lincoln (R)	1809	1865	52	Ky.	Ill.	March 4, 1861-March 4, 1865	Hannibal Hamlin
Abraham Lincoln (R)			56			March 4, 1865-April 15, 1865	Andrew Johnson
Andrew Johnson (R)	1808	1875	56	N.C.	Tenn.	April 15, 1865-March 4, 1869	
Ulysses S. Grant (R)	1822	1885	46	Ohio	Ill.	March 4, 1869-March 4, 1873	Schuyler Colfax
Ulysses S. Grant (R)			50			March 4, 1873-March 4, 1877	Henry Wilson
Rutherford B. Hayes (R)	1822	1893	54	Ohio	Ohio	March 4, 1877-March 4, 1881	William A. Wheeler
James A. Garfield (R)	1831	1881	49	Ohio	Ohio	March 4, 1881-Sept. 19, 1881	Chester A. Arthur
Chester A. Arthur (R)	1830	1886	50	Vt.	N.Y.	Sept. 20, 1881-March 4, 1885	
Grover Cleveland (D)	1837	1908	47	N.J.	N.Y.	March 4, 1885-March 4, 1889	Thomas A. Hendricks
Benjamin Harrison (R)	1833	1901	55	Ohio	Ind.	March 4, 1889-March 4, 1893	Levi P. Morton
Grover Cleveland (D)	1837	1908	55			March 4, 1893-March 4, 1897	Adlai E. Stevenson
William McKinley (R)	1843	1901	54	Ohio	Ohio	March 4, 1897-March 4, 1901	Garret A. Hobart
William McKinley (R)			58			March 4, 1901-Sept. 14, 1901	Theodore Roosevelt
Theodore Roosevelt (R)	1858	1919	42	N.Y.	N.Y.	Sept. 14, 1901-March 4, 1905	
Theodore Roosevelt (R)			46			March 4, 1905-March 4, 1909	Charles W. Fairbanks
William H. Taft (R)	1857	1930	51	Ohio	Ohio	March 4, 1909-March 4, 1913	James S. Sherman
Woodrow Wilson (D)	1856	1924	56	Va.	N.J.	March 4, 1913-March 4, 1917	Thomas R. Marshall
Woodrow Wilson (D)			60			March 4, 1917-March 4, 1921	Thomas R. Marshall
Warren G. Harding (R)	1865	1923	55	Ohio	Ohio	March 4, 1921-Aug. 2, 1923	Calvin Coolidge
Calvin Coolidge (R)	1872	1933	51	Vt.	Mass.	Aug. 3, 1923-March 4, 1925	
Calvin Coolidge (R)			52			March 4, 1925-March 4, 1929	Charles G. Dawes
Herbert Hoover (R)	1874	1964	54	Iowa	Calif.	March 4, 1929-March 4, 1933	Charles Curtis
Franklin D. Roosevelt (D)	1882	1945	51	N.Y.	N.Y.	March 4, 1933-Jan. 20, 1937	John N. Garner
Franklin D. Roosevelt (D)			55			Jan. 20, 1937-Jan. 20, 1941	John N. Garner
Franklin D. Roosevelt (D)			59			Jan. 20, 1941-Jan. 20, 1945	Henry A. Wallace
Franklin D. Roosevelt (D)			63			Jan. 20, 1945-April 12, 1945	Harry S Truman
Harry S Truman (D)	1884	1972	60	Mo.	Mo.	April 12, 1945-Jan. 20, 1949	
Harry S Truman (D)			64			Jan. 20, 1949-Jan. 20, 1953	Alben W. Barkley
Dwight D. Eisenhower (R)	1890	1969	62	Texas	N.Y.	Jan. 20, 1953-Jan. 20, 1957	Richard M. Nixon
Dwight D. Eisenhower (R)			66		Pa.	Jan. 20, 1957-Jan. 20, 1961	Richard M. Nixon
John F. Kennedy (D)	1917	1963	43	Mass.	Mass.	Jan. 20, 1961-Nov. 22, 1963	Lyndon B. Johnson
Lyndon B. Johnson (D)	1908	1973	55	Texas	Texas	Nov. 22, 1963-Jan. 20, 1965	
Lyndon B. Johnson (D)			56			Jan. 20, 1965-Jan. 20, 1969	Hubert H. Humphrey
Richard M. Nixon (R)	1913		56	Calif.	N.Y.	Jan. 20, 1969-Jan. 20, 1973	Spiro T. Agnew
Richard M. Nixon (R)			60		Calif.	Jan. 20, 1973-Aug. 9, 1974	Spiro T. Agnew / Gerald R. Ford
Gerald R. Ford (R)	1913		61	Neb.	Mich.	Aug. 9, 1974-Jan. 20, 1977	Nelson A. Rockefeller
Jimmy Carter (D)	1924		52	Ga.	Ga.	Jan. 20, 1977-Jan. 20, 1981	Walter F. Mondale
Ronald Reagan (R)	1911		69	Ill.	Calif.	Jan. 20, 1981-	George Bush

*Key to abbreviations: (D) Democrat, (D-R) Democrat-Republican, (F) Federalist, (N-R) National Republican, (R) Republican, (W) Whig

SOURCE: Joseph Nathan Kane, *Facts About the President*, revised edition, 1976

The Long Road to the White House

The choosing of a president has evolved into one of the most dramatic political events in the United States and, perhaps, in the world. Every four years for almost 200 years, the country has been offered a hectic nominating process based on rhetoric, partisan maneuvering and character analysis as ambitious politicians vie for the nation's top prize.

Although the politics, motivations and emotions underlying presidential election campaigns have remained constant, changes in the mechanisms of the battle for the presidency have occurred gradually over the course of American history, although the pace appears to have quickened since World War II.

One of the first and most important developments came about in the early part of the 19th century as more and more states decided that presidential electors should be chosen by popular vote rather than by their legislatures. As a result, the electors generally became bound by party loyalty and abandoned the practice of voting according to personal preference.

During the early years of the Republic, the parties had created an informal nominating device for choosing their presidential candidates: a caucus of each party's members in Congress. From 1796 until 1824 congressional caucuses (when a party had enough representatives to form one) chose almost all the nominees. Only twice, in 1800 and 1824, as a result of a failure of any candidate to receive a majority of electoral votes, were presidential elections decided by the House of Representatives. Even in those two cases, political parties were instrumental in the election of the president.

By 1832 all states except Maryland and South Carolina held statewide elections to choose slates of electors pledged to vote for the parties' presidential candidates.

Democratizing the Selection Process

The trend toward democratization of the presidential selection process, as evidenced by expansion of the suffrage and growing importance of the popular vote for election of the president, led to creation of the national political party nominating conventions. The convention system was begun by the Anti-Masons in 1831 and subsequently adopted by the major parties before the end of the decade.

The birth of the national conventions was a milestone in the evolution of the presidential nominating process. In his book, *Politics, Parties and Pressure Groups* (1964), political scientist V. O. Key Jr. summarized some of the major forces that brought about the rise of the convention system: "The destruction of the caucus represented more than a mere change in the method of nomination. Its replacement by the convention was regarded as the removal from power of self-appointed oligarchies that had usurped the right to nominate. The new system, the convention, gave, or so it was supposed, the mass of party members an opportunity to participate in nominations. These events occurred as the domestic winds blew in from the growing West, as the suffrage was being broadened, and as the last vestiges of the early aristocratic leadership were disappearing. Sharp alterations in the distribution of power were taking place, and they were paralleled by the shifts in methods of nomination."

The establishment of the national convention solidified the two-party system. Unlike the Founding Fathers, who were suspicious of competitive parties, some political leaders in the late 1820s and 1830s viewed favorably the existence of opposing parties. One of the most prominent of these was Martin Van Buren, a leading organizer of Democratic presidential candidate Andrew Jackson's 1828 election victory. Van Buren wrote in 1827 that "[w]e must always have party distinctions...."

Presidential Primaries

By the 1900s presidential campaigns had undergone another significant transformation as candidates began to campaign more and more on their own behalf.

At the same time the delegate selection process was revolutionized by the birth of the presidential primary election, in which delegates were elected directly by the voters. Initiated in Florida in 1904, the presidential primary by 1912 was in use in 13 states.

In his first annual message to Congress the following year, President Woodrow Wilson advocated the establishment of a national primary to select presidential candidates: "I feel confident that I do not misinterpret the wishes or the expectations of the country at which the voters of the several parties may choose their nominees for the presidency without the intervention of nominating conventions." Wilson went on to suggest the retention of conventions for the purpose of declaring the results of the primaries and formulating the parties' platforms.

Before any action was taken on Wilson's proposal, the progressive spirit that spurred the growth of presidential primaries died out. Not until after World War II, when widespread pressures for change touched both parties, especially the Democrats, was there a significant growth in presidential primaries. The most dramatic surge occurred in the 1970s. Twenty-three primaries were held in 1972, 30 in 1976 and 37 in 1980 (including the District of Columbia and Puerto Rico). While only about 40 percent of the delegates were elected from primaries to the Democratic and Republican conventions in 1968, about three-quarters of the delegates in 1980 were the product of primary elections.

The popularity of the presidential delegate selection primary had begun to wane by 1984 as several states abandoned it and no additional states adopted that method.

As presidential campaigns have lengthened, the elimination of presidential hopefuls has come earlier. It used to be that most of the candidates remained in the race until the national convention. But not since 1952 has a Democratic or Republican convention taken more than one ballot to select a nominee for president. During the opening round of the 1976 primaries, for example, six Democratic candidates withdrew from the field, while former Georgia Gov. Jimmy Carter hurdled to the front of the pack. At the same time, Republican candidate Ronald Reagan was nearly knocked out of the GOP race by a series of early primary losses. An upset victory in North Carolina rescued his flagging campaign, but it was insufficient to stop incumbent Republican President Gerald R. Ford's momentum. *(Length of presidential campaigns, box, p. 35)*

1980 Presidential Election

The 1980 primaries concluded in a manner nearly the reverse of 1976. In 1976 Jimmy Carter wrapped up the Democratic nomination in the final week of the primary season, while Republican candidate Reagan and President Ford battled on to the Republican convention. Four years later, Reagan became the almost certain nominee early in the primary campaign, while Carter — although holding more than enough delegates to win the nomination — continued to face a stiff challenge from his principal Democratic opponent, Sen. Edward M. Kennedy, D-Mass., all the way to, and even during, the party's convention in August.

The long 1980 presidential campaign ended in a landslide victory for Reagan. Official returns gave the Republican nominee an absolute majority (50.7 percent) of the popular vote and an 8,417,992-vote margin (9.7 percentage points) over Carter.

By carrying 44 states, Reagan's Electoral College advantage was even more pronounced. He won 489 electoral votes to just 49 for Carter, who carried only six states and the District of Columbia. Carter's campaign officials had feared that independent candidate John B. Anderson, R-Ill., would draw the support of enough liberal Democrats to deny the president re-election. However, Anderson did not win any states or even any state congressional districts. Even if Carter had won every vote that went to Anderson, Reagan still would have carried a majority of states, winning more than 300 electoral votes. Only 270 were needed for victory.

Magnitude of Carter Defeat

In rejecting Carter, voters for the second consecutive election turned their backs on an embattled incumbent to elect a challenger promising a fresh approach to government and a dynamic new brand of leadership. But unlike the close contest in 1976, in which Carter narrowly defeated Ford, the results in 1980 were emphatic. Since the Civil War, only two presidents — William Howard Taft in 1912 and Herbert Hoover in 1932 — had been denied re-election by larger popular vote margins than Carter. Only six incumbents in all lost re-election bids during this period.

Taft was crippled by the Republican Party split that produced the Bull Moose candidacy of Theodore Roosevelt. Taft finished third in the 1912 election, 19 percentage points behind Democratic Party winner Woodrow Wilson. Hoover unsuccessfully sought a second term in the midst of the Depression and was beaten by Democrat Franklin D. Roosevelt by 18 percentage points. Still, Hoover won more electoral votes (59) than Carter, who was the first Democratic incumbent president denied re-election since 1888. In that election Grover Cleveland was ousted by Republican Benjamin Harrison even though Cleveland ran ahead in the popular vote.

Carter's defeat underscored the Democrats' difficulty in winning presidential elections. Since the end of World War II, the Republicans had won five elections to the Democrats' four. But only twice — in 1964 and 1976 — had the Democratic candidate drawn a majority of the popular vote. Carter's percentage of the vote dropped below his 1976 share in every state by at least 2 percentage points. In nearly half the states it declined by at least 10 percentage points. Reagan easily carried every region of the country, including the keystones of Carter's triumph four years before — the industrial Northeast and the president's native South.

A variety of public opinion polls showed an unusually large number of undecided voters in the final weeks of that campaign. In addition, many Americans apparently did not vote. Only about 54 percent of the nation's voting age population of 160.5 million went to the polls, marking the fifth consecutive presidential election that the turnout had declined. The 1980 figure was less than 1 percentage point below the 1976 turnout rate of 54.4 percent, but it was the lowest turnout since 1948.

Criticism of Election Process

Many participants and observers of the U.S. presidential election process have criticized the system as much too long and expensive. Campaigns increasingly are being conducted in a media fishbowl that leaves little room for mistakes. There is little doubt that the visible, public side of campaigns has grown longer. For example, by June 1983 there already were six announced major candidates running for the Democratic nomination for president in 1984; by June 1979 there were seven announced candidates for president in the 1980 election; by June 1975 there were six announced candidates for the 1976 election; by June 1971, only one (Sen. George McGovern, D-S.D.), already was running for 1972; and by June 1967 no one had yet announced for the 1968 election.

For the 1984 presidential election, all eight Democratic candidates had announced before the campaign year began: Sen. Alan Cranston, Calif. — Feb. 2, 1983; Sen. Gary Hart, Colo. — Feb. 17; former vice president Walter F. Mondale

— Feb. 21; former Florida Gov. Reubin Askew — Feb. 23; Sen. Ernest F. Hollings, S.C. — April 18; Sen. John Glenn, Ohio — April 21; McGovern — Sept. 13; and Jesse Jackson — Nov. 3.

President Reagan announced his intention to seek another term on Jan. 29, 1984.

Observers have pointed out that the intense scrutiny may force candidates to shy away from the detailed discussion of issues, reducing the campaign to a long endurance contest that fatigues both the candidates and the voters. According to 1980 Democratic National Committee Chairman John C. White, one result has been lower and lower turnouts. "Candidates are seeking attention and are creating contrived crises," he contended. "By the time we elect a president, the people and the candidates are worn out."

White also argued that the long campaign cut into the president's ability to govern. "At some time, with this many primaries, the president must turn away from his duties" to campaign, he said.

Critics of the lengthy presidential election campaign are in general agreement that a reduction in the number of primaries, or in the length of the primary season, is needed. They argue that if there were fewer primaries there would be less incentive for the candidates to conduct such long campaigns.

Moreover, some states have discovered that primary elections are not the bonanza that they expected. Many had hoped that a primary would attract glamorous candidates and focus media attention on their states. But many of the small states that switched from caucuses to primaries in the 1970s have been disappointed. Their presidential primaries drew little attention and, when operated on a different date from the primary election for other federal as well as state offices, proved to be expensive.

GOP United Behind Reagan

Party unity during the presidential renomination process has been a consistent harbinger of success in the November general election. President Reagan in 1984 enjoyed it as much as, if not more than, any of his post-World War II predecessors.

Presidents who were secure within their own party usually got that way for a reason. Some, such as Reagan and Dwight D. Eisenhower, were father figures within their party. Others, such as Richard Nixon, managed to win rank-and-file respect without much personal popularity. Whatever the reason, it is a matter of record that the less vulnerable a president is within his own party the better his chances of winning re-election.

As the 1984 election year began, Reagan was virtually unopposed for renomination. He launched his re-election campaign Jan. 29 against the weakest primary field that any incumbent president of either party had encountered since 1956, when Eisenhower went through an entire primary season without any declared opponent appearing on a ballot against him.

Reagan's position contrasts with that of recent embattled White House incumbents. The previous two presidents, Jimmy Carter in 1980 and Gerald R. Ford in 1976, had to survive difficult primary challenges to win renomination. Nixon enjoyed a much easier time of it in 1972, but even he faced a primary challenge from two House members who represented opposite wings of the GOP. Rep. John M. Ashbrook of Ohio (1961-82) challenged Nixon

Presidents' Re-election Chances

The record of 20th century U.S. presidential elections indicates that a smooth path to renomination is essential for incumbents seeking re-election.

Every president who actively sought renomination this century was successful. And those that were virtually unopposed within their own party won another term. But all of the presidents that faced significant opposition for renomination ended up losing in the general election.

The following chart shows the presidents who sought re-election to a second term this century, whether they had "clear sailing" or "tough sledding" for renomination, and their fate in the general election.

Those with an asterisk (*) next to their name were, like Ronald Reagan, completing their first full four-year term when they sought re-election. A dash (—) indicates there were no presidential preference primaries. The primary vote for President Lyndon B. Johnson in 1964 included the vote for favorite sons and uncommitted delegate slates.

	Primary Vote	Convention Delegates	General Election Result
'Clear Sailing'			
William McKinley (1900) *	—	100%	Won
Theodore Roosevelt (1904)	—	100	Won
Woodrow Wilson (1916) *	99%	99	Won
Calvin Coolidge (1924)	68	96	Won
Franklin D. Roosevelt (1936) *	93	100	Won
" " (1940)	72	86	Won
" " (1944)	71	92	Won
Harry S Truman (1948)	64	75	Won
Dwight D. Eisenhower (1956) *	86	100	Won
Lyndon B. Johnson (1964)	88	100	Won
Richard M. Nixon (1972) *	87	99	Won
'Tough Sledding'			
William H. Taft (1912) *	34%	52%	Lost
Herbert Hoover (1932) *	33	98	Lost
Gerald R. Ford (1976)	53	53	Lost
Jimmy Carter (1980) *	51	64	Lost

from the right that year and drew 5 percent of the primary vote nationally; liberal Republican Paul N. McCloskey Jr. of California drew about 2 percent and won a lone convention delegate in New Mexico.

Party Unity and Election Success

In this century, five elected presidents have run for second terms and won. All five coasted to renomination. Four of them — William McKinley in 1900, Franklin D. Roosevelt in 1936, Eisenhower in 1956 and Nixon in 1972 — were easily re-elected. Only Woodrow Wilson, who sought re-election in 1916 — in the midst of a Republican era — had a close call. *(See box, this page)*

Presidents who were beaten for re-election nearly always had trouble first within their own party; the warning signs generally were evident long before the November election. This century's list of defeated presidents — William Howard Taft (1912), Herbert Hoover (1932), Ford (1976) and Carter — reveals that the incumbents limped into the general election campaign at the conclusion of long and bitter primary challenges.

Criticized for their supposedly incompetent leadership, Taft, Ford and Carter all drew opposition from the top names in their party. Reagan himself led the conservative opposition to Ford in 1976.

Hoover's situation in 1932 was a bit different. Saddled with the Depression, he was the unenthusiastic choice of GOP leaders. Nevertheless, an obscure former U.S. senator from Maryland, Joseph I. France, not only ran against Hoover in the primaries but actually polled more votes than the president in the preference primaries. But when France sought to use his new-found celebrity to nominate former President Calvin Coolidge at the Republican convention, party officials refused France permission to speak and had him escorted from the hall.

Reagan Decision to Run

Without a serious challenge to his renomination, Reagan could have waited much longer than Jan. 29, 1984, to declare his candidacy. Even so, Reagan's was one of the latest in years. It came almost one full year after California Sen. Alan Cranston formally became the first major Democratic contender and nearly three months after the Rev. Jesse Jackson had become the last.

Reagan launched his campaign with a four-minute nationally televised statement from the White House. In his remarks he dispelled any speculation that he might replace Vice President George Bush on the Republican ticket and laid out some of the basic themes of the forthcoming re-election campaign.

"America is back and standing tall," Reagan declared, in what was certain to be one of the major punch lines in GOP campaign speeches. The president elaborated on his re-election themes during a campaign swing in Iowa on Feb. 20, the date of the Democrats' presidential caucuses, won decisively by Mondale. In Waterloo, Reagan stressed that the country was strong again and that the nation's economic recovery was spreading "a spirit of optimism ... across our land."

Invisible Rivals

Republican Party opposition to Reagan was virtually invisible. None of the other Republicans on any of the primary ballots had the potential to cause the president any embarrassment. Reagan has four minor rivals in New Hampshire, the first primary state; in the other primary states where the filing period had ended by the beginning of March 1984 the president ran unopposed.

Reagan captured 97 percent of the vote in the party's first test of strength, a straw poll held in conjunction with the Jan. 11 precinct caucuses in Michigan. Of the rest of the vote, 2 percent went to California businessman Ben Fernandez and 1 percent to former Minnesota Gov. Harold E. Stassen. Reagan ran about as well in New Hampshire on Feb. 28.

The 76-year-old Stassen was Reagan's most recognizable rival. A perennial candidate for the White House, he mounted a serious challenge for the Republican presidential nomination in 1948 but had not won a convention delegate since 1968.

Fernandez was a fresher face, but hardly more imposing. Running in the 1980 Republican primaries as the nation's first Hispanic presidential aspirant, he had almost no impact. Conservative audiences liked to hear Fernandez tell his rags-to-riches story: from birth in a converted boxcar in the Kansas City railroad yards to a million-dollar fortune as a financial consultant. But he was hardly a hit at the polls, winning less than 25,000 of nearly 13 million votes cast in the 1980 GOP primaries.

Fernandez had claimed his campaign would mushroom into a national force if he could win at least 15 percent of the vote in New Hampshire, but Reagan loyalists had little to worry about. Not exactly one to go for the jugular, Fernandez described Reagan as one of America's greatest presidents.

Third-party Challenges

Throughout American history, the second presidential election campaign has been a disappointment for third-party and independent presidential candidates. Such movements and personalities usually have reflected momentary national or regional unease or divisions within one of the two major parties. Once the issues giving rise to these groups were resolved, and the public's interest subsided, support dropped off dramatically.

Even when conditions are ripe, third party candidates face two major hurdles in developing effective nationwide campaigns: a dearth of money — and without benefit of public financing under the Federal Election Campaign Act — and onerous state ballot access. It was a major feat, consuming enormous time and money, just for independent John B. Anderson and the Libertarian Party's presidential candidate to get on the ballot in all 50 states in 1980. In 1976 the Libertarians got their name on the presidential ballot in only 34 states. *(History of third parties, see box, p. 19)*

Anderson's Third-party Effort

In organizing his second challenge to the two-party system, Anderson hoped in 1984 to do what no significant third-party candidate had done before: maintain his popular appeal. Before Anderson, 10 third parties had drawn more than 5 percent of the vote in a presidential election. But virtually all had a quick demise after that one election.

According to Anderson, the two-party system had a "mythology and mystique" in the United States "that unfortunately has been allowed to go unchallenged." Voting habits were so entrenched that most major third-party figures, ranging from Theodore Roosevelt to George C. Wallace, bucked the system only once.

A former Republican House member from Illinois (1961-81), Anderson did not return to the GOP after his 1980 independent presidential campaign. Almost immediately he began talking about a new third party. And in 1983 he began laying the groundwork for a new campaign.

In the March-April 1983 issue of his periodic newsletter, *An Independent View*, he sketched out the reasoning for a new party. The major parties have grown sterile, he claimed — "the GOP with a narrow focus on supply-side economics and the Democrats with a preference for a reversion to old demand-side politics." Free from ties to special interests, a new party, Anderson maintained, could "dare to be different."

However, by early 1984 it was evident that Anderson would not have the impact on the presidential campaign that he had in 1980 or that Wallace had 12 years earlier. Anderson had yet to show that he could motivate a sizable constituency from the center. Even in the 1980 election, he did not come close to carrying a single state or even a single county. His best statewide showing was in Massachusetts, where he won 15.2 percent of the popular vote. His overall nationwide average was 6.6 percent of the vote.

For many voters, Anderson served merely as a handy vehicle to protest the choices offered by the two major parties. But four years later, there did not appear to be strong nationwide sentiment in favor of finding alternatives to the Republicans and the Democrats. A 1980 Election Day survey by CBS News and *The New York Times* found that 49 percent of Anderson's support came from voters who were primarily against both Reagan and President Carter, not pro-Anderson. But only 25 percent of Carter supporters and 18 percent of those who voted for Reagan said they were voting mainly against another candidate.

Less than one-third of the 5.7 million votes received by Anderson were cast by people who said they strongly favored him.

In an interview with Congressional Quarterly, Anderson dismissed the idea of another independent candidacy, saying that an isolated national campaign every four years would have a minimal influence on the governmental process. Anderson believed a third party, with candidates running at all levels, would have the opportunity to make a more significant impact on the national political scene. He tentatively named his party the National Unity Party.

One strength of an Anderson-led party was its eligibility for public financing for the presidential campaign. The Federal Election Commission (FEC) said that, on the basis of his 1980 showing, Anderson, as a third-party candidate for president, could receive up to $6 million in federal funds before the 1984 election.

The party-building process moved into full swing in June 1983. Anderson convened a group of 30 people, who constituted themselves as a steering committee for the new party. Subcommittees were formed to draft a set of principles and develop procedures for party structure, membership, funding and rules. A statement of principles was drafted and the steering committee planned to hold a convention in 1984 to choose the party's national ticket.

Anderson was expected to be the presidential nominee. No other political figure with national stature had associated himself with the new party. Anderson's running mate in 1980, former Wisconsin Gov. Patrick J. Lucey, D, endorsed the candidacy of Walter F. Mondale for the Democratic presidential nomination.

Seeking the Center

The absence of big-name support forced Anderson to talk modestly about the party's chances in 1984 and emphasize factors that might encourage its long-range success, such as the increase in recent years in the number of independent voters. Anderson also was buoyed by the British parliamentary elections in June 1983. Although it won only a handful of seats, a centrist alliance of the old Liberal and new Social Democratic parties drew 25 percent of the popular vote.

Anderson was optimistic about a similar opportunity for a centrist party in the United States. "There is an opening here like there obviously is in Great Britain," he said, "for a center party between the polar extremes of a left-wing labor party and a right-wing conservative party."

The center for Anderson meant a frugal, "pay-as-you-go" government, a restructured economy and a new concept of national security that put emphasis on the creation of a more humane society. Or, as an official in the 1980 Anderson campaign stated: "Anderson dares to wear his wallet on the right and his heart on the left."

Challenging History

But by building a party in the center, Anderson was challenging American history. Most significant third parties had occupied the fringes of the right or left, where the real passion in American politics existed.

In the 1980 general election, Anderson's support came mainly from the left. He ran best among young, well-educated, liberal Democrats and independents, with fairly strong showings in academic communities, white-collar suburbs and Yankee New England, where his roots in moderate Republicanism were more palatable to many GOP voters than Ronald Reagan's rock-ribbed conservatism.

With President Reagan's policies exerting strong emotions in the country — both for and against — Anderson was expected to have a more difficult time drawing off voters to his cause. Many of his former supporters could be expected to unite behind a Democrat with a reasonable chance of defeating Reagan, instead of forming a third party that would drain votes from the anti-Reagan effort.

Various 1983 presidential polls showed Anderson drawing 13 to 15 percent of the vote in a three-way race. But much of that support was based on familiarity with his name. In the early stages of his 1980 independent campaign Anderson had soared above 20 percent in the polls, before sinking to 6.6 percent on Election Day.

Playing the Spoiler?

One of Anderson's basic problems in 1984 is that he no longer is the "fresh face" he represented in 1980. That year he enjoyed favorable media attention after his strong showing in the early New England GOP primaries, which laid the foundation for his independent campaign. Media treatment later in 1980 was less flattering, although Anderson was viewed as the main alternative to Carter and Reagan.

But in 1984 Anderson no longer was a novel political phenomenon, and the press began to treat him more skeptically. In a June 1983 column, liberal commentator Carl T. Rowan accused Anderson of having "a lingering ego thirst" that could reduce Democratic chances of ousting Reagan. "'Spoiler,'" Rowan concluded, "is too polite a word for him."

There was little doubt that Anderson had an ample supply of political ambition. "It's exhilarating to have a national forum to express your views," he told Dartmouth political scientist Frank Smallwood in an interview published in 1983 in Smallwood's book, *The Other Candidates*. "It [the 1980 campaign] brought to a focus what I had been doing, and it gave me an outlet that I simply couldn't have found in any other way." It also was probable that another Anderson candidacy would hurt the Democrats primarily. Exit polling by ABC News on Election Day 1982 found that 67 percent of Anderson supporters voted for Democratic congressional candidates, while only 28 percent voted for Republicans.

Anderson viewed the early media reaction to his new party as totally unfair. Reagan ran for the presidency three times in 12 years without a negative media response, he claimed. "Anderson merely indicates that he will run a second time and he becomes Harold Stassen. What kind of equity is that?" Anderson asked.

Public Financing

Anderson's third-party plans were aided by two favorable developments in 1983. In February the FEC issued an advisory opinion that declared that since Anderson had received more than 5 percent of the popular vote for president in 1980 he could qualify for about $6 million in public funds in 1984, even as the nominee of a new party.

Anderson received $4.2 million in federal funds in 1980. But he got the money only after the election, when it was apparent that he had met the 5 percent threshold established by the Federal Election Campaign Act. In 1984 Anderson would receive the federal funds before the election, once his party had held its convention and won ballot positions in 10 states.

The other bit of good news came in April when the U.S. Supreme Court upheld Anderson's challenge to Ohio's early filing deadline for the general election. Although Anderson's independent campaign was launched after the state's filing deadline in 1980, he appeared on the Ohio ballot that year as a result of a favorable ruling by a U.S. district court.

The ruling was reversed by a federal appeals court after the election, causing Anderson to take his case to the Supreme Court.

Neither ruling, however, was likely to be a big help to Anderson in 1984. The Supreme Court decision clearly aided a late-starting independent — as Anderson was in 1980 — but ballot access for third parties remained difficult in many states. In North Carolina, for instance, the Legislature in 1983 raised to 37,000, from 5,000, the number of signatures needed by a third party to appear on the ballot.

And while $6 million in federal money gave Anderson the ability to mount a visible campaign, it was a drop in the bucket compared to the amount needed to compete effectively with the major parties. In 1980 the Democratic and Republican candidates each collected nearly $30 million from the federal Treasury to run their general election campaigns. The major party candidates expected to receive

Third Parties Usually Fade Rapidly

Most third-party movements are like shooting stars, shining brightly in one election and then quickly disappearing. In the last century and a half, 10 third parties — plus independent John B. Anderson in 1980 — have drawn at least 5 percent of the popular vote in a presidential election. But none of the third parties was able to maintain its foothold in the electoral process. Four had disappeared by the next election, four others drew a smaller vote total and two merged with one of the major parties.

Each of these significant third parties, except the Socialists in 1912, made its best showing in its first election. (The Socialists, led by Eugene V. Debs, first ran in 1900, winning just 0.62 percent of the vote.) The following chart lists each party's presidential candidate and the percentage of the vote the party received in that race and in the following election. A dash (—) indicates that the party had disappeared.

	Year	Percentage of Vote	Next Election
Anti-Masonic (William Wirt)	1832	7.8%	endorsed Whig
Free Soil (Martin Van Buren)	1848	10.1	4.9%
Whig-American (Millard Fillmore)	1856	21.5	—
Southern Democrats (John C. Breckinridge)	1860	18.1	—
Constitutional Union (John Bell)	1860	12.6	—
Populist (James B. Weaver)	1892	8.5	endorsed Democrat
Progressive (Bull Moose) (Theodore Roosevelt)	1912	27.4	0.2
Socialist (Eugene V. Debs)	1912	6.0	3.2
Progressive (Robert M. LaFollette)	1924	16.6	—
American Independent (George C. Wallace)	1968	13.5	1.4
John B. Anderson	1980	6.6	?

about $40 million each for the 1984 election.

Anderson denied that he would run again just to get the federal money. "It is ridiculous to run to collect about $6 million," he declared. "We raised $17 million in 1980 and we needed more." Public money in 1984 would be available to him only after his campaign was well under way. The important early groundwork would have to be funded from private contributions, which were slow in coming. Although Anderson's 1980 "National Unity Campaign" had more than 200,000 contributors, only $150,000 had been raised by his new party as of September 1983.

As an independent, Anderson talked of leading a crusade to capture the White House. As a potential third-party candidate, he talked of building a party that could have a long-range impact on the political system. "Popular acceptance comes slowly," he said. "We are making slow, steady, if unspectacular, progress."

Libertarians Fight for Respect

Although Democrats and Republicans did not begin to select their national convention delegates until early 1984, the Libertarian Party — the largest third party — by the fall of 1983 already had chosen its national ticket, adopted a platform and launched its 1984 campaign.

The party's presidential nominee was attorney David D. Bergland, 48 in 1983, of Costa Mesa, Calif. The nominee for vice president was Jim Lewis, 50 in 1983, of Old Saybrook, Conn. He was a sales representative for a bookbinding company.

The Libertarians could be forgiven if they felt like the Rodney Dangerfield of the American political system. In 1980 the Libertarian presidential ticket appeared on all 50 state ballots, raised more than $3 million and drew nearly one million votes. Yet it operated throughout the campaign in the shadow of independent presidential candidate John B. Anderson.

That could happen again in 1984. Even in the New York City hotel where their national convention was held Aug. 29-Sept. 5, 1983, the Libertarians did not enjoy top billing. The hotel marquee instead advertised a nightclub act: "La Ronde presents Paradise on Ice."

The Libertarians were following an untested route to prominence. They did not tie themselves to a famous personality or a single issue. Even the most ardent Libertarians were not sure whether the ambitious young party was on the verge of a breakthrough or was on the road to oblivion.

The party began the 1984 campaign with some obvious assets. It had a larger base of contributors (more than 20,000 names) than ever before and ballot status in 16 states, including California. The party was on the ballot in just six states at a similar stage of the 1980 campaign.

Unlike 1980, however, the Libertarians did not have anyone on the ticket who could bankroll the campaign. In 1980 one of the party's wealthiest supporters, New York chemical engineer David Koch, ran for vice president and pumped more than $2 million into the presidential campaign.

Money was not the only problem for the Libertarians. They were searching for the breakthrough that would place them in the public consciousness. In the 11-year history of the party the Libertarians had never won a governorship or any federal office. In 1982 they lost the only two state legislative seats they had held, both in Alaska.

A growing "body count" of candidates — 150 for the U.S. House in 1982 — had given the Libertarians increased visibility. But in the party's most significant 1983 race, for the Alaska governorship, the Libertarian candidate drew only 15 percent of the vote in spite of a $650,000 campaign chest. Libertarians were looking for evidence that their unconventional political philosophy would sell in a society that accepted the ambiguities and pragmatism of the two major parties.

Wide Range of Views

The keystone of libertarianism was individual liberty, but the movement encompassed a wide range of beliefs that defied easy labeling. The Libertarian hostility to taxes and devotion to a free market economy matched the most conservative Republican theme. On the other hand, their call for a sharply reduced military establishment and an end to the draft echoed the most liberal Democrat.

Distrust of the federal government was another hallmark of libertarianism. A condensed version of the party platform read: "We favor the abolition of damn near everything, we call for drastic reductions in everything else. And we refuse to pay for what's left!"

Clearly, the Libertarians were on a wavelength of their own. In no other party would Alaska have the third largest convention delegation. In no other party would a presidential contender distribute a "progressive bibliography of Austrian neo-classical free market economics."

The party was overwhelmingly white, young and middle- to upper-class. A large minority was gay, drawn by the Libertarians' accent on individual freedom and opposition to laws against victimless crimes.

Party members were well educated. According to a random sample of Libertarian activists by two Furman University political scientists, nearly half the respondents had done graduate school work. Almost one-quarter had earned doctoral degrees. The internal consistency of the Libertarian philosophy drew a wide number of adherents with backgrounds in science, mathematics and engineering.

Libertarian officials boasted of the intellectual prowess of party members. "Libertarians are by far the highest brain power group, probably in the world," said Bergland, who was the party's 1976 vice presidential candidate.

For convention delegates who wanted more than campaign clinics on public speaking and answering tough questions, there were workshops scheduled on a potpourri of

Eighth Bid for Stassen

The old political warrior Harold Stassen mounted his eighth bid for president in 1984.

His campaign, as in other recent quests for the presidency, was a far cry from the halcyon days of the 1940s when Stassen, a Republican, was the "boy wonder" of American politics and his future seemed to hold unlimited possibilities.

Stassen was elected governor of Minnesota at the age of 31, keynoted the 1940 Republican National Convention at the age of 33 and was the youngest delegate participating in the drafting of the United Nations Charter in 1945.

A major contender for the Republican presidential nomination in 1948, along with New York Gov. Thomas E. Dewey and Ohio Sen. Robert A. Taft, Stassen won four presidential primaries that year but lost the crucial Oregon primary to Dewey.

In 1948 Stassen moved his political base to Pennsylvania. He served as president of the University of Pennsylvania from 1948 to 1953. In 1952 he again entered the presidential campaign but threw his support behind Dwight D. Eisenhower at the Republican convention.

He served in top positions in the Eisenhower administration. He was in charge of the U.S. foreign aid program from 1953 to 1955 and was a special assistant to the president for disarmament questions, a position having Cabinet rank, from 1955 to 1958.

In 1956 Stassen tried unsuccessfully to have Vice President Richard Nixon removed from the ticket.

Over the next 23 years, Harold Stassen slowly became transformed into a standard political joke as he ran losing races for public office on numerous occasions. He lost bids to obtain the Pennsylvania Republican gubernatorial nomination in 1958 and 1966 and for major of Philadelphia in 1959.

He sought the Republican presidential nomination in every election since 1948 except when Presidents Eisenhower and Nixon ran for renomination (1956 and 1972). In the 1984 New Hampshire GOP presidential primary, Stassen received 2 percent of the vote.

Through all his political meanderings, Stassen achieved something that very few perennial candidates managed to do: He retained his dignity and his sense of humor. He still made good speeches, urging a moderate course for his party and accusing the Democrats of economic mismanagement.

topics ranging from an introduction to microcomputers to an exploration of the question: "Is Reagan a Keynesian?" For those party members wanting very practical information, a series of lectures were held on "How to Cut Your Taxes."

Presidential Nomination Fight

Libertarians probably had their sharpest debates on political tactics, particularly which issues to emphasize in an effort to expand the party's national base. In his quest for the 1984 nomination, Bergland accented the conservative side of the Libertarian equation. "Government is big, ugly and powerful," he told the delegates and promised to campaign throughout "Middle America" to woo disgruntled Reagan supporters.

His principal rival, Georgetown University international relations Professor Earl Ravenal, stressed the party's non-interventionist foreign policy and support of mutual nuclear disarmament. He saw a chance for the Libertarians to grab the "peace" issue and build bridges to the anti-war movement.

The 48-year-old Bergland epitomized what might be called the party's "Old Guard." A veteran party activist, he promised to adhere stricty to the platform and to concentrate on grass-roots party-building activities.

A more recent convert to the party, Ravenal argued for a bolder national campaign that would exploit his ties to major media outlets in the East. "The only issue now at stake," he told the delegates, "is the stature of our party in the American scene. Are we going to shrink to a mere parody of a political party or are we going to carry the libertarian message to a broad sweep of the American people?"

The two sides were nearly evenly divided. Boosted by a strong vote in the delegations from the Sun Belt states, Bergland won with a bare majority on the fourth ballot.

His nomination capped a hectic week of politicking. Florida radio talk show host Gene Burns had been viewed as the consensus choice for the nomination, but dropped out of the race on the eve of the convention, citing inadequate financial support from party officials.

Presidential Backgrounds

Most presidents have come to the White House with long public careers behind them, but there have been notable exceptions. Zachary Taylor's only career was the Army; he went straight from the service to the White House.

In the 19th century, men changed public jobs frequently as they prepared for the presidency. James Madison, Thomas Jefferson and Andrew Jackson each held nearly a dozen public posts before reaching the White House. In recent years, however, presidents have done fewer things. Gerald R. Ford, for example, had held no public position except U.S. representative. But he was a representative for 25 years.

The field of candidates for the 1980 presidential nomination continued a trend that first appeared in the 1976 campaign — the re-emergence of governors as leading contenders in the nomination sweepstakes.

For 16 years, starting with John F. Kennedy's ascension from the Senate to the White House in 1960 until 1976, senators dominated presidential compaigns. During that time every single major party nominee was a senator or former senator.

That represented an about-face from earlier times. In the 36 years before Kennedy, the two major parties nominated only one man who ever served in the Senate. And that man, Harry S Truman, was already president when he was nominated.

While there was no shortage of senators in the 1976 campaign it was the governors that attracted the most attention. Former California Governor Ronald Reagan came close to depriving incumbent Gerald R. Ford of the Republican presidential nomination. The Democratic nominee, former Georgia Governor Jimmy Carter, faced a dramatic last-minute challenge from the governor of California at the time, Jerry Brown.

Carter, Reagan and Brown were candidates again in 1980. Former Texas Governor John Connally, who had joined the field of those seeking the Republican nomination, dropped out of the race March 9.

The fact that Carter and Reagan emerged as the Democratic and Republican nominees was consistent with the fads and trends through American history that have marked the public's ideas about the proper training for a president.

A look backward to the 18th century shows just how often the fashion has changed. The nation has never made up its mind what background a president ought to have.

Paths of Glory

The earliest tradition developed around the secretary of state. The secretary of state was considered the preeminent Cabinet officer and thus the most important man in the executive branch after the president. Washington's first secretary of state was Thomas Jefferson. Although Jefferson left the Cabinet early in Washington's second term, he went on to become leader of the newly formed Democratic Republican Party and its candidate for president in 1796, 1800 and 1804. Losing to John Adams in 1796, Jefferson came back to win four years later.

In turn, Jefferson's secretary of state, James Madison, won the presidency in 1808. Madison had been a close ally of Jefferson's in the political struggles of the 1790s and served throughout Jefferson's two presidential terms as secretary of state (1801-09). During his first term as president, Madison appointed fellow Virginian James Monroe as his secretary of state. And following in what was rapidly becoming a tradition, Monroe went on to the presidency in 1816, serving two terms (1817-25).

Throughout Monroe's terms, the secretary of state was John Quincy Adams, son of former President John Adams. When Monroe's second term was nearing its end, five major candidates entered the race to succeed him. Three were Cabinet officers, including Adams.

None of the four remaining candidates (one had withdrawn) managed to acquire a majority in the Electoral College and the House then chose Secretary of State Adams.

Adams was the last secretary of state to go directly from his Cabinet post to the White House. After him, only two secretaries of state made it to the White House at all — Martin Van Buren, who was secretary of state from 1829 to 1831 and president from 1837 to 1841, and James Buchanan, who served as secretary of state under President James K. Polk (1845-49) and as president from 1857 to 1861.

Two other institutions died at approximately the same time as the Cabinet tradition — the Virginia dynasty and "King Caucus." After the four Virginians who occupied the presidency during the first 36 years of the Republic — Washington, Jefferson, Madison and Monroe — there have been no presidents elected who were both born in and made their careers in the state. John Tyler was a Virginian, but succeeded to the presidency from the vice presidency in 1841 and was not renominated. Three other presidents were born in Virginia but made their careers elsewhere — William Henry Harrison, Zachary Taylor and Woodrow Wilson.

"King Caucus" was a derogatory reference to the congressional party caucuses that met throughout the early 1800s to designate presidential nominees. During its heyday, the Washington-centered mentality of the caucus had virtually guaranteed that Cabinet officers should be among those most often nominated by the party in power. But the caucus came under attack as being undemocratic and unrepresentative, and ceased to function as a presidential nominating mechanism after 1824. It was replaced by the national conventions, bodies which are not connected with Congress and which have never met in the national capital.

Men on Horseback

The next cycle of American politics, from the presidency of Andrew Jackson (1829-37) to the Civil War, saw a variety of backgrounds qualify candidates for the presidency. One of the most prevalent was the military. Andrew Jackson, who ran in 1824 (unsuccessfully), 1828 and 1832, was a general in the War of 1812, gaining near-heroic stature by his defeat of the British at the Battle of New Orleans in January 1815. Like most military officers who have risen to the presidency, however, Jackson was only a part-time military man. As a politician, Jackson had served in the U.S. House during George Washington's presidency and in the Senate during John Adams' administration, as well as later, under Monroe and John Quincy Adams. Only Presidents Taylor, Grant and Eisenhower were career military officers.

Other candidates during this era who were or had been military officers included William Henry Harrison, a Whig candidate in 1836 and 1840; Zachary Taylor, the Whig nominee in 1848; Winfield Scott, the 1852 Whig candidate; Franklin Pierce, the Democratic nominee in 1852, and John Charles Fremont in 1856, the Republican Party's first presidential candidate. Thus, from 1824 through 1856, all but one presidential election featured a major candidate with a military background.

Like Jackson, Harrison had a mixed military and political career. A member of a distinguished Virginia family, Harrison was the son of a signer of the Declaration of Independence. He served in Congress during the John Adams administration and again under Madison, Monroe, and John Quincy Adams. In between, he battled the Indians and the British during the War of 1812.

Taylor and Scott were both career military men who led conquering armies in the Mexican War. Pierce also had a command in the Mexican War, although he had been primarily a politician, with service in both the House and the Senate during the 1830s and 1840s. Fremont was famous as an explorer as well as for a dashing military campaign through California during the Mexican War. Later, he was an early U.S. senator from California (1850-51).

The smoldering political conflicts of the 1840s and 1850s probably contributed to the naming of military men for the presidency. Generals had usually escaped involvement in national politics and had avoided taking stands on the issues that divided the country — slavery, expansion, the currency and the tariff. In 1840, for example, the Whigs adopted no platform or statement of principles, simply nominating Harrison and assuming his personal popularity plus the resentments against the incumbent Democratic administration of Martin Van Buren would suffice for Whig victory. They were right.

Later on, the nature of the Civil War almost automatically led at least one of the parties to choose a military officer as presidential standard-bearer every four years. To have been on the "right" side during the war — fighting to save the union and destroy slavery — was a major political asset in the North and Middle West, where tens of thousands of war veterans were effectively organized in the Grand Army of the Republic (GAR). The GAR became part of the backbone of the Republican Party during the last third of the 19th century.

Consequently, it became customary for Republicans to have a Civil War officer at the head of their ticket. With the exception of James G. Blaine in 1884, every Republican presidential nominee from 1868 to 1900 had served as an officer in the Union Army during the Civil War. Blaine, who had spent the Civil War years as a Maine state legislator and a member of the U.S. House, lost the election.

Of all the Republican nominees, however, only Grant was a professional military man. The others — Rutherford B. Hayes in 1876, James A. Garfield in 1880, Benjamin Harrison in 1888 and 1892 and William McKinley in 1896 and 1900 — were civilians who volunteered for service in the Civil War. Two of them — Hayes and Garfield — were elected to the House while serving in the Army. At the time of their presidential nominations, Hayes was governor of Ohio, Garfield was minority leader of the U.S. House and a senator-elect, Harrison was an ex-senator from Indiana and McKinley was a former governor of Ohio.

The Democrats, who had been split over the war, had few prominent military veterans to choose from. Only twice between 1860 and 1900 did the Democrats pick a Civil War officer as their nominee. In 1864, during the Civil War, the Democrats nominated Gen. George B. McClellan, the Union military commander who had fallen out with President Lincoln. And in 1880, Gen. Winfield Scott Hancock of Pennsylvania was the Democrats' choice.

The Empire State

Otherwise, Democrats tended to favor governors or former governors of New York. Their 1868 nominee was Horatio Seymour, who had been governor of New York in 1853-55 and again 1863-65. In 1876 they chose Samuel J. Tilden, New York's reform governor who was battling Tammany Hall. And in 1884, Grover Cleveland, another New York reform governor, captured the Democratic nomination. He went on to become the first Democrat to win the White House in 28 years. Cleveland was again the Democratic nominee in 1888 and 1892.

Besides being the most populous state, New York was a swing state in presidential politics. During the period from Reconstruction through the turn of the century, most Southern states voted Democratic, while the Republicans usually carried Pennsylvania, the Midwest and New England. A New Yorker appeared as the nominee for president or vice president of at least one of the major parties in every single election from 1868 through 1892.

This general tradition was maintained through the candidacy of Thomas E. Dewey, Republican governor of New York, in 1948. Only twice between 1868 and 1948 was there no New Yorker on the national ticket of at least one of the major parties — for president or vice president.

Once, in 1944, both major party presidential nominees, Democrat Franklin D. Roosevelt and Republican Dewey, were selected from New York.

Since 1948, however, the only New Yorker to be nominated by a major party for president or vice president was Rep. William E. Miller, R-N.Y. (1951-65), the Republican vice presidential nominee in 1964. Eisenhower in 1952 and Nixon in 1968 were technically residents of New York, but they were generally identified with other states. Gerald R. Ford's vice president, Nelson Rockefeller, was a former governor of New York, but he was appointed to the vice presidency. He was not asked to be on the ticket when Ford ran in 1976.

Another major swing state in the years from the Civil War through the First World War was Indiana. And in most elections, a prominent Indianan found his way onto one of the major party's national tickets. In the 13 presidential elections between 1868 and 1916, an Indianan appeared 10 times on at least one of the major parties' national tickets. However, since 1916 only one Indianan, Wendell Willkie in 1940, has been a major party's nominee.

The Governors

From 1900 to 1956, Democrats tended to favor governors for the presidential nomination, a trend that may be making a comeback. Democratic governors who received their party's presidential nomination included Woodrow Wilson of New Jersey in 1912, James M. Cox of Ohio in 1920, Alfred E. Smith of New York in 1928, Franklin D. Roosevelt of New York in 1932 and Adlai E. Stevenson of Illinois in 1952.

During the same period, 1900 to 1956, Republican presidential nominees had a wide variety of backgrounds. There were two Cabinet officers (Secretary of War William Howard Taft in 1908 and Secretary of Commerce Herbert Hoover in 1928), a Supreme Court justice (Charles Evans Hughes in 1916), a U.S. senator (Warren G. Harding in 1920), two governors (Alfred M. Landon of Kansas in 1936 and Thomas E. Dewey of New York in 1944 and 1948), a private lawyer (Wendell Willkie in 1940) and a general (Eisenhower in 1952 and 1956). Calvin Coolidge of Massachusetts, the 1924 nominee, and Theodore Roosevelt of New York, the 1904 nominee, both of whom succeeded to the presidency from the vice presidency, had been governors of their respective states. As noted, both Carter and Reagan in 1980 had been governors.

Curiously, the two world wars did not produce a plethora of military candidates for the presidency. The only general besides Eisenhower who made a strong bid for a presidential nomination was Gen. Leonard Wood, who had commands in the Spanish-American War and the First World War. Wood led on five ballots at the 1920 Republican national convention before losing out on the 10th ballot to Warren G. Harding. Otherwise, only a few military men have even been mentioned for the presidency in the 20th century — most notably Gen. Douglas MacArthur in the 1940s and 1950s — and they got little support at national conventions.

Former Vice Presidents

A sudden change took place in 1960 with the nomination of Kennedy, a senator, and Nixon, a former senator and sitting vice president. It was the first time since 1860 and only the second time in the history of party nominating conventions that an incumbent vice president was chosen for the presidency (the others were Democrat Martin Van Buren in 1836 and John C. Breckinridge, the choice of the Southern Democratic faction in 1860). And it was only the second time in the 20th century that an incumbent U.S. senator was nominated for the presidency (Republican Warren G. Harding was the first, in 1920). In the 19th century the phenomenon was also rare, with National Republican Henry Clay in 1832, Democrat Lewis Cass in 1848 and Democrat Stephen A. Douglas in 1860 the only incumbent senators nominated for president by official party conventions. Republican James A. Garfield was a senator-elect at the time of his election in 1880.

The nomination of Nixon, like the nomination of Kennedy, was a sign of things to come. Beginning in 1960 the vice presidency, like the Senate, became a presidential training ground. Vice President Hubert H. Humphrey was chosen by the Democrats for president in 1968. Vice President Spiro T. Agnew (R 1969-73) was the leading contender for the 1976 Republican presidential nomination before his resignation in October 1973. Even defeated vice presidential nominees have been considered for the nomination — witness Henry Cabot Lodge Jr. of Massachusetts in 1964, Edmund S. Muskie of Maine in 1972, Sargent Shriver of Maryland in 1976, and Bob Dole of Kansas in 1980.

What They Did Before They Became President

Most presidents have come to the White House with long public careers behind them, but there have been notable exceptions. Zachary Taylor's only career was the Army; he went straight from the service to the White House.

In the 19th century, men changed public jobs frequently as they prepared for the presidency. James Madison, Thomas Jefferson and Andrew Jackson each held nearly a dozen public posts before reaching the White House. In recent years, however, presidents have done fewer things. Gerald R. Ford, for example, had held no public position except U.S. representative. But he was a representative for 25 years. Ronald Reagan served two four-year terms as governor of California.

Following are the public jobs each president held in his pre-presidential years:

George Washington: 1759-74, Virginia House of Burgesses; 1774-75, delegate to Continental Congress; 1775, commander of colonial Army; 1787, delegate to constitutional convention; 1789-97, president.

John Adams: 1771, Massachusetts colonial legislature; 1774-75, Continental Congress; 1778, minister to France; 1779, delegate to Massachusetts constitutional convention; 1780, minister to the Netherlands; 1785, minister to Great Britain; 1785-97, vice president; 1797-1801, president.

Thomas Jefferson: 1769-74, Virginia House of Burgesses; 1775, delegate to Continental Congress; 1775, delegate to Virginia Convention; 1776, delegate to Continental

Congress; 1776-79, Virginia House of Delegates; 1779-81, governor of Virginia; 1784-89, envoy and minister to France; 1789-93, secretary of state; 1797-1801, vice president; 1801-09, president.

James Madison: 1774, Colonial Committee of Safety; 1776, delegate to Virginia Convention; 1776-77, Virginia House of Delegates; 1777, Virginia State Council; 1778, Virginia Executive Council; 1779-83, Continental Congress; 1784-86, Virginia House of Delegates; 1786-88, Continental Congress; 1787, delegate to constitutional convention; 1789-97, U.S. House of Representatives (Va.); 1801-09, secretary of state; 1809-17, president.

James Monroe: 1780, Virginia House of Delegates; 1781-83, governor's council; 1783-86, Continental Congress; 1786, Virginia House of Delegates; 1787, delegate to constitutional convention; 1790-94, U.S. Senate (Va.); 1794-96, minister to France; 1799-1803, governor of Virginia; 1803, minister to England and France; 1804, minister to Spain; 1810, Virginia House of Delegates; 1811-17, secretary of state; 1814-15, secretary of war; 1817-25, president.

John Quincy Adams: 1794, minister to Netherlands; 1796, minister to Portugal; 1797, minister to Prussia; 1802, Massachusetts Senate; 1803-08, U.S. Senate (Mass.); 1809-14, minister to Russia; 1815-17, minister to England; 1817-25, secretary of state; 1825-29, president.

Andrew Jackson: 1788, solicitor for western North Carolina; 1796, delegate to Tennessee constitutional convention; 1796-97, U.S. House (Tenn.); 1797-98, U.S. Senate; 1798-1804, Tennessee Supreme Court; 1807, Tennessee Senate; 1812, commander, U.S. militia; 1814, general U.S. Army; 1821, governor of Florida; 1823-25, U.S. Senate (Tenn.); 1829-37, president.

Martin Van Buren: 1813-20, New York Senate; 1815-19, New York attorney general; 1821-28, U.S. Senate; 1829, governor of New York; 1829, secretary of state; 1831, minister to Great Britain; 1833-37, vice president; 1837-41, president.

William Henry Harrison: 1798-99, secretary of Northwest Territory; 1799-1800, U.S. House (territorial delegate); 1801-13, territorial governor of Indiana; 1812-14, general, U.S. Army; 1816-19, U.S. House (Ohio); 1819-21, Ohio Senate; 1825-28, minister to Colombia; 1841, president.

John Tyler: 1811-16, Virginia House of Delegates; 1816, Virginia State Council; 1817-21, U.S. House (Va.); 1823-25, Virginia House of Delegates; 1825-27, governor of Virginia; 1827-36, U.S. Senate (Va.); 1839, Virginia House of Delegates; 1841, vice president; 1841-45, president.

James Knox Polk: 1821-23, chief clerk, Tennessee Senate; 1823-25, Tennessee House; 1825-39, U.S. House (Tenn.); 1839-41, governor of Tennessee; 1841-45, president.

Zachary Taylor: 1808-49, U.S. Army; 1849-50, president.

Millard Fillmore: 1828-31, New York Assembly; 1833-35, U.S. House (N.Y.); 1837-43, U.S. House (N.Y.); 1848-49, New York controller; 1849-50, vice president; 1850-53, president.

Franklin Pierce: 1829-33, New Hampshire House; 1833-37, U.S. House (N.H.); 1837-42, U.S. Senate (N.H.); 1850, New Hampshire constitutional convention; 1853-57, president.

James Buchanan: 1814-15, Pennsylvania House; 1821-31, U.S. House (Pa.); 1832-33, minister to Russia; 1834-45, U.S. Senate (Pa.); 1845-49, secretary of state; 1853, minister to Great Britain; 1857-61, president.

Abraham Lincoln: 1833, postmaster, New Salem, Illinois; 1835-36, Illinois General Assembly; 1847-49, U.S. House (Ill.); 1861-65, president.

Andrew Johnson: 1828-29, alderman, Greeneville, Tenn.; 1830-33, mayor, Greeneville, Tenn.; 1835-37, Tennessee House; 1839-41, Tennessee House; 1841, Tennessee Senate; 1843-53, U.S. House (Tenn.); 1853-57, governor of Tennessee; 1857-62, U.S. Senate (Tenn.); 1862-65, military governor of Tennessee; 1865, vice president; 1865-69, president.

Ulysses S. Grant: 1843-54, U.S. Army; 1861-65, general, U.S. Army; 1867-68, secretary of war; 1869-77, president.

Rutherford B. Hayes: 1857-59, Cincinnati city solicitor; 1865-67, U.S. House (Ohio); 1868, governor of Ohio; 1876-77, governor of Ohio; 1877-81, president.

James A. Garfield: 1859, Ohio Senate; 1863-80, U.S. House (Ohio); 1881, president.

Chester A. Arthur: 1871-78, collector for Port of New York; 1881, vice president; 1881-85, president.

Grover Cleveland: 1863-65, assistant district attorney of Erie County, N.Y.; 1871-73, sheriff of Erie County, N.Y.; 1882, mayor of Buffalo, N.Y.; 1883-85, governor of New York; 1885-89, president; 1893-97, president.

Benjamin Harrison: 1864-68, reporter of decisions, Indiana Supreme Court; 1879, member, Mississippi River Commission; 1881-87, U.S. Senate (Ind.); 1889-93, president.

William McKinley: 1869-71, prosecutor, Stark County, Ohio; 1877-83, U.S. House (Ohio); 1885-91, U.S. House (Ohio); 1892-96, governor of Ohio; 1897-1901, president.

Theodore Roosevelt: 1882-84, New York State Assembly; 1889-95, U.S. Civil Service Commission; 1895, president of New York City board of police commissioners; 1897, assistant secretary of the Navy; 1898, U.S. Army; 1899-1901, governor of New York; 1901, vice president; 1901-09, president.

William Howard Taft: 1881-82, assistant prosecutor, Cincinnati; 1887, assistant city solicitor, Cincinnati; 1887-90, Cincinnati Superior Court; 1890-92, U.S. solicitor general; 1892-1900, U.S. Circuit Court; 1900-01, president of Philippines Commission; 1901, governor general, Philippine Islands; 1904-08, secretary of war; 1907, provisional governor of Cuba; 1909-13, president.

Woodrow Wilson: 1911-13, governor of New Jersey; 1913-21, president.

Warren G. Harding: 1895, auditor of Marion County, Ohio; 1899-1903, Ohio Senate; 1904-05, lieutenant governor of Ohio; 1915-21, U.S. Senate (Ohio); 1921-23, president.

Calvin Coolidge: 1899, city council of Northampton, Mass.; 1900-01, city solicitor of Northampton, Mass.; 1903-04, clerk of the courts, Hampshire County, Mass.; 1907-08, Massachusetts House; 1910-11, mayor of Northampton, Mass.; 1912-15, Massachusetts Senate; 1916-18, lieutenant governor of Massachusetts; 1919-20, governor of Massachusetts; 1921-23, vice president; 1923-29, president.

Herbert Hoover: 1914-15, chairman of American Relief Committee in London; 1915-18, chairman, Commission for the Relief of Belgium; 1917-19, U.S. food administrator; 1919, chairman, Supreme Economic Conference in Paris; 1920, chairman, European Relief Council; 1921-28, secretary of commerce; 1929-33, president.

Franklin D. Roosevelt: 1911-13, New York Senate; 1913-20, assistant secretary of the Navy; 1929-33, governor of New York; 1933-45, president.

Harry S Truman: 1926-34, administrative judge, court of Jackson County, Missouri; 1935-45, U.S. Senate; 1945, vice president; 1945-53, president.

Dwight D. Eisenhower: 1915-48, U.S. Army; 1950-52, commander of NATO forces in Europe; 1953-61, president.

John F. Kennedy: 1947-53, U.S. House (Mass.); 1953-61, U.S. Senate (Mass.); 1961-63, president.

Lyndon B. Johnson: 1935-37, Texas director of National Youth Administration; 1937-48, U.S. House (Texas); 1949-61, U.S. Senate (Texas); 1961-63, vice president; 1963-69, president.

Richard M. Nixon: 1947-51, U.S. House (Calif.); 1951-53, U.S. Senate (Calif.); 1953-61, vice president; 1969-74, president.

Gerald R. Ford: 1949-73, U.S. House (Mich.); 1973-74, vice president; 1974-77, president.

Jimmy Carter: 1955-62, chairman, Sumter County (Ga.) Board of Education; 1963-67, Georgia Senate; 1971-75, governor of Georgia; 1977-81, president.

Ronald Reagan: 1942-46, Army Air Corps; 1967-75, governor of California; 1981- , president.

Presidential Primaries

Presidential primaries originated as an outgrowth of the progressive movement in the early 20th century. Progressives, populists, and reformers in general at the turn of the century were fighting state and municipal corruption. They objected to the links between political bosses and big business and advocated returning the government to the people.

Part of this "return to the people" was the inauguration of primary elections, wherein candidates for office would be chosen by the voters of their party rather than by what were looked upon as boss-dominated conventions. It was only a matter of time before the idea spread from state and local elections to presidential contests. Since there was no provision for a nationwide primary, state primaries were initiated to choose delegates to the national party conventions (delegate selection primaries), and to register voters' preferences on their parties' eventual presidential nominees (preference primaries).

Florida enacted the first presidential primary law in 1901. The law gave party officials an option of holding a party primary to choose any party candidate for public office, as well as delegates to the national conventions. However, there was no provision for placing names of presidential candidates on the ballot — either in the form of a preference vote or with information indicating the preference of the candidates for convention delegates.

Impact of Progressive Movement

Wisconsin's progressive Republican politician, Gov. Robert M. La Follette, gave a major boost to the presidential primary following the 1904 Republican national convention. It was at that convention that the credentials of La Follette's progressive delegation were rejected and a regular Republican delegation was seated from Wisconsin. Angered by what he considered his unfair treatment, La Follette returned to his home state and began pushing for a presidential primary law. The result was the Wisconsin law of 1905 providing for the mandatory direct election of national convention delegates. The law, however, did not include a provision for indicating delegate preference for presidential candidates.

Pennsylvania closely followed Wisconsin (in 1906) with a statute providing that each candidate for delegate to a national convention could have printed beside his name on the official primary ballot the name of the presidential candidate he would support at the convention. However, no member of either party exercised this option in the 1908 primary.

La Follette's sponsorship of the delegate selection primary helped make the concept part of the progressive political program. The growth of the progressive movement rapidly resulted in the enactment of presidential primary laws in other states.

The next step in presidential primaries — the preferential vote for president — took place in Oregon. There, in 1910, Sen. Jonathan Bourne, R (1907-13), a progressive Republican colleague of La Follette (then a senator), sponsored a referendum to establish a presidential preference primary, with delegates legally bound to support the winner of the preference primary.

By 1912, with Oregon in the lead, 12 states had enacted presidential primary laws that provided for either direct election of delegates, a preferential vote, or both. The number had expanded to 26 states by 1916.

Primaries and Conventions

The first major test of the impact of presidential primary laws — in 1912 — demonstrated that victories in the primaries did not ensure a candidate's nomination at the convention. Former President Theodore Roosevelt, campaigning in 12 Republican primaries, won nine of them, including a defeat of incumbent Republican President William Howard Taft in Taft's home state of Ohio. Roosevelt lost only three — to Taft by a narrow margin in Massachusetts and to La Follette in North Dakota and in La Fol-

---

Sources

James W. Davis. *Presidential Primaries: Road to the White House.* New York: Thomas Y. Crowell Co., 1967.

Richard M. Scammon. *America Votes 1956-57.* New York: The Macmillan Co., 1958. *America Votes 4*, Pittsburgh: University of Pittsburgh Press, 1962. *America Votes 6, America Votes 8, America Votes 10, America Votes 12.* Washington, D.C.: Congressional Quarterly Inc., 1966, 1970, 1973, 1977; *America Votes 14*, Washington, D.C.: Elections Research Center, 1981.

Types of Primaries and Procedures

Presidential primaries consist of two basic types. One is the presidential preference primary in which voters vote directly for the person they wish to be nominated for president. The second type is the delegate selection primary in which voters elect delegates to the national conventions.

States may use various combinations of these methods:

• A state may have a preference vote but choose delegates at party conventions. The preference vote may or may not be binding on the delegates.

• A state may combine the preference and delegate selection primaries by electing delegates pledged or favorable to a candidate named on the ballot. However, under this system, state party organizations may run unpledged slates of delegates.

• A state may have an advisory preference vote and a separate delegate selection vote in which delegates may be listed as either pledged to a candidate, favorable or unpledged.

• A state may have a mandatory preference vote with a separate delegate selection vote. In these cases, the delegates are required to support the preference primary winner.

For those primaries in which the preference vote is binding upon delegates, state laws may vary as to the number of ballots through which delegates at the convention may remain committed.

Most primary states hold presidential preference votes, in which voters choose among the candidates who have qualified for the ballot in their states. Although preference votes may be binding or non-binding, in most states the vote is binding on the delegates, who either are elected in the primary itself or chosen outside of it by a caucus process, by a state committee or by the candidates who have qualified to win delegates.

Delegates may be bound for as short as one ballot or as long as a candidate remains in the race. Party rules in effect in 1980 required delegates to be bound for one ballot unless released by the candidate they were elected to support. The rule was repealed for 1984.

Until 1980 the Republicans had a rule requiring delegates bound to a specific candidate by state law in primary states to vote for that candidate at the convention regardless of their personal presidential preferences. That rule was repealed at the July 1980 convention.

There are a variety of ways in which delegates from primary states are allocated to candidates.

Most of the methods are based on the preference vote — proportional representation, statewide winner-take-all (in which the candidate winning the most votes statewide wins all the delegates), congressional district and statewide winner-take-all (in which the high vote-getter in a district wins that district's delegates and the high vote-getter statewide wins all the at-large delegates) or some combination of the three. Still another method is the selection of individual delegates in a "loophole" primary. Then the preference vote is either non-binding, or there is no preference vote at all — the case in 1980 with the Republican primaries in New York, Mississippi and the District of Columbia.

In the proportional representation system, the qualifying threshold for candidates to win delegates can vary.

In 1980 Democratic rules set the threshold in congressional districts at a range of 15 to 25 percent of the vote but generally no lower than 15 percent, and for statewide at-large delegates and an expanded 10 percent "bonus" group of party and elected officials who were delegates at 15 to 20 percent of the statewide vote.

The Republicans allow the primary states to set their own thresholds, which in many states in 1980 were lower than the Democrats'. In Massachusetts, for example, a GOP candidate had to receive only 2.4 percent of the vote in order to win a delegate.

In nearly half the primary states, major candidates are placed on the ballot by the secretary of state or a special nominating committee. The consent of the candidate is required in only three states — Kentucky, Michigan and North Carolina.

Elsewhere, candidates must take the initiative to get on the ballot. The filing requirements range from sending a letter of candidacy to election officials — the case in Puerto Rico — to filing petitions signed by a specified number of registered voters and paying a filing fee — the case in Alabama.

On many primary ballots, voters have the opportunity to mark a line labeled "uncommitted" if they do not prefer any of the candidates. In 1976 an "uncommitted" line appeared on the ballot in more than a dozen primary states. Few voters marked it in the early primaries, but later it was used by supporters of Democrats Hubert Humphrey, Minn., and Edmund G. Brown Jr., Calif., to show support for them. Humphrey never entered the race, while Brown launched his drive too late to make the ballot in most primaries.

Democrats require states to set their filing deadlines 30 to 90 days before the election. Delegates must declare presidential preference or uncommitted status. Republicans have no deadline and delegates are not required to declare preference.

---

lette's home state of Wisconsin.

Despite this impressive string of primary victories, however, the Republican National Convention rejected Roosevelt in favor of Taft. The Republican National Committee, which organized the convention, and the convention's credentials committee, which ruled on contested delegates, both were dominated by Taft supporters. Moreover, Taft was backed by many state organizations, especially in the South, where most delegates were chosen by caucuses or conventions dominated by party leaders.

On the Democratic side, the primaries were more closely connected with the results of the convention. New Jersey Gov. Woodrow Wilson and Speaker of the House Champ Clark of Missouri were closely matched in total primary votes, with Wilson only 29,632 votes ahead of Clark. Wilson emerged with the nomination after a long struggle with Clark at the convention.

Likewise in 1916, Democratic primary results foreshadowed the winner of the nomination. However, Wilson was then the incumbent president and had no major opposition for renomination. But once again Republican presidential primaries had little to do with the nominating process at the convention. The eventual nominee, U.S. Supreme Court Justice Charles Evans Hughes, won only two primaries.

In 1920 presidential primaries did not play a major role in determining the winner of either party's nomination. Democrat James M. Cox, the eventual nominee, ran in only one primary, his home state of Ohio. Most of the Democratic primaries featured favorite son candidates or write-in votes. And at the convention, Democrats took 44 ballots to make their choice.

Similarly, the main entrants in the Republican presidential primaries that year failed to capture their party's nomination. Sen. Warren G. Harding of Ohio, the compromise choice, won the primary in his home state but lost badly in Indiana and garnered only a handful of votes elsewhere. The three leaders in the primaries — Sen. Hiram Johnson, of California, Gen. Leonard Wood of New Hampshire and Illinois Gov. Frank O. Lowden — all lost out in the end.

Revival of Interest

After the first wave of enthusiasm for presidential primaries in the 1910s, interest waned. By 1935 eight states had repealed their presidential primary laws.

The diminution of reform zeal during the 1920s and the preoccupation of the country with the Great Depression in the 1930s and then World War II were leading factors in this decline. Also, party leaders were not enthusiastic about primaries; the cost of conducting them was relatively high, both for the candidates and the states; many primaries were ignored by presidential candidates; and there was often low voter participation.

But after World War II, interest picked up again. Some politicians with presidential ambitions, knowing the party leadership was not enthusiastic about their candidacies, entered the primaries to try to generate a bandwagon effect. In 1948, Harold Stassen, Republican governor of Minnesota from 1939 to 1943, entered Republican presidential primaries in opposition to the Republican organization and was able to make some dramatic headway before losing to Gov. Thomas E. Dewey, R, of New York in Oregon. And in 1952 Tennessee Sen. Estes Kefauver, D (1949-63), riding a wave of public recognition as head of a Senate Organized Crime Investigating Committee, challenged Democratic Party leaders by winning several primaries, including an upset of President Truman in New Hampshire. The Eisenhower-Taft struggle for the Republican Party nomination that year also stimulated interest in the primaries.

Sen. John F. Kennedy, D-Mass., in 1960, Sen. Barry M. Goldwater, R-Ariz., in 1964, Richard M. Nixon, R, in 1968, Sen. George S. McGovern, D-S.D., in 1972, and former Georgia Gov. Jimmy Carter, D, in 1976 — all party presidential nominees — were able to use the primaries to show their vote-getting and organizational abilities.

With the growing demand for political reform in the 1960s and early 1970s, the presidential primaries became more popular as a route to the nomination. The revival of the old progressive reformist faith that primaries would allow the people to choose their own leaders made participation in primaries almost mandatory for anyone seeking a presidential nomination. By 1976 26 states plus the District of Columbia held some variation of the presidential preference primary. Also, in Alabama, New York and Texas, delegates to the national party conventions were elected in primaries, but none of these states provided for a specific expression statewide of presidential preference by the voter.

Primary Growth, Turnout

With a record 37 presidential primaries in 1980, the opportunity for mass participation in the nominating process was greater than ever before. But as in 1976 it was the voters in the early primary states who had the most impact. As the number of primaries grew, the importance of the early ones increased.

There were seven more primaries in 1980 than in 1976, with Connecticut, Kansas, Louisiana, Mississippi (Republicans only), New Mexico, Puerto Rico and South Carolina (Republicans only) joining the flock. The more than three dozen primaries were compressed into a 14-week period with most of the later elections scheduled on the same dates. As a result, it was New Hampshire and other early primary states such as Massachusetts, Florida and Illinois that were the focus of attention.

Presidential campaigns have grown so long that the first indications of candidate strength no longer were occurring in New Hampshire but in the myriad straw polls and public opinion surveys that were taken in the year before the election.

In 1984 some states reverted to caucuses, and the number of delegate selection primaries dropped to 25.

One of the major factors in the growth of primaries has been the belief that they would greatly increase mass participation in the nominating process.

But reality has not matched expectations. There were six more preference primaries in 1976 than 1972, but the nationwide turnout for Democratic contests increased by less than 200,000 votes (16 million to 16.2 million votes). The turnout for Republican primaries was up by nearly 3.8 million from 1972 to 1976, but in 1972 President Richard Nixon faced negligible opposition for the GOP nomination.

The turnout for the 1980 preference primaries was a record 32.3 million voters, compared to 26.4 million in 1976. But the figure is somewhat deceptive because more primaries were held in 1980 than ever before. The Republican primary turnout barely kept pace with the rate of population growth, while the Democratic primary turnout sagged noticeably.

Between 1976 and 1980 the national voting age population grew by about 7 percent. Comparing turnout totals for primaries that were held both in 1976 and 1980, the 1980 Republican primary turnout increased 7.7 percent from 1976, while the Democratic primary turnout in 1980 decreased 5.7 percent.

The 1980 primaries had a much lower rate of participation than the 1976 general election or even the 1978 midterm elections. Based on July 1979 voting age population estimates from the Census Bureau, only 24 percent of the eligible population in the primary states voted in either the Democratic or Republican preference primaries. In no 1980 primary did a majority of the state's voting age population participate.

1980 Primaries

President Jimmy Carter and Republican Ronald Reagan were the clear winners of the long 1980 primary season.

Although Carter received a bare majority of the cumulative Democratic primary vote, he amassed a plurality of nearly 2.7 million votes over his major rival, Sen. Edward M. Kennedy, D-Mass.

With no opposition in the late primary contests, Reagan emerged as a more one-sided choice of GOP primary voters. He finished nearly 4.6 million votes ahead of George Bush, who withdrew from the race May 26.

Carter and Reagan built up large early leads with a series of landslide primary victories in the South and industrial Midwest. Reagan ran best in closed primaries, where only Republican voters could participate. Carter was strongest in open primaries, where crossover voting was permitted. The president drew the support of 51 percent of the nearly 20 million voters who cast ballots in the Democratic primaries. He won 24 of the primary contests to 10 for Kennedy. Reagan won 28 preference primaries to Bush's six, although 11 of Reagan's primary triumphs came after Bush had withdrawn.

Both Carter and Reagan benefited significantly from their parties' delegate allocation systems. They won a far higher percentage of delegates than their comparable share of primary votes.

While Carter received 51 percent of the combined popular vote in the Democratic preference primaries, he garnered 58 percent of the primary state delegates. The disparity was even greater on the Republican side, where Reagan's 60 percent share of the GOP preference vote translated into 78 percent of his party's primary state delegates.

Both front-runners were aided by victories in winner-take-all contests. There were more of them on the Republican side, where they are permitted by party rules. Winner-take-all elections are prohibited under Democratic rules, but Illinois and West Virginia were granted exemptions to retain "loophole," or district winner-take-all primaries in 1980. Carter won in both states. *(Primary procedures, types, see boxes, pp. 28, 36)*

Proposals for Reform

Despite the growing use of primaries however, the existing system came under considerable criticism. The critics often cited the length of the primary season (nearly twice as long as the general election campaign), the expense, the physical strain on the candidates and the variations and complexities of state laws as leading problems of presidential primaries.

To deal with these problems, several states in 1974-75 discussed the feasibility of creating regional primaries, in which individual states within a geographical region would hold their primaries on the same day. Supporters of the concept believed it would reduce candidate expenses and strain and would permit concentration on regional issues.

The idea achieved some limited success when two groups of states — one in the West and the other in the South — decided to organize regional primaries in 1976 in each of their areas. However, the two groups both chose the same day, May 25, to hold their primaries, thus defeating one of the main purposes of the plan by continuing to force candidates to shuttle across the country to cover both areas. The Western states participating in the grouping were Idaho, Nevada and Oregon; the Southern states were Arkansas, Kentucky and Tennessee.

Attempts were also made in New England to construct a regional primary. But jealousy on the part of New Hampshire for its first-in-the-nation primary and hesitancy by the other New England state legislatures defeated the idea. Only Vermont joined Massachusetts, on March 2, in holding a simultaneous presidential primary.

In 1980 limited regional primaries were held again in several areas of the country — on March 4 in New England (Massachusetts and Vermont), on March 11 in the Southeast (Alabama, Florida and Georgia), and on May 27 in the South (Arkansas and Kentucky) and the West (Idaho and Nevada).

In 1984 the so-called Super Tuesday, March 13, produced regional primaries in New England (Massachusetts and Rhode Island) and in the South (Alabama, Florida and Georgia).

Other approaches to changing the primary system have been attempted at the national level. National reform proposals included a single nationwide primary, standardization of the date of primaries to shorten the campaign season, and a law mandating a regional primary system.

Since 1911 hundreds of bills have been introduced in Congress to reform the presidential primary system. The largest quantities were introduced in sessions after the 1912, 1952 and 1968 nominating campaigns. All three campaigns produced the feeling among many voters that the will of the electorate, as expressed in the primaries, had been thwarted by national conventions. But since 1911 the only legislation enacted by Congress concerned the presidential primary in the District of Columbia. Rarely did primary reform legislation even reach the hearing stage.

1984 Delegate Selection

For the third time in the last four presidential nominating campaigns, a little-known outsider threw the Democratic contest into turmoil with an unexpected string of early successes.

Like South Dakota Sen. George McGovern in 1972 and Jimmy Carter in 1976, Colorado Sen. Gary Hart vaulted from the back of the pack virtually overnight, dislodging an early front-runner whose strongest ties were to the party leadership and its traditional core elements.

None of this was supposed to happen in 1984. The Democratic establishment rewrote the delegate selection rules to blunt the possibility of a long-shot candidate winning the nomination. Democrats were expected to bring down the curtain on the period of grass-roots control of the party's nominating process begun in the early 1970s and open a new era dominated by the party regulars.

Changes in the Democrats' nominating process for 1984 were supposed to help the early front-runner, former Vice President Walter F. Mondale. A large bloc of party officials was added to the convention roster to bring an element of "peer review" — judgment of a candidate by professionals familiar with his work. Even more important, the number of caucuses was increased and the number of "mass appeal" primaries reduced, and 25 separate delegate selection events were scheduled in the 12-day period from March 13 to March 24 — a blur of primaries and caucuses expected to benefit the well-organized Mondale.

The compressed primary and caucus schedule backed by the Mondale forces ironically appeared to work to Hart's advantage after his victory in the New Hampshire primary — the nation's first. With subsequent victories in Maine, Vermont and Wyoming in early March, and a better than even split with Mondale in the nine state primaries and caucuses on "Super Tuesday" — March 13 — Hart had the momentum as the campaign for the Democratic nomination entered its second, critical stage.

The caucus states, which once seemed to provide a safety net for Mondale, no longer appeared so secure. However, the uncommitted group of party and elected officials — the so-called superdelegates who were given nearly 15 percent of the seats at the Democratic convention — remained firmly behind Mondale. The vast majority of this group initially backed the former vice president. *(U.S. House and Senate superdelegates, box, p. 40)*

The Republican precinct caucuses held in Michigan Jan. 10, 1984, and the Democratic precinct caucuses in Iowa on Feb. 20 marked the official beginning of the process to select delegates to the two major parties' national presidential nominating conventions. The Democrats' was scheduled for San Francisco July 16-19 and the Republicans' in Dallas Aug. 20-23.

Reagan in Command

Republicans began the year united behind President Ronald Reagan, who entered 1984 in a much stronger position than did President Carter four years earlier. Though the record of his first three years in office was controversial in many respects, Reagan did not have the intractable liabilities surrounding his leadership of his party and country that plagued Carter. In fact, most observers maintained that Reagan began his campaign for re-election politically stronger than any incumbent president since Dwight D. Eisenhower in 1956.

With the economy on the rebound, and no debilitating Iranian hostage crisis to divert the attention of the American people, Reagan could assume a steady presidential demeanor and quietly watch the Democrats publicly battle each other for their party's nomination.

For the Republicans, therefore, the delegate selection events promised to be pro forma affairs because Ronald Reagan did not face a serious challenge for the Republican nomination. Thus he had little reason to mount an active primary campaign. Instead, his organizers worked quietly to ensure that the delegates to the GOP convention would overwhelmingly endorse his renomination. *(GOP delegate selection rules, box, p. 42)*

The Democratic Challengers

Initially, eight major Democratic candidates vied for the right to run against President Reagan, who announced Jan. 29 that he would seek re-election.

The big question for Democrats on the eve of the first presidential caucuses and primaries was whether Mondale would be able to sew up the nomination quickly against Sen. John Glenn, D-Ohio, who was thought to be his only serious challenger. All of the other Democrats in the race were considered dark horses at best. They were: Hart, Sen. Alan Cranston of California, Sen. Ernest F. Hollings of South Carolina, former Florida Gov. Reubin Askew, McGovern, a former senator and the 1972 Democratic presidential nominee, and the Rev. Jesse Jackson.

1984 Democratic Presidential Primary, Caucus Dates

The 1984 Democratic nominating process was heavily "front-loaded," with the majority of states launching their delegate selection proceedings by early April.

The following calendar of the Democratic primary and first-stage caucus dates is based on a list compiled by the Democratic National Committee. Primaries that did not select delegates, such as the non-binding Vermont vote held on March 6, are not included. In parenthesis is each state's delegate count.

Date	Primaries	Caucuses	Date	Primaries	Caucuses
Feb. 20		Iowa (58)[1]	April 3	New York (285)	
Feb. 28	New Hampshire (22)[1]	April 7		Wisconsin (89)	
March 4		Maine (27)	April 10	Pennsylvania (195)	
March 10		Wyoming (15)[1]	April 14		
March 13	Florida (143)	Washington (70)			Arizona (40)
	Massachusetts (116)	Oklahoma (53)	April 16		Utah (27)
	Georgia (84)	Hawaii (27)	April 18		Missouri (86)
	Alabama (62)	Nevada (20)	April 24		Vermont (17)
	Rhode Island (27)	American Samoa (6)	April 28		Guam (7)
	Democrats Abroad (5)		May 1	Tennessee (76)	
March 14		Delaware (18)		District of Columbia (19)	
		North Dakota (18)[2]	May 5	Louisiana (69)[4]	Texas (200)
March 15		Alaska (14)	May 7		Colorado (51)
March 17		Michigan (155)	May 8	Ohio (175)	
		Kentucky (63)		Indiana (88)	
		South Carolina (48)		North Carolina (88)	
		Mississippi (43)		Maryland (74)	
		Arkansas (42)	May 15	Oregon (50)	
		Latin America (5)		Nebraska (30)	
March 18	Puerto Rico (53)		May 24	Idaho (22)	
March 20	Illinois (194)	Minnesota (86)	June 5	California (345)	
March 24		Kansas (44)		New Jersey (122)	
		Virginia (78)[3]		West Virginia (44)	
March 25		Montana (25)		New Mexico (28)	
March 27	Connecticut (60)			South Dakota (19)	
March 31		Virgin Islands (6)			

[1] The dates of the Iowa, New Hampshire and Wyoming delegate selection events were never formally approved by the Democratic National Committee's Compliance Review Commission.
[2] Caucuses run through March 28.
[3] Caucuses also held March 26.
[4] Ordered by a three-judge federal panel March 21. Louisiana appeal dismissed by the Supreme Court March 28.

In all, there were 25 Democratic delegate selection primaries and 32 party caucuses scheduled between Feb. 20 and June 5. There were also some non-binding primaries, called "beauty contests." The Vermont primary March 6, in which Hart took 71 percent of the vote, was one of those.

The results in the first few Democratic contests underscored the startling fluidity of the nominating process in its early stages. With voter support often determined by vague themes and impressions, sentiment changed quickly and dramatically. That had been the story of all the nominating campaigns since 1968, and it was repeated in 1984.

By March 1, after the Democratic delegate contests in Iowa and New Hampshire, three of the eight candidates — Cranston, Hollings and Askew — had taken themselves out of the race for the nomination. McGovern dropped out March 13 following his third-place finish in the Massachusetts primary. And Glenn, who finished no better than third in any of the primaries through "Super Tuesday," announced March 16 that he was ending his campaign for the presidential nomination.

Third Party Candidates

Several third-party presidential nominees also were running against Reagan. However, they were unlikely to have the impact that John B. Anderson did in 1980 or George Wallace did 12 years earlier.

Anderson, who was attempting to build a third party, had yet to prove that he could motivate a sizable constituency from the center. Even in the 1980 election, he did not come close to carrying a single state or even a single county. For many voters, Anderson served merely as a handy vehicle to protest the choices offered by the two major parties.

No great nationwide protest against the two parties was evident in 1984. The election campaign was being shaped by the conservative policies of Ronald Reagan. Most Democrats considered the 1984 election to present a clearer choice. As a result, liberals who deserted their party in 1980 to support Anderson, or did not vote at all, were less likely to do so this time because they felt the stakes were much higher. According to many political observers, the 1984 general election turnout was likely to be higher than in recent presidential elections. Because of the high degree of partisanship surrounding the Reagan administration's performance and policies, blacks and other minorities were expected to vote in larger numbers. One reason for that assessment was the turnout in the 1982 congressional contests, which broke a 20-year decline in participation in federal elections. *(Voter turnout, box, p. 6)*

The Democratic Primaries

The 1984 nominating process appeared to be much like that in use during previous election years. A party-prescribed number of delegates and alternates to the national conventions were to be selected in each state and territory, either through party primaries or in precinct and state caucuses. Important changes, however, marked the 1984 selection process on the Democratic side — the fourth consecutive convention in which the Democrats had changed their presidential primary and caucus rules.

Ever since the tumultuous convention of 1968, the party had struggled over how presidential nominees should be chosen. The reformers, whose views held sway between 1972 and 1980, believed that the delegates should represent the candidate preferences of rank-and-file party members as reflected in the primary and caucus results. Others felt that party leaders, with their greater political experience and knowledge of the candidates, should be given a major role in naming the nominee. Modifications reflecting these latter views were accepted by the Democratic National Committee (DNC) in 1982 and instituted for the 1984 nomination process.

In previous primary seasons, the lesser known Democratic presidential candidates could count on the important early events being staggered over a period of two months. The Iowa caucuses were held in late January, followed about a month later by New Hampshire's primary. Then, at weekly intervals, came crucial primaries in Massachusetts, Florida and Illinois.

This was an ideal arrangement for long shots such as McGovern in 1972 and Carter in 1976. They could concentrate virtually all their time and money on Iowa and New Hampshire, then use the publicity and sense of momentum they gained in these media fishbowl events to build a following in the states that came next.

But the primary calendar was not so favorable to dark horses in 1984. Barely three weeks separated Iowa's caucuses from the 10-state delegate selection events of "Super Tuesday," March 13. The result was a much quicker transition from the fishbowl stage — where candidates competed mainly against media expectations — into the more demanding delegate counting stage, in which "better than expected" was not enough. *(Dates of 1984 Democratic Party presidential primaries and caucuses, box, p. 32)*

As part of its 1982 revision of the delegate selection process, the DNC set the Iowa caucuses on Feb. 27 and New Hampshire's primary on March 6. But Vermont

---

National Primary Proposal

Every four years, dissatisfaction surfaces with the process for selecting presidential nominees. One suggested change was to establish a direct national primary. But a Democratic study commission as well as several academic groups that examined that idea had rejected it. The consensus was that such a process would strip the party leadership of any role in the nominating process, enable presidential candidates to run factional or regional campaigns and increase the primacy of media "image" over serious discussion of the issues. "If you go to a national primary," said Ann Lewis, political director of the Democratic National Committee, "you don't have a political process anymore, you have the 'Battle of the Network Stars,'..."

Some political scientists seemed to long for the days when the nominees were chosen in large measure by the party leaders. In 1980 Jeane J. Kirkpatrick, then a Georgetown University professor and the U.S. representative to the United Nations in the Reagan administration, called for the abolition of primaries and creation of a decision-making process restricted to party and elected officials.

Political scientist Austin Ranney also felt that the power of the party leaders should be restored: "In the old smoke-filled-room days, the people who really chose the presidential nominee were people who knew [the candidates] and saw them in action and had some idea of what they were like." Ranney did not go as far as Kirkpatrick. Instead, he advocated a process in which the consensus of political leaders would be the deciding influence in national conventions. Ranney, however, thought it unlikely that either party would return to the smoke-filled rooms. "I think it's against the whole ethos of our times," he said.

---

scheduled a non-binding primary on March 6, so New Hampshire moved its contest to Feb. 28. Iowa followed by moving its caucuses to Feb. 20.

The earlier dates provided a small break for the dark horses, such as Hart. If they were able to make a breakthrough in Iowa or New Hampshire, they would have an extra week to mobilize for the March 13 contests.

The South was given a greater role in 1984 than it ever had before in the party's early decision making on a presidential nominee. Among the states included in the March 13 primary balloting were Florida, with 143 delegates to be selected, Georgia and Alabama. With three primaries and a caucus (Oklahoma) in the region, the South ranked close behind Iowa and New Hampshire in the candidates' early strategic planning.

'Frost Belt' Impact

For the first time in years, the backbone of the Democratic Party — the "Frost Belt" industrial states — stood ready to play a pivotal role in the nominating process.

Democratic Presidential Primary Winners

Since the proliferation of presidential primaries began in the early 1970s, the Democratic nominee has always been the candidate who won the most primaries. In 1972, it was South Dakota Sen. George McGovern, who took nine out of 23 primary contests. Other winners that year were Alabama Gov. George C. Wallace, with six victories; former vice president Hubert H. Humphrey Jr., with four; Maine Sen. Edmund S. Muskie, with two; and District of Columbia Delegate Walter E. Fauntroy and New York Rep. Shirley Chisholm, with one each.

In 1976 the big winner was former Georgia Gov. Jimmy Carter, who captured 18 out of 30 primaries. Sen. Frank Church of Idaho won four primaries, California Gov. Edmund G. Brown Jr. won three, Sen. Henry M. Jackson of Washington won two, West Virginia Sen. Robert C. Byrd won one and Wallace won one.

Four years later it was Carter again, the winner of 24 out of 35 primary elections. Massachusetts Sen. Edward M. Kennedy won 10 primaries.

The following chart lists the Democratic presidential primaries in the order they were held in 1980, with the winner and his percentage of the preference vote in every primary since 1972. In primary states where there was no preference vote but delegates were elected, the candidate who won the most delegates is listed. A dash (——) indicates no primary was held.

Primary	1972	1976	1980
New Hampshire	Muskie (46%)	Carter (28%)	Carter (47%)
Massachusetts	McGovern (53%)	Jackson (22%)	Kennedy (65%)
Vermont	——	Carter (42%)	Carter (73%)
Alabama	Wallace	Wallace	Carter (82%)
Florida	Wallace (42%)	Carter (34%)	Carter (61%)
Georgia	——	Carter (83%)	Carter (88%)
Puerto Rico	——	——	Carter (52%)
Illinois	Muskie (63%)	Carter (48%)	Carter (65%)
Connecticut	——	——	Kennedy (47%)
New York	McGovern	Jackson	Kennedy (59%)
Kansas	——	——	Carter (57%)
Wisconsin	McGovern (30%)	Carter (37%)	Carter (56%)
Louisiana	——	——	Carter (56%)
Pennsylvania	Humphrey (35%)	Carter (37%)	Kennedy (46%)
Texas	——	Carter	Carter (56%)
District of Columbia	Fauntroy (72%)	Carter (32%)	Kennedy (62%)
Indiana	Humphrey (47%)	Carter (68%)	Carter (68%)
North Carolina	Wallace (50%)	Carter (54%)	Carter (70%)
Tennessee	Wallace (68%)	Carter (78%)	Carter (75%)
Maryland	Wallace (39%)	Brown (48%)	Carter (48%)
Nebraska	McGovern (41%)	Church (38%)	Carter (47%)
Michigan	Wallace (51%)	Carter (43%)	Uncommitted (46%)
Oregon	McGovern (50%)	Church (34%)	Carter (57%)
Arkansas	——	Carter (63%)	Carter (60%)
Idaho	——	Church (79%)	Carter (62%)
Kentucky	——	Carter (59%)	Carter (67%)
Nevada	——	Brown (53%)	Carter (38%)
California	McGovern (44%)	Brown (59%)	Kennedy (45%)
Montana	——	Church (59%)	Carter (51%)
New Jersey	Chisholm (67%)	Carter (58%)	Kennedy (56%)
New Mexico	McGovern (33%)	——	Kennedy (46%)
Ohio	Humphrey (41%)	Carter (52%)	Carter (51%)
Rhode Island	McGovern (41%)	Uncommitted (32%)	Kennedy (68%)
South Dakota	McGovern (100%)	Carter (41%)	Kennedy (49%)
West Virginia	Humphrey (67%)	Byrd (89%)	Carter (62%)

Presidential Candidates' Campaigns

(Announcement dates of major candidates and length of campaigns since 1972)

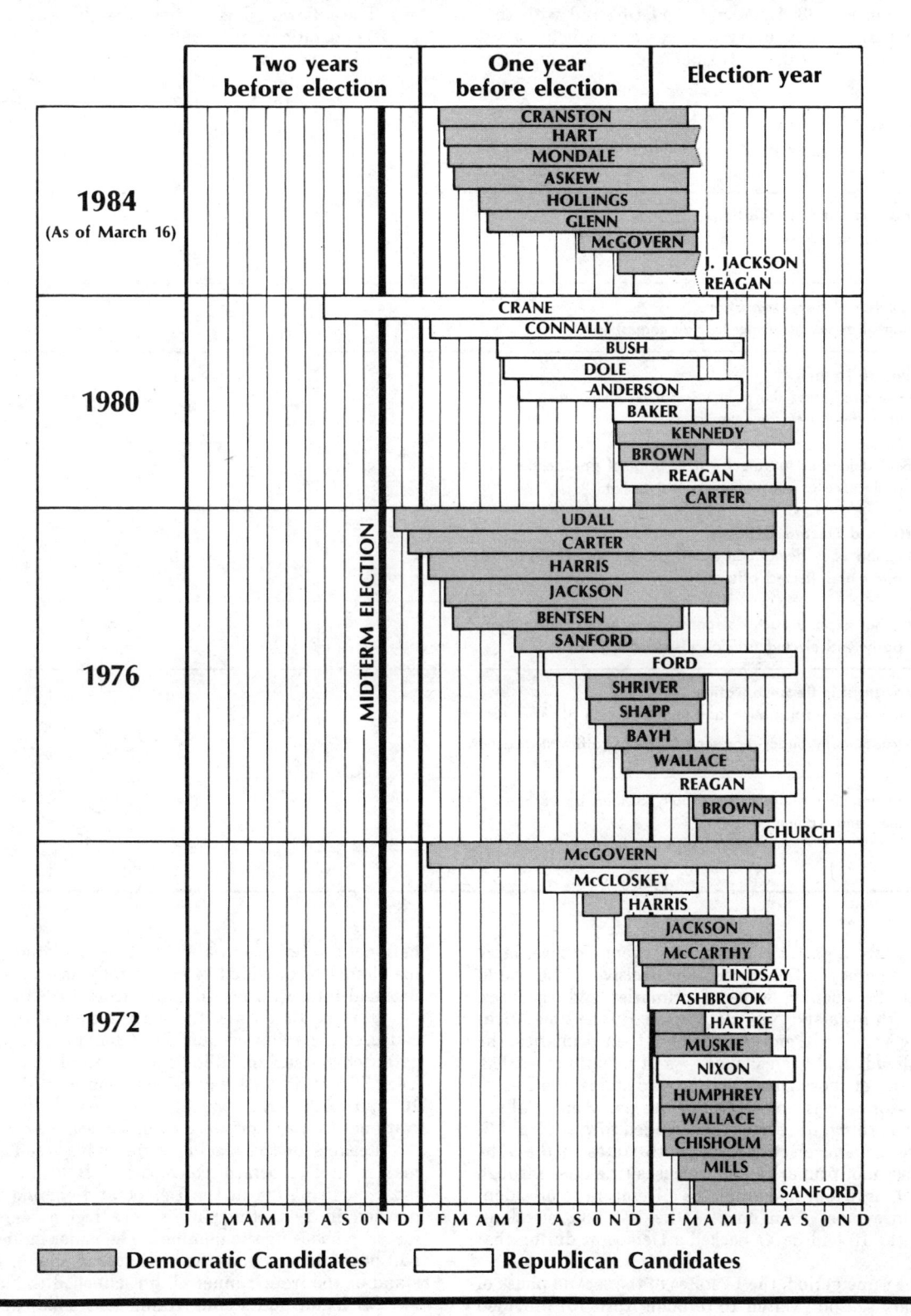

1984 (As of March 16)
- CRANSTON
- HART
- MONDALE
- ASKEW
- HOLLINGS
- GLENN
- McGOVERN
- J. JACKSON
- REAGAN

1980
- CRANE
- CONNALLY
- BUSH
- DOLE
- ANDERSON
- BAKER
- KENNEDY
- BROWN
- REAGAN
- CARTER

1976
- UDALL
- CARTER
- HARRIS
- JACKSON
- BENTSEN
- SANFORD
- FORD
- SHRIVER
- SHAPP
- BAYH
- WALLACE
- REAGAN
- BROWN
- CHURCH

1972
- McGOVERN
- McCLOSKEY
- HARRIS
- JACKSON
- McCARTHY
- LINDSAY
- ASHBROOK
- HARTKE
- MUSKIE
- NIXON
- HUMPHREY
- WALLACE
- CHISHOLM
- MILLS
- SANFORD

☐ Democratic Candidates   ☐ Republican Candidates

Democrats' Nominating Rules Keep Changing

Since 1968, Democrats had tinkered with their nominating rules every four years, producing a system that, if not better than before, was always different. The following chart shows the ebb and flow of the Democratic Party's rules changes, with a "✔" indicating the years these major rules were in effect.

	1972	1976	1980	1984
Timing: Restrict delegate selection events to a 3-month period (the "window").			✔	✔
Conditions of Participation: Restrict participation in delegate selection events to Democrats.		✔	✔	✔
Proportional Representation: Ban all types of winner-take-all contests.			✔	
Delegate Loyalty: Give candidates the right to approve delegates identifying with their candidacy.		✔	✔	✔
Bind delegates to vote for their original presidential preference at convention on first ballot.			✔	
Party and Elected Officials: Expand each delegation by 10 percent to include pledged party and elected officials.			✔	✔
Further expand each delegation to include uncommitted party and elected officials ("superdelegates").				✔
Demographic Representation: Encourage participation and representation of minorities and traditionally under-represented groups (affirmative action).	✔	✔	✔	✔
Require delegations to be equally divided between men and women.			✔	✔

In the recent past, the nominating events in these large states were largely anticlimactic. The decisive battleground had been the opening wave of primaries and caucuses, starting with Iowa and New Hampshire. By the time Michigan, New York and Pennsylvania held their primaries, the contest already had been shaped — and sometimes settled. Yet in many of those small, early-round states, the Democratic electorate was not typical of the party nationally.

For one thing, the early states tended to vote Republican in the general election. Of the 16 states in the 1984 opening wave of primaries and caucuses (the ones through March 15), only four had voted for a Democratic presidential nominee more than once in the last four elections. Seven of the 16 had never backed a Democrat during that period.

In the same period, the 14 states in the second phase of the primary season (March 16 through April 10) provided the past four Democratic nominees with nearly half their national total of electoral votes. New York and Pennsylvania alone had provided 140 electoral votes, a quarter of the national total won by the party from 1968 through 1980.

For the first time, the early round of primaries and caucuses was followed quickly by balloting in several delegate-rich states from Illinois across the Frost Belt to New York. There, in a 24-day period from mid-March to April 10, four of the seven largest delegations to the Democratic National Convention were to be chosen.

Leaders in the big industrial states used to be kingmakers at Democratic conventions. But since the era of mass participation in the Democratic nominating process dawned in 1972, the party's core region scarcely was a factor in choosing the nominee. The major industrial states had been places where the beleaguered loser made his last stand or the front-runner all but clinched the nomination.

Michigan and Pennsylvania had handicapped themselves by placing their events too late on the calendar.

How to Win a Democratic Delegate

One problem for the layman in a presidential election year was understanding the Democrats' delegate selection process. Democratic presidential candidates had to reach different thresholds in different places to qualify for a share of the national convention delegates. In a caucus state, for instance, a candidate had to win 20 percent of the vote at a congressional district convention to qualify for a delegate. But in a proportional representation primary, the district threshold was based on the percentage it would take to win one delegate. In some cases where there were a number of delegates at stake, that was barely 10 percent.

The following chart lists the thresholds that applied in 1984 in caucus and primary states at both the district and statewide levels. Most of the nearly 4,000 Democratic delegates were to be elected at the district level. Statewide delegates included at-large and pledged party and elected officials.

	District	**Statewide**
Caucus [1]	20% of vote	20% of vote
Direct Election (or Loophole) Primary [2]	No threshold; winner-take-all possible	20% of district delegates
Bonus Primary [3]	100 percent divided by the number of delegates minus one (30 percent maximum)	20% of vote
Proportional Representation Primary [4]	100 percent divided by number of delegates (25 percent maximum)	20% of vote

[1] *Delegates in caucus states were allocated by either a bonus or proportional representation method. Bonus caucus states were Arkansas, Colorado, Hawaii, Idaho, Kentucky and Montana. Proportional representation caucuses were scheduled in Alaska, Arizona, Delaware, Iowa, Kansas, Louisiana, Maine, Michigan, Minnesota, Mississippi, Missouri, Nevada, North Dakota, Oklahoma, South Carolina, Texas, Utah, Vermont, Virginia, Washington, Wisconsin, Wyoming, American Samoa, Guam, Latin America and the Virgin Islands.*

[2] *Direct election (or "loophole") primaries were to be held in California, Florida, Illinois, Maryland, New Jersey, Pennsylvania, West Virginia and the Democrats Abroad.*

[3] *Bonus primaries were scheduled in Georgia, New York, North Carolina, Ohio and Puerto Rico.*

[4] *Proportional representation primaries were to be held in Alabama, Connecticut, the District of Columbia, Indiana, Massachusetts, Nebraska, New Hampshire, New Mexico, Oregon, Rhode Island, South Dakota and Tennessee.*

From 1972 to 1980 neither state selected its delegates before late April. Both were leapfrogged by smaller states seeking to gain influence. By the time Michigan and Pennsylvania got around to voting, there was little left to decide.

New York had the same problem in 1972 when it selected its delegates in mid-June. Since then, it has held its presidential primary much earlier. But frequent changes in the state's delegate selection rules kept the event confusing, the turnout low and the nation's attention elsewhere.

Illinois reduced the importance of its primary in another way. Although in had held its primary in March in recent years, until 1980 the late Chicago Mayor Richard J. Daley effectively posted a "Keep Out" sign that sent the candidates scurrying to other states to fight their primary battles. Daley wanted the Illinois convention delegation to be loyal to himself, rather than to any candidate.

The cumulative result of party decisions in all four of those states was that the party's loyal core had little impact in the choice of the Democratic nominee.

All of that changed in 1984. Not only did the major Democratic industrial states decide to crowd their events into a short period from late March to mid-April; they also awarded delegates in ways that maximized their influence.

Illinois (March 20) and Pennsylvania (April 10) had primaries in which the first-place finisher in a given congressional district could take all the delegates at stake there. New York (April 3) adopted a bonus primary, which was a modified version of the winner-take-all method. By offering a candidate the potential of a huge one-event windfall, these primaries enhanced the power of the large states to affect the nominating process. Only Michigan, a caucus state, among the major industrial states retained a strict system of proportional representation for allocating its rich lode of delegates. *(Types of primaries, box, p. 28)*

By the end of the industrial state phase, a total of 30 states — containing about 60 percent of the presidential delegates — had expressed their preference for president.

Evolution of Delegate Selection

Following the 1968 Democratic National Convention in Chicago that saw the party nearly break apart over the Vietnam War, broader and more democratic delegate selection rules were approved for subsequent presidential conventions, including requirements for "party primary, con-

Delegates From U.S. Territories

Delegates to the Democratic convention in San Francisco July 16-19 were to include not only those from the 50 states and the District of Columbia but also from American possessions around the globe.

Besides the usual coterie of territories on the convention floor — Guam, the Virgin Islands, Puerto Rico and the Panama Canal Zone (known in recent years within the party as the Latin American Democrats) — there also was space allocated in 1984 for delegates from American Samoa.

Their presence would not guarantee them much attention, however. While virtually all the territories had joined the rush for positions near the beginning of the delegate selection calendar, they were virtually ignored by the candidates. They offered a total of only 24 delegates. "With our budget," explained Rick Ridder, field director for Colorado Sen. Gary Hart, "the telephone costs alone have deterred us from making contacts."

American Samoa, Guam, the Virgin Islands and the Latin American Democrats used the caucus process to elect their delegates. American Samoa was the first of the group to vote, joining the myriad states balloting March 13. The dates for the others were: Latin American Democrats (March 17), the Virgin Islands (March 31) and Guam (April 28).

---

vention or committee procedures open to public participation within the calendar year of the National Convention" and for minority groups, young persons and women to be represented "in reasonable relationship to their presence in the population of the state."

The rules report also called for creation of a Commission on Party Structure and Delegate Selection. The commission, headed first by McGovern and later by Rep. Donald Fraser of Minnesota (1963-79), by April 1970 had drawn up a list of reforms that were to change the nature of the Democratic Party's nominating process. Under the rules endorsed by the Democratic National Committee, all state delegate selection events — caucuses as well as primaries — were to be open to all declared Democrats. Delegate positions no longer could be reserved for state party leaders and elected officials. Increased minority and female representation at the national conventions was mandated in such a way that critics accused the party of setting "quotas."

In subsequent years the Democrats took even stronger steps to ensure that the results of the primaries and caucuses would be fully reflected at the convention. For 1976 the party banned winner-take-all primaries and mandated that delegates in each state be divided among the candidates in proportion to the vote they received in the primaries or caucuses. In 1980 the Democrats required that each delegation be equally divided between men and women. The party also bound delegates to their candidate commitments to the extent that a candidate could replace any delegate who threatened to be "unfaithful."

Members of the McGovern-Fraser commission said they did not intend their reforms to lead to an increased number of primaries. "Indeed, we hoped to prevent any such development by reforming the delegate-selection rules so that the party's non-primary processes would be open and fair, participation in them would greatly increase, and consequently the demand for primaries would fade away," wrote political scientist and commission member Austin Ranney.

An increase in the number of primaries was, however, the most noticeable result of the reforms. The number of Democratic primaries went up from 17 in 1968 to 23 in 1972, 29 in 1976 and 31 in 1980. Party leaders in several states, fearing that insurgents or candidate activists would gain access to conventions where other state party business was conducted, switched their delegate selection from a caucus to a primary system. Others did the same in the belief that they could more easily meet the party's demographic "fairness" requirements if the delegate slates were chosen by the candidates and approved by primary voters. Still others acted in hopes of sharing some of the media attention enjoyed by other primary states.

But many political scientists and party leaders found substantial fault with the new system. Because of the need for candidates to compete for mass support in many states, primary and caucus campaigning grew more and more expensive and physically taxing. With the nominating decision in the hands of the voters, the importance of media interpretation of primary results increase. Some analysts saw network news commentators taking over the "kingmaker" role long exercised by political bosses. And the ability of candidates to bypass the politicians by appealing to the people was seen as weakening the coalitions that traditionally helped candidates win and winners govern.

The reforms essentially required each candidate to set up personal campaign organizations in every state — a costly and time-consuming process that forced candidates to announce their intentions and begin fund raising earlier. Jimmy Carter announced his candidacy for the 1976 nomination in January 1975. Rep. Philip Crane, R-Ill., kicked off the 1980 race in August 1978.

Well-known, "unannounced" contenders often began their organizing and fund-raising activities just after the previous election. Reagan took that route in the years before the 1980 campaign. Mondale spent his three years after leaving the vice presidency building a nationwide campaign organization. *(Length of candidates' campaigns, box, p. 35)*

With the role of party leaders as intermediaries virtually abolished, media interpretation of early events took on greater importance. Thus, Democratic candidates felt it necessary to focus their efforts on the early caucus and primary states of Iowa and New Hampshire, both relatively small in population and demographically unrepresentative. While the front-runners hoped to lengthen or at least maintain their leads in these early events, the long-shot candidates sought to win the "perception" game. McGovern lost the 1972 New Hampshire primary to front-runner Sen. Edmund S. Muskie of Maine by 10 percentage points, but his better-than-expected performance gave him credibility. Within weeks, McGovern was the front-runner and Muskie was out of the race. In 1976 Carter won only 28 percent of the Iowa caucus votes, finishing behind the "uncommitted" category, but his margin over the other candidates made him a media "star." A victory in New

Hampshire, again with just 28 percent of the vote, made him the front-runner.

In 1984 Hart did better than expected in the Iowa caucuses by coming in second to Mondale, who easily won with 44.5 percent to Hart's 14.8 percent. Even though he received a relatively small percentage of the vote, Hart's second-place showing separated him from the other long-shot candidates and gave him the momentum he needed for the New Hampshire primary, which he went on to win with 37.3 percent; Mondale finished second there with 27.9 percent.

Advocates of proportional representation had hoped that apportioning the delegates among several candidates would keep any one candidate from clinching the nomination early in the process, possibly allowing the convention to act as a deliberative body in choosing a compromise candidate. In practice, however, candidates who did not do well in the early events often faced fund-raising and organizational difficulties that forced them out of contention. That was Glenn's fate in 1984. The delegate selection process today exercises the "winnowing" function once performed by party leaders.

Delegate binding rules also were criticized. Political scientists said the rules turned delegates into "robots," further eroding the convention's ability to act as a deliberative body. Supporters of the 1970s' reforms responded that the old system of informal commitments, enforced by local and state party organizations, often was as binding as the formal commitments. They also noted that the delegates still had an important role to play on the party platform and the rules.

The rules imposed in the 1970s also made it difficult for party and elected officials to serve as delegates. Having lost their reserved delegate slots, Democratic Party leaders were placed in the uncomfortable position of having to run against their constituents. Moreover, the binding rules made party insiders who were unwilling to commit themselves to a candidate ineligible to serve as delegates. Even a 10 percent "add-on" reserved for party and elected officials in 1980 helped little because they still had to be pledged to a candidate. Only 14 percent of all Democrats in the U.S. Senate served as delegates in 1980, down from 68 percent in 1968; 15 percent of all Democrats in the U.S. House of Representatives took part, down from 39 percent in 1968.

That trend was reversed in 1984. The Democratic Party, in reassessing its selection rules in 1982, decided to establish so-called "superdelegates" that would not be formally committed to any presidential candidates. There were 566 delegate slots reserved for party leaders and elected officials in this category, including 164 Democrats from the U.S. House and 27 from the Senate. These "superdelegates" could be decisive in a deadlocked convention. (However, the vast majority of those delegates publicly declared their preferences early in the process. *See box, p. 40)*

1984 Changes

Continuing controversy involving the nominating process prompted the 1980 Democratic convention to create yet another commission to study the party rules. The Commission on Presidential Nominations, headed by North Carolina Gov. James B. Hunt Jr., issued a report to the DNC in March 1982. Sensitive to the governance issue and dissatisfied with the minimal role party leaders played in past Democratic nominations, the commission made recommendations aimed at restoring some degree of party influence while maintaining grass-roots participation. Two of the proposals sought to increase chances that the nomination would not be sewn up before the national convention.

The first important difference was that the number of primaries in 1984 was reduced to 25, thus increasing the number of caucuses to 32. Second, the desire to minimize the impact of early campaign events motivated the creation of a truncated primary season. Under the Hunt commission's original rules, all delegate selection events were to take place between March 13 and June 12. Any delegates selected outside that period in events not approved by the party's Compliance Review Commission could be challenged at the convention.

That rules change was not entirely successful, however. Because Iowa wanted to continue to be the first Democratic caucus state and New Hampshire the first primary state, the DNC granted them limited dispensation, allowing a Feb. 27 date for the Iowa caucuses and a March 6 primary for New Hampshire. However, Vermont decided to hold its "beauty contest" presidential primary on March 6 to coincide with its town meetings, provoking New Hampshire to move up its primary to Feb. 28. Iowa legislators, who felt the publicity advantage of holding the Democrats' first event would be dampened by a primary the next day, moved its caucuses to Feb. 20.

Democrats Abroad

Not all the primaries and caucuses on March 13 — Super Tuesday — took place within the boundaries of the United States. Ballots of Democrats Abroad, in their mail-in primary, also were counted the same day.

Democrats Abroad was not a group that the candidates eagerly courted. Although any American citizen of voting age who lived overseas could participate in the group's primary, only 2,000 ballots were cast in 1980, the bulk of them from Western Europe.

The organization, nonetheless, took itself seriously. Its delegate selection plan required 10 typed, single-spaced pages to explain the choosing of eight delegates who would cast five votes.

Moreover, the Democrats Abroad had an eye for publicity by making their event an international version of Dixville Notch. Just as the northern New Hampshire hamlet got a jump on the rest of the country by casting its ballots shortly after midnight every Election Day, the Democrats Abroad were planning to count their ballots shortly after noon March 13, Greenwich Mean Time. That was early morning back in the United States.

Walter F. Mondale narrowly won the nonbinding "beauty contest" preference vote in 1984, although the group's three delegates were uncommitted. In 1980, Sen. Edward M. Kennedy, Mass., was an easy winner.

List of House and Senate 'Superdelegates'

At a House Democratic Caucus meeting in January 1984, 164 so-called superdelegates to the Democratic National Convention July 16-19 were elected. Mondale, according to an unofficial count by Congressional Quarterly based on candidates' tallies, public endorsements and news reports, won the support of 67 House members. A CQ survey taken March 21 — after many of the Democratic candidates had dropped out of the race — indicated that Mondale's support had increased to 82 members.

Sen. Gary Hart's, D-Colo., support went from five in January to nine in March, and support for Jesse Jackson went from six to seven. The remaining delegates were uncommitted. Technically, all the delegates went to the convention unpledged to any candidate.

Senate Democrats chose their superdelegates at a party caucus March 20. Only 25 of the 27 slots reserved for senators were filled. No other Democrats expressed interest in being a delegate. Of the 25, Mondale received the support of nine senators, Hart was backed by two and the other 14 remained uncommitted.

Following is a list of the delegates:

House Leadership

O'Neill, Thomas P. Jr., Mass.
Wright, Jim, Texas
Foley, Thomas S., Wash.
Long, Gillis W., La.
Ferraro, Geraldine A., N.Y.
Alexander, Bill, Ark.
Coelho, Tony, Calif.

Other House Members

Anderson, Glenn M., Calif.
Andrews, Michael A., Texas
Annunzio, Frank, Ill.
Aspin, Les, Wis.
AuCoin, Les, Ore.
Barnes, Michael D., Md.
Bedell, Berkley, Iowa
Beilenson, Anthony C., Calif.
Berman, Howard L., Calif.
Bevill, Tom, Ala.
Biaggi, Mario, N.Y.
Boggs, Lindy (Mrs. Hale), La.
Boland, Edward P., Mass.
Boner, Bill, Tenn.
Bonior, David E., Mich.
Bonker, Don, Wash.
Boucher, Frederick C., Va.
Boxer, Barbara, Calif.
Breaux, John B., La.
Britt, Robin, N.C.
Brooks, Jack, Texas
Brown, George E. Jr., Calif.
Bryant, John, Texas
Burton, Sala, Calif.
Byron, Beverly B., Md.
Chappell, Bill Jr., Fla.
Clay, William, Mo.
Collins, Cardiss, Ill.
Conyers, John Jr., Mich.
Corrada, Baltasar, Puerto Rico
Coyne, William J., Pa.
Crockett, George W. Jr., Mich.
de la Garza, E. "Kika", Texas
Dellums, Ronald V., Calif.
de Lugo, Ron, Virgin Islands
Derrick, Butler, S.C.
Dicks, Norman D., Wash.
Dingell, John D., Mich.
Dixon, Julian C., Calif.
Dowdy, Wayne, Miss.
Downey, Thomas J., N.Y.
Dwyer, Bernard J., N.J.
Dymally, Mervyn M., Calif.
Early, Joseph D., Mass.
Eckart, Dennis E., Ohio
Edgar, Bob, Pa.
Edwards, Don, Calif.
Fauntroy, Walter E., D.C.
Fazio, Vic, Calif.
Feighan, Edward F., Ohio
Flippo, Ronnie G., Ala.
Foglietta, Thomas M., Pa.
Ford, Harold E., Tenn.
Ford, William D., Mich.
Fowler, Wyche Jr., Ga.
Frank, Barney, Mass.
Frost, Martin, Texas
Garcia, Robert, N.Y.
Gejdenson, Sam, Conn.
Gephardt, Richard A., Mo.
Gibbons, Sam, Fla.
Glickman, Dan, Kan.
Gray, William H. III, Pa.
Guarini, Frank J., N.J.
Hall, Katie, Ind.
Hall, Ralph M., Texas
Hamilton, Lee H., Ind.
Harkin, Tom, Iowa
Hatcher, Charles, Ga.
Hawkins, Augustus F., Calif.
Hayes, Charles A., Ill.
Hightower, Jack, Texas
Howard, James J., N.J.
Hoyer, Steny H., Md.
Huckaby, Jerry, La.
Hughes, William J., N.J.
Jacobs, Andrew Jr., Ind.
Jenkins, Ed, Ga.
Jones, James R., Okla.
Kaptur, Marcy, Ohio
Kastenmeier, Robert W., Wis.
Kazen, Abraham Jr., Texas
Kennelly, Barbara B., Conn.
Kildee, Dale E., Mich.
Kogovsek, Ray, Colo.
Kostmayer, Peter H., Pa.
LaFalce, John J., N.Y.
Lehman, Richard H., Calif.
Lehman, William, Fla.
Leland, Mickey, Texas
Levine, Mel, Calif.
Lipinski, William O., Ill.
Luken, Thomas A., Ohio
Lundine, Stan, N.Y.
Martinez, Matthew G., Calif.
Matsui, Robert T., Calif.
McCurdy, Dave, Okla.
McHugh, Matthew F., N.Y.
Mica, Daniel A., Fla.
Mikulski, Barbara A., Md.
Miller, George, Calif.
Mineta, Norman Y., Calif.
Mitchell, Parren J., Md.
Moakley, Joe, Mass.
Murphy, Austin J., Pa.
Murtha, John P., Pa.
Neal, Stephen L., N.C.
Nelson, Bill, Fla.
Oakar, Mary Rose, Ohio
Oberstar, James L., Minn.
Ortiz, Solomon P., Texas
Owens, Major R., N.Y.
Panetta, Leon E., Calif.
Patterson, Jerry M., Calif.
Pease, Don J., Ohio
Pepper, Claude, Fla.
Perkins, Carl D., Ky.
Pickle, J. J., Texas
Price, Melvin, Ill.
Rahall, Nick J. II, W.Va.
Rangel, Charles B., N.Y.
Ratchford, William R., Conn.
Richardson, Bill, N.M.
Roe, Robert A., N.J.
Rose, Charlie, N.C.
Rostenkowski, Dan, Ill.
Roybal, Edward R., Calif.
Russo, Marty, Ill.
Sabo, Martin Olav, Minn.
St Germain, Fernand J., R.I.
Savage, Gus, Ill.
Scheuer, James H., N.Y.
Schroeder, Patricia, Colo.
Schumer, Charles E., N.Y.
Shannon, James M., Mass.
Sisisky, Norman, Va.
Skelton, Ike, Mo.
Smith, Neal, Iowa
Spratt, John M. Jr., S.C.
Stark, Fortney H. "Pete", Calif.
Stenholm, Charles W., Texas
Stokes, Louis, Ohio
Stratton, Samuel S., N.Y.
Tallon, Robin, S.C.
Torres, Esteban Edward, Calif.
Towns, Edolphus, N.Y.
Traxler, Bob, Mich.
Udall, Morris K., Ariz.
Vento, Bruce F., Minn.
Weaver, James, Ore.
Weiss, Ted, N.Y.
Wheat, Alan, Mo.
Williams, Pat, Mont.
Wilson, Charles, Texas
Wirth, Timothy E., Colo.
Wyden, Ron, Ore.
Young, Robert A., Mo.

Senate Members

Baucus, Max, Mont.
Bentsen, Lloyd, Texas
Bingaman, Jeff, N.M.
Boren, David L., Okla.
Cranston, Alan, Calif.
DeConcini, Dennis, Ariz.
Dixon, Alan J., Ill.
Dodd, Christopher J., Conn.
Eagleton, Thomas F., Mo.
Ford, Wendell H., Ky.
Glenn, John, Ohio
Hollings, Ernest F., S.C.
Inouye, Daniel K., Hawaii
Leahy, Patrick J., Vt.
Levin, Carl, Mich.
Matsunaga, Spark M., Hawaii
Melcher, John, Mont.
Metzenbaum, Howard M., Ohio
Mitchell, George J., Maine
Moynihan, Daniel Patrick, N.Y.
Nunn, Sam, Ga.
Pell, Claiborne, R.I.
Riegle, Donald W. Jr., Mich.
Sarbanes, Paul S., Md.
Sasser, Jim, Tenn.

Also not in compliance was Wyoming, which held its presidential caucuses on March 10.

DNC Chairman Charles T. Manatt at first threatened to disallow the results of the Iowa and New Hampshire events if they did not stick to the DNC-approved schedule. But there was little he could do to prevent these two states from going ahead with their own contests.

It was hoped that the media emphasis on the first events would be lessened somewhat by the unprecedented number of primaries and caucuses coming shortly afterwards. While shortening the campaign, the Hunt commission rules did not prohibit states from moving their events to the front of the schedule. The March 13 "Super Tuesday" primaries were in Alabama, Florida, Georgia, Massachusetts and Rhode Island and the caucuses that day were in Hawaii, Nevada, Oklahoma and Washington state. And in the following four days, eight other caucuses were held, including those in Michigan. On March 20 Illinois, the state with the fifth largest delegation, held its primary. Under the primary schedule, at least one-third of the delegates to the convention were to be selected by the end of March.

The 1984 rules allowed states to reward presidential candidates who finished first in the voting. It threw out the 1980 rule requiring allocation of delegates on the basis of the percentage of the popular vote each candidate received in the primary or caucus. The formula used by New Hampshire that year, and in 1984, was typical. The state had a total of 22 delegates. Six delegates represented each of the state's two congressional districts, and candidates who topped a threshold of 16.6 percent of the vote in either district qualified for a share of the delegates. Another six at-large delegates were apportioned among candidates receiving at least 20 percent of the statewide vote. The remaining four positions went to party and elected officials who were officially uncommitted.

States in 1984 also had two other options, each of which provided bonus delegates to the candidates who finished first. Six caucus states and four primary states plus Puerto Rico chose the "winner-take-more" plan. Under this system, the Democratic presidential candidate who won a congressional district automatically was awarded one delegate. The rest of the district's delegates were divided proportionally among all the candidates, including the winner.

The "winner-take-all" primary was even more victory-oriented. Voters chose among potential delegates, who were listed along with their presidential preference. Voters could choose delegates representing different candidates, but it was more likely that they would vote a straight ticket. If so, the presidential candidate who won the district likely would win all of its delegates. The seven states that used this option in 1984 included five of the largest: California, Florida, Illinois, New Jersey and Pennsylvania.

For a candidate with a strong lead in a state, the "winner-take-all" option was a big advantage. In the 1980 primary in Illinois, which was granted an exemption from that year's proportional representation rule, Carter bested Sen. Edward M. Kennedy, D-Mass., in the popular vote by 65 percent to 30 percent. However, Carter obtained all of the delegates in 20 districts, Kennedy in only one, and they broke even in three others. As a result, Carter won more than 90 percent of the state's delegates.

Of the states holding caucuses, 22 stuck with proportional representation in 1984; 12 of the 22 primary states stayed with that system. (Victory-oriented primaries also were held in Puerto Rico and by the Americans Abroad

Primary Vote by Stages

Although anyone wanting to be president today is forced to compete in the presidential primaries, there are different routes to the nomination. South Dakota Sen. George McGovern in 1972 started slowly; he first had to establish himself in the early primaries as the leading liberal contender before he emerged as the front-runner down the stretch.

Jimmy Carter, on the other hand, moved ahead of his rivals at the beginning of both the 1976 and 1980 campaigns, only to falter at the end of the primary season after his nomination had been secured.

The following chart shows the percentage of the presidential preference primary vote won by leading Democratic candidates in each stage of the nominating process since 1972. The highest percentage in each stage is indicated in boldface. An asterisk (*) indicates the Democratic nominee.

1972	Through March	April-May	June	Total
Humphrey	9%	26%	37%	**26%**
McGovern*	4	24	**43**	25
Wallace	21	**30**	8	23
Muskie	**36**	9	2	12
Others	30	11	10	14
1976				
Carter*	**38%**	**46%**	31%	**39%**
Brown	0	6	**39**	15
Wallace	27	10	4	12
Udall	5	14	9	10
Jackson	12	8	2	7
Church	0	4	10	5
Others	18	12	5	11
1980				
Carter*	**54%**	**56%**	42%	**51%**
Kennedy	40	30	**45**	38
Others	6	14	12	11

category, while proportional representation continued to be used in the District of Columbia.)

Likelihood of a Brokered Convention

One of the more visible changes in the Democratic rules for 1984 was the abolition of the binding rule. This reversal was in part a reaction to the perverse effect the binding rule had on the 1980 campaign. President Carter clinched his renomination by winning 270 more "bound" delegates in primaries and caucuses than he needed. But as public opinion of Carter fell before the convention, Sen. Kennedy kept his campaign alive by claiming that without the binding rule delegates would have rejected Carter and nominated him or someone else. Kennedy's forces unsuccessfully challenged the rule at the convention. Ann Lewis, a Kennedy delegate in 1980, admitted later that removal of the binding rule probably would not have affected the outcome of the convention. She added that most delegates in 1984 were not likely to reject their commitments either, even with elimination of the binding rule.

Recent history suggested that Lewis' assessment probably was correct. But if the leading Democrat was short of a majority, there was at least the possibility of a brokered convention. The rulemakers hoped the superdelegate slots would increase the incentive for presidential candidates to establish good relationships with party leaders. Secondly, they hoped to revive "peer review," the concept that the party leaders who had worked with and personally knew the candidates were better able to judge which one would be the best nominee.

There were indications, though, that the superdelegates were unlikely to play an independent role in judging the candidates who survived the pre-convention campaign. While nominally uncommitted, the vast majority of these delegates had endorsed Mondale. However, they remained technically uncommitted and could always change their allegiances.

Moreover, because these party leaders lacked the power they once had to force their will on their constituent delegations, many experts thought they were likely to follow the prevailing opinion in their delegations and states. "They certainly are concerned for the party, they want the party to have a good candidate ... but they're also concerned with their own political, personal status back home," said Ranney. Nevertheless, the party professionals were given a key role in creating the party platform, he noted, because "they have a selfish political stake in having a non-crazy platform, and much more of their effort is going to be spent in keeping the platform from being regarded as crazy by their voters...."

Challenges to Selection Rules

While the 1970s' McGovern-Fraser reforms had some unintended effects that the Hunt commission sought to change, they had an intended effect that was not repealed: increasing minority and female participation at the national convention. At the 1980 Democratic convention, 14 percent of the delegates were black and 49 percent were women. The affirmative action rules that guided state delegations in the 1972, 1976 and 1980 conventions remained in force. "We genuinely have a participatory party," said Lewis. "We're not going to give that up."

Jackson, a black activist in his first presidential race, criticized the way delegates had been apportioned among the presidential candidates. He said it was unfair to minority voters and long-shot candidates.

Jackson questioned the party's commitment to minority opportunity and called on national party leaders to revoke the winner-biased delegate apportionment rules and the modifications in the proportional representation system. "We want to eliminate all of the thresholds, and instead we want straight proportional allocation of delegates for all candidates," Jackson wrote in a letter to DNC Chairman Manatt in December 1983. Jackson also stated his opposition to automatic delegate slots, asserting that they were dominated by white males, who made up the majority of party and elected officials.

Manatt defended the rules in meetings with Jackson in December and January 1984. But an attempt to reach a compromise with Jackson failed, and it was conceivable

GOP Primary Rules

Any discussion of the 1984 nominating process necessarily focused on the Democrats. One reason was obvious. There was no contest on the Republican side. No one was challenging President Reagan for the GOP nomination. Another reason was almost as apparent: the Democrats were doing all the rules writing.

The Republican Party, wrote political scientist Nelson W. Polsby, "in many respects remains unreformed." Virtually anything was permitted as long as it was not baldly discriminatory. And that was the way GOP leaders wanted it. "We're happy with the rules we have," said Ernie Angelo, head of the GOP's most recent rules review panel. "The process works. The longer it stays the same, the fairer it is."

While state Democratic parties had to adhere to strict standards in devising delegate selection plans, their Republican counterparts were given wide latitude by the Republican National Committee (RNC).

The result was a nominating procedure with a simplicity and continuity that the Democrats lacked. A more homogenous party than the Democrats, the Republicans did not feel the pressure for rules reform that had engulfed the Democrats. No major rules changes were made by the Republicans during the last decade, and none was contemplated in 1984.

Republicans, however, had not been able to operate totally in their own world. The campaign finance law and the rising influence of the mass media affected Republicans as well as Democrats. And in states where legislatures accommodated the Democrats and created a presidential primary, the Republicans were dragged along.

And by an ironic turn of events, the GOP had been less hasty than the Democrats in abandoning primaries. "One of the major ironies of 1984," contended Angelo, was that "Democrats fostered primaries on the grounds that they would give more people a chance to participate. But now that they don't like the results, they're running away from them." There were a number of states, including Texas and Wisconsin, where the GOP in 1984 was expected to elect delegates through primaries while the Democrats reverted to the caucus process. Republicans were likely to end up having about the same number of binding primaries as they had in 1980.

that Jackson would take his complaint to the convention floor. Lewis also defended the new bonus delegate rules: "It's possible to say that participation is more important than winning. But I don't think you can say it's morally wrong for a political process to emphasize winning."

Democratic officials were concerned that black voters would be alienated from the party if Jackson's complaints were not resolved. Since adoption of Jackson's political agenda — seen by most officials as more liberal than that of the majority of party voters — was unlikely, an agreement to make rules changes for 1988 might be seen as the simplest solution.

Campaign Finance Laws

Like the Democratic Party reforms, federal campaign finance laws had unanticipated effects on the presidential nominating process. The Federal Election Campaign Act (FECA) of 1974 set national spending limits for presidential candidates in primary and general elections and state-by-state limitations for primary elections. Individual contributions to candidates were limited to $1,000.

To make up for the loss of funds from big contributors, presidential candidates were provided with federal funding. All contributions up to $250 were matched by the federal government up to a formula-derived spending limit, provided the candidate raised at least $5,000 in each of 20 states. *(Details, see Campaign Spending chapter)*

Federal financing probably encouraged some long-shot candidates to enter the presidential campaign because it often allowed them to mount a nationwide campaign.

Reliance on thousands of small contributions rather than on a smaller number of large contributions forced candidates to spend a greater amount of their time and resources on fund raising. This in turn influenced the decision of many candidates to begin their campaigns very early.

Although these effects were criticized, there was no outcry for reform. All of the Democratic candidates for president in 1984 applied for federal funding. Distributions began Jan. 1, with Democrats Mondale, Glenn and Cranston the biggest recipients initially.

'Outsider' Presidential Campaigns

Many political scientists believed the rise of candidate organizations and the lessening of party influence threatened the coalition-building process that helped presidential nominees to win the general election and govern the nation effectively. As evidence they cited the 1972 and 1976 Democratic nominees. Running an outsider campaign gave McGovern enough delegates to win the nomination in 1972. However, many party regulars who had been ignored or rebuffed during the nominating campaign returned the favor and did little to rescue McGovern's floundering general election campaign.

Four years later Carter ran a campaign based on an image of honesty and morality uncorrupted by Washington politics. Carter made little effort to gain the support of the party's elected leadership in Congress or the states, relying on his pluralities in the early primaries and caucuses to give him the momentum that carried him to the nomination. Many experts felt that the process that allowed Carter to ignore party leaders had serious implications for his conduct in office. "It's not just who ends up with the nomination, but it's the lessons learned by the person who wins the nomination and how well the government operates after that candidate is nominated and elected," said political scientist Thomas E. Mann, executive director of the American Political Science Association.

Carter's cold shoulder to party regulars also may have hurt get-out-the-vote efforts in the general election campaign in 1976 as his lead over incumbent Gerald R. Ford slipped from over 20 percentage points in post-convention

First-round Caucus Results

Because delegates in caucus states were elected at the end of a long, multi-tier process, participants in first-round mass meetings often felt less urgency about making a final choice among the presidential candidates than did primary voters. That was obvious in 1976, when most caucus states went uncommitted in first-round voting. But it was a different story four years later, when party leaders and teachers in the caucus states were among the first to back President Carter for re-election.

The following chart shows the first-round leaders — Carter, Minnesota Sen. Hubert H. Humphrey Jr., Washington Sen. Henry M. Jackson, Alabama Gov. George C. Wallace, Arizona Rep. Morris K. Udall and Massachusetts Sen. Edward M. Kennedy — in the 1976 and 1980 Democratic caucuses.

The states are listed in the order they held their first-round mass meetings in 1980. States that conducted caucuses only in 1976 also are included. "Unrecorded" means there was no available statewide tally of first-round caucus action. A dash (— —) indicates delegates were elected in a primary.

Caucus State	1976	1980
Iowa	Uncommitted (38%)	Carter (59%)
Maine	Uncommitted (64%)	Carter (47%)
Minnesota	Humphrey (51%)	Unrecorded (75%)
Alaska	Uncommitted (90%)	Uncommitted (63%)
Hawaii	Uncommitted (85%)	Carter (74%)
Oklahoma	Uncommitted (40%)	Carter (72%)
Washington	Jackson (58%)	Carter (53%)
Delaware	Unrecorded	Carter (60%)
Mississippi	Wallace (44%)	Carter (75%)
South Carolina	Uncommitted (48%)	Carter (62%)
Wyoming	Uncommitted (87%)	Carter (64%)
Virginia	Uncommitted (58%)	Carter (80%)
Kansas	Uncommitted (50%)	— —
Arizona	Udall (71%)	Kennedy (53%)
Idaho	— —	Carter (49%)
North Dakota	Unrecorded	Uncommitted (61%)
Missouri	Uncommitted (66%)	Carter (69%)
New Mexico	Uncommitted (37%)	— —
Vermont	Uncommitted (65%)	Kennedy (44%)
Michigan	— —	Kennedy (49%)
Louisiana	Uncommitted (46%)	— —
Texas	Unrecorded	Unrecorded
Connecticut	Carter (33%)	— —
Colorado	Uncommitted (34%)	Unrecorded
Utah	Uncommitted (41%)	Carter (50%)

Senate Voting Records of Democratic Candidates

Following are the Congressional Quarterly voting study scores for Sen. John Glenn, Ohio; Sen. Alan Cranston, Calif.; Sen. Gary Hart, Colo.; Sen. Ernest F. Hollings, S.C.; and former Sen. George McGovern, S.D.

	Presidential Support [1]		Party Unity [2]		Conservative Coalition [3]	
	Support	Opposition	Support	Opposition	Support	Opposition
1982						
Cranston	26	66	81	10	7	84
Glenn	35	45	67	17	26	51
Hart	37	56	85	12	14	79
Hollings	43	45	73	20	55	36
1981						
Cranston	38	48	77	10	10	74
Glenn	53	42	74	21	34	66
Hart	35	57	84	10	13	83
Hollings	54	38	58	35	67	30
1980						
Cranston	63	10	81	6	6	89
Glenn	72	21	77	16	29	58
Hart	66	23	68	19	25	63
Hollings	63	28	55	33	64	23
McGovern	45	15	44	7	7	44
1979						
Cranston	77	16	83	28	15	81
Glenn	77	16	79	19	34	65
Hart	79	17	79	18	23	71
Hollings	57	37	62	31	75	20
McGovern	70	18	77	9	11	78
1978						
Cranston	87	13	88	8	11	87
Glenn	87	11	86	12	18	83
Hart	84	9	87	8	20	76
Hollings	66	23	61	33	58	35
McGovern	68	11	76	4	11	68
1977						
Cranston	80	16	81	10	20	74
Glenn	83	15	63	36	59	41
Hart	74	25	80	14	19	73
Hollings	66	31	65	29	40	54
McGovern	61	22	77	5	2	82

[1] *Percentages of votes in which the member voted for and against the president's clear, personal position.*

[2] *Percentages of votes in which the member voted for and against the position taken by a majority of members of his party, in opposition to a majority of members of the other party.*

[3] *Percentages of votes in which the member voted for and against the position taken by a majority of Southern Democrats and Republicans, in opposition to a majority of Northern Democrats.*

polls to a final margin of 2 percentage points. Moreover, once in office President Carter continued his "loner" ways. Many observers blamed his inability or unwillingness to work with his party's leadership in Congress for the failure of the legislature to pass many of his key proposals.

President Reagan, on the other hand, was more successful than Carter in getting his legislative proposals passed. According to Mann, "Ronald Reagan in 1980 ran an extraordinarily party-based campaign ... unprecedented in the extent to which the presidential candidate and the congressional candidates ran together. So when he came into office, there were representatives and senators who felt that their own fates were tied up with his." Reagan also relied on personal politicking with members of Congress to get bills enacted.

Opponents of the Democrats' presidential nomination process insisted, though, that it was just as likely to produce a Carter as a Reagan because a candidate no longer needed to cultivate ties with his party's leaders to win the nomination. "You may have one who decides it's a good idea to do it ... like Ronald Reagan did, or you may get a president ... who doesn't think it's worthwhile, like Carter," said Ranney. "The present system doesn't prevent it, but it doesn't require it either."

GOP Nominating Process

Unlike the Democrats, the Republican Party in the 1960s and 1970s had never experienced the intense demands for reform of its presidential nomination process. Nonetheless, the GOP was influenced by many of the changes made by the Democrats. The most obvious modification was in delegate selection. Primaries and participatory caucuses replaced the formerly dominant party caucus/convention system in many states.

Most state Republican parties followed proportional representation rules that were similar, if not identical, to their Democratic counterparts. Often this adaptation was not by choice. Delegate selection laws passed by Democratic-controlled state legislatures were applied to both parties. Other state GOP organizations chose to go along with the prevailing political ethos of open participation in the delegate selection process.

One area of clear difference, though, was in the role of the national parties. The Republican National Committee had nothing comparable to the McGovern-Fraser commission, and it made little attempt to force its will on state parties. "The Republicans believe that the state parties are

"The Republicans believe that the state parties are independent soveregin units and that the national committee and the national convention are merely collections of these state party officers and delegates," wrote political scientists Robert J. Huckshorn and John F. Bibby. "Republican rules, therefore, permit state parties wide latitude in delegate selection procedures and maintain the essentially confederate character of the party."

There were some attempts in the 1970s to involve the national Republican Party in setting guidelines for delegate selection. In 1974 a committee headed by Rep. William A. Steiger of Wisconsin (1967-78) urged state parties to "take positive action to achieve the broadest possible participation in party affairs," particularly in the delegate selection process, by women, young people, minority and heritage groups, and senior citizens." Rule 32, passed by the 1976 convention, called for each state to "endeavor to have equal representation of men and women in its delegation."

However, adherence to these goals by state parties was voluntary, a fact reflected by the relatively low numbers of women and blacks among the delegates to Republican conventions. At the Detroit convention in 1980, 29 percent of the Republican delegates were women and 3 percent were blacks. Party officials insisted they were working hard to increase representation, especially among blacks. "We have tried through various seminars around the country to encourage blacks to become delegates," said Republican National Committee deputy chief counsel Catherine Gensior. "We are trying to encourage minority participation on every level."

However, lack of minority representation at the convention also reflected a lack of minority support for the Republican Party in general and in Reagan in particular. Reagan received only 10 percent of the national black vote in 1980, and public opinion polls indicated his popularity among this group had not increased during his years in office. "I don't think there's any question that the composition of the Republican National Convention is not going to do anything to reduce the idea that Reagan doesn't care about blacks and about minorities," said Ranney. "That isn't necessarily his fault, it's just the nature [of his support], and the Republicans are not about to adopt quotas, the kind of artificial constraints that would produce more minorities and women."

If the Republicans seemed to have a nonchalant attitude toward the nominating process in 1984 it was because Reagan was not seriously challenged for the Republican nomination. "I think any delegate that is going to be committed to another candidate is more or less committing political suicide," said Gensior.

However, since Reagan could serve only one more term as president even if he won in November, the Republicans would have to find a new nominee in 1988. And it could be assumed that prospective candidates and party officials would be examining the nominating process over the next four years to divine whether it gave an advantage to any particular candidate.

Pages 46-47 list the results of the early Democratic presidential primaries and caucuses and the Republican primary in New Hampshire.

1984 Primary and Caucus Results

(Through March)

Iowa Caucus (Feb. 20)

	Preference Vote	%	Weighted County Results*	%
Walter F. Mondale	27,896	44.5	1,444.8	48.9
Gary Hart	9,286	14.8	486.3	16.5
George McGovern	7,896	12.6	303.1	10.3
Alan Cranston	5,617	9.0	219.5	7.4
Uncommitted	4,701	7.5	277.4	9.4
John Glenn	3,310	5.3	102.2	3.5
Reubin Askew	2,084	3.3	73.7	2.5
Jesse Jackson	1,670	2.7	45.2	1.5
Ernest F. Hollings	165	0.3	1.4	0.0

Number of state convention delegates.

New Hampshire Primary (Feb. 28)

Democrats

	Vote	%
Gary Hart	37,702	37.3
Walter F. Mondale	28,173	27.9
John Glenn	12,088	12.0
Jesse Jackson	5,311	5.2
George McGovern	5,217	5.2
Ronald Reagan (write-ins)	5,056	5.0
Ernest F. Hollings	3,583	3.5
Alan Cranston	2,136	2.1
Reubin Askew	1,025	1.0
Others	752	0.7
Scattered write-ins	86	0.1

Republicans

	Vote	%
Ronald Reagan	65,033	86.2
Harold E. Stassen	1,543	2.0
David Kelley	360	0.5
Gary Arnold	252	0.3
Ben Fernandez	202	0.3
Scattered write-ins	8,094	10.7

Maine Caucus (March 4)

	State Delegates	Convention Percentage
Gary Hart	1,586	50.2
Walter F. Mondale	1,434	45.4
George McGovern	20	0.6
Jesse Jackson	13	0.4
John Glenn	5	0.2
Uncommitted	102	3.2

Vermont Primary (March 6)

	Vote	%
Gary Hart	51,703	71.1
Walter F. Mondale	14,896	20.5
Jesse Jackson	5,677	7.8
Reubin Askew	433	0.6

Other Primary Results

	Glenn Vote	%	Hart Vote	%	Jackson Vote	%	McGovern Vote	%	Mondale Vote	%	Others Vote	%	Uncommitted Vote	%
Alabama (March 13)	88,057	21.0	88,005	21.0	81,218	19.4	—	—	144,129	34.4	13,793	3.2	4,253	1.0
Florida (March 13)	126,383	10.8	458,523	39.3	142,520	12.2	17,319	1.5	388,216	33.2	34,641	3.0	—	—
Georgia (March 13)	122,739	17.9	186,825	27.3	143,622	21.0	11,464	1.7	208,191	30.4	8,270	1.2	3,056	0.5
Massachusetts (March 13)	45,299	7.3	243,227	39.1	31,452	5.0	132,409	21.3	160,101	25.8	3,628	0.6	5,630	0.9
Rhode Island (March 13)	2,225	4.9	20,419	45.2	3,550	7.9	2,160	4.8	15,871	35.2	474	1.0	436	1.0

	Hart Vote	%	Jackson Vote	%	Mondale Vote	%	Uncommitted Vote	%	Others Vote	%
Puerto Rico (March 20)	724	0.5	—	—	134,241	99.2	—	—	407	0.3
Illinois (March 20)	578,726	35.3	339,932	20.8	663,596	40.5	—	—	55,355	3.4
Connecticut (March 27)	116,076	52.7	26,044	11.8	64,136	29.1	1,985	0.9	12,059	5.5

Other Caucus Results

State	Estimated Turnout	Glenn	Hart	Jackson	McGovern	Mondale	Uncommitted
Wyoming (March 10)	3,526	0.1	60.4	0.4	0.2	35.9	3.0
Oklahoma (March 13) *	42,000	5.0	41.4	3.8	—	39.7	10.1
Washington (March 13) †	65,000	1.0	51.0	5.0	1.0	34.0	8.0
Nevada (March 13) *	5,000	2.0	52.3	0.6	0.2	37.7	7.2
Hawaii (March 13)	2,830	—	—	4.2	—	32.3	63.5
Delaware (March 14)	2,856	—	29.8	9.6	—	60.1	0.5
Alaska (March 15)	2,200	—	44.1	9.6	—	28.0	18.3

Nearly complete results.
† *Results with 50% of precincts reporting.*

1984 Delegate Selection

State	Estimated Turnout	Percentage of County Convention Delegates				
		Hart	Jackson	Mondale	Others	Uncommitted
Arkansas (March 17)	20,000	30.3	19.9	44.0	—	5.8
Kentucky (March 17)[1]	Not available	10.4	15.9	19.4	—	54.3
Michigan (March 17)[2]	132,002	32.2	16.7	50.4	0.2	0.5
Mississippi (March 17)	Not available	11.0	27.1	30.4	—	31.5
South Carolina (March 17)	40,000	12.7	25.0	9.1	—	53.2
Minnesota (March 20)[3]	Not available	7.0	2.0	62.0	—	29.0

[1] Precinct caucus results for three of Kentucky's 120 counties.
[2] Percentages reflect raw vote of caucus participants.
[3] Based on results from 150 precincts, tabulated to form a weighted sampling of the state.

State	Estimated Turnout	Percentage of Congressional District Delegates				
		Hart	Jackson	Mondale	Others	Uncommitted
Kansas (March 24)	11,553	41.8	3.3	48.7	—	6.2
Montana (March 25)[1]	13,832	49.2	5.2	35.7	0.3	9.6
Virginia (March 24 & 26)	25,505	14.7	26.7	30.4	—	28.2
North Dakota (March 14-28)[2]	5,000	35.8	2.8	29.9	—	31.5

[1] Percentages reflect raw vote of caucus participants.
[2] Percentages reflect poll taken of delegates elected to state convention.

Delegate Count
(Through March)

	Number of Pledged Delegates	Hart	Jackson	Mondale	Others	Uncommitted	Undetermined
"Hard" Count Total[1]	801	259	37	395	104	3	3
Grand Total	1,564	365	77	627	105	147	243

[1] "Hard" count includes only delegates pledged to candidates on the basis of primary or caucus results. The grand total also includes projected delegate totals on the basis of first-round caucus showings and preferences of House and Senate members; no House or Senate members are formally pledged to candidates. Caucus counts are subject to change.

National Nominating Conventions 49

Functions of Party Conventions 51
Pre-convention Era, 1789-1828 60
National Party Conventions, 1831-1980 65
National Convention Information for 1980, 1984 68

Breakdown of Convention Votes, 1964-80

The following chart shows the percentage of the Republican and Democratic convention vote that major presidential candidates with substantial opposition have received from caucus state delegates and primary state delegates from 1964 through 1980. The chart is based on first ballot votes before switches.

Republican Convention, 1964

	Caucus States	Primary States	Convention Votes	Percent of Convention
TOTAL VOTE	655	653	1,308	100.0
Goldwater	74.5%	60.5%	883	67.5
Scranton	10.7%	22.1%	214	16.4
Rockefeller	0.6%	16.8%	114	8.7
Others	14.2%	0.6%	97	7.4

Democratic Convention, 1968

	Caucus States	Primary States	Convention Votes	Percent of Convention
TOTAL VOTE	1,346	1,276	2,622	100.0
Humphrey	80.2%	53.4%	1,760.25	67.1
McCarthy	12.1%	34.4%	601	22.9
McGovern	3.8%	7.5%	146.5	5.6
Others	4.0%	4.7%	114.25	4.4

Republican Convention, 1968

	Caucus States	Primary States	Convention Votes	Percent of Convention
TOTAL VOTE	706	627	1,333	100.0
Nixon	59.6%	43.2%	692	51.9
Rockefeller	14.4%	27.9%	277	20.8
Reagan	11.2%	16.4%	182	13.7
Others	14.7%	12.4%	182	13.7

Democratic Convention, 1972

	Caucus States	Primary States	Convention Votes	Percent of Convention
TOTAL VOTE	1,009	2,007	3,016	100.0
McGovern	41.0%	64.9%	1,715.35	56.9
Jackson	30.0%	11.5%	534	17.7
Wallace	7.3%	15.5%	385.7	12.8
Others	21.7%	8.1%	380.95	12.6

Republican Convention, 1976

	Caucus States	Primary States	Convention Votes	Percent of Convention
TOTAL VOTE	693	1,566	2,259	100.0
Ford	44.9%	55.9%	1,187	52.5
Reagan	55.1%	43.9%	1,070	47.4
Others	0.0%	0.1%	2	0.1

Democratic Convention, 1976

	Caucus States	Primary States	Convention Votes	Percent of Convention
TOTAL VOTE	732	2,276	3,008	100.0
Carter	72.3%	75.1%	2,238.5	74.4
Udall	13.8%	10.0%	329.5	11.0
Brown	6.6%	11.1%	300.5	10.0
Others	7.4%	3.8%	139.5	4.6

Democratic Convention, 1980

	Caucus States	Primary States	Convention Votes	Percent of Convention
TOTAL VOTE	953	2,378	3,331	100.0
Carter	71.0 %	60.81%	2,123	63.73
Kennedy	24.3 %	38.64%	1,150.48	34.53
Others	4.66%	.54%	57.5	1.72

Functions of Party Conventions

Although the presidential nominating convention has been a target of criticism throughout its existence, it has survived to become a traditional fixture of American politics. The longevity and general acceptance of the convention is in large part due to its multiplicity of functions — functions that the convention uniquely combines.

The convention is a nominating body, used by the Democrats, Republicans and most of the principal third parties over the past 150 years. The convention writes a platform, presenting the positions of the party on issues of the campaign. The convention serves as the supreme governing body of the political party, making major decisions on party affairs that in the interim between the conventions are made by the national committee with the guidance of the party chairman. The convention also serves as the ultimate campaign rally, gathering together thousands of party leaders and rank and file members from across the country in an atmosphere that varies widely, sometimes encouraging sober discussion but often resembling a carnival. And the convention serves as a forum for compromise among the diverse elements within a party, allowing the discussion and often the satisfactory solution of differing points of view. There have been many critics of the convention process, but because it successfully combines a multiplicity of functions, the convention has endured.

The convention is an outgrowth of the American political experience. Nowhere is it mentioned in the Constitution, nor has the authority of the convention ever been a subject of congressional legislation. Rather, the convention is the evolutionary result of the American presidential selection process. The convention has been the accepted nominating method of the major political parties since the election of 1832, but internal changes within the convention system have been massive since the early, formative years.

Convention Sites

In the pre-Civil-War period, conventions were frequently held in small buildings, even churches, and attracted only several hundred delegates and a minimum of spectators. Transportation and communications were slow, so most conventions were held in the late spring in a city centrally located geographically. Baltimore, Md., was the most popular convention city in the pre-Civil-War period, hosting the first six Democratic conventions (1832 through 1852), two Whig conventions, one National Republican convention, and the 1831 Anti-Masonic gathering — America's first national nominating convention.

With the nation's westward expansion, Chicago, Ill., in the heartland of America, emerged as the most frequent convention center. Since hosting its first convention in 1860, Chicago has been the site of 24 major party conventions (14 Republican, 10 Democratic). But in recent years, other factors have emerged to be considered along with geographic centrality in the choice of a convention city. The pledge of a financial contribution by the convention city to the party is a major consideration in site selection. The contribution, made in cash and goods and services, in recent years has often been in the vicinity of $1 million and is used to help defray expenses of the party in running the convention. Adequate hotel and convention hall facilities are also of prime importance, as modern-day conventions attract thousands of delegates, party officials, spectators and media representatives. In the last decade convention security has become an increasingly important factor in site selection. A reason given for the choice of Miami Beach, Florida, by the Republicans in 1968 and by both major parties in 1972 was the city's island location, believed to be a strategic advantage in the control of any disruptive protest demonstrations. For the party that controls the White House, often the overriding factor in any site selection decision is the personal preference of the incumbent president. His choice often carries great weight in the final selection of a convention city.

The choice of the convention site is made by the national committees of the two parties about one year before the convention is to take place and is the first major step in the quadrennial convention process. It is followed several months later by announcement of the convention call, the establishment of the major convention committees — credentials, rules, and platform (resolutions), the appointment of convention officers and finally the holding of the convention itself. While these basic steps in the quadrennial process have undergone little change over the past 150 years, there have been major alterations within the nominating convention system.

The call to the convention sets the date and site of the meeting, and is issued early in each election year, if not before. The call to the first Democratic convention, held in 1832, was issued by the New Hampshire Legislature. Early Whig conventions were called by party members in Congress. With the establishment of national committees later in the 19th century, the function of issuing the convention

Democratic Conventions, 1832-1980

Year	City	Dates	Presidential Nominee	Vice Presidential Nominee	No. of Pres. Ballots
1832	Baltimore	May 21-23	Andrew Jackson	Martin Van Buren	1
1835	Baltimore	May 20-22	Martin Van Buren	Richard M. Johnson	1
1840	Baltimore	May 5-6	Martin Van Buren	—[1]	1
1844	Baltimore	May 27-29	James K. Polk	George M. Dallas	9
1848	Baltimore	May 22-25	Lewis Cass	William O. Butler	4
1852	Baltimore	June 1-5	Franklin Pierce	William R. King	49
1856	Cincinnati	June 2-6	James Buchanan	John C. Breckinridge	17
1860	Charleston	April 23-May 3	Deadlocked		57
	Baltimore	June 18-23	Stephen A. Douglas	Benjamin Fitzpatrick Herschel V. Johnson[2]	2
1864	Chicago	August 29-31	George B. McClellan	George H. Pendleton	1
1868	New York	July 4-9	Horatio Seymour	Francis P. Blair	22
1872	Baltimore	July 9-10	Horace Greeley	Benjamin G. Brown	1
1876	St. Louis	June 27-29	Samuel J. Tilden	Thomas A. Hendricks	2
1880	Cincinnati	June 22-24	Winfield S. Hancock	William H. English	2
1884	Chicago	July 8-11	Grover Cleveland	Thomas A. Hendricks	2
1888	St. Louis	June 5-7	Grover Cleveland	Allen G. Thurman	1
1892	Chicago	June 21-23	Grover Cleveland	Adlai E. Stevenson	1
1896	Chicago	July 7-11	William J. Bryan	Arthur Sewall	5
1900	Kansas City	July 4-6	William J. Bryan	Adlai E. Stevenson	1
1904	St. Louis	July 6-9	Alton S. Parker	Henry G. Davis	1
1908	Denver	July 7-10	William J. Bryan	John W. Kern	1
1912	Baltimore	June 25-July 2	Woodrow Wilson	Thomas R. Marshall	46
1916	St. Louis	June 14-16	Woodrow Wilson	Thomas R. Marshall	1
1920	San Francisco	June 28-July 6	James M. Cox	Franklin D. Roosevelt	43
1924	New York	June 24-July 9	John W. Davis	Charles W. Bryan	103
1928	Houston	June 26-29	Alfred E. Smith	Joseph T. Robinson	1
1932	Chicago	June 27-July 2	Franklin D. Roosevelt	John N. Garner	4
1936	Philadelphia	June 23-27	Franklin D. Roosevelt	John N. Garner	Acclamation
1940	Chicago	July 15-18	Franklin D. Roosevelt	Henry A. Wallace	1
1944	Chicago	July 19-21	Franklin D. Roosevelt	Harry S Truman	1
1948	Philadelphia	July 12-14	Harry S Truman	Alben W. Barkley	1
1952	Chicago	July 21-26	Adlai E. Stevenson	John J. Sparkman	3
1956	Chicago	Aug. 13-17	Adlai E. Stevenson	Estes Kefauver	1
1960	Los Angeles	July 11-15	John F. Kennedy	Lyndon B. Johnson	1
1964	Atlantic City	Aug. 24-27	Lyndon B. Johnson	Hubert H. Humphrey	Acclamation
1968	Chicago	Aug. 26-29	Hubert H. Humphrey	Edmund S. Muskie	1
1972	Miami Beach	July 10-13	George McGovern	Thomas F. Eagleton R. Sargent Shriver[3]	1
1976	New York	July 12-15	Jimmy Carter	Walter F. Mondale	1
1980	New York	Aug. 11-14	Jimmy Carter	Walter F. Mondale	1

1. The 1840 Democratic convention did not nominate a candidate for vice president.
2. The 1860 Democratic convention nominated Benjamin Fitzpatrick, who declined the nomination shortly after the convention adjourned. On June 25 the Democratic National Committee selected Herschel V. Johnson as the party's candidate for vice president.
3. The 1972 Democratic convention nominated Thomas F. Eagleton, who withdrew from the ticket on July 31. On Aug. 8 the Democratic National Committee selected R. Sargent Shriver as the party's candidate for vice president.

call fell to these new party organizations. Each national committee presently has the responsibility for allocating delegates to each state.

Delegate Selection

The method of allocating delegates to the individual states and territories has been modified by both parties in the 20th century. Throughout the existence of the convention system in the 19th century, both the Democrats and Republicans distributed votes to the states based on their Electoral College strength. The first deviation from this procedure was made by the Republicans after their divisive 1912 convention, in which President William Howard Taft won renomination over former President Theodore Roosevelt, due largely to nearly solid support from the South — a region vastly over-represented in relation to its number of

Republican Conventions, 1856-1980

Year	City	Dates	Presidential Nominee	Vice Presidential Nominee	No. of Pres. Ballots
1856	Philadelphia	June 17-19	John C. Fremont	William L. Dayton	2
1860	Chicago	May 16-18	Abraham Lincoln	Hannibal Hamlin	3
1864	Baltimore	June 7-8	Abraham Lincoln	Andrew Johnson	1
1868	Chicago	May 20-21	Ulysses S. Grant	Schuyler Colfax	1
1872	Philadelphia	June 5-6	Ulysses S. Grant	Henry Wilson	1
1876	Cincinnati	June 14-16	Rutherford B. Hayes	William A. Wheeler	7
1880	Chicago	June 2-8	James A. Garfield	Chester A. Arthur	36
1884	Chicago	June 3-6	James G. Blaine	John A. Logan	4
1888	Chicago	June 19-25	Benjamin Harrison	Levi P. Morton	8
1892	Minneapolis	June 7-10	Benjamin Harrison	Whitelaw Reid	1
1896	St. Louis	June 16-18	William McKinley	Garret A. Hobart	1
1900	Philadelphia	June 19-21	William McKinley	Theodore Roosevelt	1
1904	Chicago	June 21-23	Theodore Roosevelt	Charles W. Fairbanks	1
1908	Chicago	June 16-19	William H. Taft	James S. Sherman	1
1912	Chicago	June 18-22	William H. Taft	James S. Sherman / Nicholas Murray Butler[1]	1
1916	Chicago	June 7-10	Charles E. Hughes	Charles W. Fairbanks	3
1920	Chicago	June 8-12	Warren G. Harding	Calvin Coolidge	10
1924	Cleveland	June 10-12	Calvin Coolidge	Charles G. Dawes	1
1928	Kansas City	June 12-15	Herbert Hoover	Charles Curtis	1
1932	Chicago	June 14-16	Herbert Hoover	Charles Curtis	1
1936	Cleveland	June 9-12	Alfred M. Landon	Frank Knox	1
1940	Philadelphia	June 24-28	Wendell L. Willkie	Charles L. McNary	6
1944	Chicago	June 26-28	Thomas E. Dewey	John W. Bricker	1
1948	Philadelphia	June 21-25	Thomas E. Dewey	Earl Warren	3
1952	Chicago	July 7-11	Dwight D. Eisenhower	Richard M. Nixon	1
1956	San Francisco	Aug. 20-23	Dwight D. Eisenhower	Richard M. Nixon	1
1960	Chicago	July 25-28	Richard M. Nixon	Henry Cabot Lodge	1
1964	San Francisco	July 13-16	Barry Goldwater	William E. Miller	1
1968	Miami Beach	Aug. 5-8	Richard M. Nixon	Spiro T. Agnew	1
1972	Miami Beach	Aug. 21-23	Richard M. Nixon	Spiro T. Agnew	1
1976	Kansas City	Aug. 16-19	Gerald R. Ford	Robert Dole	1
1980	Detroit	July 14-17	Ronald Reagan	George Bush	1

1. The 1912 Republican convention nominated James S. Sherman, who died on Oct. 30. The Republican National Committee subsequently selected Nicholas Murray Butler to receive the Republican electoral votes for vice president.

Source for Data on Conventions: Bain, Richard C. and Parris, Judith H. *Convention Decisions and Voting Records*, Brookings Institution, Washington, D.C. 1973.

Republican voters. Before their 1916 convention the Republicans reduced the allocation of votes to the Southern states, marking the first major move by either party in modifying its delegate allocation method. At their 1924 convention the Republicans applied the first bonus system, by which states were awarded extra votes for supporting the Republican presidential candidate in the previous election. The concept of bonus votes, applied as a reward to the states for supporting the party ticket, has been used and expanded by both parties since that time.

The Democrats first used a bonus system in 1944, completing a compromise arrangement with Southern states for abolishing the party's controversial two-thirds nominating rule. Since then, both parties have used various delegate allocation formulas. At their 1972 convention the Republicans revised the method used in allocating delegates and added more than 900 new delegate slots. The Ripon Society, an organization of liberal Republicans, sued to have the new rules overturned. They argued that, because of the extra delegates awarded to states that voted Republican in the previous presidential election, small Southern and Western states were favored at the expense of the more populous but less Republican Eastern states. The challenge failed when the Supreme Court in February 1976 refused to hear the case and thus let stand a U.S. Court of Appeals decision upholding the rules.

Only 116 delegates from 13 states attended the initial national nominating convention held by the Anti-Masons in 1831, but with the addition of more states and the adoption of increasingly complex voting allocation formulas by the major parties, the size of conventions spiraled. The 1976 Republican convention had 2,259 delegates, while the Democrats in the same year had 3,075 delegates (casting 3,008 votes). The expanded size in part reflected the democratization of the conventions, with less command by a few party leaders and the dramatic growth of youth, women and minority delegates. Increased representation by such groups was one of the major reasons given by the

1984 Delegate Selection Rules

The rules governing delegate selection adopted by the Republicans and the Democrats differ on several key points. Following is a summary of the major differences in party delegate selection rules for 1984:

- Democrats require states to hold their primaries or the first stage of their caucus process between March 13 and June 12. Republicans leave the choice of delegate selection dates up to the state parties.
- Democrats require primary states to set filing deadlines 30 to 90 days before the election. Republicans leave any restrictions up to state stature or state party rules.
- The Democratic Party allows only publicly-declared Democrats to participate in its primaries and caucuses. Republicans allow cross-overs where state law permits.
- Democrats require delegates to declare presidential preference or uncommitted status. Republican delegates are not required to declare preference unless mandated by state law or state party regulations.
- Democratic delegates are pledged to vote "in all good conscience" for the candidate they were elected to support. Republicans require delegates bound to a candidate by state law in primary states to vote for that candidate.
- Democrats require states to elect an equal number of men and women delegates. Republicans request states to elect an equal number.

Republicans for the 60 percent increase in delegate strength authorized by the 1972 convention (and effective for the 1976 gathering). The Democrats adopted new rules in June 1978 expanding the number of delegates by 10 percent to provide extra representation for state and local officials. The new rules also required that women account for at least 50 percent of the delegates to the 1980 convention.

With the increased size of conventions has come a formalization in the method of delegate selection. In the formative years of the convention system, delegate selection was often haphazard and informal. At the Democratic convention in 1835, the state of Maryland had 188 delegates to cast the state's 10 votes. On the other hand, the 15 votes for the state of Tennessee were cast by a traveling businessman, who inadvertently happened to be in the convention city at the time of the convention. While the number of delegates and the number of votes allocated tended to be equal or nearly so later in the 19th century, domination of national conventions was frequently exercised by a few party bosses.

Two basic methods of delegate selection were employed in the 19th century and continued to be used into the 20th: the caucus method, by which delegates were chosen by meetings at the local or state level; and the appointment method, by which delegates were appointed by the governor or a powerful state leader.

A revolutionary new mechanism for delegate selection emerged during the early 1900s: the presidential primary election in which delegates were elected directly by the voters.

Initiated in Florida in 1904, the presidential primary by 1912 was used by 13 states. In his first annual message to Congress the following year, President Woodrow Wilson advocated the establishment of a national primary to select presidential candidates: "I feel confident that I do not misinterpret the wishes or the expectations of the country when I urge the prompt enactment of legislation which will provide for primary elections throughout the country at which the voters of the several parties may choose their nominees for the presidency without the intervention of nominating conventions." Wilson went on to suggest the retention of conventions for the purpose of declaring the results of the primaries and formulating the parties' platforms.

Before any action was taken on Wilson's proposal, the progressive spirit that spurred the growth of presidential primaries died out. Not until after World War II, when widespread pressures for change touched both parties, especially the Democratic, was there a rapid growth in presidential primaries. By 1980 there were a record 37 presidential primaries.

Presently in most states that use it, participation in the presidential primary is restricted to voters belonging to the party holding the primary. In some states, however, participation by voters outside the party is allowed. New rules adopted by the Democrats in 1978 prohibited this practice in Democratic primaries.

1984 Democratic Rules

In June 1982, the Democratic National Committee (DNC) adopted several changes in the presidential nominating process recommended by the party's Commission on Presidential Nominations, chaired by North Carolina Governor James B. Hunt, Jr. The Hunt Commission, as it came to be known, suggested revisions in the nominating process designed to increase the power of party regulars and give the convention more freedom to act on its own. It was the fourth time in 12 years that the Democrats, struggling to repair their nominating process without repudiating earlier reforms, had rewritten their party rules.

One major change in the Democrats' rules was the creation of a new group of "superdelegates," party and elected officials who would go to the 1984 convention uncommitted and would cast about 14 percent of the ballots. The DNC also adopted a Hunt Commission proposal to weaken the rule binding delegates to vote for their original presidential preference on the first convention ballot. The new rule allowed a presidential candidate to replace any disloyal delegate with a more faithful one.

One of the most significant revisions was the Democrats' decision to relax proportional representation at the convention and end the ban on the "loophole" primary. Proportional representation is the distribution of delegates among candidates to reflect their share of the primary or caucus vote. Mandated by party rules in 1980, it was blamed by some Democrats for the protracted primary fight between President Jimmy Carter and Massachusetts Sen. Edward M. Kennedy. Because candidates needed only about 20 percent of the vote in most places to qualify for a share of the delegates, Kennedy was able to remain in contention. But while the system kept Kennedy going, it did nothing to help his chances of winning the nomination.

Although the Democrats' 1984 rules permitted states to retain proportional representation, they also allowed states to take advantage of two options that could help a front-running candidate build the momentum to wrap up the nomination early in the year.

One was a winner-take-more system. States could elect to keep proportional representation but adopt a winner bonus plan that would award the top vote-getter in each district one extra delegate.

The other option was a return to the loophole primary — winner take all by district. This system was outlawed by party rules in 1980, although Illinois and West Virginia were granted special exemptions to maintain their loophole voting systems.

In the loophole states, voters ballot directly for delegates, with each delegate candidate identified by presidential preference. Sometimes several presidential contenders win at least a fraction of the delegates in a given district, but the most common result is a sweep by the presidential front-runner, even if he has less than an absolute majority. Loophole primaries aid the building of a consensus behind the front-runner, while still giving other candidates a chance to inject themselves back into the race by winning decisively a major loophole state.

The DNC retained the delegate selection season adopted in 1978, a three month period stretching from the second Tuesday in March to the second Tuesday in June. But, in an effort to reduce the growing influence of early states in the nominating process, the Democrats required Iowa and New Hampshire to move their highly publicized elections to late winter. Party rules maintained the privileged status of Iowa and New Hampshire before other states, but mandated that their initial nominating rounds be held only eight days apart in 1984. Five weeks intervened between the Iowa caucuses and New Hampshire primary in 1980.

The DNC also retained rules requiring primary states to set candidate filing deadlines 30 to 90 days before the election and limiting participation in the delegate selection process to Democrats only. This last rule eliminated crossover primaries where voters could participate in the Democratic primary without designating their party affiliation. Blacks and Hispanics won continued endorsement of affirmative action in the new party rules. Women gained renewed support for the equal division rule, which required state delegations at the national convention to be divided equally between men and women.

Credentials Disputes

Before the opening of a convention, the national committee compiles a temporary roll of delegates. The roll is referred to the convention's credentials committee, which holds hearings on the challenges and makes recommendations to the convention, the final arbiter of all disputes.

Some of the most bitter convention battles have concerned the seating of contested delegations. In the 20th century most of the heated credentials fights have concerned delegations from the South. In the Republican Party the challenges focused on the power of the Republican state organizations to dictate the selection of delegates. The issue was hottest in 1912 and 1952, when the party throughout most of the South was a skeletal structure whose power was largely restricted to selection of convention delegates. Within the Democratic Party the question of Southern credentials emerged after World War II on the volatile issues of civil rights and party loyalty. Important credentials challenges on these issues occurred at the 1948, 1952, 1964 and 1968 Democratic conventions.

There were numerous credentials challenges at the 1972 Democratic convention, but unlike its immediate predecessors the challenges involved delegations from across the nation and focused on violations of the party's newly adopted guidelines.

After their 1952 credentials battle, the Republicans established a contest committee within the national committee to review credentials challenges before the convention. After their divisive 1968 convention the Democrats also created a formal credentials procedure within the national committee to review all challenges before the opening of the convention.

Equally important to the settlement of credentials challenges are the rules under which the convention operates. The Republican Party adopts a completely new set of rules at every convention. Although large portions of the existing rules are enacted each time, general revision is always possible.

After its 1968 convention the Democratic Party set out to reform itself and the convention system. The Commission on Rules and the Commission on Party Structure and Delegate Selection, both created by the 1968 convention, proposed many changes that were accepted by the national committee. As a result, a formal set of rules was adopted for the first time at the party's 1972 convention.

Controversial Rules

Although not having a formal set of rules before 1972, the Democratic Party throughout the bulk of its history operated with two critical and controversial rules never used by the Republicans: the unit rule and the two-thirds nominating rule. The unit rule enabled the majority of a delegation, if authorized by its state party, to cast the

---

Democrats' Two-Thirds Rule

At their first convention in 1832, the Democrats adopted a rule requiring a two-thirds majority for nomination. Two presidential candidates — Martin Van Buren in 1844 and Champ Clark in 1912 — received majorities but failed to attain the two-thirds requirement.

In 1844, on the first ballot Van Buren received 146 of the 266 convention votes, 54.9 percent of the total. His total fell under a simple majority on succeeding roll calls and on the ninth ballot the nomination went to a dark horse candidate, former Gov. James K. Polk of Tennessee.

In 1912, from the 10th through the 16th ballots, Clark recorded a simple majority. He reached his peak on the 10th ballot, receiving 556 of the 1,094 convention votes, 50.8 percent of the total. The nomination, however, ultimately went to New Jersey Gov. Woodrow Wilson, who was selected on the 46th ballot.

At their 1936 convention, the Democrats voted to end the requirement for a two-thirds majority for nomination.

Notable Credentials Fights

1848, Democratic. Two rival New York state factions, known as the Barnburners and the Hunkers, sent separate delegations. By a vote of 126 to 125, the convention decided to seat both delegations and split New York's vote between them. This compromise suited neither faction: the Barnburners bolted the convention; the Hunkers remained but refused to vote.

1860, Democratic. Dissatisfaction with the slavery plank in the party platform spurred a walkout by several dozen southern delegates from the Charleston convention. When the tumultuous convention reconvened in Baltimore six weeks later, a credentials controversy developed on the status of the bolting delegates. The majority report of the credentials committee recommended that the delegates in question, except those from Alabama and Louisiana, be reseated. The minority report recommended that a larger majority of the withdrawing Charleston delegates be allowed to return. The minority report was defeated, 100-1/2 to 150, prompting a walkout by the majority of delegates from nine states.

1880, Republican. Factions for and against the candidacy of former President Ulysses S. Grant clashed on the credentials of the Illinois delegation. By a margin of 353 to 387, the convention rejected a minority report that proposed seating pro-Grant delegates elected at the state convention over other delegates elected at a congressional district caucus. Three other votes were taken on disputed credentials from different Illinois districts, but all were decided in favor of the anti-Grant forces by a similar margin. The votes indicated the weakness of the Grant candidacy. The nomination went to a dark horse candidate on the 36th ballot, Rep. James A. Garfield of Ohio.

1912, Republican. The furious struggle between President William Howard Taft and Theodore Roosevelt for the presidential nomination centered on credentials. The Roosevelt forces brought 72 delegate challenges to the floor of the convention, but the test of strength between the two candidates came on a procedural motion. By a vote of 567 to 507, the convention tabled a motion presented by the Roosevelt forces barring any of the delegates under challenge from voting on any of the credentials contests. This procedural vote clearly indicated Taft's control of the convention. All the credentials cases were settled in favor of the Taft delegates and the presidential nomination ultimately went to the incumbent president.

1932, Democratic. Two delegations favorable to the front runner for the presidential nomination, Franklin D. Roosevelt, came under challenge. However, in a show of strength, the Roosevelt forces won both contests: seating a Louisiana delegation headed by Sen. Huey P. Long by a vote of 638-3/4 to 514-1/4, and a Roosevelt delegation from Minnesota by an even wider margin, 658-1/4 to 492-3/4. Roosevelt won the nomination on the fourth ballot.

1952, Democratic. The refusal of three southern states — Louisiana, South Carolina and Virginia — to agree to a party loyalty pledge, brought their credentials into question. The Virginia delegation argued that the problem prompting the loyalty pledge was covered by state law. By a vote of 650-1/2 to 518, the convention approved the seating of the Virginia delegation. After Louisiana and South Carolina took positions similar to that of Virginia, they were seated by a voice vote.

1952, Republican. Sixty-eight delegates from three southern states (Georgia, Louisiana, and Texas) were the focal point of the fight for the presidential nomination between Gen. Dwight D. Eisenhower and Ohio Sen. Robert A. Taft. The national committee, controlled by forces favorable to Taft, had voted to seat delegations friendly to the Ohio Senator from these three states. But by a vote of 607 to 531 the convention seated the Georgia delegation favorable to Eisenhower and without roll calls seated the Eisenhower delegates from Louisiana and Texas. The General went on to win the presidential nomination on the first ballot.

1968, Democratic. A struggle between the anti-Vietnam war forces, led by Minnesota Sen. Eugene J. McCarthy, and the party regulars, headed by Vice President Hubert Humphrey, dominated the 17 credentials cases considered by the credentials committee. Three of the cases, involving the Texas, Georgia and Alabama delegations, required roll calls on the convention floor. All were won by the Humphrey forces. By a vote of 1,368-1/4 to 956-3/4, the regular Texas delegation headed by Gov. John B. Connally was seated. A minority report to seat the entire Georgia delegation led by black leader Julian Bond was defeated, 1,043.55 to 1,415.45. And a minority report to seat a McCarthy-backed, largely black delegation from Alabama was also rejected, 880-3/4 to 1,607. Humphrey, having shown his strength during the credentials contests, went on to an easy first ballot nomination.

1972, Democratic. The first test of strength at the convention between South Dakota Sen. George McGovern's delegates and party regulars came over credentials. Key challenges brought to the convention floor concerned the South Carolina, California and Illinois delegations. The South Carolina challenge was brought by the National Women's Political Caucus in response to alleged underrepresentation of women in the delegation. Although their position was supposedly supported by the McGovern camp, votes were withheld in order not to jeopardize McGovern's chances of winning the important California contest. The women's challenge lost 1,429.05 to 1,555.75. The California challenge was of crucial importance to McGovern, since it involved 151 delegates initially won by the South Dakota senator in the state's winner-take-all primary, but stripped from him by the credentials committee. By a vote of 1,618.28 to 1,238.22, McGovern regained the contested delegates, and thereby nailed down his nomination. With victory in hand, the dominant McGovern camp sought a compromise on the Illinois case, which pitted a delegation headed by Chicago's powerful Mayor Richard Daley against an insurgent delegation composed of party reformers. Compromise was unattainable and with the bulk of McGovern delegates voting for the reformers, a minority report to seat the Daley delegates was rejected.

entire vote of the delegation for one candidate or position. In use since the earliest Democratic conventions, the unit rule was abolished by the 1968 convention.

From its first convention in 1832 until its elimination over a century later at the 1936 convention, the Democrats employed the two-thirds nominating rule, which required any candidate for president or vice president to win not just a simple majority but a two-thirds majority. Viewed as a boon to the South since it allowed that region a virtual veto power over any possible nominee, the rule was abolished with the stipulation that the South would receive an increased vote allocation at later conventions.

In its century of use the two-thirds rule frequently produced protracted, multi-ballot conventions, often giving the Democrats a degree of turbulence the Republicans, requiring only a simple majority, did not have. Between 1832 and 1932, seven Democratic conventions took more than 10 ballots to select a presidential candidate. In contrast, in their entire convention history (1856 through 1976), the Republicans have had just one convention that required more than 10 ballots to select a presidential candidate.

One controversy that surfaced during the 1980 Democratic Party convention concerned a convention rule that bound delegates to vote on the first ballot for the candidates under whose banner they had been elected. Supporters of Sen. Edward M. Kennedy, D-Mass., had devoted their initial energies to prying the nomination from incumbent President Jimmy Carter by trying unsuccessfully to open the convention by defeating that rule. The final tally on the rule showed 1,936.42 delegates favoring the binding rule and 1,390.580 opposing it. Passage of the binding rule assured Carter's renomination, and shortly after the vote, Kennedy ended his nine-month challenge to the president by announcing that his name would not be placed in nomination Aug. 13.

Convention Officers

Credentials, rules and platform are the major convention committees, but each party has additional committees including one in charge of convention arrangements. Within the Republican Party the arrangements committee recommends a slate of convention officers to the national committee, which in turn refers the names to the committee on permanent organization for confirmation. The people the committee chooses are subject to the approval of the convention. In the Democratic Party, this function is performed by the rules committee.

Both in the Democratic and Republican parties, the presiding officer during the bulk of the convention is the permanent chairman. Over the past quarter century the position has usually gone to the party's leader in the House of Representatives. However, this loose precedent was broken in the Democratic Party by a rule adopted at the 1972 convention requiring that the position alternate every four years between the sexes.

Party Platforms

The adoption of a party platform is one of the principal functions of a convention. The platform committee is charged with the responsibility of writing a party platform to be presented to the convention for its approval.

The main problem of a platform committee is to write a platform all party candidates can use in their campaigns.

Major Platform Fights

1860, Democratic. A minority report on the slavery plank, stating that the decision on allowing slavery in the territories should be left to the Supreme Court, was approved, 165 to 138. The majority report (favored by the South) declared that no government — local, state or federal — could outlaw slavery in the territories. The acceptance of the minority report precipitated a walkout by several dozen southern delegates and the eventual sectional split in the party.

1896, Democratic. The monetary plank of the platform committee, favoring free and unlimited coinage of silver at a ratio of 16 to 1 with gold, was accepted by the convention, which defeated a proposed gold plank, 303 to 626. During debate, William Jennings Bryan made his famous "Cross of Gold" speech supporting the platform committee plank, bringing him to the attention of the convention and resulting in his nomination for president.

1908, Republican. A minority report, proposing a substitute platform, was presented by Sen. Robert M. LaFollette (Wis.). Minority proposals included increased antitrust activities, enactment of a law requiring publication of campaign expenditures, and popular election of senators. All the proposed planks were defeated by wide margins; the closest vote, on direct election of senators, was 114 for, 866 against.

1924, Democratic. A minority plank was presented that condemned the activities of the Ku Klux Klan, then enjoying a resurgence in the South and some states in the Midwest. The plank was defeated 542-7/20 to 543-3/20, the closest vote in Democratic convention history.

1932, Republican. A minority plank favoring repeal of the 18th Amendment (Prohibition) in favor of a state-option arrangement was defeated, 460-2/9 to 690-19/36.

1948, Democratic. An amendment to the platform, strengthening the civil rights plank by guaranteeing full and equal political participation, equal employment opportunity, personal security and equal treatment in the military service, was accepted, 651-1/2 to 582-1/2.

1964, Republican. An amendment offered by Sen. Hugh Scott (Pa.) to strengthen the civil rights plank by including voting guarantees in state as well as in federal elections and by eliminating job bias was defeated, 409 to 897.

1968, Democratic. A minority report on Vietnam called for cessation of the bombing of North Vietnam, halting of offensive and search-and-destroy missions by American combat units, a negotiated withdrawal of American troops and establishment of a coalition government in South Vietnam. It was defeated, 1,041-1/4 to 1,567-3/4.

1972, Democratic. By a vote of 999.34 to 1,852.86, the convention rejected a minority report proposing a government guaranteed annual income of $6,500 for a family of four. By a vote of 1,101.37 to 1,572.80, a women's rights plank focusing on the issue of abortion was defeated.

For this reason, platforms often fit the description given them by the late Wendell L. Willkie, Republican presidential candidate in 1940: "fusions of ambiguity."

Despite the best efforts of platform-builders to compromise their differences in the comparative privacy of the committee room, they sometimes encounter so controversial a subject that it cannot be compromised. Under these conditions, dissident committee members often submit a minority report to the convention floor. Open floor fights are not unusual and like credentials battles, often serve as an indicator of the strength of the various candidates.

When the party has an incumbent president, the platform is often drafted in the White House, or at least approved by the president. Rarely is a platform adopted by a party that criticizes its incumbent president.

The first platform was adopted by the Democrats in 1840. It was a short document less than 1,000 words long. Since then the platforms with few exceptions have grown longer and longer, covering more issues and making an appeal to more interest groups. The platform adopted by the Republicans in 1976 was nearly 20,000 words long. The Democrats, however, bucked the trend toward longer platforms by adopting one in 1976 that was about half the length of their 25,000-word 1972 document. However, the Democrats' 1980 platform contained a record 40,000 words, and the Republicans' was almost as long.

The Republicans' 1980 platform mirrored the convention's emphasis on party unity and generally followed front-runner Ronald Reagan's wishes, in contrast to 1976, when platform deliberations had been marked by discord between the Reagan faction and incumbent President Gerald R. Ford. The 1980 platform was more a blueprint for victory in November than a definitive statement of party views. Rather than slug it out over specifics, the party's moderate and conservative wings agreed to blur their differences in order to appear united, to broaden the party's appeal and to smooth the way to the White House for their nominee. On a few issues, platform writers veered from traditional Republican positions. On others, they went out of their way to embrace policies that meshed with Reagan's views more than their own. But for the most part, they managed to fashion a policy statement that pleased no party faction entirely but with which all could live reasonably.

In contrast to the Republicans' harmony, the 1980 Democratic convention was marked by bitter contests over the party platform that was adopted Aug. 13 after two days of prolonged and sometimes raucus debate that pitted Carter against Kennedy and a coalition of special interest groups. The final document was filled with so many concessions to the Kennedy forces that it won only a halfhearted endorsement from the president.

In many key areas the platform bore little resemblance to the document that Carter operatives took to the first platform drafting meeting June 17. During that session numerous minor changes proposed by Kennedy backers were accepted. Then, two weeks before the convention, Carter began to yield on more substantive issues. By the time the platform debate started, Carter had accepted eight of Kennedy's minority reports. During the debate, six other minority planks were adopted either with Carter's acquiescence or in spite of his opposition.

Third Party Platforms

Throughout American history, many daring and controversial political platforms adopted by third parties have been rejected as too radical in their own time by the major parties. Yet these proposals have later won popular acceptance, made their way into the major party platforms — and into law.

Ideas such as the graduated income tax, popular election of senators, women's suffrage, minimum wages, social security, day-care centers and the 18-year-old vote were advocated by Populists, Progressives and other independents long before they were finally accepted by the nation as a whole.

The radical third parties and their platforms have been anathema to the established wisdom of the day, denounced as impractical, dangerous, destructive of moral virtues and even traitorous. They have been anti-establishment and more far-reaching in their proposed solutions to problems than the major parties have dared to be.

In contrast to the third parties, Democrats and Republicans traditionally have been much more chary of adopting radical platform planks. Trying to appeal to a broad range of voters, the two major parties have tended to compromise differences or to turn down controversial planks.

The Democratic Party has been more ready than the Republicans to adopt once-radical ideas, but there is usually a considerable time lag between their origin in third parties and their eventual adoption in Democratic platforms. For example, while the Democrats by 1912 had adopted many of the Populist planks of the 1890s, the Bull Moose Progressives of that year were already way ahead of them in proposals for social legislation. Not until 1932 were many of the 1912 Progressive planks adopted by the Democrats.

Similarly, not until the 1960s did Democratic platforms incorporate many of the more far-reaching proposals put forward by the 1948 Henry Wallace Progressives.

Communications and the Media

Major changes in the national nominating convention have resulted from the massive advances in transportation and communication particularly evident in the 20th century.

A major impact of the revolution in transportation has affected the scheduling of conventions. In the 19th century, conventions were sometimes held a year or more before the election and at the latest were completed by late spring of the election year. With the ability of people to assemble quickly, conventions in recent years have been held later in the election year, usually in July or August. Advances in transportation have also affected site location. Geographic centrality is no longer the primary consideration in the selection of a convention city. Increasingly, coastal cities have been chosen as convention hosts.

The invention of new means of communication, particularly television, have had a further impact on the convention system. The changes spurred by the media have primarily been cosmetic ones, designed to give the convention a look of efficiency that was not so necessary in earlier days. As the conduct of the convention has undergone closer scrutiny by the American electorate, both parties have made major efforts to cut back the frivolity and hoopla, and to accentuate the more sober aspects of the convention process.

Radio coverage of conventions began in 1924; television coverage was initiated 16 years later. One of the first changes inspired by the media age was the termination of

Selection by Caucus Method

Although about three-fourths of the delegates to the 1980 nominating conventions were chosen in presidential primaries, party caucuses also had a share of the limelight. In 1980 15 states used the caucus method to select delegates to the nominating conventions, while 27 states used the primary method and 8 states employed a hybrid method of primaries and caucuses. Indeed, the Jan. 21, 1980, Iowa precinct caucuses assumed an importance that rivaled the traditionally important New Hampshire primary. In the process, the Iowa caucuses raised public consciousness of a delegate selection method that had been on the decline throughout the last decade.

The impact of caucuses in the 1970s decreased as the number of primaries grew dramatically. During the 1960s, a candidate sought to run well in primary states mainly to have a bargaining chip with which to deal with powerful leaders in the caucus states. Republicans Barry Goldwater in 1964 and Richard Nixon in 1968 and Democrat Hubert H. Humphrey in 1968 all built up solid majorities among caucus state delegates that carried them to their parties' nominations. Humphrey did not even enter a primary in 1968.

But since 1968 candidates have placed their principal emphasis on primary campaigning. First George McGovern, D-S.D. — and then incumbent Republican President Gerald R. Ford and Democratic challenger Jimmy Carter in 1976 — all won their parties' nominations by winning a large majority of the primary state delegates. Neither McGovern nor Ford won a majority of the caucus state delegates. Carter was able to win a majority only after his opponents' campaigns collapsed.

Complex Method

Compared to a primary, the caucus system is relatively complex. Instead of focusing on a single primary election ballot, the caucus presents a multi-tiered system that involves meetings scheduled over several weeks, sometimes even months. While there is mass participation at the first level only, meetings at this step often last several hours and attract only the most enthusiastic and dedicated party members.

The operation of the caucus varies from state to state, and each party has its own set of rules. But most use a process that begins with precinct caucuses or some other type of local mass meeting open to all party voters. Participants, often publicly declaring their votes, elect delegates to the next stage in the process.

In smaller states such as Delaware and Hawaii, delegates are elected directly to a state convention, where the national convention delegates are chosen.

In larger states like Iowa, there is at least one more step. Most frequently, delegates are elected at the precinct caucuses to county conventions, where the national convention delegates are chosen. In Iowa, Democrats hold their district conventions in April and their state convention in mid-June. Iowa Republicans hold district caucuses during the state convention in early June.

Participation, even at the first level of the caucus process, is usually much lower than in primary states. In few states did caucus turnout exceed 10 percent of those eligible to participate in 1976. Caucus participants usually are local party leaders and activists, not newcomers to the process. Many rank-and-file voters find a caucus complex and confusing; others find it intimidating.

In a caucus state the focus is on one-on-one campaigning. Time, not money, is the most valuable resource. Because organization and personal campaigning are so important, an early start is far more crucial in a caucus state than a primary. And because only a small segment of the electorate is targeted in most caucus states, candidates usually use media advertising sparingly. On the average, candidates in 1976 spent about $5 in every primary state for every $1 they spent in a caucus state.

Although the basic steps in the caucus process are the same for both parties, the rules that govern them are vastly different. Democratic rules have been revamped substantially since 1968, establishing national standards for grass-roots participation. Republican rules have remained largely unchanged with the states given wide latitude in drawing up their delegate selection plans. Democratic caucuses are open to Democrats only. Republicans allow crossovers where state law permits, creating a wide range of variations. The first step of the Democratic caucus process must be open, well-publicized mass meetings. In most states Republicans do the same. Generally, voters may only participate in the election of local party officials, who meet to begin the caucus process.

Caucus Revival

The most tangible evidence of a revival of the caucus process is found in the percentage of delegates elected from caucus states. For both parties this figure was on a sharp decline throughout the 1970s. But Democrats broke the downward trend and actually elected more delegates by the caucus process in 1980 than in 1976. The principal reason for the upward swing was that two of the largest delegations — Texas and Michigan — switched from primaries to caucuses to choose delegates. Those two switches more than offset the moves of the Democratic parties in Connecticut, Kansas, Louisiana, New Mexico and Puerto Rico from caucuses to primaries.

Throughout the 1970s, Republicans elected a larger proportion of their delegates from caucus states than did the Democrats. But that changed in 1980, with only 24 percent of the GOP convention coming from caucus states (compared to 31 percent in 1976 and 53 percent in 1968).

During the 1980 presidential campaign both Carter and Reagan reaped the harvest of early organization and grass-roots strength by garnering substantial leads in the caucus states. Carter won 64 percent of Democratic delegates in caucus states compared to 58 percent in primary states, while Reagan won 83 percent of caucus-selected delegates and 78 percent of the delegates elected in primaries.

the custom that a presidential candidate not appear at the convention, but accept his nomination in a ceremony several weeks later. Franklin D. Roosevelt was the first major party candidate to break this tradition, when, in 1932, he delivered his acceptance speech in person before the Democratic convention. Thomas E. Dewey 12 years later became the first Republican nominee to give his acceptance speech to the convention. Since then the final activity of both the Democratic and Republican conventions has been the delivery of the acceptance speeches by the vice presidential and presidential nominees.

In addition to curbing the circus-like aspects of the convention, party leaders in recent years have streamlined the schedule with the assumption that the interest level of most of the viewing public for politics is limited. The result has been shorter speeches and generally fewer roll calls than at those conventions in the pre-television era.

Showmanship

Party leaders desire to put on a good show for the viewing public with the hope of winning votes for their party in November. The convention is a showcase, designed to show the party as both a model of democracy and an efficient, harmonious body. The schedule of convention activities is drawn up with an eye on the peak evening television viewing hours. There is an attempt to put the party's major selling points — the highly partisan keynote speech, the nominating ballots, and the candidates' acceptance speeches — on in prime time. As well, with an equal awareness of the television audience, party leaders often try to keep evidence of bitter party factionalism — such as explosive credentials and platform battles — out of the peak viewing period.

In the media age, the appearance of fairness is important, and in a sense this need to look fair and open has assisted the movement in recent years for party reform. Some influential party leaders, skeptical of reform of the convention, have found resistance difficult in the glare of television.

Before the revolution in the means of transportation and communication, conventions met in relative anonymity. Today, the convention is held in all the privacy of a fishbowl, with every action and every rumor closely scrutinized. It has become a media event, and as such has become a target for political demonstrations that can be not only an embarrassment to the party but a security problem as well.

But in spite of its difficulties, the convention system has survived. As the nation has grown over the past century and a half, the convention has evolved as well, changing its form but retaining its variety of functions which accounts for the remarkable longevity of the convention system. Criticism has been leveled at the convention, but no substitute has yet been offered that would nominate a presidential ticket, adopt a party platform, act as the supreme governing body of the party and serve as a massive campaign rally and propaganda forum. In addition to these functions, a national convention is a place where compromise can take place — compromise often is mandatory in a major political party that combines viewpoints that stretch across the political spectrum and represent various regions of the country.

Pre-convention Era, 1789-1828

For nearly a century and a half, the United States has had an established two-party system. Yet such a system was never envisioned by the Founding Fathers, who viewed the existence of political parties with suspicion.

In his Farewell Address, written in 1796, President George Washington warned the American people of "the danger of parties," and went on to state: "There is an opinion that parties in free countries are useful checks upon the administration of the government, and serve to keep alive the spirit of liberty. This within certain limits is probably true; and in governments of a monarchical cast patriotism may look with indulgence, if not with favor, upon the spirit of party. But in those of the popular character, in governments purely elective, it is a spirit not to be encouraged.... A fire not to be quenched, it demands a uniform vigilance to prevent its bursting into a flame, lest, instead of warming, it should consume."

Washington's suspicion of parties was not unusual for the period and was shared by other early American leaders. Thomas Jefferson, writing in 1789, declared: "If I could not go to heaven but with a party, I would not go there at all." Even a generation later, after the establishment of an American party system, two early 19th century presidents continued to speak out against the existence of political parties. Andrew Jackson, 12 years before he was elected president, wrote in 1816: "Now is the time to exterminate the monster called party spirit." In 1822, after his unopposed 1820 election victory, President James Monroe characterized parties as "the curse of the country."

Early American leaders were heavily influenced in their attitude by a dominant anti-party theme in European political philosophy, which equated parties with factions and viewed both negatively. Thomas Hobbes (1588-1679), David Hume (1711-1776) and Jean Jacques Rousseau (1712-1778)—three European philosophers whose views strongly influenced the Founding Fathers—regarded parties as threats to state government.[1] In England there was no formal party system until the 1820s, several decades after the formation of parties in the United States. In colonial America there were no parties, and there were none in the Continental Congress or under the Articles of Confederation. *(Footnotes, p. 64)*

The Constitution did not provide either authority for or prohibitions against political parties. Historians have pointed out that most of the Founding Fathers had only a dim understanding of the function of political parties and thus were ambivalent, if not hostile, toward parties when they laid down the framework of the new government. Nevertheless, the delegates to the Constitutional Convention and their successors in Congress ensured a role for parties in the government when they gave protection to civil rights and the right to organize. The founders set up what they regarded as safeguards against excesses of party activity by providing an elaborate governmental system of checks and balances. The prevailing attitude of the convention on this matter was summed up by James Madison, who wrote in *The Federalist* that the "great object" of the new government was "to secure the public good and private rights against the danger of such a faction [party], and at the same time to preserve the spirit and the form of popular government."

Madison's greatest fear was that a party would become a tyrannical majority. This could be avoided, he believed, through the republican form of government which the proponents of the Constitution advocated. A republic, as understood by Madison, was an elected body of wise, patriotic citizens, while a democracy was equated with mob rule. In *The Federalist*, Madison dismissed the democratic form of government as a spectacle of "turbulence and contention."

Ironically, in this setting two competing parties grew up quickly. They developed as a result of public sentiment for and against adoption of the Constitution. The Federalist Party—a loose coalition of merchants, shippers, financiers and other business interests—favored the strong central government provided by the Constitution, while their opponents (at first called Anti-Federalists) were intent upon preservation of sovereignty of the states. Underlying the controversy was the desire of the interests represented by the Federalists to create a government with power to guarantee the value of the currency (and thus protect the position of creditors) and the desire of the agrarians and frontiersmen who made up the Anti-Federalists to maintain easy credit conditions and the power of state legislatures to fend off encroachments by a remote federal government.

Unlike the Federalist Party, which was never more than a loose alliance of particular interests, the Anti-Federalists achieved a high degree of organization. The Federalists, in fact, never considered themselves a political party but rather a gentlemanly coalition of interests representing respectable society. What party management there was, they kept clandestine, a reflection of their own fundamental suspicion of parties.

There is no precise date for the beginning of parties, although both Thomas Jefferson and Alexander Hamilton (a Federalist) referred to the existence of a Jeffersonian republican "faction" in Congress as early as 1792.[2]

While party organization became more formalized in the 1790s and early 1800s, particularly among the Jeffersonians, they never acquired a nationally accepted name. The Jeffersonians most commonly referred to themselves as Republicans. Their opponents labeled the Republicans as Anti-Federalists, disorganizers, Jacobins and Democrats —the latter an unflattering term in the early years of the Republic. To many Americans in the late 18th century, a democrat was considered a supporter of mob rule and revolution and often ideologically identified with the bloody French Revolution. The designation Democrat-Republican was used by the Jeffersonians in several states, but was never widely accepted as a party label. However, historians often refer to the Jeffersonians as the Democratic-Republicans, to avoid confusion with the later and unrelated Republican Party, founded in 1854.[3]

Although the early American political leaders acknowledged the development of parties, they did not foresee the emergence of a two-party system. Rather, they often justified the existence of their own party as a reaction to an unacceptable opposition. Jefferson defended his party involvement as a struggle between good and evil: "[When] the principle of difference is as substantial and as strongly pronounced as between the republicans and the Monocrats of our country, I hold it as honorable to take a firm and decided part, and as immoral to pursue a middle line, as between the parties of Honest men, and Rogues, into which every country is divided."

Presidential Politics

The rise of parties forced an alteration in the presidential selection method envisioned by the creators of the Constitution. Delegates to the Constitutional Convention of 1787 had sought a presidential selection method in which the "spirit of party" would play no part. The electoral college system they finally settled on was a compromise born of the diversity of the states—the slavery in the South, the big-state versus small-state rivalries, complexities of the separation of powers system and a basic distrust in the political abilities of the populace.

Rather than having the people vote directly for president, the choice was to be entrusted to presidential "electors"—men the Founding Fathers hoped would be wise leaders in the separate states, able to choose the one man best qualified to be president.

Caucus System

But strong political parties soon developed and quickly removed the presidential nomination from the hands of state electors. The parties created the first informal nominating device for choosing a president: a caucus of each party's members in Congress. From 1796 until 1824, congressional caucuses—when a party had enough representatives to form one—chose almost all the candidates for president; the electors then chose from the party nominees. Only twice—in 1800 and 1824—as a result of a failure of any candidate to receive a majority of electoral votes, were presidential elections decided by the House of Representatives, and even in those two cases political parties were instrumental in the election of the president.

Election of 1789

In the United States' first presidential election, held in 1789 shortly after the ratification of the Constitution, the nominating and electing process centered in the electoral college. Electors chosen in the various states were, under the Constitution, entitled to cast two votes, and required to cast each vote for a different person. The individual receiving votes of a majority of the electors was named president and the person receiving the second highest total was named vice president. There were no formal nominations in 1789, but public opinion centered on George Washington of Virginia for president. He received 69 electoral votes, the maximum possible. John Adams of Massachusetts was the leading second choice, although he did not enjoy the degree of unanimity that surrounded Washington. Adams easily won the vice presidency, receiving 34 electoral votes.

Election of 1792

The Federalists and Democratic-Republicans were emerging as competitive parties by the election of 1792, and as a result the Republic experienced the first modification

Presidents, 1789-1829

Term	President	Vice President
1789-93	George Washington (Fed.)	John Adams (Fed.)
1793-97	George Washington (Fed.)	John Adams (Fed.)
1797-1801	John Adams (Fed.)	Thomas Jefferson (D-R)
1801-05	Thomas Jefferson (D-R)	Aaron Burr (D-R)
1805-09	Thomas Jefferson (D-R)	George Clinton (D-R)
1809-13	James Madison (D-R)	George Clinton (D-R)
1813-17	James Madison (D-R)	Elbridge Gerry (D-R)
1817-21	James Monroe (D-R)	Daniel D. Tompkins (D-R)
1821-25	James Monroe (D-R)	Daniel D. Tompkins (D-R)
1825-29	John Q. Adams (D-R)	John C. Calhoun (D-R)

Fed. - Federalist; D-R - Democratic-Republican

in the presidential nominating process. No attempt was made to displace President Washington, but the Democratic-Republicans mounted a challenge to Vice President Adams. Meeting in Philadelphia in October 1792, a group of Democratic-Republican leaders from the Middle Atlantic states and South Carolina endorsed New York Governor George Clinton over New York Senator Aaron Burr for the vice presidency. While Adams emerged victorious in the electoral college, the endorsement of Clinton by a meeting of party politicians was a milestone in the evolution of the presidential nominating process and a step away from the original electoral college system.

Election of 1796

The election of 1796 brought further modifications in the nominating method, evidenced by the appearance of the congressional caucus.

There was no opposition to Thomas Jefferson as the Democratic-Republican presidential candidate, and he was considered the party's standard-bearer by a consensus of party leaders. However, a caucus of Democratic-Republican senators was unable to agree on a running mate, producing a tie vote between New York Senator Aaron Burr and South Carolina Senator Pierce Butler that ended with a walk-out by Butler's supporters. As a result, there was no formal Democratic-Republican candidate to run with Jefferson.

The Federalists held what historian Roy F. Nichols described as a "quasi caucus" of the party's members of Congress in Philadelphia in May 1796.[4] The gathering chose Vice President Adams and Minister to Great Britain Thomas Pinckney of South Carolina as the Federalist candidates.

Election of 1800

In the election of 1800 the congressional caucus for the first time was used as the nominating body by both parties. Neither party, however, desired much publicity for its meeting, gathering in secret to deliberate. The proceedings of their caucuses were sketchily described by private correspondence and occasionally referred to in newspapers of the day. Unlike the public national conventions of later years, privacy was a hallmark of the early caucuses.[5]

Although the actual dates of the 1800 caucuses are hazy, it is believed that both were held in May.[6] The Democratic-Republican caucus was held in Marache's boardinghouse in Philadelphia, where 43 of the party's members of Congress selected Aaron Burr to run with Thomas Jefferson, the latter again the presidential candidate by consensus and not formally nominated by the caucus.

Federalist members of Congress met in the Senate chamber in Philadelphia and nominated President Adams and General Charles Cotesworth Pinckney of South Carolina. Pinckney, the older brother of the Federalist vice presidential candidate in 1796, was placed on the ticket at the insistence of Alexander Hamilton, who believed one of the South Carolina Pinckneys could win. Although the deliberations of the Federalist caucus were secret, the existence of the meeting was not. It was described by the local Democratic-Republican paper, the *Philadelphia Aurora*, as a "Jacobinical conclave." Further denunciations by the paper's author, Benjamin F. Bache, earned him a personal rebuke from the United States Senate.[7]

Election of 1804

The election of 1804 was the first to be held after ratification of the 12th Amendment to the Constitution, in September 1804. The amendment altered the electoral college system by requiring the electors to cast separate votes for president and vice president. The amendment was designed to avoid the unwieldy situation which had developed in 1800, when the leading two Democratic-Republican candidates, Jefferson and Burr, both received the same number of electoral votes. The unexpected tie vote threw the presidential election into the House of Representatives, where it took 36 ballots before Jefferson finally won. With ratification of the amendment, parties in 1804 and thereafter specifically designated their presidential and vice presidential candidates.

The Democratic-Republicans retained the caucus system of nomination in 1804, as they did for the next two decades, and for the first time publicly reported their deliberations. The party caucus was held in February and attracted 108 of the party's senators and representatives. President Jefferson was renominated by acclamation, but Vice President Burr was not considered for a second term. On the first nominating roll call publicly reported in American political history, Governor George Clinton of New York was chosen to run for vice president. He received 67 votes to easily defeat Senator John Breckinridge of Kentucky, who collected 20 votes. "To avoid unpleasant discussions" no names were placed in nomination, and the vote was taken by written ballot.[8]

Before adjourning, the caucus appointed a 13-member committee to conduct the campaign. A forerunner of party national committees, the new campaign group included members of both the House and Senate, but with no two individuals from the same state.

The Federalists dropped the congressional caucus as their nominating method. Federalist leaders in 1804 informally chose Charles Cotesworth Pinckney for president and Rufus King of New York for vice president. However, exactly how they formulated this ticket is unknown. There is no record in 1804 of any Federalist meeting to nominate candidates.[9]

Election of 1808

The Democratic-Republican caucus was held in January 1808. For the first time there was a formal call issued. Vermont Senator Stephen R. Bradley, the chairman of the 1804 caucus, issued the call to all 146 Democratic-Republicans in Congress and several Federalists sympathetic to the Democratic-Republican cause. His authority to call the caucus was questioned by several party leaders, but various reports indicate that 89 to 94 members of Congress attended.[10]

As in 1804 the balloting was done without the formal

placing of names in nomination. For president, Jefferson's hand-picked successor, Secretary of State James Madison of Virginia, was an easy winner with 83 votes. Vice President Clinton and James Monroe of Virginia each received three votes. For vice president the caucus overwhelmingly renominated Clinton. He received 79 votes, while runner-up John Langdon of New Hampshire collected five. Despite his nomination, supporters of Clinton hoped that their man would be nominated by the Federalists later in the year. But their hopes were dashed when the nomination ultimately went to Pinckney.

As in 1804 the Democratic-Republican caucus appointed a campaign committee that was entrusted with the conduct of the campaign. Membership on the committee was expanded to 15 House and Senate members and it was formally called the "committee of correspondence and arrangement."[11] The committee was authorized to fill any vacancies on the national ticket, should any occur.

Before adjournment a resolution was passed defending the caucus system as "the most practicable mode of consulting and respecting the interest and wishes of all." A similar resolution was passed by later caucuses throughout the history of the system.

The resolution was meant to stem the rumblings of opposition to the caucus system. Seventeen Democratic-Republican members of Congress signed a protest against Madison's selection and questioned the authority of the caucus as a nominating body. Vice President Clinton, himself selected by the caucus, wrote of his disapproval of the caucus system.

The Federalists in 1808 again altered their presidential selection process, holding a secret meeting of party leaders in August of that year to choose the ticket. The meeting, held in New York City, was initially called by the Federalist members of the Massachusetts legislature. Twenty-five to thirty party leaders from seven states, all but South Carolina north of the Potomac River, attended the national meeting. There was some discussion of choosing Vice President George Clinton, a dissident Democratic-Republican, for the presidency, but the meeting ultimately selected the Federalist candidates of 1804: Charles Cotesworth Pinckney and Rufus King.

Election of 1812

The Democratic-Republicans held their quadrennial nominating caucus in May 1812. Eighty-three of the party's 138 members of Congress attended, with the New England and New York delegations poorly represented. The New York delegation was sympathetic to the candidacy of the state's lieutenant governor, De Witt Clinton, who was maneuvering for the Federalist nomination, while New England was noticeably upset with President Madison's foreign policy that was leading to war with England. President Madison was renominated with a near-unanimous total, receiving 82 votes. John Langdon of New Hampshire was chosen for vice president by a wide margin, collecting 64 votes to 16 for Governor Elbridge Gerry of Massachusetts. But Langdon declined the nomination, citing his age (70) as the reason. In a second caucus held in June, Gerry was a runaway winner, receiving 74 votes.

In 1812, as four years earlier, the Federalists held a secret meeting in New York City. It was over twice the size of the 1808 gathering, with 70 representatives from 11 states attending the three-day meeting in September. Delegates were sent to the conference by Federalist general committees, with all but nine of the delegates from the New England and Middle Atlantic states.

Debate centered on whether to run a separate Federalist ticket or to endorse the candidacy of DeWitt Clinton, the nephew of George Clinton. The younger Clinton had already been nominated for the presidency by the New York Democratic-Republican caucus, and the Federalists ultimately passed a resolution approving his candidacy and that of Jared Ingersoll. Ingersoll was a Pennsylvania Federalist who was initially nominated for vice president by a party legislative caucus in that state.

Election of 1816

The Federalist Party was nearly extinct by 1816 and did not hold any type of meeting to nominate candidates for president and vice president. As a result, nomination by the Democratic-Republican caucus was tantamount to election. Only 58 members of Congress attended the first caucus in the House chamber. With the expectation of better attendance, a second caucus was held several days later in mid-March, 1816, and drew 119 senators and representatives. By a vote of 65 to 54, Secretary of State James Monroe was nominated for president, defeating Secretary of War William H. Crawford of Georgia. Forty of Crawford's votes came from five states: Georgia, Kentucky, New Jersey, New York and North Carolina. The vice presidential nomination went to New York Governor Daniel D. Tompkins, who easily outdistanced Pennsylvania Governor Simon Snyder, 85 to 30. The nominations of Monroe and Tompkins revived a Virginia-New York alliance which extended back to the late 18th century. With the lone exception of 1812, every Democratic-Republican ticket since 1800 was composed of a presidential candidate from Virginia and a vice presidential candidate from New York.

While the collapse of the Federalists assured Democratic-Republican rule, it also increased intraparty friction and spurred further attacks on the caucus system. Twenty-two Democratic-Republican members of Congress were absent from the second party caucus, and at least 15 were known to be opposed to the system. Historian Edward Stanwood wrote that there were mass meetings around the country in protest to the caucus system.[12] Opponents claimed that the caucus was not envisioned by the writers of the Constitution, that presidential nominating should not be a function of Congress and that the caucus system **encouraged candidates to curry the favor of Congress.**

Election of 1820

The 1820 election came during the "Era of Good Feelings," a phrase coined by a Boston publication, the *Columbian Centinel*, to describe a brief period of virtual one-party rule in the United States. With only one candidate, President James Monroe, there was no need for a caucus. One was called, but fewer than 50 of the Democratic-Republican's 191 members of Congress attended. The caucus voted unanimously to make no nominations and passed a resolution explaining that it was inexpedient to do so. Despite the fact that Monroe and Tompkins were not formally renominated, electoral slates were filed on their behalf. They both received nearly unanimous electoral college victories.

Demise of the Caucus

In 1824 there was still only one party, but within this party there was an abundance of candidates for the presidency: Secretary of State John Quincy Adams of Massachusetts; Senator Andrew Jackson of Tennessee;

Secretary of War John C. Calhoun of South Carolina; House Speaker Henry Clay of Kentucky; and Secretary of the Treasury William H. Crawford. It was generally assumed that Crawford was the strongest candidate among members of Congress and would win a caucus if one were held; therefore, Crawford's opponents joined the growing list of caucus opponents.

In early February, 1824, 11 Democratic-Republican members of Congress issued a call for a caucus to be held in the middle of the month. Their call was countered by 24 other members of Congress from 15 states who deemed it "inexpedient under existing circumstances" to hold a caucus. They claimed that 181 members of Congress were resolved not to attend if a caucus were held.

When the caucus convened in mid-February, only 66 members of Congress were present, with three-quarters of those attending from just four states—Georgia, New York, North Carolina and Virginia. As expected, Crawford won the presidential nomination, receiving 64 votes. Selected for vice president was Albert Gallatin of Pennsylvania, who received 57 votes. The caucus passed a resolution defending their actions as "the best means of collecting and concentrating the feelings and wishes of the people of the Union upon this important subject." A committee was appointed to write an address to the people. As written, the text of the address viewed with alarm the "dismemberment" of the Democratic-Republican Party.

The caucus nomination proved to be an albatross for Crawford as his opponents denounced him as the candidate of "King Caucus." Reflecting the increasing democratization of American politics, other presidential candidates relied on nominations by state legislatures to legitimize their presidential ambitions. However, in an attempt to narrow the field, the candidates had to negotiate among themselves. Calhoun alone withdrew to become the vice presidential candidate of all the anti-caucus entries. Adams offered the vice presidency to Jackson as "an easy and dignified retirement to his old age."[13] Jackson refused. Other maneuvers were equally unsuccessful, so that four presidential candidates remained in the field to collect electoral votes, subsequently throwing the election into the House of Representatives, where Adams won.

The election of 1828 proved to be a transitional one in the development of the presidential nominating process. The caucus was dead, but the national nominating convention was not yet born. Jackson was nominated by his native Tennessee legislature and in October, 1825, three years before the election, accepted the nomination in a speech before the legislature. He accepted Vice President Calhoun as his running-mate, after it was proposed in January 1827, by the *United States Telegraph*, a pro-Jackson paper in Washington. A Pennsylvania state convention paired President Adams with Secretary of the Treasury Richard Rush of Pennsylvania, a ticket that Adams' supporters in other states accepted. Both Jackson and Adams were endosed by other legislatures, conventions and meetings.

Trend Toward Conventions

The birth of the national convention system came in 1831, seven years after the death of the caucus. The caucus system collapsed when a field of candidates appeared who would not acquiesce to the choice of one caucus-approved candidate. But other factors were present to undermine the caucus system. These included changes in voting procedures and an expansion of suffrage. Between 1800 and 1824, the number of states in which the electors were chosen by popular vote rather than by the state legislature increased from four out of 16 to 18 out of 24. In 1824 the popular vote reached 1.1 million, compared with fewer than 400,000 in 1800. A broader base of support than the congressional caucus became essential for presidential aspirants.

State legislatures, state conventions and mass meetings all emerged in the 1820s to challenge the caucus. The trend to democratization of the presidential nominating process, as evidenced by the expansion of suffrage and increased importance of the popular vote for President, led shortly to creation of the national nominating convention. The convention system was initiated by the Anti-Masons in 1831, and subsequently was adopted by the major parties before the end of the decade.

The birth of the national nominating convention was a milestone in the evolution of the presidential nominating process. Political Scientist V. O. Key Jr. summarized some of the major forces that brought about the rise of the convention system: "The destruction of the caucus represented more than a mere change in the method of nomination. Its replacement by the convention was regarded as the removal from power of self-appointed oligarchies that had usurped the right to nominate. The new system, the convention, gave, or so it was supposed, the mass of party members an opportunity to participate in nominations. These events occurred as the domestic winds blew in from the growing West, as the suffrage was being broadened, and as the last vestiges of the early aristocratic leadership were disappearing. Sharp alterations in the distribution of power were taking place, and they were paralleled by the shifts in methods of nomination."[14]

With the establishment of the national convention came the re-emergence of the two-party system. Unlike the Founding Fathers, who were suspicious of competitive parties, some political leaders in the late 1820s and 1830s favorably viewed the existence of opposing parties. One of the most prominent of these men, Martin Van Buren, a leading organizer of Jackson's 1828 election victory and himself President after Jackson, had written in 1827: "We must always have party distinctions...."

Notes

1. Arthur M. Schlesinger Jr., ed., *History of U.S. Political Parties*, volume 1 (1973), p. xxxiv.
2. *Ibid.*, p. 241; William N. Chambers, *Political Parties in a New Nation: The American Experience, 1776-1809* (1963), p. 57.
3. Schlesinger, *op. cit.*, p. 240; Roy F. Nichols, *The Invention of the American Political Parties* (1967), p. 176.
4. Nichols, *ibid.*, p. 192.
5. Schlesinger, *op. cit.*, p. 263.
6. Nichols, *op. cit.*, p. 207. Schlesinger, *op. cit.*, p. 252. George W. Stimpson, *A Book about American Politics* (1952), p. 42.
7. Nichols, *op. cit.*, p. 206; Edward Stanwood, *A History of the Presidency from 1788 to 1897* (1898), p. 59.
8. Nichols, *ibid.*, p. 226.
9. Stanwood, *op. cit.*, p. 83.
10. Nichols, *op. cit.*, p. 235.
11. Schlesinger, *op. cit.*, p. 264.
12. Stanwood, *op. cit.*, p. 110.
13. Eugene H. Roseboom, *A History of Presidential Elections* (1959), p. 83.
14. V. O. Key Jr., *Politics, Parties and Pressure Groups* (1964), p. 372.

Highlights of National Party Conventions, 1831-1980

1831   First national political convention was held in Baltimore by Anti-Masonic Party. Second such convention was held several months later by National Republican Party (no relation to modern Republicans).

1832   Democratic Party met in Baltimore for its first national political convention and nominated Andrew Jackson. The rule requiring a two-thirds majority for nominations was initiated.

1835   President Jackson called his party's convention more than a year before the election in order to prevent build-up of opposition to his choice of successor, Martin Van Buren.

1839   Whig Party held its first convention and chose the winning slate of William Henry Harrison and John Tyler. Party adopted unit rule for casting state delegations' votes.

1840   To avoid bitter battle over vice presidential nomination, Democratic Party set up a committee to select nominees, subject to approval of convention. In accordance with committee recommendations, Van Buren was nominated for president and no one for vice president.

1844   Democrats nominated James K. Polk — first "dark horse" or compromise candidate — after nine ballots. Silas Wright, convention's choice for vice president, declined the nomination. First time a convention nominee refused nomination. Convention subsequently nominated George M. Dallas.

1848   Democratic convention voted to establish continuing committee, known as "Democratic National Committee."

1852   Democrats and Whigs both adopted platforms before nominating candidates for president, setting precedent almost uniformly followed ever since.

1854   First Republican state convention held in Jackson, Mich., to nominate candidate slate. Platform denounced slavery.

1856   First Republican national convention held in Philadelphia. Kennedy sent the only Southern delegation. Nominated John C. Fremont for president.

1860   One of longest, most turbulent and mobile conventions in Democratic history. Democrats met in Charleston, S.C., April 23. After 10 days and no agreement on a presidential nominee, delegates adjourned and reconvened in Baltimore in mid-July, for what turned out to be another disorderly meeting. Delegates finally nominated Stephen A. Douglas for president.
Benjamin Fitzpatrick, the convention's choice for vice president, became the first candidate to withdraw after convention adjournment and be replaced by a selection of the national committee. Delegates who bolted the original convention later joined Baltimore dissidents to nominate Vice President John C. Breckinridge for president.
Republicans nominated Abraham Lincoln for the presidency. First Republican credentials dispute took place over seating delegates from slave states and over voting strength of delegates from states where party was comparatively weak. Party rejected unit rule for first time.
Constitutional Union Party running on a platform of national unity nominated John Bell for president.

1864   Civil War led to bitter debate within Democratic Party over candidates, including Gen. George B. McClellan, presidential nominee.
In attempt to close ranks during war, Republicans used the name "Union Party" at convention. Renominated Lincoln. Platform called for constitutional amendment outlawing slavery.

1868   Susan B. Anthony urged Democratic support for women's suffrage.
For the first time, Republicans gave a candidate (Ulysses S. Grant) 100 percent of vote on first ballot. Incumbent Andrew Johnson, who succeeded assassinated Lincoln, sought nomination unsuccessfully. First Republican convention with full Southern representation.

1872   Republicans renominated Grant at Philadelphia. Disident liberal Republicans nominated Horace Greeley in Cincinnati. Democrats also nominated Greeley. Victoria Clafin Woodhull, nominated by the Equal Rights Party, was first woman presidential candidate. Black leader Frederick Douglass was her running mate.

1876   First time either party nominated incumbent governor for president; both major parties did so that year with Rutherford B. Hayes, R-Ohio, and Samuel J. Tilden, D-N.Y. Republican convention rejected unit rule for second time.

1880   Republicans nominated James A. Garfield for President on 36th ballot — party's all-time record number of ballots. Unit rule was rejected for the third and final time. Republican convention passed loyalty pledge for nominee, binding each delegate to his support.

1884   Democrats turned back Tammany Hall challenge to unit rule.
Republicans nominated James G. Blaine (Maine) for president and John Logan (Illinois) for vice president, reversing 24-year pattern of seeking presidential candidate from the Midwest and vice presidential candidate from the East. John Roy Lynch, three-term U.S. representative from Mississippi, became first black elected temporary chairman of national nominating convention.

1888   Frederick Douglass was first black to receive a vote in presidential balloting at political convention. He received one vote on fourth ballot at Republican convention. Nineteen names were entered into Republican balloting. Benjamin Harrison won nomination on eighth ballot.

1892   Democrat Grover Cleveland broke convention system tradition by receiving third presidential nomination. People's Party (the Populists) hold first national nominating convention in Omaha, Neb., and adopt first platform.

1896   Democrats, divided over silver-gold question, repudiated Cleveland administration and nominated William J. Bryan.
Thirty-four Republican delegates against free silver walked out of convention.

1900   Each party had one woman delegate.

1904   Florida Democrats elected national convention delegates in public primary, under the first legislation permitting any recognized party to hold general primary elections.

Republicans nominated Theodore Roosevelt, first time a vice president who had succeeded a deceased president went on to be nominated in his own right.

1908 Democrats, calling for legislation terminating what they called "partnership" between Republicans and corporations, pledged to refuse campaign contributions from corporations.

Call to Republican convention provided for election of delegates by primary method introduced in some states for the first time.

1912 Increasing numbers of delegates were selected in primaries held in 13 states.

First time Republicans renominated entire ticket — William H. Taft and James S. Sherman. Malapportionment of convention seats as result of Republican decline in South killed Theodore Roosevelt's chances of nomination. Taft renominated but 349 delegates protested his nomination by refusing to vote. Roosevelt nominated for president on Progressive ticket at separate convention.

1916 Democrats renominated entire ticket — Woodrow Wilson and Thomas R. Marshall — for first time.

Hopes of reuniting Republicans diminished when Roosevelt could not secure their nomination and refused Progressive renomination.

1920 For the first time, women attended conventions in significant numbers.

1924 Republicans adopted bonus votes for first time — three bonus delegates at large allotted to each state carried by party in last preceding presidential election. Republican convention was first to be broadcast on radio.

John W. Davis was nominated by Democrats on record 103rd ballot.

Three Democratic women received one or more votes for presidential nomination.

1928 Democrat Alfred E. Smith, governor of New York was first Roman Catholic nominated for president by a major party.

1932 Republicans began tradition of appointing party leader from House of Representatives as permanent convention chairman.

Franklin D. Roosevelt appeared before Democratic convention to accept presidential nomination, the first major party candidate to do so.

1936 Democratic Party voted to end requirement of two-thirds delegate majority for nomination, a rule adopted at party's first convention and one that sometimes had led to lengthy balloting and selection of dark horse slates.

Republicans nominated Alfred M. Landon and Frank Knox in vain effort to break new Democratic coalition.

1940 Franklin D. Roosevelt was nominated for unprecedented third term. He then wrote out a refusal of his renomination because of opposition to his vice presidential choice, Henry A. Wallace. Opposition deferred and Wallace was nominated.

Republicans held first political convention to be televised.

1944 Franklin D. Roosevelt, already having broken tradition by winning third term, was nominated for fourth time. Democrats put system of bonus votes into effect for states that voted Democratic in previous presidential election.

Thomas E. Dewey became first Republican candidate to accept nomination in appearance before the convention.

1948 After Democratic convention adopted strong civil rights plank, entire Mississippi delegation and 13 of Alabama's 26 delegates walked out.

Dissidents from 13 southern states met several days later and nominated South Carolina Gov. Strom Thurmond for President.

Democrats began appointing speaker of the House as permanent chairman. Practice followed, with exception of 1960 when Sam Rayburn declined, through 1968. Since 1948 conventions, presidential nominees of both parties have appeared at their conventions. Republicans renominated Thomas E. Dewey — first time party renominated a defeated presidential candidate.

1952 Adlai E. Stevenson, who did not seek the nomination, was chosen as Democratic nominee in one of few genuine "drafts" in history of either political party. Republican women delegates wanted to nominate Sen. Margaret Chase Smith (Maine) for vice president, but Smith requested her name not be put in nomination.

1956 Democratic nominee Stevenson left choice of running mate to convention. Winner of open race was Sen. Estes Kefauver (Tenn.). First time a party loyalty provision was put into effect during delegate selection.

Dwight D. Eisenhower renominated unanimously on first ballot at Republican convention.

1960 Democrats adopted civil rights plank that was strongest in party history. Presidential nominee John F. Kennedy was second Catholic to receive presidential nomination of major party.

Republican nominee Richard M. Nixon was party's first vice president nominated for president at completion of his term.

1964 Democratic President Lyndon B. Johnson was nominated for second term by acclamation. Fight over credentials of Alabama and Mississippi delegations was overriding issue at the convention.

Sen. Margaret Chase Smith's name was placed in nomination for presidency at Republican convention — first time a woman placed in nomination by a major party. Sen. Barry Goldwater (Ariz.) won the nomination.

1968 Democratic delegates voted to end unit rule and to eliminate it from all levels of party politics for 1972 convention.

Republicans nominated Richard Nixon, who had made one of most remarkable political comebacks in American history.

1972 With newly adopted party reform guidelines, the Democratic convention included a record number of women, youth and minorities. Open debate on many issues occurred with an unprecedented 23 credentials challenges brought to the floor. George McGovern, who built up following as an antiwar candidate, nominated for president on first ballot. His choice for vice president, Thomas Eagleton, became the second candidate in American history to withdraw from the ticket and be replaced by the choice of the national committee, R. Sargent Shriver.

In a harmonious convention Republicans renominated Richard Nixon and Spiro Agnew with nearly unanimous votes.

Both Major Parties to Hold Biggest Conventions

Both the Democratic and Republican parties in 1984 planned to hold the largest presidential nominating conventions in their history.

The state-by-state Democratic delegate count included each state's share of the new group of uncommitted party and elected officials. These "superdelegates" represented between 10 and 30 percent of each state delegation. Following are the numbers of delegates allocated by the two parties to the 50 states and other U.S. jurisdictions.

STATE	DEMOCRATS	REPUBLICANS	STATE	DEMOCRATS	REPUBLICANS
Alabama	62	38	New Hampshire	22	22
Alaska	14	18	New Jersey	122	64
Arizona	40	32	New Mexico	28	24
Arkansas	42	29	New York	285	136
California	345	176	North Carolina	88	53
Colorado	51	35	North Dakota	18	18
Connecticut	60	35	Ohio	175	89
Delaware	18	19	Oklahoma	53	35
District of Columbia	19	14	Oregon	50	32
Florida	143	82	Pennsylvania	195	98
Georgia	84	37	Rhode Island	27	14
Hawaii	27	14	South Carolina	48	35
Idaho	22	21	South Dakota	19	19
Illinois	194	93	Tennessee	76	46
Indiana	88	52	Texas	200	109
Iowa	58	37	Utah	27	26
Kansas	44	32	Vermont	17	19
Kentucky	63	37	Virginia	78	50
Louisiana	69	41	Washington	70	43
Maine	27	20	West Virginia	44	19
Maryland	74	31	Wisconsin	89	46
Massachusetts	116	52	Wyoming	15	18
Michigan	155	77	Puerto Rico	53	14
Minnesota	86	32	Guam	7	4
Mississippi	43	30	Virgin Islands	6	4
Missouri	86	47	Latin American Democrats (Canal Zone)	5	—
Montana	25	20	Democrats Abroad	5	—
Nebraska	30	24	American Samoa	6	—
Nevada	20	22	**Total:**	**3,933**	**2,234**

1976 The Democrats in a unified convention nominated Jimmy Carter. The gathering was notable for the lack of bitter floor fights and credentials challenges that had characterized some of the recent conventions. Incumbent President Gerald R. Ford received the Republican nomination, narrowly surviving a challenge from Ronald Reagan.

1980 The Democrats renominated incumbent President Jimmy Carter in a convention marked by bitter contests over the party platform and rules binding delegates to vote on the first ballot for the candidates under whose banner they were elected. The struggle pitted Carter forces against supporters of Sen. Edward M. Kennedy, D-Mass., who were trying to pry the nomination away from the president and alter the party platform. While the Carter camp prevailed on the delegate binding rule, Kennedy managed to force major concessions in the Democratic platform.

In contrast, a harmonious and unified Republican convention nominated former California Gov. Ronald Reagan. Rumors abounded during the convention that former President Gerald R. Ford would serve as Reagan's vice-presidential candidate. After it became obvious that efforts to persuade Ford to join the ticket had failed, Reagan chose George Bush as his running mate.

National Convention Information for 1980, 1984

	1984 Electoral Votes	State Vote for President '80	'76	'72	'68	Presidential Primary 1984	DEMOCRATIC Votes at Convention 1984	1980	Vote at 1980 Convention Presidential Ballot	REPUBLICAN Votes at Convention 1984	1980	Vote at 1980 Convention Presidential Ballot
Alabama	9	R	D	R	AI	March 13	62	45	Carter: 43 Kennedy: 2	38	27	Reagan: 27
Alaska	3	R	R	R	R		14	11	Carter: 8.4 Kennedy: 2.6	18	19	Reagan: 19
Arizona	7	R	R	R	R		40	29	Carter: 13 Kennedy: 16	32	28	Reagan: 28
Arkansas	6	R	D	R	AI		42	33	Carter: 25 Kennedy: 6 Bumpers: 1 Uncommitted: 1	29	19	Reagan: 19
California	47	R	R	R	R	June 5	345	306	Carter: 140 Kennedy: 166	176	168	Reagan: 168
Colorado	8	R	R	R	R		51	40	Carter: 27 Kennedy: 10 Muskie: 1 Uncommitted: 2	35	31	Reagan: 31
Connecticut	8	R	R	R	D	March 27	60	54	Carter: 26 Kennedy: 28	35	35	Reagan: 35
Delaware	3	R	D	R	R		18	14	Carter: 10 Kennedy: 4	19	12	Reagan: 12
Florida	21	R	D	R	R	March 13	143	100	Carter: 75 Kennedy: 25	82	51	Reagan: 51
Georgia	12	D	D	R	AI	March 13	84	63	Carter: 62 Absent: 1	37	36	Reagan: 36
Hawaii	4	D	D	R	D		27	19	Carter: 16 Kennedy: 2 Abstain: 1	14	14	Reagan: 14
Idaho	4	R	R	R	R	May 22	22	17	Carter: 9 Kennedy: 7 Uncommitted: 1	21	21	Reagan: 21
Illinois	24	R	R	R	R	March 20	194	179	Carter: 163 Kennedy: 16	93	102	Reagan: 81 Anderson: 21
Indiana	12	R	R	R	R	May 8	88	80	Carter: 53 Kennedy: 27	52	54	Reagan: 54
Iowa	8	R	R	R	R		58	50	Carter: 31 Kennedy: 17 Culver: 2	37	37	Reagan: 37
Kansas	7	R	R	R	R		44	37	Carter: 23 Kennedy: 14	32	32	Reagan: 32
Kentucky	9	R	D	R	R		63	50	Carter: 45 Kennedy: 5	37	27	Reagan: 27
Louisiana	10	R	D	R	AI		69	51	Carter: 50 Kennedy: 1	41	31	Reagan: 31
Maine	4	R	R	R	D		27	22	Carter: 11 Kennedy: 11	20	21	Reagan: 21

68

Convention Information

	1984 Electoral Votes	State Vote for President '80	'76	'72	'68	Presidential Primary 1984	DEMOCRATIC Votes at Convention 1984	1980	Vote at 1980 Convention Presidential Ballot	REPUBLICAN Votes at Convention 1984	1980	Vote at 1980 Convention Presidential Ballot
Maryland	10	D	D	R	D	May 8	74	59	Carter: 34 Kennedy: 24 Uncommitted: 1	31	30	Reagan: 30
Massachusetts	13	R	D	D	D	March 13	116	111	Carter: 34 Kennedy: 77	52	42	Reagan: 33 Anderson: 9
Michigan	20	R	R	R	D		155	141	Carter: 102 Kennedy: 38 Abstain: 1	77	82	Reagan: 67 Bush: 13 Armstrong: 1 Not voting: 1
Minnesota	10	D	D	R	D		86	75	Carter: 41 Kennedy: 14 Proxmire: 10 Horbal: 5 Spannous: 2 Tripp: 2 Mondale: 1	32	34	Reagan: 33 Not voting: 1
Mississippi	7	R	D	R	AI	June 5 (R)	43	32	Carter: 32	30	22	Reagan: 22
Missouri	11	R	D	R	R		86	77	Carter: 58 Kennedy: 19	47	37	Reagan: 37
Montana	4	R	R	R	R	June 5	25	19	Carter: 13 Kennedy: 6	20	20	Reagan: 20
Nebraska	5	R	R	R	R	May 15	30	24	Carter: 14 Kennedy: 10	24	25	Reagan: 25
Nevada	4	R	R	R	R		20	12	Carter: 8.12 Kennedy: 3.88	22	17	Reagan: 17
New Hampshire	4	R	R	R	R	Feb. 28	22	19	Carter: 10 Kennedy: 9	22	22	Reagan: 22
New Jersey	16	R	R	R	R	June 5	122	113	Carter: 45 Kennedy: 68	64	66	Reagan: 66
New Mexico	5	R	R	R	R	June 5	28	20	Carter: 10 Kennedy: 10	24	22	Reagan: 22
New York	36	R	D	R	D	April 3	285	282	Carter: 129 Kennedy: 151 Dellums: 2	136	123	Reagan: 121 Not voting: 2
North Carolina	13	R	D	R	R	May 8	88	69	Carter: 66 Kennedy: 3	53	40	Reagan: 40
North Dakota	3	R	R	R	R	June 12	18	14	Carter: 5 Kennedy: 7 Uncommitted: 2	18	17	Reagan: 17
Ohio	23	R	D	R	R	May 8	175	161	Carter: 89 Kennedy: 72	89	77	Reagan: 77
Oklahoma	8	R	R	R	R		53	42	Carter: 36 Kennedy: 3 Carey: 1 Steed: 1 Absent: 1	35	34	Reagan: 34
Oregon	7	R	R	R	R	May 15	50	39	Carter: 26 Kennedy: 13	32	29	Reagan: 29
Pennsylvania	25	R	D	R	D	April 10	195	185	Carter: 95 Kennedy: 90	98	83	Reagan: 83

70 Elections '84

	1984 Electoral Votes	State Vote for President '80	'76	'72	'68	Presidential Primary 1984	DEMOCRATIC Votes at Convention 1984	1980	Vote at 1980 Convention Presidential Ballot	REPUBLICAN Votes at Convention 1984	1980	Vote at 1980 Convention Presidential Ballot
Rhode Island	4	D	D	R	D	March 13	27	23	Carter: 6 Kennedy: 17	14	13	Reagan: 13
South Carolina	8	R	D	R	R	March 10 (R)	48	37	Carter: 37	35	25	Reagan: 25
South Dakota	3	R	R	R	R	June 5	19	19	Carter: 9 Kennedy: 10	19	22	Reagan: 22
Tennessee	11	R	D	R	R	May 1	76	55	Carter: 51 Kennedy: 4	46	32	Reagan: 32
Texas	29	R	D	R	D	May 5 (R)	200	152	Carter: 108 Kennedy: 38 Hance: 2 Uncommitted: 3 Not voting: 1	109	80	Reagan: 80
Utah	5	R	R	R	R		27	20	Carter: 11 Kennedy: 4 Matheson: 5	26	21	Reagan: 21
Vermont	3	R	R	R	R	March 6	17	12	Carter: 5 Kennedy: 7	19	19	Reagan: 19
Virginia	12	R	R	R	R		78	64	Carter: 59 Kennedy: 5	50	51	Reagan: 51
Washington	10	R	R	R	D		70	58	Carter: 36 Kennedy: 22	43	37	Reagan: 36 Anderson: 1
West Virginia	6	D	D	R	D	June 5	44	35	Carter: 21 Kennedy: 10 Byrd: 2 Randolph: 2	19	18	Reagan: 18
Wisconsin	11	R	D	R	R	April 3	89	75	Carter: 48 Kennedy: 26 Brown: 1	46	34	Reagan: 28 Anderson: 6
Wyoming	3	R	R	R	R		15	11	Carter: 8 Kennedy: 3	18	19	Reagan: 19
American Samoa							6	—		—	—	
District of Columbia	3	D	D	D	D	May 1	19	19	Carter: 12 Kennedy: 5 Abstain: 2	14	14	Reagan: 14
Latin American Democrats							5	4	Carter: 4	—	—	
Guam							7	4	Carter: 4	4	4	Reagan: 4
Puerto Rico						March 18 (D)	53	41	Carter: 21 Kennedy: 20	14	14	Reagan: 14
Virgin Islands							6	4	Carter: 4	4	4	Reagan: 4
Democrats Abroad						March 13	5	4	Carter: 1.50 Kennedy: 2 Dellums: 0.50	—	—	
TOTAL	538 (needed to elect: 270)						3,933 (needed to nominate: 1,967)	3,331 (needed to nominate: 1,666)		2,234 (needed to nominate: 1,118)	1,994 (needed to nominate: 998)	

1984 Convention Sites, Officials

Democratic Party

1984 Democratic Convention
Dates — July 16-19, 1984
Place — Moscone Convention Center, San Francisco, California
Convention headquarters — San Francisco Hilton and Tower Hotel
Number of votes — 3,933
Needed to nominate — 1,967
Maximum number of alternates — 1,313

National Democratic Officers*
Chairman — Charles T. Manatt, Washington, D.C.
Vice chairmen —
Lynn Cutler, Washington, D.C.; Richard G. Hatcher, Indiana; Polly Baca, Colorado

Regional officers —
Eastern region — Sharon Dixon, Washington, D.C.
Midwestern region — George Gaukler, North Dakota
Southern region — Jesse Bankston, Louisiana
Western region — Wallace Albertson, California

Members-at-large —
Hannah Atkins, Oklahoma; Roland Burris, Illinois; Fran Martinez Bussie, Louisiana; Ann D. Campbell, New Jersey; Evelyn Dubrow, Washington, D.C.; Caffie Greene, California; Rachelle Horowitz, Washington, D.C.; Florine Koole, Washington, D.C.; Leon Lynch, Pennsylvania; Ray Majerus, Michigan; William Marshall, Michigan; Alice McDonald, Kentucky; Gerald McEntee, Washington, D.C.; C.J. McLin Jr., Ohio; Barbara Mikulski, Maryland; Jack Otero, Virginia; Sharon Rockefeller, West Virginia; Mark Siegal, Washington, D.C.; Elizabeth Smith, Washington, D.C.; Marc Stepp, Michigan; C. Delores Tucker, Pennsylvania; J.C. Turner, Washington, D.C.; Glenn Watts, Washington, D.C.; William Winpisinger, Washington, D.C.; Addie Wyatt, Washington, D.C.

Secretary — Dorothy Bush, Washington, D.C.
Treasurer — Paul G. Kirk, Washington, D.C.
Other officers:
Peter G. Kelley, National Finance Chair
Robert C. Byrd, Minority Leader, U.S. Senate
Thomas P. O'Neill Jr., Speaker, U.S. House
Charles S. Robb, Chairman, Democratic Governors Association
Lee Alexander, President, National Conference of Democratic Mayors
Terrance Pitts, Chairman, National Democratic County Officials
Angie M. Elkins, President, National Federation of Democratic Women

*Executive Committee of the Democratic National Committee.

Republican Party

1984 Republican Convention
Dates — August 20-23
Place — Dallas Convention Center; Dallas, Texas
Convention headquarters — Dallas Convention Center
Number of votes — 2,235
Needed to nominate — 1,118
Maximum number of alternates — 2,235

National Republican Officers
Chairman — Frank J. Fahrenkopf Jr.
Co-chairman — Betty Heitman
Vice chairmen —
Midwestern region — Ranny Riecker, Michigan; John C. McDonald, Iowa
Northeastern region — Bernard M. Shanley, New Jersey; M. Sheila Roberge, New Hampshire
Southern region — Clarke Reed, Mississippi; Paula F. Hawkins, Florida
Western region — Edith Holm, Alaska; Jack Londen, Arizona
Secretary — Jean G. Birch, Montana
Treasurer — William J. McManus, Maryland
General counsel — Roger Allan Moore, Massachusetts

Executive Committee
Don W. Adams, Illinois
Ernest Angelo Jr., Texas
Grace Boulton, Oklahoma
Gerald P. Carmen, New Hampshire
Ben J. Clayburgh, North Dakota
Jack Courtemanche, California
Michael Doud Gill, Washington, D.C.
Nora W. Hussey, South Dakota
Allan C. Levey, Maryland
Ginny C. Martinez, Louisiana
Kit Mehrtens, Arizona
Peter C. Murphy, Oregon
Mary Louise Smith, Iowa
Mary Stivers, Georgia
Eunice B. Whittlesey, New York

Ex Officio:
Howard H. Baker Jr., Majority Leader, U.S. Senate
Robert H. Michel, Minority Leader, U.S. House
Victor G. Atiyeh, Chairman, Republican Governors Association, Governor of Oregon
Mike Curb, Chairman, Republican National Finance Committee
Mrs. Harold J. Rendel, President, National Federation of Republican Women
William D. Harris, Chairman, Republican State Chairman's Advisory Committee
Stephen R. Clark, Chairman, Young Republican National Federation
Jack Abramoff, Chairman, College Republican National Committee
Michael Sotirhos, Chairman, National Republican Heritage Groups Council
Mrs. LeGree Daniels, Chairman, National Black Republican Council
Tirso del Junco, Chairman, Republican National Hispanic Assembly
Robert Isaac, Chairman, National Conference of Republican Mayors
Don Smith, President, National Conference of Republican County Officials
Fred Finlinson, President, National Republican Legislators Association

Republican Chairmen, Committeemen, Committeewomen

State	State Chairman	National Committeeman	National Committeewoman
Alabama	William D. Harris	Perry O. Hooper	Jean Sullivan
Alaska	Kenneth O. Stout	Eldon R. Ulmer	Edith Holm
Arizona	John F. Munger	Jack Londen	Kit Mehrtens
Arkansas	Robert Leslie	A. Lynn Lowe	Leona Dodds
California	Ed Reinecke	Jack Courtemanche	Gertrude McDonald
Colorado	Howard Callaway	Harold Krause	Kay Riddle
Connecticut	Thomas D'Amore	John Alsop	Mary Boatwright
Delaware	Jerome O. Herlihy	Francis DiMondi	Priscilla Rakestraw
District of Columbia	Robert S. Carter	Michael Doud Gill	Patricia Bruns
Florida	Henry B. Sayler	William C. Cramer	Paula F. Hawkins
Georgia	Robert H. Bell	Carl L. Gillis, Jr.	Mary Stivers
Guam	Peter F. Perez, Jr.	Ben Blaz	Felicia Fajardo
Hawaii	Patricia Saiki	D. G. Anderson	Carla W. Coray
Idaho	Dennis M. Olsen	Philip E. Batt	Janet Miller
Illinois	Don W. Adams	Harold B. Smith, Jr.	Crete B. Harvey (Mrs.)
Indiana	Gordon K. Durnil	James T. Neal	Margaret C. Hill
Iowa	Rolf V. Craft	John C. McDonald	Mary Louise Smith
Kansas	Dave C. Owen	McDill Boyd	Marynell D. Reece
Kentucky	Liz Thomas	James P. Bunning	Nelda L. Barton
Louisiana	George J. Despot	Frank Spooner	Ginny C. Martinez
Maine	Loyall F. Sewall	Charles L. Cragin	Mary Wold Payson
Maryland	Allan C. Levey	Richard P. Taylor	Louise Gore
Massachusetts	Andrew S. Natsios	Gordon M. Nelson	Paula Logan
Michigan	E. Spencer Abraham	Peter Secchia	Ranny Riecker
Minnesota	Leon L. Oistad	Francis Graves, Jr.	Evie Teegen
Mississippi	Ebbie Spivey	Clarke Reed	Evelyn McPhail
Missouri	Hillard Selck, Jr.	Jewett Fulkerson	Lydia J. Miller
Montana	John C. Brenden	Jack E. Galt	Jean G. Birch
Nebraska	Kermit Brashear II	Arthur L. Knox	Sallie Folsom
Nevada	Curtis C. Patrick	Ed Fike	Eileen C. Schouweiler
New Hampshire	Donna P. Syteck	Gerald P. Carmen	M. Sheila Roberge
New Jersey	Frank B. Holman	Bernard M. Shanley	Noel L. Gross
New Mexico	Edward L. Lujan	Robert C. Davidson	Christine A. Donisthorpe
New York	George Clark, Jr.	Richard Rosenbaum	Eunice Whittlesey
North Carolina	David Flaherty	John P. East	Mary Alice Warren
North Dakota	Marlys Fleck	Ben Clayburgh	Betty Lou Pyle
Ohio	Michael Colley	James A. Rhodes	Martha C. Moore
Oklahoma	Nancy Apgar	L. O. Ward	Grace Boulton
Oregon	D. F. O'Scannlain	Peter C. Murphy	Dorotha Moore
Pennsylvania	Robert Asher	Andrew L. Lewis, Jr.	Elsie Hillman
Puerto Rico	Luis Ferre	Hernan Padilla	Miriam Ramirez de Ferrer
Rhode Island	John A. Holmes	Frederick Lippitt	Elinor J. Clapp
South Carolina	George G. Graham	John E. Courson	Beverly J. Gosnell
South Dakota	Dan Parish	William F. Lenker	Nora W. Hussey
Tennessee	Susan Richardson-Williams	Mark C. Hicks, Jr.	Jeanne K. Geraghty
Texas	George W. Strake	Ernest Angelo, Jr.	Fran Chiles
Utah	Charles W. Akerlow	Wilbern McDougal	Zenda Hull
Vermont	George S. Coy	Lawrence A. Wright	Madeline Harwood
Virginia	Donald W. Huffman	William Stanhagen	Helen Obenshain
Virgin Islands	Viola I. Burgess	Melvin H. Evans	Meredith P. Clark
Washington	Jennifer B. Dunn	Edsel Hammond	Bernece Bippes
West Virginia	Kent S. Hall, Sr.	Arch A. Moore, Jr.	Priscilla Humphreys
Wisconsin	J. Michael Borden	Ody J. Fish	Helen Bie
Wyoming	Thomas Sansonetti	Sam Ratcliff	Margaret Kelly

Source: Republican National Committee

Democratic Chairmen, Chairwomen, DNC Representatives

State	State Chairman	State Chairwomen	DNC Representative
Alabama	James R. Knight	Patricia Edington	Dorothy Carmichael Louphenia Thomas
Alaska	Stanley Sobocienski	Dianne A. O'Connell	Pegge Begich William L. Hensley
American Samoa	Letalu M. Moliga	Olotoa Overland	Tuiafona Matautia Repeka M. Howland
Arizona	Samuel Goddard, Jr.	Marian Bauhs	Ronald Warner Lorraine W. Frank
Arkansas	Lilburn Carlisle	Lottie Shackelford	Jim Blair Mary Schroeder
California	Peter D. Kelly Richard Alatorre	Carmen Perez	Wallace Albertson Dina Beaumont Maxine Waters Ed Burke Bert Coffey June Degnan Anna Eshoo Bruce Lee Charles T. Manatt Justin Ostro Adolph Schuman Stephen H. Smith Norma Sublett Alice Travis Mary Warren
Colorado	Floyd Ciruli	Judy Henning	Kathy Farley Michael Muftic
Connecticut	James M. Fitzgerald	Arline Bidwell	Peter G. Kelly John J. Flynn Mary Sullivan
Delaware	Samuel Shipley	Myrtle Shockley	Ned Davis Marilyn Huthmacher
Democrats Abroad	Andrew Sundberg	Roberta Enschede	Dean Ferrier Michael J. McNulty
District of Columbia	Theodis "Ted" Gay	Barbara Clark	Sharon P. Dixon John Hechinger
Florida	Charles Whitehead	Hazel Evans	Ann M. Cramer T. Wayne Bailey William Darden Phyllis Miller Michael Shea Mayre Lutha Tillman
Georgia	Bert Lance	Maxine Goldstein Irving Kaler Herbert Mabry	Melba Williams
Guam	F. Philip Carbullido	Louise S. Cepeda	Madeleine Bordallo Frank Lujan
Hawaii	James Kumagai	Matilda Molina	Elmer F. Cravalho Momi Minn Lee
Idaho	Mel Morgan	Anna J. Wilson	John S. Chapman Carolyn Selander
Illinois	Calvin R. Sutker	Lillian Clinton	Joanne H. Alter Thomas A. Dunn Irene C. Hernandez Gwen R. Martin Earl L. Neal John Rednour Yvonne Rice Paul Schuler Grace Mary Stern
Indiana	Jerry J. Miller	Linda Hatch	Katie Wolf Richard Stoner Ruth Ruderman Mayor Robert Pastrick Julia M. Carson

Convention Information 73

State	State Chairman	State Chairwomen	DNC Representative
Iowa	Dave Nagle	Barbara Leach	Chuck Gifford
			Jean Haugland
			William Sueppel
Kansas	Charles Thompson	Pat Lehman	Joseph T. Carey
			Sherry McGowan
Kentucky	Joseph Prather	June Taylor	John Y. Brown, Jr
			Sandy Metts
			Larry Townsend
Latin American	Richard M. Koster	Marlyn O'Kane	Paul Lawson
			Sharon Dawson
Louisiana	Jesse H. Bankston	Kathleen Vick	Henry Braden, IV
			Marianne Freeman
			John W. Scott
Maine	Barry J. Hobbins	Jane Paxton	Phil Merrill
			Barbara Trafton
Maryland	Howard J. Thomas	Vera P. Hall	Clarence Blount
			Grace Connolly
			Lanny J. Davis
Massachusetts	Chester Atkins	Eva Hester	Betty Taymor
			Anna Buckley
			Thomas McGee
			David Bartley
			James Roosevelt, Jr
			Margaret Xifaras
Michigan	Richard Wiener	Helen Root	Sam Fishman
			Shirley R. Hall
			Bea Williams
			Kim Moran
			Frank Garrison
			Kathleen Johnston-Calati
			Morley A. Winograd
			Coleman Young
Minnesota	Karl Neid	Mary Monahan	Forrest Harris
			Dick Hanson
			Sue Rockne
			Nellie Stone Johnson
Mississippi	Danny E. Cupit	Unita Blackwell	Aaron Henry
			Helen Tedford
Missouri	Pat Lea	Margie Klearman	Jean Briscoe
			Louis B. Susman
			Rosemary Lowe
			Burleigh Arnold
Montana	Bruce Nelson	Donna Small	Dorothy Bradley
			James Pasma
Nebraska	Francis Moul	DiAnna Schimek	Dan Morgan
			Kathleen Kelley
Nevada	Brent T. Adams	Beverly Wilke	Didi Carson
			Grant Sawyer
New Hampshire	George C. Bruno	Holly Abrams	J. Willcox Brown
			Patricia Russel
New Jersey	James F. Maloney	Virginia Feggins	Gina Glantz
			Jerry English
			John Horn
			Jacqueline Klein
			Vincent Rigolosi
			Anthony Yelencsics
New Mexico	Fred E. Mondragon	Bea Costellano	Zora Hesse
			Ben Alexander
New York	William Hennessey	Dorothea Noonan	Joseph Crangle
			Patrick Cunningham
			Laurence Kirwan
			Dominic Baranello
			Robert Dryfoos
			Donald Manes
			Stanley Friedman
			Jerome Tarnoff
			Barbara Fife
			Michele Aisenberg
			Ada Torres
			Bella Abzug

State	State Chairman	State Chairwomen	DNC Representative
			Helen Marshall
			Hazel Dukes
			Lucille Rose
North Carolina	David Price	Betty Speir	Clarence Lightner
			Betty McCain
			Linda Ashendorf
			Wallace Hyde
North Dakota	George Gaukler	Joan Carlson	Robert Whitney
			Bea Peterson
Ohio	James M. Ruvolo	Fran Alberty	Bill Casstevens
			Gertrude Donahey
			Morris Jackson
			Vern Riffe, Jr
			Phyllis Hart
			Helen Karpinski
			Martin Hughes
			Marigene Valiquette
			Paul Tipps
Oklahoma	Jim Frasier	Betty Hall	Edna Mae Phelps
			George W. Krumme
Oregon	Dick Celsi	Leslie Moore	David McTeague
			Larryann Willis
Pennsylvania	Edward Mezvinsky	Dorothy Zug	Joseph F. Smith
			Rena Baumgartner
			Rita Wilson Kane
			Ruth Harper
			Julius Uehlein
			Ruth C. Rudy
			K. Leroy Irvis
			Evelyn Richardson
			William Myrtetus
			Cyril Wecht
Puerto Rico	Chas. Rodriguez	Marlene Gillette	Baltasar Corrada
			Nivea McClintock
Rhode Island	Julius Michaelson	Maureen Maigret	Edward Maggiacomo
			Eleanor Slater
South Carolina	Wm. J. Dorn	Marcia Duffy	Donald Fowler
			Beatrice Thompson
South Dakota	Robert Williams	Georgia Cook	Michael O'Connor
			Patricia Kenner
Tennessee	Richard Lodge	Brenda Turner	George Lewis, III
			M. Inez Crutchfield
			Trabue Lewis
Texas	Robert Slagle	Deralyn Davis	Millie Bruner
			Edgar Ball
			Billie Carr
			Jesse W. Jones
			Sue Pate
			Juan Maldonado
			Sylvia Rodriguez
			Mickey Leland
Utah	Patrick A. Shea	Janet Prazen	Calvin Rampton
			Elizabeth Vance
Vermont	Edwin C. Granai	Shirley Schommer	John Carnahan
			Maureen McNamara
Virgin Islands	St. Claire Williams	Marylyn Stapelton	Alexander Farrelly
			Joyce LeBron
Virginia	Alan Diamonstein	Jessie Rattley	Louise Cunningham
			Sandy Duckworth
			James P. Jones
			Benj. Lambert III
Washington	Darrell Beers	Karen Marchioro	Betty Drumheller
			William Ames
			Jolene Unsoeld
West Virginia	Joseph Goodwin	Shelby Leary	Emilie Holroyd
			Paul Rusen
Wisconsin	Matthew Flynn	Suellen Albrecht	Robert Friebert
			Gary Aamodt
			Elizabeth King
			Midge Miller

Convention Information 75

State	State Chairman	State Chairwomen	DNC Representative
Wyoming	David Freudenthal	Dee Arps	Leslie Peterson Don Anselmi

Members-at-Large

Hannah Atkins	Jack Otero
Roland Burris	Sharon Rockefeller
Fran Martinez Bussie	Mark Siegel
Ann D. Campbell	Elizabeth Smith
Evelyn Dubrow	Marc Stepp
Caffie Greene	C. Delores Tucker
Rachelle Horowitz	J. C. Turner
Florine Koole	Glenn Watts
Leon Lynch	William W. Winpisinger
Ray Majerus	Addie Wyatt
William Marshall	
Alice McDonald	**Designees**
Gerald McEntee	
C. J. McLin, Jr	George L. Brown
Barbara Mikulski	Louis F. Moret

Source: Democratic National Committee

Electing The President 77

The Electoral College 79
The Popular Vote 97

Electoral Votes by States — 1984, 1988 Elections

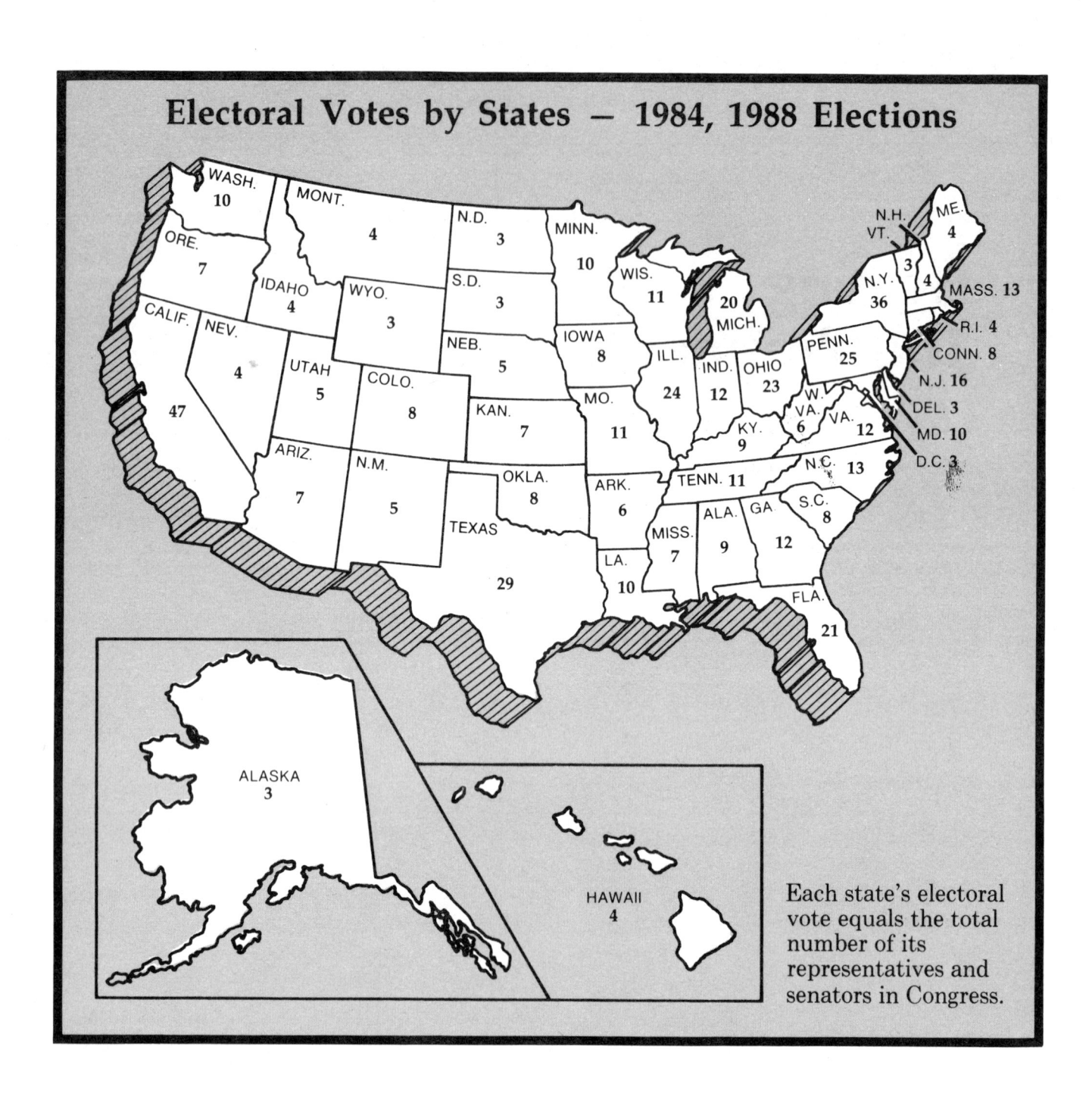

State	EV	State	EV	State	EV
WASH.	10	MONT.	4	N.D.	3
MINN.	10	ORE.	7	IDAHO	4
WYO.	3	S.D.	3	WIS.	11
N.H.	4	VT.	3	ME.	4
N.Y.	36	MASS.	13	CALIF.	47
NEV.	4	UTAH	5	COLO.	8
NEB.	5	IOWA	8	ILL.	24
IND.	12	OHIO	23	PENN.	25
MICH.	20	R.I.	4	CONN.	8
N.J.	16	DEL.	3	MD.	10
D.C.	3	ARIZ.	7	N.M.	5
KAN.	7	MO.	11	KY.	9
W.VA.	6	VA.	12	OKLA.	8
ARK.	6	TENN.	11	N.C.	13
TEXAS	29	LA.	10	MISS.	7
ALA.	9	GA.	12	S.C.	8
FLA.	21	ALASKA	3	HAWAII	4

Each state's electoral vote equals the total number of its representatives and senators in Congress.

The Electoral College

For almost two centuries, Americans have been electing their presidents through a unique method called the Electoral College. Conceived by the Founding Fathers as a compromise between electing presidents by Congress or by direct popular vote, the system has continued to function even while the United States has undergone radical transformation from an agricultural seaboard nation to a world power.

Under the Electoral College system, each state is entitled to electoral votes equal in number to its congressional delegation — i.e., the number of representatives from the state, plus two more for the state's two senators. Whichever party receives a plurality of the popular vote in a state usually wins that state's electoral votes. However, there have been numerous exceptions to that rule, including choosing of electors by district, statewide votes for each individual elector and selection of electors by state legislatures.

Constitutional Background

The method of selecting a president was the subject of long debate at the Constitutional Convention of 1787. Several plans were proposed and rejected before a compromise solution, which was modified only slightly in later years, was adopted (Article II, Section I, Clause 2).

Facing the convention when it convened May 25 was the question of whether the chief executive should be chosen by direct popular election, by the Congress, by state legislatures or by intermediate electors. Direct election was opposed, because it was generally felt that the people lacked sufficient knowledge of the character and qualifications of possible candidates to make an intelligent choice. Many delegates also feared that the people of the various states would be unlikely to agree on a single person, usually casting their votes for favorite-son candidates well known to them.

The possibility of giving Congress the power to choose the president also received consideration. However, this plan was rejected, largely because of fear that it would jeopardize the principle of executive independence. Similarly, a plan favored by many delegates, to let state legislatures choose the president, was turned down because it was feared that the president might feel so indebted to the states as to allow them to encroach on federal authority.

Unable to agree on a plan, the convention on Aug. 31 appointed a "Committee of 11" to propose a solution to the problem. The committee on Sept. 4 suggested a compromise under which each state would appoint presidential electors equal to the total number of its representatives and senators. The electors, chosen in a manner set forth by each state legislature, would meet in their own states and each cast votes for two persons. The votes would be counted in Congress, with the candidate receiving a majority elected president and the second-highest candidate becoming vice president.

No distinction was made between ballots for president and vice president. Moreover, the development of national political parties and the nomination of tickets for president and vice president created further confusion in the electoral system. All the electors of one party tended to cast ballots for their two party nominees. But with no distinction between the presidential and vice presidential nominees, the danger arose of a tie vote between the two. That actually happened in 1800, leading to a change in the original electoral system with ratification of the 12th Amendment in 1804.

The committee's compromise plan constituted a great concession to the less populous states, since they were assured of three votes (two for their two senators and at least one for their representative) however small their populations might be. The plan also left important powers with the states by giving complete discretion to state legislatures to determine the method of choosing electors.

The only part of the committee's plan that aroused serious opposition was a provision giving the Senate the

---

Sources

Petersen, Svend. *A Statistical History of the American Presidential Elections.* New York: Frederick Ungar, 1968.

Schlesinger, Arthur M. Jr., ed. *History of American Presidential Elections.* 4 vols. New York: McGraw-Hill, 1971.

Stanwood, Edward. *A History of the Presidency, 1788-1916.* 2 vols. Boston: Houghton Mifflin, vol. 1, 1889; vol. 2, 1916.

U.S. Bureau of the Census. *Historical Statistics of the United States, Colonial Times to 1957.* Washington, D.C.: U.S. Government Printing Office, 1960.

right to decide presidential elections in which no candidate received a majority of electoral votes. Some delegates feared that the Senate, which already had been given treaty ratification powers and the responsibility to "advise and consent" to all important executive appointments, might become too powerful. Therefore, a counterproposal was made and accepted to let the House decide in instances when the electors failed to give a majority of their votes to a single candidate. The interests of the small states were preserved by giving each state's delegation only one vote in the House on roll calls to elect a president.

The system adopted by the Constitutional Convention was a compromise born out of problems involved in diverse state voting requirements, the slavery problem, big- versus small-state rivalries and the complexities of the balance of power among different branches of the government. It also was apparently as close to a direct popular election as the men who wrote the Constitution thought possible and appropriate at the time.

The 12th Amendment

Only once since ratification of the Constitution has an amendment been adopted that substantially altered the method of electing the president. In the 1800 presidential election, the Democratic-Republican electors inadvertently caused a tie in the Electoral College by casting equal numbers of votes for Thomas Jefferson, whom they wished to be elected president, and Aaron Burr, whom they wished to elect vice president. The election was thrown into the House of Representatives and 36 ballots were required before Jefferson was finally elected president. The 12th Amendment, ratified in 1804, sought to prevent a recurrence of this incident by providing that the electors should vote separately for president and vice president. *(Text, box, p. 81)*

Other changes in the system evolved over the years. The authors of the Constitution, for example, had intended that each state should choose its most distinguished citizens as electors and that they would deliberate and vote as individuals in electing the president. But as strong political parties began to appear, the electors came to be chosen merely as representatives of the parties; independent voting by electors disappeared almost entirely.

Methods of Choosing Electors

In the early years of the Republic, states chose a variety of methods to select presidential electors. For the first presidential election, in 1789, four states held direct popular elections to choose their electors: Pennsylvania and Maryland (at large) and Virginia and Delaware (by district). In five states — Connecticut, Georgia, New Jersey, New York and South Carolina — the state legislatures were to make the choice.

Two states, New Hampshire and Massachusetts, adopted a combination of the legislative and popular methods. New Hampshire held a statewide popular vote for presidential electors with the stipulation that any elector would have to win a majority of the popular vote to be elected; otherwise, the Legislature would choose.

In Massachusetts, the arrangement was for the people in each congressional district to vote for the two persons they wanted to be presidential electors. From the two persons in each district having the highest number of votes, the Legislature, by joint ballot of both houses, was to choose one. In addition, the Legislature was to choose two additional electors at large.

In a dispute between the two houses of the state Legislature in New York, that state failed to choose electors. The state Senate insisted on full equality with the Assembly (lower house); that is, the Senate wanted each house to take a separate ballot and to resolve any differences between them by agreement rather than by having one house impose its will on the other. The Assembly, on the other hand, wanted a joint ballot, on which the lower house's larger numbers would prevail, or it was willing to divide the electors with the Senate. The failure to compromise cost the state its vote in the first presidential election.

The 12th and 13th states — North Carolina and Rhode Island — had not ratified the Constitution by the time the electors were chosen, and so they did not participate.

Generally similar arrangements prevailed for the election of 1792. Massachusetts, while continuing the system of choosing electors by district, changed the system somewhat to provide for automatic election of any candidate for elector who received a majority of the popular vote. New Hampshire continued the system of popular election at large, but substituted a popular runoff election in place of legislative choice, if no candidate received a majority of the popular vote.

Besides Massachusetts and New Hampshire, electors were chosen in 1792 by popular vote in Maryland and Pennsylvania (at large) and Virginia and Kentucky (by district). State legislatures chose electors in Connecticut, Delaware, Georgia, New Jersey, New York, North Carolina, Rhode Island, South Carolina and Vermont.

By 1796 several changes had occurred. New Hampshire switched back to legislative choice for those electors who failed to receive a majority of the popular vote. Tennessee entered the Union (1796) with a unique system for choosing presidential electors: The state Legislature appointed three persons in each county, who in turn chose the presidential electors. Massachusetts retained the system used in 1792. Other states chose their electors as follows: popular vote, at large: Georgia, Pennsylvania; popular vote, by district: Kentucky, Maryland, North Carolina, Virginia; state legislature: Connecticut, Delaware, New Jersey, New York, Rhode Island, South Carolina, Vermont.

Political Parties and Electors: 1800

As political parties gained power, manipulation of the system of choosing electors became increasingly widespread. For example, in 1800 Massachusetts switched from popular voting to legislative selection of electors because of recent successes by the Democratic-Republican Party in that state. The Federalists, still in firm control of the Legislature, sought to secure the state's entire electoral vote for its presidential candidate, native son John Adams. New Hampshire did likewise.

Nor were the Democratic-Republicans innocent of this kind of political maneuver. In Virginia, where that party was in control, the Legislature changed the system for choosing electors from districts to a statewide at-large ballot. That way, the expected statewide Democratic-Republican majority could overcome Federalist control in some districts and garner a unanimous vote for Democratic-Republican presidential candidate Thomas Jefferson.

In Pennsylvania, the two houses of the state Legisla-

Constitutional Provisions for Selection of the President

Article II

Section I. The executive Power shall be vested in a President of the United States of America. He shall hold his Office during the Term of four Years, and, together with the Vice President, chosen for the same term, be elected, as follows.

Each State shall appoint, in such Manner as the Legislature thereof may direct, a Number of Electors, equal to the whole Number of Senators and Representatives to which the State may be entitled in the Congress: but no Senator or Representative, or Person holding an Office of Trust or Profit under the United States, shall be appointed an Elector.

[The Electors shall meet in their respective States, and vote by Ballot for two Persons, of whom one at least shall not be an Inhabitant of the same State with themselves. And they shall make a List of all the Persons voted for, and of the Number of Votes for each; which List they shall sign and certify, and transmit sealed to the Seat of the Government of the United States, directed to the President of the Senate. The President of the Senate shall, in the Presence of the Senate and House of Representatives, open all the Certificates, and the Votes shall then be counted. The Person having the greatest Number of Votes shall be the President, if such Number be a Majority of the whole Number of Electors appointed; and if there be more than one who have such Majority, and have an equal Number of Votes, then the House of Representatives shall immediately chuse by Ballot one of them for President; and if no Person have a Majority, then from the five highest on the List the said House shall in like Manner chuse the President. But in chusing the President, the Votes shall be taken by States, the Representation from each State having one Vote; a quorum for this Purpose shall consist of a Member or Members from two thirds of the States, and a Majority of all the States shall be necessary to a Choice. In every Case, after the Choice of the President, the Person having the greatest Number of Votes of the Electors shall be the Vice President. But if there should remain two or more who have equal Votes, the Senate shall chuse from them by Ballot the Vice-President.]*

The Congress may determine the Time of chusing the Electors, and the Day on which they shall give their Votes; which Day shall be the same throughout the United States.

No person except a natural born Citizen, or a Citizen of the United States, at the time of the Adoption of this Constitution, shall be eligible to the Office of President; neither shall any Person be eligible to that Office who shall not have attained to the Age of thirty five Years, and been fourteen Years a Resident within the United States.

Amendment XII *(Ratified July 27, 1804)*

The Electors shall meet in their respective states and vote by ballot for President and Vice-President, one of whom, at least, shall not be an inhabitant of the same state with themselves; they shall name in their ballots the person voted for as President, and in distinct ballots the person voted for as Vice-President, and they shall make distinct lists of all persons voted for as President, and of all persons voted for as Vice-President, and of the number of votes for each, which lists they shall sign and certify, and transmit sealed to the seat of the government of the United States, directed to the President of the Senate; ...The person having the greatest number of votes for President, shall be the President, if such number be a majority of the whole number of Electors appointed; and if no person have such majority, then from the persons having the highest numbers not exceeding three on the list of those voted for as President, the House of Representatives shall choose immediately, by ballot, the President. But in choosing the President, the votes shall be taken by states, the representation from each state having one vote; a quorum for this purpose shall consist of a member or members from two-thirds of the states, and a majority of all the states shall be necessary to a choice. [And if the House of Representatives shall not choose a President whenever the right of choice shall devolve upon them, before the fourth day of March next following, then the Vice-President shall act as President, as in the case of the death or other constitutional disability of the President. —]† The person having the greatest number of votes as Vice-President, shall be the Vice-President, if such number be a majority of the whole number of Electors appointed, and if no person have a majority, then from the two highest numbers on the list, the Senate shall choose the Vice-President; a quorum for the purpose shall consist of two-thirds of the whole number of Senators, and a majority of the whole number shall be necessary to a choice. But no person constitutionally ineligible to the office of President shall be eligible to that of Vice-President of the United States.

Amendment XX *(Ratified January 23, 1933)*

Section 1. The terms of the President and Vice President shall end at noon on the 20th day of January . . . .

Section 3. If, at the time fixed for the beginning of the term of the President, the President elect shall have died, the Vice President elect shall become President. If a President shall not have been chosen before the time fixed for the beginning of his term, or if the President elect shall have failed to qualify, then the Vice President elect shall act as President until a President shall have qualified; and the Congress may by law provide for the case wherein neither a President elect nor a Vice President elect shall have qualified, declaring who shall then act as President, or the manner in which one who is to act shall be selected, and such person shall act accordingly until a President or Vice President shall have qualified.

Section 4. The Congress may by law provide for the case of the death of any of the persons from whom the House of Representatives may choose a President whenever the right of choice shall have devolved upon them, and for the case of the death of any of the persons from whom the Senate may choose a Vice President whenever the right of choice shall have devolved upon them.

---
* Superseded by the 12th Amendment.
† Changed to Jan. 20 by the 20th Amendment, ratified in 1933.

ture could not agree on legislation providing for popular ballots, the system used in the first three elections, so the Legislature itself chose the electors, dividing them between the parties.

In other changes in 1800, Rhode Island switched to popular election and Georgia reverted to legislative elections. The 16 states thus used the following methods of choosing presidential electors in 1800:

- By popular vote: Kentucky, Maryland, North Carolina (by district); Rhode Island, Virginia (at large).
- By the legislature: Connecticut, Delaware, Georgia, Massachusetts, New Hampshire, New Jersey, New York, Pennsylvania, South Carolina, Tennessee (indirectly, as in 1796), Vermont.

Trend to Winner-Take-All System

For the next third of a century, the states moved slowly but inexorably toward a standard system of choosing presidential electors — the statewide, winner-take-all popular ballot. The development of political parties resulted in the adoption of party slates of electors pledged to vote for the parties' presidential candidates. Each party organization saw a statewide ballot as being in its best interest, with the hope of sweeping in all its electors and preventing the opposition group from capitalizing on local areas of strength (which could result in winning only part of the electoral vote under the districting system).

From 1804 to 1832 there were three basic methods used by the states in choosing presidential electors — popular vote, at large; popular vote, by district; and election by the state legislature. The following list shows the changing methods of choosing presidential electors for each state from 1804 to 1932:

1804

Popular vote, at large: New Hampshire, New Jersey, Ohio, Pennsylvania, Rhode Island, Virginia.

Popular vote, by district: Kentucky, Maryland, Massachusetts, North Carolina, Tennessee.

State legislature: Connecticut, Delaware, Georgia, New York, South Carolina, Vermont.

1808

Popular vote, at large: New Hampshire, New Jersey, Ohio, Pennsylvania, Rhode Island, Virginia.

Popular vote, by district: Kentucky, Maryland, North Carolina, Tennessee.

State legislature: Connecticut, Delaware, Georgia, Massachusetts, New York, South Carolina, Vermont.

1812

Popular vote, at large: New Hampshire, Ohio, Pennsylvania, Rhode Island, Virginia.

Popular vote, by district: Kentucky, Maryland, Massachusetts, Tennessee.

State legislature: Connecticut, Delaware, Georgia, Louisiana, New Jersey, New York, North Carolina, South Carolina, Vermont.

1816

Popular vote, at large: New Hampshire, New Jersey, North Carolina, Ohio, Pennsylvania, Rhode Island, Virginia.

Popular vote, by district: Kentucky, Maryland, Tennessee.

State legislature: Connecticut, Delaware, Georgia, Indiana, Louisiana, Massachusetts, New York, South Carolina, Vermont.

1820

Popular vote, at large: Connecticut, Mississippi, New Hampshire, New Jersey, North Carolina, Ohio, Pennsylvania, Rhode Island, Virginia.

Popular vote, by district: Illinois, Kentucky, Maine, Maryland, Massachusetts, Tennessee.

State legislature: Alabama, Delaware, Georgia, Indiana, Louisiana, Missouri, New York, South Carolina, Vermont.

1824

Popular vote, at large: Alabama, Connecticut, Indiana, Massachusetts, Mississippi, New Hampshire, New Jersey, North Carolina, Ohio, Pennsylvania, Rhode Island, Virginia.

Popular vote, by district: Illinois, Kentucky, Maine, Maryland, Missouri, Tennessee.

State legislature: Delaware, Georgia, Louisiana, New York, South Carolina, Vermont.

1828

Popular vote, at large: Alabama, Connecticut, Georgia, Illinois, Indiana, Kentucky, Louisiana, Massachusetts, Mississippi, Missouri, New Hampshire, New Jersey, North Carolina, Ohio, Pennsylvania, Rhode Island, Vermont, Virginia.

Popular vote, by district: Maine, Maryland, New York, Tennessee.

State legislature: Delaware, South Carolina.

1832

Popular vote, at large: All states except Maryland and South Carolina.

Popular vote, by district: Maryland.

State legislature: South Carolina.

By 1836 Maryland switched to the system of choosing its electors statewide, by popular vote. This left only South Carolina selecting its electors through the state legislature. The state continued this practice through the election of 1860. Only after the Civil War was popular voting for presidential electors instituted in South Carolina.

Thus, since 1836 the statewide, winner-take-all popular vote for electors has been the almost universal practice. Exceptions include the following:

Massachusetts, 1848. Three slates of electors ran — Whig, Democratic and Free Soil — none of which received a majority of the popular vote. Under the law then in force, the state Legislature was to choose in such a case. It chose the Whig electors.

Florida, 1868. The state Legislature chose the electors.

Colorado, 1876. The state Legislature chose the electors because the state had just been admitted to the Union, had held state elections in August and did not want to go to the trouble and expense of holding a popular vote for the presidential election so soon thereafter.

Michigan, 1892. Republicans had been predominant in the state since the 1850s. However, in 1890 the Democrats managed to gain control of the Legislature and the governorship. They promptly enacted a districting system of choosing presidential electors in the expectation that the Democrats could carry some districts and thus win some electoral votes in 1892. The result confirmed their expectations, with the Republicans winning nine and the Democrats five electoral votes that year. But the Republicans soon regained control of the state and re-enacted the at-large system for the 1896 election.

Maine, 1972. In 1969 the Maine Legislature enacted a district system for choosing presidential electors. Two of the state's four electors were selected on the basis of the statewide vote, while the other two were determined by which party carried each of the state's two congressional districts. The system is still in force.

Historical Anomalies

The complicated and indirect system of electing the president has led to anomalies from time to time. In 1836, for example, the Whigs sought to take advantage of the electoral system by running different presidential candidates in different parts of the country. William Henry Harrison ran in most of New England, the mid-Atlantic states and the Midwest; Daniel Webster ran in Massachusetts; Hugh White of Tennessee ran in the South.

The theory was that each candidate could capture electoral votes for the Whig Party in the region where he was strongest. Then the Whig electors could combine on one candidate or, alternatively, throw the election into the House, whichever seemed to their advantage. However, the scheme did not work because Martin Van Buren, the Democratic nominee, captured a majority of the electoral vote.

Another quirk in the system surfaced in 1872. The Democratic presidential nominee, Horace Greeley, died between the popular vote and the meeting of the presidential electors. Thus the Democratic electors had no party nominee to vote for, and each was left to his own judgment. Forty-two of the 66 Democratic electors chose to vote for the Democratic governor-elect of Indiana, Thomas Hendricks. The rest of the electors split their votes among three other politicians: 18 for B. Gratz Brown of Missouri, the Democratic vice presidential nominee; two for Charles J. Jenkins of Georgia, and one for David Davis of Illinois. Three Georgia electors insisted on casting their votes for Greeley, but Congress refused to count them.

The provision that the Electoral College, not the people directly, is to choose the president has led to three presidents assuming the office even though they ran behind their opponents in the popular vote. In two of these instances — Republican Rutherford B. Hayes in 1876 and Republican Benjamin Harrison in 1888 — the winning candidate carried a number of key states by close margins, while losing other states by wide margins. In the third instance — Democratic-Republican John Quincy Adams in 1824 — the House chose the new president after no candidate had achieved a majority in the Electoral College.

Election by Congress

Congress under the Constitution has two key responsibilities relating to the election of the president and vice president. First, it is directed to receive and in joint session count the electoral votes certified by the states. Second, if no candidate has a majority of the electoral vote, the House of Representatives must elect the president and the Senate the vice president.

Although many of the framers of the Constitution

Information on Selecting Electors

Information on the methods of selecting presidential electors for the period 1789-1836 appears in several sources, and the sources in a number of instances are in conflict. Among the sources are *Historical Statistics of the United States, Colonial Times to 1957*, prepared by the Bureau of the Census with the cooperation of the Social Science Research Council, published by the U.S. Government Printing Office, Washington, D.C., 1960; Edward Stanwood's *A History of the Presidency, 1788-1916*, Vol. I (Houghton Mifflin, Boston, 1889); Svend Petersen's *A Statistical History of the American Presidential Elections* (Frederick Ungar, New York, 1968); and Neil R. Peirce's *The People's President: the Electoral College in American History and the Direct Vote Alternative* (Simon & Schuster, New York, 1968).

Congressional Quarterly used the Census Bureau's *Historical Statistics of the United States* as its basic source. The chart on p. 681 of *Historical Statistics* presented the most detailed information of all the sources on the various methods used for choosing electors.

---

apparently thought that most elections would be decided by Congress, the House actually has chosen a president only twice, in 1801 and 1825. But a number of campaigns have been deliberately designed to throw elections into the House, where each state has one vote and a majority of states is needed to elect.

In modern times the formal counting of electoral votes has been largely a ceremonial function, but the congressional role can be decisive when votes are contested. The pre-eminent example is the Hayes-Tilden contest of 1876, when congressional decisions on disputed electoral votes from four states gave the election to Republican Rutherford B. Hayes despite the fact that Democrat Samuel J. Tilden had a majority of the popular vote. *(Tilden-Hayes election, p. 89)*

From the beginning, the constitutional provisions governing the selection of the president have had few defenders, and many efforts at Electoral College reform have been undertaken. Although prospects for reform seemed favorable after the close 1968 presidential election, the 91st Congress (1969-71) did not take final action on a proposed constitutional amendment that would have provided for direct popular election of the president and eliminated the existing provision for contingent election by the House. Reform legislation was reintroduced in the Senate during the 94th Congress (1975-77) and the 95th Congress (1977-79).

In addition to its role in electing the president, Congress bears responsibility in the related areas of presidential succession and disability. The 20th Amendment empowers Congress to decide what to do if the president-elect and the vice president-elect both fail to qualify by the date prescribed for commencement of their terms; it also gives Congress authority to settle problems arising from the death of candidates in cases where the election devolves upon Congress. Under the 25th Amendment, Congress has ultimate responsibility for resolving disputes over presidential disability. It also must confirm presidential nominations to fill a vacancy in the vice presidency.

Jefferson-Burr Deadlock

The election of 1800 was the first in which the contingent election procedures of the Constitution were put to the test and the president was elected by the House.

The Federalists, a declining but still potent political force, nominated John Adams for a second term and chose Charles Cotesworth Pinckney as his running mate. A Democratic-Republican congressional caucus chose Vice President Thomas Jefferson for president and Aaron Burr, who had been instrumental in winning the New York Legislature for the Democratic-Republicans earlier in 1800, for vice president.

The electors met in each state on Dec. 4, and the results gradually became known throughout the country: Jefferson and Burr, 73 electoral votes each; Adams, 65; Pinckney, 64; John Jay, 1. The Federalists had lost, but because the Democratic-Republicans had neglected to withhold one electoral vote from Burr, their presidential and vice presidential candidates were tied and the election was thrown into the House.

The lame-duck Congress, with a partisan Federalist majority, was still in office for the electoral count, and the possibilities for intrigue were only too apparent. After toying with and rejecting a proposal to block any election until March 4, when Adams' term expired, the Federalists decided to support Burr and thus elect a relatively pliant politician over a man they considered a "dangerous radical." Alexander Hamilton opposed this move. "I trust the Federalists will not finally be so mad as to vote for Burr," he wrote. "I speak with intimate and accurate knowledge of his character. His elevation can only promote the purposes of the desperate and the profligate. If there be a man in the world I ought to hate, it is Jefferson. With Burr I have always been personally well. But the public good must be paramount to every private consideration."

On Feb. 11, 1801, Congress met in joint session — with Jefferson, the outgoing vice president, in the chair — to count the electoral vote. This ritual ended, the House retired to its own chamber to elect a president. When the House met, it became apparent that the advice of Hamilton had been rejected. A majority of Federalists in the House insisted on backing Burr over Jefferson, the man they despised more. Indeed, if Burr had given clear assurances that he would run the country as a Federalist, he might have been elected. But Burr was unwilling to make those assurances; and, as one chronicler put it, "No one knows whether it was honor or a wretched indecision which gagged Burr's lips."

In all, there were 106 members of the House at the time, 58 Federalists and 48 Democratic-Republicans. If the ballots had been cast per capita, Burr would have been elected, but the Constitution provided that each state should cast a single vote and that a majority of states was necessary for election.

On the first ballot Jefferson received the votes of eight states, one short of a majority of the 16 states then in the Union. Six states backed Burr, while the representatives of Vermont and Maryland were equally divided, so they lost their votes. By midnight of the first day of voting, 19 ballots had been taken, and the deadlock remained.

In all, 36 ballots were taken before the House came to a decision on Feb. 17. Predictably, there were men who sought to exploit the situation for personal gain. Jefferson wrote: "Many attempts have been made to obtain terms and promises from me. I have declared to them unequivocally that I would not receive the Government on capitulation; that I would not go in with my hands tied."

The impasse was finally broken when Vermont and Maryland switched to support of Jefferson. Delaware and South Carolina also withdrew their support from Burr by casting blank ballots. The final vote: 10 states for Jefferson, four (all in New England) for Burr. Thus Jefferson became president, and Burr, under the Constitution as it then stood, automatically became vice president.

Federalist James A. Bayard of Delaware, who had played a key role in breaking the deadlock, wrote to Hamilton: "The means existed of electing Burr, but this required his cooperation. By deceiving one man (a great blockhead) and tempting two (not incorruptible), he might have secured a majority of the states. He will never have another chance of being president of the United States; and the little use he has made of the one which has occurred gives me but an humble opinion of the talents of an unprincipled man."

The Jefferson-Burr contest clearly illustrated the dangers of the double-balloting system established by the original Constitution, and pressure began to build for an amendment requiring separate votes for president and vice president. Congress approved the 12th Amendment in December 1803, and the states — acting with unexpected speed — ratified it in time for the 1804 election.

John Quincy Adams Election

The only other time a president was elected by the House of Representatives was in 1825. There were many contenders for the presidency in the 1824 election, but four predominated: John Quincy Adams, Henry Clay, William H. Crawford and Andrew Jackson. Crawford, secretary of the Treasury under Monroe, was the early front-runner, but his candidacy faltered after he suffered an incapacitating illness in 1823.

When the electoral votes were counted, Jackson had 99, Adams 84, Crawford 41 and Clay 37. With 18 of the 24 states choosing their electors by popular vote, Jackson also led in the popular voting, although the significance of the popular vote was open to challenge. Under the 12th Amendment, the names of the three top contenders — Jackson, Adams and the ailing Crawford — were placed before the House. Clay's support was vital to either of the two front-runners.

From the start, Clay apparently intended to support Adams as the lesser of two evils. But before the House voted, a great scandal erupted. A Philadelphia newspaper printed an anonymous letter alleging that Clay had agreed to support Adams in return for being made secretary of state. The letter alleged also that Clay would have been willing to make the same deal with Jackson. Clay immediately denied the charge and pronounced the writer of the letter "a base and infamous character, a dastard and a liar." But Jackson believed the charges and found his suspicions vindicated when Adams, after the election, did appoint Clay as secretary of state. 'Was there ever witnessed such a bare-faced corruption in any country before?" Jackson wrote to a friend.

When the House met to vote, Adams was supported by the six New England states and New York and, in large part through Clay's backing, by Maryland, Ohio, Kentucky, Illinois, Missouri and Louisiana. Thus a majority of 13 delegations voted for him — the bare minimum he needed for election, since there were 24 states in the Union at the time. The election was accomplished on the first ballot, but Adams took office under a cloud from which his administration never emerged.

Jackson's successful 1828 campaign made much of his contention that the House of Representatives had thwarted

Presidential Election by the House

The following rules, reprinted from Hinds' Precedents of the House of Representatives, were adopted by the House in 1825 for use in deciding the presidential election of 1824. They would provide a precedent for any future House election of a president, although the House could change them.

1. In the event of its appearing, on opening all the certificates, and counting the votes given by the electors of the several States for President, that no person has a majority of the votes of the whole number of electors appointed, the same shall be entered on the Journals of this House.

2. The roll of the House shall then be called by States; and, on its appearing that a Member or Members from two-thirds of the States are present, the House shall immediately proceed, by ballot, to choose a President from the persons having the highest numbers, not exceeding three, on the list of those voted for as President; and, in case neither of those persons shall receive the votes of a majority of all the states on the first ballot, the House shall continue to ballot for a President, without interruption by other business, until a President be chosen.

3. The doors of the Hall shall be closed during the balloting, except against the Members of the Senate, stenographers, and the officers of the House.

4. From the commencement of the balloting until an election is made no proposition to adjourn shall be received, unless on the motion of one State, seconded by another State, and the question shall be decided by States. The same rule shall be observed in regard to any motion to change the usual hour for the meeting of the House.

5. In balloting the following mode shall be observed, to wit:

The Representatives of each State shall be arranged and seated together, beginning with the seats at the right hand of the Speaker's chair, with the Members from the State of Maine; thence, proceeding with the Members from the States, in the order the States are usually named for receiving petitions* around the Hall of the House, until all are seated.

A ballot box shall be provided for each State.

The Representatives of each State shall, in the first instance, ballot among themselves, in order to ascertain the vote of their State; and they may, if necessary, appoint tellers of their ballots.

After the vote of each State is ascertained, duplicates thereof shall be made out; and in case any one of the persons from whom the choice is to be made shall receive a majority of the votes given, on any one balloting by the Representatives of a State, the name of that person shall be written on each of the duplicates; and in case the votes so given shall be divided so that neither of said persons shall have a majority of the whole number of votes given by such State, on any one balloting, then the word "divided" shall be written on each duplicate.

After the delegation from each State shall have ascertained the vote of their State, the Clerk shall name the States in the order they are usually named for receiving petitions; and as the name of each is called the Sergeant-at-Arms shall present to the delegation of each two ballot boxes, in each of which shall be deposited, by some Representative of the State, one of the duplicates made as aforesaid of the vote of said State, in the presence and subject to the examination of all the Members from said State then present; and where there is more than one Representative from a State, the duplicates shall not both be deposited by the same person.

When the votes of the States are thus all taken in, the Sergeant-at-Arms shall carry one of said ballot boxes to one table and the other to a separate and distinct table.

One person from each State represented in the balloting shall be appointed by the Representatives to tell off said ballots; but, in case the Representatives fail to appoint a teller, the Speaker shall appoint.

The said tellers shall divide themselves into two sets, as nearly equal in number as can be, and one of the said sets of tellers shall proceed to count the votes in one of said boxes, and the other set the votes in the other box.

When the votes are counted by the different sets of tellers, the result shall be reported to the House; and if the reports agree, the same shall be accepted as the true votes of the States; but if the reports disagree, the States shall proceed, in the same manner as before, to a new ballot.

6. All questions arising after the balloting commences, requiring the decision of the House, which shall be decided by the House, voting per capita, to be incidental to the power of choosing a President, shall be decided by States without debate; and in case of an equal division of the votes of States, the question shall be lost.

7. When either of the persons from whom the choice is to be made shall have received a majority of all the States, the Speaker shall declare the same, and that that person is elected President of the United States.

8. The result shall be immediately communicated to the Senate by message, and a committee of three persons shall be appointed to inform the President of the United States and the President-elect of said election.

On Feb. 9, 1825, the election of John Quincy Adams took place in accordance with these rules.

Petitions are no longer introduced in this way. This old procedure of calling the states beginning with Maine proceeded through the original 13 states and then through the remaining states in the order of their admission to the Union.

Splitting of States' Electoral Votes...

Throughout the history of presidential elections, there have been numerous cases where a state's electoral votes have been divided between two candidates. The split electoral votes occurred for a variety of reasons.

Electoral Vote Splits, 1789-1836

Splits of a state's electoral votes cast for president before 1836 occurred for these reasons:

- For the first four presidential elections (1789-1800) held under Article II, section 1 of the Constitution, each elector cast two votes without designating which vote was for president and which for vice president. As a result, electoral votes for each state were often scattered among several candidates. The 12th Amendment, ratified in 1804, required electors to vote separately for president and vice president.

- The district system of choosing electors, in which different candidates each could carry several districts. This system is the explanation for the split electoral votes in Maryland in 1804, 1808, 1812, 1824, 1828 and 1832; North Carolina in 1808; Illinois in 1824; Maine in 1828, and New York in 1828.

- The selection of electors by the legislatures of some states. This system sometimes led to party factionalism or political deals that resulted in the choice of electors loyal to more than one candidate. This was the cause for the division of electoral votes in New York in 1808 and 1824, Delaware in 1824 and Louisiana in 1824.

- The vote of an individual elector for someone other than his party's candidate. This happened in New Hampshire in 1820 when one Democratic-Republican elector voted for John Quincy Adams instead of the party nominee, James Monroe.

Voting for Individual Electors

By 1836 all states with the exception of South Carolina, which selected its electors by the state legislature until after the Civil War, had established a system of statewide popular election of electors. The new system limited the frequency of electoral vote splits. Nevertheless, a few states still, on occasion, divided their electoral votes among different presidential candidates. This occurred because of the practice of listing on the ballot the names of all electors and allowing voters to cross off the names of any particular electors they did not like, or, alternatively, requiring voters to vote for each individual elector. In a close election, electors of different parties sometimes were chosen. An example occurred in California in 1880, when one Democratic elector ran behind the Republican thus:

Winning Votes	Party	Losing Electors	Party
80,443	Democratic	80,282	Republican
80,426	Democratic	80,252	Republican
80,420	Democratic	80,242	Republican
80,413	Democratic	80,228	Republican
80,348	Republican	79,885	Democratic

Other similar occurrences include the following:

New Jersey, 1860. Four Republican and three Douglas Democratic electors won.

California, 1892. Eight Democratic electors and one Republican won.

---

the will of the people by denying him the presidency in 1825 even though he had been the leader in popular and electoral votes.

Other Anomalies

On only one occasion has the Senate chosen the vice president. That was in 1837, when Van Buren was elected president with 170 of the 294 electoral votes while his vice presidential running mate, Richard M. Johnson, received only 147 electoral votes — one less than a majority. This discrepancy occurred because Van Buren electors from Virginia boycotted Johnson, reportedly in protest against his social behavior. The Senate elected Johnson, 33-16, over Francis Granger of New York, the runner-up in the electoral vote for vice president.

Although only two presidential elections actually have been decided by the House, a number of others — including those of 1836, 1856, 1860, 1892, 1948, 1960 and 1968 — could have been thrown into the House by only a small shift in the popular vote.

The threat of House election was most clearly evident in 1968, when Democrat George C. Wallace of Alabama ran as a strong third-party candidate. Wallace frequently asserted that he could win an outright majority in the Electoral College by the addition of key Midwestern and Mountain states to his hoped-for base in the Deep South and border states. In reality, the Wallace campaign had a narrower goal: to win the balance of power in Electoral College voting, thus depriving either major party of the clear electoral majority required for election. Wallace made it clear that he would then expect one of the major party candidates to make concessions in return for enough votes from Wallace electors to win the election. Wallace indicated that he expected the election to be settled in the Electoral College and not in the House of Representatives. At the end of the campaign it was disclosed that Wallace had obtained written affidavits from all of his electors in which they promised to vote for Wallace "or whomsoever he may direct" in the Electoral College.

In response to the Wallace challenge, both major party candidates, Republican Richard M. Nixon and Democrat Hubert H. Humphrey, maintained that they would refuse to bargain with Wallace for his electoral votes. Nixon asserted that the House, if the decision rested there, should elect the popular-vote winner. Humphrey said the representatives should select "the president they believe would be best for the country." Bipartisan efforts to obtain advance agreements from House candidates to vote for the national popular-vote winner if the election should go to the House ended in failure. Neither Nixon nor Humphrey replied to suggestions that they pledge before the election

... Factionalism and 'Faithless Electors'

North Dakota, 1892. Two Fusionists (Democrats and Populists) and one Republican won. One of the Fusion electors voted for Democrat Grover Cleveland and the other voted for Populist James B. Weaver, while the Republican elector voted for Benjamin Harrison, thus splitting the state's electoral vote three ways.

Ohio, 1892. Twenty-two Republicans and one Democratic elector won.

Oregon, 1892. Three Republicans and one Populist with Democratic support won.

California, 1896. Eight Republicans and one Democratic elector won.

Kentucky, 1896. Twelve Republicans and one Democratic elector won.

Maryland, 1904. Seven Democratic electors and one Republican won.

Maryland, 1908. Six Democratic and two Republican electors won.

California, 1912. Eleven Progressive and two Democratic electors won.

West Virginia, 1916. Seven Republicans and one Democratic elector won.

The increasing use of voting machines and straight-ticket voting — where the pull of a lever or the marking of an "X" results in automatically casting a vote for every elector — led to the decline in split electoral votes.

'Faithless Electors'

Yet another cause for occasional splits in a state's electoral vote is the so-called "faithless elector." Legally, no elector is bound to vote for any particular candidate; he may cast his ballot for whom he chooses. But in reality, electors are almost always faithful to the candidate of the party with which they are affiliated.

However, sometimes in American political history an elector has broken ranks to vote for a candidate other than his party's. In 1796 a Pennsylvania Federalist elector voted for Democratic-Republican Thomas Jefferson instead of Federalist John Adams. And some historians and political scientists claim that three Democratic-Republican electors voted for Adams. However, the fluidity of political party lines at that early date, and the well-known personal friendship between Adams and at least one of the electors, makes the claim of their being "faithless electors" one of continuing controversy. In 1820 a New Hampshire Democratic-Republican elector voted for John Quincy Adams instead of the party nominee, James Monroe.

There was no further occurrence until 1948, when Preston Parks, a Truman elector in Tennessee, voted for Gov. Strom Thurmond of South Carolina, the States Rights Democratic Party (Dixiecrat) presidential nominee. Since then, there have been the following additional instances:

● In 1956, when W. F. Turner, a Stevenson elector in Alabama, voted for a local judge, Walter E. Jones.

● In 1960, when Henry D. Irwin, a Nixon elector in Oklahoma, voted for Sen. Harry F. Byrd, D-Va.

● In 1968, when Dr. Lloyd W. Bailey, a Nixon elector in North Carolina, voted for George C. Wallace, the American Independent Party candidate.

● In 1972, when Roger L. MacBride, a Nixon elector in Virginia, voted for John Hospers, the Libertarian Party candidate.

● In 1976, when Mike Padden, a Ford elector in the state of Washington, voted for former Gov. Ronald Reagan of California.

---

to swing enough electoral votes to the popular-vote winner to assure his election without help from Wallace.

In the end Wallace received only 13.5 percent of the popular vote and 46 electoral votes (including the vote of one Republican defector), all from Southern states. He failed to win the balance of power in the Electoral College which he had hoped to use to wring policy concessions from one of the major-party candidates. If Wallace had won a few border states, or if a few thousand more Democratic votes had been cast in Northern states barely carried by Nixon, thus reducing Nixon's electoral vote below 270, Wallace would have been in a position to bargain off his electoral votes or to throw the election into the House for final settlement.

The near success of the Wallace strategy provided dramatic impetus for electoral reform efforts in the 91st Congress.

Counting the Electoral Vote

Congress has mandated a variety of dates for the casting of popular votes, the meeting of the electors to cast ballots in the various states and the official counting of the electoral votes before both houses of Congress.

The Continental Congress made the provisions for the first election. On Sept. 13, 1788, the Congress directed that each state choose its electors on the first Wednesday in January 1789. It further directed these electors to cast their ballots on the first Wednesday in February 1789.

In 1792 the 2nd Congress passed legislation setting up a permanent calendar for choosing electors. Allowing some flexibility in dates, the law directed that states choose their electors within the 34 days preceding the first Wednesday in December of each presidential election year. Then the electors would meet in their various states and cast their ballots on the first Wednesday in December. On the second Wednesday of the following February, the votes were to be opened and counted before a joint session of Congress. Provision also was made for a special presidential election in case of the removal, death, resignation or disability of both the president and vice president.

Under that system, states chose presidential electors at various times. For instance, in 1840 the popular balloting for electors began in Pennsylvania and Ohio on Oct. 30 and ended in North Carolina on Nov. 12. South Carolina, the only state still choosing presidential electors through the state Legislature, appointed its electors on Nov. 26.

Congress modified the system in 1845, providing that each state choose its electors on the same day — the Tuesday next after the first Monday in November — a provision that still remains in force. Otherwise, the days for

88 Elections '84

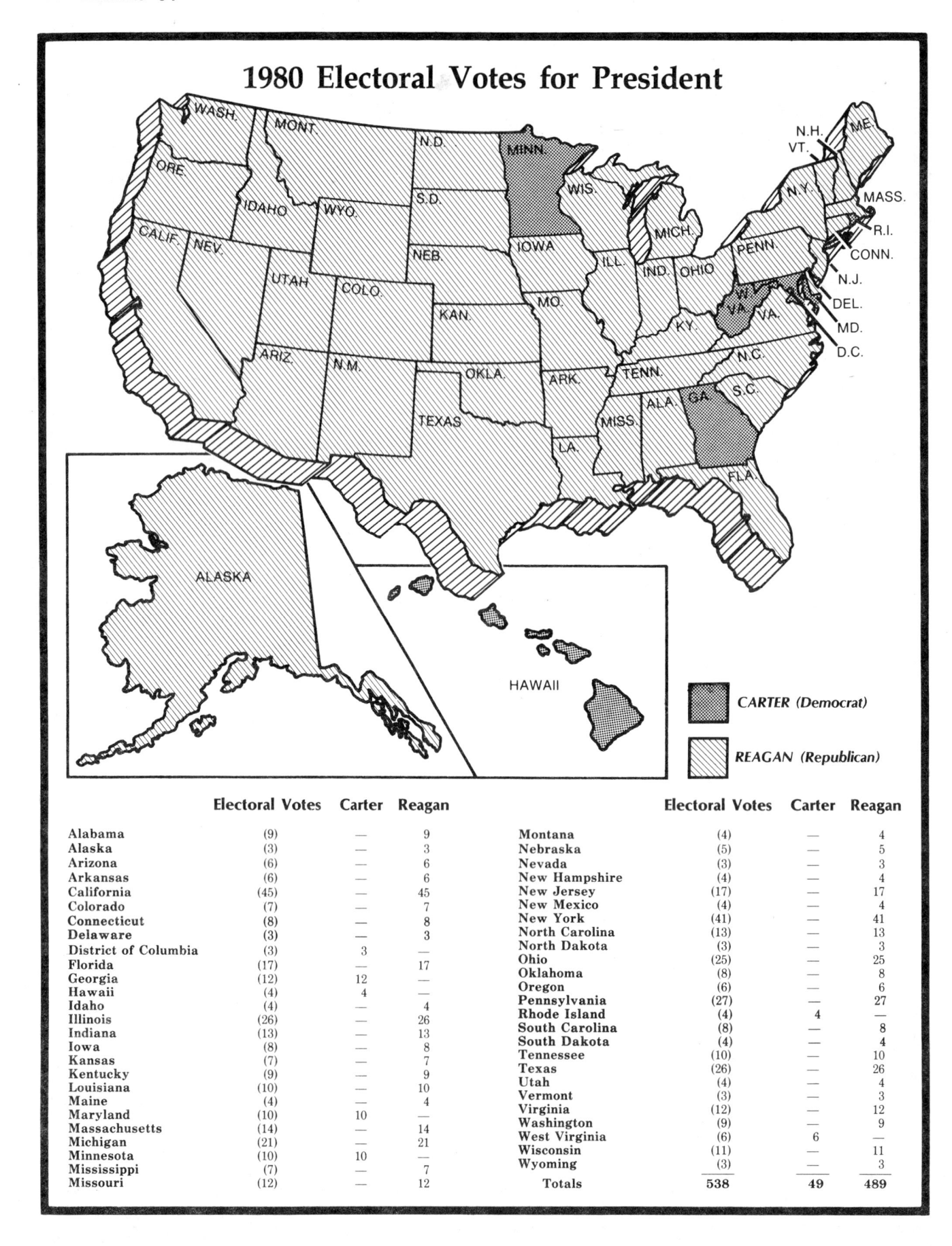

1980 Electoral Votes for President

	Electoral Votes	Carter	Reagan		Electoral Votes	Carter	Reagan
Alabama	(9)	—	9	Montana	(4)	—	4
Alaska	(3)	—	3	Nebraska	(5)	—	5
Arizona	(6)	—	6	Nevada	(3)	—	3
Arkansas	(6)	—	6	New Hampshire	(4)	—	4
California	(45)	—	45	New Jersey	(17)	—	17
Colorado	(7)	—	7	New Mexico	(4)	—	4
Connecticut	(8)	—	8	New York	(41)	—	41
Delaware	(3)	—	3	North Carolina	(13)	—	13
District of Columbia	(3)	3	—	North Dakota	(3)	—	3
Florida	(17)	—	17	Ohio	(25)	—	25
Georgia	(12)	12	—	Oklahoma	(8)	—	8
Hawaii	(4)	4	—	Oregon	(6)	—	6
Idaho	(4)	—	4	Pennsylvania	(27)	—	27
Illinois	(26)	—	26	Rhode Island	(4)	4	—
Indiana	(13)	—	13	South Carolina	(8)	—	8
Iowa	(8)	—	8	South Dakota	(4)	—	4
Kansas	(7)	—	7	Tennessee	(10)	—	10
Kentucky	(9)	—	9	Texas	(26)	—	26
Louisiana	(10)	—	10	Utah	(4)	—	4
Maine	(4)	—	4	Vermont	(3)	—	3
Maryland	(10)	10	—	Virginia	(12)	—	12
Massachusetts	(14)	—	14	Washington	(9)	—	9
Michigan	(21)	—	21	West Virginia	(6)	6	—
Minnesota	(10)	10	—	Wisconsin	(11)	—	11
Mississippi	(7)	—	7	Wyoming	(3)	—	3
Missouri	(12)	—	12	Totals	538	49	489

casting and counting the electoral votes remained the same.

The next change occurred in 1887, when Congress provided that electors were to meet and cast their ballots on the second Monday in January instead of the first Wednesday in December. Congress also dropped the provision for a special presidential election.

In 1934 Congress again revised the law. The new arrangements, still in force, directed the electors to meet on the first Monday after the second Wednesday in December. The ballots are opened and counted before Congress on Jan. 6 (the next day if Jan. 6 falls on a Sunday).

The Constitution states: "The President of the Senate shall, in the presence of the Senate and House of Representatives, open all the certificates, and the votes shall then be counted." It gives no guidance on disputed ballots.

Before counting the electoral votes in 1865, Congress adopted the 22nd Joint Rule, which provided that no electoral votes objected to in joint session could be counted except by the concurrent votes of both the Senate and House. The rule was pushed by congressional Republicans to ensure rejection of the electoral votes from the newly reconstructed states of Louisiana and Tennessee. Under this rule, Congress in 1873 also threw out the electoral votes of Louisiana and Arkansas and three from Georgia.

However, the rule lapsed at the beginning of 1876, when the Senate refused to readopt it because the House was in Democratic control. Thus, following the 1876 election, when it became apparent that for the first time the outcome of an election would be determined by decisions on disputed electoral votes, Congress had no rules to guide it.

Hayes-Tilden Contest

The 1876 campaign pitted Republican Rutherford B. Hayes against Democrat Samuel J. Tilden. Early election-night returns indicated that Tilden had been elected. He had won the swing states of Indiana, New York, Connecticut and New Jersey; those states plus his expected Southern support would give him the election. However, by the following morning it became apparent that if the Republicans could hold South Carolina, Florida and Louisiana, Hayes would be elected with 185 electoral votes to 184 for Tilden. But if a single elector in any of these states voted for Tilden, he would throw the election to the Democrats. Tilden led in the popular-vote count by more than a quarter million votes.

The situation was much the same in each of the three contested states. Historian Eugene H. Roseboom described it as follows: "The Republicans controlled the state governments and the election machinery, had relied upon the Negro masses for votes, and had practiced frauds as in the past. The Democrats used threats, intimidation, and even violence when necessary, to keep Negroes from the polls; and where they were in a position to do so they resorted to fraud also. The firm determination of the whites to overthrow carpetbag rule contributed to make a full and fair vote impossible; carpetbag hold on the state governments made a fair count impossible. Radical reconstruction was reaping its final harvest."

Both parties pursued the votes of the three states with a fine disregard for propriety or legality, and in the end double sets of elector returns were sent to Congress from all three. Oregon also sent two sets of returns. Although Hayes carried that state, the Democratic governor discovered that one of the Hayes electors was a postmaster and therefore ineligible to be an elector under the Constitution, so he certified the election of the top-polling Democratic elector. However, the Republican electors met, received the resignation of their ineligible colleague, then reappointed him to the vacancy since he had in the meantime resigned his postmastership.

Had the 22nd Joint Rule remained in effect, the Democratic House of Representatives could have objected to any of Hayes' disputed votes. But since the rule had lapsed, Congress had to find some new method of resolving electoral disputes. A joint committee was created to work out a plan, and the resulting Electoral Commission Law was approved by large majorities and signed into law Jan. 29, 1877 — only a few days before the date scheduled for counting the electoral votes.

The law, which applied only to the 1876 electoral vote count, established a 15-member electoral commission which was to have final authority over disputed electoral votes, unless both houses of Congress agreed to overrule it. The commission was to consist of five senators, five representatives and five Supreme Court justices. Each chamber was to select its own members of the commission, with the understanding that the majority party would have three members and the minority two. Four justices, two from each party, were named in the bill, and these four were to select the fifth. It was expected that they would choose Justice David Davis, who was considered a political independent, but he disqualified himself when the Illinois Legislature named him to a seat in the Senate. Justice Joseph P. Bradley, a Republican, then was named to the 15th seat on the commission. The Democrats supported his selection, because they considered him the most independent of the remaining justices, all of whom were Republicans. However, he was to vote with the Republicans on every dispute and thus assure the victory of Hayes.

The electoral count began in Congress Feb. 1 (moved up from the second Wednesday in February for this one election), and the proceedings continued until March 2. States were called in alphabetical order, and as each disputed state was reached, objections were raised to both the Hayes and Tilden electors. The question was then referred to the electoral commission, which in every case voted 8-7 for Hayes. In each case, the Democratic House rejected the commission's decision, but the Republican Senate upheld it, so the decision stood.

As the count went on, Democrats in the House threatened to launch a filibuster to block resumption of joint sessions so that the count could not be completed before Inauguration Day. The threat was never carried out, because of an agreement reached between the Hayes forces and Southern conservatives. The Southerners agreed to let the electoral count continue without obstruction. In return Hayes agreed that, as president, he would withdraw federal troops from the South, end Reconstruction and make other concessions. The Southerners, for their part, pledged to respect Negro rights, a pledge they did not carry out.

Thus, at 4 a.m. March 2, 1877, the president of the Senate was able to announce that Hayes had been elected president with 185 electoral votes, as against 184 for Tilden. Later that day Hayes arrived in Washington. The next evening he took the oath of office privately at the White House, because March 4 fell on a Sunday. His formal inauguration followed on Monday. The country acquiesced. Thus ended a crisis that could have resulted in civil war.

Not until 1887 did Congress enact permanent legislation on the handling of disputed electoral votes. The Elec-

Law for Counting Electoral Votes in Congress

Following is the complete text of Title 3, section 15 of the U.S. Code, enacted originally in 1887, governing the counting of electoral votes in Congress:

Congress shall be in session on the sixth day of January succeeding every meeting of the electors. The Senate and House of Representatives shall meet in the Hall of the House of Representatives at the hour of 1 o'clock in the afternoon on that day, and the President of the Senate shall be their presiding officer. Two tellers shall be previously appointed on the part of the Senate and two on the part of the House of Representatives, to whom shall be handed, as they are opened by the President of the Senate, all the certificates and papers purporting to be certificates of the electoral votes, which certificates and papers shall be opened, presented, and acted upon in the alphabetical order of the States, beginning with the letter A; and said tellers, having then read the same in the presence and hearing of the two Houses, shall make a list of the votes as they shall appear from the said certificates; and the votes having been ascertained and counted according to the rules in this subchapter provided, the result of the same shall be delivered to the President of the Senate, who shall thereupon announce the state of the vote, which announcement shall be deemed a sufficient declaration of the persons, if any, elected President and Vice President of the United States, and, together with a list of the votes, be entered on the Journals of the two Houses. Upon such reading of any such certificate or paper, the President of the Senate shall call for objections, if any. Every objection shall be made in writing, and shall state clearly and concisely, and without argument, the ground thereof, and shall be signed by at least one Senator and one Member of the House of Representatives before the same shall be received. When all objections so made to any vote or paper from a State shall have been received and read, the Senate shall thereupon withdraw, and such objections shall be submitted to the Senate for its decision; and the Speaker of the House of Representatives shall, in like manner, submit such objections to the House of Representatives for its decision; and no electoral vote or votes from any State which shall have been regularly given by electors whose appointment has been lawfully certified to according to section 6* of this title from which but one return has been received shall be rejected, but the two Houses concurrently may reject the vote or votes when they agree that such vote or votes have not been so regularly given by electors whose appointment has been so certified. If more than one return or paper purporting to be a return from a State shall have been received by the President of the Senate, those votes, and those only, shall be counted which shall have been regularly given by the electors who are shown by the determination mentioned in section 5† of this title to have been appointed, if the determination in said section provided for shall have been made, or by such successors or substitutes, in case of a vacancy in the board of electors so ascertained, as have been appointed to fill such vacancy in the mode provided by the laws of the State; but in case there shall arise the question which of two or more of such State authorities determining what electors have been appointed, as mentioned in section 5 of this title, is the lawful tribunal of such State, the votes regularly given of those electors, and those only, of such State shall be counted whose title as electors the two Houses, acting separately, shall concurrently decide is supported by the decision of such State so authorized by its law; and in such case of more than one return or paper purporting to be a return from a State, if there shall have been no such determination of the question in the State aforesaid, then those votes, and those only, shall be counted which the two Houses shall concurrently decide were cast by lawful electors appointed in accordance with the laws of the State, unless the two Houses, acting separately, shall concurrently decide such votes not to be the lawful votes of the legally appointed electors of such State. But if the two Houses shall disagree in respect of the counting of such votes, then, and in that case, the votes of the electors whose appointment shall have been certified by the executive of the State, under the seal thereof, shall be counted. When the two Houses have voted, they shall immediately again meet, and the presiding officer shall then announce the decision of the questions submitted. No votes or papers from any other State shall be acted upon until the objections previously made to the votes or papers from any State shall have been finally disposed of.

* Section 6 provides for certification of votes by electors by state Governors.
† Section 5 provides that if state law specifies a method for resolving disputes concerning the vote for Presidential electors, Congress must respect any determination so made by a state.

---

toral Count Act of that year gave each state final authority in determining the legality of its choice of electors and required a concurrent majority of both the Senate and House to reject any electoral votes. It also established procedures for counting electoral votes in Congress. *(Text, box, this page)*

Application of 1887 Law in 1969

The procedures relating to disputed electoral votes were utilized for the first time after the election of 1968. When Congress met in joint session Jan. 6, 1969, to count the electoral votes, Sen. Edmund S. Muskie, D-Maine, and Rep. James G. O'Hara, D-Mich., joined by six other senators and 37 other representatives, filed a written objection to the vote cast by a North Carolina elector, Dr. Lloyd W. Bailey of Rocky Mount, who had been elected as a Republican but chose to vote for George C. Wallace and Curtis LeMay, the presidential and vice presidential candidates of the American Independent Party, instead of Republicans Richard M. Nixon and Spiro T. Agnew.

Acting under the 1887 law, Muskie and O'Hara objected to Bailey's vote on the grounds that it was "not properly given" because a plurality of the popular votes in North Carolina were cast for Nixon-Agnew and the state's voters had chosen electors to vote for Nixon and Agnew only. Muskie and O'Hara asked that Bailey's vote not be counted at all by Congress.

The 1887 statute, incorporated in the U.S. Code, Title

Electoral College

> ## 25th Amendment
> (Ratified Feb. 10, 1967)
>
> **Section 1.** In case of the removal of the President from office or of his death or resignation, the Vice President shall become President.
>
> **Section 2.** Whenever there is a vacancy in the office of the Vice President, the President shall nominate a Vice President who shall take office upon confirmation by a majority vote of both Houses of Congress.
>
> **Section 3.** Whenever the President transmits to the President pro tempore of the Senate and the Speaker of the House of Representatives his written declaration that he is unable to discharge the powers and duties of his office, and until he transmits to them a written declaration to the contrary, such powers and duties shall be discharged by the Vice President as Acting President.
>
> **Section 4.** Whenever the Vice President and a majority of either the principal officers of the executive departments or of such other body as Congress may by law provide, transmit to the President pro tempore of the Senate and the Speaker of the House of Representatives their written declaration that the President is unable to discharge the powers and duties of his office, the Vice President shall immediately assume the powers and duties of the office as Acting President.
>
> Thereafter, when the President transmits to the President pro tempore of the Senate and the Speaker of the House of Representatives his written declaration that no inability exists, he shall resume the powers and duties of his office unless the Vice President and a majority of either the principal officers of the executive departments or of such other body as Congress may by law provide, transmit within four days to the President pro tempore of the Senate and the Speaker of the House of Representatives their written declaration that the President is unable to discharge the powers and duties of his office. Thereupon Congress shall decide the issue, assembling within forty-eight hours for that purpose if not in session. If the Congress, within twenty-one days after receipt of the latter written declaration, or, if Congress is not in session, within twenty-one days after Congress is required to assemble, determines by two-thirds vote of both houses that the President is unable to discharge the powers and duties of his office, the Vice President shall continue to discharge the same as Acting President; otherwise, the President shall resume the powers and duties of his office.

3, Section 15, stipulated that "no electoral vote or votes from any state which shall have been regularly given by electors whose appointment has been lawfully certified ... from which but one return has been received shall be rejected, but the two Houses concurrently may reject the vote or votes when they agree that such vote or votes have not been so regularly given by electors whose appointment has been so certified." The statute did not define the term "regularly given," although at the time of its adoption chief concern centered on problems of dual sets of electoral vote returns from a state, votes cast on an improper day or votes disputed because of uncertainty about whether a state lawfully was in the Union on the day that the electoral vote was cast.

The 1887 statute provided that if written objection to any state's vote was received from at least one member of both the Senate and House, the two legislative bodies were to retire immediately to separate sessions, debate for two hours with a five-minute limitation on speeches, and that each chamber was to decide the issue by vote before resuming the joint session. The statute made clear that both the Senate and House had to reject a challenged electoral vote (or votes) for such action to prevail.

At the Jan. 6 joint session in the House chamber, with Senate President Pro Tempore Richard B. Russell, D-Ga., presiding, the counting of the electoral vote proceeded smoothly through the alphabetical order of states until the North Carolina result was announced, at which time O'Hara rose to announce filing of the complaint. The two houses then reassembled in joint session at which the results of the separate deliberations were announced and the count of the electoral vote by state proceeded without event. At the conclusion, Russell announced the vote and declared Nixon and Agnew elected.

Although Congress did not sustain the challenge to Bailey's vote, the case of the "faithless" elector led to increased pressure for changes in the procedures. However, no reforms had cleared Congress by early 1983.

Reform Proposals

Since Jan. 6, 1797, when Rep. William L. Smith, F-S.C., introduced in Congress the first proposed constitutional amendment for reform of the Electoral College system, hardly a session of Congress has passed without the introduction of one or more resolutions of this nature. But only one — the 12th Amendment, ratified in 1804 — ever has been approved.

In recent years, public interest in a change in the Electoral College system was spurred by the close 1960 and 1968 elections, by a series of Supreme Court rulings relating to apportionment and districting and by introduction of unpledged elector systems in the Southern states.

House Approval of Amendment

Early in 1969, President Nixon asked Congress to take prompt action on Electoral College reform. He said he would support any plan that would eliminate individual electors and distribute among the presidential candidates the electoral vote of every state and the District of Columbia in a manner more closely approximating the popular vote.

Later that year the House approved, 338-70, a resolution proposing a constitutional amendment to eliminate the Electoral College and to provide instead for direct popular election of the president and vice president. The measure set a minimum of 40 percent of the popular vote as sufficient for election and provided for a runoff election between the two top candidates for the presidency if no candidate received 40 percent. Under this plan the House of Representatives could no longer be called upon to select a president. The proposed amendment also authorized Congress to provide a method of filling vacancies caused by the death, resignation or disability of presidential nominees before the election and a method of filling post-election vacancies caused by the death of the president-elect or vice president-elect.

Nixon, who previously had favored a proportional plan of allocating each state's electoral votes, endorsed the House resolution and urged the Senate to adopt it. To become effective, the proposed amendment had to be approved by a two-thirds majority in both the Senate and House and be ratified by the legislatures of three-fourths of the states.

When the proposal reached the Senate floor in September 1970, small-state and Southern senators succeeded in blocking final action on it. The resolution was laid aside Oct. 5, after two unsuccessful efforts to cut off a filibuster against the proposed constitutional amendment.

Carter Endorsement of Plan

Another major effort to eliminate the Electoral College occurred in 1977, when President Carter included such a proposal in his election reform package, unveiled March 22.

Carter endorsed the amendment approved by the House in 1969, to replace the Electoral College with direct popular election of the president and vice president, and provide for a runoff if no candidate received at least 40 percent of the vote. Because the Senate was again seen as the major stumbling block, the House waited to see what the Senate would do before beginning any deliberation of its own.

After several months of deadlock, the Senate Judiciary Committee approved Sept. 15 the direct presidential election plan by a vote of 9 to 8. But Senate opponents of the measure promised another filibuster and the Senate leadership decided it could not spare the time or effort to try to break it. The measure was never brought to the floor and died when the 95th Congress adjourned in 1978.

On Jan. 15, 1979, the opening day of the 96th Congress, Sen. Birch Bayh, D-Ind., began another effort to abolish the Electoral College through a constitutional amendment. In putting off action in the previous Congress, Senate leaders had agreed to try for early action in the 96th.

A proposed constitutional amendment to abolish the Electoral College and elect the president by popular vote did reach the Senate floor in July 1979. The Senate voted in favor of the measure, 51-48 — 15 votes short of the required two-thirds majority of those present and voting needed to approve a constitutional amendment.

Supporters of the resolution blamed defections by several Northern liberals for the margin of defeat. Major Jewish and black groups extensively lobbied the Northern senators, arguing that the voting strength of black and Jewish voters is maximized under the Electoral College system because both groups are concentrated in urban areas of the large electoral vote states.

Presidential Disability

A decade of congressional concern over the question of presidential disability was eased in 1967 by ratification of the 25th Amendment to the Constitution. The amendment for the first time provided for continuity in carrying out the functions of the presidency in the event of presidential disability and for filling a vacancy in the vice presidency.

Congressional consideration of the problem of presidential disability had been prompted by President Eisenhower's heart attack in 1955. The ambiguity of the language of the disability clause (Article II, Section 1, Clause 5) of the Constitution had provoked occasional debate ever since the Constitutional Convention of 1787. But it had never been decided how far the term "disability" extended or who would be the judge of it.

Clause 5 provided that Congress should decide who was to succeed to the presidency in the event that both the president and the vice president died, resigned or became disabled. Congress enacted succession laws three times. By the Act of March 1, 1792, it provided for succession (after the vice president) of the president pro tempore of the Senate, then of the House Speaker; if those offices were vacant, states were to send electors to Washington to choose a new president.

That law stood until passage of the Presidential Succession Act of Jan. 19, 1886, which changed the line of succession to run from the vice president to the secretary of state, secretary of the Treasury and so on through the Cabinet in order of rank. Sixty-one years later, the Act of July 18, 1947 (still in force), placed the Speaker of the House and the president pro tempore of the Senate ahead of Cabinet officers in succession after the vice president.

Before ratificiation of the 25th Amendment in 1967, no procedures had been laid down to govern situations arising in the event of presidential incapacity or of a vacancy in the office of vice president. Two presidents had had serious disabilities — James A. Garfield, shot in 1881 and confined to his bed until he died 2½ months later, and Woodrow Wilson, who suffered a stroke in 1919. In each case the vice president did not assume any duties of the presidency for fear he would appear to be usurping the powers of that office. As for a vice presidential vacancy, the United States has been without a vice president 18 times for a total of 40 years through 1980, after the elected vice president succeeded to the presidency, died or resigned.

Ratification of the 25th Amendment established procedures that clarified these areas of uncertainty in the Constitution. The amendment provided that the vice president should become acting president under either one of two circumstances. If the president informed Congress that he was unable to perform his duties, the vice president would become acting president until the president could resume his responsibilities.

If the vice president and a majority of the Cabinet, or another body designated by Congress, found the president to be incapacitated, the vice president would become acting president until the president informed Congress that his disability had ended. Congress was given 21 days to resolve any dispute over the president's disability; a two-thirds vote of both chambers was required to overrule the president's declaration that he was no longer incapacitated.

Whenever a vacancy occurred in the office of the vice president, either by death, succession to the presidency or resignation, the president was to nominate a vice president, and the nomination was to be confirmed by a majority vote of both houses of Congress.

The proposed 25th Amendment was approved by the Senate and House in 1965. It took effect Feb. 10, 1967, **after ratification by 38 states.** *(Text, box, p. 91)*

Within only eight years, the power of the president to appoint a new vice president under the terms of the 25th Amendment was used twice. In 1973, when Vice President Agnew resigned, President Nixon nominated Gerald R. Ford as the new vice president. Ford was confirmed by both houses of Congress and sworn in Dec. 6, 1973. On Nixon's resignation Aug. 9, 1974, Ford succeeded to the presidency, becoming the first unelected president in

American history. President Ford chose as his new vice president former Gov. Nelson A. Rockefeller of New York, who was sworn in Dec. 19, 1974.

With both the president and vice president holding office through appointment rather than election, members of Congress and the public expressed concern about the power of a president to, in effect, appoint his own successor. Accordingly, Sen. John O. Pastore, D-R.I., introduced a proposed constitutional amendment on Feb. 3, 1975, to provide for a special national election for president with more than one year remaining in a presidential term. Hearings were held before the Senate Judiciary Subcommittee on Constitutional Amendments, but no action was taken on the measure.

Confusion After Reagan Shooting

In the aftermath of the attempted assassination of President Ronald Reagan in 1981, there was no need to invoke the presidential disability provisions of the 25th Amendment. However, some of the public statements made by administration officials immediately after the shooting reflected continuing confusion over the issue of who is in charge when the president temporarily is unable to function. Soon after word of the shooting became known, the members of the Reagan Cabinet gathered in the White House, ready to invoke the amendment's procedures, if necessary. Vice President George Bush was on an Air Force jet returning to Washington from Texas.

At a televised press briefing later that afternoon, Secretary of State Alexander M. Haig Jr., confirmed that Reagan was in surgery. Under anesthesia, it was clear that he temporarily was unable to make presidential decisions should the occasion — such as a foreign attack or other national emergency — require them. Attempting to reassure the country, Haig stated that he was in control in the White House pending the return of Vice President Bush, with whom he was in contact.

This assertion was followed by the question, from the press, as to who was making administration decisions. Haig responded, "Constitutionally, gentlemen, you have the president, the vice president and the secretary of state in that order, and should the president decide he wants to transfer the helm to the vice president, he will do so. He has not done that."

Haig's response dealt with the old line of succession that predated the Presidential Succession Act. The Constitution does not spell out a line of succession. The law (PL 80-199) specifies that the line of succession is the vice president, the Speaker of the House, the president pro tempore of the Senate, the secretaries of state, Treasury, defense, the attorney general, the secretaries of interior, agriculture, commerce, labor, health and human services, housing and urban development, transportation, energy and education.

Electoral Votes for Vice President, 1804-1980

The following list gives the electoral votes for vice president from 1804 to 1980. Unless indicated by a *footnote*, the state-by-state breakdown of electoral votes for each vice presidential candidate was the same as for his party's presidential candidate.

Prior to 1804, under Article II, Section 1, of the Constitution, each elector cast two votes — each vote for a different person. The electors did not distinguish between votes for president and vice president.

The candidate receiving the second highest total became vice president. The 12th Amendment, ratified in 1804, required electors to vote separately for president and vice president.

Candidates

In some cases persons had received electoral votes although they had never been formally nominated. The word *candidate* is used in this section to designate persons receiving electoral votes.

Sources: Votes and Parties

The *Senate Manual* (U.S. Government Printing Office, 1977) was the source used for vice presidential electoral votes.

For political party designation, the basic source was *A Statistical History of the American Presidential Elections* (Frederick Ungar, New York, 1968) by Svend Petersen; Petersen gives the party designation of *presidential candidates only*. Congressional Quarterly adopted Petersen's party designations for the running mates of presidential candidates.

To supplement Petersen, Congressional Quarterly consulted the *Biographical Directory of the American Congress, 1774-1971*, U.S. Government Printing Office, 1971; the *Dictionary of American Biography*, Charles Scribner's, New York, 1928-1936; the *Encyclopedia of American Biography,* Harper and Row, New York, 1974, and *Who Was Who in America, 1607-1968*, Marquis Co., Chicago, 1943-1968.

Year	Candidate	Electoral Votes
1804	George Clinton (Democratic-Republican)	162
	Rufus King (Federalist)	14
1808	George Clinton (Democratic-Republican)[1]	113
	John Langdon (Democratic-Republican)	9
	James Madison (Democratic-Republican)	3
	James Monroe (Democratic-Republican)	3
	Rufus King (Federalist)	47
1812	Elbridge Gerry (Democratic-Republican)[2]	131
	Jared Ingersoll (Federalist)	86
1816	Daniel D. Tompkins (Democratic-Republican)	183
	John E. Howard (Federalist)[3]	22
	James Ross (Federalist)	5
	John Marshall (Federalist)	4
	Robert G. Harper (Federalist)	3
1820	Daniel D. Tompkins (Democratic-Republican)[4]	218
	Richard Rush (Democratic-Republican)	1
	Richard Stockton (Federalist)	8
	Daniel Rodney (Federalist)	4
	Robert G. Harper (Federalist)	1
1824	John C. Calhoun (Democratic-Republican)[5]	182
	Nathan Sanford (Democratic-Republican)	30
	Nathaniel Macon (Democratic-Republican)	24
	Andrew Jackson (Democratic-Republican)	13
	Martin Van Buren (Democratic-Republican)	9
	Henry Clay (Democratic-Republican)	2
1828	John C. Calhoun (Democratic-Republican)[6]	171

Year	Candidate	Electoral Votes
	William Smith (Independent Democratic-Republican)	7
	Richard Rush (National Republican)	83
1832	Martin Van Buren (Democratic)[7]	189
	William Wilkins (Democratic)	30
	Henry Lee (Independent Democratic)	11
	John Sergeant (National Republican)	49
	Amos Ellmaker (Anti-Masonic)	7
1836	Richard M. Johnson (Democratic)[8]	147
	William Smith (Independent Democratic)	23
	Francis Granger (Whig)	77
	John Tyler (Whig)	47
1840	John Tyler (Whig)	234
	Richard M. Johnson (Democratic)[9]	48
	L. W. Tazewell (Democratic)	11
	James K. Polk (Democratic)	1
1844	George M. Dallas (Democratic)	170
	Theodore Frelinghuysen (Whig)	105
1848	Millard Fillmore (Whig)	163
	William O. Butler (Democratic)	127
1852	William R. King (Democratic)	254
	William A. Graham (Whig)	42
1856	John C. Breckinridge (Democratic)	174
	William L. Dayton (Republican)	114
	Andrew J. Donelson (American)	8
1860	Hannibal Hamlin (Republican)	180
	Joseph Lane (Southern Democratic)	72
	Edward Everett (Constitutional Union)	39
	Herschel V. Johnson (Democratic)	12
1864	Andrew Johnson (Republican)	212
	George H. Pendleton (Democratic)	21
1868	Schuyler Colfax (Republican)	214
	Francis P. Blair (Democratic)	80
1872	Henry Wilson (Republican)	286
	Benjamin G. Brown (Democratic)[10]	47
	Alfred H. Colquitt (Democratic)	5
	John M. Palmer (Democratic)	3
	Thomas E. Bramlette (Democratic)	3
	William S. Groesbeck (Democratic)	1
	Willis B. Machen (Democratic)	1

Electoral Votes for Vice President

	Candidate	Votes
	George W. Julian (Liberal Republican)	5
	Nathaniel P. Banks (Liberal Republican)	1
1876	William A. Wheeler (Republican)	185
	Thomas A. Hendricks (Democratic)	184
1880	Chester A. Arthur (Republican)	214
	William H. English (Democratic)	155
1884	Thomas A. Hendricks (Democratic)	219
	John A. Logan (Republican)	182
1888	Levi P. Morton (Republican)	233
	Allen G. Thurman (Democratic)	168
1892	Adlai E. Stevenson (Democratic)	277
	Whitelaw Reid (Republican)	145
	James G. Field (Populist)	22
1896	Garret A. Hobart (Republican)	271
	Arthur Sewall (Democratic)[11]	149
	Thomas E. Watson (Populist)	27
1900	Theodore Roosevelt (Republican)	292
	Adlai E. Stevenson (Democratic)	155
1904	Charles W. Fairbanks (Republican)	336
	Henry G. Davis (Democratic)	140
1908	James S. Sherman (Republican)	321
	John W. Kern (Democratic)	162
1912	Thomas R. Marshall (Democratic)	435
	Hiram W. Johnson (Progressive)	88
	Nicholas M. Butler (Republican)	8
1916	Thomas R. Marshall (Democratic)	277
	Charles W. Fairbanks (Republican)	254
1920	Calvin Coolidge (Republican)	404
	Franklin D. Roosevelt (Democratic)	127
1924	Charles G. Dawes (Republican)	382
	Charles W. Bryan (Democratic)	136
	Burton K. Wheeler (Progressive)	13
1928	Charles Curtis (Republican)	444
	Joseph T. Robinson (Democratic)	87
1932	John N. Garner (Democratic)	472
	Charles Curtis (Republican)	59
1936	John N. Garner (Democratic)	523
	Frank Knox (Republican)	8
1940	Henry A. Wallace (Democratic)	449
	Charles L. McNary (Republican)	82
1944	Harry S Truman (Democratic)	432
	John W. Bricker (Republican)	99
1948	Alben W. Barkley (Democratic)	303
	Earl Warren (Republican)	189
	Fielding L. Wright (States' Rights Democratic)	39
1952	Richard M. Nixon (Republican)	442
	John J. Sparkman (Democratic)	89
1956	Richard M. Nixon (Republican)	457
	Estes Kefauver (Democratic)	73
	Herman Talmadge (Democratic)	1
1960	Lyndon B. Johnson (Democratic)	303
	J. Strom Thurmond (Democratic)[12]	14
	Henry Cabot Lodge (Republican)	219
	Barry Goldwater (Republican)	1
1964	Hubert H. Humphrey (Democratic)	486
	William E. Miller (Republican)	52
1968	Spiro T. Agnew (Republican)	301
	Edmund S. Muskie (Democratic)	191
	Curtis E. LeMay (American Independent)	46
1972	Spiro T. Agnew (Republican)	520
	R. Sargent Shriver (Democratic)	17
	Theodora Nathan (Libertarian)	1
1976	Walter F. Mondale (Democratic)	297
	Robert J. Dole (Republican)[13]	241
1980	George Bush (Republican)	489
	Walter F. Mondale (Democratic)	49

---

1. New York cast 13 presidential electoral votes for Democratic-Republican James Madison and 6 votes for Clinton; for vice president, New York cast 13 votes for Clinton, 3 votes for Madison and 3 votes for Monroe.

Langdon received Ohio's three votes and Vermont's 6 votes.

2. The state-by-state vote for Gerry was the same as for Democratic-Republican presidential candidate Madison except for Massachusetts and New Hampshire. Massachusetts cast 2 votes for Gerry and 20 votes for Ingersoll; New Hampshire cast 1 vote for Gerry and 7 votes for Ingersoll.

3. Four Federalists received vice presidential electoral votes: Howard—Massachusetts, 22 votes; Ross—Connecticut, 5 votes; Marshall—Connecticut, 4 votes; Harper—Delaware, 3 votes.

4. The state-by-state vote for Tompkins was the same as for Democratic-Republican presidential candidate James Monroe except for Delaware, Maryland and Massachusetts. Delaware cast 4 votes for Rodney; Maryland cast 10 votes for Tompkins and one for Harper; Massachusetts cast 7 votes for Tompkins and 8 for Stockton.

New Hampshire, which cast 7 presidential electoral votes for Monroe and 1 vote for John Quincy Adams, cast 7 vice presidential electoral votes for Tompkins and 1 vote for Rush.

5. The state-by-state vice presidential electoral vote was as follows:

Calhoun—Alabama, 5 votes; Delaware, 1 vote; Illinois, 3 votes; Indiana, 5 votes; Kentucky, 7 votes; Louisiana, 5 votes; Maine, 9 votes; Maryland, 10 votes; Massachusetts, 15 votes; Mississippi, 3 votes; New Hampshire, 7 votes; New Jersey, 8 votes; New York, 29 votes; North Carolina, 15 votes; Pennsylvania, 28 votes; Rhode Island, 3 votes; South Carolina, 11 votes; Tennessee, 11 votes; Vermont, 7 votes.

Sanford—Kentucky, 7 votes; New York, 7 votes; Ohio, 16 votes.

Macon—Virginia, 24 votes.

Jackson—Connecticut, 8 votes; Maryland, 1 vote; Missouri, 3 votes; New Hampshire, 1 vote.

Van Buren—Georgia, 9 votes.

Clay—Delaware, 2 votes.

6. The state-by-state vote for Calhoun was the same as for Democratic-Republican presidential candidate Jackson except for Georgia, which cast 2 votes for Calhoun and 7 votes for Smith.

7. The state-by-state vote for Van Buren was the same as for Democratic presidential candidate Jackson except for Pennsylvania which cast 30 votes for Wilkins.

South Carolina cast 11 presidential electoral votes for Independent Democratic presidential candidate Floyd and 11 votes for Independent Democratic vice presidential candidate Lee.

Vermont cast 7 presidential electoral votes for Anti-Masonic candidate Wirt and 7 vice presidential electoral votes for Wirt's running mate, Ellmaker.

8. The state-by-state vote for Johnson was the same as for Democratic presidential candidate Van Buren except for Virginia which cast 23 votes for Smith.

Granger's state-by-state vote was the same as for Whig presidential candidate Harrison except for Maryland and Massachusetts. Maryland cast 10 presidential electoral votes for Harrison and 10 vice presidential votes for Tyler; Massachusetts cast 14 presidential electoral votes for Whig candidate Webster and 14 vice presidential votes for Granger.

Tyler received 11 votes from Georgia, 10 from Maryland, 11 from South Carolina and 15 from Tennessee.

No vice presidential candidate received a majority of the electoral vote. As a result, the Senate, for the only time in history, selected the vice president under the provisions of the 12th Amendment. Johnson was elected vice president by a vote of 33 to 16 for Granger.

9. The Democratic Party did not nominate a vice presidential candidate in 1840. Johnson's state-by-state vote was the same as for presidential candidate Van Buren except for South Carolina and Virginia.

South Carolina cast 11 votes for Tazewell.

Virginia cast 23 presidential electoral votes for Van Buren, 22 vice presidential votes for Johnson and 1 vice presidential vote for Polk.

10. Liberal Republican and Democratic presidential candidate Horace Greeley died Nov. 29, 1872. As a result, 18 electors pledged to Greeley cast their presidential electoral votes for Brown, Greeley's running mate.

The vice presidential vote was as follows:

Brown—Georgia, 5 votes; Kentucky, 8 votes; Maryland, 8 votes; Missouri, 6 votes; Tennessee, 12 votes; Texas, 8 votes.

Colquitt—Georgia, 5 votes.

Palmer—Missouri, 3 votes.

Bramlette—Kentucky, 3 votes.

Groesbeck—Missouri, 1 vote.

Machen—Kentucky, 1 vote.

Julian—Missouri, 5 votes.

Banks—Georgia, 1 vote.

11. The state-by-state vote for Sewell was the same as for Democratic-Populist candidate William Jennings Bryan except for the following states which cast electoral votes for Thomas E. Watson: Arkansas—3 votes; Louisiana—4 votes; Missouri—4 votes; Montana—1 vote; Nebraska—4 votes; North Carolina—5 votes; South Dakota—2 votes; Utah—1 vote; Washington—2 votes; Wyoming—1 vote.

12. Democratic electors carried Alabama's 11 electoral votes. Five of the electors were pledged to the national Democratic ticket of John F. Kennedy and Lyndon B. Johnson. Six electors ran unpledged and voted for Harry F. Byrd for president and Thurmond for vice president.

Mississippi's 8 electors voted for Byrd and Thurmond.

In Oklahoma, the Republican ticket of Richard M. Nixon and Henry Cabot Lodge carried the state, but one of the state's 8 electors voted for Byrd for president and Goldwater for vice president.

13. One Republican elector from the state of Washington cast his presidential electoral vote for Ronald Reagan instead of the Republican nominee, Gerald R. Ford. But he voted for Robert J. Dole, Ford's running mate, for vice president. Thus Dole received one more electoral vote than Ford.

1980 Presidential Election

Total Popular Vote: 86,515,221
Reagan's Plurality: 8,420,270

STATE	RONALD REAGAN (Republican) Votes	%	JIMMY CARTER (Democrat) Votes	%	JOHN B. ANDERSON (Independent) Votes	%	ED CLARK (Libertarian) Votes	%	OTHER[1] Votes	%	PLURALITY
Alabama	654,192	48.8	636,730	47.5	16,481	1.2	13,318	1.0	21,208	1.6	17,462
Alaska	86,112	54.3	41,842	26.4	11,155	7.0	18,479	11.7	857	0.5	44,270
Arizona	529,688	60.6	246,843	28.2	76,952	8.8	18,784	2.2	1,678	0.2	282,845
Arkansas	403,164	48.1	398,041	47.5	22,468	2.7	8,970	1.1	4,939	0.6	5,123
California	4,524,858	52.7	3,083,661	35.9	739,833	8.6	148,434	1.7	90,277	1.1	1,441,197
Colorado	652,264	55.1	367,973	31.1	130,633	11.0	25,744	2.2	7,801	0.7	284,291
Connecticut	677,210	48.2	541,732	38.5	171,807	12.2	8,570	0.6	6,966	0.5	135,478
Delaware	111,252	47.2	105,754	44.8	16,288	6.9	1,974	0.8	632	0.3	5,498
D.C.	23,545	13.4	131,113	74.8	16,337	9.3	1,114	0.6	3,128	1.8	107,568
Florida	2,046,951	55.5	1,419,475	38.5	189,692	5.1	30,524	0.8	288	0.0	627,476
Georgia	654,168	41.0	890,733	55.8	36,055	2.3	15,627	1.0	112	0.0	236,565
Hawaii	130,112	42.9	135,879	44.8	32,021	10.6	3,269	1.1	2,006	0.7	5,767
Idaho	290,699	66.5	110,192	25.2	27,058	6.2	8,425	1.9	1,057	0.2	180,507
Illinois	2,358,049	49.6	1,981,413	41.7	346,754	7.3	38,939	0.8	24,566	0.5	376,636
Indiana	1,255,656	56.0	844,197	37.7	111,639	5.0	19,627	0.9	10,914	0.5	411,459
Iowa	676,026	51.3	508,672	38.6	115,633	8.8	13,123	1.0	4,207	0.3	167,354
Kansas	566,812	57.9	326,150	33.3	68,231	7.0	14,470	1.5	4,132	0.4	240,662
Kentucky	635,274	49.1	616,417	47.6	31,127	2.4	5,531	0.4	6,278	0.5	18,857
Louisiana	792,853	51.2	708,453	45.7	26,345	1.7	8,240	0.5	12,700	0.8	84,400
Maine	238,522	45.6	220,974	42.3	53,327	10.2	5,119	1.0	5,069	1.0	17,548
Maryland	680,606	44.2	726,161	47.1	119,537	7.8	14,192	0.9			45,555
Massachusetts	1,057,631	41.9	1,053,802	41.7	382,539	15.2	22,038	0.9	8,288	0.3	3,829
Michigan	1,915,225	49.0	1,661,532	42.5	275,223	7.0	41,597	1.1	16,148	0.4	253,693
Minnesota	873,268	42.6	954,174	46.5	174,990	8.5	31,592	1.5	17,956	0.9	80,906
Mississippi	441,089	49.4	429,281	48.1	12,036	1.3	5,465	0.6	4,749	0.5	11,808
Missouri	1,074,181	51.2	931,182	44.3	77,920	3.7	14,422	0.7	2,119	0.1	142,999
Montana	206,814	56.8	118,032	32.4	29,281	8.0	9,825	2.7			88,782
Nebraska	419,937	65.9	166,851	26.0	44,993	7.0	9,073	1.4			253,086
Nevada	155,017	62.5	66,666	26.9	17,651	7.1	4,358	1.8	4,193	1.7	88,351
New Hampshire	221,705	57.7	108,864	28.4	49,693	12.9	2,064	0.5	1,664	0.4	112,841
New Jersey	1,546,557	52.0	1,147,364	38.6	234,632	7.9	20,652	0.7	26,479	0.9	399,193
New Mexico	250,779	54.9	167,826	36.7	29,459	6.5	4,365	1.0	4,542	1.0	82,953
New York	2,893,831	46.7	2,728,372	44.0	467,801	7.5	52,648	0.8	59,307	1.0	165,459
North Carolina	915,018	49.3	875,635	47.2	52,800	2.8	9,677	0.5	2,703	0.1	39,383
North Dakota	193,695	64.2	79,189	26.3	23,640	7.8	3,743	1.2	1,278	0.4	114,506
Ohio	2,206,545	51.5	1,752,414	40.9	254,472	5.9	49,033	1.1	21,139	0.5	454,131
Oklahoma	695,570	60.5	402,026	35.0	38,284	3.3	13,828	1.2			293,544
Oregon	571,044	48.3	456,890	38.7	112,389	9.5	25,838	2.2	15,355	1.3	114,154
Pennsylvania	2,261,872	49.6	1,937,540	42.5	292,921	6.4	33,263	0.7	35,905	0.8	324,332
Rhode Island	154,793	37.2	198,342	47.7	59,819	14.4	2,458	0.6	660	0.2	43,549
South Carolina	441,841	49.4	430,385	48.1	14,153	1.6	5,139	0.6	2,553	0.3	11,456
South Dakota	198,343	60.5	103,855	31.7	21,431	6.5	3,824	1.2	250	0.1	94,488
Tennessee	787,761	48.7	783,051	48.4	35,991	2.2	7,116	0.4	3,697	0.2	4,710
Texas	2,510,705	55.3	1,881,147	41.4	111,613	2.5	37,643	0.8	528	0.0	629,558
Utah	439,687	72.8	124,266	20.6	30,284	5.0	7,226	1.2	2,759	0.5	315,421
Vermont	94,628	44.4	81,952	38.4	31,761	14.9	1,900	0.9	3,058	1.4	12,676
Virginia	989,609	53.0	752,174	40.3	95,418	5.1	12,821	0.7	16,010	0.9	237,435
Washington	865,244	49.7	650,193	37.3	185,073	10.6	29,213	1.7	12,671	0.7	215,051
West Virginia	334,206	45.3	367,462	49.8	31,691	4.3	4,356	0.6			33,256
Wisconsin	1,088,845	47.9	981,584	43.2	160,657	7.1	29,135	1.3	13,000	0.6	107,261
Wyoming	110,700	62.6	49,427	28.0	12,072	6.8	4,514	2.6			61,273
Totals	43,904,153	50.7	35,483,883	41.0	5,720,060	6.6	921,299	1.1	485,826	0.6	

The Popular Vote

Few elements of the American political system have changed so markedly over the years as has the electorate. Since the early days of the nation, when the voting privilege was limited to the upper economic classes, one voting barrier after another has fallen to pressures for wider suffrage. First nonproperty-holding males, then women, then black Americans and finally young people pushed for the franchise. By the early 1970s, almost every restriction on voting had been removed, and virtually every adult citizen 18 years of age and older had won the right to vote.

Actions to expand the electorate have taken place at both the state and federal levels. Voting qualifications have varied widely in the states because of a provision of the federal Constitution (Article I, Section 2) permitting the states to set their own voting standards. Early in the nation's history, the states dropped their property qualifications for voting but some retained literacy tests as late as 1970.

On the federal level, the Constitution has been amended five times to circumvent state qualifications denying the franchise to certain categories of persons. The 14th Amendment, ratified in 1868, directed Congress to reduce the number of representatives from any state that disfranchised adult male citizens for any reason other than commission of a crime. However, no such reduction was ever made. The 15th Amendment, ratified in 1870, prohibited denial of the right to vote "on account of race, color or previous condition of servitude," while the 19th Amendment in 1920 prohibited denial of that right "on account of sex." The 24th Amendment, which came into effect in 1964, barred denial of the right to vote in any federal election "by reason of failure to pay any poll tax or other tax." Finally, in 1971, the 26th Amendment lowered the voting age to 18 in federal, state and local elections.

Congress in the 1950s and 1960s enacted a series of statutes to enforce the 15th Amendment's guaranty against racial discrimination in voting. A law passed in 1970 nullified state residence requirements of longer than 30 days for voting in presidential elections, suspended literacy tests for a five-year period (the suspension was made permanent in 1975) and lowered the minimum voting age from 21 years, the requirement then in effect in most states, to 18. Subsequently, a Supreme Court ruling upheld the voting-age change for federal elections but invalidated it for state and local elections. In the same decision (*Oregon v. Mitchell*, 400 U.S. 112, 1970) the court upheld the provision on residence requirements and sustained the suspension of literacy tests with respect to both state and local elections. The 26th Amendment was ratified six months after the court's decision.

The right to vote in presidential elections was extended to citizens of the District of Columbia by the 23rd Amendment, ratified in 1961. District residents had been disfranchised from national elections except for a brief period in the 1870s when they elected a nonvoting delegate to the House of Representatives. In 1970 Congress took another step toward full suffrage for District residents by again authorizing the election of a non-voting delegate to the House, beginning in 1971.

Voting Trends

Statistics show that each major liberalization of election laws has resulted in a sharp increase in the number of persons voting. From 1824 to 1856, a period in which states gradually relaxed their property and taxpaying qualifications for voting, voter participation in presidential elections increased from 3.8 percent to 16.7 percent of the total population. In 1920, when the 19th Amendment giving women the franchise went into effect, voter participation increased to 25.1 percent of the population.

Between 1932 and 1976 both the number of voters in presidential elections and the voting-age population almost doubled. Except for the 1948 presidential election, when barely more than half the voting-age population was estimated to have gone to the polls, the turnout in the postwar years through 1968 was approximately 60 percent, according to Census Bureau surveys. This relatively high percentage was due largely to passage of new civil rights laws encouraging blacks to vote.

Despite a steady increase in the numbers of persons voting in the 1970s, voter turnout actually declined as a percentage of eligible voters who voted. Voter participation reached a modern peak of 63.1 percent in the 1960 presidential election. It declined steadily over the next decade, falling to 61.8 percent in 1964, 60.7 percent in 1968 and 55.4 percent in 1972. Voting in the off-year congressional elections, always lower than in presidential years, also declined during this period.

According to the Census Bureau, 54.4 percent of the voting-age population went to the polls in 1976. In 1980 voting declined further, with only an estimated 53 percent of the 162.8 million Americans of voting age bothering to vote. This was the fifth consecutive presidential election in which the voter turnout decreased. (Census Bureau surveys, it should be pointed out, are based on polls of eligible voters rather than on actual counts of the voting-age population or of registered voters. The bureau defines "eligible" voters as all adult civilians of voting age — 18 and older and registered or not — except persons in penal or other institutions. The number of registered voters nationwide at any given time is impossible to calculate. States have different registration deadlines before an election; persons who move may be registered in more than one state at the same time or temporarily may not be recorded in any state; and some states do not require pre-registration before voting, while others do not require towns and municipalities to keep registration records. Thus in a few states without registration requirements, the Census Bureau considers all eligible voters as registered voters as well.)

Changes in the age distribution of the electorate figured prominently in the 1970s decline. Due to the surge in the birth rate beginning in 1947, the youth population has been the most rapidly growing group. However, young adults have tended to vote in much smaller proportions than the rest of the voting-age population. When approximately 11 million young voters entered the electorate in 1972 when the voting age was lowered to 18, the percentage of eligible Americans who voted dropped sharply even though the total number of voters who cast ballots for president rose to 77,625,000, 4.4 million more than in 1968.

In addition to changes in the composition of the electorate, political scientists have attributed the decline in the percentage of Americans voting to several factors: long periods of political stability; the predictable outcome of many races; and the lack of appeal of some candidates.

Studies by the Census Bureau have shown a marked difference in participation among various classes of voters. In general, the studies have found higher participation rates among whites, persons 45 to 65 years of age, non-Southerners, persons with higher family incomes and white-collar employees and professionals. Private studies have shown repeatedly that higher voter turnout in an election generally favors Democrats while lower ones favor Republicans. Far more voters are registered as Democrats.

As the voting population grew, political parties became increasingly important in the electoral process in the 19th century. As the power of the individual's vote became more and more diluted, voters found parties a convenient mechanism for defining political issues and mobilizing the strength to push a particular policy through to enactment and execution. After the rise and fall of numerous different political parties during the first half of the 19th century, most voting strength became and remained polarized in two major parties — the Republican and the Democratic. This changed somewhat in the 20th century. The Progressive movement won a sizable following in the early years of the century, and Americans who refused to register in either of the major parties — the independent voters — increased appreciably in the post-World War II years.

Broadening the Franchise

During the first few decades of the Republic, all 13 of the original states limited the franchise to property holders and taxpayers. Seven of the states required ownership of land or a life estate as opposed to a leased estate as a qualification for voting, while the other six permitted persons to substitute either evidence of ownership of certain amounts of personal property or payment of taxes as a prerequisite to vote.

The framers of the Constitution apparently were content to have the states limit the right to vote to adult males who had a real stake in good government. This meant, in most cases, persons in the upper economic levels. Not wishing to discriminate against any particular type of property owner (uniform federal voting standards inevitably would have conflicted with some of the state standards), the Constitutional Convention adopted without dissent the recommendation of its Committee of Detail providing that qualifications for the electors of the House of Representatives "shall be the same ... as those of the electors in the several states of the most numerous branch of their own legislatures."

Under this provision fewer than one-half of the adult white men in the United States were eligible to vote at the outset in federal elections. Because no state made women eligible (although states were not forbidden to do so), only one white adult in four qualified to go to the polls. Slaves, both blacks and Indians, were ineligible, and they comprised almost one-fifth of the American population as enumerated in the census of 1790. Also ineligible were white indentured servants, whose status was little better than that of the slaves.

Actually, these early state practices represented a liberalization of restrictions on voting that had prevailed at one time in the colonial period. Roman Catholics had been disfranchised in almost every colony, Jews in most colonies, Quakers and Baptists in some. In Rhode Island, Jews remained legally ineligible to vote until 1842.

For half a century before the Civil War there was a **steady broadening of the electorate.** The new Western settlements supplied a stimulus to the principle of universal manhood suffrage, and Jacksonian democracy encouraged its acceptance. Gradually, the seven states making property ownership a condition for voting substituted a taxpaying requirement: Delaware in 1792; Maryland in 1810; Connecticut in 1818; Massachusetts in 1821; New York in 1821; Rhode Island in 1842, and Virginia in 1850. By the mid-19th century, most states had removed even the taxpaying qualifications although some jurisdictions persisted in this practice into the 20th century.

The trend toward a broadened franchise continued in the 20th century with women obtaining the vote and racial barriers to black voting slowly eliminated. Once Congress acted, the Supreme Court steadily backed its power to ensure the right to vote. In general, by the 200th anniversary of the nation the only remaining restrictions prevented voting by the insane, convicted felons and otherwise eligible voters who were unable to meet short residence requirements for voting.

Voting Behavior

A precise breakdown that shows which groups of voters (blacks, women, etc.) have higher turnout rates has never been possible. It would require an elaborate questionnaire for every eligible voter asking whether the person had participated in the election, and an honest answer from the voter.

In place of a complete survey, the Census Bureau has attempted to measure voting behavior by taking a random sample of the electorate in every election year since 1964. The Survey Research Center-Center for Political Studies at the University of Michigan also analyzes voting behavior. Again, these surveys cannot be precise because they are based on people's responses. Estimates made from the survey differ from the actual ballot count because people frequently report that they or members of their families voted when in fact they did not.

The Census Bureau reported that its preliminary survey following the 1980 election showed that the proportion of the voting-age population who said they were registered to vote in 1980 (67 percent) was the same as in 1976. This was a decrease from 1968 when 74 percent of the voting-age population reported being registered. Sixty-one percent of the white population of voting age reported they voted in 1980 compared with only 51 percent of the black population and 30 percent of the Spanish-origin population. However, the report noted that the differences in voter turnout were almost entirely the result of differences in the proportion of the population who were registered — ranging from a high of 68 percent of the white population to 60 percent of the black population and only 36 percent of the Spanish-origin population.

There was little difference in voter participation for men and women. In 1964 the reported voting rate for men (72 percent) was about 5 percent higher than for women.

The largest decline in voter turnout in the elections since 1964 occurred in the North and West where voter participation declined by 12 percentage points for whites and 19 percentage points for blacks. In the South there were relatively smaller changes in voter turnout between 1964 and 1980. Although there was an increase in the voter turnout rate for blacks from 44 percent in 1964 to 48 percent in 1980, there was a decrease for whites from 60 percent to 57 percent.

There were a number of reasons for the low voter turnout in 1980. Various surveys pointed to a growing sense of powerlessness among the electorate, a feeling that one person's vote was not important and a belief that it made no difference which party won.

Another reason for declining turnouts was that even in 1980 voting could be a time-consuming process. Citizens first must register. Though requirements have been eased, only five states — Maine, Minnesota, North Dakota, Oregon and Wisconsin — permit election day registration.

Voter turnout varies according to region. Fewer voters go to the polls in one-party regions, especially in the South. And, as mentioned earlier, the actual turnout always is lower than the numbers obtained from surveys since people are reluctant to admit they did not vote.

Ironically, in 1912, 1924, 1948 and 1980 — when there have been major third party candidates — turnout has been lower than in the previous election.

In the congressional elections of 1982, voter turnout increased for the first time in a mid-term election since the mid-60s.

According to a Gallup Poll released in April 1981, 28 percent of American voters considered themselves Republicans and 41 percent considered themselves Democrats, a decline of 4 percentage points for the Democratic Party since 1975. The number of independent voters dropped from 33 percent in 1975 to 31 percent in 1981. The 28 percent Republican figure was the highest in nine years.

The breakdown of political affiliation emerging from a Gallup Poll conducted in late 1980 indicated that blacks continued to consider themselves Democrats. Persons with a college education identified with Republicans or independents more often than with Democrats. Regionally, independents were strongest in the Midwest and weakest in the South and West, and Republicans were strongest in the West and relatively weak in the South. The Democratic Party was relatively weak in the Midwest.

'Minority' Presidents

Under the U.S. electoral college system, 15 presidents have been elected, either by the electoral college itself or by the House of Representatives, who did not receive a majority of the popular votes cast in the election. Three of them — John Quincy Adams, Rutherford B. Hayes and Benjamin Harrison — actually trailed their opponents in the popular vote.

The following table shows the percentage of the popular vote received by candidates in the 15 elections in which a "minority" president was elected:

Year Elected				
1824	Adams 30.92	Jackson 41.34	Clay 12.99	Crawford 11.17
1844	Polk 49.54	Clay 48.08	Birney 2.30	
1848	Taylor 47.28	Cass 42.49	Van Buren 10.12	
1856	Buchanan 45.28	Fremont 33.11	Fillmore 21.53	
1860	Lincoln 39.82	Douglas 29.46	Breckenridge 18.09	Bell 12.61
1876	Hayes 47.95	Tilden 50.97	Cooper .97	
1880	Garfield 48.27	Hancock 48.25	Weaver 3.32	Others .15
1884	Cleveland 48.50	Blaine 48.25	Butler 1.74	St. John 1.47
1888	Harrison 47.82	Cleveland 48.62	Fisk 2.19	Streeter 1.29
1892	Cleveland 46.05	Harrison 42.96	Weaver 8.50	Others 2.25
1912	Wilson 41.84	T. Roosevelt 27.39	Taft 23.18	Debs 5.99
1916	Wilson 49.24	Hughes 46.11	Benson 3.18	Others 1.46
1948	Truman 49.52	Dewey 45.12	Thurmond 2.40	H. Wallace 2.38
1960	Kennedy 49.72	Nixon 49.55	Others .72	
1968	Nixon 43.42	Humphrey 42.72	G. Wallace 13.53	Others .33

Source: Congressional Quarterly, Guide to U.S. Elections, Washington, D.C.: Congressional Quarterly Inc., 1975.

Congressional and Gubernatorial Elections 101

The 1984 Congressional Elections 103
Senate Membership in the 98th Congress 109
House Membership in the 98th Congress 110
Senate Elections 113
House Elections 121
House Districts for the 1980s 125
Gubernatorial Elections 129

1984 Elections for Governor, Senate, House

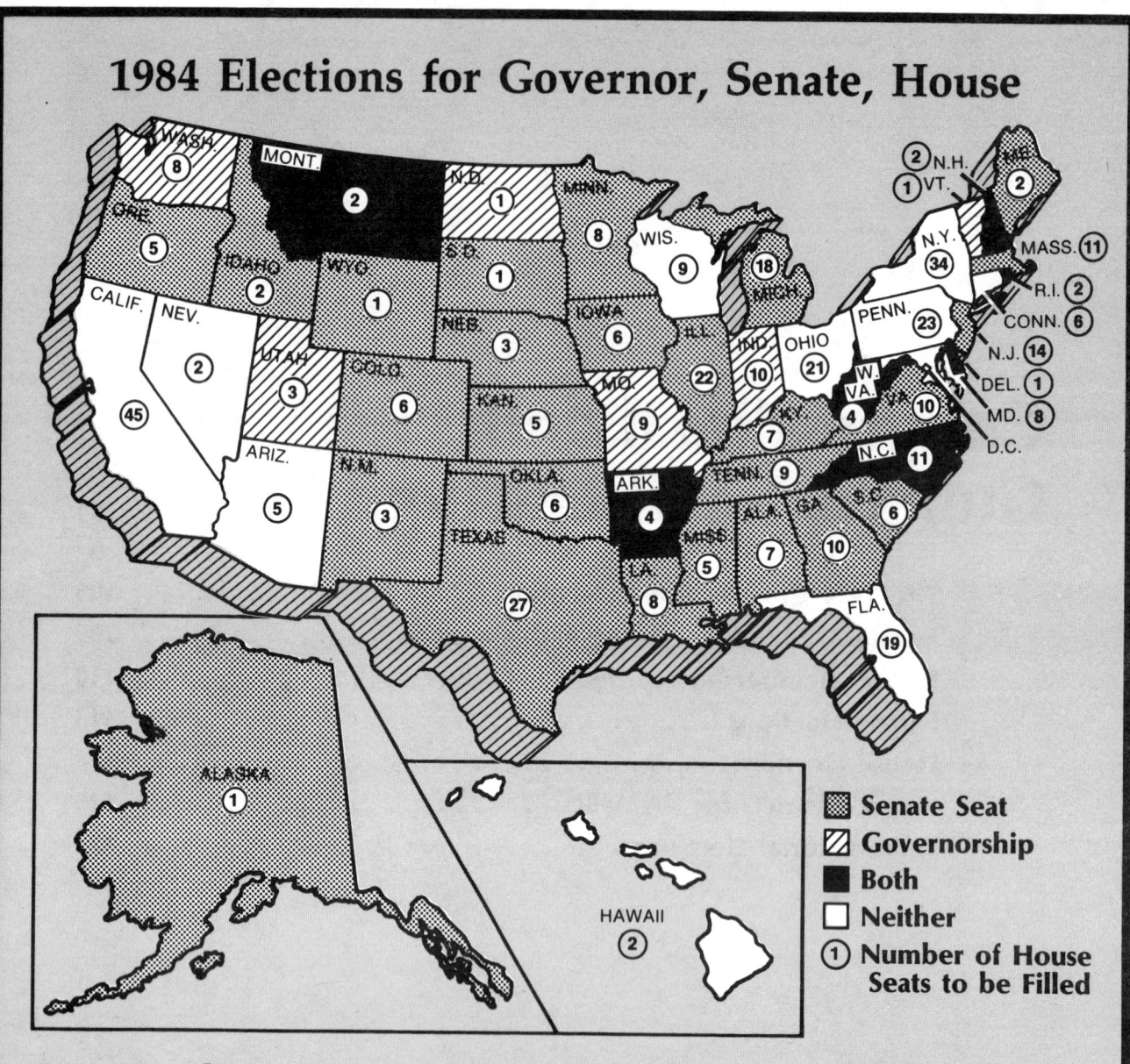

- ▨ Senate Seat
- ▨ Governorship
- ■ Both
- ☐ Neither
- ① Number of House Seats to be Filled

Governorships, Senate and House Seats to be Filled Nov. 6

To be elected
- 13 Governors
- 33 Senators
- 435 Representatives

Current Party Lineup
- Governors - 35 Democrats, 15 Republicans
- Senators - 45 Democrats, 55 Republicans
- Representatives - 268 Democrats, 166 Republicans, 1 vacancy

The 1984 Congressional Elections

Reading the newspapers and watching the news on television, it was easy to conclude that the congressional elections were little more than a sideshow to the politics of 1984. For every story about Democratic efforts to regain control of the Senate, there were a dozen about the Democrats' presidential primaries and the White House strategy for re-electing President Ronald Reagan in November.

When it comes time to chart the politics of 1985, however, the 1984 outcome in the Senate will deserve nearly equal billing with the election results for president. If President Reagan succeeded in winning a second term, in 1985 he would have either a split Congress similar to the one that enacted his economic program three years ago or an opposition Democratic Congress of the kind that left Presidents Richard Nixon and Gerald R. Ford largely impotent in domestic policy. A new Democratic administration would be able to look forward to friendly majorities in both chambers, and at least a temporary "honeymoon," or to continual trouble with a suspicious GOP-controlled Senate.

Regardless of what lawmakers accomplished in the final year of the 98th Congress, it was believed certain in Washington that 1985 would be *the* year for crucial economic decisions. Government officials and outside observers were only a little less certain that the direction of those decisions would be shaped by the Senate elections, not just the one for president.

Republicans entered the election year controlling the Senate with 55 seats. If the Democratic Party were to win the presidency in 1984, a gain of five seats would bring them a Senate majority, assuming a tie-breaking vote in their favor from a new Democratic vice president. Failure to regain the White House would require the Democrats to make a net gain of six seats because a tie vote would go against them.

Senate Races

Republicans in 1984 initially settled on a risky "51st vote" strategy for the Senate elections. Instead of discounting the idea that they could lose control of the Senate to the Democrats, Republicans intentionally publicized that possibility in the hope of focusing voters' attention on the GOP assertion that the Senate would become a liberal playground if Democrats regained control.

The point of their strategy was to turn an albatross — the Republicans' vulnerable position — into an asset. The GOP was defending 19 seats in 1984 compared to only 14 for the Democrats.

There was a risk that the "51st vote" strategy could backfire; it might seem negative and dangerous to Republicans who preferred that the party's own candidates not be spreading unflattering predictions that GOP control of the Senate might be lost.

But many Republicans felt they had to resort to some type of potentially hazardous strategy because the party faced a situation that seemed stacked against it. Although circumstances might change before the November elections that dramatically altered the nature of the Senate elections, most of the close contests at the beginning of the year were expected to be in states where Republicans were on the defensive.

Strategists at the National Republican Senatorial Committee (NRSC) hoped that the anti-liberal mood that gave the GOP a Senate majority in 1980 could be tapped to help the party retain control in 1984. NRSC Executive Director Mitchell E. Daniels maintained that even a moderate Democratic incumbent could be beaten if voters were told that "he's going to cast a devastatingly bad vote when he votes for Senator Byrd or Senator Kennedy or whoever becomes the next majority leader and brings committee and subcommittee chairmen like Metzenbaum, Tsongas, Levin *et al* with him." Sens. Robert C. Byrd of West Virginia, now Senate minority leader, Edward M. Kennedy of Massachusetts, Howard M. Metzenbaum of Ohio and Carl Levin of Michigan could occupy important leadership posts if Democrats regained control of the Senate.

Republican campaign literature echoed that theme. "Even if the reports I've received are only half right, we are still in grave danger of losing Senate control," warned NRSC Chairman Sen. Richard G. Lugar, Ind., in a fund-raising letter. "Ted Kennedy could control the Senate by 1984," Lugar wrote. The Republican strategy was similar to that used by the Nixon administration in 1970, when President Nixon and Vice President Spiro Agnew warned that the Senate had to be delivered from the hands of "radical liberal" Democratic incumbents.

1984 Congressional, State Election Calendar

State	Primary Dates †	Candidate Filing Deadline	Voter Registration Deadline ‡	U.S. Senators terms expire	Governors terms expire	Current lineup U.S. House Seats
Ala.	Sept. 4/Sept. 25	July 6	Aug. 24/Oct. 26	Heflin (D)		5 D, 2 R
Alaska	Aug. 28	June 1	July 29/Oct. 7	Stevens (R)		1 R
Ariz.	Sept. 11	June 28	July 23/Sept. 17			2 D, 3 R
Ark.	May 29/June 12	April 3	May 8/Oct. 16	Pryor (D)	Clinton (D)	2 D, 2 R
Calif.	June 5	March 9	May 7/ Oct. 8			28 D, 17 R
Colo.	Sept. 11	July 27	Aug. 10/Oct. 5	Armstrong (R)		3 D, 3 R
Conn.	Sept. 11	Aug. 10	Aug. 28/Oct. 16			4 D, 2 R
Del.	Sept. 8	July 27	Aug. 18/Oct. 20	Biden (D)	du Pont (R)#	1 D
Fla.	Sept. 4/Oct. 2	July 20	Aug. 4/Oct. 6			13 D, 6 R
Ga.	Aug. 14/Sept. 4	June 13	July 16/Oct. 9	Nunn (D)		9 D, 1 R
Hawaii	Sept. 22	July 24	Aug. 23/Oct. 9			2 D
Idaho	May 22	April 6	May 11/Oct. 26	McClure (R)		2 R
Ill.	March 20	12/19/83	Feb. 21/Oct. 9	Percy (R)		12 D, 10 R
Ind.	May 8	March 9	April 9/Oct. 8		Orr (R)	5 D, 5 R
Iowa	June 5	March 30	May 26/Oct. 27	Jepsen (R)		3 D, 3 R
Kan.	Aug. 7	June 11	July 17/Oct. 16	Kassebaum (R)		2 D, 3 R
Ky.	Aug. 28††	May 30	July 30/Oct. 12	Huddleston (D)		4 D, 3 R
La.	Sept. 29 [1]	July 20	Aug. 30/Oct. 13	Johnston (D)		6 D, 2 R
Maine	June 12	April 1	June 12/Nov. 6 [2]	Cohen (R)		2 R
Md.	May 8	Feb. 27	April 9/Oct. 8			7 D, 1 R
Mass.	Sept. 18	June 5	Aug. 21/Oct. 9	Tsongas (D)*		10 D, 1 R
Mich.	Aug. 7	July 5	July 9/Oct. 8	Levin (D)		12 D, 6 R
Minn.	Sept. 11	July 17	Aug. 21[3]/Oct. 16[3]	Boschwitz (R)		5 D, 3 R
Miss.	June 5/June 26	April 6	May 5/Oct. 6	Cochran (R)		3 D, 2 R
Mo.	Aug. 7	March 27	July 11/Oct. 10		Bond (R)#	6 D, 3 R
Mont.	June 5	April 16	May 6/Oct. 7	Baucus (D)	Schwinden (D)	1 D, 1 R
Neb.	May 15	March 16	May 4/Oct. 26	Exon (D)		3 R
Nev.	Sept. 4	July 3	Aug. 4/Oct. 6			1 D, 1 R
N.H.	Sept. 11	June 20	Sept. 1/Oct. 27	Humphrey (R)	Sununu (R)	1 D, 1 R
N.J.	June 5	April 26	May 7/Oct. 9	Bradley (D)		9 D, 4 R[4]
N.M.	June 5	Feb. 28	April 24/Sept. 25	Domenici (R)		1 D, 2 R
N.Y.	Sept. 11	July 26	July 13/Sept. 7			20 D, 14 R
N.C.	May 8/June 5	Feb. 6	April 9/Oct. 8	Helms (R)	Hunt (D)**	9 D, 2 R
N.D.	June 12	April 18	None		Olson (R)	1 D
Ohio	May 8	Feb. 23	April 9/Oct. 8			10 D, 11 R
Okla.	Aug. 28/Sept. 18	July 11	Aug. 17/Oct. 26	Boren (D)		5 D, 1 R
Ore.	May 15	March 6	May 15/Nov. 6	Hatfield (R)		3 D, 2 R
Pa.	April 10	Jan. 31	March 12/Oct. 9			13 D, 10 R
R.I.	Sept. 11	June 11	Aug. 11/Oct. 6	Pell (D)	Garrahy (D)*	1 D, 1 R
S.C.	June 12/June 26	April 30	May 12/Oct. 5	Thurmond (R)		3 D, 3 R
S.D.	June 5	April 3	May 21/Oct. 22	Pressler (R)		1 D
Tenn.	Aug. 2	June 7	July 3/Oct. 6	Baker (R)*		6 D, 3 R
Texas	May 5/June 2	Feb. 6	April 5/Oct. 7	Tower (R)*		21 D, 6 R
Utah	Aug. 21	April 16	Aug. 16/Nov. 1		Matheson (D)*	3 R
Vt.	Sept. 11	July 16	Aug. 25/Oct. 20		Snelling (R)*	1 R
Va.	June 12	April 12	May 12/Oct. 6	Warner (R)		4 D, 6 R
Wash.	Sept. 18	Aug. 3	Aug. 18/Oct. 6		Spellman (R)	5 D, 3 R
W.Va.	June 5	March 31	May 7/Oct. 8	Randolph (D)*	Rockefeller (D)#**	4 D
Wis.	Sept. 11	July 10	Aug. 29/Oct. 24			5 D, 4 R
Wyo.	Sept. 11	July 13	Aug. 11/Oct. 6	Simpson (R)		1 R

† Where two dates are listed, first is the regular primary, second is the runoff primary. Runoffs are required in these states when no candidate wins a majority in the first primary.

‡ Registration deadline before the slash applies to primary, after slash to general election.

* Retiring from office.
** Running for the Senate.
# Ineligible to seek re-election.
†† Primary may be rescheduled for May 29.

[1] Louisiana primary includes all candidates of both parties. Top two vote-getters in each race face each other in the general election, regardless of party. A candidate receiving more than 50 percent of the vote in the primary is elected without a general election.

[2] Voter registration is closed in different municipalities for a period of one to nine days prior to an election, but Election Day registration is allowed.

[3] Election Day registration is allowed.

[4] One vacant House seat, due to the death of Rep. Edwin B. Forsythe, R, on March 29.

That approach was a dismal failure. Democrats under challenge had little trouble disclaiming any contact with radical ideas and planting themselves in the middle of the political spectrum. Expected to come within a seat or two of the seven they needed for control that year, Republicans managed to win only two.

By the spring of 1984, however, it was the conventional wisdom in Washington that a Democratic Senate majority was increasingly unlikely. Republican senators once thought to be vulnerable were in a much better position than expected; Democrats were increasingly pessimistic about their chances. Strategists in both parties described the odds for a change of control as less than even.

In most election years large switches were difficult because both sides had seats they were likely to lose, and a party usually had to take away eight or nine opposition seats to guarantee a net increase of five or six. Democrats did not seem to be in that position in 1984.

The Republican Party was looking hard for Democratic seats it could steal away, but it was having a hard time finding good targets. Democratic seats in Michigan, Arkansas and Kentucky were drawing concerted Republican challenges — and the GOP also was eyeing one in West Virginia as a possibility — but all of them as of mid-March were long shots for the Republicans. The only good news for the GOP in this category was the announcement Jan. 12 by Democratic Sen. Paul E. Tsongas, Mass., that he would retire at the end of the year for health reasons. With former U.S. Attorney General Elliot L. Richardson running on the Republican side, and with Democrats locked in a multi-candidate convention battle, that seat went into the vulnerable category. *(Senate outlook summary, p. 118)*

In general, though, the Democratic Party moved toward the election reasonably confident that winning five or six Republican seats would create about that many net gains. The question was, could they do it?

The Democrats had a reasonably good chance of coming within a seat or two of control. In Tennessee, where GOP leader Howard H. Baker Jr. was retiring, Democratic Rep. Albert Gore Jr. was the clear favorite. In Texas, prospects were at least even for Democratic control of the seat held by Republican John Tower, who also was retiring.

After that, the Democrats' prospects for gaining additional Senate seats became more difficult. In 1982 GOP incumbents Jesse Helms in North Carolina and Roger W. Jepsen in Iowa trailed badly in the polls, but they gained momentum in 1983 and by the following spring showed up as virtually even with their challengers — a timely reminder of the ways any incumbent can mold his own image.

Helms gambled in 1982 by fighting the proposed national holiday in memory of the Rev. Dr. Martin Luther King Jr. At first, national political writers tended to see his unsuccessful filibuster against the King holiday bill as likely to isolate him further as a political extremist. By January, though, it was clear that Helms' position had improved his standing against his Democratic opponent, Gov. James B. Hunt Jr. Helms could not realistically hope for more than a tiny black vote anyway, and rural white voters — likely to be the decisive group in November — were not very sympathetic to the idea of a holiday for King.

Jepsen, clearly in trouble in 1983 following unfavorable press reports about his use of various perquisites of office, had rebounded with a string of attacks on his challenger, Democratic Rep. Tom Harkin. When Harkin sponsored a bill through which dairy farmers would be paid to reduce their production, Jepsen made that an issue among cattle growers, who feared a glut of dairy cows on the market. Harkin, who hoped to spend all of 1984 on the attack, had to devote part of his campaign time to defending his record.

Despite the Republican surge, a prudent observer might want to predict a Democratic victory in at least one of these two states, given the exceptional challengers who were running there. Victory in either Iowa or North Carolina would give Democrats 48 seats — within striking distance of Senate control.

At that point, though, it got harder and harder to see where other seats could be won. Gordon J. Humphrey of New Hampshire and Rudy Boschwitz of Minnesota were on every list of endangered Republican incumbents, but both proved agile and started the election year in good shape.

Humphrey, derided for most of his Senate term as an inflexible New Right ideologue, had managed to carve a different reputation for himself. By demonstrating concern over the impact of acid rain and fighting the Clinch River nuclear reactor on financial grounds, Humphrey positioned himself as a fiscal conservative and something of an environmentalist at the same time.

Boschwitz had to show some independence from the Reagan administration, especially if native son Walter F. Mondale became the Democratic presidential nominee, but he was off to a good start on that project with a proposal for a "fair play" budget that would hold federal spending increases to 5 percent per year for five years.

If Boschwitz and Humphrey remained strong in the fall, the only other potential Democratic successes probably were the seats in Illinois and Mississippi, states which had not drawn much public attention.

In Illinois, GOP incumbent Charles H. Percy faced a serious conservative challenge for renomination. Although he was able to survive it, his standing for the November general election depended on how his performance in the March 20 primary was perceived by Illinois voters, and whether he would gain the strong support of the conservative wing of his party. With the Democratic nomination going to U.S. Rep. Paul Simon, who had good statewide name recognition and a downstate Illinois political base, Percy could move from "vulnerable" to the "highly vulnerable" category.

Sen. Thad Cochran was about as strong as any Republican could be in Mississippi, but when former Democratic Gov. William Winter decided to challenge him, a competitive election was guaranteed. Despite a winning personal style and reputation as a thoughtful, pragmatic legislator, Cochran could take nothing for granted in a state that was 35 percent black and had never given a majority to any Republican candidate for statewide office. Cochran won his first Senate term with 45 percent of the vote in a three-way contest.

Winning the Close Ones

The Democrats' task seemed to be even more difficult in the context of the presidential election. It probably was going to require, among other things, a healthy Democratic victory at the presidential level. There was no mathematical reason why the country could not return Reagan to office while turning his party out of the Senate, but there was no historical precedent for it.

In the 70-year history of popular elections for the Senate, no party had lost more than three seats in a year when the country was re-electing its president. And both of those three-seat losses (under Woodrow Wilson in 1916 and Franklin Roosevelt in 1940) occurred when the majority

106 Elections '84

Election Results, Congress and Presidency, 1854-1982

Election Year	Congress Elected	HOUSE Members Elected Dem.	Rep.	Misc.	HOUSE Gains/Losses Dem.	Rep.	SENATE Members Elected Dem.	Rep.	Misc.	SENATE Gains/Losses Dem.	Rep.	PRESIDENCY Elected	Popular Vote Plurality
1854	34th	83	108	43			42	15	5			Pierce (D)	
1856	35th	131	92	14	+ 48	− 16	39	20	5	− 3	+ 5	Buchanan (D)	498,209
1858	36th	101	113	23	− 30	+ 21	38	26	2	− 1	+ 6		
1860	37th	42	106	28	− 59	− 7	11	31	7	−27	+ 5	Lincoln (R)	487,764
1862	38th	80	103		+ 38	− 3	12	39		+ 1	+ 8		
1864	39th	46	145		− 34	+ 42	10	42		− 2	+ 3	Lincoln (R)	414,299
1866	40th	49	143		+ 3	− 2	11	42		+ 1	0	Johnson (R)	
1868	41st	73	170		+ 24	+ 27	11	61		0	+19	Grant (R)	309,380
1870	42nd	104	139		+ 31	− 31	17	57		+ 6	− 4		
1872	43rd	88	203		− 16	+ 64	19	54		+ 2	− 3	Grant (R)	763,664
1874	44th	181	107	3	+ 93	− 96	29	46		+10	− 8		
1876	45th	156	137		− 25	+ 30	36	39	1	+ 7	− 7	Hayes (R)	−251,746
1878	46th	150	128	14	− 6	− 9	43	33		+ 7	− 6		
1880	47th	130	152	11	− 20	+ 24	37	37	2	− 6	+ 4	Garfield (R)	9,457
1882	48th	200	119	6	+ 70	− 33	36	40		− 1	+ 3	Arthur (R)	
1884	49th	182	140	2	− 18	+ 21	34	41		− 2	+ 2	Cleveland (D)	23,737
1886	50th	170	151	4	− 12	+ 11	37	39		+ 3	− 2		
1888	51st	156	173	1	− 14	+ 22	37	47		0	+ 8	Harrison (R)	−95,096
1890	52nd	231	88	14	+ 75	− 85	39	47	2	+ 2	0		
1892	53rd	220	126	8	− 11	+ 38	44	38	3	+ 5	− 9	Cleveland (D)	365,516
1894	54th	104	246	7	−116	+120	30	44	5	− 5	+ 6		
1896	55th	134	206	16	+ 30	− 40	34	46	10	− 5	+ 2	McKinley (R)	597,012
1898	56th	163	185	9	+ 29	− 21	26	53	11	− 8	+ 7		
1900	57th	153	198	5	− 10	+ 13	29	56	3	+ 3	+ 3	McKinley (R)	861,668
1902	58th	178	207		+ 25	+ 9	32	58		+ 3	+ 2	Roosevelt (R)	
1904	59th	136	250		− 42	+ 43	32	58		0	0	Roosevelt (R)	2,544,298
1906	60th	164	222		+ 28	− 28	29	61		− 3	− 3		
1908	61st	172	219		+ 8	− 3	32	59		+ 3	− 2	Taft (R)	1,268,449
1910	62nd	228	162	1	+ 56	− 57	42	49		+10	−10		
1912	63rd	290	127	18	+ 62	− 35	51	44	1	+ 9	− 5	Wilson (D)	2,173,466
1914	64th	231	193	8	− 59	+ 66	56	39	1	+ 5	− 5		
1916	65th	210	216	9	− 21	+ 23	53	42	1	− 3	+ 3	Wilson (D)	582,576
1918	66th	191	237	7	− 19	+ 21	47	48	1	− 6	+ 6		
1920	67th	132	300	1	− 59	+ 63	37	59		−10	+11	Harding (R)	7,020,023
1922	68th	207	225	3	+ 75	− 75	43	51	2	+ 6	− 8	Coolidge (R)	
1924	69th	183	247	5	− 24	+ 22	40	54	1	− 3	+ 3	Coolidge (R)	333,217
1926	70th	195	237	3	+ 12	− 10	47	48	1	+ 7	− 6		
1928	71st	163	267	1	− 32	+ 30	39	56	1	− 8	+ 8	Hoover (R)	6,429,579
1930	72nd	216	218	1	+ 53	− 49	47	48	1	+ 8	− 8		
1932	73rd	313	117	5	+ 97	−101	59	36	1	+12	−12	Roosevelt (D)	7,068,817
1934	74th	322	103	10	+ 9	− 14	69	25	2	+10	−11		
1936	75th	333	89	13	+ 11	− 14	75	17	4	+ 6	− 8	Roosevelt (D)	11,073,102
1938	76th	262	169	4	− 71	+ 80	69	23	4	− 6	+ 6		
1940	77th	267	162	6	+ 5	− 7	66	28	2	− 3	+ 5	Roosevelt (D)	4,964,561
1942	78th	222	209	4	− 45	+ 47	57	38	1	− 9	+ 10		
1944	79th	243	190	2	+ 21	− 19	57	38	1	0	0	Roosevelt (D)	3,594,993
1946	80th	188	246	1	− 55	+ 56	45	51		−12	+13	Truman	
1948	81st	263	171	1	+ 75	− 75	54	42		+ 9	− 9	Truman (D)	2,188,054
1950	82nd	234	199	2	− 29	+ 28	48	47	1	− 6	+ 5		
1952	83rd	213	221	1	− 21	+ 22	47	48	1	− 1	+ 1	Eisenhower (R)	6,621,242
1954	84th	232	203		+ 19	− 18	48	47	1	+ 1	− 1		
1956	85th	234	201		+ 2	− 2	49	47		+ 1	0	Eisenhower (R)	9,567,720
1958	86th	283	154		+ 49	− 47	64	34		+17	−13		
1960	87th	263	174		− 20	+ 20	64	36		− 2	+ 2	Kennedy (D)	118,574*
1962	88th	258	176	1**	− 4	+ 2	67	33		+ 4	− 4		
1964	89th	295	140		+ 38	− 38	68	32		+ 2	− 2	Johnson (D)	15,951,296
1966	90th	248	187		− 47	+ 47	64	36		− 3	+ 3		
1968	91st	243	192		− 4	+ 4	58	42		− 5	+ 5	Nixon (R)	510,314
1970	92nd	255	180		+ 12	− 12	55	45		− 4	+ 2		
1972	93rd	243	192		− 12	+ 12	57	43		+ 2	− 2	Nixon (R)	17,999,528
1974	94th	291	144		+ 43	− 43	61†	38		+ 3†	− 3		
1976	95th	292	143		+ 1	− 1	62	38		0	0	Carter (D)	1,682,970
1978	96th	277	158		− 11	+ 11	59	41		− 3	+ 3		
1980	97th	243	192		− 33	+ 33	47	53		−12	+12	Reagan (R)	8,420,270
1982	98th	269	166		+ 26	− 26	46	54		0	0		

* Includes divided Alabama elector slate votes.
** Vacancy — Rep. Clem Miller (D-Calif. 1959-62) died Oct. 6, 1962, but his name remained on the ballot and he received a plurality.

Democrats had plenty of seats to spare. For the Republicans to re-elect Reagan but lose five or six Senate seats, and their majority along with it, would be an unusual event indeed.

Republicans also took some comfort in their party's recent good fortune — or skill — at coming out ahead in most of the close Senate races. That was a crucial ingredient in 1980, when GOP candidates took an amazing 16 of the 19 Senate elections in which the winning candidate drew 55 percent or less. That record was repeated in 1982, when nine of 12 contests in that category went to the Republican candidate. Democrats actually won 54 percent of the national vote in that year's Senate elections, but the party did not gain even one seat for it because so many of the Democratic votes went to safe incumbents who did not really need them.

In 1980 some of those close Republican victories simply represented a late and unexpected swing in national mood that turned against virtually any visible Democrat in a statewide election. Republicans did not win the close ones by design. The most that could be said was that superior financial resources kept their candidates close enough for the national GOP tide to make the difference in the end.

But 1982 looked like a different matter. National Republican strategists spent heavily that year on sophisticated day-by-day polling that allowed them to respond to trouble quickly during the crucial weeks in October. When internal polls for GOP Sen. John C. Danforth showed him slipping dangerously close to defeat in Missouri a month before the election, Danforth was able to respond with carefully designed television spots in which he looked voters in the eye and told them why he felt he deserved re-election.

Danforth eventually won a second term with 50.9 percent of the vote against Democratic challenger Harriet Woods. It was impossible to prove that the day-by-day tracking or the new ads saved him, but a Democrat in the same situation would not have had Danforth's flexibility. Democrats did not have an intelligence system that allowed them to switch resources from state to state at the last minute. They were not able to afford one. That was why they had so many 62-percent winners and so many 49-percent losers in 1982.

House Races

If the Senate elections sometimes seemed like a sideshow to the presidential campaign, the House contests were something even less than that.

Nearly always a backwater in national political reporting, the House was in the spotlight in 1982 when Republicans began the election season with some hope of winning the 26 new seats that would give them a majority in that chamber and bring full congressional control to the party. In the end, the opposite happened: Democrats won 26 seats and re-established their own dominance politically as well as numerically.

Not even the professionals could summon up much excitement about the House contests in 1984. The overwhelming consensus was that when the 99th Congress convened in January 1985 there would be little change in the ratio of 267 Democrats to 168 Republicans that existed in the 98th Congress.

That could be a reckless assumption, so far in advance of Election Day. But given what most observers thought

Congressional Departures

(As of April 10, 1984)

RETIRING

	Began Service	Age
Sen. Howard H. Baker Jr. (R-Tenn.)	1967	58
Sen. Jennings Randolph (D-W.Va.)	1958	81
Sen. John Tower (R-Texas)	1961	58
Sen. Paul E. Tsongas (D-Mass.)	1979	43
Rep. Barber B. Conable Jr. (R-N.Y. 30)	1965	61
Rep. Jack Edwards (R-Ala. 1)	1965	55
Rep. John N. Erlenborn (R-Ill. 13)	1965	57
Rep. Ray Kogovsek (D-Colo. 3)	1979	42
Rep. Richard L. Ottinger (D-N.Y. 20)	1965 [1]	55
Rep. Joel Pritchard (R-Wash. 1) [2]	1973	58
Rep. J. Kenneth Robinson (R-Va. 7)	1971	67
Rep. Larry Winn Jr. (R-Kan. 3)	1967	64
Rep. Harold S. Sawyer (R-Mich. 5)	1977	64

SEEKING OTHER OFFICE

	Began Service	Age	Office
Rep. Ed Bethune (R-Ark. 2)	1979	48	Senate
Rep. Tom Corcoran (R-Ill. 14)	1977	44	Senate
Rep. Norman E. D'Amours (D-N.H. 1)	1975	46	Senate
Rep. Albert Gore Jr. (D-Tenn. 6)	1977	35	Senate
Rep. Phil Gramm (R-Texas 6)	1979	41	Senate
Rep. Kent Hance (D-Texas 19)	1979	41	Senate
Rep. Tom Harkin (D-Iowa 5)	1975	44	Senate
Rep. Edward J. Markey (D-Mass. 7)	1976	37	Senate
Rep. Dan Marriott (R-Utah 2)	1977	44	Governor
Rep. James G. Martin (R-N.C. 9)	1973	48	Governor
Rep. James L. Oberstar (D-Minn. 8)	1975	49	Senate
Rep. Ron Paul (R-Texas 22)	1976 [3]	48	Senate
Rep. James M. Shannon (D-Mass. 5)	1979	31	Senate
Rep. Paul Simon (D-Ill. 22)	1975	55	Senate

VACANT SEATS

	Date Vacated	Began Service	Age
Rep. Edwin B. Forsythe (R-N.J. 13) [4]	3/29/84	1970	68

[1] Did not serve 1971-75.
[2] Pritchard has not formally announced his retirement, but has said previously that he would not serve more than six terms.
[3] Paul served from April 1976 to January 1977 after winning a 1976 special election. Although he lost the 1976 general election, he was re-elected in 1978, and has served continuously since 1979.
[4] Died in office.

would be a relatively close presidential election, it was a good bet to make. Major change in the House was nearly always related to either a presidential landslide or a midterm election in which the electorate was in an ornery mood. In recent times at least, close elections for the presidency resulted in little turnover in the House. In 1968, when Richard M. Nixon narrowly won a first term, Republicans added five House seats; in 1976, when Jimmy Carter won in similar circumstances, his party added one.

Who Wants to Run?

The most striking thing about the House in 1984 was that there appeared to be relatively few competitive races. Strong challengers failed to emerge in dozens of districts where the incumbent looked politically healthy, but not necessarily invincible. Political action committees on both sides of the spectrum agreed that 1984 was developing into an unusually slow year at the House level.

The likely result was that the House election game would be played on a relatively confined court — 50 or 60 districts around the country where the seat was open or where the incumbent was unmistakably vulnerable.

If that assessment turned out to be true, it probably would aid the Democratic Party. Severely limited in money, national Democratic strategists could not stretch their resources to provide much help to deserving candidates in 100 competitive districts. But if there were only half that many, they could come closer to matching the funding of their amply funded opponents.

The problem for Republicans in much of the country was finding candidates good enough to make intelligent use of the money. Although the National Republican Congressional Committee was more sophisticated than ever in its recruiting operation, it still was having trouble coming up with challengers in borderline districts — ones where it might start in an underdog position but could tie up precious Democratic money with a decent GOP effort. Few ambitious politicians of either party seemed to want to make that sort of effort in 1984.

Why did so many local political figures decide not to run for the House this time? Some of them, particularly on the Democratic side, simply were delaying — waiting for 1986, when they might be able to take advantage of the historical swing against a party holding the White House for a second term.

Others might have decided, upon surveying the lines of their congressional districts, that they discouraged competition. In several of the largest states, redistricting rearranged the boundaries to make incumbents of both parties stronger. The current congressional map in California, for example, was drawn to provide 28 Democratic seats, the number it had in the 1982 elections. One way it did that was by cramming as many GOP areas as possible into the 17 remaining districts held by Republicans. The map was a crucial reason why only a handful of House elections in California promised to provide even a hint of competition in 1984. *(Redistricting status, 1982 impact, see p. 126.)*

The dearth of competition also had something to do with people's attitudes toward Congress. In conservative parts of the country, especially the South and the Mountain states, it was increasingly common to hear local political figures turn down congressional campaigns with the comment that they did not want to come to Washington — it symbolized a wasteful and ineffective government they would just as soon stay out of.

In the long run, an attitude like that would hurt Republicans more than Democrats because Republicans at the state and local level tended to be much more suspicious of Washington. Whether the shortage of House competition was a temporary development or a real symptom of political attitudes in America in the 1980s would not be known until several more congressional elections had been held.

Senate Membership in the 98th Congress

Democrats 45   Republicans 55
(As of April 10, 1984)

> Senators elected in 1982 are *italicized*
> # Freshman Senators

ALABAMA
Howell Heflin (D)
Jeremiah Denton (R)

ALASKA
Frank H. Murkowski (R)
Ted Stevens (R)

ARIZONA
Dennis DeConcini (D)
Barry Goldwater (R)

ARKANSAS
Dale Bumpers (D)
David Pryor (D)

CALIFORNIA
Alan Cranston (D)
Pete Wilson (R)#

COLORADO
Gary Hart (D)
William L. Armstrong (R)

CONNECTICUT
Christopher J. Dodd (D)
Lowell P. Weicker Jr. (R)

DELAWARE
Joseph R. Biden Jr. (D)
William V. Roth Jr. (R)

FLORIDA
Lawton Chiles (D)
Paula Hawkins (R)

GEORGIA
Sam Nunn (D)
Mack Mattingly (R)

HAWAII
Daniel K. Inouye (D)
Spark M. Matsunaga (D)

IDAHO
James A. McClure (R)
Steven D. Symms (R)

ILLINOIS
Alan J. Dixon (D)
Charles H. Percy (R)

INDIANA
Richard G. Lugar (R)
Dan Quayle (R)

IOWA
Charles E. Grassley (R)
Roger W. Jepsen (R)

KANSAS
Robert Dole (R)
Nancy Landon Kassebaum (R)

KENTUCKY
Wendell H. Ford (D)
Walter D. Huddleston (D)

LOUISIANA
J. Bennett Johnston (D)
Russell B. Long (D)

MAINE
George J. Mitchell (D)
William S. Cohen (R)

MARYLAND
Paul S. Sarbanes (D)
Charles McC. Mathias Jr. (R)

MASSACHUSETTS
Edward M. Kennedy (D)
Paul E. Tsongas (D)

MICHIGAN
Carl Levin (D)
Donald W. Riegle Jr. (D)

MINNESOTA
Rudy Boschwitz (R)
David Durenberger (R)

MISSISSIPPI
John C. Stennis (D)
Thad Cochran (R)

MISSOURI
Thomas F. Eagleton (D)
John C. Danforth (R)

MONTANA
Max Baucus (D)
John Melcher (D)

NEBRASKA
J. James Exon (D)
Edward Zorinsky (D)

NEVADA
Chic Hecht (R)#
Paul Laxalt (R)

NEW HAMPSHIRE
Gordon J. Humphrey (R)
Warren B. Rudman (R)

NEW JERSEY
Bill Bradley (D)
Frank R. Lautenberg (D)#

NEW MEXICO
Jeff Bingaman (D)#
Pete V. Domenici (R)

NEW YORK
Daniel Patrick Moynihan (D)
Alfonse M. D'Amato (R)

NORTH CAROLINA
John P. East (R)
Jesse Helms (R)

NORTH DAKOTA
Quentin N. Burdick (D)
Mark Andrews (R)

OHIO
John Glenn (D)
Howard M. Metzenbaum (D)

OKLAHOMA
David L. Boren (D)
Don Nickles (R)

OREGON
Mark O. Hatfield (R)
Bob Packwood (R)

PENNSYLVANIA
John Heinz (R)
Arlen Specter (R)

RHODE ISLAND
Claiborne Pell (D)
John H. Chafee (R)

SOUTH CAROLINA
Ernest F. Hollings (D)
Strom Thurmond (R)

SOUTH DAKOTA
James Abdnor (R)
Larry Pressler (R)

TENNESSEE
Jim Sasser (D)
Howard H. Baker Jr. (R)

TEXAS
Lloyd Bentsen (D)
John Tower (R)

UTAH
Jake Garn (R)
Orrin G. Hatch (R)

VERMONT
Patrick J. Leahy (D)
Robert T. Stafford (R)

VIRGINIA
Paul S. Trible Jr. (R)#
John W. Warner (R)

WASHINGTON
Daniel J. Evans (R)*#
Slade Gorton (R)

WEST VIRGINIA
Robert C. Byrd (D)
Jennings Randolph (D)

WISCONSIN
William Proxmire (D)
Robert W. Kasten Jr. (R)

WYOMING
Alan K. Simpson (R)
Malcolm Wallop (R)

* *Daniel J. Evans, R, was appointed Sept. 8, 1983, and elected Nov. 8, 1983, to complete the term of Henry M. Jackson, D, who died Sept. 1, 1983. Jackson was re-elected in 1982.*

House Membership in the 98th Congress

House Lineup
Democrats 268   Republicans 166
Vacancy, N. J. 13th District
(As of April 10, 1984)

ALABAMA
1. Jack Edwards (R)
2. William L. Dickinson (R)
3. Bill Nichols (D)
4. Tom Bevill (D)
5. Ronnie G. Flippo (D)
6. Ben Erdreich (D)
7. Richard C. Shelby (D)

ALASKA
AL Don Young (R)

ARIZONA
1. John McCain (R)
2. Morris K. Udall (D)
3. Bob Stump (R)
4. Eldon Rudd (R)
5. Jim McNulty (D)

ARKANSAS
1. Bill Alexander (D)
2. Ed Bethune (R)
3. John Paul Hammerschmidt (R)
4. Beryl Anthony Jr. (D)

CALIFORNIA
1. Douglas H. Bosco (D)
2. Gene Chappie (R)
3. Robert T. Matsui (D)
4. Vic Fazio (D)
5. Sala Burton (D)
6. Barbara Boxer (D)
7. George Miller (D)
8. Ronald V. Dellums (D)
9. Fortney H. "Pete" Stark (D)
10. Don Edwards (D)
11. Tom Lantos (D)
12. Ed Zschau (R)
13. Norman Y. Mineta (D)
14. Norman D. Shumway (R)
15. Tony Coelho (D)
16. Leon E. Panetta (D)
17. Charles Pashayan Jr. (R)
18. Richard Lehman (D)
19. Robert J. Lagomarsino (R)
20. William M. Thomas (R)
21. Bobbi Fiedler (R)
22. Carlos J. Moorhead (R)
23. Anthony C. Beilenson (D)
24. Henry A. Waxman (D)
25. Edward R. Roybal (D)
26. Howard L. Berman (D)
27. Mel Levine (D)
28. Julian C. Dixon (D)
29. Augustus F. Hawkins (D)
30. Matthew G. Martinez (D)
31. Mervyn M. Dymally (D)
32. Glenn M. Anderson (D)
33. David Dreier (R)
34. Esteban Torres (D)
35. Jerry Lewis (R)
36. George E. Brown Jr. (D)
37. Al McCandless (R)
38. Jerry M. Patterson (D)
39. William E. Dannemeyer (R)
40. Robert E. Badham (R)
41. Bill Lowery (R)
42. Dan Lungren (R)
43. Ron Packard (R)
44. Jim Bates (D)
45. Duncan L. Hunter (R)

COLORADO
1. Patricia Schroeder (D)
2. Timothy E. Wirth (D)
3. Ray Kogovsek (D)
4. Hank Brown (R)
5. Ken Kramer (R)
6. Daniel L. Schaefer (R)

CONNECTICUT
1. Barbara B. Kennelly (D)
2. Sam Gejdenson (D)
3. Bruce A. Morrison (D)
4. Stewart B. McKinney (R)
5. William R. Ratchford (D)
6. Nancy L. Johnson (R)

DELAWARE
AL Thomas R. Carper (D)

FLORIDA
1. Earl Hutto (D)
2. Don Fuqua (D)
3. Charles E. Bennett (D)
4. Bill Chappell Jr. (D)
5. Bill McCollum (R)
6. Kenneth H. MacKay (D)
7. Sam Gibbons (D)
8. C.W. Bill Young (R)
9. Michael Bilirakis (R)
10. Andy Ireland (D)
11. Bill Nelson (D)
12. Tom Lewis (R)
13. Connie Mack III (R)
14. Daniel A. Mica (D)
15. E. Clay Shaw Jr. (R)
16. Larry Smith (D)
17. William Lehman (D)
18. Claude Pepper (D)
19. Dante B. Fascell (D)

GEORGIA
1. Lindsay Thomas (D)
2. Charles Hatcher (D)
3. Richard Ray (D)
4. Elliott H. Levitas (D)
5. Wyche Fowler Jr. (D)
6. Newt Gingrich (R)
7. George W. "Buddy" Darden (D)
8. J. Roy Rowland (D)
9. Ed Jenkins (D)
10. Doug Barnard Jr. (D)

HAWAII
1. Cecil Heftel (D)
2. Daniel K. Akaka (D)

IDAHO
1. Larry E. Craig (R)
2. George Hansen (R)

ILLINOIS
1. Charles A. Hayes (D)
2. Gus Savage (D)
3. Marty Russo (D)
4. George M. O'Brien (R)
5. William O. Lipinski (D)
6. Henry J. Hyde (R)
7. Cardiss Collins (D)
8. Dan Rostenkowski (D)
9. Sidney R. Yates (D)
10. John Edward Porter (R)
11. Frank Annunzio (D)
12. Philip M. Crane (R)
13. John N. Erlenborn (R)
14. Tom Corcoran (R)
15. Edward R. Madigan (R)
16. Lynn Martin (R)
17. Lane Evans (D)
18. Robert H. Michel (R)
19. Daniel B. Crane (R)
20. Richard J. Durbin (D)
21. Melvin Price (D)
22. Paul Simon (D)

INDIANA
1. Katie Hall (D)
2. Philip R. Sharp (D)
3. John Hiler (R)
4. Dan Coats (R)
5. Elwood Hillis (R)
6. Dan Burton (R)
7. John T. Myers (R)
8. Francis X. McCloskey (D)
9. Lee H. Hamilton (D)
10. Andrew Jacobs Jr. (D)

IOWA
1. Jim Leach (R)
2. Tom Tauke (R)
3. Cooper Evans (R)
4. Neal Smith (D)
5. Tom Harkin (D)
6. Berkley Bedell (D)

KANSAS
1. Pat Roberts (R)
2. Jim Slattery (D)
3. Larry Winn Jr. (R)
4. Dan Glickman (D)
5. Bob Whittaker (R)

KENTUCKY
1. Carroll Hubbard Jr. (D)
2. William H. Natcher (D)
3. Romano L. Mazzoli (D)
4. Gene Snyder (R)
5. Harold Rogers (R)
6. Larry J. Hopkins (R)
7. Carl D. Perkins (D)

LOUISIANA
1. Bob Livingston (R)
2. Lindy (Mrs. Hale) Boggs (D)
3. W. J. "Billy" Tauzin (D)
4. Buddy Roemer (D)
5. Jerry Huckaby (D)
6. Henson Moore (R)
7. John B. Breaux (D)
8. Gillis W. Long (D)

MAINE
1. John R. McKernan Jr. (R)
2. Olympia J. Snowe (R)

MARYLAND
1. Roy Dyson (D)
2. Clarence D. Long (D)
3. Barbara A. Mikulski (D)
4. Marjorie S. Holt (R)
5. Steny H. Hoyer (D)
6. Beverly B. Byron (D)
7. Parren J. Mitchell (D)
8. Michael D. Barnes (D)

MASSACHUSETTS
1. Silvio O. Conte (R)
2. Edward P. Boland (D)
3. Joseph D. Early (D)
4. Barney Frank (D)
5. James M. Shannon (D)
6. Nicholas Mavroules (D)
7. Edward J. Markey (D)
8. Thomas P. O'Neill Jr. (D)
9. Joe Moakley (D)
10. Gerry E. Studds (D)
11. Brian J. Donnelly (D)

MICHIGAN
1. John Conyers Jr. (D)
2. Carl D. Pursell (R)
3. Howard Wolpe (D)
4. Mark Siljander (R)
5. Harold S. Sawyer (R)
6. Bob Carr (D)
7. Dale E. Kildee (D)
8. Bob Traxler (D)
9. Guy Vander Jagt (R)
10. Don Albosta (D)
11. Robert W. Davis (R)
12. David E. Bonior (D)
13. George W. Crockett Jr. (D)
14. Dennis M. Hertel (D)
15. William D. Ford (D)
16. John D. Dingell (D)
17. Sander Levin (D)
18. William S. Broomfield (R)

MINNESOTA
1. Timothy J. Penny (D)
2. Vin Weber (R)
3. Bill Frenzel (R)
4. Bruce F. Vento (D)
5. Martin Olav Sabo (D)
6. Gerry Sikorski (D)

House Membership in the 98th Congress

7. Arlan Stangeland (R)
8. James L. Oberstar (D)

MISSISSIPPI
1. Jamie L. Whitten (D)
2. Webb Franklin (R)
3. G. V. "Sonny" Montgomery (D)
4. Wayne Dowdy (D)
5. Trent Lott (R)

MISSOURI
1. William Clay (D)
2. Robert A. Young (D)
3. Richard A. Gephardt (D)
4. Ike Skelton (D)
5. Alan Wheat (D)
6. E. Thomas Coleman (R)
7. Gene Taylor (R)
8. Bill Emerson (R)
9. Harold L. Volkmer (D)

MONTANA
1. Pat Williams (D)
2. Ron Marlenee (R)

NEBRASKA
1. Douglas K. Bereuter (R)
2. Hal Daub (R)
3. Virginia Smith (R)

NEVADA
1. Harry Reid (D)
2. Barbara Vucanovich (R)

NEW HAMPSHIRE
1. Norman E. D'Amours (D)
2. Judd Gregg (R)

NEW JERSEY
1. James J. Florio (D)
2. William J. Hughes (D)
3. James J. Howard (D)
4. Christopher H. Smith (R)
5. Marge Roukema (R)
6. Bernard J. Dwyer (D)
7. Matthew J. Rinaldo (R)
8. Robert A. Roe (D)
9. Robert G. Torricelli (D)
10. Peter W. Rodino Jr. (D)
11. Joseph G. Minish (D)
12. Jim Courter (R)
13. Vacancy
14. Frank J. Guarini (D)

NEW MEXICO
1. Manuel Lujan Jr. (R)
2. Joe Skeen (R)
3. Bill Richardson (D)

NEW YORK
1. William Carney (R)
2. Thomas J. Downey (D)
3. Robert J. Mrazek (D)
4. Norman F. Lent (R)
5. Raymond J. McGrath (R)
6. Joseph P. Addabbo (D)
7. Gary L. Ackerman (D)
8. James H. Scheuer (D)
9. Geraldine A. Ferraro (D)
0. Charles E. Schumer (D)
11. Edolphus Towns (D)
12. Major R. Owens (D)
13. Stephen J. Solarz (D)
14. Guy V. Molinari (R)
15. Bill Green (R)
16. Charles B. Rangel (D)
17. Ted Weiss (D)
18. Robert Garcia (D)
19. Mario Biaggi (D)
20. Richard L. Ottinger (D)
21. Hamilton Fish Jr. (R)
22. Benjamin A. Gilman (R)
23. Samuel S. Stratton (D)
24. Gerald B. H. Solomon (R)
25. Sherwood L. Boehlert (R)
26. David O'B. Martin (R)
27. George C. Wortley (R)
28. Matthew F. McHugh (D)
29. Frank Horton (R)
30. Barber B. Conable Jr. (R)
31. Jack F. Kemp (R)
32. John J. LaFalce (D)
33. Henry J. Nowak (D)
34. Stanley N. Lundine (D)

NORTH CAROLINA
1. Walter B. Jones (D)
2. I. T. "Tim" Valentine Jr. (D)
3. Charles Whitley (D)
4. Ike Andrews (D)
5. Stephen L. Neal (D)
6. Charles Robin Britt (D)
7. Charlie Rose (D)
8. W. G. "Bill" Hefner (D)
9. James G. Martin (R)
10. James T. Broyhill (R)
11. James McClure Clarke (D)

NORTH DAKOTA
AL Byron L. Dorgan (D)

OHIO
1. Thomas A. Luken (D)
2. Bill Gradison (R)
3. Tony P. Hall (D)
4. Michael G. Oxley (R)
5. Delbert L. Latta (R)
6. Bob McEwen (R)
7. Michael Dewine (R)
8. Thomas N. Kindness (R)
9. Marcy Kaptur (D)
10. Clarence E. Miller (R)
11. Dennis E. Eckart (D)
12. John R. Kasich (R)
13. Don J. Pease (D)
14. John F. Seiberling (D)
15. Chalmers P. Wylie (R)
16. Ralph Regula (R)
17. Lyle Williams (R)
18. Douglas Applegate (D)
19. Edward F. Feighan (D)
20. Mary Rose Oakar (D)
21. Louis Stokes (D)

OKLAHOMA
1. James R. Jones (D)
2. Mike Synar (D)
3. Wes Watkins (D)
4. Dave McCurdy (D)
5. Mickey Edwards (R)
6. Glenn English (D)

OREGON
1. Les AuCoin (D)
2. Bob Smith (R)
3. Ron Wyden (D)
4. James Weaver (D)
5. Denny Smith (R)

PENNSYLVANIA
1. Thomas M. Foglietta (D)
2. William H. Gray III (D)
3. Robert A. Borski (D)
4. Joseph P. Kolter (D)
5. Richard T. Schulze (R)
6. Gus Yatron (D)
7. Robert W. Edgar (D)
8. Peter H. Kostmayer (D)
9. Bud Shuster (R)
10. Joseph M. McDade (R)
11. Frank Harrison (D)
12. John P. Murtha (D)
13. Lawrence Coughlin (R)
14. William J. Coyne (D)
15. Don Ritter (R)
16. Robert S. Walker (R)
17. George W. Gekas (R)
18. Doug Walgren (D)
19. Bill Goodling (R)
20. Joseph M. Gaydos (D)
21. Thomas J. Ridge (R)
22. Austin J. Murphy (D)
23. William F. Clinger Jr. (R)

RHODE ISLAND
1. Fernand J. St Germain (D)
2. Claudine Schneider (R)

SOUTH CAROLINA
1. Thomas F. Hartnett (R)
2. Floyd Spence (R)
3. Butler Derrick (D)
4. Carroll A. Campbell Jr. (R)
5. John Spratt (D)
6. Robert M. Tallon Jr. (D)

SOUTH DAKOTA
AL Thomas A. Daschle (D)

TENNESSEE
1. James H. Quillen (R)
2. John J. Duncan (R)
3. Marilyn Lloyd Bouquard (D)
4. Jim Cooper (D)
5. Bill Boner (D)
6. Albert Gore Jr. (D)
7. Don Sundquist (R)
8. Ed Jones (D)
9. Harold E. Ford (D)

TEXAS
1. Sam B. Hall Jr. (D)
2. Charles Wilson (D)
3. Steve Bartlett (R)
4. Ralph M. Hall (D)
5. John Bryant (D)
6. Phil Gramm (R)
7. Bill Archer (R)
8. Jack Fields (R)
9. Jack Brooks (D)
10. J. J. Pickle (D)
11. Marvin Leath (D)
12. Jim Wright (D)
13. Jack Hightower (D)
14. Bill Patman (D)
15. E. "Kika" de la Garza (D)
16. Ronald Coleman (D)
17. Charles W. Stenholm (D)
18. Mickey Leland (D)
19. Kent Hance (D)
20. Henry B. Gonzalez (D)
21. Tom Loeffler (R)
22. Ron Paul (R)
23. Abraham Kazen Jr. (D)
24. Martin Frost (D)
25. Mike Andrews (D)
26. Tom Vandergriff (D)
27. Solomon P. Ortiz (D)

UTAH
1. James V. Hansen (R)
2. Dan Marriott (R)
3. Howard C. Nielson (R)

VERMONT
AL James M. Jeffords (R)

VIRGINIA
1. Herbert H. Bateman (R)
2. G. William Whitehurst (R)
3. Thomas J. Bliley Jr. (R)
4. Norman Sisisky (D)
5. Dan Daniel (D)
6. James R. Olin (D)
7. J. Kenneth Robinson (R)
8. Stan Parris (R)
9. Frederick C. Boucher (D)
10. Frank R. Wolf (R)

WASHINGTON
1. Joel Pritchard (R)
2. Al Swift (D)
3. Don Bonker (D)
4. Sid Morrison (R)
5. Thomas S. Foley (D)
6. Norman D. Dicks (D)
7. Mike Lowry (D)
8. Rodney Chandler (R)

WEST VIRGINIA
1. Alan B. Mollohan (D)
2. Harley O. Staggers Jr. (D)
3. Bob Wise (D)
4. Nick J. Rahall II (D)

WISCONSIN
1. Les Aspin (D)
2. Robert W. Kastenmeier (D)
3. Steve Gunderson (R)
4. Gerald Kleczka (D)
5. Jim Moody (D)
6. Thomas E. Petri (R)
7. David R. Obey (D)
8. Toby Roth (R)
9. F. James Sensenbrenner Jr. (R)

WYOMING
AL Dick Cheney (R)

Years of Expiration of Senate Terms

— 1984 —

(33 Senators: 19 Republicans, 14 Democrats)

Armstrong, William L. (R Colo.)
Baker, Howard H. Jr. (R Tenn.)*
Baucus, Max (D Mont.)
Biden, Joseph R. Jr. (D Del.)
Boren, David L. (D Okla.)
Boschwitz, Rudy (R Minn.)
Bradley, Bill (D N.J.)
Cochran, Thad (R Miss.)
Cohen, William S. (R Maine)
Domenici, Pete V. (R N.M.)
Exon, J. James (D Neb.)

Hatfield, Mark O. (R Ore.)
Heflin, Howell (D Ala.)
Helms, Jesse (R N.C.)
Huddleston, Walter D. (D Ky.)
Humphrey, Gordon J. (R N.H.)
Jepsen, Roger W. (R Iowa)
Johnston, J. Bennett (D La.)
Kassebaum, Nancy Landon (R Kan.)
Levin, Carl (D Mich.)
McClure, James A. (R Idaho)
Nunn, Sam (D Ga.)

Pell, Claiborne (D R.I.)
Percy, Charles H. (R Ill.)
Pressler, Larry (R S.D.)
Pryor, David (D Ark.)
Randolph, Jennings (D W.Va.)*
Simpson, Alan K. (R Wyo.)
Stevens, Ted (R Alaska)
Thurmond, Strom (R S.C.)
Tower, John (R Texas)*
Tsongas, Paul E. (D Mass.)*
Warner, John W. (R Va.)

— 1986 —

(34 Senators: 22 Republicans, 12 Democrats)

Abdnor, James (R S.D.)
Andrews, Mark (R N.D.)
Bumpers, Dale (D Ark.)
Cranston, Alan (D Calif.)
D'Amato, Alfonse (R N.Y.)
Denton, Jeremiah (R Ala.)
Dixon, Alan J. (D Ill.)
Dodd, Christopher J. (D Conn.)
Dole, Robert (R Kan.)
Eagleton, Thomas F. (D Mo.)
East, John P. (R N.C.)
Ford, Wendell H. (D Ky.)

Garn, Jake (R Utah)
Glenn, John (D Ohio)
Goldwater, Barry (R Ariz.)
Gorton, Slade (R Wash.)
Grassley, Charles E. (R Iowa)
Hart, Gary (D Colo.)
Hawkins, Paula (R Fla.)
Hollings, Ernest F. (D S.C.)
Inouye, Daniel K. (D Hawaii)
Kasten, Robert W. Jr. (R Wis.)
Laxalt, Paul (R Nev.)

Leahy, Patrick J. (D Vt.)
Long, Russell B. (D La.)
Mathias, Charles McC. Jr. (R Md.)
Mattingly, Mack (R Ga.)
Murkowski, Frank H. (R Alaska)
Nickles, Don (R Okla.)
Packwood, Bob (R Ore.)
Quayle, Dan (R Ind.)
Rudman, Warren B. (R N.H.)
Specter, Arlen (R Pa.)
Symms, Steven D. (R Idaho)

— 1988 —

(33 Senators: 14 Republicans, 19 Democrats)

Bentsen, Lloyd (D Texas)
Bingaman, Jeff (D N.M.)
Burdick, Quentin N. (D N.D.)
Byrd, Robert C. (D W.Va.)
Chafee, John H. (R R.I.)
Chiles, Lawton (D Fla.)
Danforth, John C. (R Mo.)
DeConcini, Dennis (D Ariz.)
Durenberger, David (R Minn.)
Evans, Daniel J. (R Wash.)
Hatch, Orrin G. (R Utah)

Hecht, Chic (R Nev.)
Heinz, John (R Pa.)
Kennedy, Edward M. (D Mass.)
Lautenberg, Frank R. (D N.J.)
Lugar, Richard G. (R Ind.)
Matsunaga, Spark M. (D Hawaii)
Melcher, John (D Mont.)
Metzenbaum, Howard M. (D Ohio)
Mitchell, George J. (D Maine)
Moynihan, Daniel Patrick (D N.Y.)
Proxmire, William (D Wis.)

Riegle, Donald W. Jr. (D Mich.)
Roth, William V. Jr. (R Del.)
Sarbanes, Paul S. (D Md.)
Sasser, Jim (D Tenn.)
Stafford, Robert T. (R Vt.)
Stennis, John C. (D Miss.)
Trible, Paul S. Jr. (R Va.)
Wallop, Malcolm (R Wyo.)
Weicker, Lowell P. Jr. (R Conn.)
Wilson, Pete (R Calif.)
Zorinsky, Edward (D Neb.)

* Senators who announced they would not seek re-election — as of April 10, 1984.

Senate Elections

The creation of the United States Senate was a result of the so-called "great compromise" at the Constitutional Convention in 1787. The small states wanted equal representation in Congress, fearing domination by the large states under a population formula. The larger states, however, naturally wished for a legislature based on population, where their strength would prevail.

In compromising this dispute, delegates simply split the basis of representation between the two houses — population for the House of Representatives, equal representation by state for the Senate. By the terms of the compromise, each state was entitled to two senators. In a sense, they were conceived to be ambassadors from the states, representing the sovereign interests of the states to the federal government.

Election by State Legislatures

To elect these "ambassadors," the founding fathers chose state bodies — the state legislatures — instead of the people themselves. The argument was that legislatures would be able to give more sober and reflective thought than the people at large to the kind of persons needed to represent the states' interests to the federal government. Moreover, the delegates felt, the state legislatures, and thus the states, would take a greater supportive interest in the fledgling national government if they were involved in its operations this way. Also, the state legislatures had chosen the members of the Continental Congress (followed by the congress under the Articles of Confederation), as well as the members of the Constitutional Convention itself, so the procedure was not an unfamiliar one.

Discarded Proposals

In choosing the state legislatures as the instruments of election for senators, the Constitutional Convention considered and discarded several alternatives. Some delegates had suggested that the senators be elected by the House or appointed by the president from a list of nominees selected by the state legislatures. These ideas were discarded as making the Senate too dependent on another branch or section of the federal government. Also turned down was a scheme for a system of electors, similar to presidential electors, to choose the senators in each state. And popular election was rejected as being too radical and inconvenient.

Senators as State Ambassadors

So deeply entrenched was the ambassadorial aspect of a senator's duty that state legislatures sometimes took it upon themselves to instruct senators on how to vote. This sometimes raised severe problems of conscience among senators and resulted in several resignations.

For example, in 1836 future President John Tyler was serving as a U.S. senator from Virginia. That year, the Virginia state legislature instructed him to vote for a resolution to expunge the Senate censure of President Andrew Jackson for removal of the federal deposits from the Bank of the United States. Tyler had voted for the censure resolution and was a bitter opponent of Jackson. He resigned from the Senate rather than comply.

In another instance, Sen. Hugh Lawson White of Tennessee, a Whig, resigned from the Senate in 1840 after being instructed by his state legislature to vote for the sub-treasury bill, an economic measure supported by the Democratic Van Buren administration.

Length of Terms

Another problem for the founding fathers was the length of the senatorial term. The framers of the Constitution tried to balance two principles: the belief that relatively frequent elections were necessary in order to promote good behavior; and the need for steadiness and continuity in government. Delegates proposed terms of three, four, five, six, seven and nine years. They finally settled on six-year staggered terms, with one-third of the members coming up for election every two years. *(Classification of senators, terms, p. 112)*

Changing Procedures for Election

At first, states made their own arrangements regarding how their state legislatures would elect the senators. Many states required an election made by the two houses of the legislature, sitting separately. That is, each house separately had to vote for the same candidate in order for him to be elected. Other states, however, provided for election by a joint ballot of the two houses sitting together.

However, the Constitution specifically authorized Congress to regulate senatorial elections if it so chose. Article I, Section 4, Paragraph 1 states, "The times, places and

Election to the Senate

Constitutional Provisions

Article I, Section 3

The Senate of the United States shall be composed of two Senators from each State, chosen by the Legislature thereof, for six years; and each Senator shall have one Vote.

Immediately after they shall be assembled in Consequence of the first Election, they shall be divided as equally as may be into three Classes. The Seats of the Senators of the first Class shall be vacated at the Expiration of the second Year, of the second Class at the Expiration of the fourth Year, and of the third class at the Expiration of the sixth Year, so that one third may be chosen every second Year; and if Vacancies happen by Resignation, or otherwise, during the Recess of the Legislature of any State, the Executive thereof may make temporary Appointments until the next Meeting of the Legislature, which shall then fill such Vacancies.

No Person shall be a Senator who shall not have attained the Age of thirty Years, and been nine Years a Citizen of the United States, and who shall not, when elected, be an Inhabitant of that State for which he shall be chosen.

Article I, Section 4

The Times, Places and Manner of holding Elections for Senators and Representatives, shall be prescribed in each State by the Legislature thereof; but the Congress may at any time by Law make or alter such Regulations, except as to the Places of chusing Senators.

The Congress shall assemble at least once in every Year, and such Meeting shall be on the first Monday in December, unless they shall by Law appoint a different Day.

Article I, Section 5

Each House shall be the Judge of the Elections, Returns and Qualifications of its own Members, and a Majority of each shall constitute a Quorum to do Business; but a smaller Number may adjourn from day to day, and may be authorized to compel the Attendance of absent Members in such Manner, and under such Penalties as each House may provide.

Amendment XVII

(Ratified May 31, 1913)

The Senate of the United States shall be composed of two Senators from each State, elected by the people thereof, for six years; and each Senator shall have one vote. The electors in each State shall have the qualifications requisite for electors of the most numerous branch of the State legislatures.

When vacancies happen in the representation of any State in the Senate, the executive authority of such State shall issue writs of election to fill such vacancies: *Provided,* That the legislature of any State may empower the executive thereof to make temporary appointments until the people fill the vacancies by election as the legislature may direct.

This amendment shall not be so construed as to affect the election or term of any Senator chosen before it becomes valid as part of the Constitution.

---

manner of holding elections for Senators and Representatives shall be prescribed in each state by the legislature thereof; but the Congress may at any time by law make or alter such regulations, except as to the places of chusing Senators."

1866 Act of Congress, Election Deadlocks

In 1866, Congress decided to exercise its authority. Procedures in some states, particularly those requiring concurrent majorities in both houses of the state legislature for election to the Senate, had resulted in numerous delays and vacancies.

The new federal law set up the following procedure: The first ballot for senator was to be taken by the two houses of each state legislature voting separately. If no candidate received a majority of the vote in both houses — that is, if a deadlock resulted — then the two houses were to meet and ballot jointly until a majority choice emerged.

Also included in the 1866 law were provisions for roll-call votes in the state legislatures (secret ballots had prevailed in several states) and for a definite timetable. The law directed that the first vote take place on the second Tuesday after the meeting and organization of the legislature, followed by a minimum of a single ballot on every legislative day thereafter, until election resulted.

But the new uniform system did not have the desired effect. The requirement for a majority vote continued the frequency of deadlock. In fact, one of the worst deadlocks in senatorial election history happened under the new federal law.

The case occurred in Delaware at the end of the 19th century. In 1899, with the legislature divided between two factions of the Republican Party, and the Democrats in the minority, no majority selection could be made for the senatorial term beginning March 4, 1899. So bitter was the Republican factional dispute that neither side would support a candidate acceptable to the other; nor would the Democrats play kingmaker by siding with one or the other Republican group. The dispute continued throughout the life of the 56th Congress (1899-1901), leaving a seat unfilled.

Furthermore, the term of Delaware's other Senate seat ended in 1901, necessitating another election. The same pattern continued, with the legislature unable to fill either Senate seat, leaving Delaware totally unrepresented in the Senate from March 4, 1901, until March 1, 1903, when two senators finally were elected in the closing days of the 57th Congress (1901-03). The deadlock was broken when the two Republican factions split the state's two seats between them.

Abuses of Election by Legislatures

Besides the frequent deadlocks, critics pointed to what they saw as other faults in the system. They charged, for example, that the party caucuses in the state legislatures, as well as individual members, were subject to intense and unethical lobbying practices by supporters of various senatorial candidates. The relatively small size of the electing body and the high stakes involved — a seat in the Senate — often tempted the use of questionable methods in conducting the elections.

Because of the frequency of allegations of illegal methods used in securing election, the Senate found itself involved in election disputes. The Constitution makes Congress the judge of its own members. Article I, Section 5, Paragraph 1, states, "Each House shall be the judge of the elections, returns, and qualifications of its own members...."

One of the most sensational cases concerned the election of William Lorimer (R Ill.) to the Senate. Lorimer won his seat on the 99th ballot taken by the Illinois Legislature in 1909. Charges flew that he had secured election by bribery, and a year after he had taken his seat, he requested that the Senate investigate. On March 1, 1911, the Senate decided 46 to 40 against a resolution that Lorimer was "not duly and legally elected."

But the case was soon reopened, with an investigation by the Illinois Legislature revealing new evidence. After a year's inquest, the Senate agreed with the minority report of its investigating committee that Lorimer's election "reeks and teems with evidence of a general scheme of corruption." On July 13, 1912, the Senate voted 55 to 28 that Lorimer's election was invalid and he was not entitled to his seat.

Critics had still another grievance against the legislative method of choosing senators. They contended that elections to the state legislatures were often overshadowed by senatorial contests. Thus when voters went to the polls to choose their state legislators, they would sometimes be urged to disregard state and local issues and vote for a legislator who promised to support a certain candidate for the U.S. Senate. This, the critics said, led to a neglect of state government and issues. Moreover, drawn-out Senate contests tended to hold up the consideration of state business.

Demands for Popular Election

But the main criticism of legislative elections was that they distorted, or even blocked, the will of the people. Throughout the 19th century, the movement toward popular election had taken away from legislatures the right to elect governors and presidential electors in states that had such provisions. Now attention focused on the Senate.

Five times around the turn of the century, the House passed constitutional amendments for popular Senate elections — in the 52nd Congress on Jan. 16, 1893; in the 53rd Congress on July 21, 1894; in the 55th Congress on May 11, 1898; in the 56th Congress on April 13, 1900, and in the 57th Congress on Feb. 13, 1902. But each time the Senate refused to act.

Frustrated in their desire for direct popular elections to the Senate, reformers began implementing various formulas for pre-selecting Senate candidates, attempting to reduce the legislative balloting to something approaching a mere formality.

In some cases, party conventions endorsed nominees for the Senate, allowing the voters at least to know who the members of the legislature were likely to support. Southern states adopted the party primary to choose Senate nominees early in the century. However, legislators never could be legally bound to support anyone, because the Constitution gave them the unfettered power of electing whomever they chose to the U.S. Senate.

Popular Elections Before the 17th Amendment

Oregon took the lead in instituting non-binding popular elections. Under a 1901 law, voters expressed their choice for senator in popular ballots. While the results of the vote had no legal force, the law required that the election returns be formally announced to the state legislature before it proceeded to the election of a senator.

At first the law did not work — the winner of the informal popular vote in 1902 was not chosen senator by the legislature. But the reformers increased their pressure, including demands that candidates for the legislature sign a pledge to vote for the winner of the popular vote. By 1908, the plan was successful, with a Republican legislature electing to the Senate Democrat George Chamberlain, the winner of the popular contest. Several other states adopted the Oregon method, including Colorado, Kansas, Minnesota, Montana, Nevada and Oklahoma.

The 17th Amendment

However, despite these palliatives, pressures continued to mount for a switch to straight popular elections. Frustrated at the failure of the Senate to act, proponents of change began pushing for a convention to propose this, and perhaps, other, amendments. (Article V of the Constitution provides two methods of proposing amendments — either passage by two-thirds of both Houses of Congress, or through the calling of a special convention if requested by the legislatures of two-thirds of the states. In either case, any amendments proposed by Congress or a special convention must be ratified by three-fourths of the states.)

Conservatives began to fear a convention more than they did popular election of senators. There was no precedent for an amending convention, and conservatives feared that it might be dominated by liberals and progressives who would propose numerous amendments and change the very nature of the government. Consequently, their opposition to popular election of senators receded in intensity.

At the same time, progressives of both parties made strong gains in the midterm elections of 1910. Some successful Senate candidates had made pledges to work for adoption of a constitutional amendment providing for popular election. In this atmosphere, the Senate debated and finally passed the amendment on June 12, 1911, by a vote of 64-24. The House concurred in the Senate version on May 13, 1912, by a vote of 238-39. Ratification of the 17th Amendment was completed by the requisite number of states on April 8, 1913, and was proclaimed a part of the Constitution by Secretary of State William Jennings Bryan on May 31, 1913.

The first popularly elected senator was chosen in a special election in November 1913. He was Sen. Blair Lee (D Md. 1914-17), elected for the remaining three years of the unexpired term of the late Sen. Isidor Rayner (D 1905-12).

There was no wholesale changeover in membership when the 17th Amendment became effective. In fact, every one of the 23 senators elected by state legislatures for their previous terms, and running for re-election to full terms in November 1914, was successful. Seven had retired or died, and two had been defeated for renomination.

Senate Appointments and Special Elections

Governors were given specific authority in the Constitution to make temporary appointments to the Senate. Article I, Section 3, Paragraph 2 states: "If vacancies happen by resignation, or otherwise, during the recess of the legislature of any state, the executive thereof may make temporary appointments until the next meeting of the legislature, which shall then fill such vacancies."

The principle was established as early as 1794 that a vacancy created solely because a state legislature had failed to elect a new senator could not be filled by appointment, because the vacancy had not occurred "during the recess of the legislature."

For example, the term of Sen. Matthew Quay (R Pa. 1887-99, 1901-04) expired March 3, 1899. The legislature was in session but had failed to re-elect him. Nor did it elect anyone before adjourning that April 20. Thereupon, the governor appointed Quay to the vacancy; but the Senate did not allow Quay to take the seat, because the vacancy had occurred during the meeting of the legislature. In 1901, Quay was elected by the legislature for the remainder of the term.

On the other hand, if a senator's term expired and the legislature was *not* in session, a governor was able to make an appointment — but only until the legislature either elected a successor or adjourned without electing one. For example, on March 3, 1809, the term of Sen. Samuel Smith (D-R Md. 1803-15, 1822-33) expired. The legislature was not then in session and had not elected a successor. Therefore the governor appointed Smith to fill the vacancy until the next meeting of the legislature, which was scheduled for June 5, 1809. The Senate ruled that he was entitled to the seat. During the subsequent meeting of the state legislature that year, Smith was elected to a full term.

However, whatever the condition under which an appointment had been made, it was to last only through the next state legislative session. Even if a legislature failed to elect a new senator, the appointed senator's service was to expire with the adjournment of the state legislature.

This principle was confirmed in the case of Sen. Samuel Phelps (Whig Vt. 1839-51, 1853-54). Phelps was appointed in January 1853 to a vacancy caused by the death of Sen. William Upham (Whig Vt. 1843-53), whose term was to run through March 3, 1855. As the legislature was in recess, Phelps continued to serve until the expiration of the 32nd Congress on March 3, 1853, and also during a special session of the 33rd Congress in March and April 1853. The state legislature met during October and December 1853 without electing a senator to fill the unexpired term. Phelps then showed up for the regular session of the 33rd Congress in December, but the Senate in March 1854 decided he was not entitled to retain his seat, because the legislature had met and adjourned without electing a new senator.

17th Amendment and Special Elections

The adoption of the 17th Amendment in 1913, providing for popular election of senators, altered the provision for gubernatorial appointment of senators to fill vacancies. The amendment provided that in case of a vacancy, "the executive authority of such state shall issue writs of election to fill such vacancies: *Provided*, that the legislature of any state may empower the executive thereof to make temporary appointments until the people fill the vacancies by election as the legislature may direct." Under this provision, state legislatures allowed governors to make temporary appointments until the vacancy could be filled by a special election. Special elections — elections held to fill unexpired terms — were usually held in November of an even-numbered year. Some states, however, provided for special elections to be held within just a few months after the vacancy occurred.

Before ratification of the 17th Amendment the term of an appointee generally ended when a successor was elected to fill the unexpired term, or at the end of the six-year term, whichever occurred first. After the ratification of the 17th Amendment but before ratification of the 20th Amendment in 1933, senators who were elected to fill unexpired terms which had several years left to run could usually take office immediately, displacing an appointee. If an appointee was serving near the close of a six-year term, most states would usually hold simultaneous elections to fill both the six-year term and the four-month "lame duck" term. Sometimes different persons would be elected to each term. The lame-duck sessions were always full working sessions of Congress.

After the 20th Amendment took effect, senators elected to fill vacancies in terms which had several years to run would take office immediately, as before, but if a vacancy occurred near the end of a six-year term, an appointee would often serve until the Jan. 3 expiration date, eliminating the necessity for a special election.

Some states, however, still hold elections in November for the remaining two months of a term. Georgia voters in 1972, for example, found on the ballot two Senate elections — one for a six-year term, and one for a two-month term to fill the unexpired term of the late Sen. Richard B. Russell (D Ga. 1933-71).

Dates of Service

Title II, Section 36 of the U.S. Code sets the dates on which senators appointed or elected to fill unexpired terms formally begin service and go on the payroll. The service of an appointee commences the day of appointment and continues until a successor is elected and qualified. If the Senate is in *sine die* adjournment when a new senator is elected to succeed an appointee, he will take office and begin receiving his salary on the day after the election.

If the Senate is in session when a new senator is elected to succeed an appointee, the new senator may take office when he presents himself before the Senate to take the oath; the appointee may continue in office until this occurs or the Senate adjourns *sine die*, whichever happens first. The term of the newly elected senator would then begin at *sine die* adjournment.

Election Disputes

The changeover in method of electing senators ended the frequent legislative stalemates in choosing members of the Senate. Otherwise, many things remained the same. There were still election disputes, including charges of corruption, as well as miscounting of votes.

Election disputes continued to occupy the Senate. In 1926, two Republicans — William S. Vare of Pennsylvania and Frank L. Smith of Illinois — defeated incumbent Republican senators for renomination. The primary campaigns were marked by heavy expenditures and alleged corrupt practices. In both instances, the Senate voted to deny seats to the senators-elect — against Vare on Dec. 6, 1929, and against Smith on Jan. 19, 1928.

A bitter contest for a New Hampshire Senate seat in 1974 between Rep. Louis C. Wyman (R) and John A. Durkin (D) wound up in the Senate after a seesaw battle between New Hampshire authorities over who had won. The state Ballot Law Commission had finally awarded the victory to Wyman by two votes, but Durkin took his case to the Senate. After wrestling with the problem for seven months, the Senate gave up and declared the seat vacant. A new election was held Sept. 16, 1975, which Durkin won decisively.

Classes of Senators

The Senate is divided into three classes, or groups of members. A member's class depends on the year in which he was elected. Article I, Section 3, Paragraph 2 of the Constitution, relating to the classification of senators in the first and succeeding Congresses, provides that, "Immediately after they shall be assembled in consequence of the first election, they shall be divided as equally as may be into three classes. The seats of the Senators of the first class shall be vacated at the expiration of the second year, of the second class at the expiration of the fourth year and of the third class at the expiration of the sixth year, so that one-third may be chosen every second year."

Thus senators belonging to class one began their regular terms in the years 1789, 1791, 1797, 1803, etc., continuing through the present day to 1959, 1965, 1971, 1977, 1983, and coming up for re-election in 1988. Senators belonging to class two began their regular terms in 1789, 1793, 1799, 1805, etc., continuing through the present day to 1955, 1961, 1967, 1973, 1979, and coming up for re-election in 1984. And senators belonging to class three began their regular terms in 1789, 1795, 1801, 1807, etc., continuing through the present day to 1957, 1963, 1969, 1975, 1981, and coming up for re-election in 1986.

Sessions and Terms

In the fall of 1788, the expiring Continental Congress established a schedule for the incoming government under the new Constitution. The Congress decided that the new government was to commence on the first Wednesday in March 1789 — March 4. Even though the House did not achieve a quorum until April 1 and the Senate April 6, and President Washington was not inaugurated until April 30, Senate, House and presidential terms were still considered to have begun March 4. The term of the first Congress continued through March 3, 1791. Because congressional and presidential terms were fixed at exactly two, four and six years, March 4 became the official date of transition from one administration to another every four years and from one Congress to another every two years.

But the Constitution did not mandate a regular congressional session to begin March 4. Instead, Article I, Section 4, Paragraph 2 called for at least one congressional session every year, to convene on the first Monday in December unless Congress by law set a different day. Consequently, except when called by the president for special sessions, or when Congress itself set a different day, Congress convened in regular session each December, until the passage of the 20th Amendment in 1933.

The December date resulted in a long and short session. The first (long) session would meet in December of an odd-numbered year and continue into the next year, usually adjourning some time the next summer. The second (short) session began in December of an even-numbered year and continued through March 3 of the next year, when its term ran out. It also became customary for the Senate to meet in a brief special session on March 4 or March 5, especially in years when a new president was inaugurated, to act on presidential nominations.

To illustrate with an example of a typical Congress, the 29th (1845-47): President James K. Polk (D) was inaugurated on March 4, 1845. The Senate met in special session from March 4 to March 20 to confirm Polk's Cabinet and other appointments. Then the first regular session convened Dec. 1, 1845, working until Aug. 10, 1846, when it adjourned. The second, a short session, lasted from Dec. 7, 1846, through March 3, 1847.

Since it was not clear whether terms of members of Congress ended at midnight March 3 or noon March 4, the custom evolved of extending the legislative day of March 3, in odd-numbered years, to noon March 4.

The 20th Amendment

The political consequence of the short session was to encourage filibusters and other delaying tactics by members determined to block legislation that would die upon the automatic adjournment of Congress on March 3. Moreover, the Congresses that met in short session always included a substantial number of "lame duck" members who had been defeated at the polls, yet were able quite often to determine the legislative outcome of the session.

Dissatisfaction with the short session began to mount after 1900. During the Wilson administration (1913-1921), each of four such sessions ended with a Senate filibuster and the loss of important bills including several funding bills. Sen. George W. Norris, R-Neb. (1913-43), became the leading advocate of a constitutional amendment to abolish the short session by starting the terms of Congress and the president in January instead of March. The Senate approved the Norris amendment five times during the 1920s, only to see it blocked in the House each time. It was finally approved by both chambers in 1932 and became the 20th Amendment upon ratification by the 36th state in 1933.

The amendment provided that the terms of senators and representatives would begin and end at noon on the third day of January of the year following the election. However, according to the *Senate Manual* (1973 edition, pp. 755-756), "In view of the impracticality of dealing with split days, . . . it has been the long established practice for payment of salaries, computation of allowances and recording of service to credit a member for the full day of the

Wrap-up of 1984 Senate Races

State	Incumbent	First Elected	1978 Percentage	Outlook (As of March 20, 1984)
REPUBLICAN SEATS				
Highly Vulnerable				
Tenn.	Howard H. Baker Jr.	1966	56%	Baker was retiring. Democratic Rep. Albert Gore Jr. faced GOP primary winner, probably state Sen. Victor Ashe.
Texas	John Tower	1961	50%	Tower was retiring. Democratic candidates included state Sen. Lloyd Doggett, former Rep. Bob Krueger and Rep. Kent Hance. Republicans running were Reps. Phil Gramm and Ron Paul and oilman Rob Mosbacher.
Iowa	Roger W. Jepsen	1978	51%	Democratic challenger was Rep. Tom Harkin.
N.C.	Jesse Helms	1972	55%	Democratic challenger was Gov. James B. Hunt Jr.
Vulnerable				
Miss.	Thad Cochran	1978	45%	Democratic challenger was former Gov. William Winter.
Ill.	Charles H. Percy	1966	53%	Percy was challenged by GOP Rep. Tom Corcoran in the Senate primary but succeeded in winning renomination with 58.8 percent of the vote. Democratic candidate was Rep. Paul Simon.
Minn.	Rudy Boschwitz	1978	57%	Democratic challengers included Rep. James L. Oberstar, Secretary of State Joan Growe and former Sen. Wendell Anderson.
N.H.	Gordon J. Humphrey	1978	51%	Democratic challenger was Rep. Norman E. D'Amours.
Probably Secure				
N.M.	Pete V. Domenici	1972	53%	
Maine	William S. Cohen	1978	56%	
S.D.	Larry Pressler	1978	67%	
Va.	John W. Warner	1978	50%	Democrats were campaigning actively in several of these states, but the Republicans were solid favorites as of mid-March.
Ore.	Mark O. Hatfield	1966	62%	
Colo.	William L. Armstrong	1978	59%	
Alaska	Ted Stevens	1970	76%	
Idaho	James A. McClure	1972	68%	
Wyo.	Alan K. Simpson	1978	62%	
S.C.	Strom Thurmond	1954	56%	
Kansas	Nancy Landon Kassebaum	1978	54%	
DEMOCRATIC SEATS				
Vulnerable				
Mass.	Paul E. Tsongas	1978	55%	Tsongas was retiring. Democratic candidates included Reps. James M. Shannon and Edward J. Markey and former state House Speaker David M. Bartley; Republicans were former U.S. Attorney General Elliot L. Richardson and businessman Raymond Shamie.
Potentially Vulnerable				
W.Va.	Jennings Randolph	1958	50%	Randolph was retiring. Democratic candidate was Gov. John D. "Jay" Rockefeller IV, who expected a tough race if former GOP Gov. Arch Moore decided to run.
Mich.	Carl Levin	1978	52%	GOP primary pitted former Rep. Jim Dunn against retired astronaut Jack Lousma.
Probably Secure				
Ark.	David Pryor	1978	77%	
Ky.	Walter D. Huddleston	1972	61%	
R.I.	Claiborne Pell	1960	75%	
Del.	Joseph R. Biden Jr.	1972	58%	
Mont.	Max Baucus	1978	56%	Republicans had significant challengers in some of these states, but all the incumbents looked strong as of mid-March.
Ala.	Howell Heflin	1978	94%	
Neb.	J. James Exon	1978	68%	
La.	J. Bennett Johnston	1972	59%	
Okla.	David L. Boren	1978	66%	
N.J.	Bill Bradley	1978	55%	
Ga.	Sam Nunn	1972	83%	

third of January he takes office and consider his term as ended at the close of business on the second of January six years later."

The 20th Amendment also established noon Jan. 20 as the day on which the president and vice president take office. It provided also that Congress should meet annually on Jan. 3 "unless they shall by law appoint a different day." The second session of the 73rd Congress was the first to convene on the new date, Jan. 3, 1934. Franklin D. Roosevelt was the first president and John N. Garner the first vice president to be inaugurated on Jan. 20, at the start of their second terms in 1937.

The amendment was intended to permit Congress to extend its first session for as long as necessary and to complete the work of its second session before the next election, thereby obviating legislation by a "lame-duck" body.

120 Elections '84

Results of Elections in House of Representatives, 1964-1982

	64	66	68	70	72	74	76	78	80	82
NATIONAL TOTALS										
Democrats	295	248	243	255	243	291	292	277	243	269
Republicans	140	187	192	180	192	143	143	158	192	166
ALABAMA										
Democrats	3	5	5	5	4[2]	4	4	4	4	5
Republicans	5	3	3	3	3	3	3	3	3	2
ALASKA										
Democrats	1	0	0	1	1[3]	0	0	0	0	0
Republicans	0	1	1	0	0	1	1	1	1	1
ARIZONA										
Democrats	2	1	1	1	1[1]	1	2	2	2	2[1]
Republicans	1	2	2	2	3	3	2	2	2	3
ARKANSAS										
Democrats	4	3	3	3	3	3	3	2	2	2
Republicans	0	1	1	1	1	1	1	2	2	2
CALIFORNIA										
Democrats	23	21	21	20	23[1]	28	29	26	22	28[1]
Republicans	15	17	17	18	20	15	14	17	21	17
COLORADO										
Democrats	4	3	3	2	2[1]	3	3	3	3	3[1]
Republicans	0	1	1	2	3	2	2	2	2	3
CONNECTICUT										
Democrats	6	5	4	4	3	4	4	5	4	4
Republicans	0	1	2	2	3	2	2	1	2	2
DELAWARE										
Democrats	1	0	0	0	0	0	0	0	0	1
Republicans	0	1	1	1	1	1	1	1	1	0
FLORIDA										
Democrats	10	9	9	9	11[1]	10	10	12	11	13[1]
Republicans	2	3	3	3	4	5	5	3	4	6
GEORGIA										
Democrats	9	8	8	8	9	10	10	9	9	9
Republicans	1	2	2	2	1	0	0	1	1	1
HAWAII										
Democrats	2	2	2	2	2	2	2	2	2	2
Republicans	0	0	0	0	0	0	0	0	0	0
IDAHO										
Democrats	1	0	0	0	0	0	0	0	0	0
Republicans	1	2	2	2	2	2	2	2	2	2
ILLINOIS										
Democrats	13	12	12	12	10	13	12	11	10	12[2]
Republicans	11	12	12	12	14	11	12	13	14	10
INDIANA										
Democrats	6	5	4	5	4	9	8	7	6	5[2]
Republicans	5	6	7	6	7	2	3	4	5	5
IOWA										
Democrats	6	2	2	2	3[2]	5	4	3	3	3
Republicans	1	5	5	5	3	1	2	3	3	3
KANSAS										
Democrats	0	0	0	1	1	1	2	1	1	2
Republicans	5	5	5	4	4	4	3	4	4	3
KENTUCKY										
Democrats	6	4	4	5	5	5	5	4	4	4
Republicans	1	3	3	2	2	2	2	3	3	3
LOUISIANA										
Democrats	8	8	8	8	7[3]	6[5]	6	5	6	6
Republicans	0	0	0	0	1	1	2	3	2	2
MAINE										
Democrats	1	2	2	2	1	0	0	0	0	0
Republicans	1	0	0	0	1	2	2	2	2	2
MARYLAND										
Democrats	6	5	4	5	4	5	5	6	7	7
Republicans	2	3	4	3	4	3	3	2	1	1
MASSACHUSETTS										
Democrats	7	7	7	8	9[4]	10	10	10	10	10[2]
Republicans	5	5	5	4	3	2	2	2	2	1
MICHIGAN										
Democrats	12	7	7	7	7	12	11	13	12	12[2]
Republicans	7	12	12	12	12	7	8	6	7	6
MINNESOTA										
Democrats	4	3	3	4	4	5	5	4	3	5
Republicans	4	5	5	4	4	3	3	4	5	3
MISSISSIPPI										
Democrats	4	5	5	5	3	3	3	3	3	3
Republicans	1	0	0	0	2	2	2	2	2	2

	64	66	68	70	72	74	76	78	80	82
MISSOURI										
Democrats	8	8	9	9	9	9	8	8	6	6[2]
Republicans	2	2	1	1	1	1	2	2	4	3
MONTANA										
Democrats	1	1	1	1	1	2	1	1	1	1
Republicans	1	1	1	1	1	0	1	1	1	1
NEBRASKA										
Democrats	1	0	0	0	0	1	1	0	0	0
Republicans	2	3	3	3	3	2	2	3	3	3
NEVADA										
Democrats	1	1	1	1	0	1	1	1	1	1[1]
Republicans	0	0	0	0	1	0	0	0	0	1
NEW HAMPSHIRE										
Democrats	1	0	0	0	0	1	1	1	1	1
Republicans	1	2	2	2	2	1	1	1	1	1
NEW JERSEY										
Democrats	11	9	9	9	8	12	11	10	8	9[2]
Republicans	4	6	6	6	7	3	4	5	7	5
NEW MEXICO										
Democrats	2	2	0	1	1	1	1	1	0	1[1]
Republicans	0	0	2	1	1	1	1	1	2	2
NEW YORK										
Democrats	27	26	26	24	22[2]	27	28	26	22	20[2]
Republicans	14	15	15	17	17	12	11	13	17	14
NORTH CAROLINA										
Democrats	9	8	7	7	7	9	9	9	7	9
Republicans	2	3	4	4	4	2	2	2	4	2
NORTH DAKOTA										
Democrats	1	0	0	1	0[2]	0	0	0	1	1
Republicans	1	2	2	1	1	1	1	1	0	0
OHIO										
Democrats	10	5	6	7	7[2]	8	10	10	10	10[2]
Republicans	14	19	18	17	16	15	13	13	13	11
OKLAHOMA										
Democrats	5	4	4	4	5	6	5	5	5	5
Republicans	1	2	2	2	1	0	1	1	1	1
OREGON										
Democrats	3	2	2	2	2	4	4	4	3	3[1]
Republicans	1	2	2	2	2	0	0	0	1	2
PENNSYLVANIA										
Democrats	15	14	14	14	13[2]	14	17	15	13	13[2]
Republicans	12	13	13	13	12	11	8	10	12	10
RHODE ISLAND										
Democrats	2	2	2	2	2	2	2	1	1	1
Republicans	0	0	0	0	0	0	0	1	1	1
SOUTH CAROLINA										
Democrats	6	5	5	5	4	5	5	4	2	3
Republicans	0	1	1	1	2	1	1	2	4	3
SOUTH DAKOTA										
Democrats	0	0	0	2	1	0	0	1	1	1[2]
Republicans	2	2	2	0	1	2	2	1	1	0
TENNESSEE										
Democrats	6	5	5	5	3[2]	5	5	5	5	6[1]
Republicans	3	4	4	4	5	3	3	3	3	3
TEXAS										
Democrats	23	21	20	20	20[1]	21	22	20	19	22[1]
Republicans	0	2	3	3	4	3	2	4	5	5
UTAH										
Democrats	1	0	0	1	2	2	1	1	0	0[1]
Republicans	1	2	2	1	0	0	1	1	2	3
VERMONT										
Democrats	0	0	0	0	0	0	0	0	0	0
Republicans	1	1	1	1	1	1	1	1	1	1
VIRGINIA										
Democrats	8	6	5	4	3	5	4	4	1	4
Republicans	2	4	5	6	7	5	6	6	9	6
WASHINGTON										
Democrats	5	5	5	6	6	6	6	6	5	5[1]
Republicans	2	2	2	1	1	1	1	1	2	3
WEST VIRGINIA										
Democrats	4	4	5	5	4[2]	4	4	4	2	4
Republicans	1	1	0	0	0	0	0	0	2	0
WISCONSIN										
Democrats	5	3	3	5	5[2]	7	7	5	5	5
Republicans	5	7	7	5	4	2	2	3	4	4
WYOMING										
Democrats	1	0	0	1	1	1	1	0	0	0
Republicans	0	1	1	0	0	0	0	1	1	1

[1] *State gained seats due to reapportionment.*
[2] *State lost seats due to reapportionment.*
[3] *Alaska and Louisiana 1972: Total includes one Democratic candidate who died before the election but his name remained on the ballot and he was re-elected. A special election was held the next year to fill the vacancy.*
[4] *Massachusetts 1972: Democratic total includes Rep. Joe Moakley, elected as an independent but served as a Democrat.*
[5] *Louisiana 1974: One vacancy. There was no declared winner in the 6th District. A special election was held the next year to fill the vacancy.*

House Elections

The House of Representatives was designed by the Founding Fathers to be the branch of government closest to the people.

Its members, unlike the Senate or the presidency — elected by state legislatures and presidential electors — were to be chosen directly by the people. They would have two-year terms, so the people would have a chance to monitor and pass on their activities at brief intervals. And the House would be a numerous branch, with members having relatively small constituencies.

Early Models

The lower houses of the state legislatures served as a model for the U.S. House. All the states had at least one house of their legislatures elected by popular vote. Ten states had two-house legislatures; Georgia, Pennsylvania and Vermont had popularly elected unicameral legislatures.

The Constitution left the qualification of voters to the states, with one exception: the qualifications could be no more restrictive than for the most numerous branch of each of the states' own legislatures. At first, property qualifications for voting were general. Five states required ownership of real estate, five mandated either real estate or other property and three required personal wealth or payment of public taxes. But the democratic trend of the early 19th century swept away most property qualifications, producing practically universal white male suffrage by the 1830s.

Constitutional Amendments

Over the years, several changes in the Constitution have also broadened the franchise. The 15th Amendment (1870) extended the franchise to newly freed slaves; the 19th Amendment (1920) granted the right of suffrage to women; the 23rd Amendment (1961) extended the presidential vote to the District of Columbia; the 24th Amendment (1964) banned the poll tax; and the 26th Amendment (1971) lowered the voting age from 21 to 18.

Many delegates to the Constitutional Convention preferred annual elections for the House, believing that the body should reflect as closely as possible the wishes of the people. James Madison, however, argued for a three-year term, to allow representatives to gain knowledge and experience in national affairs, as well as the affairs of their own localities. They compromised on two-year terms.

Two-Year Term

The two-year term has not been universally popular. From time to time, proposals have been made to extend the term to four years. On the latest occasion, the movement to extend the term of representatives to four years gained temporary momentum early in 1966 after President Lyndon B. Johnson (D) urged the extension in his State of the Union message January 12. His proposal received more applause than any other part of his speech.

However, the proposed amendment never emerged from committee. Opponents criticized the proposal's provision that the four-year term coincide with the presidential term. This would create a House of "coattail riders," critics said, and end the minority party's traditional gains in non-presidential years. This fear of diminishing the independence of the House appeared to be the principal factor that killed the proposal.

Size of the House

The size of the original House was written into Article I, Section 2 of the Constitution, along with directions to apportion the House according to population after the first census in 1790. Until the first census and apportionment, the 13 states were to have the following numbers of representatives: New Hampshire, 3; Massachusetts, 8; Rhode Island, 1; Connecticut, 5; New York, 6; New Jersey, 4; Pennsylvania, 8; Delaware, 1; Maryland, 6; Virginia, 10; North Carolina, 5; South Carolina, 5; Georgia, 3. This apportionment of seats — 65 in all — thus mandated by the Constitution remained in effect during the First and Second Congresses (1789-93).

By act of Congress (April 14, 1792), an apportionment measure provided for a ratio of one member for every 33,000 inhabitants and fixed the exact number of representatives to which each state was entitled. The total membership of the House was to be 105. In dividing the population of the various states by 33,000, all remainders were to be disregarded. This was known as the method of rejected fractions and was devised by Thomas Jefferson. Congress enacted a new apportionment measure, including the mathematical formula to be used, every 10 years (except 1920) until a permanent law became effective in 1929.

Majority Elections

Five New England states at one time or another had a requirement for majority victory in congressional elections. But all phased them out by the end of the 19th century. The requirement provided that in order to win a seat in the

U.S. House, a candidate had to achieve a majority of the popular vote. If no candidate gained such a majority, new elections were held until one contender managed to do so.

The provision was last invoked in Maine in 1844; in New Hampshire in 1845; in Vermont in 1866; in Massachusetts in 1848; and in Rhode Island in 1892. Sometimes, multiple races were necessary because none of the candidates could achieve the required majority. In the 4th District of Massachusetts in 1848-49, for example, 12 successive elections were held to try to choose a representative. None of them were successful, and the district remained unrepresented in the House during the 31st Congress (1849-51).

Multi-Member Districts

Another anomaly of early House elections was the multi-member district. Several states had districts which elected more than one representative. For example, in 1824 Maryland's 5th District chose two representatives, while the remaining seven districts chose one each. And in Pennsylvania, two districts (the 4th and 9th) elected three representatives each, and four districts (the 7th, 8th, 11th and 17th) chose two representatives each.

As late as 1838, New York still had as many as five multi-member districts — one (the 3rd) electing four members and four (the 8th, 17th, 22nd and 23rd) choosing two each. But the practice ended in 1842 when Congress enacted a law that "no one district may elect more than one Representative." The provision was a part of the reapportionment legislation following the census of 1840.

Elections in Odd-Numbered Years

Another practice that has faded out over the years was general elections in odd-numbered years for the House. Prior to ratification of the 20th (lame duck) Amendment in 1933, regular sessions of Congress began in December of odd-numbered years. There were, therefore, 11 months in the odd-numbered years to elect members before the beginning of the congressional session. For example, in 1841, the following states held general elections for representative for the 27th Congress, convening that year: Alabama, Connecticut, Illinois, Indiana, Kentucky, Maryland, Mississippi, New Hampshire, North Carolina, Rhode Island, Tennessee and Virginia.

The practice continued until late in the century. In 1875, four states still chose their representatives in regular odd-year elections: California, Connecticut, Mississippi and New Hampshire. But by 1881, all members of the House were being chosen in even-numbered years (except for special elections to fill vacancies). One of the major problems encountered by states choosing their representatives in odd-numbered years was the possibility of a special session of the new Congress being called before the states' elections were held. Depending on the date of the election, a state could be unrepresented in the House. For example, California elected its U.S. House delegation to the 40th Congress (1867-69) on Sept. 4, 1867, in plenty of time for the first regular session scheduled for Dec. 2. But the Congress had already met in two special sessions — March 4 to March 20 and July 3 to July 20 — without any representation from California.

Southern Anomalies

Many of the anomalies in election of U.S. representatives occurred in the South. That region's experience with slavery, Civil War, Reconstruction and racial antagonisms created special problems for the regular electoral process.

Article I, Section 2 of the Constitution contained a formula for counting slaves for apportionment purposes: every five slaves would be counted as three persons. Thus, the total population of a state to be used in determining its congressional representation would be the free population plus three-fifths of the slave population.

After the Civil War and the emancipation of the slaves, blacks were fully counted for the purposes of apportionment. The 14th Amendment, ratified in 1868, required that apportionment be based on "the whole number of persons in each State...." On this basis, several southern states tried to claim immediate additional representation on their readmission to the Union. Tennessee, for example, chose an extra U.S. representative, electing him at large in 1868, and claimed that inasmuch as its slaves were now free, the state had added to its apportionment population a sufficient number to give it nine instead of eight representatives. Virginia took similar action in 1869 and 1870, and South Carolina did the same in both 1868 and 1870. But the House declined to seat the additional representatives, and declared that states would have to await the regular reapportionment following the 1870 census for any changes in their representation.

Part of the 14th Amendment (1868) affected — or was intended to affect — southern representation in the House. The second paragraph of the amendment stated, "When the right to vote at any election for the choice of electors for President and Vice President of the United States, Representatives in Congress, the executive and judicial officers of a State, or the members of the legislature thereof, is denied to any of the male inhabitants of such state, being twenty-one years of age, and citizens of the United States, or in any other way abridged, except for participation in rebellion, or other crime, the basis of representation [in the U.S. House] shall be reduced in the proportion which the number of such male citizens shall bear to the whole number of male citizens twenty-one years of age in such state."

Designed as a club to use in forcing the South to accept black voting participation, the provision was incorporated in the reapportionment legislation of 1872. According to the legislation, the number of representatives from any state interfering with the exercise of the right to vote was to be reduced in proportion to the number of inhabitants of voting age whose right to go to the polls was denied or abridged. But the provision was never put into effect because of the difficulty of determining the exact number of persons whose right to vote was being abridged, and also because of the decline of northern enthusiasm for forcing Reconstruction policies on the South.

As an alternative to invoking the difficult 14th Amendment provision, Congress often considered election challenges filed against members from the South. When Republicans were in control of the House, several Democrats from the former Confederate states found themselves unseated, often on charges that black voting rights were abused in their districts. During the 47th Congress (1881-83) five Democrats from former Confederate states were unseated; in the 51st Congress (1889-91), six; and in the 54th Congress (1895-97), seven.

Special Elections

When vacancies occur in the House, the usual procedure is for the governor of the state concerned to call a

Election to the House of Representatives

Constitutional Provisions

Article I, Section 2

The House of Representatives shall be composed of Members chosen every second Year by the People of the several States, and the Electors in each State shall have the Qualifications requisite for Electors of the most numerous Branch of the State Legislature.

No Person shall be a Representative who shall not have attained to the age of twenty five Years, and been seven Years a Citizen of the United States, and who shall not, when elected, be an Inhabitant of that State in which he shall be chosen.

Representatives and direct Taxes shall be apportioned among the several States which may be included within this Union, according to their respective Numbers, which shall be determined by adding to the whole Number of free Persons, including those bound to Service for a Term of Years, and excluding Indians not taxed, three fifths of all other Persons. The actual Enumeration shall be made within three Years after the first Meeting of the Congress of the United States, and within every subsequent Term of ten Years, in such Manner as they shall by Law direct. The Number of Representatives shall not exceed one for every thirty Thousand, but each State shall have at Least one Representative; and until such enumeration shall be made, the State of New Hampshire shall be entitled to chuse three, Massachusetts eight, Rhode-Island and Providence Plantations one, Connecticut five, New-York six, New Jersey four, Pennsylvania eight, Delaware one, Maryland six, Virginia ten, North Carolina five, South Carolina five, and Georgia three.

When vacancies happen in the Representation from any State, the Executive Authority thereof shall issue Writs of Election to fill such Vacancies.

Article I, Section 4

The Times, Places and Manner of holding Elections for Senators and Representatives, shall be prescribed in each State by the Legislature thereof; but the Congress may at any time by Law make or alter such Regulations, except as to the Places of chusing Senators.

The Congress shall assemble at least once in every Year, and such Meeting shall be on the first Monday in December, unless they shall by Law appoint a different day.

Article I, Section 5

Each House shall be the Judge of the Elections, Returns and Qualifications of its own Members, and a Majority of each shall constitute a Quorum to do Business; but a smaller Number may adjourn from day to day, and may be authorized to compel the Attendance of absent Members in such Manner, and under such Penalties as each House may provide.

Amendment XIV, Section 2

(Ratified July 28, 1868)

Representatives shall be apportioned among the several States according to their respective numbers, counting the whole number of persons in each State, excluding Indians not taxed. But when the right to vote at any election for the choice of electors for President and Vice President of the United States, Representatives in Congress, the Executive and Judicial officers of a State, or the members of the Legislature thereof, is denied to any of the male inhabitants of such State, being twenty-one years of age, and citizens of the United States, or in any way abridged, except for participation therein shall be reduced in the proportion which the number of such male citizens shall bear to the whole number of male citizens twenty-one years of age in such State.

Amendment XX

(Ratified Jan. 23, 1933)

Section 1.

The terms of the President and Vice President shall end at noon on the 20th day of January, and the terms of Senators and Representatives at noon on the 3d day of January, of the years in which such terms would have ended if this article had not been ratified; and the terms of their successors shall then begin.

Section 2.

The Congress shall assemble at least once in every year, and such meeting shall begin at noon on the 3d day of January, unless they shall by law appoint a different day.

---

special election. These may be held at any time throughout the year, and there are usually several per Congress. During the 94th Congress (1975-77), for example, there were nine special House elections held to replace members who had died or resigned.

In the 95th Congress, six special elections were held to replace members who had been appointed or elected to other offices or resigned. As of mid-March 1980, three special elections had been held for the 96th Congress.

Sometimes there are delays in the calling of a special election. One of the longest periods in recent years when a congressional district went unrepresented occurred in 1959-60. On April 28, 1959, Rep. James G. Polk (D 1931-41, 1949-59) of the Ohio 6th District died. But not until November 1960 was there an election to replace Polk. It was held simultaneously with the general election, and the winner, Ward M. Miller (R), served only the two months remaining in the term. For the full term, both Republicans and Democrats nominated different candidates than those for the short term.

In the days of the lame-duck sessions of Congress, elections for the remainder of a term were quite often held simultaneously with the general election, because the session following the election was an important, working meeting which lasted until March 4. However, since the passage of the 20th Amendment and the ending of most

House Makeup, Party Gains and Losses

	97th Congress Seats	Dem.	Rep.	98th Congress Seats	Dem.	Rep.	Gain/Loss		97th Congress Seats	Dem.	Rep.	98th Congress Seats	Dem.	Rep.	Gain/Loss
Ala.	7	4	3	7	5	2	+1D/-1R	Neb.	3	0	3	3	0	3	
Alaska	1	0	1	1	0	1		Nev.	1	1	0	2	1	1	+1R
Ariz.	4	2	2	5	2	3	+1R	N.H.	2	1	1	2	1	1	
Ark.	4	2	2	4	2	2		N.J.	15	8	7	14	9	5	+1D/-2R
Calif.	43	22	21	45	28	17	+6D/-4R	N.M.	2	0	2	3	1	2	+1D
Colo.	5	3	2	6	3	3	+1R	N.Y.	39	22	17	34	20	14	-2D/-3R
Conn.	6	4	2	6	4	2		N.C.	11	7	4	11	9	2	+2D/-2R
Del.	1	0	1	1	1	0	+1D/-1R	N.D.	1	1	0	1	1	0	
Fla.	15	11	4	19	13	6	+2D/+2R	Ohio	23	10	13	21	10	11	-2R
Ga.	10	9	1	10	9	1		Okla.	6	5	1	6	5	1	
Hawaii	2	2	0	2	2	0		Ore.	4	3	1	5	3	2	+1R
Idaho	2	0	2	2	0	2		Pa.	25	12	13	23	13	10	+1D/-3R
Ill.	24	10	14	22	12	10	+2D/-4R	R.I.	2	1	1	2	1	1	
Ind.	11	6	5	10	5	5	-1D	S.C.	6	2	4	6	3	3	+1D/-1R
Iowa	6	3	3	6	3	3		S.D.	2	1	1	1	1	0	-1R
Kan.	5	1	4	5	2	3	+1D/-1R	Tenn.	8	5	3	9	6	3	+1D
Ky.	7	4	3	7	4	3		Texas	24	19	5	27	22	5	+3D
La.	8	6	2	8	6	2		Utah	2	0	2	3	0	3	+1R
Maine	2	0	2	2	0	2		Vt.	1	0	1	1	0	1	
Md.	8	7	1	8	7	1		Va.	10	1	9	10	4	6	+3D/-3R
Mass.	12	10	2	11	10	1	-1R	Wash.	7	5	2	8	5	3	+1R
Mich.	19	12	7	18	12	6	-1R	W.Va.	4	2	2	4	4	0	+2D/-2R
Minn.	8	3	5	8	5	3	+2D/-2R	Wis.	9	5	4	9	5	4	
Miss.	5	4	1	5	3	2	+1R/-1D	Wyo.	1	0	1	1	0	1	
Mo.	10	6	4	9	6	3	-1R	TOTALS	435	243	192	435	269	166	+26D/-26R
Mont.	2	1	1	2	1	1									

lame-duck sessions, elections for the remaining two months of a term have become less usual. Miller, for example, was never sworn in because Congress was never in session during the time he was a representative.

Usually, states are more prompt in holding special House elections than was Ohio in 1959-60. One of the most rapid instances of succession occurred in Texas' 10th Congressional District in 1963. Rep. Homer Thornberry (D 1949-63) submitted his resignation on Sept. 26, 1963, to take effect Dec. 20. On the strength of Thornberry's post-dated resignation, a special election was held in his district — the first election was held Nov. 9 and the runoff on Dec. 17.

The winner, J. J. Pickle (D) was ready to take his seat as soon as Thornberry stepped down, and was sworn in the next day, Dec. 21, 1963.

House Districts for the 1980s

Republicans were supposed to do well in the 1982 elections for the U.S. House of Representatives. A popular Republican president sat in the White House, the nation seemed to be taking a rightward political turn and the reapportionment mandated by the 1980 Census shifted a large number of U.S. House seats from the Democratic North to the more conservative Sun Belt.

It did not work out that way. With a substantial edge in the number of state legislatures they controlled, particularly in those states that gained House seats, Democrats were able to draw congressional district maps that helped them and hurt their opponents. In the 1982 elections, Democrats won 26 additional House seats, including 10 of the seats created by redistricting.

The Sun Belt proved the Republicans' greatest disappointment. The GOP had hoped to take control of a dozen House seats that were shifted to that region and to the far West states. But Democratic legislative cartography and unfriendly federal court action got in the way, and in the end Democrats won 10 of the 17.

Democrats also managed to sidestep the brunt of district losses in the Northeast and Midwest. Legislative map makers eliminated Republican seats in Illinois and New Jersey, even though the population decline had been in urban Democratic areas. In the November elections, anti-Republican economic resentments took over, bringing victory to several Democrats in new districts that were nominally Democratic but had been voting conservatively in recent years.

In all, in the 10 Northern states that lost districts, Republicans came out 18 seats short of where they stood before the 1982 election.

In most of the 11 states that gained seats, the GOP seemed the natural beneficiary of demographic changes. All 11 were carried by Ronald Reagan in the 1980 presidential race and eight went for Republican Gerald R. Ford in 1976.

Nonetheless, legislatures or courts in six of the states drew new districts favoring or leaning to Democrats. And, contrary to the predictions, not one of these new constituencies nominated a conservative Democrat for a House seat. As a result, liberals, including four Hispanics, made up a large portion of the Sun Belt's House contingent in the 98th Congress.

What might have a more lasting impact on the nation and its representative government was the new use to which the Supreme Court's edict of one person, one vote was put in the redistricting that followed the 1980 Census. In California, New Jersey and points between, Republicans and Democrats justified highly partisan remaps by demonstrating respect for the 1964 Supreme Court mandate that populations of congressional districts within states had to be made as equal as possible. Other interests at stake in redistricting, such as the preservation of community boundaries and the grouping of constituencies with similar concerns, were brushed aside.

The Supreme Court itself seemed to approve this kind of partisan mapmaking. In June 1983 it overturned New Jersey's congressional district map on the ground that the population variations among the districts — the greatest of which was 0.69 percent — were too large and therefore unconstitutional. In its opinion the court ignored the fact that the map divided townships and cut up counties all across the state solely to give the Democrats a political advantage. *(Status of redistricting, see box, p. 126)*

Other states had population variations as great or greater than New Jersey's. But it appeared unlikely that many of these plans would be challenged in court. What seemed more uncertain was how the Supreme Court's decision would affect the redistricting scheduled to follow the 1990 Census.

The 1980 Census count confirmed that there was a dramatic decline in America's big city population during the 1970s. Most central city districts suffered severe shrinkage, and older suburban districts experienced slow growth or none at all.

And there was substantial movement of the population from North to South and East to West. As a result, 17 House seats shifted from states in the Northeast and Midwest, the so-called Snow Belt, to those in the Sun Belt states of the South and West. Florida was the biggest gainer, receiving four new seats. Texas picked up three additional seats; California, two; and Arizona, Colorado, Nevada, New Mexico, Oregon, Tennessee, Utah and Washington, one each.

New York, which lost almost 700,000 people in the 1970s, according to the census, was hit with a five-seat loss, the biggest one-time drop-off in House representation since New York and Virginia lost six seats each in 1840. Illinois,

Status of Congressional Redistricting

(As of March 15, 1984)

State	Redistricting Action
Alabama	Legislative plan enacted Aug. 18, 1981.
Arizona	Federal court approved legislative plan April 2, 1982.
Arkansas	Federal court plan enacted Feb. 25, 1982.
California	Voters in 1982 rejected legislative plan, which was used for that year's elections. Slightly revised plan signed by Gov. Edmund G. Brown Jr. before he left office in January 1983 is being challenged by the state's Republicans but will be used for the 1984 elections.
Colorado	Federal court plan enacted Jan. 28, 1982.
Connecticut	Special commission plan enacted Oct. 28, 1981.
Florida	Legislative plan enacted May 23, 1982.
Georgia	First plan voided by Justice Department. Second legislative plan enacted Aug. 8, 1982.
Hawaii	Federal court approved special commission plan May 5, 1982.
Idaho	Legislative plan enacted July 30, 1981.
Illinois	Federal court plan enacted Nov. 23, 1981.
Indiana	Legislative plan enacted May 5, 1981.
Iowa	Legislative plan enacted Aug. 20, 1981.
Kansas	Federal court plan enacted June 2, 1982.
Kentucky	Legislative plan enacted March 10, 1982.
Louisiana	Legislative plan approved Nov. 12, 1981. Two New Orleans districts voided by federal court Sept. 24, 1983. New legislative plan signed by Gov. David C. Treen Dec. 19, 1983.
Maine	Special commission plan enacted March 30, 1983.
Maryland	Special commission plan enacted April 9, 1982.
Massachusetts	Legislative plan enacted Dec. 16, 1981.
Michigan	Federal court plan enacted May 17, 1982.
Minnesota	Federal court plan enacted March 11, 1982.
Mississippi	First plan voided by Justice Department. Federal court enacted temporary plan June 9, 1982, for that year's election, but new plan was under populated and a permanent plan had not been finalized as of March 15, 1983.
Missouri	Federal court plan enacted Dec. 28, 1981.
Montana	Special commission plan enacted March 4, 1983.
Nebraska	Legislative plan enacted May 28, 1981.
Nevada	Legislative plan enacted June 3, 1981.
New Hampshire	Legislative plan enacted March 4, 1982.
New Jersey	Legislative plan, voided by federal court March 3, 1982, used for 1982 elections; Supreme Court upheld lower court ruling June 22, 1983. After New Jersey's Republican governor and the Democratic-controlled Legislature were unable to agree on a new plan, a three-judge federal panel on Feb. 17, 1984, handed down a new redistricting plan.
New Mexico	Legislative plan enacted Jan. 19, 1982.
New York	First plan voided by Justice Department. Second legislative plan enacted July 2, 1982.
North Carolina	First plan voided by Justice Department. Second legislative plan enacted Feb. 11, 1982.
Ohio	Legislative plan enacted March 25, 1982. Subsequently, a federal judicial panel Jan. 30, 1984, struck down the plan because of unacceptable variations in population. Ohio officials have appealed the decision.
Oklahoma	Voters approved legislative plan Nov. 2, 1982.
Oregon	Legislative plan enacted Aug. 22, 1981.
Pennsylvania	Legislative plan enacted March 3, 1982.
Rhode Island	Legislative plan enacted April 9, 1982.
South Carolina	Federal court plan enacted March 8, 1982.
Tennessee	Legislative plan enacted June 17, 1981.
Texas	First plan voided by Justice Department Jan. 29, 1982. Federal court plan overturned by Supreme Court April 11, 1982. Second legislative plan enacted June 19, 1983.
Utah	Legislative plan enacted Nov. 11, 1981.
Virginia	Legislative plan enacted June 12, 1981.
Washington	Legislative plan voided in federal court Nov. 30, 1982. Special commission plan enacted March 29, 1983.
West Virginia	Legislative plan enacted Feb. 8, 1982.
Wisconsin	Legislative plan enacted March 25, 1982.

Ohio and Pennsylvania each lost two seats, while Indiana, Massachusetts, Michigan, Missouri, New Jersey and South Dakota lost one each.

Drawing the Lines

Only 44 states went through the redistricting process. The other six — Alaska, Delaware, North Dakota, South Dakota, Vermont and Wyoming — each have only one representative elected at large.

Anticipating the apparent gains the population shifts would give the GOP — and anxious to capitalize on them — the Republicans undertook a nationwide campaign to win control of more state legislatures in preparation for the critical 1981 redistricting process. They had only scattered success in the November 1980 elections. Democrats still controlled 28 of the nation's state legislatures, while the Republicans held only 15. (The remaining legislatures were divided, except for Nebraska, which has a unicameral, nonpartisan legislature.)

Despite this nationwide disadvantage, Republicans in individual states were able to hold their own. In Florida, for example, the Democratic legislature drew only one new safe Democratic House seat; the other three were expected to be competitive. In the November 1982 elections the Democrats won two, and the Republicans won the other two.

In several states where one or the other party was firmly in control, the redistricting process was overtly partisan. In Indiana the district map passed by the Republican-controlled Legislature April 30, 1981, was a textbook case of gerrymandering. Republicans drew the plan with the help of Market Opinion Research Corp.'s sophisticated computer system at a cost of more than $250,000. Its lines wove freely in and out of counties, concentrating Democratic voting strength into the districts of just three of the state's six Democratic incumbents and damaging the reelection prospects of the other three.

The state's Republicans made no apologies for their plan. As early as December 1980 they had made it clear they would take full advantage of their control of state government to secure a majority in Indiana's U. S. House delegation in the 1982 elections. As it turned out, their elaborate schemes went for nought, at least in 1982. The line-up after the election was five Republicans and five Democrats.

Various partisan redistricting plans drawn up by Democratic-controlled legislatures were the focus of GOP attacks. For example, California's plan, crafted by Democratic Rep. Phillip Burton (1964-83), was designed to bring five more Democrats into the state's House delegation, which increased from 43 to 45 after the 1980 Census. When Rep. William M. Thomas, R-Calif., called Burton's plan "an abomination," Burton countered that the Democrats had done only what Republicans had done in Indiana and were attempting to do in Washington and Colorado.

California Republicans filed sufficient signatures to hold a referendum on Burton's redistricting plan, and in June 1982 the state's voters rejected the map. However, six months earlier the state supreme court had ruled that the Burton plan would stay in effect for the 1982 elections. A slightly revised plan then was passed by the California Legislature in December 1982 and signed into law by Gov. Edmund G. Brown just before he left office in January 1983. That plan also was challenged by the Republicans. However, a GOP-sponsored redistricting initiative, which Republicans hoped to take to the voters in a special election that December, was blocked in September 1983 by the state Supreme Court. The court's action all but assured that the revised Democratic-drawn district lines would go into effect for the 1984 elections.

Court-imposed Plans

Sometimes, states cannot come up with a plan at all. This usually happens in states where control of the legislature is split between the parties, or where the governor's party does not control the state legislature. Philosophical or personal differences sometimes can interfere, even within parties. When deadlocks occur, the task of redistricting falls to the federal courts.

In Illinois, which lost two seats, no compromise could be reached between competing Democratic and Republican redistricting plans in 1981, and both parties filed suit in federal district court in Chicago. A three-judge panel, which included two judges with Republican backgrounds, heard the case and decided in favor of the Democratic plan. The Illinois Republicans' appeal to the U.S. Supreme Court was rejected.

A sharp drop in St. Louis' population cost Missouri one congressional seat. For most of 1981 it appeared that the problem might have to be solved by placing Democratic incumbents William Clay, a veteran black legislator, and Richard A. Gephardt, a "rising star," in the same district. The Democratic-dominated Legislature rejected this plan and failed to come up with another, leaving the decision up to a federal court panel. Much to the relief of the Democrats, the judicial plan penalized the Republicans, eliminating GOP Rep. Wendell Bailey's 8th District and forcing incumbent Republican Bill Emerson into a heavily Democratic district.

After Democratic Gov. Richard D. Lamm vetoed three redistricting maps passed by the Republican majority in Colorado's Legislature, a federal judge ordered Lamm and the legislative redistricting committee to negotiate. Talks in November 1981 failed to produce a compromise plan, so a federal court in Denver was given responsibility for drawing the district lines. The state gained one House seat, which Republicans easily won.

Minorities and Maps

Several states that managed to pass redistricting plans still had to clear another hurdle. Under the Voting Rights Act of 1965, the Justice Department had to approve redistricting plans in Alabama, Arizona, Georgia, Louisiana, Mississippi, South Carolina, Texas and Virginia, and in parts of California, Colorado, Connecticut, Florida, Hawaii, Idaho, Maine, Massachusetts, Michigan, New Hampshire, New Mexico, New York, North Carolina and Oklahoma. The department could reject any redistricting plans in these states that diluted the voting strength or in any other way discriminated against blacks and other minorities.

This happened in several states in 1981. The North Carolina redistricting plan included a district that protected incumbent Democrat L. H. Fountain by curving around the heavily black community in Durham and the liberal university town of Chapel Hill. The Justice Department rejected the plan on Dec. 8, ruling that the "strangely irregular shape" of "Fountain's Fishhook" raised questions about the racial motivations of the state legislators. The legislators drew a second map, which put Durham County in Fountain's district. That map was approved, Fountain decided to retire and a black came close to winning the Democratic nomination, winning 46 percent of the vote in a runoff.

In Georgia the Justice Department ruled that the Legislature improperly divided a "cohesive black community" in the Atlanta area between the 4th and 5th districts, reducing the chances that either would elect a black candidate to the House. Legislators then drew a plan that passed Justice Department review, but the elections for those two seats were postponed nearly a month to Nov. 30, 1982.

In Mississippi, Justice Department rejection of the legislative map resulted in creation of the state's first black-majority district since 1966. But the Mississippi 2nd district was only 54 percent black, and civil rights leaders continued to pursue the matter in federal court. A federal panel in December 1983 unveiled a new map that raised the black population of the district to 58 percent. But it then was discovered that the total population of the revised district was 6,000 below the ideal district population for the state, necessitating further changes. As of March 1984, the Mississippi map still was pending in court.

In Louisiana, blacks demanded the creation of a black-majority district in New Orleans, a concept endorsed by both the state House and state Senate. Republican Gov. David Treen opposed the black-majority district because the resulting boundaries would have endangered the seat of U.S. Rep. Bob Livingston, R, who represented the New Orleans suburbs. The governor prevailed upon legislators

Voluntary Departures From Capitol Hill 1946-1984

House
- Running for Other Office (white)
- Retiring from Public Life (gray)

Senate
- Not Running for Re-election

*As of March 30, 1984

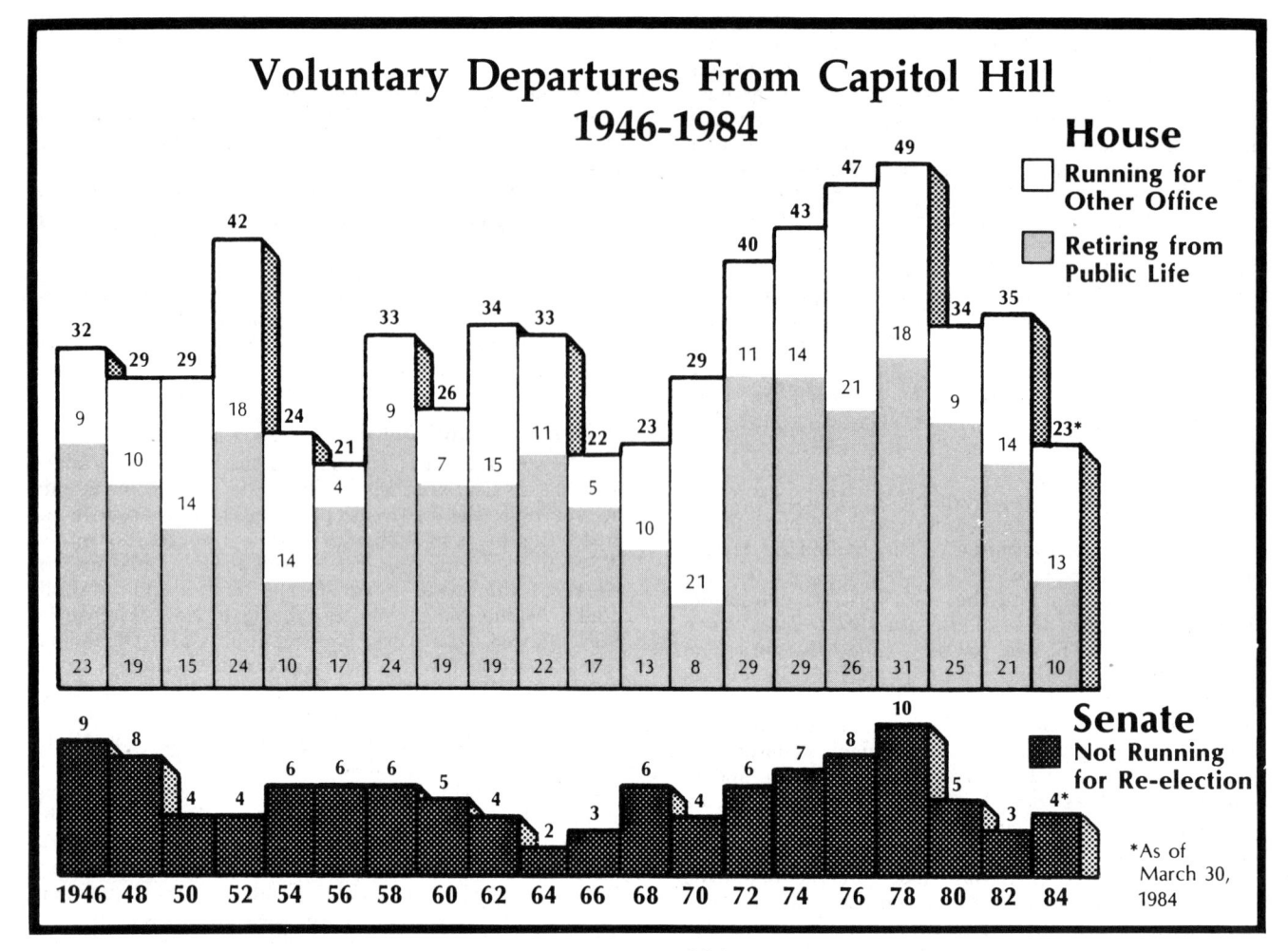

to approve a remap protecting incumbents, and the Justice Department approved that map. Blacks then went to court, which threw out the New Orleans district lines on Sept. 24, 1983.

That action forced the state Legislature to redraw the district's lines. The new boundaries, within the city of New Orleans, included a majority of blacks (58 percent). Gov. Treen signed the revised map on Dec. 19.

Hispanics were the beneficiaries of Justice Department review in Texas. In January 1982 the department ruled that the map improperly diluted the Hispanic vote in two south Texas districts by making one of them 80 percent Hispanic and the other 52 percent Hispanic.

A federal court subsequently drew a map redistributing the voters in those two districts, and Hispanics won both seats in 1982.

Ohio Reversal

In Ohio a federal judicial panel struck down the state's revised 1982 congressional district map. The three-judge panel ruled Jan. 30, 1984, that Ohio's 21 districts (a loss of two seats as a result of the 1980 Census) had constitutionally unacceptable variations in population. The state had to devise new districts by March 1984. A plan had been enacted without major controversy on March 25, 1982.

Ohio officials appealed the decision and also requested a stay to allow the November 1984 congressional elections to proceed under the existing boundaries. On Feb. 17, 1984, the judges agreed to allow Ohio to conduct its 1984 elections under the existing boundaries, giving the state a reprieve from the difficult task of redrawing its congressional district map. Meanwhile, state officials went ahead with their effort to appeal the ruling to the Supreme Court.

Gubernatorial Elections

Governors were not popular in Revolutionary days. During the colonial era, the British-appointed governors were the symbols of the mother country's control and, the revolutionaries argued, of tyranny.

During the years before the Revolutionary War, colonial assemblies were able to assert their control over appropriations and thus became the champions of colonial rights against the governors. Thus, when forming their own state constitutions, the newly-freed Americans tended to look with suspicion on the office of governor and gave most of the power to the legislative bodies.

For these reasons, early American governors found themselves hedged in by restrictions. Among such restrictions were both the length of the term of office and the method of election.

Length of Terms

As of 1789, all four New England states — Connecticut, Massachusetts, New Hampshire, and Rhode Island, (Vermont was admitted in 1791 and Maine in 1820) — held gubernatorial elections every year. Some of the Middle Atlantic states favored somewhat longer terms — New York and Pennsylvania had three-year terms for their governors, although New Jersey had a one-year term. The border and Southern states had a mix — Maryland and North Carolina governors served a one-year term, South Carolina had a two-year term, and Delaware, Virginia and Georgia had three-year terms. No state had a four-year term.

Over the years, states have changed the length of gubernatorial terms. With some occasional back and forth movement, the general trend has been toward lengthening terms. New York, for example, has changed the term of office of its governor four times. Starting in 1777 with a three-year term, the state switched to a two-year term in 1820, back to a three-year term in 1876, back to a two-year term in 1894, and to a four-year term beginning in 1938.

Maryland is another example of a state which has had several changes in its gubernatorial term. Beginning with a one-year term in 1776, the state extended the term to three years in 1838, then to four years in 1851. Regular gubernatorial elections were held every second odd year from then through 1923, when the state had one three-year term in order to hold elections in the future in even numbered years, beginning in 1926. Thus, the state held gubernatorial elections in 1919, 1923, 1926, 1930, 1934, 1938, etc.

The trend toward longer gubernatorial terms shows up clearly by comparing the length of terms in 1900 and 1980. *(Box, p. 130)* Of the 45 states in the Union in 1900, 22, almost half, had two-year terms. One (New Jersey) had a three-year term, while Rhode Island and Massachusetts were the only states left with one-year terms. The remaining 20 states had four-year gubernatorial terms.

But by 1980, 41 of those same states had four-year terms; in addition, the five states admitted to the Union since 1900 — Oklahoma (1907), Arizona and New Mexico (1912), Alaska (1958) and Hawaii (1959) — had four-year gubernatorial terms as of 1980. This left only four states with two-year terms: New Hampshire, Vermont, Rhode Island, and Arkansas.

Non-presidential Year Elections

Along with the change to longer terms for governors came another trend — away from holding gubernatorial elections in presidential election years. With the exception of North Dakota, every state in the 20th century to switch to four-year gubernatorial terms scheduled its elections in non-presidential years. Moreover, Florida, which held its quadrennial gubernatorial elections in presidential years, changed to non-presidential years in 1966. In order to make the switch, the state shortened to two years the term of the governor elected in 1964, then resumed the four-year term in 1966. Thus, Florida held gubernatorial elections in 1960, 1964, 1966, 1970 and 1974.

Illinois made a similar switch in 1976-78, leaving only nine states — Delaware, Indiana, Missouri, Montana, North Carolina, North Dakota, Utah, Washington, and West Virginia — holding quadrennial gubernatorial elections at the same time as the presidential election. (Louisiana holds its gubernatorial election in presidential years, but early in the year instead of November; Arkansas, New Hampshire, Rhode Island, and Vermont still have two-year terms, so every other gubernatorial election in

Length of Governor Terms

State	1900	1984	Year of change to longer term
Alabama	2	4	—
Alaska*	—	4	—
Arizona*	—	4	1970
Arkansas	2	2	—
California	4	4	—
Colorado	2	4	1958
Connecticut	2	4	1950
Delaware	4	4	—
Florida	4	4	—
Georgia	2	4	1942
Hawaii*	—	4	—
Idaho	2	4	1946
Illinois	4	4	—
Indiana	4	4	—
Iowa	2	4	1974
Kansas	2	4	1974
Kentucky	4	4	—
Louisiana	4	4	—
Maine	2	4	1958
Maryland	4	4	—
Massachusetts	1	4	1920, 1966†
Michigan	2	4	1966
Minnesota	2	4	1962
Mississippi	4	4	—
Missouri	4	4	—
Montana	4	4	—
Nebraska	2	4	1966
Nevada	4	4	—
New Hampshire	2	2	—
New Jersey	3	4	1949
New Mexico	—	4	1970
New York	2	4	1938
North Carolina	4	4	—
North Dakota	2	4	1964
Ohio	2	4	1958
Oklahoma*	—	4	—
Oregon	4	4	—
Pennsylvania	4	4	—
Rhode Island	1	2	1912
South Carolina	2	4	1926
South Dakota	2	4	1974
Tennessee	1	4	1954
Texas	2	4	1974
Utah	4	4	—
Vermont	2	2	—
Virginia	4	4	—
Washington	4	4	—
West Virginia	4	4	—
Wisconsin	2	4	1970
Wyoming	4	4	—

* Oklahoma was admitted to the Union in 1907, Arizona and New Mexico in 1912, Alaska in 1958 and Hawaii in 1959. Oklahoma, Alaska and Hawaii have always had four-year gubernatorial terms; Arizona started with a two-year term and switched to four years in 1970. New Mexico (1912) began with a four-year term, changed to two years in 1916, and back to four years in 1970.

† Massachusetts switched from a one- to a two-year term in 1920 and to a four-year term in 1966.

SOURCE: State secretaries of state.

these four states occurs in a presidential year.)

Methods of Election

Yet another way in which Americans of the early federal period hemmed in their governors was by the method of election. In 1789, only in New York and the four New England states (Connecticut, Massachusetts, New Hampshire and Rhode Island) did the people directly choose their governors by popular vote. In the remaining eight states, governors were chosen by the state legislatures, thus enhancing the power of the legislatures in their dealing with the governors. But the democratic trend to elect public officials directly, the diminishing distrust of the office of governor, and the need for a stronger and more independent chief executive, led to the gradual introduction of popular votes in all the states.

By the 1860s, the remaining eight original states had all switched to popular ballots. Pennsylvania was first, in 1790, and was followed by Delaware in 1792, Georgia in 1824, North Carolina in 1835, Maryland in 1838, New Jersey in 1844, Virginia in 1851, and South Carolina in 1865, after the Civil War.

All the states admitted to the Union after the original 13, with one exception, made provision from the very beginning for popular election of their governors. The exception was Louisiana, which from its admission in 1812 until a change in the state constitution in 1845 had a unique system of gubernatorial elections. The people participated, in that they voted in a first-step popular election. But then, in a second step, the Legislature was to select the governor from the two candidates receiving the highest popular vote.

Number of Terms

Another aspect of limitations placed on governors is a restriction on the number of terms they are allowed to serve. In the early years, at least three states had such limitations — governors of Maryland were eligible to serve three consecutive one-year terms, and then were required to retire for at least one year; Pennsylvania allowed its governors three consecutive three-year terms and then forced retirement for at least one term; and in New Jersey, according to the constitution of 1844, a governor could serve only one three-year term before retiring for at least one term.

In 1980, just over half the states — 27 — placed some sort of limitation on the number of consecutive terms their governors may serve. Of these 27, six prohibited their governors from serving more than one term in a row, permitting them to serve again after an interim of at least one term. The remaining 21 states allowed their governors to seek reelection once, but they must step down after two terms for an interim of at least one term. Three exceptions to that general rule — Delaware, North Carolina and Missouri — impose an absolute two-term limit. That is, a governor may serve only two terms, however spaced, in his lifetime. The remaining 23 states impose no limits on the number of consecutive terms a governor may serve. *(Box, p. 131)*

Majority Vote Requirement

A peculiarity of gubernatorial voting which has almost disappeared from the American political scene is the requirement that the winning gubernatorial candidate receive a majority of the popular vote. Otherwise, the choice devolves upon the state legislature or, in one case, necessitates a runoff between the two highest candidates. Centered in New England, this practice was used mainly in the 19th century. All six New England states, plus Georgia, had such a provision in their state constitutions at one time. New Hampshire, Vermont, Massachusetts, and Connecticut already had the provision when they entered the Union from 1789 to 1791.

Rhode Island required a majority election, but did not adopt a provision for legislative election until 1842. *(See p. 132)* Maine adopted the provision when it split off from Massachusetts to form a separate state in 1820; Georgia put the provision in its constitution when it switched from legislative to popular election of governors in 1825.

The purpose of the majority provision appears to have been to safeguard against a candidate in a multiple field winning with a small fraction of the popular vote. In most of New England, the provision was part of the early state constitutions, formed largely in the 1780s, before the development of the two party system.

The prospect of multiple-candidate fields diminished with the coming of the two party system. Nevertheless, each of these states had occasion to use the provision at least once. Sometimes, in an extremely close election, minor party candidates received enough of a vote to keep the winner from getting a majority of the total vote. And at other times, strong third party movements or disintegration of the old party structure resulted in the election being thrown into the state legislatures.

Vermont still maintains the majority vote provision, although the Legislature has not elected a governor since 1912. Georgia maintains the requirement for a majority vote for governor, but instead of legislative election, provides for a runoff between the top two contenders three weeks after the general election.[1]

Following are the states which had the majority vote provision for governor, the years in which the choice devolved on the Legislature because of it, and the year in which the requirement was repealed or changed:

No gubernatorial candidate received a majority of the popular vote, thus throwing the election into the Legislature in the following years subsequent to 1824: 1833, 1834, 1842, 1844, 1846, 1849, 1850, 1851, 1854, 1855, 1856, 1878, 1884, 1886, 1888, and 1890. Following the election of 1890, the Legislature was unable to choose a new governor, so the outgoing governor, Morgan G. Bulkeley (R) continued to serve through the entire new term (1891-93). The provision was repealed in 1901. The years prior to 1824 in which the provision was used, if any, were unavailable from the Connecticut secretary of state's office.

Although the majority vote requirement was contained in the constitution as early as 1825, it was not used until the 20th century. In 1966, with an emerging Republican Party, a controversial Democratic nominee, and an independent Democrat all in the gubernatorial race, no candidate received a majority. The Legislature chose Democrat Lester Maddox. It was the controversy surrounding this experience which led to the change from legislative choice to a runoff among the top two contenders. Earlier, in 1946, the Georgia Legislature also attempted to choose the governor, under unusual circumstances not covered by the majority vote requirement. The governor-elect, Eugene Talmadge (D) died before taking office. The Legislature, when it met, chose Talmadge's son, Herman E. Talmadge, as the new gover-

---

[1] Mississippi has a majority vote provision under the 1890 state constitution, but the provision has not been used because the Democratic Party nominee has always received a majority.

Limitations on Governor Terms
(As of 1984)

State	Maximum number of consecutive terms
Alabama	2
Alaska	2
Arizona	No limit
Arkansas	No limit
California	No limit
Colorado	No limit
Connecticut	No limit
Delaware	2*
Florida	2
Georgia	2
Hawaii	No limit
Idaho	No limit
Illinois	No limit
Indiana	2
Iowa	No limit
Kansas	2
Kentucky	0
Louisiana	2
Maine	2
Maryland	2
Massachusetts	No limit
Michigan	No limit
Minnesota	No limit
Mississippi	0
Missouri	2*
Montana	No limit
Nebraska	2
Nevada	2
New Hampshire	No limit
New Jersey	2
New Mexico	0
New York	No limit
North Carolina	2*
North Dakota	No limit
Ohio	2
Oklahoma	2
Oregon	2
Pennsylvania	2
Rhode Island	No limit
South Carolina	2
South Dakota	2
Tennessee	2
Texas	No limit
Utah	No limit
Vermont	No limit
Virginia	0
Washington	2
West Virginia	No limit
Wisconsin	No limit
Wyoming	No limit

* indicates an absolute two term limit. That is, no person may serve more than two gubernatorial terms in his lifetime. In other states with limitations, a governor may serve as many terms as he may be elected to, provided he retires after one, or two, terms, depending on the constitutional provisions of his state, and stays out of office at least one term before running again.

0 indicates the governor must retire at the end of his first term. After a one term interim, he may serve again.

2 indicates the governor must retire after two consecutive terms. After a one term interim, he may serve again.

SOURCE: *The Book of the States, 1978-79*, Vol. XX, The Council of State Governments, Lexington, Ky., 1978.

Occupants of the Nation's Statehouses

Below is a list of the governors of the 50 states as of January 1984, and the year in which each office is next up for election. The names of governors elected in 1982 or 1983 are *italicized*. Asterisks (*) denote the incumbents re-elected in either of those two years.

Alabama — *George C. Wallace (D) 1986*
Alaska — *Bill Sheffield (D) 1986*
Arizona — Bruce Babbitt (D) 1986*
Arkansas — Bill Clinton (D) 1984
California — *George Deukmejian (R) 1986*
Colorado — Richard D. Lamm (D) 1986*
Connecticut — William A. O'Neill (D) 1986*
Delaware — Pierre S. "Pete" du Pont IV (R) 1984
Florida — Robert Graham (D) 1986*
Georgia — *Joe Frank Harris (D) 1986*
Hawaii — George Ariyoshi (D) 1986*
Idaho — John V. Evans (D) 1986*
Illinois — *James R. Thompson (R) 1986*
Indiana — Robert D. Orr (R) 1984
Iowa — *Terry Branstad (R) 1986*
Kansas — John Carlin (D) 1986*
Kentucky — *Martha Layne Collins (D) 1987*
Louisiana — *Edwin Edwards (D) 1987*
Maine — *Joseph E. Brennan (D) 1986*
Maryland — *Harry R. Hughes (D) 1986*
Massachusetts — *Michael S. Dukakis (D) 1986*
Michigan — *James J. Blanchard (D) 1986*
Minnesota — *Rudy Perpich (D) 1986*
Mississippi — *Bill Allain (D) 1987*
Missouri — Christopher S. "Kit" Bond (R) 1984

Montana — Ted Schwinden (D) 1984
Nebraska — *Bob Kerrey (D) 1986*
Nevada — *Richard H. Bryan (D) 1986*
New Hampshire — *John H. Sununu (R) 1984*
New Jersey — Thomas H. Kean (R) 1985
New Mexico — *Toney Anaya (D) 1986*
New York — *Mario M. Cuomo (D) 1986*
North Carolina — James B. Hunt Jr. (D) 1984
North Dakota — Allen I. Olson (R) 1984
Ohio — *Richard F. Celeste (D) 1986*
Oklahoma — *George Nigh (D) 1986**
Oregon — *Victor G. Atiyeh (R) 1986**
Pennsylvania — *Richard L. Thornburgh (R) 1986**
Rhode Island — *J. Joseph Garrahy (D) 1984**
South Carolina — *Richard Riley (D) 1986**
South Dakota — *William J. Janklow (R) 1986**
Tennessee — *Lamar Alexander (R) 1986**
Texas — *Mark White (D) 1986*
Utah — Scott M. Matheson (D) 1984
Vermont — *Richard A. Snelling (R) 1984**
Virginia — Charles S. Robb (D) 1985
Washington — John Spellman (R) 1984
West Virginia — John D. "Jay" Rockefeller IV (D) 1984
Wisconsin — *Anthony S. Earl (D) 1986*
Wyoming — *Ed Herschler (D) 1986**

nor. Talmadge was eligible for consideration on the basis that he received enough write-in votes in the general election to make him the second-place candidate. But the state Supreme Court voided the Legislature's choice and declared that the lieutenant governor-elect, Melvin E. Thompson (D) should be governor.

Maine entered statehood in 1820 with a majority vote provision for governor and kept it until repeal in 1880. During this 60-year span, the Legislature was called on to choose the governor nine times, as follows: 1840, 1846, 1848, 1852, 1853, 1854, 1855, 1878 and 1879.

Like the other New England states, Massachusetts originally had a requirement for majority voting in gubernatorial elections. However, after six straight elections from 1848 to 1853 when the Legislature was forced to choose the governor, Massachusetts repealed the provision in 1855. The years in which it was used were as follows: 1785, 1833, 1842, 1843, 1845, 1848, 1849, 1850, 1851, 1852, 1853.

New Hampshire's mandated majority vote for governor was in force from 1784 through 1912, when it was repealed. The outcome of the following gubernatorial elections was determined by the Legislature: 1785, 1787, 1789, 1790, 1812, 1824, 1846, 1851, 1856, 1863, 1871, 1874, 1875, 1886, 1888, 1890, 1906, and 1912.

Under the constitution of 1842, Rhode Island required a majority to win the gubernatorial election. Under this mandate, the Legislature chose the governor in the years 1846, 1875, 1876, 1880, 1889, 1890, and 1891. Owing to a disagreement between the two houses of the state Legislature, the ballots for governor were not counted in 1893, and Gov. D. Russell Brown (R) continued in office for another term of one year. The provision for majority voting was then repealed.

Before 1842, there was also a requirement for a popular majority, but the Legislature was not allowed to choose a new governor if no candidate achieved a majority. Three times — in 1806, 1832 and 1839 — there was a lack of a majority in a gubernatorial election, with a different outcome each time. In 1806, the lieutenant governor-elect served as acting governor for the term. In 1832, the Legislature mandated a new election, but still no majority choice was reached; three more elections were held, all without a majority being achieved, so the same state officers were continued until the next regular election. And in 1839, when neither the gubernatorial nor lieutenant governor's race yielded a winner by majority, the senior state senator acted as governor for the term.

Vermont's provision for majority gubernatorial election resulted in the Legislature picking the governor 19 times: 1789, 1797, 1813, 1814, 1830, 1831, 1832, 1834, 1841, 1843, 1845, 1846, 1847, 1848, 1849, 1852, 1853, 1902, and 1912. On a twentieth occasion, 1835, the Legislature failed to choose a new governor because of a deadlock and the lieutenant governor-elect served as governor for the term. The Vermont provision remains in force.

Campaign Financing........ 133

Political Party Campaigning 135
Controls on Political Spending...................... 147
Incumbents' Campaign Funds — Jan. 1, 1984............ 156

Current Limits on Campaign Contributions

This table shows the limits on campaign contributions for federal elections. The figures are those in effect following the 1979 amendments to the 1971, 1974 and 1976 financing laws.

Contributions from:	To candidate or his/her authorized committee	**To national party committees[5] (per calendar year)[6]	**To any other committee (per calendar year)[6]	Total contributions (per calendar year)
Individual	$1,000 per election[3]	$20,000	$5,000	$25,000
Multicandidate committee[1]	$5,000 per election	$15,000	$5,000	No limit
Party committee	$1,000 or $5,000[4] per election	No limit	$5,000	No limit
Republican or Democratic senatorial campaign committee,[2] or the national party committee, or a combination of both**	$17,500 to Senate candidate per calendar year[6] in which candidate seeks election	Not applicable	No applicable	Not applicable
Any other committee	$1,000 per election	$20,000	$5,000	No limit

[1] A multicandidate committee is any committee with more than 50 contributors which has been registered for at least six months and with the exception of state party committees, has made contributions to five or more federal candidates.

[2] Republican and Democratic senatorial campaign committees are subject to all other limits applicable to a multicandidate committee.

[3] Each of the following elections is considered a separate election: primary election, general election, run-off election, special election and party caucus or convention which, instead of a primary, has authority to select the nominee.

[4] Limit depends on whether or not party committee is a multicandidate committee.

[5] For purposes of this limit, national party committee includes a party's national committee, the Republican and Democratic Senate and House campaign committees and any other committee established by the party's national committee, provided it is not authorized by any candidate.

[6] In 1976 only, and solely in the case of contribution limits established in the 1976 amendments (those indicated by a double asterisk), the calendar year extends from May 11 (date of enactment of the act) through Dec. 31, 1976.

[7] Calendar year extends from Jan. 1 through Dec. 31, 1976. Individual contributions made or earmarked before or after 1976 to influence the 1976 election of a specific candidate are counted as if made during 1976.

** See footnote 6.

Source: Federal Election Commission

Political Party Campaigning

In pure dollars and cents, the Democratic and Republican party organizations resemble David and Goliath. Even though Republicans have long been outnumbered by Democrats in Congress and state legislatures, the GOP towers over its rival in financial resources.

In the 1980 election cycle, the major federal-level Republican committees reportedly raised about $120 million, six times the total amount raised by their Democratic counterparts. And that degree of dominance was unlikely to end any time soon. Studies by the Citizens' Research Foundation have shown that Republican national committees have been perennially better off financially than Democratic national committees.

For example, in 1963 national Republican groups raised $3.3 million in contrast to $2.2 million raised by Democratic national committees. In 1971 the Republican committees collected $11.5 million, while the Democratic committees raised only $2.8 million.

The disparity grew even wider after passage of the Federal Election Campaign Act (FECA) amendments in 1974. The legislation placed a cap on how much individuals and Congress could contribute to national party organizations.

Under the FECA, individuals may give $20,000 a year to a national party committee and $5,000 to any state or local party committee. However, an individual's aggregate contribution in one year to parties, political action committees (PACs) and federal candidates cannot exceed $25,000.

PACs may give $15,000 a year to a national party and $5,000 to any state and local party. Their aggregate annual contribution is not limited.

The Republicans adjusted effectively to the declining influence of "fat cat" contributors by placing a heavier emphasis on direct mail contributions. By 1981 the Republican National Committee (RNC) asserted that it had a list of more than one million contributors, with most direct mail donors sending $25 or less.

The Democrats, shackled throughout the 1970s by a multimillion-dollar debt incurred in the 1968 campaign, were slow to emulate the Republicans. Without the money to launch an extensive direct mail effort, the federal-level Democratic committees were forced to rely on pre-FECA fund-raising techniques — large donor programs and special events such as $500- or $1,000-a-plate dinners. Large contributors enabled the Democratic Party to stay financially afloat, even though they could not be as generous to the party as they were before 1974. The 1980 elections pointed up the need for change to Democratic Party leaders, and slowly they began to play catch up with the Republicans.

Coping With the Laws

Each party has a welter of special committees set up to support its candidates. In all, the Republicans have six and the Democrats nine.

Most of them give relatively little money. But it is the six main national bodies — three for each party — that pack the heaviest financial weight. The Republicans' biggest givers are the RNC, the National Republican Senatorial Committee (NRSC) and the National Republican Congressional Committee (NRCC), which handles House candidates.

The Democrats have the Democratic National Committee (DNC), the Democratic Senatorial Campaign Committee (DSCC) and, for the House, the Democratic Congressional Campaign Committee (DCCC).

The DNC and the RNC have the broadest scope, dealing with both presidential and congressional races. The four other committees are dedicated solely to House or Senate candidates. In addition to giving money, the DNC and the RNC also run the national party conventions, and they push nationwide voter registration and Election Day get-out-the-vote drives.

GOP Advantage

The Democratic Party committees have portrayed themselves as poverty-stricken underdogs in an unfair battle with a money-bloated GOP. "We don't have the luxury of our Republican cousins to give the maximum to everybody," remarked DNC Treasurer Peter Kelly in 1980.

One reason the Democrats are behind financially is that their party is more prone to internal quarreling, which takes its toll. DNC fund raising was hindered in early 1980 by the divisive struggle for the Democratic presidential nomination between President Jimmy Carter and Sen. Edward M. Kennedy of Massachusetts. Although the DNC ultimately raised more than $12 million during the election year, three-quarters of it was not available until after July 1, when early planning should have been completed.

Also casting a large cloud over DNC fund-raising plans

has been the party's 16-year-old debt. Nearly all of that obligation was incurred in 1968 from the expenses of the Democratic convention and the party's assumption of the leftover debts from the presidential campaigns of Hubert H. Humphrey Jr. and Robert F. Kennedy.

But the debt was reduced only gradually. Initially $9.3 million, the indebtedness was whittled down by annual fund-raising telethons from 1972 through 1975. The DNC also settled part of its debts by paying some of its creditors 20 cents to 25 cents for each dollar owed. The Federal Election Commission (FEC) has strict regulations about how debts by political committees to corporations may be settled.

By December 1976 the DNC debt was reduced to $2.4 million. By paying off creditors — primarily airlines and telephone companies — in small increments, the DNC had trimmed the lingering debt to about $600,000 by late 1981. By 1984 the debt had been retired, according to a DNC spokesman, who explained that the committee had purchased an annuity through an insurance company. The company in turn had taken over responsibility for paying off the remaining debt.

However, the Republican financial lead has little to do with the Democratic debt or with the GOP being the so-called "party of the rich." The GOP's advantage owes more to better planning. Their committees have developed a large, ongoing direct mail solicitation program that the Democrats have been slow to emulate.

As Herbert E. Alexander, a University of Southern California political scientist, pointed out, "The Republicans are more professionalized than the Democrats at fund raising. They're able and willing to do prospecting [for mail contributors].... The Democrats haven't exploited their majority in Congress."

Ideology also is a factor in the Republican committees' financial edge. "The Republicans are a far less diverse party," explained one-time DNC political strategist Karl Struble. "The conservatives are in control there, and they can appeal to ideological zealots. Look at [President Gerald R.] Ford, who was a moderate. He did not do well at all in direct mail."

Three factors encouraged the GOP's direct mail push in the late 1970s. One was the FECA with its strict contribution limits. Another was the loss of the White House and with it access to some major donors. A third factor was congressional passage in 1978 of legislation giving national party committees special low rates on third-class bulk mail.

Fund-raising Methods

Direct mail provided much of the revenue for the three national GOP groups. In 1980 the NRSC, for example, had a base group of 350,000 donors culled from mailing lists it rented from *Business Week,* a magazine read by many corporate executives who traditionally vote Republican.

Ironically, direct mail's use as a political fund-raising device was first exploited in 1972 by a Democrat — George McGovern, the party's presidential nominee. The South Dakota senator appealed to liberals by letter and raised 40 percent, or $12 million, of his general election campaign receipts that way.

The Democrats continued to emphasize large fund-raising events, and only in the mid-1970s did the party organization begin to use direct mail. Observers attribute the delay to the man who chaired the DNC from 1972 to 1976, Robert S. Strauss, who managed President Carter's re-election campaign.

"Bob Strauss believed in those old-style fund-raisers where you go to the big contributors," said Fred Wertheimer, president of Common Cause, the public affairs lobby, and an authority on campaign finance.

According to an audit of DNC financial activity in 1980, 61 percent of the $26.5 million raised by the national committee from 1977 through 1980 came from major donors. Only 30 percent was raised through direct mail. Actually, more money was raised by the DNC through direct mail in 1976 than in 1980.

DNC Chairman Charles T. Manatt placed a new emphasis on direct mail fund raising after his election in early 1981. Manatt, a former chairman of the party's National Finance Council, hired the direct mail firm of Craver, Matthews, Smith, which had worked for independent presidential candidate John B. Anderson in 1980.

The firm's early efforts pointedly sought to tap national displeasure with the conservative policies of the Reagan administration and its allies. Large mailings decried proposed cutbacks in the Social Security system, while smaller mailings signed by former interior secretary Cecil Andrus, former Atlanta mayor Maynard Jackson and former assistant secretary of education Liz Carpenter sought to exploit liberal dissatisfaction with the new Republican administration on issues such as the environment and civil rights.

Apart from dinners and direct mail, the parties employed a variety of devices to spur donations. A popular method among Democrats was to sell paintings furnished by sympathetic artists such as Peter Max and Lowell Nesbitt.

But probably no project was more unusual than the DNC's proposed "VIP tour" of Egypt and Israel. For $10,000 an individual or $15,000 a couple, an interested Democrat would receive private meetings with Israeli Prime Minister Menachem Begin and Egyptian President Anwar Sadat. The assassination of Sadat in October 1981 forced postponement of the trip.

Both parties have elite groups of contributors who, in return for their generosity, can attend social functions and seminars hosted by party notables. At the beginning of the 1980s the DNC had the National Finance Council for individuals who give $5,000 annually and the Business Council for donations of at least $10,000 annually. Among congressional clubs was the Democratic House and Senate Council, with members paying $1,500 a year to belong.

Republicans had several groups. The top RNC club was the Republican Eagles, which cost $10,000 annually to belong. The Republican Senatorial Trust cost $5,000 to join, and the Republican Senatorial Inner Circle required a $1,000 contribution. Most of the groups had several hundred members each.

Supporting the Candidates

Under the landmark 1974 election law that established the existing campaign finance rules, party organization enjoys a privileged spot. The amount that party committees can spend on candidates is far higher than the amounts that can be spent by individuals and non-party PACs.

To many Democrats, the Republicans were circumventing the original intent of the law, passed by a Democratic Congress that believed the existing situation allowed rich Republicans to "buy" elections. The law placed a lid of $1,000 on what an individual could give to a campaign per election, and a limit of $5,000 for a PAC. National party committees, on the other hand, could spend up to $34,720 on a House election in 1980 and as much as $987,548 on a Senate race.

To assist their presidential nominees, the Democratic and Republican national party committees were each permitted to spend $4.6 million in 1980. The money could not be contributed to the candidate, but it could be spent in conjunction with him. State and local parties were allowed to spend unlimited amounts to conduct voter registration and get-out-the-vote and other grass-roots activities.

But only the Republicans have been able to capitalize on these advantages. Democratic Party committees were not able to come up with enough money to give anywhere near the maximum amounts.

To be sure, the campaign war chests of Democratic officeholders were hardly bare. The mere fact that they controlled Congress in the past gave Democrats the edge with money provided by PACs. In 1980, 93 percent of the contributions to congressional candidates by labor union PACs went to Democrats. And Democratic candidates snared about 40 percent of the political gifts made by business and trade association PACs.

Many Democratic candidates have another advantage over Republicans, GOP officials contend. "Our financial capability is not the advantage for us that incumbency is for the Democrats," remarked Charles Black, the Republican National Committee campaign director in 1978. The advantages of incumbency — use of the franking privilege for mail, public exposure, extensive staff — are significant.

Congressional Campaign Efforts

For years congressional campaign committees tended to be somnolent men's clubs that held a dinner once a year, funneled the proceeds to incumbents and did little else besides issue pronouncements of partisan optimism.

Today's campaign committees — Republican and Democratic — are very different. They are national political strategy centers that not only pump millions of dollars into campaigns but recruit House candidates, teach them campaign skills, mount national advertising efforts and conduct year-round polling. Republicans do far more of this because they have more money, but Democrats are moving in the same direction.

To some extent, the rise of the campaign committees is a story that applies to the Senate as well as the House. The National Republican Senatorial Committee and the Democratic Senatorial Campaign Committee also have grown in sophistication. But because the House organizations are so much larger, with hundreds of elections to focus on, they are the center of new ideas and the focus of the national strategy revival.

What this amounts to is a new nationalizing force in congressional elections. Every two years the local political parties seem to be less relevant in picking candidates for Congress. Nominees in many competitive districts today tend to be chosen with minimal participation by local party leaders.

But in many places the congressional committees are turning out to replace them. When the El Paso-based 16th District of Texas came open in 1982, for example, it was the National Republican Congressional Committee that guaranteed a strong GOP challenge. It found a popular Democratic city councilman, persuaded him to switch parties, watched over his nomination and made sure he had close to the legal maximum in party money. When his challenge ultimately fell 8,000 votes short in the election, the NRCC began lobbying him to try again in 1984.

Meanwhile, the party campaign committees are determining the subjects their candidates talk about. It was the Democratic Congressional Campaign Committee that developed the "fairness issue" for its candidates to use against the Reagan administration in 1982, providing speeches and press releases to many successful Democratic challengers. The NRCC introduced the Kemp-Roth tax cut into national politics in 1978, setting the stage for Ronald Reagan's adoption of it in the 1980 presidential campaign.

The NRCC succeeded brilliantly in nationalizing the issues of the 1980 campaign, forcing public attention on the failings of the Democratic Congress and tying those shortcomings to the Democratic incumbents they were trying to defeat. Two years later, though, the NRCC's "stay the course" theme probably hurt some moderate GOP candidates in the Northeastern states who would have been better off stressing local issues.

Whatever the occasional problems, however, the campaign committees are not going to return to the old-style politics of writing checks and sitting back to watch the result. The NRCC, which invested more than $7 million in its House candidates in 1982, expected to spend at least that much in 1984. It will continue to take more than a passing interest in what the candidates do with their money.

The DCCC will not even come close to its Republican counterpart in funds — it provided candidates with less than $1 million in the 1982 election — or in technical sophistication. But it is beginning to compete; by 1983 it was building a new "media center" to produce commercials for Democratic candidates.

New Democratic Strategy

By 1983 the DCCC was being reborn in Tony Coelho's image — aggressively optimistic, relentless in its fund raising and eager to make friends on all sides of the political spectrum.

The third-term House Democrat from California had

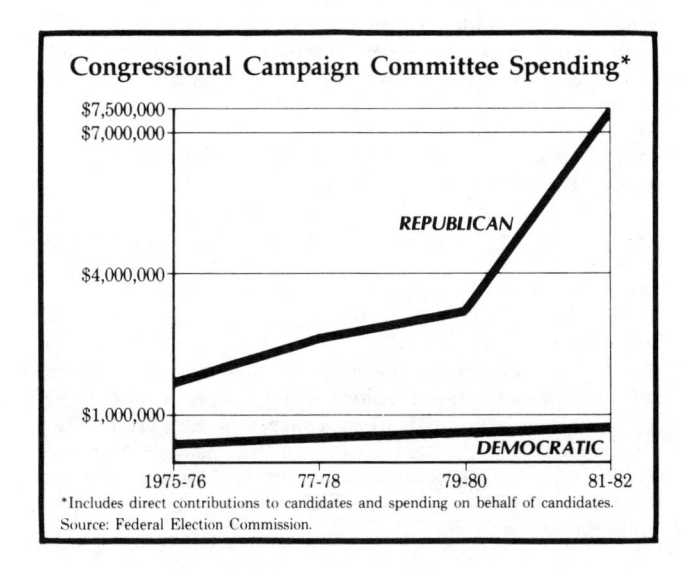

Congressional Campaign Committee Spending*

*Includes direct contributions to candidates and spending on behalf of candidates.
Source: Federal Election Commission.

not pleased everybody in his two years as campaign chairman. His fund-raising ties to business were controversial, especially to his party's left. But the tangible results of his chairmanship were easily seen.

The committee staff had grown from fewer than 10 in 1981 to a high of 39 at the time of the 1982 elections. The planned media center was expected to produce television and radio ads both for specific candidates and party messages.

The committee's financial base had changed dramatically. Coelho explained that when he became DCCC chairman in 1981 the average contribution received by the committee was $500, compared with around $45 for the Republicans. Now, Coelho said, the DCCC's average is $48, reflecting greater support from small givers. In 1983 and 1984, half of the committee's anticipated $8 million to $10 million income was expected to come from direct mail and low-level givers.

Coelho referred to all this simply as an effort to "institutionalize and professionalize" the committee, to turn it into a body capable of "fighting the Republican Party's superior resources in House races." *(Republican committee, p. 141)*

New Focus

The group's strategic focus was changing as well. In the 1970s, the DCCC existed mainly to receive donations of the wealthy guests at the party's congressional fund-raising dinner and then to give that money to incumbents.

While the GOP was building a huge fund-raising base and developing the resources to support its candidates nationwide, House Democrats relied on the $1 million to $2 million they could raise in their time-honored fashion and lagged far behind their opponents in making use of more sophisticated campaign technology. The 1980 elections — which cost Democrats the presidency, the Senate and 33 House seats — demonstrated just how far behind they were.

It was in the wake of the 1980 debacle that Coelho won the DCCC chairmanship, replacing fellow-Californian James C. Corman (1961-81), who had lost his House seat. A fund-raising whiz since his early days in the House, Coelho sold more tickets to the Democratic congressional dinner than anyone else in 1979, his first year in office.

Coelho decided, in his words, to "change the committee from a funneling committee to a targeting committee." Safe incumbents who were accustomed to receiving election-year contributions from the DCCC, regardless of need, found in 1982 that the money was much harder to get. A larger percentage of the gifts went to more vulnerable incumbents and Democratic challengers identified by the committee as possible winners.

While the committee still gave some money to members who were relatively secure, most of its incumbent contributions went to those uncertain of re-election. "Our primary goal is to save incumbents," said Coelho, "but it's to *save* incumbents, not to funnel money to them. There's an important difference."

Coelho centralized the targeting process in a way that allowed him to make decisions without subjecting himself to too much arm-twisting by colleagues hankering after funds. Not long after he took over in 1981 he disbanded the DCCC's executive committee, splitting the committee's members into 18 task forces. The full committee membership rarely met.

"Decisions are made in the Speaker's office or Tony's office or God knows where," said one House Democrat critical of the move. Coelho planned to re-establish the executive committee, with a regional makeup, to provide more consultation with other members.

The move away from an incumbent share-the-wealth committee created tensions. Coelho told the House Democratic Caucus in 1981 that "if I do this job right, most of you are going to end up hating me." But the 1982 election result — 26 new House seats for the Democrats — overcame the complaints from incumbents. Coelho was re-elected caucus chairman overwhelmingly at the start of 1983. Elected vice chairman was Dan Rostenkowski, Ill., who was the chairman of the Ways and Means Committee.

Quiet, Intense Californian

When he took over the committee at the age of 38, the youngest chairman since Lyndon B. Johnson of Texas four decades earlier, Coelho was dealing himself into broader House politics as well. Fellow House Democrats began to watch this quiet but intense Californian to see whether his destination was a higher place on the party leadership ladder. Coelho insisted on full privileges as a member of the leadership before committing himself to a second term as DCCC chairman.

The key alliance for Coelho was with Majority Leader Jim Wright of Texas. Both were traditional New Deal Democrats more inclined to public works programs than to modern social activism. Within the California delegation, Coelho rested at the center of a small group of more conservative Democrats who competed for influence with outspoken liberals such as Henry A. Waxman and Don Edwards.

Coelho's political views were largely formed during 13 years as an aide to Democratic Rep. B. F. Sisk (1955-79), whose central California district he inherited on Sisk's retirement in 1979. Sisk was a national Democrat with New Deal roots, but he also was a close friend of California business, especially agribusiness.

Coelho displayed the same leanings as a member of the House Agriculture and Interior committees beginning in 1979. He was a crucial ally for large California growers in their long effort to preserve their access to federally subsidized water.

'Quick Money' Sought

As campaign chairman, Coelho worked to spread the same message — that Democrats could be the party of business as well as the party of labor and social activism. All of Coelho's targeting changes were likely to be less controversial than his fund-raising approach, which involved courting independent oil producers and other traditionally conservative business interests.

When Coelho set out in 1981 his priority was "quick money," enough to "save us in '82," he said after the elections were over. That meant actively seeking out major donors at the same time that the committee was building its direct-mail operation. He established a "Speaker's Club" for major givers, giving individuals who contribute $5,000 and groups or political action committees that give $15,000 the chance to meet House Democratic leaders.

Coelho went after donations from business people and business PACs in a very aggressive fashion, inviting them to "candidate forums" — "cattle shows," their critics call them — to meet Democratic congressional candidates.

Congressional Campaign Funding

(Jan. 1, 1981, to Dec. 31, 1982)

The following chart, based on campaign finance figures compiled by the Federal Election Commission (FEC) for the 1981-82 election cycle, lists the top spenders among congressional incumbents and challengers, the top money-raisers and the top PAC fund recipients. *Italics denote losers in the 1982 congressional elections.*

Top Spenders

Senate

Mark B. Dayton (D Minn.)	$7,172,312
Pete Wilson (R Calif.)	7,082,651
Frank R. Lautenberg (D N.J.)	6,431,334
Edmund G. Brown Jr. (D Calif.)	5,367,931
Lloyd Bentsen (D Texas)	4,971,342
James Collins (R Texas)	4,138,736
Dave Durenberger (R Minn.)	3,969,408
Orrin G. Hatch (R Utah)	3,736,771
Richard G. Lugar (R Ind.)	2,973,791
Howard M. Metzenbaum (D Ohio)	2,792,968

House

Adam K. Levin (D N.J.)	$2,337,537
Barney Frank (D Mass.)	1,501,884
Cissy Baker (R Tenn.)	1,225,458
Tom Lantos (D Calif.)	1,192,394
Johnnie Crean (R Calif.)	1,140,863
John H. Rousselot (R Calif.)	990,236
Margaret M. Heckler (R Mass.)	966,621
Tom Vandergriff (D Texas)	948,024
Jim Cooper (D Tenn.)	905,474
Morris K. Udall (D Ariz.)	840,142

Top Money-raisers

Senate

Pete Wilson (R Calif.)	$7,190,985
Mark B. Dayton (D Minn.)	7,175,368
Frank R. Lautenberg (D N.J.)	6,491,679
Edmund G. Brown Jr. (D Calif.)	5,482,877
Lloyd Bentsen (D Texas)	4,520,553
James Collins (R Texas)	4,138,743
Dave Durenberger (R Minn.)	3,974,879
Orrin G. Hatch (R Utah)	3,825,656
Howard M. Metzenbaum (D Ohio)	3,756,651
Richard G. Lugar (R Ind.)	3,001,570

House

Adam K. Levin (D N.J.)	$2,337,882
Barney Frank (D Mass.)	1,509,239
Cissy Baker (R Tenn.)	1,229,199
Tom Lantos (D Calif.)	1,220,529
Johnnie Crean (R Calif.)	1,141,459
John H. Rousselot (R Calif.)	1,030,792
Margaret M. Heckler (R Mass.)	958,479
Tom Vandergriff (D Texas)	953,564
Jim Cooper (D Tenn.)	905,522
Milton Marks (R Calif.)	851,885

Top Recipients of PAC Money

Senate

Pete Wilson (R Calif.)	$1,187,832
Dave Durenberger (R Minn.)	1,030,239
Orrin G. Hatch (R Utah)	902,002
Lloyd Bentsen (D Texas)	800,443
Richard G. Lugar (R Ind.)	712,639
Robert C. Byrd (D W.Va.)	710,541
Paul S. Trible Jr. (R Va.)	671,016
Jim Sasser (D Tenn.)	641,970
Harrison Schmitt (R N.M.)	606,973
Donald W. Riegle Jr. (D Mich.)	602,946

House

Robert H. Michel (R Ill.)	$477,037
John H. Rousselot (R Calif.)	376,265
Phillip Burton (D Calif.)	356,144
James R. Jones (D Okla.)	334,940
James J. Howard (D N.J.)	318,238
Tony Coelho (D Calif.)	308,165
Thomas P. O'Neill Jr. (D Mass.)	299,462
Dan Rostenkowski (D Ill.)	293,175
Thomas S. Foley (D Wash.)	284,442
Bill Chappell Jr. (D Fla.)	284,116

Source: Federal Election Commission

Those steps, not surprisingly, received mixed reviews. Some Southern Democrats who avoided association with the more liberal elements of the national party were glad to work with Coelho. "I think it's important for Democrats to let the business community know that there are Democratic members who feel that 'profit' is not a dirty word," said Arkansas Rep. Beryl Anthony Jr., a DCCC member.

One of Coelho's fund-raising allies in 1982 was Texas Democrat Kent Hance, who cosponsored the Reagan tax cut in the House in 1981 but used his contacts in the oil industry to help Coelho's committee the following year. "There should be participation in the Democratic Party by labor and business, and liberals and conservatives and everyone," argued Hance.

Those sentiments were echoed by Richard A. Kline, a Washington lobbyist and executive director of the Council of Active Independent Oil and Gas Producers, a small group of producers centered on the Gulf Coast, and in Kansas, Oklahoma and Colorado. A Democratic benefactor himself, Kline helped Coelho drum up financial support from business — particularly independent oil — for the DCCC. "A great danger in America is if we go the way of the British, with a labor party and a business party," Kline contended. "And that's going to happen if the Democrats get no business money."

Buying Sympathy

Much of the criticism of Coelho's fund-raising strategy sprang from concern over the extent to which special interests were "buying" sympathy with their campaign giving. Reliance on business funding, said California Democrat Leon E. Panetta, was "planting some dangerous seeds for the future.... There's a price to be paid: the growing influence that those groups have, not just with Republicans, but with Democrats."

This influence made its first conspicuous appearance in the Ways and Means Committee's "bidding war" with the Reagan administration over the 1981 tax cut — in which Democrats avidly added sweeteners for business, and particularly independent oil.

Among many Democrats, however, the more common concern was about possible pressure on members to make themselves inoffensive to business at the expense of their personal values. As one congressional aide told a reporter in 1983: no one wants to be "fingered as the fink who cost the Democrats a contribution." Said another Democratic aide: "The problem is the extent to which ... Tony is sort of arranging marriages."

Coelho himself played down his role. "The only thing I've done is to introduce people to members in the House," he said. If a potential for a conflict of interest exists, he added, "I back out of it."

Coelho got some mileage early in 1983 out of a well-publicized spat with the U.S. Chamber of Commerce, after it had endorsed 91 Republicans in the 91 "Opportunity Races" to which it alerted its members in 1982. "The national Chamber of Commerce is one group that tried the hardest last fall to achieve a Republican majority in the House," he wrote House Democrats in February 1983, urging them not to honor the Chamber's requests to appear in its programs.

Support for Coelho

If there was criticism of Coelho's fund-raising style among House Democrats, there also was considerable support, even among those who saw themselves as reformers. They argued that the real problem was with the campaign finance system.

"The bottom line is that we shouldn't have private funding of campaigns," said Connecticut Rep. Sam Gejdenson. "We shouldn't have this insanity where we put the democratic process up for sale. I don't think that Tony does that any more than anyone else."

Coelho also liked to point out that he was using business contributions in part to establish a successful direct mail operation that would help discover small contributors and use them for years to come. "I am broadening the base of our party," he insisted, "and giving the small donors a chance to have a voice in our party they haven't had before."

The attempt to catch up with the Republicans in direct mail cost Coelho's committee $2.5 million in 1981-82. By the end of 1983 direct mail was expected to start turning a profit for House Democrats. In 1984 they expected it to give them $500,000 to use in campaigning.

While there was some concern among Democrats about the source of their new wealth, most were highly impressed with the overall result of Coelho's fund raising. The DCCC raised about $5.6 million, not counting loans, in 1981 and 1982. That was more than three times what it had taken in during any previous election cycle. No one seemed to doubt its ability to reach the projected $8 million to $10 million mark in 1984.

Nor was there much doubt that the committee's new riches had given it a chance to play a significant role in helping congressional candidates. It was not difficult to find Democrats who gladly echoed South Dakota Rep. Thomas A. Daschle when he lamented that Coelho's efforts were "10 years too late." The 1982 crop of Democratic candidates, especially the challengers, received far more help and advice than any previous Democratic group.

Still, Coelho's committee did far less for its candidates than the Republican opposition. As of early 1983 the DCCC had no full-time field operatives, for example; the RNCC had eight.

Hard Choices

With only a fraction of what Republicans had available to give to their candidates, the DCCC had to make some hard choices that the opposition did not have to confront. "We were not going to be in the business of helping someone take his losing margin from 40 to 50 percent," said Martin Franks, the DCCC executive director, "or his winning margin from 55 to 60."

So, while the committee freely provided information in 1982 about legislative issues and Republican incumbents' voting records and sent out "negative press releases" to newspapers in a targeted Republican's district, it was choosy about those to whom it would give or direct money.

In some cases, it made little difference. Bruce A. Morrison, D-Conn., noted that he got "zero dollars and zero cents" but still narrowly defeated GOP incumbent Lawrence A. DeNardis in 1982. "I would have liked to get some money," Morrison said, "but my race was one which everyone in the country thought I would lose, except for me and the people around me."

Others felt the absence of national Democratic Party support explained why they were narrow losers rather than narrow winners. "We are very grateful for their issue papers ... but they didn't even come out and look at the district," said Richard C. Bodine, who came within 4,000 votes of unseating Republican John Hiler in Indiana's economically depressed 3rd District. "We didn't have anyone come and say, 'Let's go over this and see what we can do,'" Bodine said.

"There were 10 other good seats that if we had had more money and more personnel, we could have won," says Coelho. "We did a few things very well. If we had tried to spread it out more, we would have done none of it well."

Coelho and Franks pointed to the committee's support of candidates such as Bob Wise, who defeated conservative Republican incumbent David Michael Staton in the 3rd District of West Virginia; Dick Durbin, who unseated Republican Paul Findley in the Illinois 20th; and G. Douglas Stephens, who came close to unseating House Minority Leader Robert H. Michel in the Illinois 18th. All three received substantial financial and other help from the DCCC.

Field staff and polls late in the campaign would have helped the committee catch contests it had missed the first time around, Coelho argued. "But we can't afford it," he lamented.

Spending Complaints

The committee's response that it could not afford to help all the candidates who needed help brought some complaints that the DCCC spent too much on itself in 1982. The committee devoted about $4.7 million to operating expenditures, and some $780,000 to candidates in the form of direct contributions and "coordinated expenditures," such as polls. It also channeled an estimated $300,000 in contributions from individuals and groups directly to Democrats. The committee intended to spend $2 million on candidates in 1984.

"The money that is raised for campaigns should really be there for individual campaigns, not be kept there for a support staff," argued one Democrat newly elected in 1982. "You do have to pause and ask the question of what you're raising the money for."

"It is precisely that kind of short-sighted thinking," Franks replied, "that has resulted in this committee in 1982 having a $5 million or $6 million budget, and the Republicans having a $50 million budget.... The days of making these committees passthrough organizations with six people raising money are long since gone. The Federal Election Campaign Act changed that forever."

The Federal Election Campaign Act Amendments of 1974 placed limits on the amount individuals and groups could contribute to federal campaigns and made it difficult to raise large sums of money from major donors. Frank insisted that direct mail, with all its unavoidable costs, still was "the only way you're going to get any substantial amount of money."

Franks also argued that much of the DCCC's value lies in activities other than handing out money. He cited the committee's new media center as one example.

But Coelho said that his and the committee's most important contribution in 1982 was an intangible one. "Remember what it was like around here in '81," he said. "The attitude here was that we'd lost the House.... More important than anything else I did was to change incumbents' attitudes. I basically became a cheerleader. We attacked the Republicans." The committee's active support of Stephens' challenge to Michel, he said, was central to that.

"We told the Republicans that we're willing to take on your leadership. They do it to us, but we'd never done it before," Coelho said.

GOP Eyes 1984 Elections

While Coelho was scrambling to bring money and prestige to his fragile Democratic campaign committee, Rep. Guy Vander Jagt, Mich., had the luxury of overseeing a National Republican Congressional Committee so financially well-established that it could focus on picking House Democrats to target for defeat in 1984.

The Republicans had developed a three-pronged strategy for 1984, one that combined an attack on the huge Democratic group elected in 1982, a stepped-up effort against selected members of the seemingly well-entrenched 1974 class and a search for Democratic seats that escaped competition in 1982 because the congressional district lines were drawn late in the year.

"I think the old axiom still holds," Vander Jagt said, "that the most vulnerable time for congressmen is in the first election, and if you miss them on the first election, it gets more difficult to beat them on the second time around or the third or the fourth."

By focusing on freshmen, the committee challenged recent history — the past few elections provided evidence that first-term members rarely proved vulnerable unless they had made serious political mistakes. But there was some sign of freshman vulnerability in 1982; of the 26 Republican incumbents who lost, half were freshmen. GOP strategists contended that most of the Democrats who took over these seats, many of them taking advantage of new district lines, still would be beatable in 1984.

Target: Class of 1974

Meanwhile, the NRCC was taking a fresh look at the Democrats first elected in 1974, the year the GOP took a beating at the polls because the party's image was tarnished by the Watergate break-in scandal.

"There are many of those Democrats who were elected from what we believe are essentially Republican areas, or potentially Republican areas," Vander Jagt said.

This would not be the first time the NRCC had targeted the Democratic class of 1974. Republican strategists made a concerted effort to defeat its members in 1976, but all except two of the 78 first-term Democrats seeking re-election that year were successful.

Although retirements and subsequent re-election defeats thinned the Democrats of 1974, 39 from that class — half of the original group — still were serving in Congress in 1984, and a number had moved into leadership positions on House committees. The NRCC was hoping that those members could be portrayed unfavorably as in league with the House Democratic leadership.

"The third range of target seats are several handfuls of districts out there where, because of redistricting happening so late, we didn't get the candidate or the campaign put together in 1982," explained NRCC campaign director Edward Goeas in 1983.

Redistricting was one of the Republican's biggest disappointments in the 1982 election cycle. The party was confident it would benefit from the nationwide shift in population that forced a transfer of 17 House seats from Northern states to more conservative Southern and Western states.

PAC Influence Grows...

To some, political action committees (PACs) represent a healthy new way for individuals and groups to participate financially in the political process. To others, they are an insidious outgrowth of Watergate-inspired legislation. But all sides agree that PACs are an increasingly important force in the financing of congressional races.

The term "PAC" is not precisely defined in the 1971 Federal Election Campaign Act (FECA), the law that provides the basic ground rules for financing federal election campaigns. FECA does define a nonparty political committee as any committee, club, association or other group of members that either has receipts or expenditures in a calendar year of at least $1,000, or operates a separate, segregated fund to raise or disburse money used in federal campaigns. Committees that fit this definition have come to be known as PACs.

Because corporations and labor unions are prohibited by federal law from using corporate and union treasury funds for political contributions, PACs have become a tightly regulated vehicle for political involvement by business and unions. Campaign contributions by political action committees must come from voluntary gifts to the PACs. But corporate and union funds may be used to administer PACs and solicit money for them.

Most PACs are affiliated with corporations or labor unions. But there are a large number of political action committees affiliated with trade, membership and health organizations and a growing number of independent, non-connected PACs set up by groups interested in a particular cause, such as abortion, farm subsidies and the environment.

Impetus for PACs

Labor unions began forming PACs nearly a half century ago to maximize their influence in the political process. But the real impetus for PAC formation did not come until the 1970s when the federal campaign finance laws were overhauled. Crucial were the 1974 amendments to the FECA, which clamped a $1,000 limit on the amount an individual could contribute to a House or Senate candidate in a primary or general election. PACs were permitted to give $5,000 per candidate per election, with no limit on how much a candidate could receive in combined PAC donations.

Overnight the political landscape was changed. Before 1974 there was little need for PACs outside the labor movement. Individuals — whether business executives or wealthy political philanthropists — could give unlimited amounts to the candidates of their choice. But the 1974 legislation ended this era of unbridled giving and forced wealthy individuals, corporations and other organizations to seek new outlets to remain financially involved in the political process.

For many, PACs were the answer. In the wake of the 1972 Watergate scandal and the disclosure of illegal corporate contributions, they offered a centralized and well-organized way to participate politically.

Foes of PACs, however, view them quite differently. They contend that the committees are a corrupting influence on the political process, filling a vacuum created by the strict federal limitation on contributions and the decline of political parties as basic election campaign organizations.

Legislative Background

The legislative groundwork for the PAC boom of the 1970s was laid by the 1971 act. When the decade began, the political activities of corporations and unions were tightly restricted.

Corporate gifts of money to federal candidates had been prohibited since 1907 by the Tillman Act. In 1925 the ban was extended by the Federal Corrupt Practices Act to cover corporate contributions of "anything of value." Labor unions were prohibited by the Smith-Connally Act of 1943 and the Taft-Hartley Act of 1947 from making contributions to federal candidates from their members' dues.

The 1971 act modified these bans by allowing the use of corporate funds and union treasury money for "the establishment, administration and solicitation of contributions to a separate, segregated fund to be utilized for a political purpose." Administrative units of those funds became known commonly as PACs.

But the 1971 act did not modify the ban on political contributions by government contractors. This resulted in many corporations holding back from forming PACs. Labor unions, many of which had government manpower contracts, also became concerned that they would be affected and led a move to have the law changed to permit government contractors to establish and administer PACs. That change was incorporated into the 1974 amendments to the FECA.

SunPAC Decision

Labor's efforts, however, had unexpected consequences. While the easing of the prohibition against government manpower contractors forming PACs removed a headache for organized labor, it also opened the door to the formation of corporate PACs.

Yet in the wake of Watergate many corporations remained skittish about what they were permitted to do. Not until November 1975, when the Federal Election Commission (FEC) released its landmark ruling in the case involving the Sun Oil Co.'s political com-

...Along With Controversy

mittee, SunPAC, did many businesses feel comfortable about establishing PACs.

The FEC decision was in response to a request from Sun Oil for permission to use its general treasury funds to create, administer and solicit voluntary contributions to its political action committee, SunPAC. The company also sought permission to solicit its stockholders and all employees for PAC contributions and to establish a separate "political giving program" among corporate employees that could be financed through a payroll deduction plan. Sun Oil indicated that employees would be allowed to designate the recipients of their contributions.

By a 4-2 vote, the bipartisan commission issued an advisory opinion approving the requests, although the FEC emphasized that SunPAC had to abide by guidelines ensuring that the solicitation of employees was totally voluntary.

Labor was incensed by the ruling, since it greatly enlarged the potential source of funds available to corporate PACs. The unions pressed hard to have the commission's decision overturned, and they succeeded in the 1976 FECA amendments in having the range of corporate solicitation restricted from all employees to a company's management personnel and its stockholders. Corporations and unions were given the right to solicit the other's group twice a year by mail.

The 1976 amendments also permitted union PACs to use the same method of soliciting campaign contributions as the company PACs used, such as a payroll deduction plan. And the law sought to restrict the proliferation of PACs by maintaining that all political action committees established by one company or international union would be treated as a single committee for contribution purposes. The PAC contributions of a company or an international union would be limited to no more than $5,000 overall to the same candidate in any election no matter how many PACs the company or union formed.

In the short run, the 1976 amendments were a victory for labor, because they curbed some of the benefits for corporate PACs authorized by the FEC's SunPAC decision. But the legislation did nothing to undercut the primary effect of the SunPAC ruling: abetting the formation of PACs within the business community. Moreover, the law explicitly permitted trade associations, membership organizations, cooperatives and corporations without stock to establish PACs.

Growth of Other Types of PACs

Corporate and labor units together were responsible for nearly 60 percent of all direct PAC contributions to congressional candidates in 1980. The rest of the money was provided by four other categories of PACs: cooperatives, corporations without stock, trade, membership and health as well as non-connected.

Although numbered among the cooperatives are the lucrative PACs of the Associated Milk Producers and the Mid-America Dairymen, most political committees within the cooperative and corporation-without-stock categories are relatively insignificant. Together they provided only 4 percent of all contributions to House and Senate candidates in 1980.

The large group of trade, membership and health PACs, however, is a different story. In the 1980 election campaign they contributed nearly 30 percent of all PAC gifts. Many of the committees within this diverse category — such as the PACs of the National Association of Realtors and the National Automobile Dealers Association — have ties to the business community. The health-related PACs — such as the committees affiliated with the American Medical Association (AMA) and the American Dental Association — also fall into this group. And finally, there are the membership organizations — such as the NRA and the Gun Owners of America — that are rooted in a political ideology or issue.

The 1975 SunPAC decision — which spurred a rapid increase in the number of corporate PACs — also prompted growth in the number of trade, membership and health PACs. Within six months, nearly 100 new committees were formed. But the creation of trade, membership and health PACs tapered off after that. Strict regulations on the solicitation of contributions was a major factor in discouraging faster growth.

Ideological PACs' Influence

About 500 political committees fall into a unique, catch-all category called non-connected PACs. They are independent organizations without a parent body. But the leading non-connected PACs have thousands of contributors who are regularly tapped by direct-mail, fund-raising appeals.

Unlike most other PACs, which are motivated by economic concerns, the principal interests of the leading non-connected PACs are ideological. The most successful ones have been stridently conservative, such as the National Conservative Political Action Committee (NCPAC).

Much of the money raised by the ideological PACs is plowed back into costly direct-mail programs. In addition to making direct contributions or independent expenditures, some independent committees hire national experts on polling, media and other facets of modern-day campaigning that they make available to their candidates. Other PACs sponsor candidate training schools and provide research information from their Washington offices.

But the remap process dragged on well into 1982 in several states, keeping candidates guessing about which voters they should contact. Often, clever cartography by Democratic-controlled legislatures and unfriendly federal court rulings spoiled GOP hopes. In the end, Democrats won 10 of the 17 seats that shifted. *(Details, see Redistricting, p. 125)*

Protracted redistricting struggles and bad breaks in the courts played a part in defeating numerous Republican candidates — incumbents Tom Hagedorn (1975-83) and Arlen Erdahl (1979-83) in Minnesota, Rep. Jim Dunn (1981-83) in Michigan and Rep. Harold C. Hollenbeck (1977-83) in New Jersey, to name a few.

The committee also was expected to be looking at districts that could be moving in a conservative direction demographically. Missouri's 2nd District, for example, gained more Republican areas in St. Louis County in 1981 redistricting, and the district's Democratic representative, Robert A. Young, slipped to 57 percent of the vote in 1982.

Recruitment Effort Expanded

With its large Washington staff and eight full-time field directors at work in different regions of the country, the NRCC played a much larger role in candidate recruitment than did the Democratic Congressional Campaign Committee.

For 1984, the NRCC was trying to improve its talent search by making greater use of broader-based candidate recruitment committees. "We're looking for businessmen and younger people and minorities and other people that are not normally involved in the party process to serve on these candidate recruitment committees," Goeas said. Goeas pointed out that this approach "has brought us numerous names that we wouldn't have thought of before if we just sat down with the county chair and talked about candidate recruitment."

In the past, Republicans often suffered when they nominated candidates who were supported by the local party establishment but had little base outside of it. In 1978, for example, Texas Republicans hoped to capture several districts passing from the hands of departing veteran Democrats. But weak GOP nominees such as George W. Bush (son of the vice president) in the 19th District and Leo Berman in the 24th could not match the broader-based appeal of their Democratic opponents — Reps. Kent Hance in the 19th and Martin Frost in the 24th.

Second-time Candidates

One of the focal points of NRCC recruiting efforts for 1984 was the group of Republicans who lost House elections in 1982. "This committee has historically encouraged second-time candidacies," said the group's executive director, Joseph R. Gaylord.

Several of the 1982 losers were seen by the NRCC as particularly promising prospects for 1984, among them Bill Moshofsky of Oregon, who won 46 percent of the vote against Democratic Rep. Les AuCoin.

Moshofsky was in a group invited to an April 1983 "recap session" in Washington at which the NRCC staff sought the losers' comments on the 1982 elections and discussed prospects for 1984.

New Tactics

Partly in response to competitive pressures from the DCCC, the NRCC added several new wrinkles to its 1984 tactics. First, the committee virtually doubled the number of staff members who worked to secure contributions from political action committees. One reason the PAC outreach effort was being bolstered was that Coelho and the DCCC "have made a fairly concerted effort to try to raise business PAC money for Democratic candidates, much more so than we have been able to generate union PAC funds for Republican candidates," Gaylord said.

Also, the NRCC launched a publicity campaign that aimed to cast Democratic incumbents in an unfavorable light in their districts. Republicans were still snarling that Democratic campaign rhetoric in 1982 was demagoguery; Vander Jagt said he hoped the GOP in 1984 would be "one-fifth as effective in advertising against the Democrats as they were in erroneously advertising against us on the subject of Social Security."

Among the anti-incumbent mailings the NRCC sent out was one that accused 20 Democrats who voted for the Democratic budget alternative for fiscal 1984 of favoring a $300 billion tax increase over the following three years; in another mailing, the NRCC charged certain Democrats with endorsing elimination of the tax law that allows homeowners to deduct interest paid on home mortgages from their taxes.

There was a howl of Democratic protest that the NRCC mailings were misrepresentations. The budget did not include a specific tax hike figure, Democrats said, and eliminating the mortgage interest deduction was simply an option offered by a party study group to reduce the deficit.

The NRCC also was studying records at the Federal Election Commission, and it was sending its anti-incumbent mailings to people listed by the FEC as campaign contributors to the targeted Democrats. Democrats said that practice smacked of Watergate-era "dirty tricks," but Vander Jagt scoffed at the criticism.

"I would call that making the record known. To say that is gutter politics . . . borders to me on desperation." He said the practice was proper because the NRCC was not soliciting contributions (FEC data may not be used for that purpose), but simply providing information.

The NRCC also was cataloging the televised coverage of House floor debates in an effort to discourage Democrats from using excerpts against GOP incumbents, as was done in 1982 against House Minority Leader Michel. An advertisement by Michel's opponent, G. Douglas Stephens, used TV footage of a floor debate in which Michel made a comment that Stephens said demonstrated the Republican's insensitivity to Social Security recipients.

House rules prohibit incumbents from using footage of floor proceedings in their re-election campaigns, but challengers may do so. Vander Jagt said the NRCC was cataloging the televised coverage so it would be able to deliver a quick counterpunch to Democratic incumbents if Republican members found the footage being used against them.

Building on the Past

In addition to the new programs for 1984, the NRCC was working to improve the wide array of services that were available to GOP candidates in 1982. The committee offered training schools that coach candidates and campaign staffers on planning strategy, raising money, meeting FEC reporting requirements and dealing with the media.

The NRCC hoped to develop further a program tried on an experimental basis in 1982 — a computerized information network linking the committee with individual

Politicians Feast on Fund-raisers

Although there has been much emphasis in recent years on the role in campaigns of direct-mail fund-raising wizards such as Richard Viguerie, or media consultants such as David Garth and Robert Squier, the venerable fund-raising dinner is still alive and well.

In fact, some dinners are raising as much money in one night as many candidates raised during entire campaigns a few years ago.

Consider the following:

An April 29, 1983, fund-raiser in Houston for Republican Sen. John Tower of Texas grossed $1.5 million. It was the largest amount ever raised at a single event for a Senate candidate. (Tower subsequently announced he would retire.) The second largest "take" at a fund-raising event was $1.1 million — raised for GOP Sen. Charles H. Percy of Illinois on Jan. 19, 1983, in Chicago. The previous records was $1 million raised Jan. 14, 1982, at a Dallas salute honoring Tower's 20-year Senate career.

A September fund-raiser at the Columbia, S.C., Fair Grounds for Republican Sen. Strom Thurmond of South Carolina grossed $430,000. A modest sum by national standards, it nonetheless was the largest amount raised at a single event in the Southeast. Previously, the highest amount raised by a GOP candidate in South Carolina was $70,000.

All these events were organized by political consultant Brad O'Leary, president of PM Consulting. O'Leary is a Republican fund-raiser whose technical approach to managing campaign events matches anything served up by direct-mailers, pollsters or media experts.

"People who do a dinner right will find the dinner brings in a lot more money," O'Leary says. And doing it right means planning it six to nine months in advance, he says.

O'Leary's events are not stuffy — he likes to make them fun. A fund-raiser for ex-astronaut and former Sen. Harrison Schmitt, R-N.M., featured actors Buster Crabbe and Gil Gerard, both of whom played spaceman Buck Rogers in the movies, and the actors who portrayed Scotty and Lt. Uhuru in television's "Star Trek." The master of ceremonies was an actor who specialized in impersonating President Jimmy Carter.

An O'Leary fund-raiser a few years ago — again for Tower — erupted when a shotgun-toting John Wayne rode a stagecoach drawn by four horses around the auditorium where the dinner was held.

Politicians, of course, are the main draw. President Ronald Reagan and 11 senators attended the record-breaking Tower event. Reagan and nine Senate committee chairmen attended the Percy dinner.

O'Leary tries to involve as many people as possible in the dinners. He aims to have 150 to 300 co-chairmen for his dinners. Co-chairmen "sell" tables for a price they think they can handle. Donations for the Percy dinner, for example, were $1,000, $400 and $200. Thurmond dinner prices were $500, $200 and $100. Between 2,800 and 3,000 people attended Tower's Houston fund-raiser, 2,200 attended Percy's.

The more money a contributor pays, the closer he or she is to the main table. O'Leary also scatters VIPs — celebrities and politicians — among the crowd to make donors feel they are getting something for their money.

O'Leary sees an advantage to dinner fund raising. It attracts what he calls "fresh money" to a campaign. Dividing tables among so many co-chairmen brings in new donors. Making events enjoyable also attracts more money from past contributors.

The special event can also serve as a way of keeping large contributors happy. In September, O'Leary helped the National Republican Senatorial Committee entertain its Inner Circle of contributors — those who give $5,000 a year to the committee.

Some 1,300 contributors visited Washington for a briefing from senior politicians and government officials. They went to a reception at Vice President Bush's home and then split up to attend one of about 65 separate dinners that O'Leary termed intimate.

Some dinners were held at the homes of senators and Cabinet officers. (One ended with contributors getting a private, late-night tour of the Capitol from Sen. Thurmond.)

Special fund-raising events can be much more cost-efficient than direct mail. Practitioners estimate that the cost of hosting large events eats up about a third of the money raised, while a proven, successful direct-mail list can cost one-half to two-thirds of the money it brings in. An untried list (one in which the fund-raiser "prospects" for contributors) may only break even, or may lose money.

Successful dinners are not just the prerogative of Republicans. The Democrats, too, have learned that a well-fed audience can fill campaign coffers.

The Democratic Senatorial Campaign Committee (DSCC), the fund-raising vehicle for Senate Democrats, did just that Oct. 25, 1983, at the Washington Hilton. A dinner tribute to Democratic Sen. Russell B. Long of Louisiana grossed nearly $1 million from about 900 people paying $1,000 (some sent checks but did not attend). Long would be chairman of the Senate Finance Committee in 1985 if the Democrats recapture the Senate — the DSCC's goal for 1984.

Among the co-chairmen for the Long dinner were the chief executive officers of General Motors, Chrysler and AT&T. VIPs included former senator and secretary of state Edmund S. Muskie, D-Maine, and former senator Richard S. Schweiker, R-Pa., President Reagan's first secretary of health and human services, now a life insurance executive.

The DSCC also held a $1,000-a-plate fund-raiser at the Helmsley Palace, in New York City. The dinner was chaired by New York Sen. Daniel Patrick Moynihan, Gov. Mario M. Cuomo and Mayor Edward Koch.

campaigns. Gaylord said that the committee hoped to set aside $8 million for direct cash contributions to candidates and for coordinated expenditures, which were services paid for by the committee on behalf of candidates.

In the 1981-82 election cycle, the NRCC raised $54 million and spent $7.5 million on cash contributions and coordinated expenditures; $3 million of that went to GOP incumbents and the remainder to challengers and candidates for open seats. In contrast, the total amount raised by the DCCC in 1981-82 was about $5.6 million.

1982 Assessment

One key question was why, with so much money at its disposal, the NRCC could not prevent the GOP from losing 26 House seats. Gaylord responded by offering a different premise: "I have a tendency to think that the committee did an awful lot to prevent the election from being a lot worse than it was.

"We had about 42 percent of the vote nationwide, if you add up the totals in every congressional district. That usually translates into about 144 seats, when you look at most models. We ended up with 166.... It's not that we're grateful for that, but it could have been worse."

Some Republicans questioned the wisdom of the NRCC's 1982 slogan, "Stay the Course." The committee spent $14 million on national advertising touting that theme, hoping it would be as effective as the NRCC's 1980 slogan, "Vote Republican: For a Change," which was credited with helping the GOP gain 36 House seats as it took control of the White House and the Senate.

Critics of "Stay the Course" said it forced the debate in the House contests to focus on one topic — the wisdom of Reagan's controversial economic policies — and made it difficult for GOP candidates to stress other issues.

A former North Carolina representative, Eugene Johnston (1981-83), a Republican who lost his House seat in 1982 to Democrat Robin Britt, said the NRCC had a tendency "to view the nation as an amorphous, homogeneous mass rather than 435 congressional districts" each of which "have a unique personality.... To put out one theme and expect it to play in 435 different districts is like Ford making one color car — black."

Gaylord had a different view. "Our own post-election research shows that 'Stay the Course' was a helpful theme." He said NRCC surveys showed that in markets where advertisements stressing the slogan were run, there was a relatively high turnout of Republican voters.

Few Republican candidates had trouble with the NRCC approach. Mike Faubion, who lost in a newly created Texas district, the blue-collar 25th, said, "I let the NRCC know my position on the issues at the first. They did not encourage us to take any particular theme."

Catherine Bertini, defeated by Democratic Rep. Sidney R. Yates in Illinois' 9th District, recalled one dispute with the NRCC over what message her television commercials should carry. "They wanted to talk about national issues, and I wanted to talk about local issues. It was a long discussion, and I disagreed with them, but they gave me money anyway."

Unemployment to Blame

Gaylord said 1982 NRCC surveys showed that GOP chances of significantly holding down its House losses were torpedoed by the announcement on Oct. 8, 1982, that the unemployment rate had hit 10.1 percent — its highest level since 1940.

"The announcement had a devastating impact on Republican challengers. We saw people who in their survey research were within two or three points of a Democrat drop 15 or 18 points behind," Gaylord recalled.

"The same held true in a lot of incumbent areas, where we had members with 20- and 25-point leads who watched those evaporate down to six, seven, three," he added.

The October GOP hemorrhage forced the NRCC into a defensive posture. In Washington, according to Gaylord, "we went through the process of just sitting on the phone with incumbent campaigns and saying, 'Is there anything that we can do?' And in some instances there was.... We spent in the last 16 days about $2.5 million dollars" to help incumbents.

One of the NRCC's emergency actions was on behalf of freshman Rep. Hiler's campaign in Indiana's 3rd District. Hiler had not requested NRCC assistance earlier because he did not anticipate trouble winning re-election. But he got jittery in October and asked the committee to bolster his support by paying for a first-class mailing to Republican households in Hiler's home county of LaPorte.

The NRCC paid for the mailing, which cost $14,000. Gaylord said that the last-minute action was "one of the things that could have made the difference" in Hiler's narrow, 3,912-vote victory over Democrat Bodine.

Controls on Political Spending

Money and politics in America have mixed about as smoothly over the years as oil and water. While many European democracies have adopted tightly regulated systems of campaign finance, politicians in the United States still are struggling to define the relationship between money and their craft.

Until the 1970s, campaign finance, American style, was freewheeling, a shadowy area with virtually toothless legislation covering the disclosure of campaign contributions and expenditures.

But in the early 1970s the pendulum began to swing sharply in the other direction. Spiraling media costs provided the first impetus for reform. The Watergate scandal accelerated the movement. By the middle of the decade, three major pieces of campaign finance legislation had been passed, transforming the practically unregulated "industry" into one with strict controls.

By the late 1970s, however, the push for reform clearly was weakening. Criticism was growing that the law was an overreaction to Watergate that stifled contributors, candidates and political parties alike. Whereas throughout the 1970s the impetus for campaign finance legislation came from the political left, during the early 1980s the conservatives had the power in Congress to seize the initiative. By 1984 liberal reforms such as congressional public financing and political action committee (PAC) spending curbs were being considered side by side with conservative alternatives such as loosening restrictions on party giving.

Campaign Spending Controversy

One of the major difficulties politicians have faced in molding campaign finance legislation has been an absence of consensus.

There is no national system of campaign finance that covers all political races. The legislation of the 1970s dramatically overhauled presidential elections, establishing a system of partial public financing for the nominating process and virtually complete federal funding for the general election. But Congress never extended public financing to its own contests, which remain privately financed. Races at the state and local levels are a mixture of the two systems.

The lack of a national system of campaign finance reflects disagreement on what constitutes an appropriate level of campaign spending. For every person who believes that too much money is being spent on political campaigns, there is another who feels the amount is too low.

Reformers wanting tight federal controls on spending point to the escalating costs of U.S. elections since the technological boom after World War II. Campaign expenditures quadrupled from $200 million in 1964 to about $900 million in 1980, an increase nearly double the rate of inflation as measured by the Consumer Price Index.

And, reformers warn, as the costs of campaigns increase, candidates are more apt to be "bought" by special interest groups and wealthy contributors and less likely to serve the people who elected them.

But critics of lower spending maintain that charges of influence-buying are rarely substantiated, and that the costs of all political campaigns in 1980 were still less than the price tag of one nuclear-powered, missile-launching Trident submarine.

Critics also can point to the conclusions of a 1979 study of federal campaign finance legislation by the Harvard University Institute of Politics. "The most competitive elections," the report stated, "where the voters have the most information about candidates, are those in which the most money is spent. Election contests in which spending is comparatively high are also those in which voter participation tends to be highest."

Reformers and critics would agree that campaigns are growing more and more expensive. With the escalating costs of the staples of political campaigns — such as candidate staff and travel, media advertising and public opinion polling — it is expensive for a candidate to run even a competitive race.

And unless a candidate is an incumbent, a wealthy challenger or a contender in a closely contested open-seat race, fund raising can be difficult. For every House or Senate candidate whose expenses run in six or seven figures, there are dozens of "mom and pop" campaigns that cannot afford any professional help.

The extent to which an election can be won by outspending the opposition is debated during and after almost every political contest. Generally, there has always been a strong link between incumbency, money and electoral success.

The stringent controls of the new campaign finance system do not appear to have broken that link in House races. In 1978 House contests, for example, a Congressional Quarterly study found that 95 percent of all incumbents won re-election and 87 percent of incumbents outspent their challengers. In races for open seats, where there were no incumbents, the winners also tended to be the big spenders.

But in Senate and presidential races, the new system may be having a different impact. The number of incumbent senators winning re-election declined from 77 percent in 1970 to 55 percent in 1980. And in both publicly financed presidential elections (1976 and 1980) administered under the new system, the incumbents lost.

Campaign spending figures relating to the 1982 elections seem to confirm that the costs of getting elected — or re-elected — are still on the rise. Candidates for the House and Senate spent a combined total of $343.9 million during the 1981-82 political season, according to the Federal Election Commission (FEC). It was the most expensive in history, representing an increase of 43.9 percent over the 1979-80 season. PAC contributions to 1981-82 congressional campaigns rose to $83.1 million, up 50.5 percent from $55.2 million given to 1979-80 campaigns.

Legislative Goals

Campaign finance reformers over the years have sought to curb campaign spending by limiting and regulating campaign expenditures and donations made to candidates as well as by informing voters of the amounts and sources of the donations, and the amounts, purposes and payees of the expenditures. Disclosure was intended to reveal which candidates, if any, were unduly indebted to interest groups, in time to forewarn the voters. But more than a century of legislative attempts to regulate campaign financing resulted in much controversy and minimal control.

PAC Contributions To Federal Candidates
Jan. 1, 1981 - Dec. 31, 1982
(in millions of dollars)

- Corporations $29.4 (33.5%)
- Trade, membership, health $22.9 (26.2%)
- Labor $20.9 (23.9%)
- No-connected organizations $11.0 (12.6%)
- Corporations without stock $1.1 (1.3%)
- Cooperatives $2.2 (2.5%)

Total contributions — $87.55 million

Note: Each category's percentage of total PAC contributors to federal candidates during the 1981-82 election cycle is listed in parentheses.
Source: Federal Election Commission.

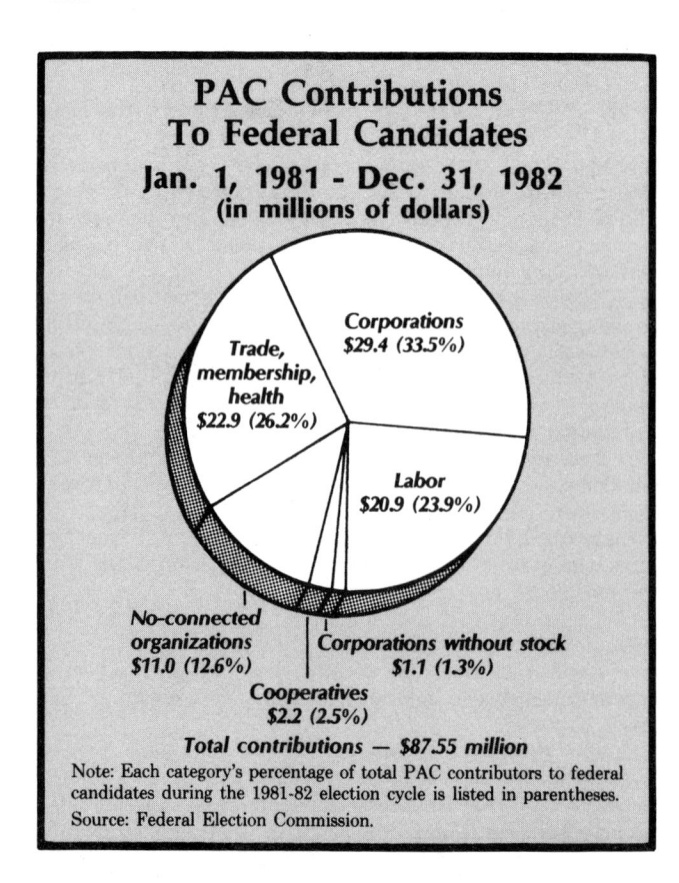

Until the 1970s, the basic federal law regulating campaign spending and requiring public disclosure was the Corrupt Practices Act of 1925, described by some as "more loophole than law." The act set a statutory maximum of $25,000 in expenditures for a Senate campaign and $10,000 for a House race. But it was not enforced.

Watergate, though, changed all that. The scandal became the code word in the 1970s for government corruption. Although there were many aspects to the scandal, money in politics was at its roots.

Included in Watergate's catalog of misdeeds were specific violations of campaign spending laws, violations of other criminal laws facilitated by the availability of virtually unlimited campaign contributions and still other instances where campaign funds were used in a manner that strongly suggested influence peddling.

Legal Changes in the 1970s

Faced with escalating media costs, Congress had begun to move on campaign finance legislation even before the June 1972 break-in at the Democratic national headquarters in Washington, D.C. In 1971 it worked hard to pass two separate pieces of legislation: 1) the Federal Election Campaign Act (FECA) of 1971, which for the first time set a ceiling on the amount federal candidates could spend on media advertising and required full disclosure of campaign contributions and expenditures, and 2) the Revenue Act of 1971, a tax checkoff bill to allow taxpayers to contribute to a general public campaign fund for eligible presidential and vice presidential candidates.

But Watergate focused public attention on campaign spending at all levels of government and produced a mood in Congress that even the most reluctant legislators found difficult to resist. In the aftermath of the scandal came the most significant overhaul in campaign finance legislation in the nation's history. Major legislation passed in 1974 and 1976, coming on the heels of the 1971 legislation, radically altered the system of financing federal elections.

Almost two and a half years after it passed the FECA of 1971 — a factor in breaking open the Watergate scandal — Congress, reacting to presidential campaign abuses, enacted another landmark campaign reform bill that substantially overhauled the existing system of financing election campaigns. Technically, the 1974 law was a set of amendments to the 1971 legislation, but in fact it was the most comprehensive campaign spending measure ever passed.

The new law, which President Gerald R. Ford signed Oct. 15, established the first spending limits ever for candidates in presidential primary and general elections and in primary campaigns for the House and Senate. It set new expenditure ceilings for general election campaigns for Congress to replace the limits established by the 1925 Federal Corrupt Practices Act that were never effectively enforced and were repealed in the 1971 law.

The 1974 law also introduced the first use of public money to pay for political campaign costs by providing for optional public financing in presidential general election campaigns and establishing federal matching grants to cover up to one-half of the costs of presidential primary campaigns. The final bill did not contain Senate-passed provisions for partial public financing of congressional campaigns. It also repealed the media spending limitations introduced in the 1971 FECA and established the Federal Election Commission.

As soon as the 1974 law took effect, it was challenged

Presidential Candidates' 1983 Fund Raising
(Jan. 1, 1983, to Dec. 31, 1983)

Candidate	Raised	Spent	Cash-on-hand	Debts
Walter F. Mondale	$11,448,263	$11,062,006	$386,257	$775,301
John Glenn	6,417,720	6,318,045	99,674	1,029,841
Alan Cranston	4,385,880	4,432,355	27,001	—0—
Ronald Reagan	3,769,467	1,692,181	2,077,285	166,965
Gary Hart	1,874,086	1,876,318	—0—	1,046,514
Reubin Askew	1,836,276	1,738,105	107,025	22,417
Ernest F. Hollings	1,581,577	1,527,001	62,611	338,152
Jesse L. Jackson	280,632	183,085	98,547	—0—
George S. McGovern	249,828	147,793	102,034	44,857

Source: Federal Election Commission

in court. The plaintiffs argued that the law's new limits on campaign contributions and expenditures curbed the freedom of contributors and candidates to express themselves in the political marketplace and that the public financing provisions discriminated against minor parties and lesser-known candidates in favor of the major parties and better-known candidates.

The case went to the Supreme Court, which handed down its historic *Buckley v. Valeo* decision on Jan. 30, 1976. In its decision, the court upheld the provisions of the statute that:
- Set limits on how much individuals and political committees could contribute to candidates.
- Provided for the public financing of presidential primary and general election campaigns.
- Required the disclosure of campaign contributions of more than $10 and campaign expenditures on behalf of the candidate of more than $100.

But the court overturned other features of the law, ruling that the campaign spending limits were unconstitutional violations of the First Amendment guarantee of free expression. For presidential candidates who accepted federal matching funds, however, the ceiling on expenditures remained intact. The court also struck down the method for selecting members of the FEC.

Responding to the Supreme Court decision, the 1976 amendments to FECA reconstituted the watchdog commission and revised some contribution limits. In 1979 legislation was passed by Congress that reduced paperwork requirements for candidates and political committees and encouraged more volunteer as well as grass-roots activity.

Unexpected Repercussions

The reform measures of the 1970s were supposed to curtail drastically the role of money in campaigns. Candidates were expected to devote less effort to wooing contributors. Overall campaign spending was expected to be reduced. Challengers and incumbents were supposed to be placed on a more equal footing than in previous campaigns because big money at last had been de-emphasized and the spending and fund-raising advantages of incumbents had been curbed.

But it didn't work out that way. While the reforms drew high marks for disclosure provisions that for the first time tracked the flow of money in federal elections, other aspects of the legislation drew criticism. Many candidates complained that to comply with the strict new disclosure requirements they had to hire an accountant or a lawyer before picking their campaign manager. Campaign funds had to be diverted from communicating with the voters to complying with the law.

Challengers complained that the law was a boon to incumbents and was responsible for longer and longer campaigns. Challengers could no longer offset the established fund-raising sources of incumbents by tapping several wealthy supporters. They had to begin their campaigns earlier to raise money in the small chunks available under the law, with expensive direct-mail drives emerging for many as the prime source of funds.

And there were complaints that, rather than accenting the small individual giver, the law was encouraging the growth of PACs, a new force in American politics. PACs are the political arms of labor unions, corporations and trade associations, in particular, although they are also a vehicle for groups espousing a particular cause or viewpoint to become financially involved in political campaigns. PACs blossomed, particularly in the corporate world, after the 1974 legislation and have proliferated at a rapid pace ever since. They have become somewhat slimmer replacements for the large individual givers in the old system, known as "fat cats." *(Political action committee spending, table, p. 154)*

Part of the problem with the new campaign finance

1984 State Spending Limits

Below are the amounts that the 1984 Democratic presidential contenders, all of whom chose to receive matching federal funds, were permitted to spend in each state in seeking their party's nomination.

There also was a nationwide spending ceiling of $20,200,000 for 1984. Amounts spent in each state counted against the nationwide ceiling. In addition to the $20.2 million, a candidate was permitted to spend up to 20 percent of that figure for fund-raising ($4,040,000) and an unlimited amount for legal and accounting fees.

State	1984 State Spending Limits
Alabama	$ 919,504.00
Alaska	404,000.00
Arizona	688,092.80
Arkansas	542,006.40
California	6,342,476.80
Colorado	741,097.60
Connecticut	768,569.60
Delaware	404,000.00
Florida	2,658,320.00
Georgia	1,328,352.00
Hawaii	404,000.00
Idaho	404,000.00
Illinois	2,707,769.60
Indiana	1,278,902.40
Iowa	684,537.60
Kansas	574,649.60
Kentucky	864,883.20
Louisiana	996,102.40
Maine	404,000.00
Maryland	1,038,118.40
Massachusetts	1,418,524.80
Michigan	2,117,606.40
Minnesota	974,771.20
Mississippi	577,558.40
Missouri	1,182,588.80
Montana	404,000.00
Nebraska	404,000.00
Nevada	404,000.00
New Hampshire	404,000.00
New Jersey	1,809,273.60
New Mexico	404,000.00
New York	4,281,107.20
North Carolina	1,448,259.20
North Dakota	404,000.00
Ohio	2,532,595.20
Oklahoma	769,216.00
Oregon	631,209.60
Pennsylvania	2,892,640.00
Rhode Island	404,000.00
South Carolina	432,118.40
South Dakota	404,000.00
Tennessee	1,110,838.40
Texas	3,582,025.60
Utah	404,000.00
Vermont	404,000.00
Virginia	1,333,523.20
Washington	1,019,372.80
West Virginia	460,560.00
Wisconsin	1,119,241.60
Wyoming	404,000.00
District of Columbia	404,000.00
Guam	404,000.00
Puerto Rico	654,480.00
Virgin Islands	404,000.00

system was that the Supreme Court decision in 1976 opened two loopholes by eliminating spending ceilings for congressional campaigns and allowing individuals to spend unlimited amounts of their own money on candidates so long as those expenditures were not coordinated with the candidate or the campaign organization.

These two loopholes placed a new premium on wealthy candidates and opened the door for individuals and PACs to make millions of dollars in independent expenditures, a tactic generally derided by candidates and party leaders as unwelcome "loose cannons" in the political process.

Throughout the late 1970s, reformers sought to curb campaign spending by pressing for the extension of public financing to congressional races. But the post-Watergate mood in Congress was less amenable to major campaign finance reforms. Legislative drives in 1977, 1978 and 1979 all failed. In late 1979 — with public financing all but buried — Congress was only able to approve non-controversial, paperwork-reducing changes in the law.

The 1979 revisions enabled the nation's campaign finance system to operate a little more smoothly. The controversy over campaign finance continued into the 1980s, however, with countless reform bills introduced each year. During the first half of 1983 alone, more than 20 campaign finance bills, spurred by Senate Rules Committee hearings on the issue, had been introduced. But there was no certainty as to whether the years ahead would see more minor tinkering or a massive overhaul.

Defenders argued that imperfections should be expected in legislation that rapidly transformed campaign finance at the federal level from a largely unregulated field to one that was strictly regulated. They contended that critics of the system were guilty of overexpectations.

In an article entitled "Reform as Bogeyman: The Law Without a Constituency," former Federal Election Commission Deputy Staff Director Bill Loughrey wrote: "It was not the intent of this legislation to: reverse the long-term decline of the political parties, assure that campaigns (which have been historically underfunded) are adequately financed, prevent the direct bribery of public officials, or allow campaigns to continue their unregulated, free-wheeling ways of raising and spending funds. Not unexpectedly, observers and critics who erroneously assumed that campaign reform legislation would achieve these goals or cure these ills have been disillusioned."

But defenders such as Loughrey have been in the minority. Critics have become increasingly visible, including some longtime supporters of campaign finance reform who had hoped the law would increase citizen participation and reduce the advantages of the well known and well heeled. Instead, the loopholes that dotted the law had created a system that many felt was something less.

Two former FEC staff members — Carol Darr and Susan Tifft — wrote in an April 1981 issue of *Legal Times of Washington* that "The election law has become in effect like tax code, manipulated by those who have the most to gain or lose. The unhappy consequence is a statute that is more loophole than law, and a campaign finance system that gives the American voter the worst of both worlds: the appearance of reform with little of the substance."

Initiatives for More Change

In the wake of the 1982 election, the most expensive in history, the 98th Congress took a serious look at federal election laws and in particular at the role of money in campaigns. Both the House and Senate held extensive hearings on the issue in 1983. The year ended without any new legislation, however, and it looked highly unlikely in early 1984 that any changes would take place before the upcoming elections. The issues considered were expected to resurface in 1985, after what promised to be an even more expensive election.

Differing Opinions

There was general agreement among members of Congress involved in the debate that the existing law performed a valuable function by requiring disclosure of campaign contributions and expenditures. But there were widely varying opinions on the limits the election law placed on receiving and spending funds and on how the law might be improved. But partisan conflicts and the controversy surrounding public campaign financing made quick action impossible. PACs and most other groups involved with campaign finance were convinced that there would be little movement in 1983, so they had not done much lobbying on the issue.

'Off the Auction Block'

Central to any campaign finance debate were the contribution limits. In 1984 an individual could give no more than $1,000 to a federal candidate in any primary, runoff or general election. An individual also could not exceed an aggregate $25,000 in contributions per year to all federal campaigns. A PAC could not give more than $5,000 to a candidate per election.

These limits were set in 1974. Ten years later inflation had lowered the ceilings by more than 50 percent. One result of this, observers contended, was increasing independent expenditures. No limit existed on independent spending. The only restriction was that an independent spender have no contact with the candidate he sought to aid. Independent expenditures surged in the 1980 election season. Low contribution limits also increased the importance of personal wealth. With individual contributions by outsiders severely limited, the person of independent means becomes a more potent candidate.

HR 2490, which sought to curb campaign spending by placing a cap on the amount of money a candidate could accept from PACs and on the amount he could spend of his own personal wealth, was introduced by a bipartisan coalition led by Rep. David R. Obey, D-Wis. The bill carried more than 100 cosponsors. Obey was concerned that special interest groups, through sizable campaign contributions, exercised an unhealthy influence on members of Congress. "It's time Congress is taken off the auction block and influence in the political process is returned to regular citizens who are more committed to the public interest than they are to special interests," he said. "I detest what money and the candidates' need for money is doing to the House."

Rep. Jim Leach, R-Iowa, a cosponsor and leading spokesman for HR 2490, agreed. "It is a simple fact of life that when big money enters the political arena, big obligations are entertained," he said.

The bill was backed by Common Cause, the only group to undertake vigorous lobbying on campaign finance in 1983. After "declaring war" on PACs in February of that year, the public interest lobby worked hard to develop grass-roots support for campaign finance changes. "We are

---

Federal Matching Funds

Presidential candidates that accepted the federal matching fund system for financing their campaigns in 1984 were able to receive up to $10.1 million in public money during the primary, or pre-convention, season. The following amounts of federal funds for the eight Democratic presidential candidates were certified by the Federal Election Commission through March 7, 1984.

Reubin Askew	$ 897,480.40
Alan Cranston	1,740,029.86
John Glenn	2,797,848.40
Gary Hart	938,904.56
Ernest F. Hollings	753,683.98
Jesse Jackson	388,355.23
George McGovern	209,337.38
Walter F. Mondale	5,268,763.28

To be eligible to receive federal matching funds, a candidate first must raise $100,000 in contributions from individuals: $5,000-plus in 20 different states, in amounts of no more than $250 from any one contributor. Candidates also must agree to abide by spending limits, keep certain records, and submit those records for audit.

The FEC in 1984 also certified $6,060,000 to the Democratic National Committee and $6,060,000 to the Republican National Committee for the two major political parties' 1984 presidential nominating conventions.

---

working to build local coalitions and support to ensure that representatives have to go deal with the issue at home," said Fred Wertheimer, president of the group.

The bill proposed to:

● Limit to $90,000 per two-year election cycle the total amount of money House candidates could accept from PACs.

● Limit to $20,000 the amount of money House candidates could spend from personal and family sources.

● Provide House candidates with the option of receiving partial public financing. Candidates would be eligible to receive a dollar-for-dollar match in public funds for contributions of $100 or less, up to $100,000. The bill required that 75 percent of the contributions come from in-state sources. If a candidate agreed to take the public financing option and his opponent did not, he was released from the other limits prescribed in the bill and would be eligible for a 2-1 match in public funds.

● Guarantee to House candidates who were the targets of independent expenditure campaigns of $5,000 or more the option of receiving free broadcast time or additional public funding equal to the amount of the independent expenditure.

● Limit total spending by House candidates in the general election to $200,000 each. Obey estimated his public financing provisions would cost approximately $40 million in the first election year in which they were used.

PACs: Controversial Election Force

One of the most vocal critics of political action committees (PACs) has been the self-styled citizens lobby, Common Cause. For years it has fought against PACs and lobbied equally strenuously for publicly financed congressional campaigns. Early in 1983 Common Cause took the lead in an attack on PACs that, temporarily at least, had corporate representatives in Washington on the defensive. Common Cause declared "war" on PACs Feb. 1, 1983, with a nationally broadcast radio speech at the National Press Club by Fred Wertheimer, the group's president. The group followed up with a full-page critique in *The New York Times* on Feb. 6

The stakes in the war are high. They concern the way members of Congress are elected and, perhaps even more importantly, what influences are brought to bear upon them once they are sworn in.

To their detractors, PACs — the legally mandated vehicles by which corporations, trade associations, labor unions and ideological groups may channel funds to candidates for federal office — have been viewed as special interest groups that distort congressional decision making. Supporters consider them a basic expression of First Amendment rights. The fight over PACs had evolved by 1983 into a fight over the sources and means of political influence. The debate focused on whether PACs are a healthy way for individuals and groups to participate financially in the political process and whether PAC contributions are a corrupting influence.

The biggest gun in Common Cause's arsenal may turn out to be the computer. The group has been collecting campaign data from the Federal Election Commission, the government's campaign finance watchdog, and produced PAC studies designed to show how the PACs of an interest group influence members of Congress through contributions.

A study of AMPAC, political action committee of the American Medical Association (AMA), entitled "Take $2,000 and Call Me in the Morning," listed AMPAC contributions since 1978 to each member of Congress. Among Common Cause's findings were that 87 percent of senators and 85 percent of representatives accepted some money from AMPAC during their careers on Capitol Hill between 1977 and 1982. "What kind of independent judgment can citizens really expect when an AMA position comes up for a vote from members who have become deeply obligated through cumulative PAC contributions?" Wertheimer asked in an accompanying press release.

Common Cause was not alone in focusing attention on PACs. *The New York Times* ran 41 stories about PACs in 1982 and 31 in 1981, compared to just four stories about PACs in 1980. *Newsweek*, *Time*, and *U.S. News and World Report* ran lengthy stories on PACs and the growing cost of political campaigning. *Business Week* and the *Wall Street Journal* surprised many by printing editorials unfavorable to PACs. Journalist Elizabeth Drew wrote a two-part series on campaign finance for *The New Yorker* magazine in December 1982.

One of the major defenders of PACs in Congress has been Bill Frenzel, R-Minn., ranking Republican on the House Administration Committee. "I think PACs are a very positive influence," Frenzel said. "I see them as the best way of increasing political participation that has occurred in my political lifetime. The typical PAC participant is one who has not given money to political parties, campaigns or candidates in the past. The political action committee has given him or her a rallying point."

After first reeling at the press criticism and the Common Cause campaign, business PACs began to fight back. The Public Affairs Council, a Washington-based association of corporate public relations officers, held a two-day conference entitled "PACs Under Fire: Meeting the Challenge" in January 1983, a few days before the Common Cause campaign got under way. The focus of the conference was on ways of rebutting criticisms of PACs. The council followed up with a six-page brochure, "Attacks on PACs Mount: Counter-Action Needed." One of the council's most powerful tools was a monograph, *The Case for PACs*, written by Herbert E. Alexander, director of the Citizens' Research Foundation.

The council joined with the Business-Industry PAC (BIPAC), the National Association of Business PACs and the National Association of Manufacturers in co-sponsoring a speakers bureau of corporate spokesmen in individual companies.

The anti-PAC campaign also brought together strange political bedfellows. The Committee for Free and Open Elections was created to head off proposals providing for publicly funded campaigns. Heading the group were John T. "Terry" Dolan, National Conservative Political Action Committee chairman; Stewart R. Mott, a wealthy liberal activist; and former Minnesota Sen. Eugene J. McCarthy, who ran for president both as an independent and as a Democrat.

In Congress, Rep. David R. Obey, D-Wis., one of the most outspoken PAC critics, in 1979 steered a bill restricting PACs through the House, only to have it die in the Senate. Obey and 90 other House members reintroduced PAC-limiting legislation in 1983. A compromise version of an earlier measure, that bill would set a spending limit of $240,000 for House campaigns, place a $90,000 limit on the amount all House candidates could accept from PACs and provide a 100 percent tax credit — up to $100 — for contributions to a qualified candidate.

Source: Adapted from Jeremy Gaunt, "The PAC Wars," *Election Politics*, Winter 1983.

At the time the bill was proposed, Wertheimer, a veteran of campaign finance reform debate, remained hopeful that public financing of congressional campaigns would soon be a reality. "If it's not going to happen now the stage is being set for 1985. The time is coming," he said. "I really do think we're closer to a firm date on serious consideration of comprehensive changes in the congressional [campaign] system than we have been since the mid-1970s."

Public financing of congressional campaigns had been controversial ever since the 1974 Federal Election Campaign Act authorized federal funding for presidential contests. There were three major attempts in the late 1970s to extend the financing provisions of the law to congressional races, but none was successful.

"The problem with public financing is that it has been around so long that people have dug in their heels," said one House Democratic staffer long active in efforts to change campaign financing.

One traditional argument against public financing was that it would aid incumbents. "All the proposals that I have seen for taxpayer-financed congressional elections appear to be very useful devices for the re-election of the incumbent officeholder," said Sen. Paul Laxalt, R-Nev., general chairman of the Republican National Committee (RNC).

Republican leaders also argued that public financing would undermine the two-party system. "Any taxpayer-financed system for congressional elections would require access to candidates other than Republicans and Democrats," Laxalt contended. "There is no way, constitutionally, to have a taxpayer-financed system that does not have a triggering mechanism for access by third party and independent candidates," he said.

"Public finance strikes at the heart of political parties' functions," said Rep. William M. Thomas, Calif., senior Republican on the House elections task force. "If you can get financing through the public sector, there will be no need for political parties."

The most vigorous opposition to public financing came from the Committee for Free and Open Elections. The group included National Conservative Political Action Committee Chairman John T. "Terry" Dolan, former Minnesota Democratic Sen. Eugene J. McCarthy and liberal philanthropist Stewart R. Mott. It targeted the districts of Obey and Leach for newspaper and television ads decrying a proposal the committee asserted would help channel taxpayers' money to candidates they did not necessarily support.

Expanded Party Role

Instead of providing public financing or limiting PACs, the Republican leadership wanted to loosen restrictions on party spending that were embedded in existing election law. The GOP proposal was grounded in the belief that money in congressional campaigns was a necessary and desirable element, according to RNC Chairman Frank J. Fahrenkopf Jr. "Money is the equivalent of communications," he said. "We need more communication in the [political] system, not less. Campaigns need more money, not less."

Supporters also believed that an enhanced role for the parties would help curb the influence of campaign contributions from special interests. "If you increase the importance of political parties, you decrease the importance of PACs," Laxalt said.

The Republican plan was embodied in S 1350, introduced by Laxalt, and HR 3081, sponsored by Rep. Bill Frenzel, Minn. The measure was endorsed by Fahrenkopf, Sen. Richard G. Lugar, Ind., chairman of the National Republican Senatorial Committee, and Rep. Guy Vander Jagt, Mich., who headed the National Republican Congressional Committee.

The legislation proposed to:

● Loosen existing restrictions on party contributions by raising the amount a party could give to a candidate to $15,000, from $5,000, per election. Limits on the amount a party's senatorial or national committee could give, either separately or in any combination, to senatorial candidates would be lifted to $30,000, from $17,500.

● Remove limits on the amount party committees could spend on behalf of House and Senate candidates through coordinated expenditures, separate from direct contributions.

● Allow parties to receive contributions from corporations and labor unions to defray costs of solicitation and administrative activities.

The bill also proposed to raise the limits on what publicly financed presidential candidates could spend for primaries and the general election and to remove state-by-state limits.

Level Playing Field?

But the Republican approach faced strong opposition from Democrats, who feared that it would further the GOP's already sizable financial advantage over them. The RNC collected $79.8 million in 1982, far outdistancing the $15.5 million taken in by the Democratic National Committee (DNC). The Democrats said they would like to close that gap before loosening the bonds on party spending.

"I buy a lot of the pure merits of the party approach," said Washington Democratic Rep. Al Swift, chairman of the House Administration Committee's Elections Task Force. "But until the playing field in fund raising is more level, to do what Frenzel is proposing would mean we'd start every game on the goal line, and they'd start every game on the 40-yard line."

Lugar replied that "The Democrats are fearful that the Republicans are better organized and better prepared.... They have a feeling that this is not the time to take off the shackles. The Democrats are spending time — profitably — trying to catch up. The limits [on party contributions] help compress the time for the catch-up."

Others had more philosophical reservations about the legislation. "The proposal has a tendency to encourage dependency on political parties," said Illinois Democratic Sen. Alan J. Dixon, who had introduced a bill (S 85) offering public funding for senatorial candidates. "I would prefer things that encourage independent, individual members."

"I don't want my party ... to wind up having the same kind of leverage over me ... as you can have by implication with a lot of other groups around here," Obey said.

Compromise Proposal

Obey and 90 other members of Congress introduced in late 1983 a compromise proposal designed, according to its sponsors, to "break the logjam on campaign finance reform." The bill retained the PAC-limiting language of HR 2490 but dropped public financing provisions in favor of giving tax credits for campaign contributions. Chief spon-

Political Action Committee (PAC) Spending

(Jan. 1, 1981, to Dec. 31, 1982)

Top Spenders

National Congressional Club	$10,404,521
National Conservative PAC	10,118,891
Realtors PAC	3,144,475
Fund for a Conservative Majority	2,945,883
National Committee for an Effective Congress	2,512,682
American Medical Association PAC	2,491,214
Citizens for the Republic	2,480,629
Committee for the Survival of a Free Congress	2,394,782
Fund for a Democratic Majority	2,207,305
UAW-V-CAP (United Auto Workers)	2,204,645

Corporate PACs

Tenneco Employees Good Government Fund	$499,651
Amoco Political Action Committee	445,899
Bear, Stearns & Co. Political Campaign Committee	439,153
American Family Political Action Committee	335,613
Sunbelt Good Government Cmte. of Winn-Dixie Stores	319,863
General Dynamics Corp. Voluntary Political Contributions	315,392
Grumman Political Action Committee	307,064
Non-Partisan Pol. Support Cmte. for General Electric Co. Employees	290,038
Harris Corporation-Federal Political Action Committee	272,134
Rockwell International Corp. Good Government Cmte.	266,688

Labor PACs

UAW-V-CAP (United Auto Workers)	$2,204,645
Machinists Non-Partisan Political League	1,613,118
National Education Association PAC	1,442,722
Transportation Political Education League	1,348,236
AFL-CIO COPE Political Contributions Committee	1,156,805
ILGWU Campaign Cmte. (Int. Ladies' Garment Workers' Union)	1,119,776
Active Ballot Club (United Food & Commercial Workers)	1,072,099
Seafarers Political Activity Donation	1,042,485
United Steelworkers of America Political Action Fund	1,031,046
CWA-COPE Political Contributions Committee	919,710

Trade/Membership/Health PACs

Realtors PAC	$3,144,475
American Medical Association PAC	2,491,214
California Medical PAC	1,369,171
NRA Political Victory Fund	1,349,726
League of Conservation Voters	1,255,082
Automobile and Truck Dealers Election Action Committee	1,202,475
Build PAC of the National Association of Home Builders	1,197,738
National Association of Life Underwriters PAC	1,085,638
Texas Medical Association PAC-TEXPAC	1,061,845
American Bankers Association BANKPAC	1,042,095

Non-connected PACs

National Congressional Club	$10,404,521
National Conservative PAC	10,118,891
Fund for a Conservative Majority	2,945,883
National Committee for an Effective Congress	2,512,682
Citizens for the Republic	2,480,629
Committee for the Survival of a Free Congress	2,394,782
Fund for a Democratic Majority	2,207,305
Committee for the Future of America	2,170,295
Republican Majority Fund	2,023,794
Independent Action	1,182,516

Cooperative PACs

Committee for Thorough Agricultural Political Education of Associated Milk Producers Inc.	$1,611,630
Dairymen Inc.-Special Political Agricultural Community Education	690,519
Mid-America Dairymen Inc. Agricultural & Dairy Educational Political Trust	667,383
Farmland Industries PAC	65,698
Diamond Walnut Growers Inc. Political Action Cmte.	60,365

Corporations Without Stock PACs

Commodity Futures Pol. Fund of the Chicago Mercantile Exchange	$501,854
Commodity Exchange, Inc. PAC	184,516
Handgun Control Inc. PAC	157,642
Akin, Gump, Strauss, Hauer & Feld Civic Action Cmte	108,758
Health & People PAC of Blue Cross/Blue Shield of Michigan	96,911

Source: Federal Election Commission

sors of the compromise bill were Obey, Leach, and Reps. Mike Synar, D-Okla., Martin Frost, D-Texas, Gillis Long, D-La., and Dan Glickman, D-Kan. Long, Synar and Frost did not endorse Obey's earlier 1983 proposal.

The tax credit idea was first raised by Reps. Barber B. Conable Jr., R-N.Y., and Matthew F. McHugh, D-N.Y., who introduced a bill to boost public participation in elections by creating a larger credit. Neither lawmaker appeared on the initial cosponsor list for the compromise proposal.

As of spring 1984 no action had been taken on any of the proposed campaign finance reform bills. Reconsideration of the issue was expected to be delayed until after the November 1984 elections, after which more information on the costs of conducting presidential and congressional campaigns under the existing laws would be available.

Incumbents' Campaign Cash On Hand — Jan. 1, 1984

Alabama
Senators
Howell Heflin (D) $1,058,463
Jeremiah Denton (R) 3,746
Representatives
1. Jack Edwards (R)[1] 21,258
2. William L. Dickinson (R) 173,208
3. Bill Nichols (D) 170,965
4. Tom Bevill (D) 226,299
5. Ronnie G. Flippo (D) 226,616
6. Ben Erdreich (D) 6,242
7. Richard C. Shelby (D) 233,243

Alaska
Senators
Ted Stevens (R) 586,842
Frank H. Murkowski (R) 37,489
Representative
AL Don Young (R) 30,756

Arizona
Senators
Barry Goldwater (R)[1] 1,416
Dennis DeConcini (D) 22,679
Representatives
1. John McCain (R) 111,361
2. Morris K. Udall (D) 3,441
3. Bob Stump (R) 50,402
4. Eldon Rudd (R) 181,079
5. James F. McNulty Jr. (D) 62,739

Arkansas
Senators
Dale Bumpers (D) 32,945
David Pryor (D) 432,022
Representatives
1. Bill Alexander (D) 84,393
2. Ed Bethune (R)[2] 7,719
3. J. P. Hammerschmidt (R) 43,527
4. Beryl Anthony Jr. (D) 56,303

California
Senators
Alan Cranston (D)[3] 7,705
Pete Wilson (R) 44,065
Representatives
1. Douglas H. Bosco (D) 6,601
2. Gene Chappie (R) 13,254
3. Robert T. Matsui (D) 217,892
4. Vic Fazio (D) 77,252
5. Sala Burton (D)[4] 67,743
6. Barbara Boxer (D) 66,063
7. George Miller (D) 135,615
8. Ronald V. Dellums (D) 31,829
9. Fortney H. Stark (D) 3,144
10. Don Edwards (D) 15,956
11. Tom Lantos (D) 229,258
12. Ed Zschau (R) 10,207
13. Norman Y. Mineta (D) 175,063
14. Norman D. Shumway (R) 20,733
15. Tony Coelho (D) 136,569
16. Leon E. Panetta (D) 136,896
17. Charles Pashayan Jr. (R) 24,115
18. Richard H. Lehman (D) 13,489
19. Robert J. Lagomarsino (R) 240,485
20. William M. Thomas (R) 175,745
21. Bobbi Fiedler (R) 81,819
22. Carlos J. Moorhead (R) 235,024
23. Anthony C. Beilenson (D) 483
24. Henry A. Waxman (D) 47,763
25. Edward R. Roybal (D) 141,250
26. Howard L. Berman (D) 5,781
27. Mel Levine (D) 92,828
28. Julian C. Dixon (D) 32,089
29. Augustus F. Hawkins (D) 27,560
30. Matthew G. Martinez (D) 9,375
31. Mervyn M. Dymally (D) 236
32. Glenn M. Anderson (D) 58,964
33. David Dreier (R) 357,980
34. Esteban Edward Torres (D) 13,140
35. Jerry Lewis (R) 141,942
36. George E. Brown Jr. (D) 29,965
37. Al McCandless (R) 8,691
38. Jerry M. Patterson (D) 30,710
39. William E. Dannemeyer (R) 127,985
40. Robert E. Badham (R) 56,253
41. Bill Lowery (R) 65,465
42. Dan Lungren (R) 56,422
43. Ron Packard (R) 21,432
44. Jim Bates (D) 17,584
45. Duncan L. Hunter (R) 90,410

Colorado
Senators
Gary Hart (D)[3] 45
William L. Armstrong (R) 56,969
Representatives
1. Patricia Schroeder (D) 122,967
2. Timothy E. Wirth (D) 98,661
3. Ray Kogovsek (D)[1] 36,824
4. Hank Brown (R) 137,152
5. Ken Kramer (R) 42,412
6. Daniel L. Schaefer (R)[4] 39,885

Connecticut
Senators
Lowell P. Weicker Jr. (R) 0
Christopher J. Dodd (D) 111,792
Representatives
1. Barbara B. Kennelly (D) 72,656
2. Sam Gejdenson (D) 31,729
3. Bruce A. Morrison (D) 9,234
4. Stewart B. McKinney (R) 61,785
5. William R. Ratchford (D) 16,711
6. Nancy L. Johnson (R) 8,587

Delaware
Senators
William V. Roth Jr. (R) 44,673
Joseph R. Biden Jr. (D) 249,260
Representative
AL Thomas R. Carper (D) 8,958

Florida
Senators
Lawton Chiles (D) 41,784
Paula Hawkins (R) 136,805
Representatives
1. Earl Hutto (D) 64,173
2. Don Fuqua (D) 28,766
3. Charles E. Bennett (D) 70,164
4. Bill Chappell Jr. (D) 26,291
5. Bill McCollum (R) 136,128
6. Kenneth H. MacKay (D) 57,705
7. Sam Gibbons (D) 96,649
8. C. W. Bill Young (R) 127,948
9. Michael Bilirakis (R) 0
10. Andy Ireland (D) 63,365
11. Bill Nelson (D) 91,017
12. Tom Lewis (R) 46,924
13. Connie Mack III (R) 35,590
14. Daniel A. Mica (D) 2,970
15. E. Clay Shaw Jr. (R) 31,918
16. Larry Smith (D) 78,107
17. William Lehman (D) 63,498
18. Claude Pepper (D) 23,842
19. Dante B. Fascell (D) 67,606

Georgia
Senators
Sam Nunn (D) 799,230
Mack Mattingly (R) 192,320
Representatives
1. Lindsay Thomas (D) 19,653
2. Charles Hatcher (D) 4,521
3. Richard Ray (D) 34,080
4. Elliott H. Levitas (D) 13,482
5. Wyche Fowler Jr. (D) 213,779
6. Newt Gingrich (R) 25,301
7. George W. Darden (D)[4] 19,480
8. J. Roy Rowland (D) 16,996
9. Ed Jenkins (D) 131,110
10. Doug Barnard Jr. (D) 209,626

Hawaii
Senators
Daniel K. Inouye (D) 470,219
Spark M. Matsunaga (D) 304,206
Representatives
1. Cecil Heftel (D) 51,023
2. Daniel K. Akaka (D) 37,672

Idaho
Senators
James A. McClure (R) 248,002
Steven D. Symms (R) 40,858
Representatives
1. Larry E. Craig (R) 20,145
2. George Hansen (R) 5,385

Illinois
Senators
Charles H. Percy (R) 541,321
Alan J. Dixon (D) 49,712
Representatives
1. Charles A. Hayes (D)[4] ———
2. Gus Savage (D) 91
3. Marty Russo (D) 11,304
4. George M. O'Brien (R) 40,345
5. William O. Lipinski (D) 2,813
6. Henry J. Hyde (R) 133,440
7. Cardiss Collins (D) 32,511

156

Campaign Cash on Hand 157

8. Dan Rostenkowski (D)	612,980
9. Sidney R. Yates (D)	9,177
10. John Edward Porter (R)	6,637
11. Frank Annunzio (D)	123,184
12. Philip M. Crane (R)	243,783
13. John N. Erlenborn (R)[1]	16,491
14. Tom Corcoran (R)[2]	0
15. Edward R. Madigan (R)	60,195
16. Lynn Martin (R)	60,198
17. Lane Evans (D)	5,938
18. Robert H. Michel (R)	217,126
19. Daniel B. Crane (R)	64,372
20. Richard J. Durbin (D)	71,740
21. Melvin Price (D)	38,444
22. Paul Simon (D)[2]	—

Indiana
Senators
Richard G. Lugar (R)	122,548
Dan Quayle (R)	44,280

Representatives
1. Katie Hall (D)	2,749
2. Philip R. Sharp (D)	62,313
3. John Hiler (R)	117,886
4. Dan Coats (R)	82,861
5. Elwood Hillis (R)	35,229
6. Dan Burton (R)	25,024
7. John T. Myers (R)	88,747
8. Francis X. McCloskey (D)	17,924
9. Lee H. Hamilton (D)	30,241
10. Andrew Jacobs Jr. (D)	695

Iowa
Senators
Roger W. Jepsen (R)	400,603
Charles E. Grassley (R)	126,015

Representatives
1. Jim Leach (R)	18,435
2. Tom Tauke (R)	40,206
3. Cooper Evans (R)	1,058
4. Neal Smith (D)	49,825
5. Tom Harkin (D)[2]	106,450
6. Berkley Bedell (D)	93,787

Kansas
Senators
Robert Dole (R)	49,646
Nancy Landon Kassebaum (R)	163,104

Representatives
1. Pat Roberts (R)	95,010
2. Jim Slattery (D)	7,077
3. Larry Winn Jr. (R)[1]	36,632
4. Dan Glickman (D)	48,968
5. Bob Whittaker (R)	139,998

Kentucky
Senators
Walter D. Huddleston (D)	677,934
Wendell H. Ford (D)	0

Representatives
1. Carroll Hubbard Jr. (D)	136,939
2. William H. Natcher (D)	—
3. Romano L. Mazzoli (D)	14,752
4. Gene Snyder (R)	223,693
5. Harold Rogers (R)	27,090
6. Larry J. Hopkins (R)	161,911
7. Carl D. Perkins (D)	4,996

Louisiana
Senators
Russell B. Long (D)	37,724
J. Bennett Johnston (D)	1,302,570

Representatives
1. Bob Livingston (R)	344,751
2. Lindy Boggs (D)	14,417
3. W. J. Tauzin (D)	227,483
4. Buddy Roemer (D)	11,636
5. Jerry Huckaby (D)	296,325
6. Henson Moore (R)	466,671
7. John B. Breaux (D)	233,526
8. Gillis W. Long (D)	418,024

Maine
Senators
Wililam S. Cohen (R)	192,668
George J. Mitchell (D)	838

Representatives
1. John R. McKernan Jr. (R)	57,723
2. Olympia J. Snowe (R)	32,209

Maryland
Senators
Charles McC. Mathias Jr. (R)	4,565
Paul S. Sarbanes (D)	11,917

Representatives
1. Roy Dyson (D)	22,096
2. Clarence D. Long (D)	192,430
3. Barbara A. Mikulski (D)	45,780
4. Marjorie S. Holt (R)	129,400
5. Steny H. Hoyer (D)	105,791
6. Beverly B. Byron (D)	57,456
7. Parren J. Mitchell (D)	404
8. Michael D. Barnes (D)	61,107

Massachusetts
Senators
Edward M. Kennedy (D)	7,357
Paul E. Tsongas (D)[1]	82,667

Representatives
1. Silvio O. Conte (R)	177,549
2. Edward P. Boland (D)	48,691
3. Joseph D. Early (D)	31,166
4. Barney Frank (D)	13,868
5. James M. Shannon (D)[2]	93,027
6. Nicholas Mavroules (D)	1,187
7. Edward J. Markey (D)[2]	160,275
8. Thomas P. O'Neill Jr. (D)	138,042
9. Joe Moakley (D)	82,655
10. Gerry E. Studds (D)	25,595
11. Brian J. Donnelly (D)	137,472

Michigan
Senators
Donald W. Riegle Jr. (D)	322,133
Carl Levin (D)	670,180

Representatives
1. John Conyers Jr. (D)	5,626
2. Carl D. Pursell (R)	40,087
3. Howard Wolpe (D)	0
4. Mark Siljander (R)	13,389
5. Harold S. Sawyer (R)	20,981
6. Bob Carr (D)	33,842
7. Dale E. Kildee (D)	16,436
8. Bob Traxler (D)	48,978
9. Guy Vander Jagt (R)	66,889
10. Don Albosta (D)	66,004
11. Robert W. Davis (R)	57,509
12. David E. Bonior (D)	17,800
13. George W. Crockett Jr. (D)	21,730
14. Dennis M. Hertel (D)	35,647
15. William D. Ford (D)	670
16. John D. Dingell (D)	45,437
17. Sander Levin (D)	15,558
18. William S. Broomfield (R)	254,815

Minnesota
Senators
Dave Durenberger (R)	128,571
Rudy Boschwitz (R)	1,321,444

Representatives
1. Timothy J. Penny (D)	69,483
2. Vin Weber (R)	83,524
3. Bill Frenzel (R)	165,375
4. Bruce F. Vento (D)	59,653
5. Martin Olav Sabo (D)	53,927
6. Gerry Sikorski (D)	138,234
7. Arlan Stangeland (R)	71,787
8. James L. Oberstar (D)[2]	11,416

Mississippi
Senators
John C. Stennis (D)	0
Thad Cochran (R)	442,338

Representatives
1. Jamie L. Whitten (D)	127,034
2. Webb Franklin (R)	12,171
3. G. V. Montgomery (D)	105,359
4. Wayne Dowdy (D)	5,494
5. Trent Lott (R)	167,745

Missouri
Senators
Thomas F. Eagleton (D)	13,532
John C. Danforth (R)	4,500

Representatives
1. William Clay (D)	15,502
2. Robert A. Young (D)	77,434
3. Richard A. Gephardt (D)	36,402
4. Ike Skelton (D)	29,189
5. Alan Wheat (D)	11,284
6. E. Thomas Coleman (R)	74,997
7. Gene Taylor (R)	246,754
8. Bill Emerson (R)	16,552
9. Harold L. Volkmer (D)	29,905

Montana
Senators
John Melcher (D)	3,987
Max Baucus (D)	61,158

Representatives
1. Pat Williams (D)	22,267
2. Ron Marlenee (R)	28,732

Nebraska
Senators
Edward Zorinsky (D)	51,889
J. James Exon (D)	51,932

Representatives
1. Douglas K. Bereuter (R)	72,143
2. Hal Daub (R)	65,932
3. Virginia Smith (R)	61,201

158 Elections '84

Nevada
Senators
Paul Laxalt (R)	6,397
Chic Hecht (R)	43,898

Representatives
1. Harry Reid (D)	735
2. Barbara Vucanovich (R)	17,809

New Hampshire
Senators
Gordon J. Humphrey (R)	77,875
Warren B. Rudman (R)	10,316

Representatives
1. Norman E. D'Amours (D)[2]	—
2. Judd Gregg (R)	26,420

New Jersey
Senators
Bill Bradley (D)	1,847,091
Frank R. Lautenberg (D)	12,271

Representatives
1. James J. Florio (D)	10,359
2. William J. Hughes (D)	36,590
3. James J. Howard (D)	73,375
4. Christopher H. Smith (R)	6,901
5. Marge Roukema (R)	45,536
6. Bernard J. Dwyer (D)	28,663
7. Matthew J. Rinaldo (R)	162,128
8. Robert A. Roe (D)	33,706
9. Robert G. Torricelli (D)	42,851
10. Peter W. Rodino Jr. (D)	67,790
11. Joseph G. Minish (D)	223,444
12. Jim Courter (R)	120,230
13. Edwin B. Forsythe (R)	40,567
14. Frank J. Guarini (D)	65,155

New Mexico
Senators
Pete V. Domenici (R)	535,904
Jeff Bingaman (D)	27,698

Representatives
1. Manuel Lujan Jr. (R)	99,775
2. Joe Skeen (R)	42,304
3. Bill Richardson (D)	29,899

New York
Senators
Daniel Patrick Moynihan (D)	69,324
Alfonse M. D'Amato (R)	1,383,417

Representatives
1. William Carney (R)	68,141
2. Thomas J. Downey (D)	110,733
3. Robert J. Mrazek (D)	24,978
4. Norman F. Lent (R)	101,525
5. Raymond J. McGrath (R)	21,058
6. Joseph P. Addabbo (D)	431,411
7. Gary L. Ackerman (D)[4]	13,294
8. James H. Scheuer (D)	3,074
9. Geraldine A. Ferraro (D)	1,711
10. Charles E. Schumer (D)	383,183
11. Edolphus Towns (D)	—
12. Major R. Owens (D)	5,909
13. Stephen J. Solarz (D)	596,495
14. Guy V. Molinari (R)	102,606
15. Bill Green (R)	125,390
16. Charles B. Rangel (D)	64,496
17. Ted Weiss (D)	14,362
18. Robert Garcia (D)	51
19. Mario Biaggi (D)	143,205
20. Richard L. Ottinger (D)[1]	3,011
21. Hamilton Fish Jr. (R)	18,619
22. Benjamin A. Gilman (R)	19,968
23. Samuel S. Stratton (D)	36,820
24. Gerald B. H. Solomon (R)	48,159
25. Sherwood L. Boehlert (R)	34,110
26. David O'B. Martin (R)	23,174
27. George C. Wortley (R)	8,714
28. Matthew F. McHugh (D)	12,461
29. Frank Horton (R)	50,678
30. Barber B. Conable Jr. (R)[1]	74
31. Jack F. Kemp (R)	198,042
32. John J. LaFalce (D)	243,609
33. Henry J. Nowak (D)	53,887
34. Stan Lundine (D)	231

North Carolina
Senators
Jesse Helms (R)	146,992
John P. East (R)	—

Representatives
1. Walter B. Jones (D)	150,370
2. Tim Valentine (D)	5,645
3. Charles Whitley (D)	25,894
4. Ike Andrews (D)	4,602
5. Stephen L. Neal (D)	21,973
6. Robin Britt (D)	10,575
7. Charlie Rose (D)	92,775
8. W. G. "Bill" Hefner (D)	27,147
9. James G. Martin (R)[5]	875
10. James T. Broyhill (R)	119,157
11. James McClure Clarke (D)	893

North Dakota
Senators
Quentin N. Burdick (D)	122,023
Mark Andrews (R)	106,373

Representative
AL Byron L. Dorgan (D)	126,239

Ohio
Senators
John Glenn (D)[3]	2,335
Howard M. Metzenbaum (D)	894,260

Representatives
1. Thomas A. Luken (D)	75,988
2. Bill Gradison (R)	82,353
3. Tony P. Hall (D)	104,166
4. Michael G. Oxley (R)	80,626
5. Delbert L. Latta (R)	99,912
6. Bob McEwen (R)	11,397
7. Michael DeWine (R)	1,465
8. Thomas N. Kindness (R)	16,901
9. Marcy Kaptur (D)	39,218
10. Clarence E. Miller (R)	32,489
11. Dennis E. Eckart (D)	9,930
12. John R. Kasich (R)	51,625
13. Don J. Pease (D)	62,669
14. John F. Seiberling (D)	5,413
15. Chalmers P. Wylie (R)	46,412
16. Ralph Regula (R)	48,953
17. Lyle Williams (R)	3,313
18. Douglas Applegate (D)	48,385
19. Edward F. Feighan (D)	20,659
20. Mary Rose Oakar (D)	53,342
21. Louis Stokes (D)	28,347

Oklahoma
Senators
David L. Boren (D)	567,025
Don Nickles (R)	304,558

Representatives
1. James R. Jones (D)	105,513
2. Mike Synar (D)	89,296
3. Wes Watkins (D)	120,947
4. Dave McCurdy (D)	7,875
5. Mickey Edwards (R)	11,538
6. Glenn English (D)	96,693

Oregon
Senators
Mark O. Hatfield (R)	84,248
Bob Packwood (R)	138,480

Representatives
1. Les AuCoin (D)	30,851
2. Bob Smith (R)	26,001
3. Ron Wyden (D)	130,003
4. James Weaver (D)	53,165
5. Denny Smith (R)	36,931

Pennsylvania
Senators
John Heinz (R)	448,331
Arlen Specter (R)	215,090

Representatives
1. Thomas M. Foglietta (D)	9,535
2. William H. Gray III (D)	5,431
3. Robert A. Borski (D)	32,465
4. Joseph P. Kolter (D)	13,288
5. Richard T. Schulze (R)	182,302
6. Gus Yatron (D)	37,411
7. Robert W. Edgar (D)	17,744
8. Peter H. Kostmayer (D)	2,490
9. Bud Shuster (R)	109,090
10. Joseph M. McDade (R)	125,476
11. Frank Harrison (D)	825
12. John P. Murtha (D)	42,834
13. Lawrence Coughlin (R)	54,672
14. William J. Coyne (D)	20,145
15. Don Ritter (R)	40,912
16. Robert S. Walker (R)	16,071
17. George W. Gekas (R)	7,333
18. Doug Walgren (D)	31,357
19. Bill Goodling (R)	6,584
20. Joseph M. Gaydos (D)	7,706
21. Thomas J. Ridge (R)	29,377
22. Austin J. Murphy (D)	65,998
23. William F. Clinger Jr. (R)	58,506

Rhode Island
Senators
Claiborne Pell (D)	238,284
John H. Chafee (R)	136,306

Representatives
1. Fernand J. St Germain (D)	366,051
2. Claudine Schneider (R)	76,588

South Carolina
Senators
Strom Thurmond (R)	30,450
Ernest F. Hollings (D)[3]	62,746

Representatives
1. Thomas F. Hartnett (R) — 56,047
2. Floyd Spence (R) — 44,272
3. Butler Derrick (D) — 83,756
4. Carroll Campbell Jr. (R) — 109,793
5. John Spratt (D) — 24,728
6. Robert M. Tallon Jr. (D) — 40,049

South Dakota
Senators
Larry Pressler (R) — 300,723
James Abdnor (R) — 47,329
Representative
AL Thomas A. Daschle (D) — 17,735

Tennessee
Senators
Howard H. Baker Jr. (R)[1] — 0
Jim Sasser (D) — 7,433
Representatives
1. James H. Quillen (R) — 162,401
2. John J. Duncan (R) — 220,254
3. Marilyn Lloyd (D) — 16,199
4. Jim Cooper (D) — 7,944
5. Bill Boner (D) — 59,929
6. Albert Gore Jr. (D)[2] — 0
7. Don Sundquist (R) — 67,687
8. Ed Jones (D) — 64,987
9. Harold E. Ford (D) — 7,010

Texas
Senators
John Tower (R)[1] — 1,170,344
Lloyd Bentsen (D) — 77,101
Representatives
1. Sam B. Hall Jr. (D) — 97,731
2. Charles Wilson (D) — 19,499
3. Steve Bartlett (R) — 101,373
4. Ralph M. Hall (D) — 117,929
5. John Bryant (D) — 17,784
6. Phil Gramm (R)[2,4] — ——
7. Bill Archer (R) — 426,010
8. Jack Fields (R) — 119,907
9. Jack Brooks (D) — 81,068
10. J. J. Pickle (D) — 388,469
11. Marvin Leath (D) — 287,494
12. Jim Wright (D) — 34,770
13. Jack Hightower (D) — 74,446
14. Bill Patman (D) — 60,470
15. E. "Kika" de la Garza (D) — 101,730
16. Ronald Coleman (D) — 11,234
17. Charles W. Stenholm (D) — 164,096
18. Mickey Leland (D) — 5,929
19. Kent Hance (D)[2] — ——
20. Henry B. Gonzalez (D) — 1,061
21. Tom Loeffler (R) — 409,325
22. Ron Paul (R)[2] — 67,071
23. Abraham Kazen Jr. (D) — 17,907
24. Martin Frost (D) — 147,165
25. Mike Andrews (D) — 781
26. Tom Vandergriff (D) — 8,980
27. Solomon P. Ortiz (D) — 64,540

Utah
Senators
Jake Garn (R) — 2,383
Orrin G. Hatch (R) — 34,186
Representatives
1. James V. Hansen (R) — 12,375
2. Dan Marriott (R)[5] — 290
3. Howard C. Nielson (R) — 1,940

Vermont
Senators
Robert T. Stafford (R) — 8,518
Patrick J. Leahy (D) — 63,115
Representative
AL James M. Jeffords (R) — 37,704

Virginia
Senators
John W. Warner (R) — 370,822
Paul S. Trible Jr. (R) — 33,435
Representatives
1. Herbert H. Bateman (R) — 42,665
2. G. William Whitehurst (R) — 30,414
3. Thomas J. Bliley Jr. (R) — 44,872
4. Norman Sisisky (D) — 25,317
5. Dan Daniel (D) — 75,677
6. James R. Olin (D) — 1,543
7. J. Kenneth Robinson (R)[1] — ——
8. Stan Parris (R) — 34,235
9. Frederick C. Boucher (D) — 15,980
10. Frank R. Wolf (R) — 22,724

Washington
Senators
Slade Gorton (R) — 114,912
Daniel J. Evans (R)[4] — 194,518
Representatives
1. Joel Pritchard (R)[1] — 12,620
2. Al Swift (D) — 29,404
3. Don Bonker (D) — 45,151
4. Sid Morrison (R) — 2,067
5. Thomas S. Foley (D) — 114,444
6. Norman D. Dicks (D) — 88,794
7. Mike Lowry (D) — 65,465
8. Rod Chandler (R) — 28,821

West Virginia
Senators
Jennings Randolph (D)[1] — 42
Robert C. Byrd (D) — 169,431
Representatives
1. Alan B. Mollohan (D) — 15,089
2. Harley O. Staggers Jr. (D) — 3,069
3. Bob Wise (D) — 7,624
4. Nick J. Rahall II (D) — 2,341

Wisconsin
Senators
William Proxmire (D) — ——
Robert W. Kasten Jr. (R) — 118,289
Representatives
1. Les Aspin (D) — 13,569
2. Robert W. Kastenmeier (D) — 9,443
3. Steven Gunderson (R) — 3,914
4. Vacant
5. Jim Moody (D) — 7,794
6. Thomas E. Petri (R) — 70,329
7. David R. Obey (D) — 121,477
8. Toby Roth (R) — 82,567
9. James Sensenbrenner (R) — 102,815

Wyoming
Senators
Malcolm Wallop (R) — 21,099
Alan K. Simpson (R) — 241,891
Representative
AL Dick Cheney (R) — 63,922

Key:
* Source: Unverified Federal Election Commission reports
[1] Retiring at end of term
[2] Running for Senate
[3] Running for president
[4] Elected 1983
[5] Running for governor
—— No end-of-year report available

Appendix.. 161

1980 Presidential Primaries......................... 163
1980 Presidential Conventions 170
Results of Presidential Elections, 1860-1980 183
Victorious Party in Presidential Elections............... 185
1982 Election Results for Governor, Senate, House........ 186
Selected Bibliography 195

1980 Presidential Primaries

Republican / Democratic

February 17 Puerto Rico

Republican

	Votes	%
George Bush (Texas)[2]	111,940	60.1
Howard H. Baker Jr. (Tenn.)[3]	68,934	37.0
Benjamin Fernandez (Calif.)	2,097	1.1
John B. Connally (Texas)[4]	1,964	1.1
Harold Stassen (N.Y.)	672	0.4
Robert Dole (Kan.)	483	0.3
Others	281	0.1

Democratic — March 16

	Votes	%
Jimmy Carter (Ga.)	449,681	51.7
Edward M. Kennedy (Mass.)	418,068	48.0
Edmund G. Brown Jr. (Calif.)[5]	1,660	0.2
Others	826	0.1

February 26 New Hampshire

	Votes	%
Ronald Reagan (Calif.)	72,983	49.6
Bush	33,443	22.7
Baker	18,943	12.1
John B. Anderson (Ill.)[6]	14,458	9.8
Philip M. Crane (Ill.)	2,618	1.8
Connally	2,239	1.5
Others*	1,876	1.3

	Votes	%
Carter	52,692	47.1
Kennedy	41,745	37.3
Brown	10,743	9.6
Lyndon LaRouche (N.Y.)	2,326	2.1
Richard Kay (Ohio)	566	0.5
Others*	3,858	3.4

March 4 Massachusetts

	Votes	%
Bush	124,365	31.0
Anderson	122,987	30.7
Reagan	115,334	28.8
Baker	19,366	4.8
Connally	4,714	1.2
Crane	4,669	1.2
Gerald R. Ford (Mich.)*	3,398	0.8
Fernandez	374	0.1
Stassen	218	0.1
Others*	2,581	0.6
No preference	2,243	0.6

	Votes	%
Kennedy	590,393	65.1
Carter	260,401	28.7
Brown	31,498	3.5
Others*	5,368	0.6
No preference	19,663	2.2

March 4 Vermont

	Votes	%
Reagan	19,720	30.1
Anderson	19,030	29.0
Bush	14,226	21.7
Baker	8,055	12.3
Ford*	2,300	3.5
Crane	1,238	1.9
Connally	884	1.3
Stassen	105	0.2
Others*	53	

	Votes	%
Carter	29,015	73.1
Kennedy	10,135	25.5
Brown*	358	0.9
LaRouche*	6	
Others	189	0.5

March 8 South Carolina

	Votes	%
Reagan	79,549	54.7
Connally	43,113	29.6
Bush	21,569	14.8
Baker	773	0.5
Fernandez	171	0.1
Stassen	150	0.1
Dole	117	0.1
Others*	59	

164 Elections '84

	Republican				**Democratic**	
		Votes	%		Votes	%

March 11 Alabama

	Votes	%		Votes	%
Reagan	147,352	69.7	Carter	193,734	81.6
Bush	54,730	25.9	Kennedy	31,382	13.2
Crane	5,099	2.4	Brown	9,529	4.0
Baker	1,963	0.9	Others	1,149	0.5
Connally	1,077	0.5	Unpledged delegates	1,670	0.7
Stassen	544	0.3			
Dole	447	0.2			
Others	141				

March 11 Florida

	Votes	%		Votes	%
Reagan	345,699	56.2	Carter	666,321	60.7
Bush	185,996	30.2	Kennedy	254,727	23.2
Anderson	56,636	9.2	Brown	53,474	4.9
Crane	12,000	2.0	Kay	19,160	1.7
Baker	6,345	1.0	No preference	104,321	9.5
Connally	4,958	0.8			
Stassen	1,377	0.2			
Dole	1,086	0.2			
Fernandez	898	0.1			

March 11 Georgia

	Votes	%		Votes	%
Reagan	146,500	73.2	Carter	338,772	88.0
Bush	25,293	12.6	Kennedy	32,315	8.4
Anderson	16,853	8.4	Brown	7,255	1.9
Crane	6,308	3.2	Cliff Finch (Miss.)	1,378	0.4
Connally	2,388	1.2	Kay	840	0.2
Baker	1,571	0.8	LaRouche	513	0.1
Fernandez	809	0.4	Unpledged delegates	3,707	1.0
Dole	249	0.1			
Stassen	200	0.1			

March 18 Illinois

	Votes	%		Votes	%
Reagan	547,355	48.4	Carter	780,787	65.0
Anderson	415,193	36.7	Kennedy	359,875	30.0
Bush	124,057	11.0	Brown	39,168	3.3
Crane	24,865	2.2	LaRouche	19,192	1.6
Baker	7,051	0.6	Anderson*	1,643	0.1
Connally	4,548	0.4	Others*	402	
Dole	1,843	0.2			
Ford*	1,106	0.3			
Others	4,063	0.1			

March 25 Connecticut

	Votes	%		Votes	%
Bush	70,367	38.6	Kennedy	98,662	46.9
Reagan	61,735	33.9	Carter	87,207	41.5
Anderson	40,354	22.1	LaRouche	5,617	2.7
Baker	2,446	1.3	Brown	5,386	2.6
Crane	1,887	1.0	Unpledged delegates	13,403	6.4
Connally	598	0.3			
Dole	333	0.2			
Fernandez	308	0.2			
Unpledged delegates	4,256	2.3			

1980 Primaries

	Republican			**Democratic**		
		Votes	%		Votes	%

March 25 New York

	Votes	%
Kennedy	582,757	58.9
Carter	406,305	41.1

April 1 Kansas

Republican	Votes	%	Democratic	Votes	%
Reagan	179,739	63.0	Carter	109,807	56.6
Anderson	51,924	18.2	Kennedy	61,318	31.6
Bush	35,838	12.6	Brown	9,434	4.9
Baker	3,603	1.3	Finch	629	0.3
Connally	2,067	0.7	Others	1,567	0.8
Fernandez	1,650	0.6	None of the names shown	11,163	5.8
Crane	1,367	0.5			
Stassen	383	0.1			
Others	2,101	0.4			
None of the names shown	6,726	2.4			

April 1 Wisconsin

Republican	Votes	%	Democratic	Votes	%
Reagan	364,898	40.2	Carter	353,662	56.2
Bush	276,164	30.4	Kennedy	189,520	30.1
Anderson	248,623	27.4	Brown	74,496	11.8
Baker	3,298	0.4	LaRouche	6,896	1.1
Crane	2,951	0.3	Finch	1,842	0.3
Connally	2,312	0.3	Others*	509	0.1
Fernandez	1,051	0.1	None of the names shown	2,694	0.4
Stassen	1,010	0.1			
Others*	4,951	0.5			
None of the names shown	2,595	0.3			

April 5 Louisiana

Republican	Votes	%	Democratic	Votes	%
Reagan	31,212	74.9	Carter	199,956	55.7
Bush	7,818	18.8	Kennedy	80,797	22.5
Stassen	126	0.3	Brown	16,774	4.7
Fernandez	84	0.2	Finch	11,153	3.1
Others	222	0.5	Kay	3,362	0.9
None of the names shown	2,221	5.3	Others	5,085	1.4
			Unpledged delegates	41,614	11.6

April 22 Pennsylvania

Republican	Votes	%	Democratic	Votes	%
Bush	626,759	50.5	Kennedy	736,854	45.7
Reagan	527,916	42.5	Carter	732,332	45.4
Baker	30,846	2.5	Brown	37,669	2.3
Anderson	26,890	2.1	Anderson*	9,182	0.6
Connally	10,656	0.9	Bush*	2,074	0.1
Stassen	6,767	0.5	Reagan*	1,097	0.1
Fernandez	2,521	0.2	Ford*	150	
Others	9,056	0.8	No preference	93,865	5.8

May 3 Texas

Republican	Votes	%	Democratic	Votes	%
Reagan	268,798	51.0	Carter	770,390	55.9
Bush	249,819	47.4	Kennedy	314,129	22.8
Unpledged delegates	8,152	1.5	Brown	35,585	2.6
			Unpledged delegates	257,250	18.7

Republican

Democratic

	Votes	%		Votes	%

May 6 District of Columbia

	Votes	%		Votes	%
Bush	4,973	66.1	Kennedy	39,561	61.7
Anderson	2,025	26.9	Carter	23,697	36.9
Crane	270	3.6	LaRouche	892	1.4
Stassen	201	2.7			
Fernandez	60	0.8			

May 6 Indiana

	Votes	%		Votes	%
Reagan	419,016	73.7	Carter	398,949	67.7
Bush	92,955	16.4	Kennedy	190,492	32.3
Anderson	56,342	9.9			

May 6 North Carolina

	Votes	%		Votes	%
Reagan	113,854	67.6	Carter	516,778	70.1
Bush	36,631	21.8	Kennedy	130,684	17.7
Anderson	8,542	5.1	Brown	21,420	2.9
Baker	2,543	1.5	No preference	68,380	9.3
Connally	1,107	0.7			
Dole	629	0.4			
Crane	547	0.3			
No preference	4,538	2.7			

May 6 Tennessee

	Votes	%		Votes	%
Reagan	144,625	74.1	Carter	221,658	75.2
Bush	35,274	18.1	Kennedy	53,258	18.1
Anderson	8,722	4.5	Brown	5,612	1.9
Crane	1,574	0.8	Finch	1,663	0.6
Baker*	16		LaRouche	925	0.3
Ford*	14		Others*	49	
Connally*	1		Unpledged delegates	11,515	3.9
Others*	8				
Unpledged delegates	4,976	2.5			

May 13 Maryland

	Votes	%		Votes	%
Reagan	80,557	48.2	Carter	226,528	47.5
Bush	68,389	40.9	Kennedy	181,091	38.0
Anderson	16,244	9.7	Brown	14,313	3.0
Crane	2,113	1.3	Finch	4,891	1.0
			LaRouche	4,388	0.9
			Unpledged delegates	45,879	9.6

May 13 Nebraska

	Votes	%		Votes	%
Reagan	155,995	76.0	Carter	72,120	46.9
Bush	31,380	15.3	Kennedy	57,826	37.6
Anderson	11,879	5.8	Brown	5,478	3.6
Dole	1,420	0.7	LaRouche	1,169	0.8
Crane	1,062	0.5	Others*	1,247	0.8
Stassen	799	0.4	Unpledged delegates	16,041	10.4
Fernandez	400	0.2			
Others*	2,268	1.1			

	Republican			Democratic		
	Votes	%		Votes	%

May 20 Michigan

	Votes	%		Votes	%
Bush	341,998	57.5	Brown	23,043	29.4
Reagan	189,184	31.8	LaRouche	8,948	11.4
Anderson	48,947	8.2	Others*	10,048	12.8
Fernandez	2,248	0.4	Unpledged delegates	36,385	46.4
Stassen	1,938	0.3			
Others*	596	0.1			
Unpledged delegates	10,265	1.7			

May 20 Oregon

	Votes	%		Votes	%
Reagan	170,449	54.0	Carter	208,693	56.7
Bush	109,210	34.6	Kennedy	114,651	31.1
Anderson	32,118	10.2	Brown	34,409	9.3
Crane	2,324	0.7	Anderson*	5,407	1.5
Others*	1,265	0.4	Reagan*	2,206	0.6
			Bush*	1,838	0.5

May 27 Arkansas

				Votes	%
			Carter	269,375	60.1
			Kennedy	78,542	17.5
			Finch	19,469	4.3
			Unpledged delegates	80,904	18.0

May 27 Idaho

	Votes	%		Votes	%
Reagan	111,868	82.9	Carter	31,383	62.2
Anderson	13,130	9.7	Kennedy	11,087	22.0
Bush	5,416	4.0	Brown	2,078	4.1
Crane	1,024	0.8	Unpledged delegates	5,934	11.8
Unpledged delegates	3,441	2.6			

May 27 Kentucky

	Votes	%		Votes	%
Reagan	78,072	82.4	Carter	160,819	66.9
Bush	6,861	7.2	Kennedy	55,167	23.0
Anderson	4,791	5.1	Kay	2,609	1.1
Stassen	1,223	1.3	Finch	2,517	1.0
Fernandez	764	0.8	Unpledged delegates	19,219	8.0
Unpledged delegates	3,084	3.3			

May 27 Nevada

	Votes	%		Votes	%
Reagan	39,352	83.0	Carter	25,159	37.6
Bush	3,078	6.5	Kennedy	19,296	28.8
None of the names shown	4,965	10.5	None of the names shown	22,493	33.6

June 3 California

	Votes	%		Votes	%
Reagan	2,057,923	80.3	Kennedy slate	1,507,142	44.8
Anderson	349,315	13.6	Carter slate	1,266,276	37.6
Bush	125,113	4.9	Brown slate	135,962	4.0
Crane	21,465	0.8	LaRouche slate	71,779	2.1
Fernandez	10,242	0.4	Others*	51	
Others*	14		Unpledged slate	382,759	11.4

Republican | Democratic

	Votes	%		Votes	%

June 3 New Mexico

Reagan	37,982	63.8	Kennedy	73,721	46.3
Anderson	7,171	12.0	Carter	66,621	41.8
Bush	5,892	9.9	LaRouche	4,798	3.0
Crane	4,412	7.4	Finch	4,490	2.8
Fernandez	1,795	3.0	Unpledged delegates	9,734	6.1
Stassen	947	1.6			
Unpledged delegates	1,347	2.3			

June 3 New Jersey

Reagan	225,959	81.3	Kennedy	315,109	56.2
Bush	47,447	17.1	Carter	212,387	37.9
Stassen	4,571	1.6	LaRouche	13,913	2.5
			Unpledged delegates	19,499	3.5

June 3 Montana

Reagan	68,744	86.6	Carter	66,922	51.5
Bush	7,665	9.7	Kennedy	47,671	36.7
No preference	3,014	3.8	No preference	15,466	11.9

June 3 Ohio

Reagan	692,288	80.8	Carter	605,744	51.1
Bush	164,485	19.2	Kennedy	523,874	44.2
			LaRouche	35,268	3.0
			Kay	21,524	1.8

June 3 Rhode Island

Reagan	3,839	72.0	Kennedy	26,179	68.3
Bush	993	18.6	Carter	9,907	25.8
Stassen	107	2.0	LaRouche	1,160	3.0
Fernandez	48	0.9	Brown	310	0.8
Unpledged delegates	348	6.5	Unpledged delegates	771	2.0

June 3 South Dakota

Reagan slate	72,861	82.2	Kennedy slate	33,418	48.6
Bush slate	3,691	4.2	Carter slate	31,251	45.4
Stassen slate	987	1.1	Uncommitted slate	4,094	6.0
No preference slate	5,366	6.1			

June 3 West Virginia

Reagan	115,407	83.6	Carter	197,687	62.2
Bush	19,509	14.1	Kennedy	120,247	37.8
Stassen	3,100	2.2			

June 3 Mississippi

Reagan slate	23,028	89.4
Bush slate	2,105	8.2
Unslated	618	2.4

Republican

	Votes	%
TOTALS[7]		
Reagan	7,709,793	60.8
Bush	2,958,093	23.3
Anderson	1,572,174	12.4
Baker	112,219	0.9
Crane	97,793	0.8
Connally	80,661	0.6
Stassen	24,753	0.2
Fernandez	23,423	0.2
Dole	7,298	0.1
Unpledged delegates	38,708	0.3
No preference	15,161	0.1
None of the names shown	14,286	0.1
Others[a]	36,089	0.3
	12,690,451	

Democratic

	Votes	%
Carter	9,593,335	51.2
Kennedy	6,963,625	37.1
Brown	573,636	3.1
LaRouche	177,784	1.0
Kay	48,061	0.3
Finch	48,032	0.3
Unpledged delegates	950,378	5.1
No preference	301,695	1.6
None of the names shown	36,350	0.1
Others[9]	54,929	0.3
	18,747,825	

[a] Write-in vote

1. In 1980 35 states, the District of Columbia and Puerto Rico held presidential primaries. California Democrats and South Dakota Republicans and Democrats held state-type preference primaries. In New York, Democrats had a presidential preference, but Republicans held primaries for the selection of delegates only, without indication of presidential preference. In Mississippi, Republicans elected delegates by congressional districts pledged to candidates and the vote indicated is for the highest of each slate's candidates in each congressional district. In Arkansas, the Republicans did not hold a primary although Democrats did. In South Carolina, the Democrats did not hold a primary but Republicans did. The vote in Ohio is for delegates at-large pledged to specific candidates and elected as a group. The Republican and Democratic primaries in Puerto Rico were held on two different dates: February 17 and March 16, respectively.

2. Bush withdrew May 26.
3. Baker withdrew March 5.
4. Connally withdrew March 9.
5. Brown withdrew April 1.
6. Anderson withdrew April 24.
7. Totals exclude Puerto Rico, where citizens are unable to vote in the general election.
8. Other vote includes: 4,357 for Alvin J. Jacobsen; 3,757 for V. A. Kelley; 1,063 for R. W. Yeager; 483 for Alvin G. Carris; 355 for Nick Belluso; 311 for William E. Carlson; 244 for Donald Badgley; 67 for C. Leon Pickett; and 25,452 scattered.
9. Other vote includes: 4,022 for Bob Maddox; 609 for William L. Nuckols; 571 for Frank Ahern; 364 for Ray Rollinson, and 47,128 scattered.

1980 Republican, Democratic and Independent Presidential Conventions

Democrats

President Jimmy Carter emerged victorious from a deeply divided Democratic National Convention unsure whether his plea for unity to supporters of rival Sen. Edward M. Kennedy of Massachusetts had succeeded. Kennedy had been Carter's main opponent in his quest for renomination throughout the spring primary season. When it became apparent that Kennedy had not won in the primaries and caucuses the delegate support he needed, he turned his efforts to prying the nomination away from the president at the convention.

Kennedy's presence was strong throughout the convention week and expressions of support for the senator sometimes upstaged those for the incumbent president. Chants of "We want Ted" rocked off the walls of New York's Madison Square Garden during the convention's four days, Aug. 11-14. And their echo faintly followed the president as he left the podium following his acceptance speech. It was a stark reminder that although Carter had captured the nomination and engaged in a series of reconciliation gestures with his rival, he still faced the difficult task of rallying a divided party behind his candidacy.

Kennedy's efforts to wrest the nomination from Carter centered around a convention rule that bound delegates to vote on the first ballot for the candidates under whose banner they were elected. When the convention opened, Carter could count 315 more votes than he needed for the nomination — votes that he had won in nominating caucuses and presidential primaries. As a result, Kennedy's only chance to gain the nomination was to defeat the binding rule.

In the week before the convention, negotiators for Carter and Kennedy agreed to one hour of debate on the rules question to begin at 6:30 p.m. Monday, Aug. 11. Kennedy forces had wanted a Tuesday night rules vote, which would have given them an extra day to lobby delegates. But they settled instead for the Monday night debate, which enabled them to argue their case before a prime-time nationwide television audience.

Opponents of the binding rule tried to present a broad-based front. Arguing against the rule on the convention floor were a Carter delegate, two Kennedy backers and two leading uncommitted delegates — New York Gov. Hugh L. Carey and prominent Washington attorney Edward Bennett Williams, the chief spokesman of the Committee for an Open Convention.

They argued that political conditions had changed since the delegates were elected months earlier and that to bind them would break with a century and a half of Democratic tradition. "For the first time in 150 years, delegates to the national convention are being asked to deliver their final freedom of choice, and to vote themselves into bondage to a candidate," Williams contended. To adopt the binding rule, other speakers added, would make the delegates little more than robots.

But most Carter supporters scoffed at that contention, stressing that delegates were free to vote their conscience on all roll calls but the one for president. Passage of the rule was simply fair play, they added. It had been adopted in 1978 without opposition by the party's last rules review commission and the Democratic National Committee. Only when it was apparent that Carter was winning, claimed Atlanta Mayor Maynard Jackson, did the Kennedy camp want to change the rules to allow a "fifth ball, a fourth out or a tenth inning."

When the measure finally came to a vote, Carter forces turned back the attempt to overturn the proposed rule. The vote was 1,390.580 to 1,936.418 against Kennedy's position.

Shortly after the vote, Kennedy ended his nine-month challenge to the president by announcing that his name would not be placed in nomination Aug. 13. Passage of the binding rule assured Carter's renomination.

In addition to its binding-rule objection, the Kennedy camp filed four other minority rules reports, but all were withdrawn before the Aug. 11 session. Three originally had been filed in response to Carter efforts to streamline the convention schedule. At its July meeting in Washington, D.C., the convention rules committee approved proposals to increase the number of signatures required on nominating petitions for president, vice president and convention chairman; to limit to two the number of speakers on each side of each issue of debate; and to allow every roll call, except for president and vice president, to be conducted by telephone while convention business proceeded.

In return for Kennedy's withdrawal of the minority reports, the Carter camp did consent to raise the number of speakers on each issue to three. They also agreed to a Kennedy proposal to add a platform accountability rule that would require each presidential candidate to submit his written views on the party platform along with his pledge to carry it out. The statement would have to be presented shortly after convention consideration of the platform was completed. The Kennedy proposal also called for the candidates' statements to be distributed and read to the delegates.

Despite the loss on the binding rule, the Kennedy camp succeeded in molding the party platform more to their liking. The final document was filled with so many concessions to the Kennedy forces that it won only a half-hearted endorsement from the president. The platform battle, one of the longest in party history, filled 17 hours of debate and roll calls that stretched over two days, Aug. 12 and 13.

Most of Carter's concessions and outright defeats came on the economic and human needs sections of the 40,000-word document. It was these revisions that Carter rejected — as diplomatically as possible — in a statement issued several hours after the debate wound to a close.

In the debate on social issues, Carter lost two roll-call votes — one on adoption of Kennedy's plank calling for jobs to be "our single highest domestic priority," and the other supporting Medicaid funding for abortions. The president also lost a voice vote on a minority report to withhold all party funds and campaign assistance to candidates who did not support the then-pending Equal Rights Amendment to the Constitution.

The only victory posted by Carter in the human needs chapter was over a Kennedy minority report calling for a single, comprehensive national health insurance plan with gradually phased-in benefits. That report was defeated on a 1,409.9-to-1,623.8 vote that came at the start of the platform debate.

It had been clear since the platform was drafted in late June that the economic plank, which contained the major Carter-Kennedy differences, would be the focus of dispute. When the hour for debate arrived, it was evident that the control Carter had exercised the previous evening on the question of binding delegates had evaporated.

Before the convention began, Carter had yielded to Kennedy language on several issues, including one of the senator's four minority economic reports. That report asserted that a policy of high interest rates and unemployment should not be used to fight inflation. White House domestic affairs adviser Stuart E. Eizenstat announced Aug. 10 that Carter would go along with that amendment — but none of the others in the economy section — because it stated a broad goal while the others called for specific legislation.

The marathon platform debate reached its high point on Tuesday evening, Aug. 12, when Kennedy addressed the delegates on behalf of his minority report on the economic chapter. Kennedy's speech provided the Democratic convention with its most exciting moments. The address, which sparked a 40-minute emotional demonstration when it was over, called for Democratic unity and laced into the Republican nominee, Ronald Reagan.

Kennedy defended his liberal ideology, supporting national health insurance and federal spending to restore deteriorated urban areas. He lashed out at Reagan's proposal for a massive tax cut, labeling it as beneficial only to the wealthy. "For all those whose cares have been our concern the work goes on, the cause endures, the hope still lives and the dream shall never die," concluded Kennedy. Buoyed by the Kennedy oratory, the convention went on to pass by voice vote three liberal Kennedy platform planks on the economy, thereby rejecting the more moderate versions favored by Carter.

The first of the Kennedy-sponsored planks was a statement pledging that fairness would be the overriding principle of the Democrats' economic policy and that no actions would be taken that would "significantly increase" unemployment. The convention next approved a Kennedy plank seeking a $12 billion anti-recession jobs program, a $1 billion rail renewal plan and an expanded housing program for low- and moderate-income families. The final Kennedy economic plank was a statement of opposition to fighting inflation through a policy of high interest rates and unemployment. Carter had agreed to this plank the day before the convention opened.

Carter floor managers realized that it would be difficult to block passage of the Kennedy economic proposals. After the senator's emotion-filled speech, Carter advisers — realizing their position could not prevail — quickly sought to change from a roll call to a voice vote on the economic planks.

During the floor demonstration that followed Kennedy's speech, a series of telephone calls ricocheted between the podium and the senator's campaign trailer located off the convention floor. The negotiations involved how many elements of the Kennedy program would be accepted by voice vote. In the end, Carter prevailed on only one of Kennedy's economic minority reports, the call for an immediate wage and price freeze followed by controls.

Prior to the 1980 convention, Democratic presidential nominees had been able to gloss over their distaste for objectionable portions of the platform. But Kennedy made that difficult to do. In his carefully worded statement following the platform debate, Carter did not flatly reject any of Kennedy's amendments, but he did not embrace them either.

Of Kennedy's $12 billion anti-recession jobs program, Carter said he would "accept and support the intent" of the program but he refused to commit himself to a specific dollar amount. Responding to Kennedy language that placed a jobs program above all other domestic priorities, Carter wrote, "We must make it clear that to acheive full employment, we must also be successful in our fight against inflation."

Carter treated two women's issues the same way. Responding to adopted language that endorsed federal funding for abortion, the president repeated his personal opposition but said he would be guided by court decisions on the questions. He also reiterated his support for ratification of the Equal Rights Amendment but did not directly comment on the platform language adopted on the floor that prevented the Democratic Party from giving campaign funds to candidates who did not back the amendment.

Carter concluded his statement with the unity refrain that had become the hallmark of every official White House comment on the platform since the drafting process began: "The differences within our party on this platform are small in comparison with the differences between the Republican and Democratic Party platforms." Kennedy apparently agreed. And shortly after Carter's renomination Aug. 13, Kennedy issued a statement endorsing the platform and pledging his support for Carter. In the final moments before adjournment, Kennedy made a stiff and brief appearance on the platform with Carter, Mondale and a host of Democratic officeholders. But the coolness of his appearance — accompanied by the warmest reception of the night — left questionable the commitment of the senator and his supporters to work strenuously for Carter's reelection.

Carter won the Democratic nomination with 2,123 votes compared with Kennedy's 1,150.5. Other candidates split 54.5 votes.

In his acceptance speech, Carter alluded to the convention's divisions. He led off with praise for Kennedy's tough campaign, thanks for his concessions during the convention and an appeal for future help. "Ted, your party needs — and I need — you, and your idealism and dedication working for us." Carter spent much of the speech characterizing Reagan's programs as a disastrous "fantasy world" of easy answers. He avoided detailed comments on the economic issues over which he and Kennedy had split, confining himself to statements that he wanted jobs for all who needed them.

As expected, Walter F. Mondale was renominated for vice president. Two other party members had their names placed in nomination so they could raise the issues of homosexual rights and Carter's decision to reinstitute draft registration. Activist Patricia Simon of Newton, Mass., withdrew after delivering a plea that "we be known as a party of peace." The other candidate was Melvin Boozer of Washington, D.C. Boozer, a number of favorite sons and others received only a smattering of votes and Mondale was nominated by acclamation before that roll call had been completed.

The vice president's acceptance speech set delegates chanting "Not Ronald Reagan" as Mondale reeled off a list of liberal values and programs that, he said, most Americans agreed with. Mondale was one of the few speakers to unequivocally praise Carter's record, which he did at some length. The speech ended with a warning not to "let anyone make us less than what we can be."

Jimmy Carter lost the election to Ronald Reagan by more than eight million votes. Carter won 35,483,820 votes, 41.0 percent of the total. Since Carter carried just six states and the District of Columbia, he managed to win only 49 electoral votes.

Following are excerpts from the Democratic party platform of 1980:

Employment. We specifically reaffirm our commitment to achieve all the goals of the Humphrey-Hawkins Full Employment Act within the currently prescribed dates in the Act, especially those relating to a joint reduction in unemployment and inflation. Full employment is important to the achievement of a rising standard of living, to the pursuit of sound justice, and to the strength and vitality of America.

Anti-Recession Assistance. A Democratic anti-recession program must recognize that Blacks, Hispanics, other minorities, women, and older workers bear the brunt of recession. We pledge a $12 billion anti-recession jobs program, providing at least 800,000 additional jobs, including full funding of the counter-cyclical assistance program for the cities, a major expansion of the youth employment and training program to give young people in our inner cities new hope, expanded training programs for women and displaced homemakers to give these workers a fair chance in the workplace, and new opportunities for the elderly to contribute their talents and skills.

Tax Reductions. We commit ourselves to targeted tax reductions designed to stimulate production and combat recession as soon as it appears so that tax reductions will not have a disproportionately inflationary effect. We must avoid untargeted tax cuts which would increase inflation.

Federal Spending. Spending restraint must be sensitive to those who look to the federal government for aid and assistance, especially to our nation's workers in times of high unemployment. At the same time, as long as inflationary pressures remain strong, fiscal prudence is essential to avoid destroying the progress made to date in reducing the inflation rate.

Fiscal policy must remain a flexible economic tool. We oppose a Constitutional amendment requiring a balanced budget.

Interest Rates.... [W]e must continue to pursue a tough anti-inflationary policy which will lead to an across-the-board reduction in interest rates on loans.

In using monetary policy to fight inflation, the government should be sensitive to the special needs of areas of our economy most affected by high interest rates.

Expanding American Exports. To create new markets for American products and strengthen the dollar, we must seek out new opportunities for American exports; help establish stable, long-term commercial relationships between nations; offer technical assistance to firms competing in world markets; promote reciprocal trading terms for nations doing business here; and help ensure that America's domestic retooling is consistent with new opportunities in foreign trade.

We must intensify our efforts to promote American exports and to ensure that our domestic industries and workers are not affected adversely by unfair trade practices, such as dumping.... We must ensure that our efforts to lower tariff barriers are reciprocated by our trading partners. We recognize the superior productivity of American agriculture and the importance of agricultural exports to the balance of trade.

Worker Protection. The Democratic Party will not pursue a policy of high interest rates and unemployment as the means to fight inflation. We will take no action whose effect will be a significant increase in unemployment, no fiscal action, no monetary action, no budgetary action. The Democratic Party remains committed to policies that will not produce high interest rates or high unemployment.

OSHA protections should be properly administered, with the concern of the worker being the highest priority; legislative or administrative efforts to weaken OSHA's basic worker protection responsibilities are unacceptable.

We will continue to oppose a sub-minimum wage for youth and other workers and to support increases in the minimum wage so as to ensure an adequate income for all workers.

Small Business.... [T]he Democratic Party commits itself to the first comprehensive program for small business in American history. That program will include the following measures:

... Allocation of a fair percentage of federal research funds to small business.

Protection of small and independent businesses against takeover by giant conglomerates.

Continued efforts to end federal regulations which reinforce barriers to entry by new and small firms, and which thereby entrench the dominance of market leaders.

A review of regulations and requirements which impose unnecessary burdens upon smaller firms. We will adopt regulatory requirements to meet the needs of smaller firms, where such action will not interfere with the objectives of the regulation.

Minority Business. The Democratic Party pledges itself to advance minority businesses, including Black, Hispanic, Asian/Pacific Americans, Native Americans and other minorities to:

- Increase the overall level of support and the overall level of federal procurement so that minority groups will receive additional benefits and opportunities.
- Triple the 1980 level of federal procurement from minority-owned firms as we have tripled the 1977 levels in the past three years.
- Increase substantially the targeting of Small Business Administration loans to minority-owned businesses.
- Increase ownership of small businesses by minorities, especially in those areas which have traditionally been closed to minorities, such as communications and newspapers.
- Expand management, technical, and training assistance for minority firms, and strengthen minority capital development....

Women and The Economy. The Democratic Party ... commits itself to strong steps to close the wage gap between men and women, to expand child care opportunities for families with working parents, to end the tax discrimination that penalizes married working couples, and to ensure that women can retire in dignity.

We will strictly enforce existing anti-discrimination laws with respect to hiring, pay and promotions. We will adopt a full employment policy, with increased possibilities for part-time work.... [W]e will ensure that women in both the public and private sectors are not only paid equally for work which is identical to that performed by men, but are also paid equally for work which is of comparable value to that performed by men.

Consumer Protection. Over the next four years, we must continue to guarantee and enhance the basic consumer rights to safety, to information, to choice and to a fair hearing.

We must continue our support of basic health, safety, environmental and consumer protection regulatory programs....

Human Needs. While we recognize the need for fiscal restraint ... we pledge as Democrats that for the sole and primary purpose of fiscal restraint alone, we will *not* support reductions in the funding of any program whose purpose is to serve the basic human needs of the most needy in our society — programs such as unemployment, income maintenance, food stamps, and efforts to enhance the educational, nutritional or health needs of children.

Health. The answer to runaway medical costs is not, as Republicans propose, to pour money into a wasteful and inefficient system. The answer is not to cut back on benefits for the elderly and eligibility for the poor. The answer is to enact a comprehensive, universal national health insurance plan.

To meet the goals of a program that will control costs and provide health coverage to every American, the Democratic Party pledges to seek a national health insurance program....

Social Security. The Democratic Party will oppose any effort to tamper with the Social Security system by cutting or taxing benefits as a violation of the contract the American government has made with its people. We hereby make a covenant with the elderly of America that as we have kept the Social Security trust fund sound and solvent in the past, we shall keep it sound and solvent in the years ahead.... We oppose efforts to raise the age at which Social Security benefits will be provided.

Finally, the Democratic Party vehemently opposes all forms of age discrimination and commits itself to eliminating mandatory retirement.

Welfare Reform. As a means of providing immediate federal fiscal relief to state and local governments, the federal government will assume the local government's burden of welfare costs. Further, there should be a phased reduction in the states' share of welfare costs in the immediate future.

We strongly reject the Republican Platform proposal to transfer the responsibility for funding welfare costs entirely to the states. Such a proposal would not only worsen the fiscal situation of state and local governments, but would also lead to reduced benefits and services to those dependent on welfare programs. The Democratic policy is exactly the opposite — to provide greater assistance to state and local governments for their welfare costs and to improve benefits and services....

Education. ... [W]e will continue to support the Department of Education and assist in its all-important educational enterprise....

... The federal government and the states should be encouraged to equalize or take over educational expenses, relieving the overburdened ... taxpayer.

The Democratic Party continues to support programs aimed at achieving communities integrated both in terms of race and economic class.... Mandatory transportation of students beyond their neighborhoods for the purpose of desegregation remains a judicial tool of last resort.

The Party reaffirms its support of public school education and would not support any program or legislation that would create or promote economic, sociological or racial segregation.

The Party accepts its commitment to the support of a constitutionally acceptable method of providing tax aid for the education of all pupils in schools which do not racially discriminate, and excluding so-called segregation academies.

The Democratic Party is committed to a federal scholarship program adequate to meet the needs of all the underprivileged who could benefit from a college education.

We support efforts to provide for the basic nutritional needs of students. We support the availability of nutritious school breakfast, milk and lunch programs.

Equal Rights Amendment. ... [T]he Democratic Party must ensure that ERA at last becomes the 27th Amendment to the Constitution. We oppose efforts to rescind ERA in states which have already ratified the amendment, and we shall insist that past rescissions are invalid.

Civil Rights and Liberties. We oppose efforts to undermine the Supreme Court's historic mandate of school desegregation, and we support affirmative action goals to overturn patterns of discrimination in education and employment.

Our commitment to civil rights embraces not only a commitment to legal equality, but a commitment to economic justice as well. It embraces a recognition of the right of every citizen ... to a fair share in our economy.

We call for passage of legislation to charter the purposes, prerogatives, and restraints on the Federal Bureau of Investigation, the Central Intelligence Agency, and other intelligence agencies of government with full protection for the civil rights and liberties of American citizens living at home or abroad. Under no circumstances should American citizens be investigated because of their beliefs.

Abortion. The Democratic Party recognizes reproductive freedom as a fundamental human right. We therefore oppose government interference in the reproductive decisions of Americans, especially those government programs or legislative restrictions that deny poor Americans their right to privacy by funding or advocating one or a limited number of reproductive choices only. Specifically, the Democratic Party opposes ... restrictions on funding for health services for the poor that deny poor women especially the right to exercise a constitutionally-guaranteed right to privacy.

Tax Reform. Capital formation is essential both to control inflation and to encourage growth. New tax reform efforts are needed to increase savings and investment, promote the principle of progressive taxation, close loopholes, and maintain adequate levels of federal revenue.

Gun Control. The Democratic Party affirms the right of sportsmen to possess guns for purely hunting and target-shooting purposes. However, handguns simplify and intensify violent crime.... The Democratic Party supports enactment of federal legislation to strengthen the presently inadequate regulations over the manufacture, assembly, distribution, and possession of handguns and to ban "Saturday night specials."

Energy. We must make energy conservation our highest priority, not only to reduce our dependence on foreign oil, but also to guarantee that our children and grandchildren have an adequate supply of energy.

Major new efforts must be launched to develop synthetic and alternative renewable energy sources.

The Democratic Party regards coal as our nation's greatest energy resource. It must play a decisive role in America's energy future.

Oil exploration on federal lands must be accelerated, consistent with environmental protections.

Offshore energy leasing and development should be conditioned on full protection of the environment and marine resources.

Solar energy use must be increased, and strong efforts, including continued financial support, must be undertaken to make certain that we achieve the goal of having solar energy account for 20% of our total energy by the year 2000.

A stand-by gasoline rationing plan must be adopted for use in the event of a serious energy supply interruption.

... Through the federal government's commitment to renewable energy sources and energy efficiency, and as alternative fuels become available in the future, we will retire nuclear power plants....

We must give the highest priority to dealing with the nuclear waste disposal problem.... [E]fforts to develop a safe, environmentally sound nuclear waste disposal plan must be continued and intensified.

Environment. We must move decisively to protect our countryside and our coastline from overdevelopment and mismanagement. ... [P]rotection must be balanced with the need to properly manage and utilize our land resources during the 1980s.

We must develop new and improved working relationships among federal, state, local, tribal, and territorial governments and private interests, to manage effectively our programs for increased domestic energy production and their impact on people, water, air, and the environment in general.

Grain Embargo. Recognizing the patriotic sacrifices made by the American farmer during the agricultural embargo protesting the invasion of Afghanistan, we commend the agricultural community's contribution in the field of foreign affairs. Except in time of war or grave threats to national security, the federal government should impose no future embargoes on agricultural products.

Foreign Policy. The Democratic Administration sought to reconcile ... two requirements of American foreign policy — principle and strength.... We have tried to make clear the continuing importance of American strength in a world of change. Without such strength, there is a genuine risk that global change will deteriorate into anarchy to be exploited by our adversaries' military power. Thus, the revival of American strength has been a central pre-occupation of the Democratic Administration.

The use of American power is necessary as a means of shaping not only a more secure, but also a more decent world.... [W]e must pursue objectives that are moral, that make clear our support for the aspirations of mankind and that are rooted in the ideals of the American people.

That is why the Democrats have stressed human rights. That is why America once again has supported the aspirations of the vast majority of the world's population for greater human justice and freedom.

.. In meeting the dangers of the coming decade the United States will consult closely with our Allies to advance common security and political goals. As a result of annual summit meetings, coordinated economic policies and effective programs of international energy conservation have been fashioned.

... [W]e must continue to improve our relations with the Third World by being sensitive to their legitimate aspirations. The United States should be a positive force for peaceful change in responding to ferment in the Third World.

Our third objective must be peace in the Middle East.... Our nation feels a profound moral obligation to sustain and assure the security of Israel.... Israel is the single democracy, the most stable government, the most strategic asset and our closest ally in the region.

To fulfill this imperative, we must move towards peace in the Middle East. Without peace, there is a growing prospect, indeed inevitability, that this region will become radicalized, susceptible to foreign intrusion, and possibly involved in another war. Thus, peace in the Middle East also is vital for our national security interests.... Our goal is to make the Middle East an area of stability and progress in which the United States can play a full and constructive role.

National Security. Our fourth major objective is to strengthen the military security of the United States and our Allies at a time when trends in the military balance have become increasingly adverse. America is now, and will continue to be, the strongest power on earth. It was the Democratic Party's greatest hope that we could, in fact, reduce our military effort. But realities of the world situation, including the unremitting buildup of Soviet military forces, required that we begin early to reverse the decade-long decline in American defense efforts.

Arms Control. ... [T]he Democrats have been and remain committed to arms control, especially to strategic arms limitations, and to maintain a firm and balanced relationship with the Soviet Union.

To avoid the danger to all mankind from an intensification of the strategic arms competition, and to curb a possible acceleration of the nuclear arms race while awaiting the ratification of the SALT II Treaty, we endorse the policy of continuing to take no action which would be inconsistent with its object and purpose, so long as the Soviet Union does likewise.

Arms control and strategic arms limitation are of crucial importance to us and to all other people. The SALT II Agreement is a major accomplishment of the Democratic Administration. It contributes directly to our national security, and we will seek its ratification at the earliest feasible time.

Republicans

Ronald Reagan, the 69-year-old former California governor, was installed as the Republican presidential nominee at the party's national convention in Detroit, but his moment of glory nearly was overshadowed by an unusual flap over the number-two spot. The choosing of Reagan's running mate provided the only suspense at the GOP convention, held July 14-17, 1980, in Detroit's Joe Louis Arena.

Who would fill the number-one spot had been determined long before when Reagan won 28 out of the 34 Republican presidential primaries and eliminated all of his major rivals. The last to withdraw — George Bush — was tapped by Reagan July 16 as his ticket mate in a dramatic post-midnight appearance before the delegates.

For most of the evening of July 16, it looked as though Gerald R. Ford would occupy the second spot on the ticket, which would have made him the first former president to run for vice president. Private polls reportedly had shown that Ford was the only Republican who would enhance Reagan's chances in November. And a number of Republicans had described the combination as a "dream ticket." Groups described as "friends of Ronald Reagan" and "friends of Gerald Ford" had met four times to "discuss" the possibility of forging a Reagan-Ford ticket.

The Ford group consisted of former Secretary of State Henry A. Kissinger, Alan Greenspan, former chairman of the Council of Economic Advisers, and Ford aides Robert Barnett and John Marsh. The Reagan group was the nucleus of his primary campaign staff: Edwin Meese, campaign director, and Richard Wirthlin, Reagan's pollster. Reagan and Ford first discussed Ford's joining the ticket at a meeting July 15, although no formal offer was made, according to a source close to Reagan. "'I want you to think this over and then we'll discuss it tomorrow,'" the source quoted Reagan as telling Ford.

The pair met again the following day to continue their discussions, but nothing was resolved. When the convention reconvened at 6:30 p.m., reports began swirling about the floor, many of them spawned by Ford himself, who in two televised interviews gave strong indications that he would accept the second spot if certain conditions were met.

In an interview with Walter Cronkite of CBS about 7:30 p.m., Ford said, "I would not go to Washington and be a figurehead vice president. If I go to Washington I have to be there in the belief that I would play a meaningful role." Later, in an interview with Barbara Walters of ABC, Ford said he did not want the job unless his role would be "non-ceremonial, constructive and responsive." Such an arrangement, he said, would require a "far different structure" from the duties performed by other vice presidents. Asked whether it would be difficult to be a vice president again after having had the top job, Ford said, "Not at all. I'd be more interested in substance than glamor."

Ford declined to spell out what his conditions for taking the job would be, but descriptions of his requirements would have made him in effect co-president with Reagan. The discussions reportedly centered around providing a role for Ford somewhat akin to the White House chief of staff's. In this kind of post he would have had responsibility for agencies such as the Office of Management and Budget, the National Security Council, the domestic policy staff and the Council of Economic Advisers.

Ford further fed the speculation, offering a simple solution to the temporary problem that would have been posed by the 12th Amendment to the Constitution. The amendment would have had the effect of prohibiting the members of the electoral college from California from voting for both Reagan and Ford because both were California residents. The amendment says that the electors from any state must vote for at least one person who is not from that state.

However, nothing in the Constitution would have excluded two residents of the same state from serving as president and vice president or prevented electors from states other than their home state from voting for those two individuals. Ford said Reagan's lawyers had researched the residency question and determined that legally there would be no problem if the former president changed his residence to Michigan, which he represented in the House for 25 years, or to Colorado, where he owned a home.

But Ford expressed reservations about how such a move might be interpreted. "I think it could create in the minds of the American people that we're trying to do something a little cute," he said. "Well, I've never done that in politics. I've got a good reputation and I'm worried about it. . . . I think it would be construed to be to some extent a gimmick."

As the evening of July 16 wore on, the speculation heightened. "The expectation, as it is presently being reported is it's going through," Michigan Gov. William G. Milliken said of the Ford candidacy. "I have it on very reliable sources within the Ford camp that it is put together," said Gov. Pierre S. (Pete) du Pont of Delaware.

About 9:15 p.m. Reagan telephoned Ford to ask him to make up his mind whether he wanted the vice president's job. Meanwhile, convention officials proceeded to call the roll of the states. When Reagan received enough votes to become the official nominee, the arena erupted into a cheering, hornblowing, flag-waving, foot-stomping, band-playing demonstration. The noise abated a bit while the roll call was finished, but continued for more than an hour.

But at about 11:15 p.m. the Reagan-Ford arrangement fell apart. Ford went to Reagan's suite in the Detroit Plaza Hotel and the two men agreed that it would be better for Ford to campaign for the GOP ticket rather than be a member of it. "His [Ford's] instinct told him it was not the thing to do," Reagan said later.

When it became apparent that efforts to persuade Ford to join the ticket had failed, Reagan turned to Bush, a moderate with proven vote-getting ability. The Reagan camp refused to acknowledge that Bush was the second choice, even though it was widely perceived that way. "There was everybody else and then the Ford option," Edwin Meese, Reagan's chief of staff, said later.

Bush had been Reagan's most persistent competitor through the long primary season, but he won only six primaries — Michigan, Massachusetts, Connecticut, Pennsylvania, the District of Columbia and Puerto Rico. Bush was one of the vice presidential possibilities favored by those in the party who believed that Reagan had to reach outside the GOP's conservative wing if he were to have broad appeal in November.

Bush supporters said that Bush's background would balance the ticket geographically and that his extensive government service would overcome criticism that Reagan did not have any Washington experience. Bush served from 1967 to 1971 in the U.S. House from Texas and had been ambassador to the United Nations, head of the U.S. liaison office in Peking and director of the Central Intelligence Agency.

Bush's first appearance at the convention earlier had produced a rousing demonstration from supporters throughout the hall, but his strongest support on the floor was in delegations from the Midwest and Northeast, such as New Jersey and the states where he won primary victories.

Reagan's choice of the moderate George Bush was viewed as his first major choice between political pragmatism and ideological purity. Throughout the primary season, Reagan had drawn a large measure of his support from the right wing of the Republican Party and had pledged himself to support conservative economic, social and defense policies. During the convention, Sen. Jesse Helms of North Carolina, the most vocal leader of the GOP's right wing, masterminded the rightward tilt of the party platform to reflect conservative viewpoints. Helms, concerned about the nomination of a moderate such as Bush, threatened to place his own name in nomination to put pressure on the GOP standardbearers to abide by conservative and "moral" principles. In the end, Helms supported the Reagan-Bush ticket, but warned that it had better support the party's conservative platform. Though Helms was not nominated for vice president, his supporters nonetheless gave him 54 votes. He finished second behind Bush, who got 1,832 votes.

The Republican Party's 1980 platform was more a blueprint for victory in November than a definitive statement of party views. Rather than slug it out over specifics, the party's moderate and conservative wings agreed to blur their differences to appear united, to broaden the party's appeal and to smooth Reagan's way to the White House.

Platform writers veered from traditional Republican positions on a few issues. On others they went out of their way to embrace policies that meshed with Reagan's views more than their own. For the most part, they managed to fashion a policy statement that pleased no party faction entirely but with which all could live reasonably.

Overwhelmingly, platform committee members agreed the document should be basically consistent with Reagan's positions. Thus, though one media poll found delegates overwhelmingly in favor of resuming a peacetime draft, the platform bowed to the view of its nominee and stated its opposition to a renewal of the draft "at this time." In the same manner, the party's platform took no position on ratification of the Equal Rights Amendment (ERA) to the Constitution. Since 1940 Republican platforms had supported an ERA amendment. Reagan, however, opposed ratification, and ERA opponents far outnumbered the amendment's supporters on the platform committee. Yet Reagan, in a gesture to moderates, suggested that the platform not take a position on the issue, and the committee agreed.

Most of the platform document consisted of policy statements on which most Republicans agreed. There were calls for tax cuts, pleas for less government regulation and harsh criticisms of the Carter administration. In two areas, however, the platform took a particularly hard-line position. The platform supported a constitutional amendment that would outlaw abortion and called on a Reagan administration to appoint federal judges who opposed abortion. On defense, platform writers took an already hard-line plank that had been drafted by party staff and moved it sharply to the right. The platform called for massive increases in defense spending and scoffed at the Carter administration's proposed strategic arms limitation treaty (SALT II).

On the other hand, to pick up votes from organized labor, blacks and the poor, the platform made some new overtures to those traditionally non-Republican groups. It pledged to strengthen enforcement of the civil rights laws, made overtures to U.S. workers put out of their jobs by competition from foreign imports and promised to save America's inner cities.

The platform was adopted by the convention July 15 without change, but not before an attempt was made to reopen on the floor one of its more controversial sections. Although party moderates such as Sens. Charles H. Percy, Ill., Charles McC. Mathias Jr., Md., and Jacob K. Javits, N.Y., made little secret of their unhappiness with the platform's failure to reaffirm the party's support for ratification of the ERA, they were particularly chagrined by the section suggesting that Reagan appoint federal judges who oppose abortion. Percy called the section "the worst plank I have ever seen in any platform by the Republican Party." The moderates July 14 sought to round up support for reopening the platform on the floor, but their efforts failed. In caucuses held early July 15, a number of state delegations including New York and Illinois voted down motions to change the platform's position on abortion.

Nonetheless, as Chairman John J. Rhodes, Ariz., proposed that the convention adopt the platform, Hawaii delegate John Leopold leaped onto a chair to seek Rhodes' recognition. When Rhodes ordered the Hawaii delegation's microphone turned on, Leopold said the group unanimously proposed a motion to suspend the convention rules to permit delegates to "discuss" the platform on the floor. If the rules were suspended, Leopold told reporters, he intended to propose that the language on federal judges be deleted. Not to allow floor discussion of the platform, he said, would be to "railroad" the document through the convention.

Rhodes explained that under convention rules a majority of the members of six state delegations was required to bring a motion to suspend the rules to a vote. He asked if a majority of the delegates from any other state supported Leopold's motion. Only Rep. Silvio O. Conte, chairman of the Massachusetts delegation, rose. But rather than announce support for Leopold's motion, Conte stated only that a majority of his delegation supported a recorded vote on the platform, something Leopold had not proposed. To the applause of many of the delegates, Rhodes then declared that Leopold's motion had failed. The platform subsequently was approved by voice vote.

Ronald Reagan received the Republican nomination on the first ballot.

In his acceptance speech, Reagan combined sharp jabs at the alleged shortcomings of the Carter administration with a reaffirmation of his own conservative credo. Reagan cited three grave threats to the nation's existence — "a disintegrating economy, a weakened defense and an energy policy based on the sharing of scarcity." The culprits, Reagan contended, were President Carter and the Democratic Congress. He said they had preached that the American people needed to tighten their belts. "I utterly reject that view," he declared. Reagan was especially critical of the Democratic administration's conduct of foreign policy. He ridiculed it as weak, vacillating and transparently hypocritical.

Reagan went on to win the presidential election in November with an absolute majority of the popular vote — 43,901,812 votes or 50.7 percent. His electoral victory over Carter was more pronounced. Reagan carried 44 states for a total of 489 electoral votes to just 49 for Carter, who carried only six states and the District of Columbia.

Following are excerpts from the Republican Party's platform of 1980:

> **Taxes.** ... [W]e believe it is essential to cut personal tax rates out of fairness to the individual....
>
> Therefore, the Republican Party supports across-the-board reductions in personal income tax rates, phased in over three years, which will reduce tax rates from the range of 14 to 70 percent to a range of from 10 to 50 percent.
>
> ... Republicans will move to end tax bracket creep caused by inflation. We support tax indexing to protect

taxpayers from the automatic tax increases caused when cost-of-living wage increases move them into higher tax brackets.

Welfare. We pledge a system that will:
- provide adequate living standards for the truly needy;
- end welfare fraud by removing ineligibles from the welfare rolls, tightening food stamp eligibility requirements, and ending aid to illegal aliens and the voluntarily unemployed;
- strengthen work incentives, particularly directed at the productive involvement of able-bodied persons in useful community work projects;
- provide educational and vocational incentives to allow recipients to become self-supporting; and
- better coordinate federal efforts with local and state social welfare agencies and strengthen local and state administrative functions.

We oppose federalizing the welfare system; local levels of government are most aware of the needs in their communities. We support a block grant program that will help return control of welfare programs to the states.

Black Americans. During the next four years we are committed to policies that will:
- encourage local governments to designate specific enterprise zones within depressed areas that will promote new jobs, new and expanded businesses and new economic vitality;
- open new opportunities for black men and women to begin small businesses of their own by, among other steps, removing excessive regulations, disincentives for venture capital and other barriers erected by the government;
- bring strong, effective enforcement of federal civil rights statutes, especially those dealing with threats to physical safety and security which have recently been increasing; and
- ensure that the federal government follows a non-discriminatory system of appointments ... with a careful eye for qualified minority aspirants.

Women's Rights. We acknowledge the legitimate efforts of those who support or oppose ratification of the Equal Rights Amendment.

We reaffirm our Party's historic commitment to equal rights and equality for women.

We support equal rights and equal opportunities for women, without taking away traditional rights of women such as exemption from the military draft. We support the enforcement of all equal opportunity laws and urge the elimination of discrimination against women.

We reaffirm our belief in the traditional role and values of the family in our society.... The importance of support for the mother and homemaker in maintaining the values of this country cannot be over-emphasized.

Abortion. While we recognize differing views on this question among Americans in general — and in our own Party — we affirm our support of a constitutional amendment to restore protection of the right to life for unborn children. We also support the Congressional efforts to restrict the use of taxpayers' dollars for abortion.

Education. ... [T]he Republican Party supports de-regulation by the federal government of public education, and encourages the elimination of the federal Department of Education.

We support Republican initiatives in the Congress to restore the right of individuals to participate in voluntary, non-denominational prayer in schools and other public facilities.

... [W]e condemn the forced busing of school children to achieve arbitrary racial quotas.... It [busing] has failed to improve the quality of education, while diverting funds from programs that could make the difference between success and failure for the poor, the disabled, and minority children.

[W]e reaffirm our support for a system of educational assistance based on tax credits that will in part compensate parents for their financial sacrifices in paying tuition at the elementary, secondary, and post-secondary level.

Health. Republicans unequivocally oppose socialized medicine, in whatever guise it is presented by the Democratic Party. We reject the creation of a national health service and all proposals for compulsory national health insurance.

Older Americans. Social Security is one of this nation's most vital commitments to our senior citizens. We commit the Republican Party to first save, and then strengthen, this fundamental contract between our government and its productive citizens.

... [W]e proudly reaffirm our opposition to mandatory retirement and our long-standing Republican commitment to end the Democrats' earnings limitation upon Social Security benefits. In addition, the Republican Party is strongly opposed to the taxation of Social Security benefits and we pledge to oppose any attempts to tax these benefits.

Crime. We believe that the death penalty serves as an effective deterrent to capital crime and should be applied by the federal government and by states which approve it as an appropriate penalty for certain major crimes.

We believe the right of citizens to keep and bear arms must be preserved. Accordingly, we oppose federal registration of firearms. Mandatory sentences for commission of armed felonies are the most effective means to deter abuse of this right.

Foreign Competition. The Republican Party recognizes the need to provide workers who have lost their jobs because of technological obsolescence or imports the opportunity to adjust to changing economic conditions. In particular, we will seek ways to assist workers threatened by foreign competition.

The Republican Party believes that protectionist tariffs and quotas are detrimental to our economic well-being. Nevertheless, we insist that our trading partners offer our nation the same level of equity, access, and fairness that we have shown them.

Training and Skills. ... [T]he success of federal employment efforts is dependent on private sector participation. It must be recognized as the ultimate location for unsubsidized jobs, as the provider of means to attain this end, and as an active participant in the formulation of employment and training policies on the local and national level.

We urge a reduction of payroll tax rates, a youth differential for the minimum wage, and alleviation of other costs of employment until a young person can be a productive employee.

Fairness to the Employer. The Republican Party declares war on government overregulation.

While we recognize the role of the federal government in establishing certain minimum standards designed to improve the quality of life in America, we reaffirm our conviction that these standards can best be attained through innovative efforts of American business without the federal government mandating the methods of attainment.

OSHA. OSHA should concentrate its resources on encouraging voluntary compliance by employers and monitoring situations where close federal supervision is needed and serious hazards are most likely to occur. OSHA should be required to consult with, advise, and assist businesses in coping with the regulatory burden before imposing any penalty for non-compliance. Small businesses and employers with good safety records should be exempt from safety inspections, and penalties should be increased for those with consistently poor performance.

Agriculture. Republicans will ensure that:

- international trade is conducted on the basis of fair and effective competition and that all imported agricultural products meet the same standards of quality that are required of American producers....
- the future of U.S. agricultural commodities is protected from the economic evils of predatory dumping by other producing nations and that the domestic production of these commodities ... is preserved.

...We believe that agricultural embargoes are only symbolic and are ineffective tools of foreign policy.... The Carter grain embargo should be terminated immediately.

Big Government. The Republican Party reaffirms its belief in the decentralization of the federal government and in the traditional American principle that the best government is the one closest to the people. There, it is less costly, more accountable, and more responsive to people's needs....

Energy. We are committed to ... a strategy of aggressively boosting the nation's energy supplies; stimulating new energy technology and more efficient energy use; restoring maximum feasible choice and freedom in the marketplace for energy consumers and producers alike; and eliminating energy shortages and disruptions....

Republicans support a comprehensive program of regulatory reform, improved incentives, and revision of cumbersome and overly stringent Clean Air Act regulations.

We support accelerated use of nuclear energy through technologies that have been proven efficient and safe.

We reject unequivocally punitive gasoline and other energy taxes designed to artificially suppress energy consumption.

A Republican policy of decontrol, development of our domestic energy resources, and incentives for new supply and conservation technologies will substantially reduce our dependence on imported oil.

Republicans will move toward making available all suitable federal lands for multiple use purposes including exploration and production of energy resources.

Environment. We believe that a healthy environment is essential to the present and future well-being of our people, and to sustainable national growth.

At the same time, we believe that it is imperative that environmental laws and regulations be reviewed, and where necessary, reformed to ensure that the benefits achieved justify the costs imposed.

Balanced Budget. If federal spending is reduced as tax cuts are phased in, there will be sufficient budget surpluses to fund the tax cuts, and allow for reasonable growth in necessary program spending.

...We believe a Republican President and a Republican Congress can balance the budget and reduce spending through legislative actions, eliminating the necessity for a Constitutional amendment to compel it. However, if necessary, the Republican Party will seek to adopt a Constitutional amendment to limit federal spending and balance the budget, except in time of national emergency as determined by a two-thirds vote of Congress.

Inflation. The Republican Party believes inflation can be controlled only by fiscal and monetary restraint, combined with sharp reductions in the tax and regulatory disincentives for savings, investments, and productivity. Therefore, the Republican Party opposes the imposition of wage and price controls and credit controls.

National Security. Republicans commit themselves to an immediate increase in defense spending to be applied judiciously to critically needed programs. We will build toward a sustained defense expenditure sufficient to close the gap with the Soviets. Republicans approve and endorse a national strategy of peace through strength.... The general principles and goals of this strategy would be:

- to inspire, focus, and unite the national will and determination to achieve peace and freedom;
- to achieve overall military and technological superiority over the Soviet Union;
- to create a strategic and civil defense which would protect the American people against nuclear war at least as well as the Soviet population is protected;
- to accept no arms control agreement which in any way jeopardizes the security of the United States or its allies, or which locks the United States into a position of military inferiority;
- to reestablish effective security and intelligence capabilities;
- to pursue positive nonmilitary means to roll back the growth of communism;
- to help our allies and other non-Communist countries defend themselves against Communist aggression; and
- to maintain a strong economy and protect our overseas sources of energy and ... raw materials.

Nuclear Forces. ...We reject the mutual-assured-destruction (MAD) strategy of the Carter Administration.... We propose, instead, a credible strategy which will deter a Soviet attack by the clear capability of our forces to survive and ultimately to destroy Soviet military targets.

A Republican Administration will strive for early modernization of our theater nuclear forces so that a seamless web of deterrence can be maintained against all levels of attack, and our credibility with our European allies is restored.

Defense Manpower and the Draft. The Republican Party is not prepared to accept a peacetime draft at this time.... We will not consider a peacetime draft unless a well-managed, Congressionally-funded, full-scale effort to improve the all-volunteer force does not meet expectations.

National Intelligence. A Republican Administration will seek adequate safeguards to ensure that past abuses will not recur, but we will seek the repeal of ill-considered restrictions sponsored by Democrats, which have debilitated U.S. intelligence capabilities while easing the intelligence collection and subversion efforts of our adversaries.

Arms Control The Republican approach to arms control has been ... based on three fundamental premises:

- first, before arms control negotiations may be undertaken, the security of the United States must be assured by the funding and deployment of strong military forces sufficient to deter conflict at any level or to prevail in battle should aggression occur;
- second, negotiations must be conducted on the basis of strict reciprocity of benefits — unilateral restraint by the U.S. has failed to bring reductions by the Soviet Union; and
- third, arms control negotiations, once entered, represent an important political and military undertaking that cannot be divorced from the broader political and military behavior of the parties.

U.S.-Soviet Relations. Republicans believe that the United States can only negotiate with the Soviet Union from a position of unquestioned principle and unquestioned strength.

A Republican Administration will continue to seek to negotiate arms reductions in Soviet strategic weapons, in Soviet bloc force levels in Central Europe, and in other areas that may be amenable to reductions or limitations. We will pursue hard bargaining for equitable, verifiable, and enforceable agreements.

We reaffirm our commitment to press the Soviet Union to implement the United Nations Declaration on Human Rights and the Helsinki Agreements which guarantee rights such as the free interchange of information and the right to emigrate.

NATO and Western Europe. A Republican Administration, as one of its highest priorities and in close concert with our NATO partners, will ... ensure that the United States leads a concerted effort to rebuild a strong, confident Alliance....

In pledging renewed United States leadership, cooperation, and consultation, Republicans assert their expectation that each of the allies will bear a fair share of the common defense effort and that they will work closely together in support of common Alliance goals.

Middle East, Persian Gulf. With respect to an ultimate peace settlement, Republicans reject any call for involvement of the PLO as not in keeping with the long-term interests of either Israel or the Palestinian Arabs. The imputation of legitimacy to organizations not yet willing to acknowledge the fundamental right to existence of the State of Israel is wrong.

The sovereignty, security, and integrity of the State of Israel is a moral imperative and serves the strategic interests of the United States. Republicans reaffirm our fundamental and enduring commitment to this principle.

While reemphasizing our commitment to Israel, a Republican Administration will pursue close ties and friendship with moderate Arab states.

The Americas. We deplore the Marxist Sandinista takeover of Nicaragua and the Marxist attempts to destabilize El Salvador, Guatemala, and Honduras. We do not support United States assistance to any Marxist government in this hemisphere and we oppose the Carter Administration aid program for the government of Nicaragua. However, we will support the efforts of the Nicaraguan people to establish a free and independent government.

Asia and the Pacific. A new Republican Administration will restore a strong American role in Asia and the Pacific. We will make it clear that any military action which threatens the independence of America's allies and friends will bring a response sufficient to make its cost prohibitive to potential adversaries.

China. We will strive for the creation of conditions that will foster the peaceful elaboration of our relationship with the People's Republic of China.

At the same time, we deplore the Carter Administration's treatment of Taiwan, our long-time ally and friend. We pledge that our concern for the safety and security of the 17 million people of Taiwan will be constant.

Africa. The Republican Party supports the principle and process of self-determination in Africa. We reaffirm our commitment to this principle and pledge our strong opposition to the effort of the Soviet Union ... to subvert this process.

Foreign Aid. No longer should American foreign assistance programs seek to force acceptance of American governmental forms. The principal consideration should be whether or not extending assistance to a nation or group of nations will advance America's interests and objectives.

Decisions to provide military assistance should be made on the basis of U.S. foreign policy objectives. Such assistance to any nation need not imply complete approval of a regime's domestic policy.

International Economic Policy. Under a Republican Administration, our international economic policy will be harmonized with our foreign and defense policies to leave no doubt as to the strategy and purpose of American policy.

Republicans will conduct international economic policy in a manner that will stabilize the value of the dollar at home and abroad.

The Republican Party believes the United States must adopt an aggressive export policy. Trade, especially exporting, must be high on our list of national priorities. The Republicans will ... promote trade to ensure the long-term health of the U.S. economy.

National Unity Campaign

Illinois Republican Rep. John B. Anderson declared himself an independent candidate for the presidency April 24, 1980 after it became clear that he could not obtain his party's presidential nomination. Anderson created the National Unity Campaign as the vehicle for his third-party candidacy. No party convention was held to select Anderson or to ratify the selection.

On Aug. 25 Anderson announced he had tapped former Wisconsin Gov. Patrick J. Lucey, a Democrat, to be his running mate. The selection of Lucey was seen as a move by Anderson to attract liberal Democrats disgruntled by President Jimmy Carter's renomination. Anderson's choice of a running mate and the Aug. 30 release of a National Unity Campaign platform helped establish him as a genuine contender in the presidential race.

The 317-page platform put forth specific proposals on a variety of national issues, emphasizing domestic questions. The positions taken generally were fiscally conservative and socially liberal, remaining true to Anderson's "wallet on the right, heart on the left" philosophy.

The platform made clear that Anderson's primary goal was to restore the nation's economic health by adopting fiscal and tax policies that would "generate a substantial pool of investment capital," which then would be used to increase productivity and create jobs. Anderson proposed countercyclical revenue sharing to direct federal funds to areas hardest hit by the election year recession. He rejected mandatory wage and price controls as a cure for inflation, proposing instead a program under which the government would encourage labor and management to work toward agreement on proper levels for wages and prices and use tax incentives to encourage compliance with the standards set. In contrast to both Carter and Reagan, Anderson opposed tax cuts for individuals. He also criticized constitutional amendments to balance the federal budget, saying that while the budget should be balanced "in ordinary times," it could be expected to run a deficit in times of "economic difficulty."

Anderson's energy policy made reducing oil imports the top priority. His platform proposed a 50-cent-a-gallon excise tax on gasoline to discourage consumption, with the revenue to be used to cut Social Security taxes. Anderson favored the decontrol of oil prices begun under Carter and proposed a 40-mile-per-gallon fuel economy standard for new autos.

For American cities, Anderson proposed using about 90 percent of alcohol and tobacco taxes to help build mass transit systems and fight deterioration of public facilities. He also favored offering tax incentives to encourage businesses to locate in blighted urban areas.

In foreign policy, Anderson emphasized strengthening alliances with Western Europe and Japan, resisting Soviet expansion while negotiating "whenever possible" and respecting the sovereignty of Third World nations. His platform supported human rights and humanitarian aid for refugees and disaster victims abroad. He pledged to support the Middle East peace process, but opposed the creation of a Palestinian state between Israel and Jordan or U.S. recognition of the Palestine Liberation Organization until the PLO recognized Israel's right to exist.

On defense issues, Anderson opposed development of the MX missile, B-1 bomber and neutron bomb, criticized the arms race and opposed a peacetime draft registration. He pledged to seek ratification of the SALT II treaty negotiated with the Soviet Union, saying that "essential equivalence" existed between U.S. and Soviet missile forces. He opposed a strategy of nuclear superiority, emphasizing instead the beefing up of conventional military forces.

Anderson finished the 1980 presidential race a distant third behind Jimmy Carter with 5,719,722 votes, 6.6 percent.

Following are excerpts from the National Unity Campaign Platform of 1980:

Economy. We will construct a Wage-Price Incentives Program. Our administration will invite labor and management leaders to agree upon fair and realistic guidelines and to determine appropriate tax-based incentives to encourage compliance....

In the absence of sharp and prolonged increases in the rate of inflation, we will oppose mandatory wage and price standards.

Youth Unemployment. To deal with the critical problem of youth unemployment, particularly among minorities, we propose: enactment of the proposed Youth Act of 1980 to provide over $2 billion a year for job training and state and local educational programs designed to improve the employability of disadvantaged and out-of-school youth; increased funding for youth career intern programs; a youth opportunity wage incentive that would exempt eligible youths and employers from Social Security taxes during the first months of employment.

Gasoline Tax. We would couple decontrol of oil and gas prices with an excise tax of 50 cents per gallon on gasoline, the full revenues of that tax being returned to individuals through reductions in payroll taxes and increased Social Security benefits.... We will employ tax credits and other incentives to promote substitution of non-petroleum energy for oil, adoption of energy-efficient systems in industry and elsewhere, improvements in transportation and energy production technologies, and development of less wasteful structures for home and commerce.

Nuclear Power. ... [W]e will act on the recommendations of the Rogovin and Kemeny Commissions to make certain that installation of any future plants is preceded by demonstration of satisfactory standards and action on the nuclear waste question. We will assess nuclear power in light of its dependence on public subsidy and of the possibility that slower growth in demand may enable us to phase in other energy supplies in preference to nuclear systems.

Cities. ... [A]n Anderson-Lucey Administration will propose an Urban Reinvestment Trust Fund. Funded through ... revenues from the Federal alcohol and tobacco excise taxes and phased in over three years, it will disburse approximately $3.9 billion annually. It will be used for upgrading, repair and replacement of [urban] capital plant and equipment.

Within our distressed older cities, there are zones of devastation, blighted by crime, arson and population flight.... We favor legislation that would create "enterprise zones" in these areas, by lowering corporate, capital gains, payroll and property taxes and by furnishing new tax incentives....

Environment. We will guard and consolidate the achievements in every field of environmental protection and preservation. We will insist, however, that economic impact studies, assessing not only direct costs but employment and energy implications, accompany proposals for major changes in environmental standards.

Social Issues. We are committed to ratification of the Equal Rights Amendment. We oppose government intrusion in the most intimate of family decisions — the right to bear or not to bear children — and will fight against any constitutional amendment prohibiting abortion. We support public funding of family planning services and other efforts to enable women to find ... alternatives to abortion.

National Defense and Arms Control. In strategic forces, we will maintain a stable balance by preserving essential equivalence with the Soviet Union. To meet an evolving threat to our deterrent, we will modernize and diversify our strategic arsenal.

The growing concern over the threat to fixed, land-based missiles poses an urgent problem to both the United States and the Soviet Union. Economically, environmentally and strategically, the ... cure proposed by the Carter Administration — the MX system — is unsound.

Arms control agreements must enhance our basic security and must not compromise our ability to protect our national interests. Agreements must preserve and reinforce the stability of the strategic balance.... Arms control must be based on adequate, effective verification.

The Western alliance should proceed with its plans to modernize its theater nuclear arsenal; at the same time, we should keep open the possibility of negotiations with the Soviet Union to limit theater nuclear forces.

We favor ... a short-term ... nuclear test ban treaty between the United States, the Soviet Union and the United Kingdom....

For a more effective defense, we will rely heavily on collective security arrangements with our principal allies in NATO and Japan. We will work to reinforce and enhance our historic partnership with our Western European allies.

We will propose to Moscow supplementary measures that could make possible the ratification of the SALT II Treaty and the start of SALT III negotiations. These proposals will respond to concerns expressed in the U.S. Senate regarding such issues as verification and future force reductions.

Middle East. The establishment and maintenance of peace in the Middle East will be an urgent objective.... A lasting settlement must encompass the principles affirmed in the Camp David accords.

Our administration will support the recognition of Palestinian rights as embodied in the Camp David accords, but will oppose the creation of a Palestinian state between Israel and Jordan.

The United States will not recognize or negotiate with the Palestine Liberation Organization unless that organization repudiates terrorism, explicitly recognizes Israel's right to exist in peace and accepts U.N. Security Council Resolutions 242 and 338....

China. ... [T]he Anderson-Lucey Administration would work to discourage antagonism between Russia and China. We should not become an arms supplier to China. We should work for better understanding by China's leaders of the consequences of nuclear war, of measures that should be taken to guard against accidental war and of ways to make the nuclear balance more stable.

Finally, our administration would abide by both the letter and spirit of the Taiwan Relations Act. We would maintain our contacts with Taiwan but would not establish official relations with its government.

1980 Conventions 181

1980 Democratic Convention Ballots

		Minority Rule #5 [1]		First Presidential [2]		
Delegation	Total Votes	Yea	Nay	Carter	Kennedy	Others [3]
Alabama	45	3	42	43	2	—
Alaska	11	6.11	4.89	8.4	2.6	—
Arizona	29	16	13	13	16	—
Arkansas	33	9	24	25	6	2
California	306	171	132 [4]	140	166	—
Colorado	40	24	16	27	10	3
Connecticut	54	28	26	26	28	—
Delaware	14	6.5	7.5	10	4	—
District of Columbia	19	12	7	12	5	2
Florida	100	25	75	75	25	—
Georgia	63	1	62	62	—	1
Hawaii	19	4	15	16	2	1
Idaho	17	9	8	9	7	1
Illinois	179	26	153	163	16	—
Indiana	80	27	53	53	27	—
Iowa	50	21	29	31	17	2
Kansas	37	17	20	23	14	—
Kentucky	50	12	38	45	5	—
Louisiana	51	15	36	50	1	—
Maine	22	12	10	11	11	—
Maryland	59	27	32	34	24	1
Massachusetts	111	81	30	34	77	—
Michigan	141	71	70	102	38	1
Minnesota	75	30	45	41	14	20
Mississippi	32	—	32	32	—	—
Missouri	77	20	57	58	19	—
Montana	19	9	10	13	6	—
Nebraska	24	11	13	14	10	—
Nevada	12	6.47	5.53	8.12	3.88	—
New Hampshire	19	9	10	10	9	—
New Jersey	113	68	45	45	68	—
New Mexico	20	11	9	10	10	—
New York	282	163	118	129	151	2
North Carolina	69	13	56	66	3	—
North Dakota	14	10	4	5	7	2
Ohio	161	81	80	89	72	—
Oklahoma	42	9	33	36	3	2
Oregon	39	14	25	26	13	—
Pennsylvania	185	102	83	95	90	—
Puerto Rico	41	20	21	21	20	—
Rhode Island	23	17	6	6	17	—
South Carolina	37	6	31	37	—	—
South Dakota	19	10	9	9	10	—
Tennessee	55	8	47	51	4	—
Texas	152	47	105	108	38	6
Utah	20	12	8	11	4	5
Vermont	12	7.5	4.5	5	7	—
Virginia	64	7	57	59	5	—
Washington	58	24	34	36	22	—
West Virginia	35	16	19	21	10	4
Wisconsin	75	26	49	48	26	1
Wyoming	11	3.5	7.5	8	3	—
Virgin Islands	4	—	4	4	—	—
Guam	4	—	4	4	—	—
Latin American	4	4	—	4	—	—
Democrats Abroad	4	2.5	1.5	1.5	2	0.5
Total	3,331	1,390.58	1,936.42	2,123	1,150.5	54.5 [5]

1. The vote was on a minority report by supporters of Sen. Edward M. Kennedy to overturn a proposed rule that would bind all delegates to vote on the first ballot for the presidential candidate under whose banner they were elected. A "yes" vote supported the Kennedy position while a "no" supported the Carter view that delegates should be bound.

2. Other votes: Uncommitted, 10 (3 in Texas, 3 in Colo., 2 in N.D., 1 in Ark., 1 in Md., 1 in Idaho); Sen. William Proxmire, 10 (all in Minn.); Gov. Scott M. Matheson, D-Utah, 5 (all in Utah); Koryne Horbal of Minn., U.S. representative on the U.N. Commission on the Status of Women, 5 (all in Minn.); abstentions, 4 (2 in D.C., 1 in Hawaii, 1 in Mich.); Rep. Ronald V. Dellums, D-Calif., 2.5 (2 in N.Y., 0.5 from Democrats Abroad.)

Receiving 2 votes each were: Sen. John C. Culver, D-Iowa (Iowa); Minnesota Attorney General Warren Spannous (Minn.); Alice Tripp (Minn.); Rep. Kent Hance, D-Texas (Texas); Senate Majority Leader Robert C. Byrd, D-W.Va. (W.Va.).

Receiving one vote each were: Sen. Dale Bumpers, D-Ark. (Ark.) Secretary of State Edmund S. Muskie (Colo.); Vice President Walter F. Mondale (Minn.); Gov. Hugh L. Carey, D-N.Y. (Okla); Rep. Tom Steed, D-Okla. (Okla.); Gov. Edmund G. Brown Jr., D-Calif. (Wis.)

3. At the conclusion of the roll call Del. switched to 14 for Carter and none for Kennedy. Iowa switched to 33 for Carter and 17 for Kennedy. After the switches, Carter was nominated by acclamation following a motion to that effect by the Mass. delegation.

4. One abstention.

5. This figure does not include: asbsent, 2 (1 in Ga., 1 in Okla.); 1 not voting (Texas).

1980 Republican Convention Ballot

First Presidential

State	Total Votes	Reagan	Anderson	Bush	Other	Abstentions
Alabama	27	27	—	—	—	—
Alaska	19	19	—	—	—	—
Arizona	28	28	—	—	—	—
Arkansas	19	19	—	—	—	—
California	168	168	—	—	—	—
Colorado	31	31	—	—	—	—
Connecticut	35	35	—	—	—	—
Delaware	12	12	—	—	—	—
District of Columbia	14	14	—	—	—	—
Florida	51	51	—	—	—	—
Georgia	36	36	—	—	—	—
Guam	4	4	—	—	—	—
Hawaii	14	14	—	—	—	—
Idaho	21	21	—	—	—	—
Illinois	102	81	21	—	—	—
Indiana	54	54	—	—	—	—
Iowa	37	37	—	—	—	—
Kansas	32	32	—	—	—	—
Kentucky	27	27	—	—	—	—
Louisiana	31	31	—	—	—	—
Maine	21	21	—	—	—	—
Maryland	30	30	—	—	—	—
Massachusetts	42	33	9	—	—	—
Michigan	82	67	—	13	1[1]	1
Minnesota	34	33	—	—	—	1
Mississippi	22	22	—	—	—	—
Missouri	37	37	—	—	—	—
Montana	20	20	—	—	—	—
Nebraska	25	25	—	—	—	—
Nevada	17	17	—	—	—	—
New Hampshire	22	22	—	—	—	—
New Jersey	66	66	—	—	—	—
New Mexico	22	22	—	—	—	—
New York	123	121	—	—	—	2
North Carolina	40	40	—	—	—	—
North Dakota	17	17	—	—	—	—
Ohio	77	77	—	—	—	—
Oklahoma	34	34	—	—	—	—
Oregon	29	29	—	—	—	—
Pennsylvania	83	83	—	—	—	—
Puerto Rico	14	14	—	—	—	—
Rhode Island	13	13	—	—	—	—
South Carolina	25	25	—	—	—	—
South Dakota	22	22	—	—	—	—
Tennessee	32	32	—	—	—	—
Texas	80	80	—	—	—	—
Utah	21	21	—	—	—	—
Vermont	19	19	—	—	—	—
Virginia	51	51	—	—	—	—
Virgin Islands	4	4	—	—	—	—
Washington	37	36	1	—	—	—
West Virginia	18	18	—	—	—	—
Wisconsin	34	28	6	—	—	—
Wyoming	19	19	—	—	—	—
Total	**1,994**	**1,939**	**37**	**13**	**1**	**4**

1. One vote for Anne Armstrong. Four not voting.

Results of Presidential Elections, 1860-1980

YEAR	NO OF STATES	CANDIDATES DEM.	CANDIDATES GOP	ELECTORAL VOTE DEM.	ELECTORAL VOTE GOP	POPULAR VOTE DEM.	POPULAR VOTE GOP
1860[a]	33	Stephen A. Douglas / Herschel V. Johnson	Abraham Lincoln / Hannibal Hamlin	12 / 4%	180 / 59%	1,380,202 / 29.5%	1,865,908 / 39.8%
1864[b]	36	George B. McClellan / George H. Pendleton	Abraham Lincoln / Andrew Johnson	21 / 9%	212 / 91%	1,812,807 / 45.0%	2,218,388 / 55.0%
1868[c]	37	Horatio Seymour / Francis P. Blair Jr.	Ulysses S. Grant / Schuyler Colfax	80 / 27%	214 / 73%	2,708,744 / 47.3%	3,013,650 / 52.7%
1872[d]	37	Horace Greeley / Benjamin Gratz Brown	Ulysses S. Grant / Henry Wilson	(d)	286 / 78%	2,834,761 / 43.8%	3,598,235 / 55.6%
1876	38	Samuel J. Tilden / Thomas A. Hendricks	Rutherford B. Hayes / William A. Wheeler	184 / 50%	185 / 50%	4,288,546 / 51.0%	4,034,311 / 47.9%
1880	38	Winfield S. Hancock / William H. English	James A. Garfield / Chester A. Arthur	155 / 42%	214 / 58%	4,444,260 / 48.2%	4,446,158 / 48.3%
1884	38	Grover Cleveland / Thomas A. Hendricks	James G. Blaine / John A. Logan	219 / 55%	182 / 45%	4,874,621 / 48.5%	4,848,936 / 48.2%
1888	38	Grover Cleveland / Allen G. Thurman	Benjamin Harrison / Levi P. Morton	168 / 42%	233 / 58%	5,534,488 / 48.6%	5,443,892 / 47.8%
1892[e]	44	Grover Cleveland / Adlai E. Stevenson	Benjamin Harrison / Whitelaw Reid	277 / 62%	145 / 33%	5,551,883 / 46.1%	5,179,244 / 43.0%
1896	45	William J. Bryan / Arthur Sewall	William McKinley / Garret A. Hobart	176 / 39%	271 / 61%	6,511,495 / 46.7%	7,108,480 / 51.0%
1900	45	William J. Bryan / Adlai E. Stevenson	William McKinley / Theodore Roosevelt	155 / 35%	292 / 65%	6,358,345 / 45.5%	7,218,039 / 51.7%
1904	45	Alton B. Parker / Henry G. Davis	Theodore Roosevelt / Charles W. Fairbanks	140 / 29%	336 / 71%	5,028,898 / 37.6%	7,626,593 / 56.4%
1908	46	William J. Bryan / John W. Kern	William H. Taft / James S. Sherman	162 / 34%	321 / 66%	6,406,801 / 43.0%	7,676,258 / 51.6%
1912[f]	48	Woodrow Wilson / Thomas R. Marshall	William H. Taft / James S. Sherman	435 / 82%	8 / 2%	6,293,152 / 41.8%	3,486,333 / 23.2%
1916	48	Woodrow Wilson / Thomas R. Marshall	Charles E. Hughes / Charles W. Fairbanks	277 / 52%	254 / 48%	9,126,300 / 49.2%	8,546,789 / 46.1%
1920	48	James M. Cox / Franklin D. Roosevelt	Warren G. Harding / Calvin Coolidge	127 / 24%	404 / 76%	9,140,884 / 34.2%	16,133,314 / 60.3%
1924[g]	48	John W. Davis / Charles W. Bryant	Calvin Coolidge / Charles G. Dawes	136 / 26%	382 / 72%	8,386,169 / 28.8%	15,717,553 / 54.1%
1928	48	Alfred E. Smith / Joseph T. Robinson	Herbert C. Hoover / Charles Curtis	87 / 16%	444 / 84%	15,000,185 / 40.8%	21,411,991 / 58.2%
1932	48	Franklin D. Roosevelt / John N. Garner	Herbert C. Hoover / Charles Curtis	472 / 89%	59 / 11%	22,825,016 / 57.4%	15,758,397 / 39.6%
1936	48	Franklin D. Roosevelt / John N. Garner	Alfred M. London / Frank Knox	523 / 98%	8 / 2%	27,747,636 / 60.8%	16,679,543 / 36.5%
1940	48	Franklin D. Roosevelt / Henry A. Wallace	Wendell L. Willkie / Charles L. McNary	449 / 85%	82 / 15%	27,263,448 / 54.7%	22,336,260 / 44.8%
1944	48	Franklin D. Roosevelt / Harry S Truman	Thomas E. Dewey / John W. Bricker	432 / 81%	99 / 19%	25,611,936 / 53.4%	22,013,372 / 45.9%
1948[h]	48	Harry S Truman / Alben W. Barkley	Thomas E. Dewey / Earl Warren	303 / 57%	189 / 36%	24,105,587 / 49.5%	21,970,017 / 45.1%
1952	48	Adlai E. Stevenson / John J. Sparkman	Dwight D. Eisenhower / Richard M. Nixon	89 / 17%	442 / 83%	27,314,649 / 44.4%	33,936,137 / 55.1%
1956[i]	48	Adlai E. Stevenson / Estes Kefauver	Dwight D. Eisenhower / Richard M. Nixon	73 / 14%	457 / 86%	26,030,172 / 42.0%	35,585,245 / 57.4%
1960[j]	50	John F. Kennedy / Lyndon B. Johnson	Richard M. Nixon / Henry Cabot Lodge	303 / 56%	219 / 41%	34,221,344 / 49.7%	34,106,671 / 49.5%
1964	50*	Lyndon B. Johnson / Hubert H. Humphrey	Barry Goldwater / William E. Miller	486 / 90%	52 / 10%	43,126,584 / 61.1%	27,177,838 / 38.5%
1968[k]	50*	Hubert H. Humphrey / Edmund S. Muskie	Richard M. Nixon / Spiro T. Agnew	191 / 36%	301 / 56%	31,274,503 / 42.7%	31,785,148 / 43.4%

183

YEAR	NO OF STATES	CANDIDATES DEM.	CANDIDATES GOP	ELECTORAL VOTE DEM.	ELECTORAL VOTE GOP	POPULAR VOTE DEM.	POPULAR VOTE GOP
1972(l)	50*	George McGovern Sargent Shriver	Richard M. Nixon Spiro T. Agnew	17 3%	520 97%	29,171,791 37.5%	47,170,179 60.7%
1976(m)	50*	Jimmy Carter Walter F. Mondale	Gerald R. Ford Robert Dole	297 55%	240 45%	40,830,763 50.1%	39,147,793 48.0%
1980	50*	Jimmy Carter Walter F. Mondale	Ronald Reagan George Bush	49 9%	489 91%	35,483,820 41.0%	43,901,812 50.7%

(a) 1860: John C. Breckinridge, Southern Democrat, polled 72 electoral votes. John Bell: Constitutional Union, polled 39 electoral votes.
(b) 1864: 81 electoral votes were not cast.
(c) 1868: 23 electoral votes were not cast.
(d) 1872: Horace Greeley died after election, 63 Democratic electoral votes were scattered, 17 were not voted.
(e) 1892: James B. Weaver, People's Party, polled 22 electoral votes.
(f) 1912: Theodore Roosevelt, Pogressive Party polled 86 electoral votes.
(g) 1924: Robert M. LaFollette, Progressive Party, polled 13 electoral votes.
(h) 1948: J. Strom Thurmond States' Rights Party, polled 39 electoral votes.
(i) 1956: Walter B. Jones, Democrat, plled 1 electoral vote.
(j) 1960: Harry Flood Byrd, Democrat, polled 15 electoral votes.
(k) 1968: George C. Wallace, American Independent, polled 46 electoral votes.
(l) 1972: John Hospers, Libertarian Party, polled 1 electoral vote.
(m) 1976: Ronald Reagan, Republican, polled 1 electoral vote.
* Fifty states plus District of Columbia.

Victorious Party in Presidential Races, 1860-1980

State	1860	1864	1868	1872	1876	1880	1884	1888	1892	1896	1900	1904	1908	1912	1916	1920	1924	1928	1932	1936	1940	1944	1948	1952	1956	1960	1964	1968	1972	1976	1980	Dem.	Rep.	Other
Ala.	SD	[2]	R	D	D	D	D	D	D	D	D	D	D	D	D	D	D	D	D	D	D	D	SR	D	D[18]	D[19]	R	AI	R	D	R	22	5	3
Alaska																										R	D	R	R	R	R	1	5	0
Ariz.												D	D	D	R	R	R	D	D	D	D	D	R	R	R	R	R	R	R	R	R	7	11	0
Ark.	SD	[2]	R	[4]	D	D	D	D	D	D	D	D	D	D	D	D	D	D	D	D	D	D	D	D	D	D	D	AI	R	D	R	24	3	2
Calif.	R	R	R	R	R	D[6]	R	R	D[7]	R[12]	R	R	R	PR	D	R	R	R	D	D	D	D	D	R	R	D	D	R	R	R	R	9	21	1
Colo.				R	R	R	R	R	PP	D	R	D	D	D	D	R	R	R	D	D	D	R	D	R	R	D	D	R	R	R	R	9	17	1
Conn.	R	R	R	R	D	R	D	R	D	R	R	R	R	D	R	R	R	R	D	D	D	D	R	R	R	D	D	R	R	D	R	11	20	0
Del.	SD	D	D	R	D	D	D	D	D	R	R	R	R	R	D	R	R	R	D	D	D	D	R	R	R	D	D	R	R	D	R	14	16	1
D.C.																										D	D	D	D	D	D	5	0	0
Fla.	SD	[2]	R	R	R	D	D	D	D	D	D	D	D	D	D	D	D	D	D	D	D	D	D	R	R	D	R	R	R	D	R	19	10	1
Ga.	SD	[2]	D	D[5]	D	D	D	D	D	D	D	D	D	D	D	D	D	D	D	D	D	D	D	D	D	D	R	AI	D	D	R	26	2	2
Hawaii																										D	D	D	R	D	D	5	1	0
Idaho									PP	D	R	R	D	D	R	R	R	R	D	D	D	D	D	R	R	R	D	R	R	R	R	10	12	1
Ill.	R	R	R	R	R	R	R	R	D	R	R	R	R	D	R	R	R	R	D	D	D	D	R	R	R	D	D	R	R	R	R	9	22	0
Ind.	R	R	R	R	D	R	D	R	D	R	R	R	R	D	R	R	R	R	D	D	R	R	R	R	R	D	R	R	R	R	R	7	24	0
Iowa	R	R	R	R	R	R	R	R	R	R	R	R	R	R	R	R	R	R	D	R	R	R	R	R	R	D	R	R	R	R	R	5	26	0
Kan.		R	R	R	R	R	R	R	PP	D	R	R	R	D	R	R	R	R	D	D	R	R	R	R	R	D	R	R	R	R	R	6	23	1
Ky.	CU	D	D	D	D	D	D	D	D	R[13]	D	D	D	D	D	R	R	D	D	D	D	D	D	R	R	D	R	R	R	D	R	22	8	1
La.	SD	[2]	D	[4]	R	D	D	D	D	D	D	D	D	D	D	D	D	D	D	D	D	D	SR	D	D	R	D	AI	R	D	R	21	5	3
Maine	R	R	R	R	R	R	R	R	R	R	R	R	R	D	R	R	R	R	R	R	R	R	R	R	R	D	D	R	R	D	R	3	28	0
Md.	SD	R	D	D	D	D	D	D	D	R	R	D[14]	D[15]	D	D	R	R	D	D	D	D	D	R	R	R	D	D	D	R	D	D	20	10	1
Mass.	R	R	R	R	R	R	R	R	R	R	R	R	R	D	R	R	R	R	D	D	D	D	D	R	R	D	D	D	R	D	R	12	19	0
Mich.	R	R	R	R	R	R	R	R	R[8]	R	R	R	R	PR	R	R	R	R	D	D	R	R	R	R	R	D	D	R	R	D	R	6	24	1
Minn.	R	R	R	R	R	R	R	R	R	R	R	R	R	PR	R	R	R	R	D	D	D	D	D	R	R	D	D	D	R	D	D	10	20	1
Miss.	SD	[2]	[3]	R	D	D	D	D	D	D	D	D	D	D	D	D	D	D	D	D	D	D	SR	D	D	[20]	R	AI	R	D	R	21	4	3
Mo.	D	R	R	D	D	D	D	D	D	D	D	D	D	D	D	R	R	R	D	D	D	D	D	R	D	D	D	R	R	R	R	20	11	0
Mont.							R	D	D	R	R	R	D	D	R	R	R	R	D	D	D	D	D	R	R	D	D	R	R	R	R	10	13	0
Neb.		R	R	R	R	R	R	R	PP	R	R	R	D	D	D	R	R	R	D	D	R	R	R	R	R	D	R	R	R	R	R	7	22	0
Nev.		R	R	R	R	D	R	R	PP	D	D	R	D	D	D	R	R	R	D	D	D	D	R	R	R	D	D	R	R	R	R	13	16	1
N.H.	R	R	R	R	R	R	R	R	R	R	R	R	R	D	R	R	R	R	D	D	R	R	R	R	R	D	D	R	R	R	R	6	25	0
N.J.	R[1]	D	D	R	D	R	D	D	D	R	R	R	R	D	R	R	R	R	D	D	D	R	R	R	R	D	D	R	R	D	R	14	17	0
N.M.												D	D	D	R	R	R	D	D	D	D	D	R	R	R	D	D	R	R	R	R	9	9	0
N.Y.	R	R	D	R	D	R	D	R	D	R	R	R	D	D	R	R	R	R	D	D	D	D	R	R	R	D	D	D	R	D	R	13	18	0
N.C.	SD	[2]	R	R	D	D	D	D	D	D	D	D	D	D	D	D	R	R	D	D	D	D	D	D	D	D	R[22]	R	R	D	R	23	6	1
N.D.									[9]	R	R	R	R	D	R	R	R	R	D	D	R	R	R	R	R	R	D	R	R	R	R	5	17	1
Ohio	R	R	R	R	R	R	R	R	R[10]	R	R	R	R	D	R	R	R	R	D	D	D	D	R	R	R	D	D	R	R	D	R	8	23	0
Okla.													D	D	D	R	R	D	D	D	D	D	D	R	R	D	R[21]	D	R	R	R	10	9	0
Ore.	R	R	D	R	R	R	R	R	R[11]	R	R	R	R	D	R	R	R	R	D	D	D	D	R	R	R	D	D	R	R	R	R	7	24	0
Pa.	R	R	R	R	R	R	R	R	R	R	R	R	R	PR	R	R	R	R	R	D	D	D	R	R	R	D	D	D	R	D	R	7	23	1
R.I.	R	R	R	R	R	R	R	R	R	R	R	R	R	R	R	R	R	R	D	D	D	D	D	R	R	D	D	D	R	D	D	12	19	0
S.C.	SD	[2]	R	R	D	D	D	D	D	D	D	D	D	D	D	D	D	D	D	D	D	D	SR	D	D	D	R	R	R	D	R	21	7	2
S.D.							R	D	R	R	PR	R	R	R	R	R	R	R	R	R	R	R	R	R	D	R	R	R	R	R	R	4	18	1
Tenn.	CU	[2]	R	D	D	D	D	D	D	D	D	D	D	D	R	R	D	R	D	D	D	D	D	R	R	D[17]	R	R	R	D	R	20	9	1
Texas	SD	[2]	[3]	D	D	D	D	D	D	D	D	D	D	D	D	D	D	D	D	D	D	D	R	R	D	D	D	R	R	D	R	23	5	1
Utah										D	R	R	R	D	D	R	R	R	D	D	D	D	D	R	R	R	R	R	R	R	R	8	14	0
Vt.	R	R	R	R	R	R	R	R	R	R	R	R	R	R	R	R	R	R	R	R	R	R	R	R	R	R	R	R	R	D	R	1	30	0
Va.	CU	[2]	[3]	R	D	D	D	D	D	D	D	D	D	D	D	D	D	D	D	D	D	D	R	R	R	D	R	R	R[23]	R	R	19	9	1
Wash.							R	D	R	R	R	R	R	PR	D	R	R	R	D	D	D	D	D	R	R	D	D	R	R	R[24]	R	9	13	1
W.Va.			R	R	R	D	D	D	D	R	R	D	R[16]	R	R	R	R	R	D	D	D	D	D	R	R	D	D	R	R	D	R	17	13	0
Wis.	R	R	R	R	R	R	R	R	D	R	R	R	R	PR	R	D	PR	R	D	D	D	D	D	R	R	D	D	R	R	D	R	8	22	1
Wyo.									R	D	R	R	R	D	D	R	R	R	D	D	D	D	D	R	R	D	D	R	R	R	R	8	15	0
Winning Party	R	R	R	R	R	D	D	R	D	R	R	R	R	D	D	R	R	R	D	D	D	D	D	R	R	D	D	R	R	D	R	12	19	0

[1] Four electors voted Republican; Three Democratic.
[2] Confederate States did not vote in 1864.
[3] Did not vote in 1868.
[4] Votes were not counted.
[5] Three votes for Greeley not counted.
[6] Five electors voted Democratic; one Republican.
[7] Eight electors voted Democratic; one Republican.
[8] Nine electors voted Republican; five Democratic.
[9] One vote each for Democratic, Republican and People's Party.
[10] 22 electors voted Republican, one Democratic.
[11] Three electors voted Republican; one People's Party.
[12] Eight electors voted Republican; one Democratic.
[13] Twelve electors voted Republican; one Democratic.
[14] Seven electors voted Democratic; one Republican.
[15] Six electors voted Democratic; two Republican.
[16] Seven electors voted Republican; one Democratic.
[17] Eleven electors voted Democratic; one States' Rights.
[18] One elector voted for Walter Jones.
[19] Six of 11 electors voted for Harry F. Byrd.
[20] Eight independent electors voted for Byrd.
[21] One vote cast for Byrd.
[22] Twelve electors voted Republican; one American Independent.
[23] One elector voted Libertarian.
[24] One elector voted for Ronald Reagan.

With the exception of the District of Columbia, blanks indicate states not yet admitted to the Union. The District of Columbia received the presidential vote in 1961.

A — American Party
AI — American Union Party
CU — Constitutional Union Party
D — Democratic Party
PP — People's Party
PR — Progressive (Bull Moose) Party
R — Republican Party
SD — Southern Democratic Party
SR — States' Rights Party

1982 Elections: Governor, Senate, House

Following are final 1982 vote returns for the Senate, House and governorships, compiled by Congressional Quarterly from results furnished by the secretaries of state or election boards in the 50 states.

All candidates are included who were listed on the ballot. Due to the exclusion of scattered write-in votes from this chart and the results of rounding numbers in computing percentages, the totals do not always equal 100 percent. The box below shows party designation symbols.

* indicates incumbents.

X denotes unopposed candidates.

- denotes minor parties for which the vote was not available.

ALABAMA

	Vote Total	Percent
Governor		
George C. Wallace (D)	650,538	57.6
Emory Folmar (R)	440,815	39.1
John Dyer (P)	4,364	0.4
Leo Suiter (C)	17,936	1.6
Henri Klingler (LIBERT)	7,671	0.7
John L. Jackson (NDPA)	4,693	0.4
Martin Boyers (S)	2,578	0.2
House		
1 Steve Gudac (D)	54,315	37.2
Jack Edwards (R)*	89,901	61.6
Bill Springer (LIBERT)	1,812	1.2
2 Billy Joe Camp (D)	81,904	49.6
William L. Dickinson (R)*	83,290	50.4
3 Bill Nichols (D)*	100,864	96.3
Richard Landers Jr. (LIBERT)	3,920	3.7
4 Tom Bevill (D)*	X	100.0
5 Ronnie G. Flippo (D)*	108,807	80.7
Leopold Yambrek (R)	24,593	18.2
Kenneth Ament (LIBERT)	1,474	1.1
6 Ben Erdreich (D)	88,029	53.2
Albert Lee Smith Jr. (R)*	76,726	46.4
Charles Ewing (LIBERT)	632	0.4
7 Richard C. Shelby (D)*	124,070	96.8
James Jones (LIBERT)	4,058	3.2

ALASKA

	Vote Total	Percent
Governor		
Bill Sheffield (D)	89,918	46.1
Tom Fink (R)	72,291	37.1
Joseph Vogler (AKI)	3,235	1.7
Richard L. Randolph (LIBERT)	29,067	14.9
House		
AL Dave Carlson (D)	52,011	28.7
Don Young (R)*	128,274	70.8

ARIZONA

	Vote Total	Percent
Governor		
Bruce Babbitt (D)*	453,795	62.5
Leo Corbet (R)	235,877	32.5
Sam Steiger (LIBERT)	36,649	5.0
Senator		
Dennis DeConcini (D)*	411,970	56.9
Pete Dunn (R)	291,749	40.3
Randall Clamons (LIBERT)	20,100	2.8
House		
1 William E. Hegarty (D)	41,261	30.5
John McCain (R)	89,116	65.9
Richard K. Dodge (LIBERT)	4,850	3.6
2 Morris K. Udall (D)*	73,468	70.9
Roy B. Laos (R)	28,407	27.4
Jessica Sampson (YSA)	1,799	1.7
3 Pat Bosch (D)	58,644	36.7
Bob Stump (R)*	101,198	63.3
4 Wayne O. Earley (D)	44,182	30.4
Eldon Rudd (R)*	95,620	65.7
Richard A. Stauffer (LIBERT)	5,664	3.9
5 Jim McNulty (D)	82,938	49.7
Jim Kolbe (R)	80,531	48.3
Richard D. Auster (LIBERT)	3,332	2.0

ARKANSAS

	Vote Total	Percent
Governor		
Bill Clinton (D)	431,855	54.7
Frank D. White (R)*	357,496	45.3
House		
1 Bill Alexander (D)*	124,208	64.8
Chuck Banks (R)	67,427	35.2
2 Charles L. George (D)	82,913	46.1
Ed Bethune (R)*	96,775	53.9
3 Jim McDougal (D)	69,089	34.0
John Paul Hammerschmidt (R)*	133,909	66.0
4 Beryl Anthony Jr. (D)*	121,256	65.6
Bob Leslie (R)	63,661	34.4

Abbreviations for Party Designations

AD	—Anti-Drug	LIBERT	—Libertarian
AKI	—Alaskan Independence	LU	—Liberty Union
AM	—American	NA	—New Alliance
AMI	—American Independent	NDPA	—National Democratic Party of Alabama
BGG	—Bipartisan Good Government	NF	—Nuclear Freeze
C	—Conservative	NP	—Nonpartisan
CIT	—Citizens	NU	—New Union
COM	—Communist	P	—Prohibition
CONSU	—Consumers	PFP	—Peace and Freedom Party
CST	—Constitution	R	—Republican
D	—Democratic	RTL	—Right to Life
DFL	—Democratic Farmer-Labor	SOC	—Socialist
F LIBERT	—Free Libertarian	SOC LAB	—Socialist Labor
FP	—Free People's	SOC WORK	—Socialist Workers
I	—Independent	TAX	—Taxpayers
I-D	—Independent-Democrat	UN	—Unity
I-R	—Independent-Republican	WF	—World Federalist
JI	—Jeffersonian Independent	WL	—Workers League
L	—Liberal	YSA	—Young Socialist Alliance

CALIFORNIA

Governor

	Vote Total	Percent
Tom Bradley (D)	3,787,669	48.1
George Deukmejian (R)	3,881,014	49.3
James C. Griffin (AMI)	56,249	0.7
Dan P. Dougherty (LIBERT)	81,076	1.0
Elizabeth Martinez (PFP)	70,327	0.9

Senator

	Vote Total	Percent
Edmund G. Brown Jr. (D)	3,494,968	44.8
Pete Wilson (R)	4,022,565	51.5
Theresa "Tena" Dietrich (AMI)	83,809	1.1
Joseph Fuhrig (LIBERT)	107,720	1.4
David Wald (PFP)	96,388	1.2

House

	Vote Total	Percent
1 Douglas H. Bosco (D)	107,749	49.8
Don H. Clausen (R)*	102,043	47.2
David Redick (LIBERT)	6,374	3.0
2 John A. Newmeyer (D)	81,314	40.5
Gene Chappie (R)*	116,172	57.9
Howard Fegarsky (PFP)	3,126	1.6
3 Robert T. Matsui (D)*	194,680	89.6
Bruce A. Daniel (LIBERT)	16,222	7.5
John C. Reiger (PFP)	6,294	2.9
4 Vic Fazio (D)*	118,476	63.9
Roger B. Canfield (R)	67,047	36.1
5 Phillip Burton (D)*	103,268	57.9
Milton Marks (R)	72,139	40.5
Justin Raimondo (LIBERT)	2,904	1.6
6 Barbara Boxer (D)	96,379	52.4
Dennis McQuaid (R)	82,128	44.6
Howard C. Creighton (LIBERT)	3,191	1.7
Timothy-Allen Albertson (PFP)	2,366	1.3
7 George Miller (D)*	126,952	67.2
Paul E. Vallely (R)	56,960	30.2
Terry L. Wells (AMI)	2,205	1.2
Rich Newell (LIBERT)	2,752	1.4
8 Ronald V. Dellums (D)*	121,537	55.9
Claude B. Hutchison Jr. (R)	95,694	44.1
9 Fortney H. "Pete" Stark (D)*	104,393	60.7
Bill J. Kennedy (R)	67,702	39.3
10 Don Edwards (D)*	77,263	62.7
Bob Herriott (R)	41,506	33.7
Edmon V. Kaiser (AMI)	2,109	1.7
Dale Burrow (LIBERT)	2,403	1.9
11 Tom Lantos (D)*	109,812	57.1
Bill Royer (R)	76,462	39.7
Nicholas W. Kudrovzeff (AMI)	1,250	0.7
Chuck Olson (LIBERT)	2,920	1.5
Wilson Branch (PFP)	1,928	1.0
12 Emmett Lynch (D)	61,372	33.5
Ed Zschau (R)	115,365	63.0
Bill White (LIBERT)	6,471	3.5
13 Norman Y. Mineta (D)*	110,805	65.9
Tom Kelly (R)	52,806	31.4
Al Hinkle (LIBERT)	4,553	2.7
14 Baron Reed (D)	77,400	36.6
Norman D. Shumway (R)*	134,225	63.4
15 Tony Coelho (D)*	86,022	63.7
Ed Bates (R)	45,948	34.0
Stephen L. Gerringer (LIBERT)	3,073	2.3
16 Leon E. Panetta (D)*	142,630	85.4
G. Richard Arnold (R)	24,448	14.6
Anne Nixon Ball (R write-in)	—	—
17 Gene Tackett (D)	68,364	46.0
Charles Pashayan Jr. (R)*	80,271	54.0
18 Richard Lehman (D)	92,762	59.5
Adrian C. Fondse (R)	59,664	38.3
Marshall William Fritz (LIBERT)	3,501	2.2
19 Frank Frost (D)	66,042	35.8
Robert J. Lagomarsino (R)*	112,486	61.1
R. C. Gordon-McCutchan (LIBERT)	4,198	2.3
Charles J. Zekan (PFP)	1,520	0.8
20 Robert J. Bethea (D)	57,769	31.9
William M. Thomas (R)*	123,312	68.1
21 George Henry Margolis (D)	46,412	24.1
Bobbi Fiedler (R)*	138,474	71.8
Daniel Wiener (LIBERT)	7,881	4.1
22 Harvey L. Goldhammer (D)	46,521	23.5
Carlos J. Moorhead (R)*	145,831	73.6
Robert T. Gerringer (LIBERT)	5,870	2.9
23 Anthony C. Beilenson (D)*	120,788	59.6
David Armor (R)	82,031	40.4
24 Henry A. Waxman (D)*	88,516	65.0
Jerry Zerg (R)	42,133	31.0
Jeff Mandel (LIBERT)	5,420	4.0
25 Edward R. Roybal (D)*	71,106	85.5
Daniel John Gorham (LIBERT)	12,060	14.5
26 Howard L. Berman (D)	97,383	59.6
Hal Phillips (R)	66,070	40.4
27 Mel Levine (D)	108,347	59.5
Bart W. Christensen (R)	67,479	37.0
Zack Richardson (LIBERT)	6,391	3.5
28 Julian C. Dixon (D)*	103,469	78.9
David Goerz (R)	24,473	18.7
David W. Meleney (LIBERT)	3,210	2.4
29 Augustus F. Hawkins (D)*	97,028	79.8
Milton R. MacKaig (R)	24,568	20.2
30 Matthew G. "Marty" Martinez (D)	60,905	53.9
John H. Rousselot (R)*	52,177	46.1
31 Mervyn M. Dymally (D)*	86,718	72.4
Henry C. Minturn (R)	33,043	27.6
32 Glenn M. Anderson (D)*	84,663	58.0
Brian Lungren (R)	57,863	39.6
Eugene E. Ruyle (PFP)	3,473	2.4
33 Paul Servelle (D)	55,514	32.2
David Dreier (R)*	112,362	65.2
Phillips P. Franklin (LIBERT)	2,251	1.3
James Michael Noonan (PFP)	2,223	1.3
34 Esteban Torres (D)	68,316	57.2
Paul R. Jackson (R)	51,026	42.8
35 Robert E. Erwin (D)	52,349	31.7
Jerry Lewis (R)*	112,786	68.3
36 George E. Brown Jr. (D)*	76,546	54.3
John Paul Stark (R)	64,361	45.7
37 Curtis P. "Sam" Cross (D)	68,510	38.5
Al McCandless (R)	105,065	59.1
Marc R. Wruple (LIBERT)	4,297	2.4
38 Jerry M. Patterson (D)*	73,914	52.4
William F. Dohr (R)	61,279	43.4
Anita K. Barr (LIBERT)	5,989	4.2
39 Frank G. Verges (D)	46,681	26.0
William E. Dannemeyer (R)*	129,539	72.2
Frank Boeheim (PFP)	3,152	1.8
40 Paul Haseman (D)	52,546	26.1
Robert E. Badham (R)*	144,228	71.5
Maxine Bell Quirk (PFP)	4,826	2.4
41 Tony Brandenburg (D)	58,677	28.8
Bill Lowery (R)	140,130	68.9
Everett Hale (LIBERT)	4,654	2.3
42 James P. Spellman (D)	58,690	28.3
Dan Lungren (R)*	142,845	69.0
John S. Donohue (PFP)	5,514	2.7
43 Roy "Pat" Archer (D)	57,995	32.1
Johnnie R. Crean (R)	56,297	31.1
Ron Packard (R write-in)	66,444	36.8
44 Jim Bates (D)	78,474	65.0
Shirley M. Gissendanner (R)	38,447	31.8
Jim Conole (LIBERT)	3,904	3.2
45 Richard Hill (D)	50,148	29.2
Duncan L. Hunter (R)*	117,771	68.6
Jack R. Sanders (LIBERT)	3,839	2.2

COLORADO

Governor

	Vote Total	Percent
Richard D. Lamm (D)*	627,960	65.7
John D. Fuhr (R)	302,740	31.7
Paul Grant (LIBERT)	19,349	2.0
Earl F. Dodge (P)	3,496	0.4
Alan Gummerson (SOC WORK)	2,476	0.2

House

	Vote Total	Percent
1 Patricia Schroeder (D)*	94,969	60.3
Arch Decker (R)	59,009	37.4
Robin White (LIBERT)	3,619	2.3
2 Timothy E. Wirth (D)*	101,194	61.8
John C. Buechner (R)	59,580	36.4
Charles Jackson (LIBERT)	2,862	1.8
3 Ray Kogovsek (D)*	92,384	53.4
Tom Wiens (R)	77,409	44.8
Stormy Mon (LIBERT)	2,439	1.4
Henry John Olshaw (I)	656	0.4
4 Charles L. "Bud" Bishopp (D)	45,750	30.2
Hank Brown (R)*	105,550	69.8
5 Tom Cronin (D)	57,392	40.5
Ken Kramer (R)*	84,479	59.5
6 Steve Hogan (D)	56,598	35.6
Jack Swigert (R)†	98,909	62.1
J. Craig Green (LIBERT)	3,605	2.3

CONNECTICUT

Governor

	Vote Total	Percent
William A. O'Neill (D)*	578,264	53.4
Lewis B. Rome (R)	497,773	45.9
Walter J. Gengarelly (LIBERT)	7,839	0.7

Senator

	Vote Total	Percent
Toby Moffett (D)	499,146	46.1
Lowell P. Weicker Jr. (R)*	545,987	50.4
Lucien DiFazio (C)	30,212	2.8
James A. Lewis (LIBERT)	8,163	0.7

House

	Vote Total	Percent
1 Barbara B. Kennelly (D)*	126,798	68.1
Herschel A. Klein (R)	58,075	31.2
Daniel Landerfen (LIBERT)	1,237	0.7
2 Sam Gejdenson (D)*	95,254	55.8
Tony Guglielmo (R)	74,294	43.5
Donald W. Wood (LIBERT)	1,255	0.7
3 Bruce A. Morrison (D)	90,638	50.0
Lawrence J. DeNardis (R)*	88,951	49.0
Joelle R. Fishman (COM)	696	0.4
Michael R. Cohen (LIBERT)	1,164	0.6
4 John A. Phillips (D)	71,110	42.9
Stewart B. McKinney (R)*	93,660	56.4
Lothar Frank (LIBERT)	1,127	0.7
5 William R. Ratchford (D)*	101,362	58.5
Neal B. Hanlon (R)	70,808	40.8
Jerry Brennan (LIBERT)	1,203	0.7

† Died Dec. 27, 1982

188 Elections '84

	Vote Total	Percent
6 William E. Curry Jr. (D)	92,178	47.7
Nancy L. Johnson (R)	99,703	51.7
Monte Dunn (LIBERT)	1,091	0.6

DELAWARE

Senator

David N. Levinson (D)	84,413	44.2
William V. Roth Jr. (R)*	105,357	55.2
Charles A. Baker (AM)	537	0.3
Lawrence D. Sullivan (LIBERT)	653	0.3

House

AL Thomas R. Carper (D)	98,533	52.4
Thomas B. Evans Jr. (R)*	87,153	46.3
Mary D. Gise (AM)	1,109	0.6
David Nuttall (CIT)	558	0.3
Richard A. Cohen (LIBERT)	711	0.4

FLORIDA

Governor

Robert Graham (D)*	1,739,553	64.7
L. A. "Skip" Bafalis (R)	949,023	35.3

Senator

Lawton Chiles (D)*	1,636,857	61.7
Van Poole (R)	1,014,551	38.3

House

1 Earl Hutto (D)*	82,482	74.5
J. Terry Bechtol (R)	28,285	25.5
2 Don Fuqua (D)*	79,096	61.7
Ron McNeil (R)	49,084	38.3
3 Charles E. Bennett (D)*	73,713	84.1
George Grimsley (R)	13,921	15.9
4 Bill Chappell Jr. (D)*	83,830	66.9
Larry Gaudet (R)	41,399	33.1
5 Dick Batchelor (D)	49,042	41.2
Bill McCollum (R)*	69,939	58.8
6 Kenneth H. "Buddy" MacKay (D)	85,799	61.3
Ed Havill (R)	54,058	38.7
7 Sam Gibbons (D)*	85,317	74.2
Ken Ayers (R)	29,624	25.8
8 C. W. Bill Young (R)*	X	100.0
9 George H. Sheldon (D)	90,673	48.8
Michael Bilirakis (R)	94,993	51.2
10 Andy Ireland (D)*	X	100.0
11 Bill Nelson (D)*	101,625	70.6
Joel Robinson (R)	42,323	29.4
12 Brad Culverhouse (D)	73,886	47.4
Tom Lewis (R)	81,864	52.6
13 Dana N. Stevens (D)	71,206	34.9
Connie Mack III (R)	132,906	65.1
14 Daniel A. Mica (D)*	128,627	73.0
Steve Mitchell (R)	47,542	27.0
15 Edward J. Stack (D)	67,058	42.9
E. Clay Shaw Jr. (R)*	89,128	57.1
16 Larry Smith (D)	91,869	67.9
Maurice Berkowitz (R)	43,343	32.1
17 William Lehman (D)*	X	100.0
18 Claude Pepper (D)*	72,137	71.2
Ricardo Nunez (R)	29,156	28.8
19 Dante B. Fascell (D)*	74,274	58.9
Glenn Rinker (R)	51,925	41.1

GEORGIA

Governor

Joe Frank Harris (D)	734,090	62.8
Bob Bell (R)	434,496	37.2

House

1 Lindsay Thomas (D)	65,625	64.1
Herb Jones (R)	36,799	35.9
2 Charles Hatcher (D)*	X	100.0
3 Richard Ray (D)	74,626	71.0
Tyron Elliott (R)	30,537	29.0
4 Elliott H. Levitas (D)*	38,758	65.5
Dick Winder (R)	20,418	34.5
5 Wyche Fowler Jr. (D)*	53,264	80.8
Paul Jones (R)	3,633	5.5
J. E. "Billy" McKinney (I)	9,049	13.7
6 Jim Wood (D)	50,459	44.7
Newt Gingrich (R)*	62,352	55.3
7 Larry P. McDonald (D)*	71,647	61.1
Dave Sellers (R)	45,569	38.9
8 J. Roy Rowland (D)	X	100.0
9 Ed Jenkins (D)*	86,514	77.0
Charles Sherwood (R)	25,907	23.0
10 Doug Barnard Jr. (D)*	X	100.0

HAWAII

Governor

George Ariyoshi (D)*	141,043	45.2
D. G. Anderson (R)	81,507	26.2
Frank F. Fasi (I-D)	89,303	28.6

Senator

Spark M. Matsunaga (D)*	245,386	80.1
Clarence J. Brown (R)	52,071	17.0
E. F. Bernier-Nachtwey (I-D)	8,953	2.9

House

1 Cecil Heftel (D)*	134,779	89.9
Rockne H. Johnson (LIBERT)	15,128	10.1
2 Daniel K. Akaka (D)*	132,072	89.2
Amelia Oy Fritts (LIBERT)	6,856	4.6
Gregory B. Mills (NP)	9,080	6.2

IDAHO

Governor

John V. Evans (D)*	165,365	50.6
Philip E. Batt (R)	161,157	49.4

House

1 Larry LaRocco (D)	74,388	46.3
Larry E. Craig (R)*	86,277	53.7
2 Richard Stallings (D)	76,608	47.7
George Hansen (R)*	83,873	52.3

ILLINOIS

Governor

Adlai E. Stevenson III (D)	1,811,027	49.3
James R. Thompson (R)*	1,816,101	49.4
Bea Armstrong (LIBERT)	24,417	0.7
John E. Roche (TAX)	22,001	0.6

House

1 Harold Washington (D)*	172,641	97.3
Charles Allen Taliaferro (R)	4,820	2.7
2 Gus Savage (D)*	140,827	87.0
Kevin Walker Sparks (R)	20,670	12.8
Joseph Zvonkovach (write-in)	288	0.2
3 Marty Russo (D)*	137,391	74.0
Richard D. Murphy (R)	48,268	26.0
4 Michael A. Murer (D)	66,323	45.4
George M. O'Brien (R)*	79,842	54.6
5 William O. Lipinski (D)	110,351	75.4
Daniel J. Partyka (R)	35,970	24.6
6 Leroy E. Kennel (D)	45,237	31.6
Henry J. Hyde (R)*	97,918	68.4
7 Cardiss Collins (D)*	133,978	86.5
Dansby Cheeks (R)	20,994	13.5
8 Dan Rostenkowski (D)*	124,318	83.4
Bonnie Hickey (R)	24,666	16.6
9 Sidney R. Yates (D)*	114,083	66.5
Catherine Bertini (R)	54,851	32.0
Sheila Jones (AD)	2,595	1.5
10 Eugenia S. Chapman (D)	63,115	41.0
John Edward Porter (R)*	90,750	59.0
11 Frank Annunzio (D)*	134,755	72.6
James F. Moynihan (R)	50,967	27.4
12 Daniel G. DeFosse (D)	40,108	30.7
Philip M. Crane (R)*	86,487	66.2
Joan T. Jarosz (LIBERT)	4,101	3.1
13 Robert Bily (D)	49,105	30.2
John N. Erlenborn (R)*	113,423	69.8
14 Dan McGrath (D)	53,914	35.4
Tom Corcoran (R)*	98,262	64.6
15 Tim L. Hall (D)	53,303	33.7
Edward R. Madigan (R)*	105,038	66.3
16 Carl R. Schwerdtfeger (D)	66,877	42.8
Lynn Martin (R)*	89,405	57.2
17 Lane Evans (D)	94,483	52.8
Kenneth G. McMillan (R)	84,347	47.2
18 G. Douglas Stephens (D)	91,281	48.4
Robert H. Michel (R)*	97,406	51.6
19 John Gwinn (D)	87,231	47.9
Daniel B. Crane (R)*	94,833	52.1
20 Richard J. Durbin (D)	100,758	50.4
Paul Findley (R)*	99,348	49.6
21 Melvin Price (D)*	89,500	63.6
Robert H. Gaffner (R)	46,764	33.3
Sandra L. Climaco (BGG)	4,344	3.1
22 Paul Simon (D)*	123,693	66.2
Peter G. Prineas (R)	63,279	33.8

INDIANA

Senator

Floyd Fithian (D)	828,400	45.6
Richard G. Lugar (R)*	978,301	53.8
Raymond James (AM)	10,586	0.6

House

1 Katie Hall (D)	89,369	56.9
Thomas H. Krieger (R)	66,921	42.6
Jesse Smith (SOC WORK)	806	0.5
2 Philip R. Sharp (D)*	107,298	56.2
Ralph W. Van Natta (R)	83,593	43.8
3 Richard C. Bodine (D)	83,046	48.8
John Hiler (R)*	86,958	51.2
4 Roger M. Miller (D)	60,054	35.1
Dan Coats (R)*	110,155	64.3
John B. Cameron (AM)	1,029	0.6
5 Allen B. Maxwell (D)	67,238	38.9
Elwood Hillis (R)*	105,469	61.1
6 George E. Grabianowski (D)	70,764	35.1
Dan Burton (R)	131,100	64.9
7 Stephen S. Bonney (D)	70,249	37.7
John T. Myers (R)*	115,884	62.3
8 Francis X. McCloskey (D)	100,592	51.4
Joel Deckard (R)*	94,127	48.1
Robert F. Arnove (CIT)	1,006	0.5
9 Lee H. Hamilton (D)*	121,094	67.1
Floyd E. Coates (R)	58,532	32.4
Stephen Arnold (CIT)	913	0.5
10 Andrew Jacobs Jr. (D)*	114,674	66.7

	Vote Total	Percent
Michael A. Carroll (R)	56,992	33.2
David W. Ellis (SOC WORK)	197	0.1

IOWA

Governor
Roxanne Conlin (D)	483,291	46.5
Terry Branstad (R)	548,313	52.8
Marcia J. Farrington (LIBERT)	3,307	0.3
Jim Bittner (SOC)	2,767	0.3

House
1	William E. Gluba (D)	61,734	40.8
	Jim Leach (R)*	89,585	59.2
2	Brent Appel (D)	69,539	41.1
	Tom Tauke (R)*	99,478	58.9
3	Lynn G. Cutler (D)	83,581	44.5
	Cooper Evans (R)*	104,072	55.5
4	Neal Smith (D)*	118,849	66.1
	Dave Readinger (R)	60,534	33.6
	Bill Douglas (SOC)	584	0.3
5	Tom Harkin (D)*	93,333	58.9
	Arlyn E. Danker (R)	65,200	41.1
6	Berkley Bedell (D)*	101,690	64.3
	Al Bremer (R)	56,487	35.7

KANSAS

Governor
John Carlin (D)*	405,772	53.2
Sam Hardage (R)	339,356	44.4
Frank W. Shelton Jr. (AM)	6,136	0.8
James H. Ward (LIBERT)	7,595	1.0
Warren C. Martin (P)	4,404	0.6

House
1	Kent Roth (D)	51,079	30.2
	Pat Roberts (R)*	115,749	68.4
	Kent Earnest (LIBERT)	2,305	1.4
2	Jim Slattery (D)	86,286	57.4
	Morris Kay (R)	63,942	42.6
3	William L. Kostar (D)	53,140	38.3
	Larry Winn Jr. (R)*	82,117	59.2
	Gene R. Blair (LIBERT)	3,439	2.5
4	Dan Glickman (D)*	107,326	73.9
	Gerald Caywood (R)	35,478	24.5
	Karl Peterjohn (LIBERT)	2,363	1.6
5	Lee Rowe (D)	47,676	31.1
	Bob Whittaker (R)*	103,551	67.6
	John L. Conger (LIBERT)	1,894	1.3

KENTUCKY

House
1	Carroll Hubbard Jr. (D)*	X	100.0
2	William H. Natcher (D)*	49,571	73.8
	Mark T. Watson (R)	17,561	26.2
3	Romano L. Mazzoli (D)*	92,849	65.1
	Carl Brown (R)	45,900	32.2
	Dan Murray (LIBERT)	608	0.4
	Craig Honts (SOC)	400	0.3
	Norbert D. Leveronne (I)	2,840	2.0
4	Terry L. Mann (D)	61,937	45.3
	Gene Snyder (R)*	74,109	54.2
	Paul Thiel (LIBERT)	704	0.5
5	Doye Davenport (D)	28,285	34.8
	Harold Rogers (R)*	52,928	65.2
6	Don Mills (D)	49,839	41.4
	Larry J. Hopkins (R)*	68,418	56.8
	Ken Ashby (LIBERT)	1,185	1.0
	Don B. Pratt (I)	917	0.8

		Vote Total	Percent
7	Carl D. Perkins (D)*	82,463	79.4
	Tom Hamby (R)	21,436	20.6

LOUISIANA

House
1	Bob Livingston (R)*	X	100.0
2	Lindy (Mrs. Hale) Boggs (D)*	X	100.0
3	W. J. "Billy" Tauzin (D)*	X	100.0
4	Buddy Roemer (D)	X	100.0
5	Jerry Huckaby (D)*	X	100.0
6	Henson Moore (R)*	X	100.0
7	John B. Breaux (D)*	X	100.0
8	Gillis W. Long (D)*	X	100.0

MAINE

Governor
Joseph E. Brennan (D)*	281,066	61.1
Charles L. Cragin (R)	172,949	37.6
J. Martin Bachon (I)	2,573	0.5
Vern Warren (I)	3,650	0.8

Senator
George J. Mitchell (D)*	279,819	60.9
David F. Emery (R)	179,882	39.1

House
1	John M. Kerry (D)	118,884	47.9
	John R. McKernan Jr. (R)	124,850	50.4
	Gregory J. Fleming (I)	4,221	1.7
2	James Patrick Dunleavy (D)	68,086	33.4
	Olympia J. Snowe (R)*	136,075	66.6

MARYLAND

Governor
Harry R. Hughes (D)*	705,910	62.0
Robert A. Pascal (R)	432,826	38.0

Senator
Paul S. Sarbanes (D)*	707,356	63.5
Lawrence J. Hogan (R)	407,334	36.5

House
1	Roy Dyson (D)*	89,503	69.3
	C. A. Porter Hopkins (R)	39,656	30.7
2	Clarence D. Long (D)*	83,318	52.6
	Helen Delich Bentley (R)	75,062	47.4
3	Barbara A. Mikulski (D)*	110,042	74.2
	H. Robert Scherr (R)	38,259	25.8
4	Patricia O'Brien Aiken (D)	47,947	38.8
	Marjorie S. Holt (R)*	75,617	61.2
5	Steny H. Hoyer (D)*	83,937	79.6
	William P. Guthrie (R)	21,533	20.4
6	Beverly B. Byron (D)*	102,596	74.4
	Roscoe Bartlett (R)	35,321	25.6
7	Parren J. Mitchell (D)*	103,496	87.9
	M. Leonora Jones (R)	14,203	12.1
8	Michael D. Barnes (D)*	121,761	71.3
	Elizabeth W. Spencer (R)	48,910	28.7

MASSACHUSETTS

Governor
Michael S. Dukakis (D)	1,219,109	59.4
John W. Sears (R)	749,679	36.6
Rebecca Shipman (LIBERT)	17,918	0.9
Frank Rich (I)	63,068	3.1

Senator
Edward M. Kennedy (D)*	1,247,084	60.8
Raymond Shamie (R)	784,602	38.3

1982 Elections 189

		Vote Total	Percent
	Howard Katz (LIBERT)	18,878	0.9

House
1	Silvio O. Conte (R, D)*	X	100.0
2	Edward P. Boland (D)*	118,215	72.6
	Thomas P. Swank (R)	44,544	27.4
3	Joseph D. Early (D)*	X	100.0
4	Barney Frank (D)*	121,802	59.5
	Margaret M. Heckler (R)*	82,804	40.5
5	James M. Shannon (D)*	140,177	84.7
	Angelo Laudani (LIBERT)	25,224	15.2
6	Nicholas Mavroules (D)*	117,723	57.8
	Thomas H. Trimarco (R)	85,849	42.2
7	Edward J. Markey (D)*	151,305	77.8
	David Basile (R)	43,063	22.2
8	Thomas P. O'Neill Jr. (D)*	123,296	74.9
	Frank Luke McNamara Jr. (R)	41,370	25.1
9	Joe Moakley (D)*	102,665	64.1
	Deborah R. Cochran (R)	55,030	34.3
	Valerie Eckart (SOC WORK)	2,527	1.6
10	Gerry E. Studds (D)*	138,418	68.7
	John E. Conway (R)	63,014	31.3
11	Brian J. Donnelly (D)*	X	100.0

MICHIGAN

Governor
James J. Blanchard (D)	1,561,291	51.4
Richard H. Headlee (R)	1,369,582	45.1
James Phillips (AMI)	7,356	0.2
Richard Jacobs (LIBERT)	15,603	0.5
Tim Crane (SOC WORK)	3,682	0.1
Martin McLaughlin (WL)	1,980	0.1
Robert Tisch (I)	80,288	2.6

Senator
Donald W. Riegle Jr. (D)*	1,728,793	57.7
Philip E. Ruppe (R)	1,223,288	40.9
Daniel Eller (AMI)	12,660	0.4
Bette Erwin (LIBERT)	19,131	0.6
Steve Beumer (SOC WORK)	4,335	0.2
Helen Halyard (WL)	6,085	0.2

House
1	John Conyers Jr. (D)*	125,517	96.7
	Bill Krebaum (LIBERT)	3,186	2.4
	Eddie Benjamin (WL)	1,140	0.9
2	George Wahr Sallade (D)	53,040	32.5
	Carl D. Pursell (R)*	106,960	65.4
	Barbara J. McKenna (LIBERT)	3,412	2.1
3	Howard Wolpe (D)*	96,842	56.3
	Richard L. Milliman (R)	73,315	42.6
	Lizzie M. Hudson (AMI)	693	0.4
	Robert S. Holderbaum (LIBERT)	1,111	0.7
4	David A. Masiokas (D)	56,877	38.8
	Mark Siljander (R)*	87,489	59.7
	Robert C. Drenkhahn (AMI)	690	0.5
	Richard Wagner (LIBERT)	1,544	1.0
5	Stephen V. Monsma (D)	87,229	46.9
	Harold S. Sawyer (R)*	98,650	53.1
6	Bob Carr (D)	84,778	51.4
	Jim Dunn (R)*	78,388	47.5
	James E. Hurrell (LIBERT)	1,818	1.1
7	Dale E. Kildee (D)*	118,538	75.4
	George R. Darrah (R)	36,303	23.1
	Dennis L. Berry (LIBERT)	1,842	1.2
	David Freund (WL)	568	0.3
8	Bob Traxler (D)*	113,515	91.0
	Sheila M. Hart (LIBERT)	11,219	9.0
9	Gerald D. Warner (D)	60,932	35.1

	Vote Total	Percent
Guy Vander Jagt (R)*	112,504	64.9
10 Don Albosta (D)*	102,048	60.1
Lawrence W. Reed (R)	66,080	39.0
William Spiers (LIBERT)	1,558	0.9
11 Kent Bourland (D)	69,181	39.5
Robert W. Davis (R)*	106,039	60.5
12 David E. Bonior (D)*	103,851	65.9
Ray Contesti (R)	52,312	33.2
Keith P. Edwards (LIBERT)	1,501	0.9
13 George W. Crockett Jr. (D)*	108,351	88.0
Letty Gupta (R)	13,732	11.1
Fred Mazelis (WL)	1,107	0.9
14 Dennis M. Hertel (D)*	116,421	95.0
Harold H. Dunn (LIBERT)	6,175	5.0
15 William D. Ford (D)*	94,950	72.8
Mitchell Moran (R)	33,904	26.0
Guy R. Collins (AMI)	1,555	1.2
16 John D. Dingell (D)*	114,006	73.7
David K. Haskins (R)	39,227	25.3
Susan Apstein (SOC WORK)	1,071	0.7
Paul Scherrer (WL)	450	0.3
17 Sander Levin (D)	116,901	66.6
Gerald E. Rosen (R)	55,620	31.7
Virginia L. Cropsey (LIBERT)	2,955	1.7
18 Allen J. Sipher (D)	46,545	25.7
William S. Broomfield (R)*	132,902	73.3
Joseph Cote (LIBERT)	1,813	1.0

MINNESOTA

Governor
Rudy Perpich (DFL)	1,049,104	58.8
Wheelock Whitney (I-R)	711,796	39.9
Franklin H. Haws (LIBERT)	6,323	0.3
Kathy Wheeler (SOC WORK)	10,332	0.6
Tom McDonald (I)	7,984	0.4

Senator
Mark Dayton (DFL)	840,401	46.6
David Durenberger (I-R)*	949,207	52.6
Fred G. Hewitt (LIBERT)	5,870	0.3
Jeffrey M. Miller (NU)	3,300	0.2
Bill Onasch (SOC WORK)	5,897	0.3

House
1 Timothy J. Penny (DFL)	109,257	51.2
Tom Hagedorn (I-R)*	102,298	47.9
Clare H. Jarvis (LIBERT)	1,965	0.9
2 James W. Nichols (DFL)	103,243	45.5
Vin Weber (I-R)*	123,508	54.5
3 Joel Saliterman (DFL)	60,993	26.4
Bill Frenzel (I-R)*	166,891	72.1
Richard Laybourn (CIT)	3,427	1.5
4 Bruce F. Vento (DFL)*	153,494	73.2
Bill James (I-R)	56,248	26.8
5 Martin Olav Sabo (DFL)*	136,634	65.5
Keith W. Johnson (I-R)	61,184	29.4
Kathryn Anderson (CIT)	8,143	3.9
Thomas Wicklund (LIBERT)	2,491	1.2
6 Gerry Sikorski (DFL)	109,246	50.8
Arlen Erdahl (I-R)*	105,734	49.2
7 Gene Wenstrom (DFL)	107,062	49.7
Arlan Stangeland (I-R)*	108,254	50.3
8 James L. Oberstar (DFL)*	176,392	76.7
Marjory L. Luce (I-R)	53,467	23.3

MISSISSIPPI

Senator
John C. Stennis (D)*	414,099	64.2
Haley Barbour (R)	230,927	35.8

House
1 Jamie L. Whitten (D)*	79,726	70.9
Fran Fawcett (R)	32,750	29.1
2 Robert G. Clark (D)	71,536	48.4
Webb Franklin (R)	74,450	50.3
William V. Harris (I)	1,887	1.3
3 G. V. "Sonny" Montgomery (D)*	114,530	93.1
James Bradshaw (I)	8,519	6.9
4 Wayne Dowdy (D)*	79,977	52.6
Liles Williams (R)	69,469	45.6
Eddie L. McBride (I)	2,770	1.8
5 Arlon "Blackie" Coate (D)	22,634	21.5
Trent Lott (R)*	82,884	78.5

MISSOURI

Senator
Harriett Woods (D)	758,629	49.1
John C. Danforth (R)*	784,876	50.9

House
1 William Clay (D)*	102,656	66.1
William E. White (R)	52,599	33.9
2 Robert A. Young (D)*	100,770	56.5
Harold L. Dielmann (R)	77,433	43.5
3 Richard A. Gephardt (D)*	131,566	77.9
Richard Foristel (R)	37,388	22.1
4 Ike Skelton (D)*	96,388	54.8
Wendell Bailey (R)*	79,565	45.2
5 Alan Wheat (D)	96,059	57.9
John A. Sharp (R)	66,664	40.1
Kathie A. Fitzgerald (SOC WORK)	1,141	0.7
Alan H. Deright (I)	2,125	1.3
6 Jim Russell (D)	79,053	44.7
E. Thomas Coleman (R)*	97,993	55.3
7 David A. Geisler (D)	89,549	49.5
Gene Taylor (R)*	91,391	50.5
8 Jerry Ford (D)	76,413	46.9
Bill Emerson (R)	86,493	53.1
9 Harold L. Volkmer (D)*	99,228	60.8
Larry E. Mead (R)	63,942	39.2

MONTANA

Senator
John Melcher (D)*	174,861	54.4
Larry Williams (R)	133,789	41.7
Larry Dodge (LIBERT)	12,412	3.9

House
1 Pat Williams (D)*	100,087	59.7
Bob Davies (R)	62,402	37.2
Don Doig (LIBERT)	5,113	3.1
2 Howard Lyman (D)	65,815	44.2
Ron Marlenee (R)*	79,968	53.7
Westley F. Deitchler (LIBERT)	3,154	2.1

NEBRASKA

Governor
Bob Kerrey (D)	277,436	50.7
Charles Thone (R)*	270,203	49.3

Senator
Edward Zorinsky (D)*	363,350	66.6
Jim Keck (R)	155,760	28.5
Virginia Walsh (I)	26,443	4.9

House
1 Curt Donaldson (D)	45,676	24.9
Douglas K. Bereuter (R)*	137,675	75.1
2 Richard M. Fellman (D)	70,431	43.1
Hal Daub (R)*	92,639	56.7
3 Virginia Smith (R)*	X	100.0

NEVADA

Governor
Richard H. Bryan (D)	128,132	53.4
Robert F. List (R)*	100,104	41.8
Dan Becan (LIBERT)	4,621	1.9
None of the Above	6,894	2.9

Senator
Howard W. Cannon (D)*	114,720	47.7
Chic Hecht (R)	120,377	50.1
None of the Above	5,297	2.2

House
1 Harry Reid (D)	61,901	57.5
Peggy Cavnar (R)	45,675	42.5
2 Mary Gojack (D)	52,265	41.3
Barbara Vucanovich (R)	70,188	55.5
Teresa Vuceta (LIBERT)	4,043	3.2

NEW HAMPSHIRE

Governor
Hugh Gallen (D)*	132,287	46.4
John H. Sununu (R)	147,774	51.9
Meldrim Thomson Jr. (I)	4,785	1.7

House
1 Norman E. D'Amours (D)*	76,281	54.9
Robert C. Smith (R)	61,876	44.6
William C. Mackenzie (I)	752	0.5
2 Robert L. Dupay (D)	37,854	29.1
Judd Gregg (R)*	92,098	70.9

NEW JERSEY

Senator
Frank R. Lautenberg (D)	1,117,549	50.9
Millicent Fenwick (R)	1,047,626	47.7
Henry Koch (LIBERT)	9,934	0.5
Julius Levin (SOC LAB)	5,580	0.3
Claire Moriarty (SOC WORK)	3,726	0.2
Robert T. Bastien (I)	2,955	0.1
Rose Zeidwerg Monyek (I)	1,830	0.1
Martin E. Wendelken (I)	4,745	0.2

House
1 James J. Florio (D)*	110,570	73.3
John A. Dramesi (R)	39,501	26.2
Jerry Zeldin (LIBERT)	493	0.3
Patrick J. McCann (SOC LAB)	327	0.2
2 William J. Hughes (D)*	102,826	68.0
John J. Mahoney (R)	47,069	31.2
Bruce Powers (LIBERT)	1,233	0.8
3 James J. Howard (D)*	104,055	62.3
Marie Sheehan Muhler (R)	60,515	36.2
John Kinnevy III (CIT)	785	0.5
Lee A. Gesner Jr. (LIBERT)	701	0.4
Lawrence D. Erickson (SOC)	436	0.3
Joseph B. Hawley (I)	504	0.3
4 Joseph P. Merlino (D)	75,658	46.5
Christopher H. Smith (R)*	85,660	52.7
Bill Harris (LIBERT)	662	0.4
Eugene A. Creech (WF)	241	0.2
Paul B. Rizzo (I)	374	0.2
5 Fritz Cammerzell (D)	53,659	33.5
Marge Roukema (R)*	104,695	65.3
William J. Zelko Jr. (LIBERT)	2,004	1.2
6 Bernard J. Dwyer (D)*	100,418	68.1
Bertram L. Buckler (R)	46,093	31.3
Charles M. Hart (LIBERT)	920	0.6

	Vote Total	Percent
7 Adam K. Levin (D)	70,978	43.2
Matthew J. Rinaldo (R)*	91,837	56.0
Donald B. Siano (LIBERT)	1,294	0.8
8 Robert A. Roe (D)*	89,980	70.7
Norm Robertson (R)	36,317	28.5
Sidney J. Pope (LIBERT)	1,000	0.8
9 Robert G. Torricelli (D)	99,090	53.0
Harold C. Hollenbeck (R)*	86,022	46.0
Robert Shapiro (LIBERT)	1,767	1.0
10 Peter W. Rodino Jr. (D)*	76,684	82.6
Timothy Lee Jr. (R)	14,551	15.7
Katherine Florentine (LIBERT)	958	1.0
Christine Keno (I)	659	0.7
11 Joseph G. Minish (D)*	105,607	64.3
Rey Redington (R)	57,099	34.8
Richard Roth (LIBERT)	1,531	0.9
12 Jeff Connor (D)	57,049	32.3
Jim Courter (R)*	117,793	66.8
Harold F. Leiendecker (LIBERT)	1,610	0.9
13 George Callas (D)	65,820	39.1
Edwin B. Forsythe (R)*	100,061	59.5
Paula Volpe (CIT)	955	0.6
Don Smith (CST)	651	0.4
Leonard T. Flynn (LIBERT)	769	0.4
14 Frank J. Guarini (D)*	94,021	74.3
Charles J. Catrillo (R)	28,257	22.3
Louis J. Sicilia (LIBERT)	471	0.4
Kenneth Famularo (I)	921	0.7
Jack Murphy (I)	1,704	1.3
Herbert H. Shaw (I)	1,232	1.0

NEW MEXICO

Governor
Toney Anaya (D)	215,840	53.0
John B. Irick (R)	191,626	47.0

Senator
Jeff Bingaman (D)	217,682	53.8
Harrison "Jack" Schmitt (R)*	187,128	46.2

House
1 Jan Alan Hartke (D)	67,534	47.6
Manuel Lujan Jr. (R)*	74,459	52.4
2 Caleb Chandler (D)	50,599	41.6
Joe Skeen (R)*	71,021	58.4
3 Bill Richardson (D)	84,669	64.5
Marjorie Bell Chambers (R)	46,466	35.4
David Arturo Fernandez (write-in)	158	0.1

NEW YORK

Governor
Mario M. Cuomo (D, L)	2,675,213	50.9
Lew Lehrman (R, C, I)	2,494,827	47.5
John J. Northrup (F LIBERT)	16,913	0.3
Nancy Ross (NA)	5,277	0.1
Diane Wang (SOC WORK)	3,766	0.1
Robert J. Bohner (RTL)	52,356	1.0
Jane Benedict (UN)	6,353	0.1

Senator
Daniel Patrick Moynihan (D,L)*	3,232,146	65.1
Florence Sullivan (R, C, RTL)	1,696,766	34.1
James J. McKeown (F LIBERT)	23,379	0.5
Steven Wattenmaker (SOC WORK)	15,206	0.3

House
1 Ethan C. Eldon (D)	49,787	36.1
William Carney (R, C, RTL)*	88,234	63.9
2 Thomas J. Downey (D)*	80,951	63.9
Paul G. Costello (R, C)	42,790	33.8
Lewis VanDenEssen (RTL)	2,971	2.3
3 Robert J. Mrazek (D)	93,846	51.8
John LeBoutillier (R, C)*	83,238	46.0
Richard Horan (RTL)	4,049	2.2
4 Robert P. Zimmerman (D, L)	63,390	36.3
Norman F. Lent (R, C)*	105,241	60.4
John J. Dunkle (RTL)	5,717	3.3
5 Arnold J. Miller (D, L)	67,002	38.8
Raymond J. McGrath (R, C)*	100,485	58.1
Thomas J. Boyle (RTL)	4,911	2.8
Richard Horan (F LIBERT)	490	0.3
6 Joseph P. Addabbo (D, R, L)*	95,483	95.9
Mark E. Scott (C)	4,074	4.1
7 Benjamin S. Rosenthal (D, L)*	84,013	77.2
Albert Lemishow (R, C, RTL)	24,832	22.8
8 James H. Scheuer (D, L)*	91,830	89.5
John T. Blume (C)	10,741	10.5
9 Geraldine A. Ferraro (D)*	75,286	73.2
John J. Weigandt (R)	20,352	19.8
Ralph G. Groves (C, RTL)	6,011	5.9
Patricia A. Salargo (L)	1,171	1.1
10 Charles E. Schumer (D, L)*	89,852	79.2
Stephen Marks (R, C)	21,726	19.1
Alice J. Bertolotti (RTL)	1,873	1.7
11 Edolphus Towns (D)	39,357	83.7
James W. Smith (R)	4,449	9.5
Joseph N. O. Caesar (C, RTL)	1,357	2.9
Patrick W. Giagnacova (L)	1,488	3.2
Susan C. Zarate (SOC WORK)	359	0.7
12 Major R. Owens (D, L)	44,586	90.5
David Katan Sr. (R)	3,215	6.5
David E. Rosenstroch (C)	1,005	2.1
Jahn-Clymer Francis (RTL)	453	0.9
13 Stephen J. Solarz (D, L)*	68,549	80.5
Leon F. Nadrowski (R, RTL)	14,257	16.8
James M. Gay (C)	2,324	2.7
14 Leo C. Zeferetti (D)*	51,728	42.9
Guy V. Molinari (R, C, RTL)*	67,626	56.1
Carl F. Grillo (L)	1,276	1.0
15 Betty G. Lall (D, L)	55,483	44.8
Bill Green (R)*	66,262	53.6
Henry Van Rossem (C)	1,953	1.6
16 Charles B. Rangel (D, R, L)*	76,626	97.5
Michael T. Berns (C)	1,261	1.6
Veronica Cruz (SOC WORK)	718	0.9
17 Ted Weiss (D, L)*	113,172	85.0
Louis S. Antonelli (R, C, RTL)	19,928	15.0
18 Robert Garcia (D, R, L)*	57,009	98.9
Rafael Perez (POPULAR)	655	1.1
19 Mario Biaggi (D, R, L, RTL)*	118,803	93.7
Michael P. McSherry (C)	7,438	5.9
Eva Chertov (SOC WORK)	584	0.4
20 Richard L. Ottinger (D)*	98,425	56.5
Jon S. Fossel (R, C)	72,005	41.3
Florence T. O'Grady (RTL)	3,798	2.2
21 J. Morgan Strong (D)	38,664	24.8
Hamilton Fish Jr. (R, C)*	117,460	75.2
22 Peter A. Peyser (D)*	73,124	42.0
Benjamin A. Gilman (R)*	92,266	52.9
Charles C. Beck (C)	4,877	2.8
Richard Bruno (RTL)	4,019	2.3
23 Samuel S. Stratton (D)*	164,427	76.1
Frank Wicks (R, NF)	41,386	19.2
Mark A. Dunlea (CIT)	1,119	0.5
John G. Dow (L)	8,492	3.9
Patricia A. Mayberry (SOC WORK)	659	0.3
24 Roy Esiason (D)	49,441	26.1
Gerald B. H. Solomon (R, C, RTL)*	140,296	73.9
25 Anita Maxwell (D)	70,793	42.4
Sherwood L. Boehlert (R)	93,071	55.8
Donald J. Thomas (RTL)	2,963	1.8
26 David P. Landy (D)	43,208	28.4
David O'B. Martin (R, C)*	108,962	71.6
27 Elaine Lytel (D, L)	79,209	44.2
George C. Wortley (R)*	95,290	53.2
Thomas M. Hunter (C)	2,783	1.5
George Hyrcza (RTL)	1,904	1.1
28 Matthew F. McHugh (D, L)*	100,665	56.4
David F. Crowley (R, C)	75,991	42.5
Mark Masterson (RTL)	2,003	1.1
29 William C. Larsen (D)	47,463	30.2
Frank Horton (R)*	104,412	66.4
Edwin Lundberg (C)	5,370	3.4
30 Bill Benet (D)	48,764	27.9
Barber B. Conable Jr. (R)*	119,105	68.2
Richard G. Baxter (C)	3,853	2.2
David J. Valone (RTL)	2,898	1.7
31 James A. Martin (D, L)	43,843	24.7
Jack F. Kemp (R, C)*	133,462	75.3
32 John J. LaFalce (D, L)*	116,386	91.4
Raymond R. Walker (R, C)	8,638	6.8
Timothy J. Hubbard (RTL)	2,359	1.8
33 Henry J. Nowak (D, L)*	126,091	84.1
Walter J. Pillich (R, C)	19,791	13.2
James Gallagher (RTL)	4,095	2.7
34 Stanley N. Lundine (D)*	99,502	60.2
James J. Snyder (R, C)	63,972	38.7
Genevieve F. Ronan (RTL)	1,806	1.1

NORTH CAROLINA

House
1 Walter B. Jones (D)*	79,954	81.3
James F. McIntyre III (R)	17,478	17.8
Bobby Yates Emory (LIBERT)	910	0.9
2 I. T. "Tim" Valentine Jr. (D)	59,617	53.5
John W. Marin (R)	34,293	30.8
Sue Lamm (LIBERT)	1,426	1.3
H. M. Michaux Jr. (write-in)	15,990	14.4
3 Charles Whitley (D)*	68,936	63.5
Eugene "Red" McDaniel (R)	39,046	36.0
Marshall Sprague (LIBERT)	491	0.5
4 Ike Andrews (D)*	70,369	51.3
William Cobey Jr. (R)	64,955	47.4
Fritz Prochnaw (LIBERT)	1,720	1.3
5 Stephen L. Neal (D)*	87,819	60.3
Anne Bagnal (R)	57,083	39.2
Naudeen Beek (LIBERT)	631	0.4
Merly Lynn Farber (SOC WORK)	174	0.1
6 Charles Robin Britt (D)	68,696	53.8
Eugene Johnston (R)*	58,244	45.7
J. Erik Christensen (LIBERT)	679	0.5
7 Charlie Rose (D)*	68,529	71.0
Edward Johnson (R)	27,015	28.0
Richard Hollenbeak (LIBERT)	990	1.0
8 W. G. "Bill" Hefner (D)*	71,691	57.4
Harris D. Blake (R)	52,417	41.9
Don Scoggins (LIBERT)	830	0.7
9 Preston Cornelius (D)	47,258	41.9
James G. Martin (R)*	64,297	57.0
David Braatz (LIBERT)	1,231	1.1
10 James T. Broyhill (R)*	80,904	92.7
Jhon Rankin (LIBERT)	6,360	7.3

192 Elections '84

	Vote Total	Percent
11 James McClure Clarke (D)	85,410	49.9
Bill Hendon (R)*	84,085	49.2
Linda Janka (LIBERT)	1,552	0.9

NORTH DAKOTA

Senator

Quentin N. Burdick (D)*	164,873	62.8
Gene Knorr (R)	89,304	34.0
Anna Bourgois (I)	8,288	3.2

House

AL Byron L. Dorgan (D)*	186,534	71.6
Kent H. Jones (R)	72,241	27.7
Don J. Klingensmith (P)	1,724	0.7

OHIO

Governor

Richard F. Celeste (D)	1,981,882	59.0
Clarence J. Brown (R)	1,303,962	38.9
Phyllis Goetz (LIBERT)	39,114	1.2
Kurt O. Landefeld (I)	14,279	0.4
Erwin J. Reupert (I)	17,484	0.5

Senator

Howard M. Metzenbaum (D)*	1,923,767	56.7
Paul E. Pfeifer (R)	1,396,790	41.1
Philip Herzing (LIBERT)	36,103	1.1
Alicia Merel (I)	38,803	1.1

House

1 Thomas A. Luken (D)*	99,143	63.5
John "Jake" Held (R)	52,658	33.7
James A. Berns (LIBERT)	4,386	2.8
2 William J. Luttmer (D)	53,169	34.2
Bill Gradison (R)*	97,434	62.7
Charles K. Shrout Jr. (LIBERT)	2,948	1.9
Joseph I. Lombardo (I)	1,827	1.2
3 Tony P. Hall (D)*	119,926	87.7
Kathryn E. Brown (LIBERT)	16,828	12.3
4 Robert W. Moon (D)	57,564	35.4
Michael G. Oxley (R)*	105,087	64.6
5 James R. Sherck (D)	70,120	44.8
Delbert L. Latta (R)*	86,450	55.2
6 Lynn Alan Grimshaw (D)	63,435	40.8
Bob McEwen (R)*	92,135	59.2
7 Roger D. Tackett (D)	65,543	42.0
Michael Dewine (R)	87,842	56.2
John B. Winer (LIBERT)	2,761	1.8
8 John W. Griffin (D)	49,877	33.6
Thomas N. Kindness (R)*	98,527	66.4
9 Marcy Kaptur (D)	95,162	57.9
Ed Weber (R)*	64,459	39.3
David Muir (LIBERT)	1,217	0.7
Susan A. Skinner (I)	1,785	1.1
James J. Somers (I)	1,594	1.0
10 John M. Buchanan (D)	57,983	36.7
Clarence E. Miller (R)*	100,044	63.3
11 Dennis E. Eckart (D)*	93,302	60.9
Glen W. Warner (R)	56,616	36.9
Jim Russell (LIBERT)	3,324	2.2
12 Bob Shamansky (D)*	82,753	47.3
John R. Kasich (R)	88,335	50.5
Russell A. Lewis (LIBERT)	3,939	2.2
13 Don J. Pease (D)*	92,296	61.2
Timothy Paul Martin (R)	53,376	35.4
James S. Patton (LIBERT)	5,053	3.4
14 John F. Seiberling (D)*	115,629	70.5

	Vote Total	Percent
Louis A. Mangels (R)	48,421	29.5
15 Greg Kostelac (D)	47,070	29.8
Chalmers P. Wylie (R)*	104,678	66.3
Steve Kender (LIBERT)	6,139	3.9
16 Jeffrey R. Orenstein (D)	57,386	34.2
Ralph Regula (R)*	110,485	65.8
17 George D. Tablack (D)	80,375	44.9
Lyle Williams (R)*	98,476	55.1
18 Douglas Applegate (D)*	X	100.0
19 Edward F. Feighan (D)	111,760	58.8
Richard G. Anter II (R)	72,682	38.3
Thomas Pekarek (LIBERT)	3,129	1.6
Kevin G. Killeen (I)	2,371	1.3
20 Mary Rose Oakar (D)*	133,603	85.6
Paris T. LeJeune (R)	17,675	11.3
Milton R. Norris (LIBERT)	2,844	1.8
Louise Haberbush (I)	1,930	1.3
21 Louis Stokes (D)*	132,544	86.1
Alan G. Shatteen (R)	21,332	13.9

OKLAHOMA

Governor

George Nigh (D)*	548,159	62.1
Tom Daxon (R)	332,207	37.6
Allah-U Akbar Allah-U Wahid (I)	2,764	0.3

House

1 James R. Jones (D)*	76,379	54.1
Richard C. Freeman (R)	64,704	45.9
2 Mike Synar (D)*	111,895	72.6
Lou Striegel (R)	42,298	27.4
3 Wes Watkins (D)*	121,670	82.2
Patrick K. Miller (R)	26,335	17.8
4 Dave McCurdy (D)*	84,205	65.0
Howard Rutledge (R)	44,351	34.3
Charles T. Emerson (I)	507	0.4
Marshall A. Luse (I)	441	0.3
5 Dan Lane (D)	42,453	28.9
Mickey Edwards (R)*	98,979	67.2
Paul E. Trent (I)	5,777	3.9
6 Glenn English (D)*	102,811	75.4
Ed Moore (R)	33,519	24.6

OREGON

Governor

Ted Kulongoski (D)	374,316	35.9
Victor G. Atiyeh (R)*	639,841	61.4
Paul J. Cleveland (LIBERT)	27,394	2.7

House

1 Les AuCoin (D)*	118,638	53.8
Bill Moshofsky (R)	101,720	46.2
2 Larryann Willis (D)	85,495	44.4
Bob Smith (R)	106,912	55.6
3 Ron Wyden (D)*	159,416	78.3
Thomas H. Phelan (R)	44,162	21.7
4 James Weaver (D)*	115,448	59.1
Ross Anthony (R)	80,054	40.9
5 J. Ruth McFarland (D)	98,952	48.8
Denny Smith (R)*	103,906	51.2

PENNSYLVANIA

Governor

Allen E. Ertel (D)	1,772,353	48.1
Richard L. Thornburgh (R)*	1,872,784	50.8
Lee Frissell (CONSU)	13,101	0.4

	Vote Total	Percent
Richard D. Fuerle (LIBERT)	10,252	0.3
Mark Zola (SOC WORK)	15,495	0.4

Senator

Cyril H. Wecht (D)	1,412,965	39.2
John Heinz (R)*	2,136,418	59.3
Liane Norman (CONSU)	16,530	0.5
Barbara I. Karkutt (LIBERT)	19,244	0.5
Kipp M. Dawson (SOC WORK)	18,951	0.5

House

1 Thomas M. Foglietta (D)*	103,626	72.3
Michael Marino (R)	38,155	26.6
Lisa Brannan (CONSU)	1,063	0.7
Ralph Mullinger (LIBERT)	572	0.4
2 William H. Gray III (D)*	120,744	76.1
William C. Saunders (LIBERT)	2,726	1.7
Milton Street (I)	35,205	22.2
3 Robert A. Borski (D)	97,161	50.1
Charles F. Dougherty (R)*	94,497	48.7
Carolyn Berger (CONSU)	980	0.5
Bruce Bishkin (LIBERT)	435	0.2
Mike Finley (SOC WORK)	881	0.5
4 Joseph P. Kolter (D)	100,481	60.1
Eugene V. Atkinson (R)*	64,539	38.6
Sam Blancato (CONSU)	2,082	1.3
5 Bob Burger (D)	44,170	32.8
Richard T. Schulze (R)*	90,648	67.2
6 Gus Yatron (D)*	108,230	72.0
Harry B. Martin (R)	42,155	28.0
7 Robert W. Edgar (D)*	105,775	55.4
Steve Joachim (R)	85,023	44.6
8 Peter H. Kostmayer (D)	83,242	50.3
Jim Coyne (R)*	80,928	48.9
Hans G. Schroeder (LIBERT)	483	0.3
Albert H. Reef (I)	882	0.5
9 Eugene V. Duncan (D)	49,583	34.9
Bud Shuster (R)*	92,322	65.1
10 Robert J. Rafalko (D)	49,868	32.5
Joseph M. McDade (R)*	103,617	67.5
11 Frank Harrison (D)	90,371	53.5
James L. Nelligan (R)*	78,485	46.5
12 John P. Murtha (D)*	96,369	61.1
William N. Tuscano (R)	54,212	34.4
Joseph E. Krill (I)	7,059	4.5
13 Martin J. Cunningham Jr. (D)	59,709	35.2
Lawrence Coughlin (R)*	109,198	64.3
Nicholas Kyodnieus (LIBERT)	917	0.5
14 William J. Coyne (D)*	120,980	74.9
John R. Clark (R)	32,780	20.3
Richard E. Calligiuri (LIBERT)	5,437	3.3
William R. Kalman (SOC WORK)	2,380	1.5
15 Richard J. Orloski (D)	58,002	42.2
Don Ritter (R)*	79,455	57.8
16 Jean D. Mowery (D)	37,364	28.7
Robert S. Walker (R)*	93,034	71.3
17 Larry J. Hochendoner (D)	61,974	42.4
George W. Gekas (R)	84,291	57.6
18 Doug Walgren (D)*	101,807	54.2
Ted Jacob (R)	84,428	45.0
William A. Lewis Jr. (LIBERT)	1,448	0.8
19 Larry Becker (D)	41,787	29.2
Bill Goodling (R)*	101,163	70.8
20 Joseph M. Gaydos (D)*	127,281	76.0
Terry T. Ray (R)	38,212	22.8
David L. Travis (LIBERT)	1,935	1.2
21 Anthony "Buzz" Andrezeski (D)	79,451	49.8
Thomas J. Ridge (R)	80,180	50.2
22 Austin J. Murphy (D)*	123,716	78.7

	Vote Total	Percent
Frank J. Paterra (R)	32,176	20.5
Deann Rathbun (SOC WORK)	1,323	0.8
23 Joseph J. Calla Jr. (D)	49,297	34.8
William F. Clinger Jr. (R)*	92,424	65.2

RHODE ISLAND

Governor
J. Joseph Garrahy (D)*	247,208	73.3
Vincent Marzullo (R)	79,602	23.6
Hilary Salk (CIT)	7,033	2.1
Peter Van Daam (JI)	3,405	1.0

Senator
Julius C. Michaelson (D)	167,283	48.8
John H. Chafee (R)*	175,495	51.2

House
1 Fernand J. St Germain (D)*	97,254	60.7
Burton Stallwood (R)	61,253	38.3
Gertrude M. Jayne Fowler (I)	1,624	1.0
2 James V. Aukerman (D)	76,769	44.4
Claudine Schneider (R)*	96,282	55.6

SOUTH CAROLINA

Governor
Richard Riley (D)*	468,819	69.8
William D. Workman Jr. (R)	202,806	30.2

House
1 W. Mullins McLeod (D)	52,916	44.9
Thomas F. Hartnett (R)*	63,945	54.3
Walter Smith (LIBERT)	971	0.8
2 Ken Mosely (D)	50,749	41.5
Floyd Spence (R)*	71,569	58.5
3 Butler Derrick (D)*	77,125	90.4
Gordon T. Davis (LIBERT)	8,214	9.6
4 Marion E. Tyus (D)	40,394	36.7
Carroll A. Campbell Jr. (R)*	69,802	63.3
5 John Spratt (D)	69,345	67.6
John S. Wilkerson (R)	33,191	32.4
6 Robert M. Tallon Jr. (D)	62,582	52.5
John L. Napier (R)*	56,653	47.5

SOUTH DAKOTA

Governor
Mike O'Connor (D)	81,136	29.1
William J. Janklow (R)*	197,426	70.9

House
AL Thomas A. Daschle (D)*	142,122	51.6
Clint Roberts (R)*	133,530	48.4

TENNESSEE

Governor
Randy Tyree (D)	500,937	40.4
Lamar Alexander (R)*	737,963	59.6

Senator
Jim Sasser (D)*	780,113	61.9
Robin L. Beard (R)	479,642	38.1

House
1 Jessie J. Cable (D)	27,580	22.8
James H. Quillen (R)*	89,497	74.1
James B. "Peppy" Fields (I)	3,778	3.1
2 John J. Duncan (R)*	X	100.0
3 Marilyn Lloyd Bouquard (D)*	84,967	61.8
Glen Byers (R)	49,885	36.3
Henry Ford Brock (I)	2,640	1.9

	Vote Total	Percent
4 Jim Cooper (D)	93,453	66.1
Cissy Baker (R)	47,865	33.9
5 Bill Boner (D)*	109,282	80.2
Laural Steinhice (R)	27,061	19.8
6 Albert Gore Jr. (D)*	X	100.0
7 Bob Clement (D)	72,359	49.5
Don Sundquist (R)	73,835	50.5
8 Ed Jones (D)*	93,945	74.9
Bruce Benson (R)	31,527	25.1
9 Harold E. Ford (D)*	112,143	72.4
Joe Crawford (R)	40,812	26.4
Isaac Richmond (I)	1,874	1.2

TEXAS

Governor
Mark White (D)	1,697,870	53.2
William Clements (R)*	1,465,937	45.9
Bob Poteet (CIT)	8,065	0.3
David Hutzelman (LIBERT)	19,143	0.6

Senator
Lloyd Bentsen (D)*	1,818,223	58.6
James M. Collins (R)	1,256,759	40.5
Lineaus Hooper Lorette (CIT)	4,564	0.1
John E. Ford (LIBERT)	23,494	0.8

House
1 Sam B. Hall Jr. (D)*	100,685	97.5
John Traylor (LIBERT)	2,598	2.5
2 Charles Wilson (D)*	91,762	94.3
Ed Richbourg (LIBERT)	5,584	5.7
3 James L. McNees Jr. (D)	28,223	21.8
Steve Bartlett (R)	99,852	77.1
Jerry R. Williamson (LIBERT)	1,453	1.1
4 Ralph M. Hall (D)*	94,134	73.8
Peter J. Collumb (R)	32,221	25.3
Bruce Iiams (LIBERT)	1,141	0.9
5 John Bryant (D)	52,214	64.8
Joe Devaney (R)	27,121	33.7
John Richard Bridges (CIT)	459	0.6
Richard Squire (LIBERT)	732	0.9
6 Phil Gramm (D)*	91,546	94.5
Ron Hard (LIBERT)	5,288	5.5
7 Dennis Scoggins (D)	17,866	14.0
Bill Archer (R)*	108,718	85.0
Bill Ware (LIBERT)	1,338	1.0
8 Henry E. Allee (D)	38,041	42.6
Jack Fields (R)*	50,630	56.8
Mike Angwin (LIBERT)	547	0.6
9 Jack Brooks (D)*	78,965	67.6
John W. Lewis (R)	35,422	30.3
Dean Allen (LIBERT)	2,510	2.1
10 J. J. Pickle (D)*	121,030	90.1
Bradley Louis Rockwell (CIT)	4,511	3.4
William G. Kelsey (LIBERT)	8,735	6.5
11 Marvin Leath (D)*	83,236	96.4
Tom Kilbride (LIBERT)	3,136	3.6
12 Jim Wright (D)*	78,913	68.9
Jim Ryan (R)	34,879	30.5
Ed Olson (LIBERT)	743	0.6
13 Jack Hightower (D)*	86,376	63.6
Ron Slover (R)	47,877	35.2
Rod Collier (LIBERT)	1,567	1.2
14 Bill Patman (D)*	76,851	60.7
Joe Wyatt Jr. (R)	48,942	38.6
Glenn Rasmussen (LIBERT)	919	0.7
15 E. "Kika" de la Garza (D)*	76,544	95.7
Frank L. Jones III (LIBERT)	3,458	4.3
16 Ronald Coleman (D)	44,024	53.9
Pat B. Haggerty (R)	36,064	44.2

1982 Elections 193

	Vote Total	Percent
Catherin A. McDivitt (LIBERT)	1,583	1.9
17 Charles W. Stenholm (D)*	109,359	97.1
James Cooley II (LIBERT)	3,271	2.9
18 Mickey Leland (D)*	68,014	82.6
C. Leon Pickett (R)	12,104	14.7
Thomas P. Bernhardt (LIBERT)	2,215	2.7
19 Kent Hance (D)*	89,702	81.6
E. L. Hicks (R)	19,062	17.3
Mike Read (LIBERT)	1,206	1.1
20 Henry B. Gonzalez (D)*	68,544	91.5
Roger V. Gary (LIBERT)	4,163	5.6
Benedict D. La Rosa (I)	2,213	2.9
21 Charles S. Stough (D)	35,112	24.6
Tom Loeffler (R)*	106,515	74.5
Jeffrey J. Brown (LIBERT)	1,243	0.9
22 Ron Paul (R)*	X	100.0
23 Abraham Kazen Jr. (D)*	51,690	55.3
Jeff Wentworth (R)	41,363	44.2
Parker Abell (LIBERT)	475	0.5
24 Martin Frost (D)*	63,857	72.8
Lucy P. Patterson (R)	22,798	26.1
David Guier (LIBERT)	998	1.1
25 Mike Andrews (D)	63,974	60.4
Mike Faubion (R)	40,112	37.9
Barbara Coldiron (CIT)	963	0.9
Jeff Calvert (LIBERT)	864	0.8
26 Tom Vandergriff (D)	69,782	50.1
Jim Bradshaw (R)	69,438	49.9
27 Solomon P. Ortiz (D)*	66,604	64.0
Jason Luby (R)	35,209	33.8
Steven R. Roberts (LIBERT)	2,231	2.2

UTAH

Senator
Ted Wilson (D)	219,482	41.3
Orrin G. Hatch (R)*	309,332	58.3
Lawrence R. Kauffman (AM)	953	0.2
George Mercier (LIBERT)	1,035	0.2

House
1 A. Stephen Dirks (D)	66,006	37.2
James V. Hansen (R)*	111,416	62.8
2 Frances Farley (D)	78,981	46.2
Dan Marriott (R)*	92,109	53.8
3 Howard C. Nielson (R)	108,478	76.9
Henry A. Huish (I-D)	32,661	23.1

VERMONT

Governor
Madeleine M. Kunin (D)	74,394	44.0
Richard A. Snelling (R)*	93,111	55.0
John L. Buttolph (LIBERT)	801	0.5
Richard F. Gottlieb (LU)	850	0.5

Senator
James A. Guest (D)	79,340	47.2
Robert T. Stafford (R)*	84,449	50.3
Ion Laskaris (CIT)	897	0.5
Bo Adlerbert (LIBERT)	892	0.5
Jerry Levy (LU)	774	0.5
Michael Hackett (I)	1,463	0.9

House
AL Mark A. Kaplan (D)	38,296	23.2
James M. Jeffords (R)*	114,191	69.2
Robin Lloyd (CIT)	6,409	3.9
George Trask (LIBERT)	1,407	0.9
Peter Diamondstone (LU)	2,794	1.7
Morris Earle (I)	1,733	1.1

194 Elections '84

	Vote Total	Percent
VIRGINIA		
Senator		
Richard J. Davis (D)	690,839	48.8
Paul S. Trible Jr. (R)	724,571	51.2
House		
1 John J. McGlennon (D)	62,379	43.7
Herbert H. Bateman (R)	76,926	53.9
2 G. William Whitehurst (R)*	X	100.0
3 John A. Waldrop Jr. (D)	63,946	40.8
Thomas J. Bliley Jr. (R)*	92,928	59.2
4 Norman Sisisky (D)	80,695	54.4
Robert W. Daniel Jr. (R)*	67,708	45.6
5 Dan Daniel (D)*	X	100.0
6 James R. Olin (D)	68,192	49.7
Kevin G. Miller (R)	66,537	48.5
Robert L. Fariss (I)	2,395	1.8
7 Lindsay G. Dorrier Jr. (D)	46,514	36.3
J. Kenneth Robinson (R)*	76,752	59.8
David J. Toscano (I)	4,950	3.9
8 Herbert E. Harris II (D)	68,071	48.6
Stan Parris (R)*	69,620	49.7
Austin W. Morrill Jr. (I)	2,373	1.7
9 Frederick C. Boucher (D)	76,205	50.4
William C. Wampler (R)*	75,082	49.6
10 Ira M. Lechner (D)	75,361	46.0
Frank R. Wolf (R)*	86,506	52.7
Scott R. Bowden (I)	2,162	1.3

WASHINGTON		
Senator		
Henry M. Jackson (D)*	943,655	68.9
Doug Jewett (R)	332,273	24.3
Jesse Chiang (I)	20,251	1.5
King Lysen (I)	72,297	5.3
House		
1 Brian Long (D)	59,444	32.4
Joel Pritchard (R)*	123,956	67.6
2 Al Swift (D)*	101,383	59.6
Joan Houchen (R)	68,622	40.4
3 Don Bonker (D)*	97,323	60.1
J. T. Quigg (R)	59,686	36.8
O'Dean Williamson (I)	5,049	3.1

	Vote Total	Percent
4 Charles D. Kilbury (D)	45,990	28.6
Sid Morrison (R)*	112,148	69.8
Michael Leroy Burns (FP)	2,530	1.6
5 Thomas S. Foley (D)*	109,549	64.3
John Sonneland (R)	60,816	35.7
6 Norman D. Dicks (D)*	89,985	62.5
Ted Haley (R)	47,720	33.2
Jayne H. Anderson (I)	6,193	4.3
7 Mike Lowry (D)*	126,313	70.9
Bob Dorse (R)	51,759	29.1
8 Beth Bland (D)	59,824	43.0
Rodney Chandler (R)	79,209	57.0

WEST VIRGINIA		
Senator		
Robert C. Byrd (D)*	387,170	68.5
Cleve Benedict (R)	173,910	30.8
William B. Hovland (SOC WORK)	4,234	0.7
House		
1 Alan B. Mollohan (D)	79,529	53.2
John F. McCuskey (R)	70,069	46.8
2 Harley O. Staggers Jr. (D)	87,904	64.0
J. D. Hinkle Jr. (R)	49,413	36.0
3 Bob Wise (D)	84,619	57.9
David Michael Staton (R)*	60,844	41.6
Adrienne Benjamin (SOC WORK)	787	0.5
4 Nick J. Rahall II (D)*	91,184	80.5
Homer L. Harris (R)	22,054	19.5

WISCONSIN		
Governor		
Anthony S. Earl (D)	896,812	56.8
Terry J. Kohler (R)	662,838	41.9
James P. Wickstrom (CST)	7,721	0.5
Larry Smiley (LIBERT)	9,734	0.6
Peter Seidman (I)	3,025	0.2
Senator		
William Proxmire (D)*	983,311	63.7
Scott McCallum (R)	527,355	34.1
Sanford G. Knapp (CST)	4,463	0.3

	Vote Total	Percent
George Liljenfeldt (LIBERT)	7,947	0.5
William Osborne Hart (I)	21,807	1.4
House		
1 Les Aspin (D)*	95,055	61.0
Peter N. Jannson (R)	59,309	38.1
Arthur F. Jackson (LIBERT)	1,438	0.9
2 Robert W. Kastenmeier (D)*	112,677	60.6
Jim Johnson (R)	71,989	38.7
David Beito (LIBERT)	1,368	0.7
3 Paul Offner (D)	75,132	42.8
Steve Gunderson (R)*	99,304	56.6
Kenneth P. Van Doren (LIBERT)	1,027	0.6
4 Clement J. Zablocki (D)*	129,557	94.5
John Gudenschwager (CST)	946	0.7
Nicholas P. Youngers (LIBERT)	4,064	3.0
John F. Baumgartner (I)	2,421	1.8
5 Jim Moody (D)	99,713	63.6
Rod K. Johnston (R)	54,826	34.9
William G. McCuen Jr. (LIBERT)	1,498	1.0
Walter G. Beach (I)	526	0.3
Cheryll Y. Hidalgo (I)	353	0.2
6 Gordon E. Loehr (D)	59,922	35.0
Thomas E. Petri (R)*	111,348	65.0
7 David R. Obey (D)*	122,124	68.0
Bernard A. Zimmerman (R)	57,535	32.0
8 Ruth C. Clusen (D)	74,436	42.0
Toby Roth (R)*	101,379	57.2
Anthony Theisen (LIBERT)	1,336	0.8
9 F. James Sensenbrenner Jr. (R)*	X	100.0

WYOMING		
Governor		
Ed Herschler (D)*	106,427	63.1
Warren A. Morton (R)	62,128	36.9
Senator		
Rodger McDaniel (D)	72,466	43.3
Malcolm Wallop (R)*	94,725	56.7
House		
AL Ted Hommel (D)	46,041	28.9
Dick Cheney (R)*	113,236	71.1

Selected Bibliography

Books

Abramson, Paul R., Aldrich, John H., and Rohde, David N. *Change and Continuity in the 1980 Elections.* Washington, D.C.: CQ Press, 1982.

Adamany, David. *Campaign Financing In America.* North Scituate, Mass.: Duxbury Press, 1972.

___, and Agree, George E., eds. *Political Money: A Strategy for Campaign Financing in America.* Baltimore: Johns Hopkins University Press, 1975.

Alexander, Herbert E. *Campaign Money: Reform and Reality in the States.* New York: Free Press, 1976.

___. *Financing Politics: Money, Elections and Political Reform.* Washington, D.C.: CQ Press; 2d edition, 1976.

___. *Financing the 1968 Election.* Lexington, Mass.: D. C. Heath, 1971.

___. *Financing the 1972 Election.* Lexington, Mass.: Lexington Books, 1976.

___. *Financing the 1976 Election.* Washington, D.C.: CQ Press, 1979.

___. *Money In Politics.* Washington, D.C.: Public Affairs Press, 1972.

___. *Money, Politics and Public Reporting.* Princeton, N.J.: Citizens' Research Foundation, 1960.

___. *Political Financing.* Minneapolis, Minn.: Burgess, 1973.

___, and Lambert, Richard E., eds. *Political Finance: Reform and Reality.* Philadelphia, Pa.: American Academy of Political and Social Science, 1976.

Altschuler, Bruce E. *Keeping a Finger on the Public Pulse: Private Polling and Presidential Elections.* Westport, Conn.: Greenwood Press, 1982.

Asher, Herbert. *Presidential Elections and American Politics.* Homewood, Ill.: Dow Jones-Irwin, 1980.

Bain, Richard C., and Parris, Judith H. *Convention Decisions and Voting Records.* Washington, D.C.: Brookings Institution, 1973.

Barber, James D., ed. *Choosing the President.* Englewood Cliffs, N.J.: Prentice-Hall, 1974.

___. James David. *The Pulse of Politics: Electing Presidents in the Media Age.* New York. W. W. Norton, 1980.

___. *Race for the Presidency: The Media and the Nominating Process.* Englewood Cliffs, N.J.: Prentice-Hall, 1978.

Best, Judith. *The Case Against Direct Election of the President: A Defense of the Electoral College.* Ithaca, N.Y.: Cornell University Press, 1975.

Bickel, Alexander M. *The New Age of Political Reform: The Electoral College, the Convention and the Party.* New York: Harper & Row, 1968.

___. *Reform and Continuity: The Electoral College, the Convention, and the Party System.* New York: Harper & Row, 1971.

Brams, Steven J. *The Presidential Election Game.* New Haven, Conn.: Yale University Press, 1978.

Brereton, Charles. *First Step to the White House: The New Hampshire Primary, 1952-1980.* Hampton, New Hampshire: The Wheelabrator Foundation Inc., 1979.

Burnham, Walter D. *Critical Elections and the Mainsprings of American Politics.* New York: Norton, 1970.

Caeser, James W. *Reforming the Reforms: A Critical Analysis of the Presidential Selection Process.* Cambridge, Mass.: Ballinger, 1982.

Campbell, Angus et al. *The American Voter.* New York: Wiley, 1960.

Chagall, David. *The New Kingmakers.* New York: Harcourt Brace Jovanovich, 1982.

Committee for Economic Development. *Financing a Better Election System.* New York: 1968.

Congressional Quarterly. *Candidates '80.* Washington, D.C.: 1980.

___. *Congressional Districts in the 1970s.* 2d ed. Washington, D.C.: 1974.

___. *Dollar Politics: The Issue of Campaign Spending.* Washington, D.C.: 1st ed, 1971; 2d ed, 1974; 3d ed, 1982.

___. *Guide to 1976 Elections.* Washington, D.C.: 1977.

___. *Guide to U.S. Elections.* Washington, D.C.: 1975.

___. *National Party Conventions 1831-1976.* Washington, D.C.: 1979.

___. *Politics in America.* Washington, D.C.: 1979.

Crotty, William J. *Political Reform and the American Experiment.* New York: Crowell, 1977.

David, Paul T. *The Politics of National Party Conventions.* Washington, D.C.: Brookings Institution, 1960.

Davis, James W. *Presidential Primaries: Road to the White House.* New York: Crowell, 1967.

___. *Springboard to the White House: Presidential Primaries, How They Are Fought and Won.* New York: Thomas Y. Crowell, 1967.

De Vries, Walter, and Tarrance, Lance, Jr. *The Ticket-Splitter: A New Force in American Politics.* Grand Rapids, Mich.: Eerdmans Publishing Co., 1972.

Drew, Elizabeth. *American Journal: The Events of 1976.* New York: Random House, 1977.

___. *Portrait of An Election: The 1980 Presidential Campaign.* New York: Simon & Schuster, 1981.

Dunn, Delmer D. *Financing Presidential Campaigns.* Washington, D.C.: Brookings Institution, 1972.

Fairlie, Henry. *The Parties: Republicans and Democrats in this Century.* New York: St. Martin's Press, 1978.

Ferguson, Thomas, and Rogers, Joel, eds. *The Hidden Election: Politics and Economics in the 1980 Presidential Campaign.* New York: Pantheon Books, 1981.

Fishel, Jeff. *Parties and Elections in an Anti-Party Age: American Politics and the Crisis of Confidence.* Bloomington: Indiana University Press, 1978.

Germond, Jack W., and Witcover, Jules. *Blue Smoke and Mirrors: How Reagan Won and Why Carter Lost the Election of 1980.* New York: Penguin Books, 1981.

Greenfield, Jeff. *The Real Campaign: How the Media Missed the Story of the 1980 Campaign.* New York: Summit Books, 1981.

Hadley, Arthur T. *The Empty Polling Booth.* Englewood Cliffs, N.J.: Prentice-Hall, 1978.

___. *The Invisible Primary.* Englewood Cliffs, N.J.: Prentice-Hall, 1976.

Heard, Alexander E. *The Costs of Democracy.* Chapel Hill, N.C.: University of North Carolina Press, 1960.

Hess, Stephen. *The Presidential Campaign: The Leadership Selection Process After Watergate.* Washington, D.C.: Brookings Institution, 1978.

Johnson, Donald B., and Porter, Kirk H. *National Party Platforms.* 2 vols. Urbana, Ill.: University of Illinois Press, 1978.

Keech, William R., ed. *Winners Take All: Report of the Twentieth Century Task Force on Reform of the Presidential Election Process.* New York: Holmes & Meier, 1978.

Keech, William R., and Matthews, Donald R. *The Party's Choice: With An Epilogue on the 1976 Nominations.* Washington, D.C.: Brookings Institution, 1976.

Kessel, John. *Presidential Campaign Politics.* Homewood, Ill.: Dow Jones-Irwin, 1980.

Key, V. O. *Responsible Electorate: Rationality in Presidential Voting, 1936-1960.* Cambridge, Mass.: Harvard University Press, 1966.

Ladd, Everett C. *Where Have All the Voters Gone?* New York: W. W. Norton, 1978.

Ladd, Everett C., and Hadley, Charles D. *Transformation of the American Party System: Political Coalitions from the New Deal to the 1970s.* New York: W. W. Norton, 1978.

Lazarsfeld, Paul F. *The People's Choice: How the Voter Makes Up His Mind in a Presidential Campaign.* New York: Columbia University Press, 1968.

Lengle, James I. *Representation and Presidential Primaries: The Democratic Party in the Post-Reform Era.* Westport, Conn.: Greenwood Press, 1981.

Lipset, Seymour M., ed. *Emerging Coalitions in American Politics.* San Francisco: Institute for Contemporary Studies, 1978.

Littlewood, Thomas B. *The 1980 Carter-Kennedy Primary in Illinois.* Institute of Government and Public Affairs, University of Illinois, December 1981.

Longley, Lawrence D. *The Politics of Electoral College Reform.* New Haven, Conn.: Yale University Press, 1972.

Malbin, Michael J. *Parties, Interest Groups, and Campaign Finance Laws.* Washington, D.C.: American Enterprise Institute for Public Policy Research, 1980.

Matthews, Donald R., ed. *Perspectives on Presidential Selection.* Washington, D.C.: Brookings Institution, 1973.

Mazmanian, Daniel A. *Third Parties in Presidential Elections.* Washington, D.C.: Brookings Institution, 1974

Michener, James A. *Presidential Lottery: The Reckless Gamble In Our Electoral System.* New York: Random House, 1969.

Nichols, David. *Financing Elections: The Politics of an American Ruling Class.* New York: New Viewpoints, 1974.

Nie, Norman H., et al. *The Changing American Voter.* Cambridge, Mass.: Harvard University Press, 1976.

Novak, Michael. *Choosing Our King: Powerful Symbols In Presidential Politics.* New York: Macmillan, 1974.

Overacker, Louise. *Money in Elections.* New York: Arno Press, 1974.

———. *The Presidential Primary.* New York: Arno Press, 1974.

Page, Benjamin I. *Choices and Echoes in Presidential Elections: Rational Man and Electoral Democracy.* Chicago: University of Chicago Press, 1978.

Parris, Judith H. *The Convention Problem: Issues in Reform of Presidential Procedures.* Washington, D.C.: Brookings Institution, 1972.

Peirce, Neal R. *The People's President: The Electoral College and the Emerging Consensus for a Direct Vote.* New York: Simon & Schuster, 1968.

Petersen, Svend. *A Statistical History of the American Presidential Elections.* New York: Frederick Ungar, 1968.

Phillips, Kevin P. *The Emerging Republican Majority.* New York: Arlington House, 1969.

Plissner, Martin, et al. eds. *Campaign '76.* New York: Arno Press, 1977.

Polsby, Nelson, and Wildavsky, Aaron. *Presidential Elections: Strategies of American Electoral Politics.* New York: Scribner, 1980.

Pomper, Gerald M. *Elections in America: Control and Influence in Democratic Politics.* New York: Dodd, Mead & Co., 1968.

———. *Nominating the President: The Politics of Convention Choice.* Evanston, Ill.: Northwestern University Press, 1963.

———. *Voters' Choice: Varieties of American Electoral Behavior.* New York: Dodd, Mead & Co., 1975.

Pomper, Marlene M., ed. *The Election of 1976: Reports and Interpretations.* New York: David McKay Co., 1977.

Ranney, Austin, ed. *The American Elections of 1980.* Washington, D.C.: American Enterprise Institute for Public Policy Research, 1981.

———. *The Past and Future of Presidential Debates.* Washington, D.C.: American Enterprise Institute for Public Policy Research, 1979.

Roseboom, Eugene H. *History of Presidential Elections: From George Washington to Richard M. Nixon.* New York: Macmillan, 1970.

Runyon, John H. *Source Book of American Presidential Campaign and Election Statistics, 1948-1968.* New York: Frederick Ungar, 1971.

Sanford, Terry. *A Danger to Democracy: The Presidential Nominating Process.* Boulder, Colo.: Westview Press, 1981.

Sayre, Wallace S. *Voting for President: The Electoral College and the American Political System.* Washington, D.C.: Brookings Institution, 1970.

Scammon, Richard M., ed. *America at the Polls: A Handbook of American Presidential Election Statistics 1920-1964.* Pittsburgh, Pa.: University of Pittsburgh Press, 1965.

———. *America Votes: A Handbook of Contemporary Election Statistics.* Washington, D.C.: Congressional Quarterly, 1956-.

Schlesinger, Arthur M. Jr., ed. *The Coming to Power: Critical Presidential Elections in American History.* New York: McGraw-Hill, 1972.

———, ed. *History of American Presidential Elections.* 4 vols. New York: McGraw-Hill, 1971.

Schram, Martin. *Running for President 1976: The Carter Campaign.* Briarcliff Manor, New York: Stein & Day, 1977.

Singer, Aaron, ed. *Campaign Speeches of American Presidential Candidates, 1928-1972.* New York: Frederick Ungar, 1976.

Shoup, Laurence H. *The Carter Presidency and Beyond: Power and Politics in the 1980s.* Palo Alto, Calif.: Ramparts Press, 1980.

Stacks, John F. *Watershed: The Campaign for the Presidency, 1980.* New York: Times Books, 1981.

Stroud, Kandy. *How Jimmy Won: The Victory Campaign from Plains to the White House.* New York: William Morrow, 1977.

Thayer, George. *Who Shakes the Money Tree?* New York: Simon & Schuster, 1974.

Wallace, David. *First Tuesday.* Garden City, N.Y.: Doubleday, 1964.

Wayne, Stephen J. *The Road to the White House: The Politics of Presidential Elections.* New York: St. Martin's Press, 1980.

White, F. Clifton and Gill, William J. *Why Reagan Won: A Narrative History fo the Conservative Movement, 1964-1981.* Chicago, Ill.: Regenery Gateway, 1981.

White, Theodore H. *The Making of the President, 1960.* New York: Atheneum, 1961.

———. *The Making of the President, 1964.* New York: Atheneum, 1965.

———. *The Making of the President, 1968.* New York: Atheneum, 1969.

———. *The Making of the President, 1972.* New York: Atheneum, 1973.

Winter, Ralph K. *Campaign Financing and Political Freedom.* Washington, D.C.: American Enterprise Institute for Public Policy Research, 1974.

Witcover, Jules. *Marathon: The Pursuit of the Presidency, 1972-1976.* New York: Viking Press, 1977.

Yunker, John H., and Longley, Lawrence D. *The Electoral College: Its Biases Newly Measured for the 1960s and 1970s.* Beverly Hills, Calif.: Sage Publications, 1976.

Zeidenstein, Harvey. *Direct Election of the President.* Lexington, Mass.: D. C. Heath, 1973.

Articles

Abramson, Paul R. "Class Voting in the 1976 Presidential Election." *Journal of Politics,* November 1978, pp. 1066-1072.

Alexander, Herbert E. "Financing American Politics." *Political Quarterly,* October/December 1974, pp. 439-448.

Axelrod, Robert. "Where the Votes Come From: An Analysis of Electoral Coalitions, 1952-1968." *American Political Science Review,* March 1972, pp. 15-17.

Bayh, Birch. "Electing a President: The Case for Direct Popular Election." *Harvard Journal on Legislation,* January 1969, pp. 1-12.

Biden, Joseph R., Jr. "Public Financing of Elections: Legislative Proposals and Constitutional Questions." *Northwestern University Law Review,* March/April 1974, pp. 1-70.

Black, Merle and Black, Earl. "Republican Party Development in the South: The Rise of the Contested Primary." *Social Science Quarterly,* December 1976, pp. 566-578.

Cronin, Thomas E. "Choosing a President." *Center Magazine,* September/October 1978, pp. 5-15.

Declerq, Eugene et al. "Voting in American Presidential Elections: 1952-1972." *American Politics Quarterly,* July 1975, pp. 222-246.

de Lesseps, Suzanne, "Electoral College Reform." *Editorial Re-*

search Reports, November 19, 1976, pp. 845-862.

Douglas, James. "Was Reagan's Victory a Watershed in American Politics?" *Political Quarterly*, April/June 1981, pp. 171-183.

Eshelman, Edwin D. "Congress and Electoral Reform: An Analysis of Proposals for Changing Our Method of Selecting a President." *Christian Century*, February 5, 1969, pp. 178-181.

Glantz, Stanton A. et al. "Election Outcomes: Whose Money Matters." *Journal of Politics*, November 1976, pp. 1033-1038.

Glen, Maxwell, "The PACs are Back, Richer and Wiser, to Finance the 1980 Elections." *National Journal*, November 24, 1979, pp. 1982-1984.

Goldstein, Joel H. "The Influence of Money on the Pre-Nomination Stage of the Presidential Selection Process: The Case of the 1976 Election." *Presidential Studies Quarterly*, Spring 1978, pp. 164-179.

Hardesty, Rex. "Elections '80: A Pivotal Decision for America." *American Federationist*, October 1980, pp. 1-5.

Hedlund, Ronald D. "Cross-Over Voting in a 1976 Open Presidential Primary." *Public Opinion Quarterly*, Winter 1977-1978, pp. 498-514.

Hodgson, Godfrey. "American Presidential and Party Politics: Changes in Spirit and Machine." *World Today*, September 1976, pp. 317-327.

Kirkpatrick, Samuel A. "American Electoral Behavior: Change and Stability." *American Politics Quarterly*, July 1975, pp. 219-352.

Ladd, Everett C. "The Brittle Mandate: Electoral Realignment and the 1980 Presidential Election." *Political Science Quarterly*, Spring 1982, pp. 1-25.

Lanouette, William J. "Complex Financing Laws Shape Presidential Campaign Strategies." *National Journal*, August 4, 1979, pp. 1281-1286.

Lechner, Alfred J. "Direct Election of the President: The Final Step in the Constitutional Evolution of the Right to Vote." *Notre Dame Lawyer*, October 1971, pp. 122-151.

Lengle, James I. "Divisive Presidential Primaries and Party Electoral Prospects, 1932-1976." *American Politics Quarterly*, July 1980, pp. 261-277.

Lobel, Martin. "Federal Control of Campaign Contributions." *Minnesota Law Review*, 1966, pp. 1-62.

McDonald, Kimberly. "The Impact of Political Action Committees." *Economic Forum*, Summer 1981, pp. 94-103.

"The Major Issues of the 1980 Campaign: Pro and Con." *Congressional Digest*, October 1980, pp. 225-256.

Mansfield, Harvey C. Jr. "The American Election: Towards Constitutional Democracy?" *Government and Opposition*, Winter 1981, pp. 3-18.

Menendez, Albert J. "Religion and Presidential Politics 1980." *Worldview*, November 1979, pp. 11-14.

———. "Religion at the Polls, 1980." *Church and State*, December 1980, pp. 15-18.

Mervin, David. "Personality and Ticket Splitting in U.S. Federal and Gubernatorial Elections, 1946-1972." *Political Studies*, September 1973, pp. 306-310.

Miller, Arthur H. "Partisanship Reinstated?" A Comparison of the 1972 and 1976 U.S. Presidential Elections." *British Journal of Political Science*, April 1978, pp. 129-152.

———. "Realignment in the 1980 Election." *Economic Outlook USA*, Autumn 1981, pp. 88-90.

———, and Wattenberg, Martin P. "The Politics from the Pulpit: Religiosity in the 1980 Elections." *Economic Outlook USA*, Summer 1982, pp. 61-64.

Olson, David M. "The Structure of Electoral Politics." *Journal of Politics*, May 1967, pp. 352-367.

Orren, Gary and Dionne, E. J. "The Next New Deal: Progressives and Democrats Won't Find It by Moving Right; a Second Look at the 1980 Election...." *Working Papers for a New Society*, May/June 1981, pp. 24-35.

Pomper, Gerald M. "From Confusion to Clarity: Issues and American Voters, 1956-1968." *American Political Science Review*, June 1972, pp. 415-428.

"Pulpits and Politics, 1980." *Church and State*, November 1980.

Reiter, Howard L. "Why Is Turnout Down?" *Public Opinion Quarterly*, Fall 1979, pp. 297-311.

Roper, Burns W. "Making More Meaningful Choices: A Proposed New System for Selecting Presidential Candidates." *Freedom at Issue*, September/October 1980, pp. 3-5.

Shafer, Byron E. "Anti-Party Politics." *Public Interest*, Spring 1981, pp. 95-111.

Staats, Elmer B. "Impact of the Federal Election Campaign Act of 1971." *Annals of the American Academy of Political and Social Science*, May 1976, pp. 98-113.

Thomas, William V. "Choosing Presidential Candidates." *Editorial Research Reports*, June 6, 1980, pp. 407-424.

Tyler, Gus. "Gauging the Republican Tide: A New Age or An Interregnum?" *New Leader*, November 17, 1980, pp. 3-5.

Waldman, Loren K. "Liberalism of Congressmen and the Presidential Vote in Their District." *Midwest Journal of Political Science*, February 1967, pp. 73-85.

Walker, Jack. "Presidential Campaigns: Reforming the Reforms." *Wilson Quarterly*, Autumn, 1981, pp. 88-101.

Ware, Alan. "The 1980 U.S. Elections: Party Revival or Continuing Party Decline?" *Parliamentary Affairs*, Spring 1981, pp. 174-190.

Weisberg, Harold, and Rusk, Jerrold. "Perceptions of Presidential Candidates: Implications for Electoral Change." *Midwest Journal of Political Science*, August 1972, pp. 388-410.

Wildavsky, Aaron. "The Three Party System-1980 and After." *Public Interest*, Summer 1981, pp. 47-57.

Zikmund, Joseph. "Suburban Voting in Presidential Elections: 1948-1964." *Midwest Journal of Political Science*, May 1968.

Documents

U.S. Congress. Clerk of the U.S. House of Representatives. *Statistics of the Presidential and Congressional Elections*. Washington, D.C.: Government Printing Office, 1981.

U.S. Congress. House. Committee on House Administration. *Presidential Matching Payments Regulations*. H. Doc. 96-57. 96th Cong., 1st sess. Washington, D.C.: Government Printing Office, 1979.

U.S. Congress. House. Committee on House Administration. *Presidential Primary Matching Payment Account: Revised Regulations*. H. Doc. 96-216. 96th Cong., 1st sess. Washington, D.C.: Government Printing Office, 1979.

U.S. Congress. House. Committee on House Administration. *The Presidential Campaign, 1976*. 2 vols. 95th Cong., 2d sess. Washington, D.C.: Government Printing Office, 1978.

U.S. Congress. Secretary of the U.S. Senate. *Nomination and Election of the President and Vice President of the United States Including the Manner of Selecting Delegates to National Political Conventions*. Washington, D.C.: Government Printing Office, 1980.

U.S. Congress. Senate. Committee on Rules and Administration. *Federal Election Campaign Act Amendments, 1979: Hearings, July 13, 1979*. 96th Cong., 1st sess. Washington, D.C.: Government Printing Office, 1979.

U.S. Congress. Senate. *Report of the Federal Election Commission Receipt and Use of Federal Funds by Candidates Who Accepted Public Financing for the 1980 Presidential Primary and General Elections*. H. Doc. 91-24, February 8, 1982. 97th Cong. 2d sess. Washington, D.C.: Government Printing Office, 1982.

U.S. Congress. Senate. Select Committee on Presidential Campaign Activities. *Election Reform: Basic References*. 93d Cong., 1st sess. Washington, D.C.: Government Printing Office, 1973.

U.S. Congress. Senate Library. *Factual Campaign Information*. Washington, D.C.: Government Printing Office, 1982.

U.S. Department of Commerce. Bureau of the Census. *Voter Participation*. Current Population Reports: Series P-20. Washington, D.C.: Government Printing Office, 19- .

U.S. Federal Election Commission. *FEC Annual Report*. Washington, D.C.: 1976-.

Index

Alabama
   Primaries - 29
   Primary returns, 1980 - 164
American Federation of Teachers (AFT) - 8-9
Anaya, Toney - 5
Anderson, John B. - 14, 17-19
Arkansas
   Primary returns, 1980 - 167
Armstrong, William L., R-Colo. - 10
Ashbrook, John M. - 15
Askew, Reubin - 15

Bayh, Birch - 92
Bergland, David D. - 19, 21
Boschwitz, Rudy, R-Minn. - 10, 105
Brown, Edmund G., Jr. (Jerry) - 22
Burton, Phillip - 127

California
   Congressional redistricting - 108, 125, 126 (box), 127
   Primary returns, 1980 - 167
Campaign finance
   Congressional campaign committee spending - 137, 139 (box)
   Contributions limit - 43, 134 (chart)
   Democratic Party - 135-138, 140-141, 145 (box), 153
   Federal matching funds - 43, 151 (box), 153
   Incumbents' cash on hand (table) - 156-159
   Legislative goals - 148-150
   PAC contributions - 148 (box), 149, 154 (box)
   Presidential candidates - 43, 149 (box), 151 (box), 153
   Public funds - 18-19
   Republican Party - 135-138, 141, 144, 145 (box), 146, 153
   Spending controversy - 147-148
   State spending limits (box) - 150
Carter, Jimmy
   Election, 1980 - 14, 15, 57
   Electoral College reform proposal - 92
   Presidential background - 22, 26
   Presidential campaign - 43, 45
   Primaries - 16, 29, 30
Caucus system. *See also* Delegates.
   Demise of caucus - 63-64
   Democratic results (box) - 43
   Election, 1984 - 39, 46-47 (table)
   Party origins - 61-63
   Selection of convention delegates (box) - 59
Chafee, John H., R-R.I. - 10
Chamber of Commerce, U.S. - 9, 140
Cochran, Thad, R-Miss. - 105
Coelho, Tony, D-Calif. - 9, 137-138, 140-141
Collins, Cardiss, D-Ill. - 8
Colorado
   Congressional redistricting - 127
Commission on Party Structure and Delegate Selection (McGovern-Fraser commission) - 39, 42

Commission on Presidential Nominations (Hunt commission) - 39, 41, 42, 54
Common Cause - 151, 152 (box)
Congress. *See also* House of Representatives; Senate.
   20th Amendment - 83
   25th Amendment - 83, 92
   Campaign funding. *See* Campaign finance.
   Departing members (box) - 107
   Election calendar (box) - 104
   Election results, 1854-1982 (table) - 106
   Election results, 1982 - 186-194
   Electoral College - 83-84, 85 (box), 86-87
   Electoral College reform proposals - 91-92
   Incumbents' cash on hand (chart) - 156-159
   Redistricting - 108, 125-128, 144
   Voluntary departures, 1946-1984 (box) - 128
Connecticut
   Gubernatorial elections - 131
   Primary returns, 1980 - 164
Constitution
   12th Amendment - 80, 81 (box), 86, 91, 94
   17th Amendment - 115, 116 (box)
   20th Amendment - 81 (box), 83, 116 (box), 117, 119
   25th Amendment - 83, 91 (box), 92
   Electoral College - 79-80, 81 (box), 86 (box), 91, 94
   Franchise laws — 97, 98, 121
   House of Representatives election - 123 (box)
   Presidential selection (box) - 81
   Senate elections (box) - 114
Conventions. *See also* Delegates.
   Binding rule - 41-42
   Credentials disputes - 55, 56 (box)
   Democratic Party - 50 (box), 52 (box), 58, 68-70 (table), 71, 170-174, 181
   Information for 1980, 1984 (table) - 68-70
   National party highlights (table) - 65-67
   Party officials - 72, 73-76 (table)
   Party origins - 13, 64
   Party platforms - 57-58
   Primary impact - 27-29
   Republican Party - 50 (box), 53 (box), 58, 68-70 (table), 71, 174-179, 182
   Sites - 51-52, 71
Corcoran, Tom, R-Ill. - 10
Cranston, Alan, D-Calif. - 14, 16

D'Amours, Norman E., D-N.H. - 10
Danforth, John C., R-Mo. - 107
DCCC. *See* Democratic Congressional Campaign Committee.
Delegates
   Primaries - 27, 28 (box)
   Selection - 37-39, 41-43, 52-55
   Selection rules, 1984 (box) - 54
   'Superdelegates' - 31, 39, 40 (box), 42
   U.S. territories (box) - 38
Democratic Congressional Campaign Committee (DCCC) - 137, 138, 140-141

Democratic National Committee (DNC)
   Campaign financing - 135-136
   Voter registration drives - 4, 54, 55
Democratic Party. *See also* Parties, political.
   Binding rule - 41-42
   Campaign finance - 135-138, 140-141, 145 (box), 153
   Caucus results - 43 (box), 46-47 (chart)
   Convention information for 1980, 1984 - 68-70 (table), 170-174, 181
   Convention platforms - 58
   Conventions, 1832-1980 (box) - 52
   Convention sites, 1984 - 71
   Convention votes, 1964-1980 (box) - 50
   Delegate count, 1984 - 47, 67 (box)
   Delegate selection - 37 (box), 54-55
   Democrats Abroad (box) - 39
   Party officials (table) - 73-76
   Platform fights (box) - 57
   Presidential candidate voting records (box) - 44
   Presidential challengers - 31-32
   Primaries, 1984 - 32 (box), 33, 34 (box), 36-37, 38, 46 (chart)
   Primary winners, 1972-1980 (box) - 34
   Rules - 36 (box), 55, 57
   Senate races - 105, 107
   'Superdelegates' - 31, 39, 40 (box), 42
   Voter turnout — 3, 4, 99
District of Columbia
   Primary returns, 1980 - 166
DNC. *See* Democratic National Committee.
Durbin, Dick, D-Ill. - 7

East, John P., R-N.C. - 5
Eisenhower, Dwight D. - 15, 26
Elections
   Criticism of process - 14-15
   Party unity - 15-16
   Voter turnout - 2 (box), 3-6, 97-99
   Voting laws changes - 97-98
Electoral College
   12th Amendment - 80, 81 (box), 86 (box), 91, 94
   25th Amendment (box) - 91
   Constitutional background - 79-80, 81 (box)
   Election by Congress - 83-84, 85 (box), 86-87
   Historical anomalies - 83, 86-87
   Law for counting votes (box) - 90
   Methods of choosing electors - 80, 82-83
   Reform proposals - 91-92
   Vice president votes, 1804-1980 - 94-95
   Vote count - 87, 89-91
   Vote splits (box) - 86-87
   Votes by states - 78, 88
   Winner-take-all system - 82-83

Falwell, Rev. Jerry - 5
Federal Election Campaign Act (FECA) - 17, 43, 135, 142-143, 148
Federal Election Commission (FEC) - 17, 18

Fernandez, Ben - 16
Florida
  Gubernatorial elections - 129
  Primaries - 29
  Primary returns, 1980 - 164
Ford, Gerald R.
  Presidential background - 24, 26
  Re-election bid - 15, 16
Franks, Martin - 140, 141
Fund raising. See Campaign finance.

Gaylord, Joseph R. - 144, 146
Georgia
  Congressional redistricting - 127
  Gubernatorial elections - 131-132
  Primary returns, 1980 - 164
Glenn, John, D-Ohio - 15
Goldsmith, Judy - 7, 8
Goldwater, Barry M., R-Ariz. - 29
Goode, W. Wilson - 5
Governors
  Election, 1984 (box) - 102
  Election methods - 130
  Election returns, 1982 - 186-194
  Length of terms - 129, 130 (box)
  Majority vote requirement - 130-131
  Non-presidential year elections - 129
  Number of terms - 130, 131 (box)
  Presidential nominees - 24
  States' list (box) - 132

Haig, Alexander M. Jr. - 93
Hance, Kent, D-Texas - 140
Harkin, Tom, D-Iowa - 105
Hart, Gary, D-Colo.
  Presidential campaign, 1984 - 14, 31
  Primaries, 1984 - 39
Helms, Jesse, R-N.C. - 5, 10, 105
Hiler, John, R-Ind. - 10, 146
Hollings, Ernest F., D-S.C. - 15
House of Representatives. See also Congress.
  Constitutional provisions for election (box) - 123
  Electing the president - 83-84, 85 (box), 86-87
  Election results, 1964-1982 (table) - 120
  Elections - 102 (box), 107-108, 121-124
  Length of terms - 121
  Membership in 98th Congress (chart) - 110-111
  Political party makeup, 1983 (box) - 124
Humphrey, Gordon J., R-N.H. - 10, 105
Humphrey, Hubert H. Jr. - 86
Hunt commission. See Commission on Presidential Nominations.

Idaho
  Primary returns, 1980 - 167
Illinois
  Congressional redistricting - 127
  Primaries - 29
  Primary returns, 1980 - 164
Indiana
  Congressional redistricting - 127
  Presidential nominees - 24
  Primary returns, 1980 - 166
Iowa
  Caucuses - 41
  Primaries - 38, 39

Jackson, Rev. Jesse
  Delegate selection - 42, 43
  Presidential candidate - 15, 16
  Voter registration - 4
Jepsen, Roger W., R-Iowa - 7, 10, 105
Johnson, Lyndon B. - 26

Kansas
  Primary returns, 1980 - 165
Kennedy, Edward M., D-Mass. - 57
Kennedy, John F.
  Presidential background - 22, 26
  Primaries - 29
Kentucky
  Primary returns, 1980 - 167
Kline, Richard A. - 140

Lamm, Richard D. - 127
Lewis, Jim - 19
Libertarian Party - 19-21
Long, Russell B., D-La. - 9
Louisiana
  Congressional redistricting - 127-128
  Method of electing governors - 130, 131 (box)
  Primary returns, 1980 - 165

McCloskey, Paul N. Jr. - 15
McGovern-Fraser commission. See Commission on Party Structure and Delegate Selection.
McGovern, George S.
  Presidential campaign - 15, 43
  Primaries - 29
Maine
  Gubernatorial elections - 132
Maryland
  Governor's length of term - 129
  Primary returns, 1980 - 166
Massachusetts
  Gubernatorial elections - 132
  Primaries - 29
  Primary returns, 1980 - 163
Media and convention coverage - 58, 60
Michel, Robert H., R-Ill. - 144
Michigan
  Primary returns, 1980 - 167
Mississippi
  Congressional redistricting - 127
  Primary returns, 1980 - 168
Missouri
  Congressional redistricting - 127
Mondale, Walter F.
  Presidential campaign, 1984 - 14, 31
  Primaries, 1984 - 39
  Special interest groups - 7, 8, 9
Montana
  Primary returns, 1980 - 168
Moral Majority - 5
Moshofsky, Bill - 144

National Education Association (NEA) - 8-9
National Federation of Independent Business (NFIB) - 9-10
National Organization for Women (NOW) - 7, 8
National Republican Congressional Committee (NRCC) - 108, 141, 144, 146
National Republican Senatorial Committee (NRSC) - 103, 137
National Unity Party - 17, 179-180. See also Anderson, John B.
Nebraska
  Primary returns, 1980 - 166

Nevada
  Primary returns, 1980 - 167
New Hampshire
  Gubernatorial elections - 132
  Primaries - 29, 30, 38, 39, 41
  Primary returns, 1980 - 163
New Jersey
  Congressional redistricting - 125
  Primary returns, 1980 - 168
New Mexico
  Primary returns, 1980 - 168
New York
  Governor's length of term - 129
  Presidential nominees - 23-24
  Primaries - 29
  Primary returns, 1980 - 165
NFIB. See National Federation of Independent Business.
Nixon, Richard M.
  Electoral College anomalies - 86-87
  Electoral College reform proposals - 92
  Presidential backgrounds - 26
  Primaries - 29
Nominating conventions. See Conventions.
North Carolina
  Congressional redistricting - 127
  Primary returns, 1980 - 166
NOW. See National Organization for Women.
NRCC. See National Republican Congressional Committee.
NRSC. See National Republican Senatorial Committee.

Ohio
  Congressional redistricting - 128
  Primary returns, 1980 - 168
O'Leary, Brad - 145
Oregon
  Primary returns, 1980 - 167

PACs. See Political Action Committees.
Parties, political. See also Conventions; Democratic Party; Republican Party; Third Parties.
  Caucus demise - 63-64
  Electors - 80, 82
  Origins of the system - 13, 60-63
  Victorious party in presidential races, 1860-1980 - 185
Peña, Federico - 5
Pennsylvania
  Primary returns, 1980 - 165
Percy, Charles H., R-Ill. - 10, 105
Political Action Committees (PACs)
  Campaign finance - 148 (box), 149, 154 (box)
  Growth and controversy - 142-143, 152 (box)
Presidency
  12th Amendment (box) - 81
  20th Amendment (box) - 81
  25th Amendment - 91 (box), 92-93
  Backgrounds of presidents - 22-24, 25-26
  Campaign finance - 43, 149 (box), 151 (box), 153
  Campaign length (chart) - 35
  Disability - 91 (box), 92-93
  Election by House - 83-84, 85 (box), 86-87
  Election results, 1854-1982 (table) - 106

Election results, 1860-1980 - 183-184
Election results, 1980 (table) - 96
Electoral College - 79-80, 81 (box), 82-84, 85 (box), 86-87, 88, 89-93, 99 (box)
History of selection - 13-14
Presidents, 1789-1829 (box) - 62
Presidents of the U.S. (chart) - 12
Primaries - 27-30
Re-election chances (box) - 15
Presidential Succession Act - 92, 93
Primaries
Delegate selection - 37-39, 41-43, 52-55
Democratic Party, 1984 - 32 (box), 33, 34 (box), 36-37, 38, 46 (chart)
History - 13-14
Presidential - 27-30
Presidential returns, 1980 - 163-169
Reform proposals - 30, 33 (box)
Republican Party rules - 42 (box)
Results, 1984 (chart) - 46
'Superdelegates' - 31, 39, 40 (box), 42
Types (box) - 28
Votes by stages (box) - 41
Puerto Rico
Primary returns, 1980 - 163

Reagan, Ronald
Election, 1980 - 14
Presidential background - 22, 24, 26
Presidential campaign, 1980 - 45
Presidential campaign, 1984 - 6, 31
Presidential disability - 93
Primaries - 30
Republican support - 15, 16
Special interest groups - 7, 8, 9
Voter turnout - 3, 4
Republican National Committee - 45
Republican Party. See also Parties, political.
Campaign finance - 135-138, 141, 144, 145 (box), 146, 153
Convention ballots, 1980 - 182
Convention delegates, 1984, by state (box) - 67
Convention information for 1980, 1984 - 68-70 (table), 174-179
Convention platforms - 58
Conventions, 1856-1980 (box) - 53
Convention sites, 1984 - 71
Convention votes, 1964-1980 (box) - 50
Nominating process - 45
Party officials (table) - 72
Platform fights (box) - 57
Primary rules - 42 (box)
Senate races - 103, 105, 107
Voter identification - 99
Revenue Act - 148
Rhode Island
Gubernatorial elections - 132
Primary returns, 1980 - 168
Ritter, Don, R-Pa. - 7, 10
Rizzo, Frank L. - 5

Secretaries of State - 22
Senate. See also Congress.
17th Amendment - 115, 116 (box)
20th Amendment - 116 (box), 117, 119
Appointments and special elections (box) - 116
Constitutional provisions for election (box) - 114
Election, 1984 - 102 (box), 103, 105, 107, 118 (box)
Election by state legislatures - 113
Election procedure changes - 113-115, 117
Expiration dates of senators' terms (box) - 112
Membership in 98th Congress (chart) - 109
Sessions and terms - 117, 119
Simon, Paul, D-Ill. - 105
Smith, Denny, R-Ore. - 10
South Carolina
Primary returns, 1980 - 163
South Dakota
Primary returns, 1980 - 168

Special interest groups - 7-10. See also Political Action Committees (PACs).
Stafford, Robert T., R-Vt. - 10
Stassen, Harold E.
Bid for presidency (box) - 20
Primaries - 29
Stephens, G. Douglas - 144
'Superdelegates' - 31, 39, 40 (box), 42

Teamsters union - 8
Tennessee
Primary returns, 1980 - 166
Texas
Congressional redistricting - 128
Primaries - 29
Primary returns, 1980 - 165
Third parties
Anderson - 17-19
Convention platforms - 58
Election, 1984 - 32-33
History (box) - 19
Libertarian Party - 19-21
National Unity Party - 17, 179-180
Treen, David - 127-128
Tsongas, Paul E., D-Mass. - 105

Vander Jagt, Guy, R-Mich. - 141
Vermont
Gubernatorial elections - 132
Primaries - 39
Primary returns, 1980 - 163
Vice Presidency
Electoral votes, 1804-1980 - 94-95
Presidential nominees - 24
Vice presidents of the U.S. (chart) - 12
Voter registration and turnout - 2 (box), 3-6, 97-99

Wallace, George C. - 86-87
Washington, Harold - 4, 5
Wertheimer, Fred - 151, 153
West Virginia
Primary returns, 1980 - 168
Wisconsin
Primary returns, 1980 - 165

JK 526 .E53 1984b

	DATE DUE		